T0305241

Economic Regulation and Its Reform

A National Bureau
of Economic Research
Conference Report

Economic Regulation and Its Reform
What Have We Learned?

Edited by   **Nancy L. Rose**

The University of Chicago Press

Chicago and London

NANCY L. ROSE is the Charles P. Kindleberger Professor of Applied
Economics and associate department head for economics at the
Massachusetts Institute of Technology. She is a research associate
of the National Bureau of Economic Research and director of its
Program on Industrial Organization.

The University of Chicago Press, Chicago 60637
The University of Chicago Press, Ltd., London
© 2014 by the National Bureau of Economic Research
All rights reserved. Published 2014.
Printed and bound by CPI Group (UK) Ltd, Croydon, CR0 4YY

23 22 21 20 19 18 17 16 15 14   1 2 3 4 5
ISBN-13: 978-0-226-13802-2 (cloth)
ISBN-13: 978-0-226-13816-9 (e-book)
DOI: 10.7208/chicago/9780226138169.001.0001

Library of Congress Cataloging-in-Publication Data
Economic regulation and its reform : what have we learned? / edited by
    Nancy L. Rose.
        pages cm. — (National Bureau of Economic Research
    conference report)
    Includes bibliographical references and index.
        ISBN 978-0-226-13802-2 (cloth : alkaline paper) — ISBN
    978-0-226-13816-9 (e-book) 1. Industrial policy—United States—
    Congresses. 2. Trade regulation—United States—Congresses.
    3. Deregulation—United States—Congresses. I. Rose, Nancy L.,
    editor. II. Series: National Bureau of Economic Research conference
    report.
        HD3616.U46E3125 2014
        338.0973—dc23
                                                          2013040451

♾ This paper meets the requirements of ANSI/NISO Z39.48-1992
(Permanence of Paper).

**Relation of the Directors to the
Work and Publications of the
National Bureau of Economic Research**

1. The object of the NBER is to ascertain and present to the economics profession, and to the public more generally, important economic facts and their interpretation in a scientific manner without policy recommendations. The Board of Directors is charged with the responsibility of ensuring that the work of the NBER is carried on in strict conformity with this object.

2. The President shall establish an internal review process to ensure that book manuscripts proposed for publication DO NOT contain policy recommendations. This shall apply both to the proceedings of conferences and to manuscripts by a single author or by one or more co-authors but shall not apply to authors of comments at NBER conferences who are not NBER affiliates.

3. No book manuscript reporting research shall be published by the NBER until the President has sent to each member of the Board a notice that a manuscript is recommended for publication and that in the President's opinion it is suitable for publication in accordance with the above principles of the NBER. Such notification will include a table of contents and an abstract or summary of the manuscript's content, a list of contributors if applicable, and a response form for use by Directors who desire a copy of the manuscript for review. Each manuscript shall contain a summary drawing attention to the nature and treatment of the problem studied and the main conclusions reached.

4. No volume shall be published until forty-five days have elapsed from the above notification of intention to publish it. During this period a copy shall be sent to any Director requesting it, and if any Director objects to publication on the grounds that the manuscript contains policy recommendations, the objection will be presented to the author(s) or editor(s). In case of dispute, all members of the Board shall be notified, and the President shall appoint an ad hoc committee of the Board to decide the matter; thirty days additional shall be granted for this purpose.

5. The President shall present annually to the Board a report describing the internal manuscript review process, any objections made by Directors before publication or by anyone after publication, any disputes about such matters, and how they were handled.

6. Publications of the NBER issued for informational purposes concerning the work of the Bureau, or issued to inform the public of the activities at the Bureau, including but not limited to the NBER Digest and Reporter, shall be consistent with the object stated in paragraph 1. They shall contain a specific disclaimer noting that they have not passed through the review procedures required in this resolution. The Executive Committee of the Board is charged with the review of all such publications from time to time.

7. NBER working papers and manuscripts distributed on the Bureau's web site are not deemed to be publications for the purpose of this resolution, but they shall be consistent with the object stated in paragraph 1. Working papers shall contain a specific disclaimer noting that they have not passed through the review procedures required in this resolution. The NBER's web site shall contain a similar disclaimer. The President shall establish an internal review process to ensure that the working papers and the web site do not contain policy recommendations, and shall report annually to the Board on this process and any concerns raised in connection with it.

8. Unless otherwise determined by the Board or exempted by the terms of paragraphs 6 and 7, a copy of this resolution shall be printed in each NBER publication as described in paragraph 2 above.

Contents

	Preface	ix
	Learning from the Past: Insights for the Regulation of Economic Activity Nancy L. Rose	1
1.	**Antitrust and Regulation** Dennis W. Carlton and Randal C. Picker	25
2.	**How Airline Markets Work . . . or Do They? Regulatory Reform in the Airline Industry** Severin Borenstein and Nancy L. Rose	63
3.	**Cable Regulation in the Internet Era** Gregory S. Crawford	137
4.	**Regulating Competition in Wholesale Electricity Supply** Frank A. Wolak	195
5.	**Incentive Regulation in Theory and Practice: Electricity Distribution and Transmission Networks** Paul L. Joskow	291
6.	**Telecommunications Regulation: Current Approaches with the End in Sight** Jerry Hausman and J. Gregory Sidak	345
7.	**Regulation of the Pharmaceutical-Biotechnology Industry** Patricia M. Danzon and Eric L. Keuffel	407

8.   **Regulation and Deregulation of the US
            Banking Industry: Causes, Consequences, and
            Implications for the Future**   485
            Randall S. Kroszner and Philip E. Strahan

9.   **Retail Securities Regulation in the Aftermath
            of the Bubble**   545
            Eric Zitzewitz

            Contributors   589
            Author Index   591
            Subject Index   601

Preface

The chapters in this volume grew out of a conference on economic regulation sponsored by the National Bureau of Economic Research in the fall of 2005. This conference brought together a group of leading scholars of regulation to discuss the history of regulation and its reform across a variety of sectors, and to assess what lessons could be drawn for regulatory policy going forward. The papers underwent a number of revisions following the conference, with the final chapters coming together just as the financial crisis of 2008 was gathering steam. In this environment, commentators and policymakers heaped blame for the financial crisis on "deregulation," and regulatory reforms across broad swaths of the economy came under increasing criticism. Given the volatility of the debate, the volume editor paused the publication process. In 2012, a review of the volume in the postcrisis context suggested that the lessons in these chapters not only remained relevant but were sorely needed as a number of regulatory reforms seemed in danger of repeating the mistakes of history. The editor approached the chapter authors with a request to review their contributions, assess the continuing relevance of their key conclusions in the postcrisis policy world, and freshen their texts where appropriate. The authors responded to this challenge with enthusiasm, and the chapters in this volume reflect the results of those efforts.

Learning from the Past
Insights for the Regulation
of Economic Activity

Nancy L. Rose

The past thirty-five years have witnessed an extraordinary transformation of government economic intervention across broad sectors of the economy throughout the world. State-owned enterprises were privatized. Price and entry controls were largely or entirely dismantled in many industries, particularly those with multifirm competition, ranging from natural gas production, to trucking and airlines, to stock exchange brokerage and retail banking. Traditional "natural monopoly" sectors such as electricity, telecommunications, and oil and gas pipelines were restructured, as more market-based institutions replaced traditional cost-of-service regulation or state ownership in many jurisdictions. Although government intervention that focused on risk, product quality, health, or environmental impact was rarely "deregulated," there was some diffusion of more market-based instruments, such as tradable permits to regulate power plant sulfur dioxide emissions and nitrous oxide emissions, the European Union Emissions Trading System for greenhouse gases, and global capital requirements for banks that "priced" the risk associated with different asset classes.

   The political economy of the reform movement has been heavily debated. Policy entrepreneurs, ideological shifts, and macroeconomic dislocations undoubtedly played a role in the torrent of reform over the late 1970s

Nancy L. Rose is the Charles P. Kindleberger Professor of Applied Economics and associate department head for economics at the Massachusetts Institute of Technology. She is a research associate of the National Bureau of Economic Research and director of its Program on Industrial Organization.
   For acknowledgments, sources of research support, and disclosure of the author's material financial relationships, if any, please see http://www.nber.org/chapters/c12564.ack.

1

and 1980s.[1] But a rich economics literature also had much to contribute. Studies demonstrated that regulation increased costs both directly and by reducing firm incentives to pursue more efficient operations, impeded the efficient allocation of goods and services to their highest value use, and often retarded innovation.[2] Many of the policy changes were bolstered by empirical analyses that documented the costs of regulation within a particular industry, and suggested the prospect of substantial gains from its reform.[3] Early studies of the aftermath of reforms confirmed many of the anticipated benefits, particularly in structurally competitive industries, and may have spurred extension to other settings.[4] Theoretical advances in understanding optimal regulation, particularly in the presence of asymmetric information, stimulated more effective policy design in some of the sectors subject to continuing regulation.[5]

The movement toward less intrusive economic regulation was far from linear or universal, however. For example, cable television in the United States underwent a relatively rapid succession of price deregulation, re-regulation, and deregulation between 1984 and 1996, as Congress grappled with the implications of price, service, and technological changes in that industry. The US intervention in the pharmaceutical industry has continued to focus on product-level entry regulation to ensure product safety and efficacy, with no direct price oversight for purchases outside government Medicaid and Medicare systems. That stands in sharp contrast to pharmaceutical controls in most other developed economies, where governments determine not only which products may be sold but also at what price, with regular price review and resetting. The electricity sector exhibits considerable heterogeneity in regulatory institutions. Many countries, led by England and Wales in 1990, and some US states have aggressively restructured this sector, creating competitive wholesale generation and retailing markets and implementing incentive regulation of remaining monopoly segments. At the other extreme are the many US states that retain vertically integrated monopoly electric utilities, subject to cost-of-service regulation that has changed only modestly over the past several decades.

Some of this variability reflects ambivalence by policymakers and various interests. The wisdom of the regulatory restructuring movement has been challenged from a number of directions, often from its earliest days.

---

1. Derthick and Quirk (1985), Noll (1989), and Peltzman (1989) analyze the politics of reform from a roughly contemporaneous perspective. See Landy, Levin, and Shapiro (2007) for a more recent analysis and assessment of successes and failures of the reform movement.

2. See, for example, Joskow and Rose (1989). Winston (1993) provides a critical review of much of this literature.

3. See, for example, Bailey (2010) on the role of academic economists and their research in airline deregulation, and Derthick and Quirk (1985) on the broader US deregulation movement.

4. Joskow and Rose (1989) and Joskow and Noll (1994) discuss much of the early literature.

5. See, for example, the body of theoretical work developed and inspired by Jean-Jacques Laffont and Jean Tirole (e.g., Laffont and Tirole 1993), and the discussion of incentive-based regulatory theory and practice by Paul Joskow in this volume.

Much of the most vocal criticism originated with groups that had benefitted from the regulations and saw these gains dissipate with the policy shift. These included executives of firms confronting unfamiliar management challenges and uncertain profitability, labor unions dealing with downward pressure on wages or employment resulting from intensified competition, and subsets of customers who had benefitted from regulated price structures. But there also has been recurrent dissatisfaction with the turbulence of market-driven outcomes, at times fueled by a conviction that reimposition of (possibly smarter) regulation would lead to more orderly markets characterized by low prices, plentiful service, generous wages, and assured returns on investments (e.g., Longman and Khan 2012).

Disparagement of reforms substantially broadened and intensified after the turn of the twenty-first century. Tumult in electricity markets, particularly the California electricity crisis of 2000 and 2001 and the Northeast blackout of 2003, was blamed on rising market power in the aftermath of utility deregulation and inadequate incentives for infrastructure investment in this setting. The bailout of individual airlines and wave of airline bankruptcies following precipitous declines in revenue and traffic subsequent to the September 11 terrorist attacks reinvigorated calls for restoring "order" through regulation of capacity, service, and even prices.[6] Broad indictments of regulatory reforms reached a crescendo with the 2008 financial crisis and its aftermath, whose roots were argued to lie in the deregulation of the financial sector, the elimination of the Glass-Steagall prohibition on investment banking activities by commercial banks, and the failure of regulators to adequately monitor and discipline bank activities.

Today, mistrust of markets abounds, and a popular credo attributes many of our current economic problems to "deregulation."[7] Concerns about conflicts of interest and the inability of regulators to monitor and control "too big to fail" financial institutions, apparently chronic financial instability in the airline industry, market power in restructured electricity markets, wage and work condition pressures in interstate trucking, rising rates for some railroad customers, failures in workplace and product safety, and myriad other issues have led to calls for renewed government oversight and intervention across a wide range of industries.

With the economy still languishing in the years following the 2008 financial crisis, attention has focused particularly on the financial sector, which some commentators argue might have avoided the crisis had more stringent and effective regulation been implemented earlier.[8] A number of economists

6. This was implemented on a limited scale in the Hawaiian intrastate air market; see Kamita (2010).

7. See, for example, Lazarus (2013). At the same time, "regulation" is criticized by others for slowing recovery and job creation, though these criticisms generally concern broader business regulation and tax policies than those issues analyzed in this volume.

8. Lo (2012) provides an assessment of the academic, policy, and media debate over the role of financial regulation in the crisis.

have called for renewed invigoration of regulation, arguing that when markets deviate from conditions of perfect competition, as they often do, outcomes will be improved by corrective government intervention. Acknowledging past regulatory failings, they argue that we can regulate better than we have in the past, in part by adopting clearer legislation, delegating less to agencies, employing some version of smarter regulators, and better insulating regulators from "capture" by the groups they regulate.[9]

How should one assess these critiques, and what lessons should one take away from the history of regulation and its reform? These questions invoke a number of others: What have been the costs and benefits of economic regulation? When might "light-handed" incentive regulation, or oversight of firms through the general antitrust or tort litigation framework, effectively substitute for more intrusive intervention in firm decision making, and when won't this work? What new challenges are raised when regulated monopolies are restructured into structurally competitive sectors that must interface with regulated monopoly network providers downstream? Are there lessons from regulation of other industries that could inform current debates about financial sector regulation?

This volume brings together a panel of distinguished scholars to discuss what we have learned from the history of economic regulation, in an effort to answer questions such as these. The research spans a range of industries, with particular attention to those historically subject to control of competition through "price and entry" regulation (most common in the United States) or state ownership (more common elsewhere in the world). These papers were selected to highlight a diverse set of salient issues in the evaluation of economic regulation through the early twenty-first century. The work in this volume describes the origins of regulation of economic activity, assesses the consequences of regulatory reforms over the past three decades, and discusses the implications of academic research and policy experience for many of the most significant contemporary concerns in restructured and deregulated industries. While the primary focus of this volume is on the regulation of competition, a number of the chapters also address risk and product quality concerns, which have been at the center of some recent policy debates. Many of the insights gained from the regulation of competition have broad applicability to these debates over the design of health, risk, and environmental regulatory policies.[10]

9. For example, Stiglitz (2009, 18) describes a rationale for the Bureau of Consumer Financial Protection, created by the 2010 Dodd-Frank legislation: "One of the arguments for a financial product safety commission . . . is that it would have a clear mandate, and be staffed by people whose only concern would be protecting the safety and efficacy of the products being sold. It would be focused on the interests of the ordinary consumer and investors, not the interests of the financial institutions selling the products." See also various chapters in Balleisen and Moss (2010).

10. For discussions of these debates, and more in-depth analysis of risk, product quality, and environmental regulation, see, for example, the National Bureau of Economic Research

The studies open in chapter 1 with an assessment by Dennis Carlton and Randall Picker of the two key instruments, apart from state ownership, that government has to influence the quality and terms of competition: antitrust (or competition) policy and regulation.[11] As governments have reduced their use of economic regulation and state ownership to control competition, there has been increased global reliance on oversight of markets by competition policy authorities, who are charged with jurisdiction over broad sectors (or all) of industry. In the United States, these responsibilities are shared at the federal level by the antitrust division of the Department of Justice and the Federal Trade Commission; state attorneys general also may intervene in areas of specific concern to their state. Where economic regulatory agencies have been dismantled (or never existed), competition policy is the primary means to control the nature of competitive interactions and to influence market structure and hence performance. Where regulatory agencies have economic oversight of an industry, lines of authority may be more blurred. As regulatory reform and industry restructuring has gained traction, understanding how best to demarcate these responsibilities has become increasingly important.

Attention in a number of industries has shifted from trying to ensure an adequate number of "horizontal" competitors (in the same market) to mediating "vertical" interactions. These are particularly relevant in network industries, where authorities may wish to prevent the owner of an essential or "bottleneck" facility in one market from impeding or foreclosing competition in a related market, using an intervention that minimizes distortions in both markets. But relying on competition to discipline markets has limitations when competition is imperfect. Carlton and Picker draw on a rich history from the origins of federal antitrust and regulatory policy to the present. They discuss a framework for considering both the positive and normative rationales for choosing between these two policy instruments, and highlight conditions under which competition policy and regulation may be complements rather than substitutes in the policy arsenal. They draw upon examples from the airline and telecommunications industries surveyed in this volume, as well as from the railroad and trucking sectors, to illustrate these arguments.

Chapter 2 turns to the airline industry, to which has been ascribed credit—or in some circles, blame—for setting off the economic deregulation movement in the 1970s (e.g., Kahn 1988, 22). Severin Borenstein and Nancy Rose

---

conference volumes on *Regulation vs. Litigation* (Kessler 2010) and *The Design and Implementation of US Climate Policy* (Fullerton and Wolfram 2012); Surowiecki (2010); and Coglianese (2012). For discussions of regulatory issues across a broad spectrum, see also Landy, Levin, and Shapiro (2007) and Balleisen and Moss (2010).

11. Antitrust, or competition policy, focuses on remediation of imperfect competition and harms that result primarily from monopoly power. Kessler's (2010) volume focuses attention on the choice of regulation versus litigation in the context of mediating health, safety, and risk choices by firms, addressed largely through tort law.

begin by documenting the evolution of airline regulation and the assessment of its operation through the early 1970s. This chapter describes the movement to deregulate the industry, and the impact of those reforms on prices, operations, service, and performance of the industry. In the airline industry, as has been common across other deregulated sectors, the transition from a regulated to competitive marketplace has been long, and the path far from smooth. Some adjustments, such as changes in the level and structure of prices, were rapid. Others, including network reconfiguration and entry of new carriers, took place over several years. And some changes, such as effective penetration of low-cost carriers at the national level, have taken decades.

While the Airline Deregulation Act of 1978 discontinued domestic price and entry regulation and dismantled the Civil Aeronautics Board, government intervention in this sector remains ubiquitous, even beyond the Federal Aviation Administration's ongoing regulation of aircraft and airline safety. Borenstein and Rose discuss the continuing dependence of performance in this sector on a variety of government policies, a pattern that is quite common among other "deregulated" industries. Since 1988, the Antitrust Division of the Department of Justice has had jurisdiction over airline mergers, alliances, and code sharing agreements. The Department of Transportation has responsibilities for administration of the program of subsidies for air service to small communities; monitoring service quality from flight on-time performance to passenger overbookings; and fare disclosure, most recently involving (chronically postponed) plans for a rulemaking on disclosure requirements for ancillary fees on global distribution systems (GDS). Local airport regulation and investments in both airport and public air traffic control system infrastructure have significant implications for capacity, and hence congestion, at both local and national levels. And competition in many international air service markets remains restricted by treaty more than three decades after domestic US airline deregulation.

This chapter tackles several concerns that dominate discussions of the contemporary airline industry: the financial viability of unregulated airline markets, the ongoing role of market power, and the adequacy of infrastructure investment and capacity allocation mechanisms. The conclusion that markets are "messy" and competition is flawed, but nonetheless may yield benefits over bureaucratic regulation of a dynamic industry, establishes an important theme that recurs throughout the volume.

Gregory Crawford's chapter on cable television regulation (chapter 3) expounds on a striking contrast to the "once and for all" nature of airline deregulation. Cable provides a rich laboratory for economists in search of policy variation, as Crawford carefully chronicles in his history of regulation, deregulation, re-regulation, and deregulation once again in this sector. He notes that the wealth of empirical evidence on the effects of these policies is discouraging for those who seek to limit prices through regulatory intervention in an industry with a rich strategy space for firms. Crawford concludes that regulation of cable prices generally (though not always) reduces price, but also appears to be associated with reduced product quality and investment. He notes suggestive evidence that despite popular complaints about rising cable rates, consumers may on net prefer the higher price, higher-quality offerings associated with unregulated markets. This highlights a pervasive difficulty confronting regulators who try to use a simple regulatory instrument such as price caps to influence outcomes when firms operate in multidimensional strategy space. In another nod to the critical importance of measuring regulation against dynamic efficiency, Crawford's analysis suggests that entry into multichannel video programming by satellite systems and local telephone providers may provide more compelling benefits to consumers than did price regulation, by encouraging both price and quality competition. Crawford closes with a discussion of the dangers of mandatory à la carte channel offerings and the ongoing threats to a more competitive landscape posed by bundling in the programming market, vertical integration of content and distribution, and the potential for foreclosure in both traditional and online video distribution.

In a number of network industries where only part of the vertical chain of production has been carved out from economic regulation, new policy challenges have emerged. These comprise many of the "natural monopoly" sectors that were liberalized in the wave of policy reform following the early transportation and energy deregulation movement. The challenges posed by these new industry structures are discussed in the next group of chapters, which include Frank Wolak's analysis of wholesale electricity markets, Paul Joskow's treatise on incentive regulation in electricity distribution and transmission, and Jerry Hausman and Gregory Sidak's discussion of telecommunications policy.

The 1990s witnessed substantial restructuring of electric utilities throughout the world and in many US states.[12] In these jurisdictions, vertically integrated monopoly state-owned or investor-owned regulated utilities were divided into separate generation, transmission, and distribution sectors. Ownership of generating assets often was divested to create competitors in a newly designed wholesale generation market. Operation of the wholesale generation market and transmission network generally was assigned to an independent system operator, and responsibility for the distribution network was assigned to a regulated utility. In many liberalized markets, customer-facing retailing and billing functions are now distinct from electricity distribution, and open to competitive entry. This movement confronted regulators with the challenge of how to design and mediate the interface between

12. In the United States, electric utilities generally are regulated at the state level, so regulatory reforms must be decided by individual state legislatures. This has led to considerable variation in regulatory structures across the contemporary US electric utility sector. In other countries, this sector typically was restructured at the national level, often as an accompaniment to privatization of state-owned utilities.

newly competitive generation and retail sectors and continuing monopoly transmission and distribution services, in addition to that of monitoring the behavior of competitors in the deregulated sector and efficiently regulating the ongoing monopoly services.

Recent studies of the generation sector suggest that competition improves operating efficiency relative to regulated monopoly (e.g., Fabrizio, Rose, and Wolfram 2007; Davis and Wolfram 2012). But these benefits come with the cost of greater complexity in market design and monitoring. As Frank Wolak's chapter on wholesale generation markets emphasizes, getting each of these right is much more difficult in the vertically disintegrated markets at the heart of electricity restructuring than in the traditional regulated monopoly utility setting. Errors may involve considerable transfers of rents, as highlighted by the California electricity crisis of 2000 and 2001. Moreover, seemingly modest differences in institutions across markets may yield substantial differences in their relative performance. For example, markets in which a significant fraction of wholesale generation is sold under forward contracts, or is vertically integrated into distribution at fixed retail prices, restrict the exercise of market power and can moderate equilibrium prices (Wolak 2007; Bushnell, Mansur, and Saravia 2008). This can be especially important when demand is near capacity. Wolak argues that the failure to appreciate the role of vertical relationships was one of the key contributors to the magnitude of California price spikes in 2000 and 2001. The trade-off between imperfect regulation and imperfect markets[13] and the importance of understanding the pivotal role played by market institutions are at the heart of this analysis, and establish vital lessons for the design and study of regulatory frameworks in general.

In market sectors subject to ongoing government oversight and control, advances in regulatory design create the potential for improving upon traditional regulatory price setting. Paul Joskow's chapter describes the theory and implementation of one of the great contributions of economic research on regulation: insight on how to incorporate incentives to design more efficient economic regulation in the context of asymmetric information between firms and their regulators. Joskow begins by laying out the evolution of models of optimal regulation in the presence of asymmetric information when regulators care about both efficiency (encouraging firms to minimize costs) and rent extraction (keeping profits, and hence prices, as low as possible consistent with firms covering their costs); see, for example, Laffont and Tirole (1993). This theory has been at the heart of reforms implemented by the UK's Office of Gas and Electricity Markets (OFGEM), which has not only pioneered the use of sophisticated incentive mechanisms in its regulation, but also has demonstrated the inherently dynamic nature of effective regulation. For example, when early implementation revealed

13. See, for example, Joskow (2010).

that firms responded to strong incentives to cut costs by both increasing efficiency and reducing spending on quality, OFGEM reacted by incorporating quality of service metrics into its next round of incentive schemes, and has continued to expand and refine its use of quality-mediated incentive mechanisms. Had regulators not been monitoring the industry and appropriately adapted their policies, the move to incentive regulation might well have been labeled a failure. The importance of sufficient resources, attention, and agility in the regulatory system to adapt to unanticipated firm responses is a theme that echoes across regulatory experiences in many industries.

Joskow's analysis also describes the complexities involved in translating the theory into practice, and the many nuanced ways in which the actual implementation often differs from its stylized discussion. For example, the "RPI-X" price cap regulation of utilities in the United Kingdom often is described as less information intensive than traditional cost-of-service regulation in the United States. Instead of building up allowable prices from detailed analysis of costs, including capital costs and allowed rates of return, stylized price cap regulation fixes a maximum allowed price, which changes over time by a formula based on the rate of inflation ("RPI") less a targeted productivity improvement rate ("X"). But Joskow describes how the institutions of price cap regulation have much in common with the practice of cost-of-service regulation, including the detailed cost accounting systems and data collection for use in benchmarking analysis, the separation of operating and capital cost allowances in determining the level of the price cap, decisions by regulators on the target capital expenditures for the future period that drive much of the X factor in these capital intensive industries, and the periodic reviews and resets of the cap. Thus, the real advantage of incentive-based regulation is not that it requires less to implement; it may well require greater collection of data and analysis. Rather, as Joskow notes, it is that these systems use the information they collect in a more forward-looking way. He urges more study of their ex post performance to assess whether the reality of incentive regulation lives up to its promise.

While mediating partially deregulated sectors poses significant regulatory challenges, if handled well, both the challenges and some of the residual regulation may prove transitory. Jerry Hausman and Greg Sidak argue that designing mechanisms that encourage investment and viable long-term entry can speed the transition to competition in local telephone markets, while rules that impede investment by requiring incumbents to grant entrants access to their network at artificially low prices may hinder such a transition, and force reliance on regulatory adjudication indefinitely. They focus on access regulation in the United States, United Kingdom, and New Zealand, with particular attention to the rationale for "total element long-run incremental cost" (TELRIC)—or "total service long-run incremental cost" (TSLRIC)—style pricing rules, which have been argued to provide new entrants with access to elements of the local telephone network at "as if competitive" prices. Hausman and Sidak argue that determining "as if competitive" prices is fraught with pitfalls, with significant damage occurring when regulators fail to account for the sunk nature of physical investment in local telephone networks. They conclude that while TSLRIC-based prices might increase the market share of new entrants, by pricing access below its economic cost, such regulations are likely to discourage investment in physical networks. Without true facilities-based competition, local carriers will retain their monopoly over the physical network and regulators will find themselves in a "regulation forever" regime—or at least until new technologies, such as wireless communications, invent around the landline systems to provide effective substitutes. This study draws attention to the importance of considering the dynamic nature of firm responses to regulation: static costs and benefits may dramatically understate the true costs or benefits of regulatory systems after effects on investment and innovation are properly accounted for.

Although the bulk of this volume focuses on economic (price and entry) regulation, regulators are charged with oversight of risk, product safety, or product quality decisions in many industries. Few of those responsibilities have been diminished by reforms over the past thirty-five years, and many have increased. Patricia Danzon and Eric Keuffel's chapter highlights the challenge of regulating safety and efficacy in the pharmaceutical industry while encouraging productive innovation. They also describe a variety of approaches countries use to mitigate the incentives insurance or single-party payer systems create for increasing pharmaceutical rents through higher markups and greater promotional activity. Their analysis highlights the complexities introduced when regulating a highly dynamic industry with multiple dimensions of performance that consumers and regulators care about, but may observe only imperfectly, echoing a theme in Joskow's incentive regulation chapter. For example, safety and efficacy regulation by agencies such as the Food and Drug Administration (FDA) can substitute expert judgment for costly and imperfect assessment of product quality by individual consumers or their doctors. But the FDA evaluation process currently requires an average of eight to twelve years of research, preclinical testing and human clinical trials, and an estimated mean cost in the range of $1 billion (Danzon and Keuffel, chapter 7, this volume; Adams and Brantner 2010)—costs that may discourage R&D investment in drugs with smaller potential markets, less wealthy patient populations (such as those targeting disease in developing economies), or for which effective patent lives would be short. Prices for pharmaceuticals vary considerably across markets, due both to price discrimination and price regulation in many markets. Historically, prices in the United States have been market based, while those in most other developed countries were controlled by governments in an effort to mitigate the moral hazard in pricing created by price inelastic demand that arises from patients' insurance coverage or national health systems. Finding the balance between mitigating market power and encouraging pharmaceutical innovation can be difficult, and the global market for many pharmaceuticals may create incentives for some countries to "free ride" on the investment incentives created by others.

Recognizing that the economic regulatory environment may interact—perhaps in unexpected ways—with product quality and risk choices by firms may be especially important for understanding the past three decades in the banking sector. Myriad government agencies at both federal and state levels exercise oversight of the balance sheet, lending activities, and risk profile of depository institutions, yet were unable—or some claim, unwilling—to avoid the catastrophic failures that gave rise to the 2008 financial crisis. Randall Kroszner and Phillip Strahan's narrative on banking regulation (chapter 8) provides an alternative perspective to the regulatory incompetence or capture views that have been advanced postcrisis, particularly in the popular media. Their chapter reviews the history of banking regulation from the 1930s through the early 2000s, describes its political economy, and assesses the economic impact of liberalization over the 1980s and 1990s.

This analysis emphasizes the dynamic nature of the industry and its regulation, and the difficulty regulators have in keeping up with the rapid evolution of behavior in this sector (see also Romano, forthcoming 2014). Kroszner and Strahan's discussion of the relaxation of price and entry restrictions on depository institutions over the 1970s and 1980s suggests that some of these changes may have been dictated by changes in the economic climate. For example, elimination of Regulation Q controls on deposit interest rates responded to the inflation-induced disintermediation occurring in the banking and savings and loan sectors in the late 1970s, which threatened widespread insolvency. This policy change may have reflected both public interest and private objectives, as "a regulation that at one point helped the industry may later become a burden and sow the seeds of its own demise" (Kroszner and Strahan, chapter 8, this volume). Kroszner and Strahan cite evidence that relaxing entry restrictions on banks permitted them to expand geographically and increase their scale, reducing their riskiness and increasing their efficiency relative to the industry of the 1970s. However, increased competition, by reducing bank charter values, also may have created incentives that in the long run work against the objectives of risk regulation.

The chapter highlights the difficulty regulators have had in keeping up with new sources of risk. For example, banks responded to new risk-based capital regulations in ways that minimized their cost of those regulations, such as changing their portfolio mix and shifting activities off-balance sheet and therefore beyond the view of regulators. Unlike the OFGEM regulators described in Joskow's chapter, depository institution regulators appear to have been slow to recognize and adapt to the rapid evolution of industry behavior. The contribution of regulation to the 2008 financial crisis may have been driven more by misjudging incentives created by particular regulations and failing to anticipate or react to innovations by firms to minimize the cost of regulatory constraints, than from "deregulation" per se.

The closing chapter, by Eric Zitzewitz, discusses regulation of the retail securities and investments industry. The Securities and Exchange Commission (SEC), created early in the Great Depression, is the primary federal regulator; competition policy authorities at the state and federal level share overlapping jurisdiction in some areas. Unlike the sectors analyzed in the earlier chapters, price and entry regulation have played no real role in this industry. Instead, regulation historically has focused on market failures arising primarily from costly and imperfect information or free rider problems, and more recently has begun to incorporate the impact of cognitive limits on investor decision making. Regulation has been most concerned with leveling the playing field across investors, ensuring the disclosure and quality of information, and mitigating conflicts of interest ("agency problems") that may arise between investors and financial advisors or between investors and security issuers or investment managers. Zitzewitz describes the challenges inherent in pursuing these objectives under the best conditions. He also details the institutions that may lead the SEC to identify with the interests of industry it regulates, noting that these may function better in disciplining the behavior of rogue individuals (the Madoff scandal notwithstanding) than in "correcting systemic market failures that are also sources of economic rents" (chapter 9, this volume). The lessons in Zitzewitz's chapter may prove especially helpful as the government shifts its general regulatory focus from industries where market power in pricing is of primary concern toward greater regulation of risk, health and safety, and externality regulation.

Before turning to the individual chapters that comprise this study, it is instructive to note several broad themes that emerge from these studies of regulation, and that may be of value in considering regulatory policies going forward (see also Rose 2012).

Institutions Matter

One of the impediments to forming generalizations about regulation (e.g., "price controls reduce quality," or "entry restrictions generate supranormal rents for firms and labor") is that seemingly modest differences in institutional settings can lead to dramatically different impacts of otherwise similar regulations. The centrality of this was recognized by Fred Kahn in titling his encyclopedic treatise on *The Economics of Regulation: Principles and Institutions* (1970–71). Paul Joskow's classic 1974 *Journal of Law and Economics* paper on utility regulation exemplifies the importance of this lesson for researchers. Regulatory economists in the late 1960s and early 1970s were engaged in a spirited debate over the Averch-Johnson (A-J) model, which highlighted the distortionary effect of rate-of-return regulation on capital choices by utilities. Amid a burgeoning theoretical and empirical literature devoted to proving or disproving the effect, Joskow (1974) stepped back from the debate to ask "what do regulators actually do?" He noted that regulators do not set a rate of return that continuously binds, as in the model. Rather, regulators adjudicate the allowed rate of return as an input to determining the cost of capital, which itself is a component of costs that utilities are entitled to recover. Then regulators fix the price firms may charge, not the rate of return, until the next rate review. Moreover, Joskow highlighted consumer antipathy to rising nominal prices, presaging concerns now common in behavioral economics, as a factor that may lead to considerable stickiness in regulated rates. Joskow showed that this simple insight—grounded in the basic institutions of the sector—turned many of the implications of the A-J model on their head, and he fixed by example an important standard for empirical work in regulatory economics.

The studies in this volume highlight relevant regulatory and market institutions, their interactions, and why they matter. For example, Carlton and Picker highlight the significance of institutional assignment of priority when regulatory agencies and antitrust authorities share jurisdiction, such as over merger policy. Regulatory agencies charged with oversight of a single industry or sector are likely, by design or evolution, to favor the interests of incumbent firms. Antitrust authorities, in contrast, enforce competition policy across the entire economy (apart from designated carve-outs), with enforcement mediated by the courts. Mergers that increase industry concentration and restrict competition are more likely to be approved when a single-sector agency— such as the Federal Communications Commission, Surface Transportation Board, or Department of Transportation—has been given final authority over merger approvals, often over the objections of the relevant antitrust authority. Such patterns dominated the early post-deregulation experience in airlines and railroads. Carlton and Picker argue that the assignment, and resulting concentration in railroads, may have been intended given the poor financial condition of railroads prior to deregulation (see chapter 1).

Wolak describes how differences in the institutional structure of wholesale generation markets—including characteristics such as horizontal market concentration, vertical contracting, the degree of excess capacity in transmission networks, and whether consumers face retail prices linked to wholesale prices—can interact to yield substantially different outcomes relative to competitive benchmarks. He argues that failure to appreciate these interactions was a substantial contributor to the severity of the 2000 and 2001 California electricity crisis. This insight is important not only for market design of wholesale generation markets, but also for ongoing oversight. For example, neglecting the vertical structure of electricity generation and distribution markets suggests that the lower prices in the PJM (Pennsylvania-New Jersey-Maryland) market during the early 2000s, relative to those in

California, reflected more competitive behavior by generators in PJM (Bushnell, Mansur, and Saravia 2008). Relying on this apparent competitiveness to keep prices low could be quite misleading, as Bushnell, Mansur, and Saravia demonstrate that generators in both regions exercise market power, and that it is the incentives created by significant distribution company ownership of generation assets combined with fixed retail prices that led to lower wholesale generation prices in PJM. Changes to either of those institutions, all else constant, could result in substantially higher prices of electricity in PJM.

Danzon and Keuffel's analysis of the pharmaceutical market is rich with institutional detail and the implications of those details for the behavior of firms and performance of the market. Consider, for example, the market for generic pharmaceuticals. In the United States, the combination of laws that allow pharmacists to substitute generic equivalents to prescribed branded pharmaceuticals and insurer pricing policies that reimburse pharmacists based on a generic reference price for the drug leads to intense price competition among generic manufacturers, particularly for the business of large buyers (pharmacy chains, wholesale distributors, etc.) who purchase on price and keep the difference between the reference price and their acquisition cost as profit. By contrast, many EU countries restricted pharmacies to fill prescriptions as written (distinguishing brands from the generic chemical name), and some reimbursed pharmacies a markup on the price of the drug. In those countries, generic manufacturers developed branded generic products that were promoted intensively to physicians. As predicted by models of differentiated products, this softened price competition among generic manufacturers, leading to higher prices and lower generic sales, relative to the United States. Recognizing how incentives differ across institutional settings is critical to predicting the impact of regulation, and leads to the second general theme of this volume.

Incentives Drive Behavior—and Perhaps Unintended Consequences

Firms respond to incentives. An effort to harness the power of this insight fueled the surge in incentive-based regulation that Joskow's chapter describes in detail. For example, to the extent that traditional cost-of-service utility regulation or state ownership of utilities fully reimbursed firms for their incurred costs—which varied in effect over time and space—it dulled incentives to improve efficiency and reduce operating costs. Adoption of regulatory schemes that gave firms explicit rights to some share of cost savings resulted in reductions—some quite significant—in the cost of producing electricity. The power of properly aligned incentives to affect desired outcomes is one of the great insights, and contributions, of the economic literature on regulation.

But firms also respond to incentives even when regulators do not fully appreciate the inducements they have created. Recent experience with prolonged electricity outages following natural disasters and system failures has led policymakers in a number of US states to question whether firms have responded to rewards for cost reduction by underproviding reliability and recovery services. Joskow describes in depth the challenges for incorporating standards for quality into incentive-based regulation, particularly where data on service quality metrics are not readily available for benchmarking exercises. Borenstein and Rose recall the spiral of ever-increasing flight frequency and falling load factors in response to the futile attempt of the Civil Aeronautics Board (CAB) to increase industry profits by increasing air fares during the 1960s and early 1970s. While the CAB could eliminate price competition through regulatory degree, the attractiveness of gaining another passenger at a price far above the incremental cost of serving them simply redirected competition to other channels, leaving airline profitability no higher than before. Hausman and Sidak point out that TSLRIC-style pricing of access to local telephone infrastructure gives potential entrants a free option to test a market and exit without paying for sunk investment costs. Not surprisingly, few choose to build their own networks when they can instead "rent" at lower cost, a conclusion reinforced in a recent econometric analysis of similar access regulations and telecommunications investment across twenty European countries (Grajek and Röller 2012).

The pharmaceutical market is rife with examples of unintended incentive effects, as discussed in depth in Danzon and Keuffel's chapter. As an example, they note that strategic responses by firms to reference pricing regulation, in which the allowed price of a drug in one jurisdiction is pegged to its price at introduction, in another location, or in another channel, may change behavior in referenced setting. For example, 1990 Medicaid "best price" rules linked the price Medicaid paid for pharmaceuticals from the average private sector price in the United States, ensuring the Medicaid program sizable discounts *relative to* the average private sector price. But the linkage also created incentives to moderate or eliminate discounts to large private sector buyers, as doing so would raise prices paid by both the private channel and Medicaid purchasers. Consistent with that incentive, private sector prices for drugs with significant Medicaid market shares were higher following adoption of this policy (Duggan and Scott Morton 2006). In Japan, biannual price reviews that ratchet prices to keep markups low interact with manufacturer competition and physician dispensing of drugs to distort the R&D process toward more frequent incremental innovation of existing drugs that enables manufacturers to restart prices at a new higher level.

Understanding incentives and how firms respond to them is critical to financial services regulation, given the complexity of the sector, the many dimensions of firm choices, and the rapid rate of innovation in this industry. Kroszner and Strahan note, for example, that the implementation of risk-based capital requirements may have had a significant role in the subsequent rise of off-balance sheet activities beginning in the 1980s, and the explosion of securitization and derivative products, such as credit default swaps, in the 1990s and 2000s. Under these rules, mortgages required one-half the capital that banks were required to hold against commercial loans; asset-backed securities with AA or AAA ratings required just one-fifth. By shifting their portfolio away from commercial debt and toward mortgages and mortgage-backed securities, banks could reduce their costs of complying with capital requirement regulation. Unfortunately, such actions also appear to have played a critical role in setting the stage for the shock of the 2008 global financial crisis. Regulatory policies that address the "cause" of the last crisis may treat the symptom without curing the ill, if underlying incentives are not recognized and changed (see Romano, forthcoming 2014).

Innovation Changes the Game

Innovation can change the regulatory calculus in at least two ways. First, regulatory systems can distort incentives for innovation in products and services, leading to dynamic effects that may swamp static costs and benefits. Reductions in innovative activity are commonly—but not always—associated with regulation. This may arise directly from the slowness of regulatory systems to respond to firms' requests to enter new markets, introduce new products, or change the way they organize their activity. Hausman and Sidak argue that Federal Communications Commission regulation delayed innovations in telecommunication both directly by slowing their approval (for example, cellular, and enhanced voice services such as voicemail), and indirectly, discouraging investment (e.g., Hausman 1997). Crawford points to suggestive evidence that cable systems reduced investment and innovation in service offerings during periods of binding price regulation, and expanded both when price caps were removed. Innovation can cover a multitude of sins, and retarding innovation can multiply them greatly. Markets may be imperfect, but if those imperfect markets adopt productive innovations faster than would a more perfect regulated sector, the benefits of regulation may be far less than its costs.

Delay may have both costs and benefits, such as delay required to complete clinical trials used to vet the safety and efficacy of new drugs. Some may be driven by limited regulatory resources that require "queuing" applications for review. But even those delays are rarely exogenous to the regulatory system. Danzon and Keuffel point out that the length of Food and Drug Administration (FDA) reviews appears responsive to past crises—FDA reviews tend to be more intensive and longer following well-publicized problems with new drugs, or shorter for those that treat conditions (such as HIV/AIDS) that have generated stronger political interest in speeding drugs to market. Harnessing this insight to design procedures that allocate resources to minimize the expected social cost of regulatory delay could improve welfare; witness the impact of the "fast track" for FDA reviews and the increased use of postlaunch monitoring on drug approval times, as discussed by Danzon and Keuffel.

Regulation does not always impede innovation, however. Borenstein and Rose note that airline regulation, by suppressing price competition, channeled competition to nonprice dimensions, including innovation. The introduction and diffusion of jet aircraft was likely accelerated by price regulation that precluded airlines with turbo-prop equipment from charging a lower fare for their slower service relative to their jet-equipped rivals, and hence forced their investment in new aircraft as the only way to compete for passengers.

The second sense in which innovation matters involves the game between regulators and regulated firms. As Allan Meltzer wrote in 2009, "[T]he first law of regulation is: Lawyers and bureaucrats write regulations. Markets learn to circumvent the costly ones." When firms respond to the incentives that regulations create, outcomes may be quite different from those intended, particularly if regulators fail to adapt the regulatory structures. Some innovations may be privately profitable but socially inefficient. Especially when these are motivated by the gains of circumventing regulation, failing to adapt regulatory structures to the changing industry dynamics can render them ineffective or even counterproductive. Although this behavior is ubiquitous, its implications for regulatory policy are far too often overlooked.

Examples of apparently unanticipated firm responses to regulations abound. Crawford's discussion of cable systems padding their basic service tier with low-value program offerings to relax per channel price cap constraints, and shifting more popular programming to higher, unregulated service tiers, is a stark example of Meltzer's "law." Borenstein and Rose note that in regulated airline markets, increased schedule frequency was the most effective tool airlines had to capture share from rivals when price competition was forbidden. But in international markets where capacity and service frequency often were also regulated, carriers added piano bars, expanded gourmet meal service, and hired attractive young women in designer flight attendant uniforms. And on many of the highest price international routes, nonscheduled air carriers changed the game. These charter carriers, who typically operated outside the constraints imposed by international air service agreements, expanded to capture a substantial share of traffic with low-price, low-amenity charter flight service.

Kroszner and Strahan describe a long and checkered history of this behavior in the banking sector. From this vantage, the crisis in 2008 was notable for its breadth, depth, and impact, but the regulatory failures that contributed to it were far from novel. For example, when inflation induced high nominal interest rates in the 1970s and Regulation Q limits on deposit account rates became too binding for free toasters to offset its cost to depositors, innovations such as NOW (negotiated order of withdrawal) accounts, cash management sweep accounts, and money market mutual funds siphoned a huge share of deposits out of these regulated savings and checking accounts. While these may have improved consumer welfare, the resulting disintermediation destabilized banks and savings and loans institutions with large portfolios of illiquid, long-term loans (including thirty-year fixed-rate mortgages), planting the seeds for a wave of failures in the late 1970s and early 1980s. Well before the 2008 financial crisis, the incentives that risk-based capital regulations under the Basel II Accord created for banks to move lending activities off-balance sheet shifted the growing risk exposures to a channel largely beyond the sight of the regulators. Distinguishing innovation that increases social welfare from innovation that may be solely or primarily for the purpose of evading or escaping some of the regulatory constraints is a considerable challenge. History may be repeating itself, as a raft of new regulations following the 2008 financial crisis reinvigorates the game of regulatory "Whac-a-Mole" (e.g., Romano, forthcoming 2014).

The value of nimble regulators is highlighted in Paul Joskow's chapter on incentive regulation, particularly in his discussion of the British OFGEM regulation of electricity and natural gas. Given the difficulty of ascertaining ex ante the full breadth of responses to regulation, ex post adaptation seems essential. As Fred Kahn wrote in 1979, "The regulatory rule is: each time the dike springs a leak, plug it with one of your fingers; just as dynamic industry will perpetually find ways of opening new holes in the dike, so an ingenious regulator will never run out of fingers" (Kahn 1979,11). Joskow points out that this can be a double-edged sword—knowing that regulators will respond to firm choices can dampen incentives for certain behavior, such as efficiency improvements, in the first place. This analysis highlights the inevitable trade-offs among objectives when executing regulatory strategies.

Imperfect Markets Meet Imperfect Regulation

One of the most important themes to emerge from the studies in this volume is that markets and regulation both tend toward flaws, and neither may operate as the neoclassical ideal would dictate. Microeconomics courses detail a litany of "market failures" that cause market equilibria to be inefficient: too few sellers to ensure competitive prices, externalities that create a wedge between private and social costs, public goods that are underprovided in the absence of collective action, and information asymmetries or transactions costs that impede efficient trade. Yet even where regulation might be intended to restore imperfect markets to a competitive ideal, outcomes frequently are associated with higher production costs and, in some cases, higher prices, distorted product offerings, and significant rent redistribution. Responding to market imperfections with government regulation may trade one set of costs for another, perhaps even greater, set of costs, as recognized by generations of regulatory economists.[14] Choices are squarely in the economists' world of the "second-best," which dictates careful consideration of the cost and benefit trade-offs.

Economists have documented the tendency of regulation to increase costs in the regulated sector. Regulations may impede efficiency by distorting management's incentives to pursue aggressively lower cost production, as discussed in depth in Joskow's chapter. Regulators may introduce rules that directly increase costs, as for example, restrictions on the operating authorities of trucking companies that led to high incidence of empty backhauls, or entry and merger restrictions that kept banks in many states at an inefficiently small scale. By suppressing price competition, regulation may induce firms to compete on nonprice dimensions, escalating the quality and cost of providing service. This was a well-recognized problem in the regulated airline industry by the early 1970s (see Borenstein and Rose). Reforms that substitute market outcomes for regulatory decision making have led to improvements in the efficiency of generating power plants facing competitive markets instead of regulated prices (Wolak, chapter 4, this volume; Fabrizio, Rose, and Wolfram 2007; Davis and Wolfram 2012), reduced freight costs through elimination of empty backhauls and circuitous routing in trucking and increased railroad efficiency (e.g., Ellig 2002; Winston 1998), and increased airline productivity through both lower operating costs per available seat mile and higher load factors (Borenstein and Rose, chapter 2, this volume).

Regulated price structures may distort consumption decisions. "Allocative efficiency" results when prices signal consumers to use goods or services when their value to the consumer is above the production cost of the good but not otherwise, and allocate scarce goods to their highest value use. In some settings, including many of the deregulated transportation sectors, regulated prices were higher than competitive levels, and it was easy to convince consumers (though perhaps not other stakeholders) that reform was desirable. In other settings, the efficient price may be higher than the regulated price. It is hard to convince consumers who otherwise would have been able to purchase at a lower price that a postreform price increase was, in fact, beneficial for the overall economy. Finally, regulation may alter the structure of prices, affecting transfers across customer groups and distorting consumption patterns and entry decisions (e.g., Davis and Muehlegger 2010).

The welfare loss from allocative inefficiency can be large. For example, Lucas Davis and Lutz Kilian (2011) analyze the impact of natural gas wellhead price ceilings, which were in place through 1989. These ceilings reduced prices for consumers lucky enough to have access to natural gas, but also

14. See, for example, discussions from Kahn (1970–71, 1979) to Joskow (2009, 2010).

discouraged natural gas exploration and production, and led to shortages and rationing of access to natural gas. Davis and Kilian show that the economic dislocations caused by these regulations persisted long after the price ceilings were abandoned, and estimate that the welfare cost of these artificially low prices averaged $3.6 billion *per year* (in 2000 dollars) between 1950 and 2000.

The dynamic impact of regulation on the economy may swamp static costs and benefits. As noted earlier, economic regulation may distort incentives for investment and innovation by regulated firms, shift risks from investors to consumers or other stakeholder groups, and substitute bureaucratic oversight for managerial judgment in investment and new product introduction decisions. This theme appears throughout the studies in this volume, as highlighted in Crawford's discussion of cable regulation, Hausman and Sidak's analysis of telecommunications reform, and Danzon and Keuffel's examination of pharmaceutical regulation.

This may not be surprising: regulating well is very difficult. Regulators typically have far less information on the markets they regulate than do the firms whose activities they oversee, confront limited resources in executing their oversight roles, and may themselves have weak incentives to achieve the outcomes that generate the greatest social welfare. As Civil Aeronautics Board chairman and regulatory scholar Fred Kahn recalled saying in the 1978 debate over airline deregulation, "If I knew what was the most efficient configuration of routes in the airline system, then I could continue to regulate. But since I can't tell you whether it's going to be a Delta kind of operation or . . . more like the Eastern shuttle or Southwest Airlines it doesn't make sense to leave it to an ignorant person like me to tell airlines how they can best configure their routes" (Kahn 2000). The dramatic changes in airline network and pricing structures that followed deregulation substantiate his argument.

Moreover, once the "coercive power" of the state (Stigler 1971) has been invoked to regulate an industry, the injection of politics into the process may yield outcomes far from those envisioned by the social welfare maximizing economist. Carlton and Picker describe the process of regulatory rent-seeking across a number of industries, from railroads to trucking to telecommunications. They note that antitrust jurisdiction over regulated sectors may help to check agencies' temptation to align with the interests of the industry they regulate, citing, for example, MCI's successful monopolization challenge against AT&T in the 1970s. Zitzewitz echoes this message in his discussion of retail securities industry regulation, noting a long-standing criticism of the Securities and Exchange Commission (SEC), that identification with the industry it is charged with regulating has led it to focus "more aggressive enforcement action against misconduct by rogue individuals (broker fraud, insider trading) than against more systemic forms of misconduct (analyst conflicts, mutual fund compliance issues, earnings management)" (chapter 9, this volume).

Political capture may not be the only, or even primary, concern. Regulatory rulemaking is intentionally cumbersome, in part to ensure some stability of the political bargain, enfranchise competing interests with a voice in the process, and counteract capture by the regulated industry. But as noted earlier, that stolidity makes regulators far from agile in responding to changing conditions or challenges. The more dynamic is the industry, the greater the potential cost of these frictions.

Determining the desirability of government intervention therefore requires a careful assessment of the costs of imperfect markets relative to the costs and benefits of imperfect regulation, with full recognition of the inevitable shortcomings in each. As the studies in this volume reveal, this calculus may reveal gains from more performance-based regulations in some settings, such as the distribution utilities Joskow analyzes. In other settings, exemplified by the airline and cable television industries, a market mediated primarily by competition policy can yield benefits over the more intrusive direction of price, product characteristic, or entry decisions by government agencies. And whenever some form of regulatory intervention is chosen, the returns to having a stable cadre of professional regulators with sufficient resources, knowledge, and skill to adapt efficiently to changes in the environment can be substantial.

The regulatory and policy responses subsequent to the 2008 financial crisis and the work in this volume suggest that many of the lessons elucidated here have yet to be fully recognized and embraced. This may reflect in significant part the political economy of regulation. But it may also arise in part from the lack of familiarity with or appreciation of the lessons accumulated in the study of decades of experience with regulation and regulatory reform across a multitude of sectors of the economy. It is our hope that the studies in this volume will help to fill this gap.

References

Adams, Christopher P., and Van Vu Brantner. 2010. "Spending on New Drug Development." *Health Economics* 19:130–41.

Bailey, Elizabeth E. 2010. "Air Transportation Deregulation." In *Better Living through Economics*, edited by John J. Siegfried, 188–202. Cambridge, MA: Harvard University Press.

Balleisen, Edward J., and David A. Moss, eds. 2010. *Government and Markets: Toward a New Theory of Regulation*. The Tobin Project. Cambridge: Cambridge University Press.

Bushnell, James B., Erin T. Mansur, and Celeste Saravia. 2008. "Vertical Arrangements, Market Structure, and Competition: An Analysis of Restructured US Electricity Markets." *American Economic Review* 98 (1): 237–66.

Coglianese, Gary, ed. 2012. *Regulatory Breakdown: The Crisis of Confidence in US Regulation.* Philadelphia: University of Pennsylvania Press.

Davis, Lucas, and Lutz Kilian. 2011. "The Allocative Cost of Price Ceilings in the US Residential Market for Natural Gas." *Journal of Political Economy* 119 (2): 212–41.

Davis, Lucas, and Erich Muehlegger. 2010. "Do Americans Consume Too Little Natural Gas? An Empirical Test of Marginal Cost Pricing." *RAND Journal of Economics* 41 (4): 791–810.

Davis, Lucas, and Catherine Wolfram. 2012. "Deregulation, Consolidation, and Efficiency: Evidence from US Nuclear Power." *American Economic Journal: Applied Economics* 4 (4): 194–225.

Derthick, Martha, and Paul J. Quirk. 1985. *The Politics of Deregulation.* Washington, DC: Brookings Institution.

Duggan, Mark, and Fiona Scott Morton. 2006. "The Distortionary Effects of Government Procurement: Evidence from Medicaid Prescription Drug Purchasing." *The Quarterly Journal of Economics* 121 (1): 1–30.

Ellig, Jerry. 2002. "Railroad Deregulation and Consumer Welfare." *Journal of Regulatory Economics* 21 (2): 143–67.

Fabrizio, Kira, Nancy L. Rose, and Catherine Wolfram. 2007. "Do Markets Reduce Costs? Assessing the Impact of Regulatory Restructuring on US Electric Generation Efficiency." *American Economic Review* 97 (5): 1250–77.

Fullerton, Don, and Catherine Wolfram, eds. 2012. *The Design and Implementation of US Climate Policy.* National Bureau of Economic Research Conference Report. Chicago: University of Chicago Press.

Grajek, Michał, and Lars-Hendrik Röller. 2012. "Regulation and Investment in Network Industries: Evidence from European Telecoms." *Journal of Law and Economics* 55 (1): 189–216.

Hausman, Jerry A. 1997. "Valuing the Effect of Regulation on New Services in Telecommunications." *Brookings Papers on Economic Activity, Microeconomics*: 1–54.

Joskow, Paul L. 1974. "Inflation and Environmental Concern: Structural Change in the Process of Public Utility Price Regulations." *Journal of Law and Economics* 17 (2): 291–327.

———. 2009. *Deregulation: Where Do We Go from Here?* Washington, DC: AEI Press.

———. 2010. "Market Imperfections versus Regulatory Imperfections." *CESifo DICE Report* 8 (3): 3–7.

Joskow, Paul L., and Roger G. Noll. 1994. "Economic Regulation during the 1980s." In *Economic Policy during the 1980s*, edited by Martin Feldstein, 367–462. Chicago: University of Chicago Press.

Joskow, Paul L., and Nancy L. Rose. 1989. "The Effects of Economic Regulation." In *Handbook of Industrial Organization*, vol. 2, edited by Richard L. Schmalensee and Robert Willig, 1449–506. Amsterdam: North-Holland.

Kahn, Alfred E. 1970–71. *The Economics of Regulation: Principles and Institutions.* 2 vols. New York: John Wiley & Sons. Reprinted with a new introduction in one volume in 1988. Cambridge, MA: MIT Press.

———. 1979. "Applications of Economics to an Imperfect World." *The American Economic Review* 69 (2): 1–13.

———. 1988. "I Would Do It Again." *Regulation* 22 (2): 22–28.

———. 2000. "Interview with A. E. Kahn." Public Broadcasting System *First Mea-*

sured Century: A Look at American History by the Numbers. Ben Wattenberg, host. Accessed January 1, 2012. http://www.pbs.org/fmc/interviews/kahn.htm.

Kamita, Rene Y. 2010. "Analyzing the Effects of Temporary Antitrust Immunity: The Aloha-Hawaiian Immunity Agreement." *Journal of Law and Economics* 53 (2): 239–61.

Kessler, Daniel P., ed. 2010. *Regulation vs. Litigation: Perspectives from Economics and Law.* National Bureau of Economic Research Conference Report. Chicago: University of Chicago Press.

Laffont, Jean-Jacques, and Jean Tirole. 1993. *A Theory of Incentives in Regulation and Procurement.* Cambridge, MA: MIT Press.

Landy, Mark K., Martin A. Levin, and Martin Shapiro. 2007. *Creating Competitive Markets: The Politics of Regulatory Reform.* Washington, DC: Brookings Institution.

Lazarus, David. 2013. "The Myth of Deregulation's Consumer Benefits." *Los Angeles Times.* February 14. http://articles.latimes.com/print/2013/feb/14/business/la-fi-lazarus-20130215.

Lo, Andrew W. 2012. "Reading about the Financial Crisis: A Twenty-One-Book Review." *Journal of Economic Literature* 50 (1): 151–78.

Longman, Phillip, and Lina Khan. 2012. "Terminal Sickness." *Washington Monthly,* March/April. Accessed October 12, 2012. http://www.washingtonmonthly.com/magazine/march_april_2012/features/terminal_sickness035756.php?page=3.

Meltzer, Allan. 2009. "Regulation Usually Fails." In *The American, the Online Magazine of the American Enterprise Institute.* February 11. http://www.american.com/archive/2009/february-2009/regulation-usually-fails/article_print.

Noll, Roger. 1989. "Economic Perspectives on the Politics of Regulation." In *Handbook of Industrial Organization,* vol. 2, edited by Richard L. Schmalensee and Robert Willig, 1253–87. Amsterdam: North-Holland.

Peltzman, Sam. 1989. "The Economic Theory of Regulation after a Decade of Deregulation." *Brookings Papers on Economic Activity, Microeconomics:* 1–60.

Romano, Roberta. 2014. "Regulating in the Dark." *Hofstra Law Review,* forthcoming.

Rose, Nancy L. 2012. "After Airline Deregulation and Alfred E. Kahn." *American Economic Review Papers and Proceedings* 102 (May): 376–80.

Stigler, George. 1971. "The Theory of Economic Regulation." *Bell Journal of Economics* 2 (2): 3–21.

Stiglitz, Joseph E. 2009. "Regulation and Failure." In *New Perspectives on Regulation,* edited by David Moss and John Cisternino, 11–23. Cambridge: The Tobin Project.

Surowiecki, James. 2010. "The Regulation Crisis." *The New Yorker,* June 14. http://www.newyorker.com/talk/financial/2010/06/14/100614ta_talk_surowiecki.

Winston, Clifford. 1993. "Economic Deregulation: Days of Reckoning for Microeconomists." *Journal of Economic Literature* 31 (3): 1263–89.

———. 1998. "US Industry Adjustment to Economic Deregulation." *Journal of Economic Perspectives* 12 (3): 89–110.

Wolak, Frank. 2007. "Quantifying the Supply-Side Benefits from Forward Contracting in Wholesale Electricity Markets." *Journal of Applied Econometrics* 22:1179–209.

Antitrust and Regulation

Dennis W. Carlton and Randal C. Picker

Within a brief span of time, Congress adopted the Interstate Commerce Act (1887) and the Sherman Act (1890). In imposing federal regulation on railroads, the Interstate Commerce Act inaugurated the era of substantial federal regulation of individual industries, while the Sherman Act created a baseline for the control of competition in the United States by generally barring contracts in restraint of trade and forbidding monopolization. The rise of the railroads and the great trusts raised concerns about economic power and spurred politicians to formulate a national policy toward competition. Since 1890, policymakers have been forced repeatedly to work through how to interleave a fully general approach to competition under the antitrust laws with industry-specific approaches to competition under regulatory statutes.

This has been a learning process, but even without learning, shifting political winds would naturally lead to fits and starts as antitrust and specific regulatory statutes have jostled and combined and sometimes even competed in establishing a framework for controlling competition. After more

Dennis W. Carlton is the David McDaniel Keller Professor of Economics at the University of Chicago Booth School of Business and a research associate of the National Bureau of Economic Research. Randal C. Picker is the James Parker Hall Distinguished Service Professor of Law at the University of Chicago Law School and a senior fellow at the Computation Institute of the University of Chicago and Argonne National Laboratory.

Randal C. Picker thanks the Paul Leffmann Fund, the Russell J. Parsons Faculty Research Fund, and the John M. Olin Program in Law and Economics at the University of Chicago Law School for their generous research support, and through the Olin Program, Microsoft Corporation and Verizon. We thank Andrew Brinkman for research assistance and Thomas Barnett, Timothy Bresnahan, Richard Epstein, Jacob Gersen, Al Klevorick, Lynette Neumann, Gregory Pelnar, Sam Peltzman, Richard Posner, Nancy Rose, and the participants of the NBER conference on regulation for their helpful comments. For acknowledgments, sources of research support, and disclosure of the authors' material financial relationships, if any, please see http://www.nber.org/chapters/c12565.ack.

than a century of effort, it is possible to advance a few general conclusions. Antitrust can say no, but struggles with saying yes. Less cryptically, antitrust is a poor framework for price setting or for establishing affirmative duties toward rivals. Price setting in a nonmarket context often requires detailed industry knowledge and often turns on political decisions about levels of service and the rate of return to capital needed to provide those services. The virtue and vice of federal judges is they are generalists, not industry specialists, and, once appointed, they are insulated from the political process. If there is a natural monopoly and prices need to be set or we are going to create a duty to, say, share an incumbent's phone network with an entrant, the evidence suggests that it is generally best to do that, if at all, through (enlightened) regulation, not antitrust, though obviously poor regulation can impose enormous costs.

However, antitrust says no very well, while regulators often have a hard time saying no. Area-specific regulation through special agencies gives rise to the fear that the regulators will be captured by the regulated industry (or other interest groups). Regulators will have come from industry or will dream of exiting to private sector salaries. Regulators will not say no often enough to proposals that benefit special interests. But federal judges are genuinely independent (or, at least, more so than regulators) and the docket of the federal judiciary is completely general. A general antitrust statute, implemented by independent federal judges—limited to issues within their competence—can protect the competitive process, especially with the rise of economic reasoning in antitrust.

Our main conclusion is that in the century-long seesaw battle over how to design competition policy, the Sherman Act has turned out to be more enduring than regulation. As the difficulties of regulation have emerged and as economic reasoning has improved the effectiveness of the Sherman Act, enforcement of the Sherman Act through an independent judiciary has shown itself to deliver lower prices and less promotion of special interests than regulation, causing a shift away from regulation. This does not, of course, mean that all regulation should vanish, especially for industries with natural monopoly characteristics, but rather that, when necessary, regulation should try to allow as much competition as possible, constrained only by antitrust law. Where activities in an industry remain partially regulated, antitrust and regulation can be used together in a complementary way to control competition and, in some cases, it is possible to use antitrust as a constraint on regulators.

This chapter is divided into three sections. First, we consider the general question of how competition policy should be implemented. We do this by considering possible roles for courts and regulatory agencies as set out in the modern political science literature on legislative bargaining. We analyze the relative advantages and disadvantages of regulation versus antitrust as a means of formulating competition policy. Industries will frequently seek to establish a sharp boundary between the industry and antitrust by obtaining a legislative antitrust immunity for the industry. Being outside of antitrust means that the industry members can act without fear of antitrust liability. But the industry might want more; it might want a federal regulator's help in enforcing cartel deals or in blocking entry by potential competitors. In those cases, industries may want more than mere exclusion from antitrust; they will want affirmative industry regulation and a regulator with enforcement power.

Second, we return to the beginning of the formulation of competition policy by considering the period starting with the Interstate Commerce Act and the Sherman Act. This history illustrates the initial view of regulation and antitrust as two competing alternatives to control competition, but with some recognition that the two would interact in unforeseen ways. We pursue the central question that dominated early competition policy and remains a central policy question, namely, how should prices be set?

Third, we turn our attention to a group of industries that have been a focus of regulation for over one hundred years—network industries—and analyze their recent development. In many of these industries—particularly the transportation industries, such as airlines, trucking, and railroads—we have moved powerfully away from regulation and have largely deregulated those industries. Deregulation effectively shifts relative authority for regulating competition away from industry regulators and, absent a legislative antitrust immunity, toward general antitrust enforcement. In these industries, deregulation has lifted artificial barriers to integration, and we have seen these industries respond by moving toward greater vertical integration, thereby eliminating interconnection and other dealings difficulties and possible double marginalization. In the network industries that remain heavily regulated—for example, electricity and telecommunications—we address the fundamental question that has occupied and continues to occupy regulatory and antitrust decisions in those industries: how should those markets be structured and specifically what sort of mandatory access rights should be established? We use this recent history to illustrate the movement away from regulation toward antitrust, with the two being used as complements to control competition in some industries.

1.1 Assigning Responsibility for Controlling Competition

We begin by framing the general problem faced by Congress and the president in choosing whether and to what extent to delegate implementation of a policy to a third party. The delegation will take the form of legislation and the scope of the delegation may be determined in part by the specificity of the language used in the statute. We want to address that problem generally and then turn to what that means for the interaction of antitrust and regulation.

1.1.1 The General Setting

Under the US Constitution, laws are enacted when the Senate, the House, and the president each vote in favor of a proposed bill. This is a simplified statement in that it ignores the possibility that Congress has sufficient votes (two-thirds in each chamber) to override a veto by the president. It also skips over the interesting and tricky issue of the extent to which domestic legislation can be set through the treaty-making power, where the president is empowered to make treaties, provided that two-thirds of the Senate vote in favor.

Following McCubbins, Noll, and Weingast (1989), we treat the process of creating legislation as a principal/agent problem or, more precisely and more interestingly, as a three principal/multiple agents problem. It is conventional (see, e.g., Shepsle and Bonchek 1997, 358–68) in the rational choice literature in political science to model legislation as a principal delegating power to an agent, where either a court or an agency acts as the agent in implementing the legislation. In the principal/agent problem faced in creating legislation, Congress and the president typically delegate to one of two agents: Article III courts or specialized agencies subject to court oversight. By institutional design, Congress and the president have relatively weak controls against the judiciary—we call this separation of powers—but, together and separately, the House, Senate, and president can choose to retain stronger control over agencies.

Focus on a standard principal/agent problem; namely, that the agent will depart from the principal's goals and pursue his own. In the political science literature, this is labeled as the problem of bureaucratic drift. For legislation to get passed, the House, Senate, and president negotiate over potential policies. But delegation is inevitable: judges decide actual cases, not Congress or the president, and with the rise of the administrative state, implementation of legislation can be delegated directly to courts or first to agencies with appeals to courts (and judicial review of agency action need not be a given).

The negotiation process that results in unanimous agreement by the House, Senate, and president on new legislation has to take into account what will happen in the subsequent delegation to courts or agencies. Each player in the negotiation game should do backwards induction looking forward to see how the agent will actually implement the enacted legislation, and in light of that, design the legislation. (The players could just care about enactment and not about implementation if that is how their constituencies keep score, but we will assume that all participants are interested in actual results, and not just appearances.) To match the political science literature, treat the House (H), Senate (S), president (P), and agent as each having preferences over the particular policy in question and focus on the essential dynamic that takes place among our four players. After negotiation, unanimity is reached and a bill is passed (absent unanimity nothing happens). The agent now implements the legislation.

What constrains how the agent does so? Consider possible sources of restrictions: the original legislation, oversight and monitoring, internal agency norms, and the threat of subsequent legislation. Focus initially on the possibility of constraint through subsequent legislation that overturns the decision of the agent. Note that this legislation requires a unanimous vote among H, S, and P, as any one of them has the power to block a change from the new status quo defined by the agent's decision. As an initial cut, the agent then has a free hand to implement her policy preferences rather than implement with fidelity the deal struck among H, S, and P. So if the agent's policy preferences matched P more closely, the agent could implement a policy that P would find superior to the deal captured in the negotiated legislation, and P would veto any subsequent legislative effort to overturn the agent's decision.

This does not mean that the new status quo would remain, but any new law negotiated among H, S, and P would need to make P better off than he is under the agent's decision. And in the face of that law, the agent could once again refuse to implement the deal negotiated and instead implement her policy preferences. Of course, none of this should be lost on H, S, and P when they negotiate the original law. Again, they will care about how the legislation is actually implemented, not the deal cut. H, S, and P can anticipate bureaucratic drift. If H and S know that the agent will deviate from the original statute in the direction of P with the agent's action protected by P's veto, H and S will never make the deal in the first place. A little bit of backwards induction goes a long way.

We quickly see the complexities of having a process involving delegation. The agent can try to implement his own agenda, deviating from the original intent, but not enough to induce intervention by the principals. Moreover, if H has been delegated control over the agent, H can cheat on the agreement with HSP and deviate from the original agreement. If a congressman wants to try to cheat on the original legislative deal, he can do so if he can exert power over his agent. As Landes and Posner (1979) argued in their explanation of the role of an independent judiciary, the congressman can commit to not cheating by relinquishing his power over the agent. At the same time, giving up control over the agent means that the agent now has freedom to implement her own policy preferences. If someone's hands are tied at the front end, it equals loss of control at the back end. If the agent does not face meaningful discipline, why should the agent pay much (any?) attention to the statute at all?

But at the same time, independence means that the agent can implement her preferences in the veto zone; that is, the spots in the policy space where Congress and the president will not agree unanimously to overturn the agent's decision. And the fact will be anticipated by the institutional players who will be disadvantaged by the deviation. They will not want independence in their agent and will instead want to design controls over the agent that make fidelity to the original deal possible.

This would be true if H, S, and P were just seeking to implement their own independent policy preferences, but it would also be true if we think of the lawmakers as just selling off legislation to the highest bidder (or as having preferences that value both legislative outcomes and transfers from legislation buyers). H, S, and P will also want controls on themselves, at least as a group, so that they can ensure that their control over the agent does not allow them to cheat on the original deal that was cut amongst themselves or with the legislation purchaser. After the fact, they would like to cheat, either individually or as a group, but that too will be anticipated by the legislation purchaser, so H, S, and P need a commitment mechanism to maximize the amount that they can charge legislation purchasers.

We can sketch out what such a system might look like. Consider a basic public choice model with an interested party simply purchasing legislation that will be implemented by an agent. We can offer H, S, and P each some levers of oversight over the agent. That may be enough to solve the problem of the agent cheating. H needs to have sufficient individual power to block moves by the agent away from the original law, and so too for S and P. Or we need to make sure that the legislation purchaser can exercise oversight powers against H, S, and P to make sure that they faithfully implement the original deal bought and paid for by the legislation purchaser.

What should our legislation purchaser fear more, cheating by the principal or cheating by the agent? Purchasers have little control over Article III judges and much more control over congressional principals and agency agents. Both of these should push the legislation purchaser toward favoring a captive agency. Legislation purchasers are well situated to punish a member of Congress who cheats on the original deal by imposing her will on the agency. Members of Congress run every two years (House) or six years (Senate) and are constantly raising money for reelection (the best way to discourage competing candidates is to amass a large pile of money). A member who cheats on a deal with a legislation purchaser reveals himself to be a poor candidate for future deals and future campaign contributions. The need to return to the market for campaign funds disciplines members of Congress from using their influence on agents to cheat on the original deal that was cut. In contrast, legislation buyers can exercise little indirect or direct control over judges, since Congress and the president both lack control over Article III judges.

We should make one other point about this structure. Agency decisions are typically subject to appeals to independent federal judges. This would seem to make the judges the ultimate authority, but that largely depends upon what judges do with agency actions. Under the Supreme Court's *Chevron* doctrine (*Chevron, Inc. v. Natural Resources Defense Council*, 467 U.S.

837, 1984), judges give agencies wide latitude in interpreting federal statutes. Not unlimited latitude, but *Chevron* is a policy of substantial deference to agencies. *Chevron* deference creates an agent largely outside of judicial control, and therefore subject to meaningful congressional control. This in turn means that Congress and the president can more credibly commit to those seeking legislation by delegating to independent agencies than it can to Article III courts. *Chevron* preserves broad independence for agencies as against the courts—thereby making them into actors that elected officials can control—while appeals to courts operate as a hedge against agents who have deviated too far from what their principals wanted.

1.1.2 Agent Choice in Antitrust and Regulated Industries

On July 2, 1890, Congress passed the Sherman Act and in so doing created a baseline for the control of competition in the United States. To the modern eye, the Sherman Act is notable for its simultaneous brevity and comprehensiveness. The entire statute is set forth in eight sections and barely covers more than one page in the *Statutes at Large*. Section 1 condemned every contract in restraint of trade and Section 2 made a criminal of every person who monopolized.

The Sherman Act: Court or Agency?

Why was the Sherman Act implemented in the federal courts and not through a federal agency? Consider a little history. At the time that the Sherman Act was passed, the Interstate Commerce Commission was still a baby, a bold experiment in a highly specialized but central industry. It would have been a sizable leap of faith to apply the same mechanism to the entire economy. The natural, conservative move was to use the federal courts. Moreover, to fast-forward twenty-five years to 1914, we did take a step in that direction when we created the Federal Trade Commission (more on that at the end of section 1.2).

The agency choice literature (Fiorina 1982; Stephenson 2005) compares the relative stability of decision making in agencies and courts. Commissions typically are small and are controlled by the party of the president; the president also chooses the chair of the commission (this was roughly how the ICC worked and is how the FCC and FTC work today). Turnover of the presidency means turnover of the commission. Commissions therefore may exhibit high variance across periods of time—a Democratic FTC looks different from a Republican FTC—but greater coherence among related decisions made within a particular window. By contrast, the federal courts are quite stable over time, but are subject to very little control at any point in time. But the sheer number of judges means that two contemporaneous decisions may reach quite different outcomes.

This helps to explain why in 1887 an agency was a relatively more attractive choice for railroads than it was for the general economy. The railroads were the first great network industry (we could fight about canals). The nature of a network is that regulatory decisions in one part of the network can have large effects in other parts of the network. That is true whether the inconsistent decisions are about technical matters or about rate decisions and what those decisions mean for the recovery of fixed costs. So if one regulator sets a track gauge of 5 feet, while another sets it at 4 feet, 6 inches, the network will operate inefficiently given the inconsistent technical standards.

In a similar fashion, inconsistent rate structures across parts of a network can make it quite difficult to recover fixed costs. In the early days of railroad regulation, state regulators were setting low rates for intrastate shipments, hoping to keep the railroads solvent on the back of interstate rates. The Supreme Court understood that fully when it decided *Smyth v. Ames* in 1898 (169 U.S. 466, 1898). In *Smyth*, the Court addressed the scope of constitutional protection for rate setting for railroads and limited state rate making that the Court concluded could be confiscatory. The same tracks would be used for intrastate and interstate shipments, and giving state rate setters free reign for intrastate state rates would force up interstate rates or push the railroads toward insolvency. For network industries, piecemeal regulation can create expensive and even insurmountable inconsistencies.

But outside of railroads, in the rest of the economy around the beginning of the twentieth century, regional inconsistencies in industry practices were less important. If the Second Circuit reached one antitrust outcome and the Seventh Circuit another, the greater the extent to which economic activity was local or regional, the less that these regulatory differences mattered. Local (uncoordinated) antitrust enforcement, whether federally at the circuit level or by states, was less costly to the economy when the economy was more of a local economy than it is today.

When many parts in the economic system need to move at the same time—when we are speaking of coevolution, as it were, rather than just evolution—it may be very hard for lower federal courts to coordinate decision making, and Supreme Court decisions are rare and slow to come. The inefficiency in a network industry of having uncoordinated decision making could be very high. Plus courts are passive when it comes to agenda setting: they can only decide the cases that come before them. In contrast, agencies expressly control their own agendas, subject to the original statute to be sure, but tied down often by nothing more than a public interest standard. The ability to set agendas means that agencies can push forward on all parts of the economic system at the same time. Agencies can change a number of policies simultaneously and can do so sharply—moving from the existing framework to a substantially different spot in a process of punctuated equilibria—while courts have little control over agendas, can only decide the issues directly before them, and are normally limited to smaller moves consistent with judicial precedent. Our logic predicts that as policy concerns with competition arise in particular industries, all else being equal, network industries are more likely than nonnetwork industries to see their competition regulated by agencies, rather than the courts.

Boundary Definition in Regulation and Antitrust

After the ICC and Sherman Act were established, how did the evolution of competition policy in particular industries proceed? What guided assignments of tasks between regulation and antitrust? Every attempt to control competition after 1890—whether within antitrust proper or outside of antitrust in the form of area-specific regulation—must be understood in the context of the Sherman Act. Given its breadth, we might ask why weren't the antitrust laws sufficient to regulate all industries? The prevailing—but, to be sure, not universally held—view of antitrust law in the United States is that it is designed to promote efficiency by protecting the competitive process to benefit society. Why shouldn't that be enough?

Boundary definition should turn on the comparative advantages of regulation and antitrust. To grossly simplify, while both antitrust and regulation are a mix of economics and politics, antitrust is now organized around an economic core, while regulation is frequently shaped by the political process. To prolong this, while the decision by the Antitrust Division in the Department of Justice or by the Federal Trade Commission to bring a case may be influenced by politics, once a case is brought, the ultimate decision regarding the case is made by a federal judge.

If we believe that the agent making a decision should reflect public welfare, agencies (and the regulation that comes with them) are a superior tool to broad antitrust statutes implemented by federal judges. Judges have no particular ability or accountability in establishing quality standards of the sort that will inevitably be required in, for example, the electricity industry or telecommunications. Pricing in electricity, for example, will depend on our willingness to endure blackouts, and if we think that at least parts of the electricity system are a natural monopoly—the transmission grid itself—the government will almost certainly be involved in price setting. Judges have little if any ability to determine the public's tolerance for blackouts and we should want that to be determined as part of a political process. And we should expect that price setting here will require the consideration of huge amounts of specialized data. All of that suggests industry-specific regulation and accountable regulators, and not general rules for competition implemented by judges separated from overall social preferences.

At the same time, we need to recognize that regulatory carve-outs from antitrust can create risks to competition. These carve-outs define sharp boundaries between antitrust and regulation. Industries will often display two natural patterns in defining the boundaries between antitrust and regulation: antitrust immunity or affirmative regulation coupled with agency enforcement power, especially enforcement power directed at implementing industry agreements on prices or at blocking new entrants. One sharp boundary is a legislative antitrust immunity for a particular industry. The immunity effectively empowers the industry to implement voluntary agreements among the industry members. The immunity replaces antitrust control through courts not with a separate agency and new industry-specific regulation but instead with self-regulation by the industry. A naked antitrust immunity means no government competition regulation at all.

But an industry might want more. The antitrust immunity itself does not give the industry a means of enforcing deals within the industry nor does it offer a means of blocking new entry into the industry. It is one thing to have an industry cartel that is free of the fear of federal antitrust enforcement; it is quite another to have a cartel that is enforced either by federal legislation or by a federal regulator so as to allow the cartel to be more effective and one that ensures that no new competitors will emerge to boot. Cartel members have powerful incentives to cheat on the cartel and we expect cheating to put natural pressure on the sustainability of an anticompetitive agreement. But if federal regulation itself will help to sustain a cartel, then we should expect the industry to seek not just an antitrust immunity—a guarantee of no federal antitrust enforcement actions against the cartel—but instead to seek legislation or a federal regulator to guarantee the enforcement of the cartel agreement and to further limit possible competition by excluding entry.

We therefore expect that where an interest group is powerful but cannot control entry on its own it will combine an antitrust exemption with legislation that restricts entry, either directly in the statute, or in the face of uncertainty about the ways to preserve the cartel or about the ability to obtain future legislation, through an agency regulator. Failing that, the industry may prefer regulation to competition, with the regulator controlling entry and perhaps price. But as we know from the theory of political regulation, there are many interest groups that will have a voice in the regulatory process. Different groups of consumers and firms will have their own interests and compromises amongst them will be up to the regulator. It is unusual for a regulator to favor one group to the exclusion of all others, as Peltzman (1976) especially has shown (see also Stigler 1971; Posner 1974; and Becker 1983). Therefore, a very powerful interest group with clear goals on how to achieve cartelization would likely have a preference to obtain exemption with legislative entry restrictions rather than rely on regulation.

1.1.3   Antitrust Immunities

An unregulated industry subject only to the antitrust laws might seek an exemption from these laws for one of two reasons. The industry might want to avoid inefficiencies that the antitrust laws create. Alternatively, the industry might want to avoid the constraints of the antitrust laws and want to engage in anticompetitive behavior such as cartelization. Policing that line—separating good antitrust immunities from the bad—can be tricky.

In some circumstances, collective action might be required to achieve efficiency, but Section 1 flatly forbids any contract in restraint of trade. Many R&D and information gathering activities, as well as sports leagues organized as joint ventures, create a high risk of antitrust liability, as the history of antitrust cases demonstrates.[1] Farmer cooperatives are another example of how small firms may be able to achieve some economies by collective action but still remain independent firms that compete against each other. Often, these collaborative activities created no market power and only efficiencies but these could have faced Sherman Act actions, especially in the early days of antitrust. Indeed Bittlingmayer (1985) has argued that the Sherman Act created antitrust liability for cooperative activities among horizontal competitors and thereby encouraged the massive merger wave around 1900.

We may be able to solve this problem within antitrust proper through careful development of doctrine, but beneficial activity that is close to the antitrust line risks treble damages. Plus firms face individual liability if they end up on the wrong side of the line, while an improvement in antitrust doctrine benefits the industry as a whole. This mismatch between private costs and industry benefits means that for a particular industry, exemption from antitrust might be easier to implement than internal reform of antitrust doctrine through the courts.

Antitrust immunities also serve a channeling function for activities to influence competition policy. Absent the immunity, activity that influences competition policy takes place in the courts, before the Federal Trade Commission, and in Congress through the pursuit of new legislation. Immunity channels this competition, mainly to Congress. We can think of antitrust immunity as a commitment about how the policy game will be played, a commitment about where the next move will be made. It means that courts and agencies do not get to move, and that instead the next move will be made by the legislature, though, of course, that could be a future legislature, rather than the current legislature.

There are many important parts of the economy that have received exemptions from the antitrust laws. The major areas are:

- *Agriculture and Fishing.* The exemption allows cooperatives to form and even have joint marketing. Section 6 of the Clayton Act (15 U.S.C. § 17) protected certain labor, agricultural, and horticultural organizations, and the 1922 Capper-Volstead Act (7 U.S.C. §§ 291–292) addressed joint marketing associations. Section 1 of the Sherman Act is odd in that it does not allow two firms, each with no market power, to set price, even though together they have no ability to raise price. The per se treatment of such price fixing is presumably justified by the belief that such price setting can have no procompetitive purpose. An antitrust exemption

---

1. See, for example, *Maple Flooring Manufacturers Association v. United States*, 268 U.S. 563 (1925); and Carlton, Frankel, and Landes (2004).

for a particular industry allows this type of price-fixing to go forward without the fear of liability.

- *R&D Joint Ventures*. Similar to the case of agricultural cooperatives, the cooperation of rivals to achieve efficiencies in R&D can raise antitrust issues. Under the National Cooperative Research Act of 1984 (15 U.S.C. §§ 4301–4306) certain of those activities are exempt from challenge as per se illegal and antitrust's treble damage rule is called off.
- *Sports Leagues*. Sport leagues consist of competing teams that must cooperate in order to have a viable league. There have been numerous antitrust cases in sports because of the peculiar combination of competition and cooperation needed for a successful league. Today sports leagues often start as a separate single firm so as to avoid antitrust challenge. When Curt Flood sued baseball commissioner Bowie Kuhn to try to end baseball's reserve clause, the Supreme Court confirmed that the antitrust laws did not apply to baseball (though they apply to other sports) (*Flood v. Kuhn*, 407 U.S. 258, 1972). Congress later brought professional baseball's dealings with the players into antitrust, while leaving baseball's prior antitrust exemption otherwise in place (Curt Flood Act of 1998, Pub.L. 105-297). The Sports Broadcasting Act of 1961 (15 U.S.C. § 1291) allows leagues to act as one entity in negotiations with television without antitrust liability.
- *Ocean Shipping*. International cartels set rates for certain ocean shipping routes. Entry is not typically controlled, though on some routes entry is unlikely. The industry's antitrust exemption (46 U.S.C. § 40307) is sometimes defended (Pirrong 1992) on the grounds that the core does not exist and that, without the cartel, chaos would reign with frequent bankruptcies and unreliable service.
- *Webb-Pomerene*. Added in 1918, this act allows cartels to set the price for exports, presumably on the logic that the antitrust laws do not protect foreign consumers (15 U.S.C. § 61).
- *Colleges*. In response to an antitrust suit alleging that the top colleges agreed on a financial aid formula to use to give out scholarship aid, Congress passed the Higher Education Amendments of 1992 (Pub.L. 102-235) to allow colleges to agree on a common formula for financial aid free of possible antitrust liability without allowing colleges to discuss aid for any particular applicant.
- *Professional Societies*. Many societies such as those involving doctors and lawyers have the ability to influence entry into their profession. Although *Professional Engineers* (435 U.S. 679, 1978) has limited the scope of the exemption, it is still the case, for example, that medical societies control the number of doctors by specialty and limit the number of medical schools that can receive accreditation. The professional societies are given this exemption because they are also regulating the quality of the profession. In a recent antitrust attack on parts of the

medical profession, a group of residents brought an antitrust suit aimed at the medical schools, teaching hospitals, and professional societies for the medical residency system. In that system, doctors seeking advanced training are assigned one hospital to work at. There is limited competition for the resident. Legislation (Section 207 of the Pension Funding Equity Act of 2004 [Pub. L. 108-218]) was passed to declare that no antitrust liability results from the administration of the medical residency system, and the original lawsuit was dismissed (Robinson 2004).

- *Labor*. Unfavorable court decisions toward labor led eventually to the labor exemption. In 1908, the Supreme Court found a union liable under the antitrust laws for organizing a boycott of a particular firm's product (*Lowe v. Lawlor*, 208 U.S. 274, 1908). This decision caused labor to pressure Congress to declare in 1914 in the Clayton Act that labor organizations were exempt from the antitrust laws. A subsequent decision (*Duplex Printing Company v. Deering*, 254 U.S. 433, 1920) found that the unions could still be liable if they assisted other unions at another firm. This led to pressure to pass the Norris-La Guardia Act in 1932, which removed virtually all jurisdiction over labor from the federal courts (Benson, Greenhut, and Holcombe 1987).[2] As if that were not enough, since then, the federal courts have added a nonstatutory labor exemption to further limit the scope of potential antitrust liability in labor situations (*Brown v. Pro Football, Inc.*, 518 U.S. 231, 1996).

As a mechanism to establish an efficient competition policy, the use of immunities may be socially desirable in those instances where some collective action is needed for efficiency. Although some immunities may be described that way, others confer market power on the exempted industries to the detriment of society.

1.2   Control over Rates: The Rise of Antitrust and the Regulation of Railroads

We return to the early period of antitrust and regulation because it illustrates the interaction between explicit regulation and the Sherman Act. The Sherman Act was passed three years after the Commerce Act. The interaction between the two and the results of that interaction not only illustrate

2. This pattern of legislation and antitrust interacting—and specifically an antitrust case being a stimulus for either immunity or regulation—applies also to other industries that we do not discuss herein. For example, the *Southeastern Underwriters* case (322 U.S. 533, 1944) found that insurance companies had antitrust liability for rate agreements even in states that regulated rates. This discussion led to the passage of the McCarran-Ferguson Act, granting antitrust immunity where states regulated insurance. Similarly, *Otter Tail* (410 U.S. 366, 1973) found antitrust liability for an electric utility company for failure to interconnect with another utility even though the Federal Power Commission (FPC) could order such interconnection. The Court ruled that the FPC's powers were too limited. This decision led to legislation giving the Federal Energy Regulatory Commission (the renamed FPC) greater powers to force interconnection.

the economic forces at work that we have discussed, but also have shaped the subsequent development of competition policy for the century. The history highlights the early view of regulation and antitrust as substitutes for each other with a recognition that the two might interact through unforeseen ways.

The Interstate Commerce Act was adopted on February 4, 1887. The new law addressed the operation of interstate railroads and limited rates to those that were "reasonable and just." The statute barred more general "unjust discrimination" and "undue or unreasonable preferences," and made unlawful long-haul/short-haul discrimination. The act also addressed directly competition among railroads by barring contracts among competing railroads for the pooling of freight traffic.

Pools dividing freight and profit had been common before the passage of the Commerce Act and indeed had been created openly in an effort to control competition among railroads (Grodinsky 1950). The structure of the railroad business prior to the Commerce Act created incentives to raise and stabilize rates through cartels and pools (Hilton 1966). The number of railroads competing on a particular route was usually small and fixed costs were high. The former meant that the costs of agreeing and monitoring that agreement were relatively low. The irreversibility of the investments in the track meant that competitors were locked into place and could not move elsewhere if the level of demand would not support multiple competitors. Absent cartels, the incentive to have rate wars was great.

We can think of the initial regulation of railroads as a search for an institutional structure that protected shippers from monopoly power and discrimination while making it possible for railroad investors to earn competitive rates of return. The Interstate Commerce Act limited competition among railroads, while also protecting local shippers against perceived discrimination in rates. (Whether this was a net plus or minus for the railroads is an issue we do not address here—for a discussion of this issue see Gilligan, Marshall, and Weingast 1989.) The Sherman Act was passed three years after the Commerce Act, without a clear indication of how the two acts should interact. We now turn to that interaction and its consequences.

1.2.1 The Interaction of the Sherman Act with the Interstate Commerce Act: The Problem of *Trans-Missouri*

The Sherman Act said nothing specific about railroads. Did the Sherman Act cover railroads, too, or should we think that the more specific, if somewhat earlier, provisions of the Interstate Commerce Act controlled railroads? These questions were posed to the courts in January of 1892, when the United States brought an action to dissolve the Trans-Missouri Freight Association. The Trans-Missouri Association had been formed in March of 1889 as a joint rate setting organization. While Section 5 of the Interstate Commerce Act barred contracts regarding pooling of freight or division of profits, it said nothing about rate setting organizations. Indeed, the Trans-Missouri group filed its agreement with the ICC as required by Section 6 of the Commerce Act.

The Supreme Court decided *Trans-Missouri* on March 22, 1897. In a 5–4 decision, the Court rejected both the idea that railroads were somehow exempt from the Sherman Act given the more direct regulatory structure set forth in the Commerce Act and that the Sherman Act condemned only unreasonable restraints of trade. Understanding the language of the Sherman Act to have meant what it "plainly imports"—condemning all restraints of trade—the Court condemned the private rate setting of the railroad association and squarely inserted the Sherman Act into the everyday economic life of the country.

Where did that leave rate setting for railroads? Two months later, on May 24, 1897, the Court announced its opinion in *Cincinnati, New Orleans, and Texas Pacific Railway* (167 U.S. 479, 1897). This case considered whether the ICC had the power to set rates. Yes, the Commerce Act required rates to be "reasonable and just" and declared unreasonable and unjust rates unlawful. Yes, the Interstate Commerce Commission was to enforce the act, but the statute only expressly authorized the commission to issue a cease-and-desist order. The Supreme Court held that the ICC could do no more than that and that the ICC lacked the affirmative power to set rates. The power to set rates, said the Court, was "a legislative, and not an administrative or judicial, function" and given the stakes, this meant that "Congress has transferred such a power to any administrative body is not to be presumed or implied from any doubtful and uncertain language."

Thus *Trans-Missouri* turned private collective railroad rate setting into an antitrust violation, and under the *Cincinnati* ruling, the ICC could do no more than reject rates. Where would rate-setting authority lie? The Sherman Act was to be enforced in the courts, and through its decisions, the Supreme Court had severely constrained the ICC (Rabin 1986). At one level, the *Trans-Missouri* decision dominated railroad and antitrust policy for the next decade; at another level, the decision was largely irrelevant. As to the latter, the Interstate Commerce Commission stated in its 1901 annual report:

> It is not the business of this Commission to enforce the antitrust act, and we express no opinion as to the legality of the means adopted by these associations. We simply call attention to the fact that the decision of the United States Supreme Court in the Trans-Missouri case and the Joint Traffic Association case has produced no practical effect upon the railway operations of the country. Such associations, in fact, exist now as they did before those decisions, and with the same general effect. In justice to all parties we ought probably to add that it is difficult to see how our interstate railways could be operated, with due regard to the interests of the shipper and the railway, without concerted action of the kind afforded to these associations. (15th Annual ICC Report, January 17, 1902, p. 16)

But in another way, the *Trans-Missouri* decision framed the country's consideration of the trust question and the related question of how to grapple with large agglomerations of capital, as Sklar (1988) demonstrates in his history of the period. This decision seemingly satisfied no one.

1.2.2   Solving *Trans-Missouri*

If the ICC was right—if the economic structure of railroads required coordinated rate setting, either privately or through the government—the path forward was through revised legislation. Theodore Roosevelt became president when McKinley was assassinated in September 1901. In February 1903, Roosevelt moved forward on two fronts. The Elkins Act of 1903 gave the Interstate Commerce Commission the independent authority to seek relief in federal courts in situations in which railroads were charging less than published rates or were engaging in forbidden discrimination. Under the original Commerce Act, the ICC could act only on the petition of an injured party. The Elkins Act increased the ICC's power, but it still did not have an independent rate-setting power. Three years later, the Hepburn Act of 1906 took a first step in that direction. It added oil pipelines to the substantive scope of the act, and gave the ICC the power to set maximum rates, once it had found a prior rate unjust and unreasonable.

But Roosevelt, unwilling to rely solely on the Sherman Act to control general competition policy, was also looking for a way to exert more regulatory pressure on the rest of the economy. On February 14, 1903, Congress created a new executive department to be known as the Department of Commerce and Labor. Within the new department, the statute created the Bureau of Corporations. The bureau was designed to be an investigatory body with power to subpoena whose mission was to investigate any corporation engaged in interstate commerce to produce information and recommendations for legislation. But all of this information was to flow through the president, who in turn had the power to release industries from scrutiny. Railroads were expressly excluded. The design of the Bureau of Corporations matched Roosevelt's conception of the presidency as the bully pulpit. The bureau would give Roosevelt the information that he needed to go to the public or to Congress, plus the fact that the release of the information was within Roosevelt's power gave him leverage in negotiations with corporations.

After winning the presidency in 1904, Roosevelt continued to pursue his progressive agenda. Roosevelt called for an expansion of federal control over railroads—greater control over entry and issuance of securities, while allowing private railroad agreements on rates subject to approval by the Interstate Commerce Commission. At the same time, Roosevelt wanted a broad expansion in federal powers over large corporations engaged in interstate activities. He called for a federal incorporation law, or a federal licensing act, or some combination of the two. But by 1909, the Hepburn Bill, Roosevelt's vehicle for these changes, was dead in committee, and with it died Roosevelt's attempt for greater direct federal regulation of competition policy.

William Howard Taft succeeded Roosevelt as president in 1909. Taft supported the Mann-Elkins Act of 1910, which created a new, limited subject matter jurisdiction court, the United States Court of Commerce. It was staffed with five judges from the federal judiciary. The new Commerce Court was given exclusive jurisdiction of all appeals from ICC orders and appeals from the Commerce Court went to the Supreme Court.

Consider the Commerce Court in light of our prior general analysis of the choice between agencies and courts. Our earlier discussion suggested that federal courts of general jurisdiction would be poorly situated to deal with network industries. As Frankfurter and Landis (1928, 154) recognized, federal courts of general jurisdiction resulted in "conflicts in court decisions begetting territorial diversity where unified treatment of a problem is demanded, nullification by a single judge, even temporarily, of legislative or administrative action affecting whole sections of the country." A federal court of specialized jurisdiction would make possible many of the benefits of agencies—in particular, the ability to make coherent, contemporaneous decisions—while creating more independence than an agency would have.

The new Commerce Court took over a large number of cases then spread throughout the federal judiciary. The court was instantly busy and, almost as quickly, reviled by the public (Ripley 1913). The Commerce Court became the flashpoint for the "railroad problem"; as Frankfurter and Landis (1928, 164) put it, "[p]robably no court has ever been called upon to adjudicate so large a volume of litigation of as far-reaching import in so brief a time."

The Commerce Court failed. The public saw the ICC as protecting shippers from the power of the railroads, while the Commerce Court frequently overturned ICC decisions to the detriment of shippers. As Kolko (1965, 199) puts it in describing a series of Commerce Court decisions that were seen to benefit the railroads, "the Commerce Court proceeded to make itself the most unpopular judicial institution in a nation then in the process of attacking the sanctity of the courts." When Woodrow Wilson became president, he quickly signed legislation ending the Commerce Court, which came to final death on December 31, 1913. Its demise illustrates the power of shippers to protect themselves in ways that antitrust could not.

Wilson's presidency brings the process of structural reform to a close. The Supreme Court's 1911 decision in *Standard Oil* had already muted some of the pressure for antitrust reform. That decision abandoned the literalism of *Trans-Missouri* and introduced (restored?) the common law distinction between reasonable and unreasonable restraints of trade. (And, by the way, also broke up Standard Oil.) Early in his first term, on January 20, 1914, Wilson delivered a special message to Congress on antitrust. Wilson had two principal aims. First he wanted to make explicit the nature of antitrust violations:

> Surely we are sufficiently familiar with the actual processes and methods of monopoly and of the many hurtful restraints of trade to make definition possible—at any rate up to the limits of what practice has disclosed. These practices, being now abundantly disclosed, can be explicitly and item by item forbidden by statute in such terms as will practically eliminate uncertainty, the law itself and the penalty being made equally plain.

Wilson then turned to the idea of an interstate trade commission:

> And the business men of the country desire something more than that the menace of legal process in these matters be made explicit and intelligible. They desire the advice, the definite guidance and information which can be supplied by administrative body, an interstate trade commission. ("President Wilson's Message on Trusts," *New York Times*, January 21, 1914, p. 2.)

Later that year, Wilson got exactly what he wanted with the enactment of the Federal Trade Commission Act (FTCA) and the Clayton Act. Adopted on September 26, 1914, the FTCA brought to a close Roosevelt's efforts to extend the Interstate Commerce Act to the general economy. The Bureau of Corporations, designed by Roosevelt as the president's private investigatory arm, was to become the back office of the new Federal Trade Commission. The commission itself was to parallel the Interstate Commerce Commission: an independent agency of five commissioners appointed by the president on the advice and consent of the Senate.

Section 5 of the FTCA declared unlawful "unfair methods of competition" and empowered the FTC to prevent the use of such methods other than by banks, subject to the new banking act, and common carriers subject to the Commerce Act. In so doing, Section 5 tracked the Commerce Act in two ways: the FTCA focused on unfairness—typically measured by comparing the treatment of two similarly situated market participants—while denying broader rate-setting power to the FTC. And the Clayton Act forbade specific practices, including tying and price discrimination. So Wilson got the specificity he wanted through the Clayton Act, and a general regulatory agency devoted to all industry through his new Federal Trade Commission. Industry would have a regulatory agency that it could turn to and perhaps even influence, though without the power to enforce industry cartels through the setting of rates or through limitations on entry, many of the critical anticompetitive harms that might result from capture were taken off of the table. The FTC, unlike industry-specific regulatory bodies, deals with industry in general. Perhaps this explains why, at least today, we are unaware of claims that the FTC has been captured by any industry or special interest group. Its structure raises the issue as to whether a combination of antitrust and industry-specific regulation in one agency, as occurs today in Australia or Europe for certain functions, is desirable—an issue we leave for future research.

With the 1914 legislation, the key institutional features that still dominate US antitrust law were established: the Sherman Act, the Clayton Act, and the FTC Act. The balance between antitrust and regulation still had to be worked out. The resolution of the issue of *Trans-Missouri* would take some time. The Transportation Act of 1920—finally—gave the Interstate Commerce Commission full control over rates, requiring the commission to ensure that rates permitted carriers to receive "a fair return upon the aggregate value of the railway property of such carriers held for and used in the service of transportation." As to the fight over whether antitrust or regulation ultimately controlled rate setting for railroads, in 1948, more than a half century after the Supreme Court's original decision in *Trans-Missouri*, Congress finally put the decision to rest by exempting joint setting of railroad rates from the antitrust laws, so long as the ICC approved the rates (Pub. L. 80-662, 62 Stat. 472 [June 17, 1948]).

1.3   Modern Approaches to Network Industries

We now jump from the formative years of the creation of competition policy to more recent times. Just as the initial battles between regulation and the Sherman Act illustrate the battle between antitrust and regulation as two methods to control competition, so too do more recent events—particularly the recent shift away from regulation to reliance on the Sherman Act. We focus our attention on network industries, since those are the ones where the case for regulation was often thought to be the strongest. If rate setting was the first great issue of competition policy for network industries, the leading issues today in network industries that continue to be heavily regulated are interconnection and mandatory access.

This recent history highlights a move away from regulation toward antitrust as a means to control competition and reveals how regulation and antitrust can be both substitutes and, in some settings, complements. The substitution involves the complete replacement of regulation with antitrust, as occurs when industries become deregulated (e.g., airlines and trucks). The complementarity between regulation and antitrust can arise in two ways. In an industry that becomes partially deregulated, antitrust can be used to control the unregulated segments, while regulation controls the rest. Indeed, partial deregulation of an industry can increase the importance to a rival of continuing rules of interconnection.

In structuring an efficient partial deregulation of an industry, the assignment of tasks to antitrust versus regulation is key. We should not ask antitrust and federal judges to perform tasks for which they are ill suited— namely price setting and crafting affirmative duties because those tasks require specialized industry knowledge that judges lack. If we need government involvement in those tasks, they should be assigned to regulators with specialized industry knowledge, though in making that judgment we need to recognize the inefficiencies that can arise as regulators cater to special interests or make mistakes. This is an especially serious problem in industries undergoing rapid technological change, where mistakes can impose huge costs. But it may be a mistake to just trump antitrust entirely, as we should fear capture of regulators, and that leads to a second type of complementarity.

The second form of complementarity between antitrust and regulation involves the use of antitrust as a constraint on how regulation is implemented. This is often implemented through a double filter or double-veto process, as we see in telecommunications mergers. The FCC evaluates telecom mergers under a public interest standard and that empowers the FCC to consider a wider range of issues than we typically entrust to federal judges. This would include, for example, whether and how to implement cross subsidies. But given the fear of regulatory capture, we apply a second, antitrust filter to these mergers by allowing the Department of Justice to sue under the antitrust laws to block an anticompetitive merger that the FCC has approved. Exactly how much scrutiny should be applied to regulatory decisions turns on a trade-off between allowing expertise to work—FCC expertise and knowledge—versus fearing biased decision making from an agency subject to capture. Even if no antitrust suit occurs, the threat of such a suit can influence FCC policy.

In this section, we address the fundamental question that has occupied and continues to occupy regulatory and antitrust decisions in network industries: How should those markets be structured and specifically how should firms interact in those industries? We focus our analysis on telecommunications and transportation (planes, trains, and trucks), though we note that interconnection issues are important in other industries such as electricity, where generators must have access to the transmission grid.

As already explained, a regulation may allow elevated pricing in return for some other objective that the regulator is likely to have to satisfy, such as a cross subsidy to different customer groups. But in order to achieve its objectives, the regulator may need to also control entry. Otherwise there may be no way to maintain the elevated price. This means that the regulator wants to limit competition and for that reason will be hostile to being constrained by the antitrust laws.

The regulators' concern with entry is especially acute in network industries in which firms may interconnect with each other, such as airlines, trucking, electricity, railroads, and telecommunications. In such industries, the regulator needs to administer the price and quality of the interconnection. If two firms compete in the end market and one competitor supplies the other a key input, the regulator must worry that the supplier will misuse its control over the input to harm his rival. This concern vanishes if the regulated firms are not allowed to vertically integrate. Moreover, when regulated firms must interconnect, the price of interconnection will typically be regulated to be above marginal cost. If so, there will be an efficiency motivation for a firm to vertically integrate to avoid double marginalization. But such mergers would eliminate firms and ultimately lead to one firm. Regulators might prefer to avoid this outcome to prevent one firm from becoming a potent political force in regulatory battles.[3]

By observing what happens when regulations are lifted, we can get a sense for why it was important to the regulators to constrain the forces of competition. We look at a few regulated network industries in the following. They all show a similar pattern: after either partial or complete deregulation, there is massive consolidation, increased industry concentration, an end to cross subsidy, often a decline in employment or wages, and a fall in price. Deregulation can be seen as the result of a consensus that regulation imposed high costs on the economy and that courts are sensibly applying the antitrust laws. Indeed, there is a recognition that the use of economics has revolutionized and made more sensible the antitrust laws.[4] In light of the costs of regulation and the improvement in antitrust, a movement away from regulation toward antitrust has occurred. In this view, regulation and antitrust are substitutes. But in some cases we also see regulation and antitrust being used together in an industry, illustrating the possible complementarity use of the two.

1.3.1   Telecommunications

Early Interconnection Battles

The telephone system is about interconnection, as a single-phone phone system is worthless. In the early days of the industry, as Mueller (1997) describes, different local companies competed with each other. A customer of one company could reach other customers of only that company; you might need to have multiple phones to reach everyone. (This is very much like instant messaging several years ago, where America Online resisted

---

3. In an industry with high sunk costs but low marginal costs, interconnection fees based on models of contestability fail to reward carriers adequately for risk, since contestability ignores sunk costs. In such situations, not only is price above marginal cost, but investment is deterred. This may have been the case in telecommunications. See Pindyck (2008).

4. As Posner (2003) explains in the preface to the second edition of his primer *Antitrust Law*:

Much of antitrust law in 1976 was an intellectual disgrace. Today, antitrust law is a body of economically rational principles largely though not entirely congruent with the principles set forth in the first edition. The chief worry at present is not doctrine or direction, but implementation.(viii)

attempts by Yahoo, Microsoft, and others to create a unified IM system [Festa 2000].) American Telephone and Telegraph—the Bell System—was the dominant firm of the day, but local competition was widespread; indeed, during the early 1900s, half of the cities with populations larger than 5,000 had competing local firms (Mueller 1997, 81). This competition almost certainly had benefits—on price and service—but came with a loss of network externalities. AT&T set out to build a universal system and started by purchasing competing telephone companies.

In 1912, that led to an antitrust suit in Portland, Oregon, and to calls by the postmaster general to nationalize the telephone and telegraph system— presumably to unify the messaging systems of the day (postal, telegraph, and phone) into one set of hands. Faced with these two threats, AT&T agreed to, in the words of N. C. Kingsbury, an AT&T vice president, "set its house in order." In what is now known as the Kingsbury Commitment, AT&T agreed to divest itself of control over Western Union; to stop acquisitions of competing lines; and to give access to Bell's long-distance lines to competing local phone companies, that is, to interconnect the Bell system's long distance lines with the local competitor's network.[5]

The Kingsbury Commitment might be framed as a victory for local phone competition but for two factors. First, few phone users made long-distance calls, so the local line/long-distance line interconnection may not have been an important competitive factor. Second, the size of the local network did matter, and AT&T aggressively moved forward on local interconnection, something outside the scope of the Kingsbury Commitment.

As is so often the case, antitrust action—here, the settlement—sets the stage for the next round of legislation, and that emerged in the form of the Willis-Graham Act of 1921. The new law entrusted telephone mergers to the Interstate Commerce Commission and authorized approval if doing so would "be of advantage to the persons to whom service is rendered and in the public interest." The act also added a sharp boundary between antitrust and regulation: once the ICC had said yes, the Department of Justice and the Federal Trade Commission could do nothing. With the new act in place, AT&T moved swiftly to create local interconnection through acquisition, with the ICC approving 271 of 274 AT&T acquisitions over a thirteen-year period (Starr 2004, 209).[6]

Interconnection Again: MCI's Entry into Long Distance

We jump ahead to consider the entry of MCI into long distance. We start with a single integrated phone system, with local and long distance controlled by AT&T. MCI entered in a very limited way, by building microwave

5. See "Government Accepts an Offer of Complete Separation," *New York Times*, Dec. 20, 1913, 1 (setting forth terms of the Kingsbury Commitment).
6. For a more detailed look at the early history of the telecommunications industry, see Weiman and Levin (1994).

towers to enable private within-firm phone calls between St. Louis and Chicago (say, between Walgreens's home office in Chicago and a district office in St. Louis). MCI did not need access to the public network to make this work. Even this limited entry required an initial 1959 order and a subsequent 1969 ruling from the Federal Communications Commission.

Unlike entry into private lines, entry into the public market for long distance required MCI to interconnect with AT&T, or in the alternative, simultaneous entry by MCI into local and long distance. And if MCI had been forced to build the entire network, it could not likely have entered the market. The local network was seen as a natural monopoly. It clearly would have been inefficient to build a second local network—that just says again that the local network was a natural monopoly—and it was also probably the case that it was a money-losing proposition for MCI to build a local network.

Bundling entry—forcing MCI to enter on the scale of having to build a local network if it wanted to enter the long-distance business—would probably have prevented the long-distance entry. Unbundling entry—giving MCI access to the local network while allowing entry only in long distance—meant that MCI could just compare the much more limited capital costs of building the second piece with the profits associated with that piece rather than the costs of both pieces with the profits associated with both pieces.

MCI moved against AT&T on both regulatory and antitrust fronts. In 1970, the FCC had concluded that some entry was appropriate, but when push came to shove, the FCC backtracked. In February 1978, the FCC rejected MCI's request that AT&T be ordered to provide local physical interconnections for MCI's intended public long-distance service. AT&T successfully persuaded the FCC that MCI would target high-profit routes and that that would destabilize the existing structure of rates, contrary to the public interest. MCI successfully appealed to the DC Circuit, which concluded that the consequences of entry could be dealt with on a case-by-case basis. In a subsequent proceeding, in 1978, the DC Circuit ordered AT&T to make interconnection for MCI's long-distance service.

MCI filed a private antitrust suit against AT&T in 1974. That case eventually went to a jury trial in the first half of 1980. The jury ultimately found AT&T liable on ten of fifteen charges, and awarded $600 million in actual damages, then trebled to $1.8 billion under Section 4 of the Clayton Act. On interconnection, MCI successfully argued that AT&T's refusal to interconnect constituted an impermissible refusal of access to an essential facility. The Seventh Circuit sustained the jury finding that this refusal constituted monopolization in violation of Section 2 of the Sherman Act.

We should step back from the details of this fight over entry and interconnection to focus on the interaction between regulation and antitrust. In general we know that regulation can lead to cross subsidy. Cross subsidies create entry incentives. General antitrust law will often facilitate entry but will do so with little regard for the cross-subsidy issues. MCI's entry into long distance probably fits in this framework. The DC Circuit expressly considered the cross-subsidy issues as part of its review of the FCC's regulatory proceedings, but concluded that those issues could be dealt with in subsequent proceedings. In contrast, the Seventh Circuit, faced with antitrust claims (and not regulatory claims) could not consider what its interconnection ruling might mean for the existing set of cross-subsidized rates. This is an excellent illustration of the use of antitrust in a regulated industry to control competition, where antitrust constrains what regulation can do.

Whether we should have welcomed MCI's entry is a separate question. To assess that, we need to assess what goals the regulators were pursuing and if those goals were sensible. MCI's entry precipitated a decline in long-distance rates. If prior to that decline, the regulators were pursuing the "public interest," then MCI's entry constrained the regulators from pursuing their desired policy. If we start with a regulated monopolist offering services to different customers, the regulator will need to set prices for each group of customers. The standard response in theory is Ramsey pricing. The regulator sets a series of prices—prices for long distance and for local service, for business customers and consumers, for urban and rural users—to minimize social loss while hitting a revenue target. The Ramsey approach is about allocating the fixed costs of production among the different groups using the service. The simple theory says that inelastic demanders should pay a larger share of the fixed costs. Inelastic demanders will not change their purchases much in the face of higher charges, and it is the reduced consumption when we push prices above marginal cost that causes the social loss. In order for elastic demanders to not bear too many fixed costs, inelastic demanders should pay a big chunk of those costs.

Now assume that we have put Ramsey prices into place. Those prices can create arbitrage opportunities: indeed, the whole vision behind Ramsey pricing is that inelastic demanders bear the brunt of fixed costs, while elastic demanders bear few of those costs. Ramsey pricing is precisely about price discrimination. If the regulators get the prices "right" in the first instance, we may nonetheless see entry that emerges because of regulator-created price gaps that are eliminated by the entry (see Faulhaber 1975). This entry would be undesirable if we accept the regulators' goals. This concern with "cream skimming" was prevalent in contemplating long-distance entry.

The regulators may not have implemented Ramsey prices in the first instance, but they clearly had created an elaborate pattern of cross subsidies, and that pattern would become more difficult to sustain after entry. How should we evaluate entry, whether facilities-based competition or otherwise, where the entry opportunity is created by cross-subsidy-driven pricing? To some extent, this requires a political account—a public choice account— about the nature of subsidies. If we thought that the subsidies were appropriate, then we should bar entry occurring just because of the opportunity created by the cross subsidy. So if the incumbent charges a higher price in urban areas than costs would warrant but does so because of a requirement that the price structure force urban users to subsidize rural users, entry targeted at urban users should be seen as problematic. In contrast, if we think of cross subsidies as inappropriate, entry may be useful in that it may make those subsidies unsustainable.

The 1996 Act's Access Rules and Trinko[7]

With the rise of AT&T's dominance, despite the passage of the Communications Act of 1934, antitrust became the main vehicle for altering the structure of AT&T. In 1949, the federal government brought an antitrust action against AT&T, which, in turn, resulted in a 1956 consent decree and final judgment. In 1974, the government brought a new action against AT&T, and in 1982, a new consent decree emerged as a modification of the 1956 decree. That decree resulted in the break up of AT&T: long distance was separated from local and regional local companies were established. (Though we will not discuss it, the breakup of AT&T has received much attention. See Noll and Owen [1989].)

We want to focus on the next important event, namely the Telecommunications Act of 1996. The 1996 act is wide ranging, but we address only its efforts to produce local competition through a strong access policy and focus on the interaction of antitrust and regulation. The 1996 act seeks to facilitate competition in local telephone markets by making it easier for entrants to compete with incumbents. It does so by creating a series of mandatory dealing obligations; that is, ways in which the incumbent is required to share its facilities with an entrant. This includes an obligation of interconnection; a requirement to sell telecommunications services to an entrant at wholesale prices, so that the entrant can resell those services at retail; and an obligation to unbundle its local network and sell access to pieces of the network at a cost-based price.

As to the intersection of the 1996 act and antitrust, the 1996 act contains a "savings" clause:

> Nothing in this Act or the amendments made by this Act . . . shall be construed to modify, impair, or supersede the applicability of any of the antitrust laws. (47 U.S.C. § 152, Historical and Statutory Notes.)

In January 2004, the Supreme Court announced its opinion in *Trinko*. AT&T wanted to enter Verizon's local markets in New York and sought access pursuant to the terms of the then-applicable rules under the 1996 act. When the access granted was seen as inadequate, both state and federal communications regulators acted and monetary penalties were imposed against Verizon. Enter Curtis Trinko, a New York lawyer. He brought an antitrust

---

7. Carlton has served as an expert for major telecommunications companies including AT&T and Verizon, and consulted on *Trinko*.

class action against Verizon alleging that, as a local customer of AT&T, he was injured by Verizon's actions and that those actions violated Section 2 of the Sherman Act. The federal district court would have none of that and booted the complaint, but the Second Circuit reversed.

Justice Scalia, for the Court, noted that the situation seemed to call for an implicit antitrust immunity. The 1996 act created access duties and those duties could be enforced—and were enforced here—through the appropriate regulators. That would seem to suffice, and there would be some risk that additional antitrust enforcement would interfere with the regulatory scheme. So the Court might have held, but for the savings clause, which precluded such a claim of implicit immunity.

Instead, the Court turned to the question of whether antitrust law, as distinct from regulation, imposed on Verizon a duty to deal with entrants. Antitrust rarely imposes mandatory obligations, other than as a remedy for an independent antitrust violation. The *Aspen Skiing* case represents one prominent exception to that statement, and whatever the merits of *Aspen* (see Carlton [2001] for criticism), the Court saw little reason to expand mandatory obligations here. Indeed, just the opposite: "The 1996 Act's extensive provision for access makes it unnecessary to impose a judicial doctrine of forced access." The Court ruled that the antitrust laws imposed no duty to deal on Verizon.

The savings clause reflects the idea of antitrust and regulation as complementary mechanisms to control competition. As suggested in the introduction to this section, Congress might want to implement complementarity as a way of imposing a check on the regulatory agents that implement particular industry legislation. The continuing applicability of antitrust law notwithstanding, the existence of industry-specific legislation imposes limits on how far industry regulators can deviate from the principles at stake in antitrust. The difficulty is in implementing that idea in a particular situation. In *Trinko* itself, the Court recognized that antitrust has only weakly embraced affirmative duties, with *Aspen Skiing* seemingly representing the outer limits for antitrust itself. Given antitrust's own deficits in the area of affirmative dealing, the Court wisely decided that *Trinko* would have represented a particularly poor situation to try to use antitrust to police errant telecom regulators.

1.3.2   Airlines

The airline industry, analyzed in great detail by Severin Borenstein and Nancy Rose in chapter 2 of this volume, provides another interesting case study of the interplay of regulation and antitrust policy. Congress established the Civil Aeronautics Administration, which later became the Civil Aeronautics Board (CAB), in 1938. The CAB regulated fares and entry. They cross-subsidized low-density short-haul routes with revenues from low-cost long-haul routes. The CAB rarely allowed mergers unless bankruptcy was imminent (Morrison and Winston 2000, 9). By the 1970s, the CAB began to allow entry. Several airlines were in the process of initiating lawsuits against the CAB for violating its congressional mandate, when the Airline Deregulation Act of 1978 was passed. (Interestingly, the largest domestic carrier at the time, United, favored deregulation.) Airline regulation was phased out and the CAB was abolished in 1984 (see Carlton and Perloff 2005).

In response to widespread criticism of regulation, airline competition was deregulated and controlled only by antitrust. As documented in chapter 2 by Borenstein and Rose, deregulation set in motion forces that are still working their way through the airline system. Fares fell substantially after deregulation with typical estimates being 20 percent or more (see also Morrison and Winston 2000, 2). The menu of fares on a typical route grew. Cross subsidies were eliminated (the CAB had eliminated cross subsidies based on distance in the 1970s). There has been a virtual flood of entry and exit since deregulation. For example, of the fifty-eight carriers that began operations between 1978 and 1990, only one (America West) was still operating by 2000 (Morrison and Winston 2000, 9).

Airlines developed hub-and-spoke networks (with Southwest being a notable exception) through merger and internal expansion, and as a result reduced their need to rely on another airline for interconnection. For example, in 1979 25 percent of trips involved connections, and of those, 39 percent involved another airline. By 1989, there were more connecting flights as a result of the hub-and-spoke system, with the effect being that 33 percent of trips involved connections, and of those, less than 5 percent involved an interconnection with another airline.

There was considerable merger activity and agreements among airlines to cooperate on flight schedules and the setting of through-fares when a passenger travels on two airlines to reach his final destination. (These agreements are called alliances or code-sharing agreements.) The Department of Justice challenged several mergers and alliances in the period between 2000 and 2010.[8] For example, its opposition ended the attempt of United to merge with US Airways.

As a result of mergers and firm expansion, concentration has risen nationally since deregulation. According to Borenstein (1992), the national four-firm concentration ratio rose from 56 percent in 1977 to 62 percent in 1990. As of 2011, it was 66 percent according to the US Department of Transportation (2011), but concentration at hubs has behaved very differently than concentration at nonhubs. At hub airports, the Herfindahl-Hirschman Index (HHI) rose from a median of under 2,200 pre-deregulation to a median of 3,700 by 1989, while at nonhub airports, the HHI fell from 3,200 in 1979 to about 2,200 in 1989 (Bamberger and Carlton 2003). As of 2011,

---

8. Carlton has served as an expert for the major airlines in mergers and other proceedings.

median HHI at hub airports was 5,400, while median HHI at nonhub airports was 2,300.[9]

Despite regulation, airlines proved to be a poor investment. During regulation, especially the 1970s, service competition eroded a significant portion of airline earnings. Since deregulation, fierce price competition has led to the bankruptcy of several airlines and indeed several major airlines were recently either in bankruptcy or are close to it. ("As of 1992 . . . , the money that has been made since the dawn of aviation by all of this country's airline companies was zero. . . . I like to think that if I'd been at Kitty Hawk in 1903, I would have been farsighted enough and public spirited enough—I owed this to future capitalists—to shoot him down" [Warren Buffet, as reported in Loomis (1999)]). The US domestic airline industry lost, in 2009 dollars, $10 billion from 1979 to 1989, made $5 billion in the 1990s, and lost $54 billion from 2000 to 2009 (Borenstein 2011). Deregulation also led to lower wages for employees and increased productivity.

The behavior of the airline industry post-deregulation illustrates that a once-regulated industry may be prone to antitrust violations in the aftermath of regulation. This could occur because collective action is needed for efficiency or simply because firms in the industry have gotten used to acting in concert during regulation. We think the airline industry illustrates well the heightened antitrust liability that can attend a network industry when it is deregulated.

Prior to deregulation, airlines relied on each other to interconnect passengers. That meant that airlines would have to set some fares jointly and decide how to split the revenue. So, for example, if airline 1 flies from A to B, and airline 2 flies from B to C, the two airlines could coordinate their flight times so that a traveler could conveniently go from A to C (with a change of plane at B). The two airlines would collectively set a fare for A to C travel and share it in some way. Also, airlines, postregulation, developed sophisticated pricing methods requiring booking agents to keep track of multiple fares and seat availability.

This created two problems. First, travel agents needed complex software to allow them to book tickets. Second, travel agents had to have up-to-date information on pricing and seat availability. Thousands of fares existed and many changed daily. The pricing of airlines sometimes involved large swings in price and its pricing is more complicated than pricing in many other markets. These characteristics created the incentive for certain acts that could achieve efficiencies but might also be used to harm competition. Significant antitrust litigation against the airlines ensued post-deregulation.

The tendency of airlines to cooperate in the setting of through-fares when traffic is shared can be a natural and desirable way for two airlines to provide a service to consumers that neither airline, on its own, could provide. It could

9. Data from Database Products Inc. These calculations for hub and nonhub airports are limited to the top 100 US airports.

also be a ploy by which one airline bribes another to prevent expansion of competing routes. (For example, if you do not enter route BC, where I fly, I will interline with your AB route and let you keep a large fraction of the through-fare from A to C. In that way, you have no incentive to enter BC and compete with me on that route.) This last concern motivates the Department of Justice to investigate proposed domestic airline alliances for possible antitrust harm.

The need for software to book tickets led to several cases and investigations into computer reservation systems (CRS), where the concern was that the CRS used by a travel agent favored the airline that produced the CRS. So, for example, if a travel agent used the Sabre system originally developed by American Airlines, that system displayed information about American Airlines flights more prominently than other airlines. As a result of the government investigation, detailed rules on "unbiasedness" were agreed to (see Guerin-Calvert and Noll 1991) but are no longer in force. Today, CRSs are no longer privately owned by the airlines.[10]

The need to have updates of the massive number of daily fare changes led to a Department of Justice investigation of information sharing amongst the airlines. Most of the airlines would provide information each day on all their fares by route. The information in a "notes section" would contain relevant fare restrictions (e.g., weekend stays, advance purchase requirements) as well as the date the fare became effective and expired. This information on fares was transmitted to the Airline Tariff Publishing Company (ATPCO) which then made a master computer tape and distributed it to all airlines and travel agents. The ATPCO was owned by the airlines.

The Department of Justice alleged that the ATPCO was being used as a mechanism to coordinate pricing. One allegation was that the notes section was used to communicate price signals. So, for example, if airline 1 cut price on an important route of airline 2, airline 2 would retaliate and cut price on an important route of airline 1. To make sure airline 1 understood why it had cut fares, airline 2 could put a note to indicate why it had cut price in an attempt to convince airline 1 to withdraw its low fares on airline 2's routes.

A related allegation was that the first effective and last effective ticket date were used to make it easier to coordinate pricing. So, for example, if airline 1 wanted to raise fares, it would announce an increase to take effect in, say, two weeks. If other airlines did not match, or only partly matched, airline 1 could rescind or revise its fare increase and not suffer any loss of business because the fare increase had not yet gone into effect. The airlines denied the government allegations.[11] The airlines settled the case by agreeing to

---

10. There have been antitrust suits in which biasing, among other issues, has been alleged. See, for example, *American Airlines, Inc., vs. Travelport Inc., Sabre, Inc., Sabre Holdings Inc., and Sabre Travel International Ltd.* in the District Court of Tarrant County, 67th District Court, Cause No. 67-249214-10. Carlton has served as an expert for American Airlines.

11. Carlton served as an expert for the airlines.

eliminate extraneous notes and by abandoning the use of first ticket dates. Interestingly, analyses of fares shows no lasting effect from the investigation and settlement (Borenstein [2004] and Miller [2010], though Miller [2010] finds some evidence of a temporary improvement in competition).

The sometimes wild price swings that occur when new entrants start servicing a route has led to both litigation and government investigations. In a city pair that can support only one or a few carriers, competition from a new rival not only can expand capacity a lot but can induce reactions from the incumbents. In response to an aggressive price and output reaction by an incumbent, allegations of predation are often made. The precise definition of predation in an industry such as airlines with large fixed costs on a route but small variable costs is not well established, especially on a route where only one carrier can survive (Edlin and Farrell 2004). But the observation that fares frequently plummet below levels that are financially viable has led to demands for government intervention.

In *U.S. v. AMR et al.* (140 F. Supp. 2d 1141 [2001], aff'd, 335 F.3d 1109 [10th Cir. 2003]), the Department of Justice accused American Airlines of practicing price predation. American Airlines competed out of Dallas Fort Worth with several low-cost airlines (Vanguard, Western Pacific, Sun Jet). American lowered its fares, and increased its seat availability in response to these low-cost airlines, causing them to abandon their routes. After the low-cost airlines exited, American reduced the number of flights and raised prices to roughly their initial levels. American responded that its prices exceeded average variable costs, and moved for summary judgment, which was granted.

Just prior to the Department of Justice case, the Department of Transportation initiated an investigation of predation in the airline industry. It investigated several incidents in which it was alleged that incumbents routinely responded to entry of low-cost carriers by lowering fares, expanding output, and driving them out of business, at which point fares rose. In a detailed study of entry and exit patterns (submitted to the Department of Transportation on behalf of United), Bamberger and Carlton (2006) found that entry and exit on routes were extremely common amongst both low-cost carriers and established carriers. Moreover, with the exception of Southwest Airlines, there were very high exit rates amongst both low-cost and regular carriers. The Department of Transportation dropped its attempt to define predation standards. Between 2000 and 2011, the share of passengers served by Southwest Airlines rose from 12 percent to 17 percent. (As an aside, between 2000 and 2011, the share of passengers served by low-cost airlines rose from 18 percent to 27 percent.)[12]

---

12. Low-cost carriers include: Airtran, America West, JetBlue, Midway, Southwest, Spirit, Sun Country, Virgin America, Allegiant, USA3000, National, and World. Data from US Department of Transportation, T1 US Air Carrier Traffic Statistics.

1.3.3   Railroads[13]

As Gilligan, Marshall, and Weingast (1989) note, the consequences of the Interstate Commerce Act are complex. One view is that it was a mechanism to benefit the railroads. But as with most regulated industries the regulators had other interest groups to satisfy, and they did. Cross subsidy to high-cost, low-density routes and to short-haul shippers emerged. Price discrimination in which high value-added products had higher rates than bulk also emerged to placate certain shipper interest groups. In what was to be important later, regulators controlled not only entry but also exit from a route. The emergence of the truck (and airplanes) complicated the regulatory calculations.

Control of trucking became necessary to protect railroads and did occur in the Motor Carrier Act of 1935. As trucking (especially its union, the Teamsters) developed as its own powerful interest group, the interest of railroads waned and railroads got clobbered financially, resulting in numerous bankruptcies. Trucks siphoned off the profitable high value-added shipments and eroded this source of revenue that railroads used for cross subsidy. The restrictions on abandonment of routes created enormous inefficiencies. The deregulation of the railroads in 1976 (4R Act) and in 1980 (Staggers Act) removed most regulations but placed merger control in the hands of the Surface Transportation Board (STB), not the Department of Justice. It streamlined the process for merging.

After deregulation, there was massive abandonment of track, reductions in employment, decline in certain rates, and massive consolidation that is still ongoing. Roughly one-third of tracks were abandoned, real operating costs fell in the twenty-year period following deregulation by about 60 percent, employment has been estimated to be about 60 percent lower as a result of deregulation (Davis and Wilson 1999), rail volumes started to grow again, and industry profitability improved. Rates fell (Burton 1993), especially for high value-added products, and service improved.

"Before deregulation, mergers typically involved railroads with substantial parallel trackage. . . . In contrast, mergers in the post-Staggers period have been primarily end-to-end" (Vellturo et al. 1992, 341–42). Mergers in the first six years of deregulation reduced the number of large railroads (Class I) from thirty-six to sixteen (Grimm and Winston 2000, 45–46, citing Chaplin and Schmidt 1999). Continued merger activity has left only two railroads servicing the West and also the East (see also Ivaldi and McCullough 2010). Using figures from the Association of American Railroads, the number of Class I railroads declined from thirty-six in 1978 to seven in 2002, where it remains. The industry's HHI, calculated on a national basis with car miles as the output, rose from 589 in 1978 to 2,262 in 2006 (Ivaldi and MCullough 2010). According to a study by the Department of Agriculture,

---

13. This section draws heavily from Peltzman (1989) and Grimm and Winston (2000).

the HHI of railroads in the East increased from 1,364 in 1980 to 4,297 in 1999 and in the West from 1,364 to 4,502.[14]

Despite opposition from the Department of Justice to many of the major mergers, STB has approved them. We believe that the reason the STB was given merger authority rather than the Department of Justice is precisely because mergers were anticipated that would lead to increased rates from reduced competition, and this was perceived as a benefit by the proponents of deregulation (which included the railroads). "The railroad industry is perhaps the only US industry that has been, or ever will be, deregulated because of its poor financial performance under regulation" (Grimm and Winston 2000, 41). Indeed, although railroads' rates in general have declined, captive shippers now have much less protection than before deregulation and pay substantial rate differentials compared to noncaptive shippers.

In March 2000, the STB issued a moratorium on mergers. In June 2001, it issued new merger regulations in which merged carriers would have an increased burden to show that the proposed merger would not harm competition. There have been no mergers among Class I railroads since. There have been congressional attempts to remove the antitrust immunity of railroads regarding mergers and other pricing matters (Gallagher 2006).

1.3.4   Trucks

As already discussed, trucking regulation emerged under the Motor Carrier Act of 1935 partly as an attempt to control competition with railroads. The trucking industry, especially its unions, was able to become a powerful interest group whom regulators protected from competition. (Estimates are that wages were 30 percent higher or more than otherwise and that this premium accounted for the bulk of the regulatory rents to trucking; see Rose 1987 and Moore 1978.) Entry was controlled with carriers needing certificates to carry certain commodities on particular routes. Rates were regulated.

The trucking industry is composed of two very different segments, truck load (TL) and less than truck load (LTL). The TL segment consists of firms that ship in truckloads from origin to destination. In contrast, the LTL segment consists of firms that will pick up several small shipments, and deliver them to their final destinations after making several stops to either pick up or drop off other shipments. Therefore, the LTL segment is a network industry where scale (or geographic scope) matters, while the TL segment is not. Deregulation had very different effects on these two segments.

Deregulation led to an increase in the total number of trucking firms. For example, the number of certified carriers rose from about 18,000 in 1980 to about 40,000 by the end of the 1980s (Nebesky, McMullen, and Lee

14. Data from comments of the US Department of Agriculture before the Surface Transportation Board, STB Docket No. 34000, Canadian National Railway Co. et al.—Control— Wisconsin Central Railway Co., June 25, 2001.

1995). In sharp contrast, the number of LTL carriers fell from around 600 firms in the late 1970s to 237 firms in the late 1980s, and to 135 firms by the early 1990s (Feitler, Corsi, and Grimm 1997). Moreover, there was evidence that pre-deregulation, LTL carriers earned rents that were eliminated after deregulation.

Although LTL carriers have increased in size, they did not rely on mergers but rather on expansion of the territory of individual carriers, often achieved through the purchase of a bankrupt carrier. (Mergers were not used in order to prevent the acquirer from being stuck with unfunded pension liabilities.) After deregulation, the market value of a trucking firm could become negative after the value of its operating certificate fell (Boyer 1993, 485). Although the evidence seems to confirm that regulation forced the LTL sector to have too many firms, evidence on scale in the LTL sector (Giordano 1997) supports the view that there will remain a sufficient number of efficient LTL carriers to preserve competition. Moreover, one factor limiting the rise in concentration was the growth in nonunion regional carriers at the expense of the unionized national carriers.

The deregulation of trucking applied to interstate but not intrastate shipments. States were able to, and some did, regulate rates and entry of intrastate trucking. Some states explicitly granted antitrust immunity, while others did not. (In the thirty-eight states that regulated trucking under 500 pounds, twenty-two had granted antitrust immunity to truckers as of 1987.) Econometric analysis (Daniel and Kleit 1995) of rates in the states that still regulated trucking showed that in the LTL segment, entry regulation raised rates by over 20 percent, rate regulation by over 5 percent, and antitrust immunity by about 12 percent. In the TL segment, only rate regulation had a statistically significant effect on price—more than 32 percent. As of 1994, congressional legislation forbids states from regulating trucking rates, except for moving companies.

Although employment in trucking continued to grow after deregulation, one estimate finds that deregulation caused a reduction of 250,000 to 300,000 union jobs, or about 20 percent of total workers in trucking (Hunter and Mangum 1995). This is further evidence that trucking regulation was heavily influenced by the powerful Teamsters Union. Moreover, the wage effect in the LTL segment was small but wages declined significantly in the TL sector (Belzer 1995).

Although we have not examined all regulated industries, we have looked at several. Regulation created numerous inefficiencies and benefited special groups. In response to criticisms of regulation, antitrust either completely or partially replaced regulation and antitrust was used as a complement and sometimes as a constraint on regulators in many industries. The deregulated network industries that we examined all show a similar pattern: after deregulation, there is massive consolidation, a lessening of the reliance on interconnection from other firms, a decline in either wages or employment or both, and a fall in prices with a reduction or end to any cross subsidy. Consumers benefit, special interests are harmed.

1.4 Conclusion

More than a century ago, the federal government started controlling competition, first railroads through the Interstate Commerce Act and then the general economy under the Sherman Act. The Commerce Act assigned primary responsibility to the first great federal agency, the Interstate Commerce Commission, while the Sherman Act relied for its implementation on federal courts of general jurisdiction. Since that time, there has been an ongoing struggle to formulate the appropriate policy for controlling competition and to determine the right balance between antitrust and regulation for implementing that policy.

Regulation and antitrust are two competing mechanisms to control competition. The early history in which special courts were established and then abolished and in which the FTC was created illustrate this point. The relative advantages and disadvantages of each mechanism became clearer over time. Regulation produced cross subsidies and favors to special interests, but was able to specify prices and specific rules of how firms should deal with each other. Antitrust, especially when it became economically coherent within the past thirty years or so, showed itself to be reasonably good at promoting competition, avoiding the favoring of special interests, but not good at formulating specific rules for particular industries. The partial and full deregulation movement was a response to the recognition of the relative advantages of regulation and antitrust. This does not mean that no sector will be regulated, but rather that competition, constrained only by antitrust, will be used over more activities, even in regulated industries.

Aside from being viewed as substitutes, antitrust and regulation can also be viewed as complements in which the activities of an industry can be subject to both regulatory and antitrust scrutiny. In this way, the complementary use of regulation and antitrust can assign control of competition to courts and regulatory agencies based on their relative strengths and, in some settings, antitrust can act as a constraint on what regulators can do. The trends in network industries indicate that regulators, not antitrust courts, will bear the responsibility for formulating interconnection policies in partially deregulated industries, but antitrust will remain in the background as a club that firms can use if regulators allow incumbents to acquire market power either through merger or predatory acts.

The history shows that at least for the United States, the increased use of the Sherman Act instead of regulation to control competition, and when necessary, the complementary use of the two, has brought benefits to consumers.

References

Bamberger, Gustavo, and Dennis Carlton. 2003. "Airline Networks and Fares." In *Handbook of Airline Economics*, second edition, edited by Darryl Jenkins, 269–88. New York: Aviation Week, a Division of McGraw-Hill.
———. 2006. "Predation and the Entry and Exit of Low-Fare Carriers." In *Advances in Airline Economics: Competition Policy and Antitrust*, edited by Darin Lee, 1–23. North Holland: Elsevier.
Becker, Gary. 1983. "A Theory of Competition among Pressure Groups for Political Influence." *Quarterly Journal of Economics* 98:371–400.
Belzer, Michael. 1995. "Collective Bargaining After Deregulation: Do the Teamsters Still Count?" *Industrial and Labor Relations Review* 48:636–55.
Benson, Bruce, M. Greenhut, and Randall Holcombe. 1987. "Interest Groups and the Antitrust Paradox." *Cato Journal* 6:801–17.
Bittlingmayer, George. 1985. "Did Antitrust Policy Cause the Great Merger Wave?" *Journal of Law & Economics* 28:77–118.
Borenstein, Severin. 1992. "The Evolution of US Airline Competition." *Journal of Economic Perspectives* 6:45–73.
———. 2004. "Rapid Price Communication and Coordination: The Airline Tariff Publishing Case." In *The Antitrust Revolution*, fourth edition, edited by John E. Kwoka and Lawrence J. White, 233–51. New York: Oxford University Press.
———. 2011. "Why Can't US Airlines Make Money?" *American Economic Review* 101:233–37.
Boyer, Kenneth. 1993. "Deregulation of the Trucking Sector: Specialization, Concentration, Entry and Financial Distress." *Southern Economic Journal* 59:481–95.
Burton, Mark. 1993. "Railroad Deregulation, Carrier Behavior, and Shipper Response: A Disaggregated Analysis." *Journal of Regulatory Economics* 5:417–34.
Carlton, Dennis. 2001. "A General Analysis of Exclusionary Conduct and Refusal to Deal: Why Aspen and Kodak Are Misguided." *Antitrust Law Journal* 68:659–83.
Carlton, Dennis, Alan Frankel, and Elisabeth Landes. 2004. "The Control of Externalities in Sports Leagues: An Analysis of Restrictions in the National Hockey League." *Journal of Political Economy* 112:S268–88.
Carlton, Dennis, and Jeffrey Perloff. 2005. *Modern Industrial Organization*, fourth edition. Pearson.
Chaplin, Alison, and Stephen Schmidt. 1999. "Do Mergers Improve Efficiency? Evidence from Deregulated Rail Freight." *Journal of Transport Economics and Policy* 33:147–62.
Daniel, Timothy, and Andrew Kleit. 1995. "Disentangling Regulatory Policy: The Effects of State Regulations on Trucking Rates." *Journal of Regulatory Economics* 8:267–84.
Davis, David, and Wesley Wilson. 1999. "Deregulation, Mergers, and Employment in the Railroad Industry." *Journal of Regulatory Economics* 15:5–22.
Edlin, Aaron, and Joseph Farrell. 2004. "The American Airlines Case: A Chance to Clarify Predation Policy (2001)." In *The Antitrust Revolution*, fourth edition, edited by John E. Kwoka and Lawrence J. White, 502–07. New York: Oxford University Press.
Faulhaber, Gerald R. 1975. "Cross-Subsidization: Pricing in Public Enterprises." *American Economic Review* 65:966–77.
Feitler, Jane, Thomas Corsi, and Curtis Grimm. 1997. "Measuring Strategic Change in the Regulated and Deregulated Motor Carrier Industry: An 18 Year Evaluation." *Transportation Research Part E, Logistics and Transportation Review* 33:159–69.

Festa, Paul. 2000. "AOL Instant Messaging Efforts May Be at Cross Purposes." *CNET News*, May 15.

Fiorina, Morris. 1982. "Legislative Choice of Regulatory Forms: Legal Process or Administrative Process?" *Public Choice* 39:33–66.

Frankfurter, Felix, and James M. Landis. 1928. *The Business of the Supreme Court: A Study in the Federal Judicial System*. New York: Macmillan.

Gallagher, John. 2006. "Justice for the Railroads." *Traffic World* 27, July 17.

Gilligan, Thomas W., William J. Marshall, and Barry R. Weingast. 1989. "Regulation and the Theory of Legislative Choice." *Journal of Law and Economics* 32:35–61.

Giordano, James. 1997. "Return to Scale and Market Concentration among the Largest Survivors of Deregulation in the US Trucking Industry." *Applied Economics* 29:101–10.

Grimm, Curtis, and Clifford Winston. 2000. "Competition in the Deregulated Railroad Industry: Sources, Effects, and Policy Issues." In *Deregulation of Network Industries: What's Next?*, edited by Sam Peltzman and Clifford Winston, 41–72. Washington, DC: AEI-Brookings Joint Center for Regulatory Studies.

Grodinsky, Julius. 1950. *The Iowa Pool: A Study in Railroad Competition, 1870–84*. Chicago: University of Chicago Press.

Guerin-Calvert, Margaret, and Roger G. Noll. 1991. "Computer Reservation Systems and Their Network Linkages to the Airline Industry." In *Electronic Service Networks: A Business and Public Policy Challenge*, edited by Margaret E. Guerin-Calvert and Steven S. Wildman, 145–87. New York: Praeger.

Hilton, George W. 1966. "The Consistency of the Interstate Commerce Act." *Journal of Law and Economics* 9:87–114.

Hunter, Natalie J., and Stephen L. Mangum. 1995. "Economic Regulation, Employment Relations, and Accident Rates in the US Motor Carrier Industry." *Labor Studies Journal* 20:48–63.

Ivaldi, Marc, and Gerard McCullough. 2010. "Welfare Tradeoffs in US Rail Mergers." TSE Working Paper 10-196, Toulouse School of Economics, Toulouse.

Kolko, Gabriel. 1965. *Railroads and Regulation, 1877–1916*. Princeton, NJ: Princeton University Press.

Landes, William, and Richard Posner. 1979. "Adjudication as a Private Good." *Journal of Legal Studies* 8:235–84.

Loomis, Carol. 1999. "Mr. Buffett on the Stock Market." *Fortune*, vol. 1, issue 10, November 22, 212–20.

McCubbins, Matthew, Roger Noll, and Barry Weingast. 1989. "Structure and Process, Politics and Policy: Administrative Arrangements and the Political Control of Agencies." *Virginia Law Review* 75:431–82.

Miller, Amalia R. 2010. "Did the Airline Tariff Publishing Case Reduce Collusion?" *Journal of Law and Economics* 53:569–86.

Moore, Thomas Gale. 1978. "The Beneficiaries of Trucking Regulation." *Journal of Law and Economics* 21:327–43.

Morrison, Steven, and Clifford Winston. 2000. "The Remaining Role for Government Policy in the Deregulated Airline Industry." In *Deregulation of Network Industries: What's Next?*, edited by Sam Peltzman and Clifford Winston, 1–40. Washington, DC: AEI-Brookings Joint Center for Regulatory Studies.

Mueller, Milton L. 1997. *Universal Service: Competition, Interconnection, and Monopoly in the Making of the American Telephone System*. Cambridge, MA: MIT Press.

Nebesky, William, B. Starr McMullen, and Man-Keung Lee. 1995. "Testing for Market Power in the US Motor Carrier Industry." *Review of Industrial Organization* 10:559–76.

Noll, Roger, and Bruce Owen. 1989. "The Anticompetitive Uses of Regulation: United States v. AT&T." In *The Antitrust Revolution*, first edition, edited by John E. Kwoka and Lawrence J. White, 328–75. New York: Scott, Foresman.

Peltzman, Sam. 1976. "Toward a More General Theory of Regulation." *Journal of Law and Economics* 19:211–40.

———. 1989. "The Economic Theory of Regulation after a Decade of Deregulation." *Brookings Papers on Economic Activity: Microeconomics* no. 3, 1–41.

Pindyck, Robert. 2008. "Sunk Costs and Real Options in Antitrust Analysis." In *Issues in Competition Law and Policy*, edited by W. Collins, 619–40. ABA Monograph.

Pirrong, Stephen Craig. 1992. "An Application of Core Theory to the Analysis of Ocean Shipping Markets." *Journal of Law and Economics* 35:89–131.

Posner, Richard. 1974. "Theories of Economic Regulation." *The Bell Journal of Economics and Management Science* 5:335–58.

——— 2003. *Antitrust Law: An Economic Perspective*, second edition. Chicago: University of Chicago Press.

Rabin, Robert L. 1986. "Federal Regulation in Historical Perspective." *Stanford Law Review* 38:1189–326.

Ripley, William Z. 1913. *Railroads: Rates and Regulation*, 2nd ed. New York: Longmans, Green, and Co.

Robinson, Sara. 2004. "Antitrust Lawsuit Over Medical Residency System Is Dismissed." *New York Times*, August 14.

Rose, Nancy. 1987. "Labor Rent Sharing and Regulation: Evidence from the Trucking Industry." *Journal of Political Economy* 95:1146–78.

Shepsle, Kenneth, and Mark Bonchek. 1997. *Analyzing Politics: Rationality, Behavior, and Institutions*. New York: Norton.

Sklar, Martin J. 1988. *The Corporate Reconstruction of American Capitalism, 1890–1917*. Cambridge: Cambridge University Press.

Starr, Paul. 2004. *The Creation of the Media: Political Origins of Modern Communications*. New York: Basic Books.

Stephenson, Matthew. 2005. "Legislative Allocation of Delegated Power: Uncertainty, Risk, and the Choice between Agencies and Courts." Harvard Law and Economics Discussion Paper No. 506.

Stigler, George. 1971. "The Theory of Economic Regulation." *The Bell Journal of Economics and Management Science* 2:3–21.

US Department of Transportation. Various years. T1 US Air Carrier Traffic Statistics.

Vellturo, Christoper, Ernst Berndt, Ann Friedlander, Judy Chiang, and Mark Showalter. 1992. "Deregulation, Mergers and Cost Savings in Class I U.S. Railroads, 1974–1986." *Journal of Economics and Management Strategy* 1:339–69.

Weiman, David F., and Richard C. Levin. 1994. "Preying for Monopoly? The Case of Southern Bell Telephone Company, 1894–1912." *Journal of Political Economy* 102:103–26.

2

How Airline Markets Work . . . or Do They?
Regulatory Reform in the Airline Industry

Severin Borenstein and Nancy L. Rose

2.1 Introduction

Government policy, rather than market forces, shaped the development and operation of scheduled passenger air service in almost all markets for the first six decades of the airline industry's history. Intervention in commercial aviation coincided with the industry's inception in the aftermath of World War I, with many governments keenly cognizant of the potential military benefits of a robust domestic aviation sector. During these early days, interest in aviation outpaced the financial viability of fledging airlines. Government support intensified worldwide as financial instability was exacerbated by the global economic depression in the 1930s and military interest in aviation was fortified by increasing geopolitical tensions. Relatively low entry barriers, combined with the lure of government subsidies, led to many small providers of passenger air transportation, and to concern over fragmentation and "destructive competition."

Pressure to rationalize the industry and promote the development of

Severin Borenstein is the E. T. Grether Professor of Business Administration and Public Policy at the Haas School of Business, University of California, Berkeley, and a research associate of the National Bureau of Economic Research. Nancy L. Rose is the Charles P. Kindleberger Professor of Applied Economics and associate department head for economics at the Massachusetts Institute of Technology. She is a research associate of the National Bureau of Economic Research and director of its Program on Industrial Organization.

Nancy L. Rose gratefully acknowledges fellowship support from the John Simon Guggenheim Memorial Foundation and MIT. We thank Andrea Martens, Jen-Jen L'ao, Yao Lu, Michael Bryant, and Gregory Howard for research assistance on this project. For helpful comments and discussions, we thank Jim Dana, Joe Farrell, Michael Levine, Steven Berry, and participants in the NBER conference on regulatory reform, held September 2005, and in seminars at University of Toronto, Northwestern University, University of Michigan, UC Berkeley, and UC Davis. For acknowledgments, sources of research support, and disclosure of the authors' material financial relationships, if any, please see http://www.nber.org/chapters/c12570.ack.

strong national air carriers became manifest in subsidies and regulation of privately owned firms in the United States, and in state ownership nearly everywhere else. In the United States, Post Office control through airmail contract awards ultimately gave way to direct economic regulation of prices and entry by an independent regulatory agency in 1938, though both direct and indirect subsidies through airmail rates continued as part of that regulation.[1] In Europe, state subsidies quickly evolved into consolidation and state ownership of domestic "flag" carriers. Restrictions on foreign ownership of domestic air carriers were universal.

International service was governed by tightly controlled bilateral agreements, which specified the cities that could be served and which carriers were authorized to provide service, typically a single carrier from each country. In many cases, these agreements negotiated market allocations across carriers that were enforced through capacity restrictions or revenue division agreements. Prices generally were established jointly by the airlines themselves, under the auspices of the International Air Transport Association (IATA), subject to approval by each carrier's government.

The transition to a more market-based aviation industry began in the United States in the mid-1970s. The Airline Deregulation Act of 1978 eliminated price and entry regulation of the domestic airline industry and provided for ultimate closure of its regulatory agency, the Civil Aeronautics Board (CAB). Subsequent privatization efforts elsewhere transferred many carriers from state-owned enterprises to the private sector, though the United States and most other countries continue to claim a national interest in domestic ownership of airlines operating within their borders. While there has been relaxation of regulation in some international markets, restrictive bilateral agreements continue to limit competition in many important markets and most nations continue to limit foreign ownership of domestic airlines. The notable exceptions are within the European Union (EU), where formal restraints on commercial aviation have been liberalized considerably over the past fifteen years, with the creation of an open intra-EU aviation market, and a limited number of "open skies" agreements.[2] Apart from the

1. The 1938 legislation also provided for federal authority over airline and airport operations. Ultimately, system operations, certification, and safety regulation were concentrated in the Federal Aviation Authority, leaving the Civil Aeronautics Board (CAB) responsible for the economic (price and entry) regulation that is the focus of this chapter.

2. The US State Department lists 107 U.S. Open Skies partners since the first agreement was signed with the Netherlands in 1992, though some agreements are provisional or not yet in force. See http://www.state.gov/e/eb/rls/othr/ata/114805.htm, accessed January 15, 2013. The multilateral US-EU open skies agreement was negotiated following the European Commission's nullification of bilateral open skies agreements between the United States and individual EU member countries, with a substantial liberalization taking effect in March 2008 and modest additional liberalization agreed to in a 2010 extension. Its breadth has been extended as some non-EU countries, such as Iceland and Norway, have since joined the US-EU open skies agreement. Continued US limits on foreign ownership of domestic air carriers and denial of EU carrier rights to cabotage within the United States remain contentious, however.

EU market, however, carriers continue to be prohibited from competing for passengers on flights entirely within another country (so-called cabotage rights).

In this chapter, we analyze government regulation and deregulation primarily in the context of US. domestic airline markets. This choice is dictated by three considerations. First, intervention in passenger aviation took place through an explicit formal regulatory system in the United States, rather than through the more opaque operation of state-owned enterprise as elsewhere. Focusing on the United States enables a clearer discussion of government policies, their changes, and effects. From the inception of air travel, the United States has led the world in incorporating market incentives into its airline policies. While nearly every other country operated one or two state-owned airlines that dominated service, the United States relied on privately owned carriers and even under regulation allowed the airlines substantial autonomy in their operations. Second, until the EU changes in the late 1990s, policy reform has taken place primarily within domestic aviation markets. As the United States has had the largest domestic passenger aviation market in the world, it provides a substantial "laboratory" for observing the effects of policy changes. The United States also was the first to deregulate airline pricing and entry, leading nearly all other countries by more than a decade, thereby providing a longer postreform period in which to study the transition across regimes. Finally, and perhaps most importantly, the US government has collected and published detailed financial, operational, and market data at the individual-carrier, and in many cases, carrier-route, level from the regulated era and continuing through to the present. These unique data resources facilitate detailed econometric analyses that typically cannot be duplicated with the data that are publicly available on airlines in other countries. The availability of these data over much of the past thirty or more years has facilitated a wealth of analysis of regulatory reform and its impact.[3]

In this chapter, we first describe briefly the inception, institutions, and operation of US airline regulation. We then turn to a discussion of the events leading to deregulation of the industry and evaluate the impact of those reforms. A brief discussion of international aviation regulation and reform follows. Finally, we study the key issues of ongoing contention in the industry and assess their implications for the continuing debate over government intervention in passenger aviation markets.

---

3. These data are now used to study aspects of firm behavior not directly related to regulation, but of broad interest to industrial organization economists, firms, and policymakers. See, for example, studies of entry determinants and incumbent responses (e.g., Berry 1990, 1992; Whinston and Collins 1992; Goolsbee and Syverson 2008) and price level and structure determinants (e.g., Borenstein 1989; Hurdle et al. 1989; Borenstein and Rose 1994; Gerardi and Shapiro 2009; Morrison 2001; Berry and Jia 2010).

2.2   Airline Regulation

The US federal government began using private air carriers to supplement military airmail carriage in 1918, with early payloads devoted primarily to mail, not passengers. The Kelly Air Mail Act of 1925 (43 Stat. 805, 1925) established a competitive bidding system for private air mail carriage, and subsequent amendments provided explicit subsidies by enabling the Post Office to award contracts with payments exceeding anticipated air mail revenues on the routes.[4] These subsidies, along with Ford Motor Company's introduction of a twelve-seat aircraft in 1926, facilitated the expansion of passenger air service in the nascent US air carrier industry. By the 1930s, reports of the postmaster general's efforts to "rationalize" the route system and encourage the "coordination" of vertically integrated, national firms in the bidding process led to congressional censure and 1934 legislation to establish regulatory oversight by the Interstate Commerce Commission (ICC). This was soon replaced by the Civil Aeronautics Act of 1938, in which the industry succeeded in establishing a system of protective economic regulation under what eventually became the Civil Aeronautics Board, and operational and safety oversight under what was to become the Federal Aviation Administration (FAA).[5] Our analysis focuses on economic regulation and deregulation.[6] FAA operational and safety functions have not been deregulated, and there is little evidence of significant interactions between economic and safety regulation in this setting (see Rose 1990, 1992; Kanafani, Keeler, and Sathisan 1993, and the citations therein).

As in many other industries during the Great Depression, airline policymakers and executives alike were eager to trade the "chaos" of market determination of pricing and network configuration for government "coordination" across air carriers, elimination of "unfair or destructive competitive practices," and restriction of entry to that required by the "public convenience and necessity."[7] Perceived national defense interests in a robust

4. See Wolfram (2004) for an analysis of the performance of the early airmail contract award process.
5. Civil Aeronautics Act of 1938, 52 Stat. 977 (1938), amended in 1958 by the Federal Aviation Act of 1958, 72 Stat. 731, 49 U.S.C. §1341 (1958). In addition to economic regulation, these acts extended government oversight to aircraft certification, safety regulation of airline operations, airport development, and the air traffic control system. The safety functions were unaffected by changes in economic regulation, and are beyond the scope of the present analysis. We discuss infrastructure policy in section 2.5.
6. This section is not intended to duplicate the many excellent treatises on the history of airline regulation. See Caves (1962) and Levine (1965) for detailed discussions of the early airline industry and its regulation in the United States. These sources, along with Jordan (1970), Eads (1975), Douglas and Miller (1974a), Bailey, Graham, and Kaplan (1985), and many others, provide excellent analyses of the regulated era. See Rose (2012) for a discussion of some lessons from airline regulation highlighted by Fred Kahn.
7. 49 U.S.C. §1302, 1371 (1958). The exchange of government coordination and regulation for the "destructive competition" of the market was echoed in the origin of trucking regulation under the Motor Carrier Act of 1935, for example. See Kahn (1971, vol. 2, chap. 5).

domestic airline industry added to the appeal. To this end, the CAB was charged with "the promotion, encouragement and development of civil aeronautics," and given authority to accomplish this through control of entry, rate levels and structures, subsidies, and merger decisions.[8]

Economic regulation of the US airline industry persisted over the subsequent four decades in largely unchanged form. Two elements of regulation are most salient for this analysis: entry restrictions and rate determination.

When the CAB was formed in 1938, existing carriers were given "grandfathered" operating authority over their existing markets, as is typical in regulatory legislation. The CAB interpreted the public interest in avoiding destructive competition as implying a high hurdle for proposed new entry, effectively ruling out de novo entry of any new national ("trunk") scheduled passenger service carrier after 1938. During World War II and its immediate aftermath, the CAB bowed to pressure to authorize entry by carriers providing service to and from smaller communities. These "local service" carriers were sparingly certified and restricted largely to "feeder" routes that avoided competition with existing trunk carriers. By 1978, they still accounted for fewer than 10 percent of domestic revenue passenger miles (RPMs).[9] Mergers led to gradual consolidation in the market, with eleven of the sixteen original grandfathered trunk airlines and a dozen local service and regional carriers still operating in the late 1970s (Bailey, Graham, and Kaplan 1985, 15). This consolidation occurred against a backdrop of explosive traffic growth, with compounded annual growth rates of 14 percent to 16 percent in passenger enplanements and revenue passenger miles between 1938 and 1977 (see figure 2.1).

Expansion by incumbent carriers was similarly subject to strict oversight. As the Federal Aviation Report of 1935 argued: "To allow half a dozen airlines to eke out a hand-to-mouth existence where there is enough traffic to support one really first-class service and one alone would be a piece of folly" (in Meyer et al. 1981, 19). Trunk carriers wishing to expand onto routes served by an existing airline were required to show that their entry would not harm the incumbent carrier. The CAB only gradually allowed expansion of the trunk carriers to erode the highly concentrated route structure preserved in the grandfathered route networks. Growth of the local service carriers was largely stifled until the mid-1960s, when political pressure against the rising subsidies they were receiving convinced the CAB to allow them to enter into some profitable higher-density trunk markets. This system resulted in no more than one or two carriers authorized to provide service in all but the largest markets. In 1958, for example, twenty-three of the hundred largest city-pair markets were effectively monopolies; another fifty-seven were

8. 49 U.S.C. §1302 (1958).
9. A revenue passenger mile is one paying passenger flying one mile on a commercial flight.

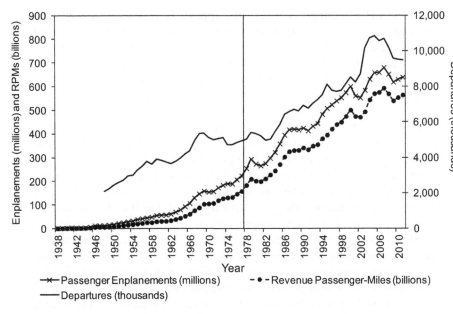

Fig. 2.1   US airlines domestic passenger traffic, 1938–2011

Sources: Data for 1938 to 1995 are from Airlines for America, Inc., "Annual Traffic and Ops: US Airlines," last modified June 7, 2008, accessed September 16, 2008, http://www.airlines .org/economics/traffic/Annual+US+Traffic.htm. Data for 1996 to 2011 are from Bureau of Transportation Statistics, RITA BTS, "US Air Carrier Traffic Statistics through September 2012" (Customize Table-Operating Statistics-System Scheduled Passenger Services), accessed January 15, 2013, http://apps.bts.gov/xml/air_traffic/src/index.xml.

Notes: Domestic scheduled revenue passenger miles and passenger enplanements, system-wide departures (includes international operations).

effectively duopolies; and in only two did the three largest carriers have less than a 90 percent share.[10]

The CAB's authority over route-level entry gave it control over airline network configurations. Over time, the CAB used this authority to generate implicit cross subsidies, awarding lucrative new routes to financially weaker carriers and using these awards as "carrots" to reward carriers for providing service on less-profitable routes (Caves 1962, chap. 9). Thus, carrier networks were optimized to maintain industry stability and minimize subsidies, but had no necessary connection to cost-minimizing or profit-maximizing design. Though there were concentrations of flight activity in airports at large population centers, the resulting networks were generally "point-to-point" systems, as illustrated in trunk carrier route maps (see figure 2.2 for an example). Moreover, the regulatory route award process largely

10. Caves (1962, 20). This defines monopoly markets as a single carrier with 90 percent or greater market share; duopoly as two carriers with a combined 90 percent or greater market share.

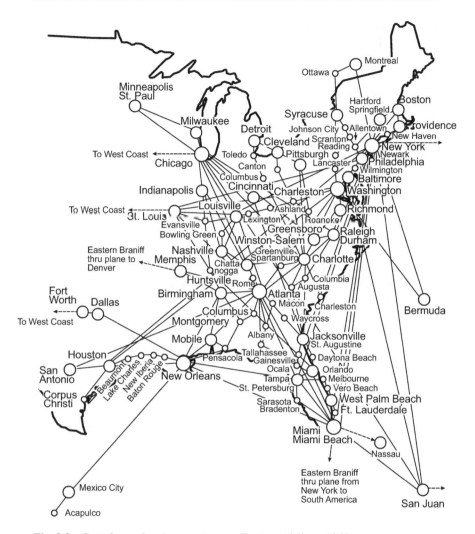

Fig. 2.2   Sample regulated era route map, Eastern Airlines, 1965

Source: www.airchive.com (http://airchive.com/html/timetable-and-route-maps/-eastern-air
lines-timetables-route-maps-and-history/1965-june-1-eastern-airlines-timetables-route
-maps-and-history/6842, accessed January 15, 2013).

prevented airlines from reoptimizing their networks to reduce operation
costs or improve service as technology and travel patterns changed.

Rate regulation was the second key component of government control.
The CAB was authorized to restrict entry in order to prevent destructive
competition, but monopoly routes raised the specter of monopoly pricing,
another concern of legislators during the 1920s and early 1930s. Authority
over rates was therefore deemed essential. An interesting transition occurred
between the 1934 act, which focused on maximum rates and elimination of

excess profits, and the 1938 act, which gave the CAB authority over minimum, maximum, and actual fares, at its discretion. Attention shifted from restraining market power in rate setting toward ensuring profit adequacy. Control over fares was one tool given to the Board; another was authority to set airmail rates "sufficient to insure the performance of such service, *and together with all other revenue of the air carrier*, to . . . maintain and continue the development of air transportation to the extent and of the character and quality required for the commerce of the United States, the Postal Service, and the national defense" (italics added, 72 Stat. 763, 49 U.S.C.A. 1376, in Caves 1962, 129).

In keeping with this focus, the Board approved general fare increases initiated by carriers and used the level of airmail rates and selective route awards to adjust profits toward implicit, and later explicit, target levels. Proposed discounts were viewed with skepticism and typically disallowed on the grounds that they disadvantaged competitors or were unduly discriminatory across passengers, even if the discounts were associated with lower quality service characteristics. Over time, the fare structure across markets became increasingly distorted in its relationship to cost structures, and resulted in fares substantially above efficient levels in many markets.

Not until the 1970–1974 Domestic Passenger Fare Investigation did the Board develop a formal cost-based standard for judging the reasonableness of fares. The resulting Standard Industry Fare Level (SIFL) formula provided a nonlinear distance-based formula for calculating fares based roughly on industry-level costs, a "reasonable" 12 percent rate of return, and target load factor of 55 percent. SIFL-based fares were intended to better align the cross-market fare structure with the distance-based economies of modern jet aircraft and mitigate the escalation of regulated fares as airline competition eroded profits through reduced load factors. The Board also returned to its historic preference for relatively level fare structures within markets, opposing a variety of promotional fares within markets on grounds of both discriminatory pricing and administrative complexity.

A starkly different industry structure developed in some intrastate markets, which were exempt from federal economic regulation by virtue of not crossing state lines and therefore provided a glimpse of the possibilities of unregulated air travel.[11] California became the poster child for advocates of regulatory reform, as large "lightly regulated" intrastate California markets could be compared to CAB-regulated interstate markets of comparable distance and density on the East Coast.[12] Similar comparisons ultimately were drawn for markets in Florida and, following the certification of Southwest

11. The CAB attempted various legal arguments to bring intrastate markets under its jurisdiction, most creatively and successfully in the case of intra-Hawaiian markets.
12. The California Public Utilities Commission had oversight authority for intrastate airline markets, but until mid-1965 could not regulate entry and exercised little control over fares. See Levine (1965).

Airlines in 1971, in Texas as well. Michael Levine (1965) and William Jordan (1970) focused attention on California. Levine argued that the scale of the air market between Los Angeles and San Francisco-Oakland—the largest market in the world at that time—was attributable in large part to the higher growth rates stemming from dynamic competition among a number of carriers that kept frequencies and load factors relatively high and fares remarkably low: "Although the lowest fare between Boston and Washington, served only by CAB-certificated trunk carriers, is $24.65, [the intrastate carrier] Pacific Southwest Airlines, using the same modern turbo-prop equipment, carries passengers between Los Angeles and San Francisco, only 59 miles closer together, for $11.43. The jet fare is only $13.50" (Levine 1965, 1433).

Keeler (1972) reached a similar conclusion based on his estimates of long-run competitive costs for airline service. His structural model, which predicted observed prices on unregulated intrastate routes to within about 3 percent of actual fares, suggested that regulated fares were substantially above competitive long-run costs—with 1968 margins ranging from 20 percent to nearly 100 percent over costs, generally increasing with distance.

High CAB-regulated fares did not translate into supranormal profits for the industry, however. This contrasted to the experience in regulated sectors such as interstate trucking.[13] Keeler (1972, 422) argued that high fares in conjunction with apparent normal rates of return to capital for airlines suggested that "airline regulation extracts high costs in inefficiency on high-density routes." Carriers responded to high margins with behavior that increased costs, reduced realized returns, and raised the cost of meeting a given level of demand for air service. As Kahn (1971, 2:209) argued: "If price is prevented from falling to marginal cost . . . then, to the extent that competition prevails, it will tend to raise cost to the level of price." Carriers continued to compete for passengers; with the suppression of price competition, they focused on schedule competition and other aspects of service quality.

Recognizing the potential significance of quality competition, the CAB over its history attempted direct control of some nonprice dimensions of competition. These included enforcement of connecting flight requirements on many route awards (to restrict nonstop competition) and limits on the use of first-class and sleeper-seat configurations (or imposition of fare surcharges for such configurations). Largely unregulated dimensions of service quality included a litany of amenities: interior aircraft configuration including seat spacing, inflight amenities including food and beverage service and entertainment, even flight attendant appearance and services.[14]

13. See Caves (1962) and Keeler (1972). Rose (1985, 1987) estimated rents for regulated less-than-truckload motor carriers in the range of 15 percent of total revenues.
14. See Braniff's "Air Strip" advertising campaign built around its designer flight attendant uniforms, viewable on Mary Wells Lawrence's "author's desktop" at http://www.random house.com/knopf/authors/lawrence/desktop.html\hb, accessed January 15, 2013.

The most costly forms of nonprice competition, however, focused on air-craft type, capacity, and scheduling. Here, regulatory action was mixed. Competition through new aircraft introduction was explicitly encouraged by the Board. The CAB consistently refused to allow airlines operating older, slower, and less comfortable aircraft to charge lower fares than competitors offering service on newer aircraft, even when these lower fares were argued to be necessary to preserve demand for the lower-quality service. This policy pushed carriers toward faster adoption and diffusion of new aircraft.

Capacity costs were further increased by airline scheduling responses to fixed prices. With passenger demand a function of price, schedule convenience, and expected seat availability (the latter also increasing in-flight quality by raising the probability of being next to an empty seat, and hence, more interior space), suppression of price competition encouraged carriers to increase flight frequency and capacity to compete for passengers. The intensity of flight competition was exacerbated by the apparent S-curve relationship between passenger share and flight share: a carrier with the majority of capacity on a route received a disproportionately high share of passengers (Fruhan 1972; Douglas and Miller 1974b; Eads 1975).

As Douglas and Miller (1974a) pointed out, however, competing in flight frequency is largely a zero-sum game across carriers. Given fixed prices and rivals' flight schedules, most of a carrier's expected increase in passenger volume from adding another flight comes from business stealing, not demand expansion. With high price-cost margins and the CAB legally prohibited from restricting carriers' flight schedules, the equilibrium of the noncooperative game is greater flight frequency and capacity, lower load factors (seats sold divided by seats available), and higher average costs per passenger mile. For example, average load factors in unregulated California intrastate markets exceeded 71 percent over 1960 to 1965, more than 15 percentage points higher than overall average load factors for trunk airlines in regulated markets over the same period (Keeler 1972, 414). Load factors in regulated airline markets not only decreased with the number of competitors on a route, but also declined with distance (Douglas and Miller 1974a; Eads 1975, 28–30). Observed load factors appeared to be lower than optimal load factors based on reasonable estimates of passengers' time valuations for all but relatively short monopoly markets (Douglas and Miller 1974a, 91; Eads 1975, 30).

Moreover, when the CAB attempted to increase rates of return by increasing prices, as it did at various points in its history, service competition intensified, leading to even lower load factors and higher average costs. As Douglas and Miller (1974a, 54) argued, "the fare level and structure, instead of determining or controlling profit rates, should be viewed principally as determining . . . the relative level of excess capacity and the associated level of service quality." Board efforts to raise carrier profits by increasing fares led to what became known as the "ratchet effect," as airlines responded to

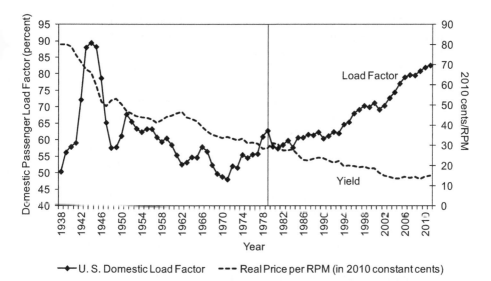

Fig. 2.3   Airline industry average domestic load factors and real yield, 1938–2011

Source: Domestic passenger yields are from Airlines for America, Inc., accessed January 10, 2013, http://www.airlines.org/Pages/Annual-Round-Trip-Fares-and-Fees-Domestic.aspx. For the domestic passenger load factor, see figure 2.1 sources.

Notes: Yields are scaled to include additional fees (primarily baggage and booking fee revenue) using authors' calculations. Adjusted to 2010 constant dollars using the CPI all-urban annual price deflator.

higher fares with increased flight frequency and declining load factors, and ultimately raised average costs rather than profitability.[15] By the early 1970s, average load factors had fallen below 50 percent for the first time since CAB regulation (see figure 2.3).

While rent dissipation through scheduling competition is well documented, there is less clear evidence on whether labor also extracted a share of the profits. In some industries, regulatory rents were shared with labor, either through increased employment, increased wages, or some combination of both (e.g., see Rose [1987] for estimates of labor rent sharing in the regulated trucking industry, and Hendricks [1994] and Peoples [1998] for cross-industry comparisons). There is some reason to think airline workers would similarly benefit from regulation: airlines were heavily unionized and union relations often were contentious. Dependence on key occupations such as pilots, FAA certification requirements that made it difficult or impossible for airlines to replace flight operations personnel during strikes, interunion rivalry for members of a given occupation class across firms, cooperation across unions representing different occupations within a firm,

15. See Paul Joskow's chapter in this volume for a discussion of the general phenomenon of strategic responses to regulatory incentives.

and CAB limits on airline entry and price competition all tended to enhance labor's ability to capture rents. But not all factors tilted in the direction of labor strength: labor union gains were limited by the ability of firms to use the Railway Labor Act provisions to delay or block strikes stemming from contract disputes, the lack of national bargaining units, and the 1958 creation of the Mutual Aid Pact, under which airlines agreed to cross-firm strike insurance payments.[16] In addition, while regulated prices prevented airlines with lower labor costs from capturing market share by underpricing higher-cost rivals, regulated prices were set on the basis of industry rather than firm-specific costs, implying possible high-powered profit incentives for firms to reduce costs relative to industry norms.[17]

Empirical evidence suggests that pilots, in particular, were effective in negotiating pay and work rule agreements that captured a significant share of productivity enhancements due to adoption of larger, faster aircraft (Caves 1962, 110). Comparisons of pilot wages and productivity levels between regulated carriers and intrastate carrier PSA are consistent with this pattern, although much of the productivity difference may be attributed directly to differential scheduling and fleet use resulting from PSA's focus on price rather than quality competition (Eads 1975). Empirical estimates of the extent of regulatory labor wage gains based on wage responses to airline deregulation suggest relatively modest effects, on the order of 10 to 15 percent of wages (Card 1997; Peoples 1998; Hirsch and Macpherson 2000; Hirsch 2007). Hendricks, Feuille, and Szerszen (1980) argue that estimates based on wage declines after deregulation may understate rent capture. They point out that deregulation increased the airlines' cost of strikes due to mandated elimination of the Mutual Aid Pact and the greater competitive disadvantage of firms that faced strikes in deregulated markets, while providing little immediate change in unionization rates or in market structure. Some support for their view is provided by Hirsch and Macpherson (2000) and Hirsch (2007), who find larger relative airline wage declines over time, and some evidence that wages follow firm profitability cycles.

16. The Mutual Aid Pact established a system of strike insurance among participating airlines. By 1970, amendments to the pact elicited participation by all trunk airlines but nonunion carrier Delta. The initial pact provided that "each party will pay over to the party suffering the strike an amount equal to its increased revenue attributable to the strike during the term thereof, less applicable direct expenses" (Unterberger and Koziara 1975, 27). Revisions over time specified guaranteed minimum payments at a specified fraction of the struck carrier's "normal air operating expenses." Unterberger and Koziara (1975) argue that the terms made some airlines more profitable during a strike than they were under normal operations, increasing the number and duration of observed strikes.

17. Setting prices independent of an individual carrier's cost would seem to yield high-powered incentives for cost minimization and technical efficiency by individual carriers (Laffont and Tirole 1993). This incentive was undermined, however, by the CAB's implicit policy of assigning profitable new routes to struggling carriers and unprofitable new routes to carriers that were highly profitable.

2.3   Airline Deregulation in the United States

In the mid-1970s, airline regulation began a drastic transformation.[18] Hearings held by Senator Edward Kennedy's Judiciary Committee in early 1975 dramatized the costs and inconsistencies of CAB regulation, and seem to have pushed airline regulation onto the national agenda.[19] Over the next three years, congressional hearings on the industry paralleled administrative reforms.

The appointment of pro-reform chairmen to the CAB heralded a dramatic departure in the Board's attitude toward regulation. The CAB became increasingly receptive to reform, approving discount fares and expanded charter operations under chair John Robson in 1976. This accelerated with the appointment of economist Alfred Kahn as chair in 1977 and Elizabeth Bailey as CAB member. Kahn—whose 1971 book remains today the preeminent analysis of the origins, principles, and effects of economic regulation—led the Board through a series of administrative reforms that reversed the agency's traditional preference for regulation over market determination of outcomes.

Political forces coalesced around legislative deregulation in 1978, with industry opposition splintering and eventually giving way with the passage of the Airline Deregulation Act by Congress, signed into law by President Carter in October 1978. The act provided for a phaseout of regulatory authority by January 1983, and elimination of the CAB itself by 1985. The most significant regulatory legacy was a continuing program of subsidies and oversight of service to small communities under the "Essential Air Service" program. The EAS was supposed to phase out in the 1980s, but political forces have kept it alive to this day. For service to all but these very small airports, however, the transition to deregulated markets occurred quite rapidly.

The confluence of several factors in the mid-1970s contributed to this reexamination and eventual repudiation of federal airline regulation in the United States. These included the contrast of CAB-set fares with fares in the intrastate California, Texas, and Florida markets; an increasing body of research documenting the problems with federal airline regulation; and political concern with rising price levels economy wide and stagnant eco-

18. Hundreds, if not thousands, of books and articles have been written on the politics and economics of airline passenger deregulation, with detail we cannot begin to replicate here. For a brief introduction, see Breyer (1982); Bailey, Graham, and Kaplan (1985); Kahn (1988); Borenstein (1992); Joskow and Noll (1994); Morrison and Winston (1986, 1995, 2000); and the references cited therein. Much less studied was the deregulation of air cargo, which preceded air passenger deregulation in the United States (see Bailey's [2010] discussion).

19. Breyer (1982, chap. 16), who was instrumental in focusing Kennedy's attention on airline regulation, provides a superb history and analysis of these events, and argues for Kennedy's role as a catalyst for eventual reform.

nomic growth, exacerbated by the 1973 and 1974 OPEC (Organization of the Petroleum Exporting Countries) oil price shock.[20] None of this, however, provides an entirely satisfactory explanation for why the airline industry was deregulated, or why it happened in 1978 and not earlier (or later). Though an important role must be assigned to political entrepreneurship by Senator Ted Kennedy and administrative reforms implemented by Alfred Kahn, these were probably not the only determinants, particularly given the coincidence of airline deregulation with regulatory reform across such disparate industries as trucking, natural gas, and banking, among others (Joskow and Rose 1989; Joskow and Noll 1994). Peltzman (1989) argues that changing economic interests in regulation were an important contributor (but see the comments on his paper in the same volume); Joskow and Noll (1994) and their commentators argue for a more multifaceted political economy interpretation. With few such deregulatory events, however, it is difficult to disentangle the complex interactions that lead to such major changes in the role government plays in the business economy.

The CAB moved quickly to implement provisions of the Airline Deregulation Act of 1978 and accelerated the shift from government to market decision making in the industry. Many entrepreneurs were quick to respond to the new opportunities—new entrants proliferated and some incumbents expanded rapidly—while management at some of the "legacy" airlines proved to be much less nimble. The impact of deregulation became evident in several areas: removing regulatory price controls was followed by lower average prices, a substantial increase in price variation, and efforts to soften price competition through differentiation and increases in brand loyalty. Lifting entry restrictions altered market structure at the industry, airport, and route levels, and led to reorganization of incumbent airline networks. The industry also developed new organizational forms, including code sharing and alliances across airlines, particularly in the aftermath of tighter merger policy. Shifting from nonprice to price competition reduced many aspects of service quality, although the quality declines of most concern to customers are most likely attributable not to deregulation but to government infrastructure policy, as we discuss later. While some of these impacts were anticipated during the debate over deregulation, others were quite unexpected (see Kahn 1988).

2.3.1   Price Levels, Dispersion, and Loyalty Programs

The aftermath of US airline deregulation seemed to confirm the forecasts of academic economists and others who predicted substantial fare reductions and concomitant traffic growth. In the first decade of deregulation, between 1978 and 1988, average domestic yield (revenue per passenger mile), as shown in figure 2.3, declined in real terms at an average compound rate

---

20. See the discussion by Bailey (2010).

of 2.0 percent per year, while domestic revenue passenger miles, shown in figure 2.1, increased at an average compound rate of 6.1 percent per year. In the subsequent twenty-three years, real yields declined at 1.9 percent per year, and traffic grew at an annual compounded rate of 2.4 percent.

Such figures are often presented to argue the success of airline deregulation. A comparison to the pre-deregulation era, however, demonstrates that the argument for deregulation must be made much more thoughtfully: in the decade *prior* to the onset of deregulation, 1968 to 1978, real domestic yield declined at a rate of 2.1 percent per year and traffic growth outpaced the post-deregulation decade, at an annual rate of 7.6 percent. Thus, attribution to deregulation requires a more carefully constructed counterfactual.

Price Levels

In examining airline prices, one appealing counterfactual is the regulatory cost-based Standard Industry Fare Level (SIFL) formula created by the CAB to determine fares just prior to deregulation. The Department of Transportation (DOT) continues to update this formula based on input cost and productivity changes in part for use in US-Canada fare negotiations.[21] Figure 2.4 presents a comparison of passenger mile weighted average yields and SIFL-based yields for tickets in Databank 1A's 10 percent sample of all airline tickets.[22] Actual fares were about 26 percent lower than SIFL-formula fares in 2011, suggesting a consumer welfare increase in the range of $31 billion in that year.[23]

Even this comparison merits closer scrutiny, however. Three underlying assumptions are critical. First, the SIFL calculation takes productivity gains in the industry as exogenous. If deregulation brought about some of these gains, and they would not have occurred under regulation, then the SIFL is understating the counterfactual fares and understating the benefits of deregulation.[24] Second, the SIFL assumes a 55 percent load factor, while planes are much more crowded than that, with domestic load factors hitting 83 percent in 2011. If, for a given schedule of flights, 80 percent of costs are

21. See US Department of Transportation Standard Industry Fare Level at http://www.dot .gov/policy/aviation-policy/standard-industry-fare-level accessed January 15, 2013.

22. The calculation reported here includes free travel tickets in the DB1A, most of which are frequent flyer bonus trips. Excluding all tickets with fares of $10 and below raises the actual yields by about 4 percent. Dollar savings are scaled up from the 10 percent sample in the DB1A. Baggage and ticket change fees are also included in the scaled calculation of average ticket prices. DB1A data are not available prior to 1979.

23. We arrive at this number by assuming constant quality and a constant elasticity demand with long-run elasticity of −1, then calculating the difference in consumer surplus from the actual 2011 average yield and domestic RPMs and the counterfactual SIFL price level and associated quantity along the same demand curve.

24. Morrison and Winston (1995, 12–14), performing a similar analysis of actual to SIFL fares for 1976 through 1993, argue that deregulation increased productivity, and therefore adjust the SIFL index upward by 1.2 percent per year over 1978 and 1983, and by a constant 8.7 percent thereafter, to remove estimated deregulation-related productivity gains.

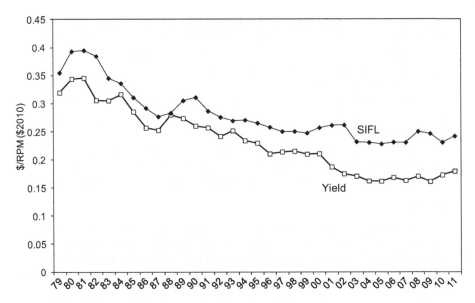

Fig. 2.4   Real yield (rev/passenger mile) versus DOT standard industry fare level, 1979–2011

Notes: Authors' calculations are from DOT Databank 1A/1B. The SIFL formula is available at http://www.dot.gov/policy/aviation-policy/standard-industry-fare-level (accessed January 15, 2013).

assumed to be invariant to changes in the load factor (i.e., to the number of passengers flown) over this range,[25] then adjusting for the change in load factor would spread those costs over 51 percent more passengers (83 percent divided by 55 percent). The effect would be to lower the SIFL for 2011 by 27 percent $(1 - (0.2 + 0.8/1.51)$ and the change in consumer surplus from deregulation would be slightly *negative*. Third and finally, the SIFL formula was for full-fare coach tickets, but even prior to deregulation limited discounting was permitted. Richards (2007) presents evidence that actual average coach fares were about 15 percent below SIFL in 1977, just prior to deregulation, though significant relaxation of fare controls had already occurred by then. Obviously, if actual average coach fares would have been 15 percent below SIFL under regulation, that alone would eliminate about half of the benefits typically calculated.

These potential changes highlight the difficulty in calculating a true counterfactual against which to judge airline deregulation. Much more important than these technical corrections, however, is the underlying assumption

25. This number comes from assuming that all costs are invariant to number of passengers except 25 percent of labor costs, 50 percent of advertising costs, 100 percent of food costs, and 100 percent of passenger commissions, all of which are assumed to increase linearly in the number of passengers.

that airline regulation would not have changed. For example, it is quite possible that incentive mechanisms, as have become common in electricity regulation, would have been adopted under continued airline regulation and led to some of the productivity improvements that have occurred under deregulation. On the other hand, the continuation of regulatory control would have made it easier for politicians, or even the airlines themselves, to subvert the regulatory process to their own advantage.[26] Similarly, more than three decades of deregulation has taught lessons about antitrust and consumer protection that would likely influence and, one hopes, improve public policy toward a less regulated airline industry.

Regardless of exactly how one calculates the fare declines attributable to deregulation, it is clear that the gains from those lower prices have not been distributed uniformly across customers. While deregulation advocates argued that the CAB may have allowed too little variation in fares—failing to account for difference across carriers in their service amenities, not permitting off-peak discounts in order to align fares with variations in the shadow costs of capacity, and not recognizing differential costs across leisure and business customers—few, if any, people predicted the resulting enormous range of prices, both across and within routes.[27] Relative to the SIFL (and pre-deregulation prices), fares have fallen more on long routes than on short routes. Fares have also remained higher in concentrated markets and on flights in and out of airports dominated by a single carrier, all else equal. And although average fares were 26 percent below SIFL in 2011, nearly one-third of economy class passengers paid a fare greater than the SIFL for the route on which they were flying.

Variation in Prices across Routes

There is considerable variation in average price levels across routes, and this variation has not been stable over time. The lower line in figure 2.5 shows the coefficient of variation of route average fares after controlling for route distance.[28] Cross-route price variation peaked in 1996 at a level that was nearly twice the variation in 1979 and 66 percent higher than in 2011.

The identity of competitors, in addition to the presence of competition,

26. An interesting and unknowable question is how a regulator would have handled the airlines' post–9/11 financial crisis. Would, for instance, the airlines have been able to push through regulated fare increases to compensate for weak demand even though the industry had massive excess capacity?

27. Through most of the regulated era, fare structures typically consisted of a standard coach and first-class fare on each route with very limited exceptions, such as a youth or family discount fare. A significant deviation from this policy was the Board's 1966 approval of "Discover America" excursion fares for leisure markets and off-season transcontinental flights.

28. This calculation is done by dividing all routes into fifty-mile distance categories. The coefficient of variation of route-averaging fares is calculated for each distance category, where each route is weighted by revenue passenger-miles. The measure shown in figure 2.5 is the weighted average of these measures across all distance categories, where the weights are total revenue passenger miles in each distance category.

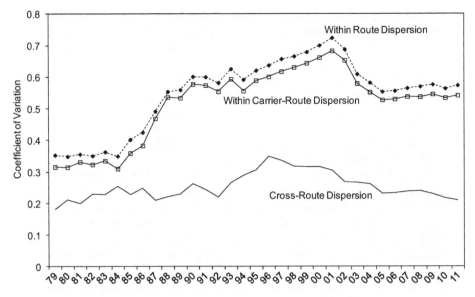

Fig. 2.5   Within-route and cross-route price dispersion, 1979–2011

Notes: Authors' calculations are from domestic tickets in Databank 1A/1B using only tickets of 4-coupons or fewer. (See "Translation of Domestic DB1A into More Usable Form," http://faculty.haas.berkeley.edu/borenste/airdata.html.) This analysis drops all fares less than zero and greater than four times SIFL for observed route, and drops all fares labeled first-class except for Southwest, Jet Blue, Spirit, Frontier, and ATA, which report all or nearly all seats as first-class during some quarters. Cross-route dispersion excludes 1980 data from the fourth quarter because Eastern and Delta massively underreported to the DOT 10 percent ticket sample. Annual data are the average of quarterly calculations, weighted by revenue passenger miles.

appears to be an important determinant of route average price levels. Since before airline deregulation, there have been "no-frills" or "low-cost" carriers that have operated with much lower costs than the regulated legacy airlines, though they operated solely intrastate before 1978. The best known of these today is Southwest, but many others have entered and most have exited over the thirty-five years since deregulation. This failure rate is puzzling given the enormous cost advantages they seemed to maintain. Figure 2.6 tracks the standard industry cost measure of cents per available seat mile (ASM),[29] in constant 2010 dollars, for the legacy carriers (and their successor companies) and for the largest low-cost entrants that have operated since deregulation, many of which did not survive or have made trips through bankruptcy court.[30] The presence of these low-cost competitors

29. An available seat mile is one seat flown one mile on a commercial flight.
30. The figure does not adjust for average flight distance, which is inversely related to cost per ASM. Adjusting for flight distance expands the cost advantage of the low-cost carriers, because most fly shorter flights than industry average.

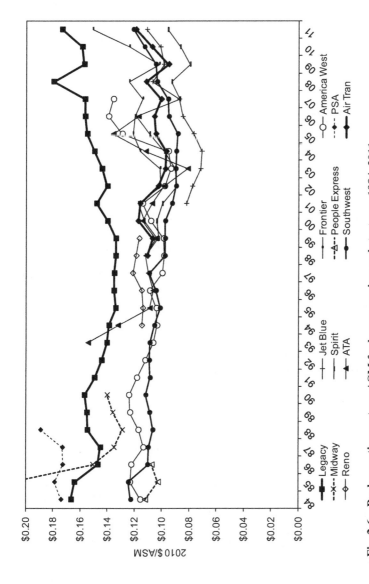

Fig. 2.6 Real operating cost per ASM for legacy carriers and start-ups, 1984–2011

Note: Authors' calculations are from DOT Form 41, Schedule P6.

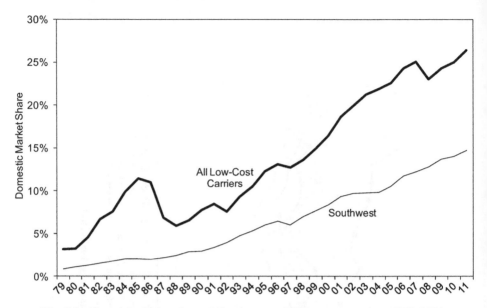

Fig. 2.7   Domestic market share of Southwest and all low-cost carriers, 1979–2011

Notes: Authors' calculations are from DOT Form 41, Schedule P6. Low-Cost Carriers are defined as Air Tran, America West, ATA, Frontier, Jet Blue, Midway, People Express, PSA, Reno, Southwest, Spirit, and ValuJet. Share based on domestic revenue passenger miles.

on a route substantially dampens average fare levels (e.g., for analyses, see Borenstein 1989, 2013; Morrison 2001; Goolsbee and Syverson 2008). Low-cost carriers have expanded substantially since the late 1980s, due in part to continued expansion of Southwest and in part to the rapid growth of some other low-cost airlines (see figure 2.7).

Variation in Prices across Passengers on the Same Route

Despite the CAB's historic reluctance to deviate from very simple fare structures, some price variation is undoubtedly efficient in the airline industry. With fixed capacity, a nonstorable product, and demand that varies both predictably and stochastically, efficient prices will vary intertemporally with demand realizations. Even tickets on the same flight purchased at different times may efficiently carry different prices (see Prescott 1975; Salop 1978; Dana 1999a, 1999b). Moreover, Ramsey-Boiteux prices yield differential markups across customers based on relative price elasticities of demand as the constrained welfare-maximizing solution to compensating firms with substantial fixed costs. While these considerations suggest deviations from the relatively level regulated fare structure, however, few observers were prepared for the often-bewildering array of fares available (and prices actually paid by different passengers) on any given airline route.

The CAB's "administrative deregulation" push over 1976 to 1978 encouraged airlines to experiment with pricing. Airlines were quick to use pricing flexibility to introduce fare variation. In 1977, American Airlines took advantage of the CAB's new push toward fare flexibility to introduce a menu of "Super Saver" fare schedules. These were targeted at increasing air travel among leisure travelers, with ticket restrictions that included both advanced purchase (fourteen or twenty-one days) and minimum stay (seven days or longer, generally). With deregulation in 1978, discount fares flourished. Airlines soon recognized that Saturday-night stay restrictions were nearly as effective as minimum-stay requirements in excluding low-elasticity business travelers from discount fare purchases, and imposed lower costs on the high-elasticity discretionary customers at whom the low fares were aimed. The Saturday-night stay restriction replaced minimum stay on discount tickets in most markets, and became the standard self-selection device for major airlines over the next twenty-five years.

The effect of this was an almost immediate boost in fare dispersion. The highest (dashed) line in figure 2.5 shows the average within-route coefficient of variation of fares. Such a measure of dispersion aggregates within carrier-route dispersion with variation in average prices across carriers on a route. The slightly lower solid line (with boxes) in figure 2.5 shows the average within carrier-route dispersion, demonstrating that most of the price variation is due to individual airlines charging different prices to different customers on the same route (and on the same flight).

Average levels of fare dispersion mask significant differences across carriers and routes, however. Some carriers, particularly among the low-cost and entrant airlines, have relatively few ticket categories, and relatively low gradients of fare increases as restrictions are removed. Others may have twenty or more different ticket restriction/price combinations available for purchase on a given route. Moreover, there appear to be substantial differences across routes in dispersion. Borenstein and Rose (1994) analyze the determinants of price dispersion, with particular attention to the impact of competition, using a cross-section of carrier routes in 1987. That work suggests that dispersion increased with the move from monopoly to duopoly to more competitive route structures. This finding is consistent with price discrimination based not only on customer heterogeneity in their overall elasticity of demand for air travel (e.g., across business and leisure travelers), but also on heterogeneity in cross-brand price elasticities, such as might result from differences in airline loyalty. Gerardi and Shapiro (2009) argue that relationship is not robust to alternative identification strategies, and evidence on the relationship between price dispersion and competition varies across studies in both the US and EU markets (e.g., Stavins 2001; Giaume and Guillou 2004; Gaggero and Piga 2011; Orlov 2011).

Over time, however, fare structures grew even more complex, with an increasing variety of advanced purchase durations (three, seven, fourteen, and twenty-one days being most common), discounts for low travel-demand days or times, temporary price promotions, negotiated corporate discounts, upgradeable economy tickets, and more recently, web-only, auction-determined, and "buyer offer" prices. The spread between the top unrestricted fares and lowest discounted fares also increased. This was accompanied by the development and increasing sophistication of management systems that monitor the evolution of demand relative to forecast demand, set overbooking limits, and allocate seats to each fare "bucket" to maximize expected revenue for the airline (Belobaba 1987). American Airlines, which was in the vanguard of developing these systems, reported that yield management systems added approximately \$500 million, or roughly 5 percent, to annual revenue for the airline in the early 1990s (Smith, Leimkuhler, and Darrow 1992). This is an enormous effect, of the same order of magnitude as the total net income/sales ratios for the industry. Revenue management systems have become an important management and strategic tool, with simulation estimates suggesting "the potential for revenue gains of 1 to 2 percent from advanced network revenue management methods, above and beyond the 4 to 6 percent gains realized from conventional leg-based fare class control" (Barnhart, Belobaba, and Odoni 2003, 383).

As illustrated by the closeness of the two higher curves in figure 2.5, cross-carrier variation in mean prices contributes relatively little to within-route dispersion; most is attributable to the enormous variation in prices any one carrier charges in a given market. The pattern illustrated in this figure is consistent with increasing concern over fare structure complexity and price dispersion through the 1990s. Price dispersion within carrier routes more than doubled between 1979 and 2001. The 2001 coefficient of variation of 0.72 implies a standard deviation that is nearly three-quarters of the mean fare. Since 2001, within-route dispersion has declined to levels not seen since the late 1980s, though still much higher than in the earliest years of deregulation. This has been accompanied by declines in cross-route price dispersion; as discussed later, both may reflect the impact of greater penetration by low-cost carriers.

Loyalty Programs

American Airlines led the industry into the use of loyalty programs with its introduction of the first frequent flyer program in 1980. Other airlines quickly followed. Since then, airlines have offered loyalty programs not only for individual customers in the form of frequent flyer programs, but also for travel agents who steer clients their way, and to corporations in the form of quantity-based discounts. Frequent flyer programs evolved into businesses on their own in the late 1980s as airlines began to sell frequent flyer points to other retailers—hotels, supermarkets, and credit cards, for example—to then be given to customers. While other retail sectors have followed suit with their own loyalty programs, airline frequent flyer programs remain by far the most successful.[31]

Loyalty programs typically reward travelers or travel agents with a non-linear schedule of potential rewards, generating an increasing return to incremental purchases. The programs for individuals and travel agents also take advantage of an incentive conflict that may exist between the entity paying for the ticket (often the individual's employer or the agent's customer) and the person receiving the loyalty bonus (the traveler or travel agent).[32] Loyalty programs soften price competition across carriers, as they induce a switching cost for travelers (or travel agents) by raising net cost if travel is spread over several airlines rather than concentrated on a single airline over time.[33] The programs also link service across markets, basing rewards on the total amount purchased from the airline in all markets, not just one city pair, and providing greater redemption opportunities on airlines with substantial service in a passenger's home market. In this way, they potentially further insulate large network carriers from competition on individual routes, particularly out of their hubs (see Lederman 2008). Over time, refinements to the programs leveraged the effect by offering enhanced access to benefits such as preferential boarding, seating, upgrades, and free travel availability to the highest volume travelers flying 50,000, 100,000 or more miles on the airline within a calendar year.

During the 1980s, policymakers became concerned that some airlines used distribution systems to unfairly insulate themselves from price competition. Until the late 1990s, travel agents issued more than 80 percent of all airline tickets, with the bulk of the remainder issued directly by the airlines. In the 1980s, agents started using computer reservation systems (CRSs) that allowed them to directly access airline availability and fare information. CRSs grew out of airlines' internal computer systems and were originally owned by the airlines. This raised the potential for airline owners to bias the systems' response to information queries in a way that advantaged them and limited price competition. Concern about bias of information displays in favor of one carrier became a competitive issue for much of the 1980s and

31. Changes to these programs have greatly devalued the frequent flyer points as flight currency over the past several years, increasing the miles needed to redeem award travel and reducing the number of seats available for those awards. This strategy seems to have reduced the concerns some analysts have voiced about the airlines' liability represented by the billions of outstanding points. For many frequent flyers, the chief value of loyalty programs now lies in the preferential boarding and upgrades accorded to the high mileage elite tier card-holders.

32. The most obvious manifestation of agency problems were short-lived promotions in late 1988 and 1989, such as the Eastern shuttle promotion—they handed passengers $50 American Express gift checks as they boarded—and Continental's promotion—they gave a $50 bill (distributed at the airport) to customers traveling on high-fare tickets.

33. Borenstein (1996) presents a model of repeat-buyer programs in network industries and discusses their use in many industries throughout the twentieth century.

1990s, ultimately leading to formal regulatory restrictions on CRS display criteria in 1984 and 1992.[34]

This concern has faded with the second major innovation in the distribution: use of the Internet. As users of sophisticated electronic reservation and ticketing interfaces with travel agents, the airlines were well prepared to move into Internet sales of their product, and airline and independent travel agencies were early adopters of Internet marketing and sales. This had particular appeal to airlines, who saw the Internet as a way to bypass the traditional sales channel—travel agents—in favor of lower-cost electronic ticketing methods. For years, airlines had complained about inefficiency of travel agency distribution and the high cost of travel agent commissions, at 10 percent or more of ticket prices. No single airline was willing to reduce their commission rate unilaterally, however, fearing that travel agents would "book away" from them. With the diffusion of Internet sales, carriers saw an alternative.

In the last fifteen years, online ticketing has skyrocketed, comprising more than 30 percent of sales in 2002 and an estimated 40 to 50 percent as of 2006 (GAO 2003; Brunger 2009; Barnes 2012). Airlines have gradually eliminated travel agent commissions on domestic tickets and reduced commissions on international tickets. They now generally charge higher distribution fees for tickets not sold electronically, even for those booked directly with the airline over the phone. While reduced travel agency commissions and online ticketing have dramatically reduced airlines' distribution costs, the Internet also has made it easier for customers to shop for low fares, find alternative airlines and routings, and generally become better informed about travel options and their costs. Some have argued that the greater transparency of airline fare structures to final consumers may have contributed substantially to reduced bookings for full-fare, unrestricted tickets, and explain at least part of the collapse in intracarrier price dispersion. This also may be an important factor in the dramatic rise of ancillary fees for services that began with reservation changes and checked baggage and now may include advance seat reservations, preferred boarding status and seating, onboard food and entertainment, and even carry-on bags. While online travel search engines could be susceptible to display bias of various kinds (an issue that has attracted considerable attention with respect to their hotel listings, for example), the largest systems claim to present neutral airline displays, and allow consumers to re-sort search results according to a variety of criteria.

---

34. These restrictions were lifted in 2004 based on the argument that there are now many more competing sources of fare, schedule, and seat-availability information.

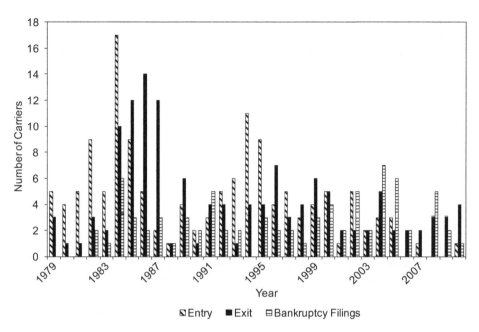

Fig. 2.8   Airline entry, exit, and bankruptcy filings, 1979–2011

Notes: See Jordan (2005) for events through 2003. Carrier entry and exit after 2003 updated from BTS carrier annual carrier reporting groups, see, for example, http://www.rita.dot.gov /bts/sites/rita.dot.gov.bts/files/subject_areas/airline_information/accounting_and_reporting _directives/pdf/number_304a.pdf. Bankruptcies updated with information from Airlines for America, Inc., http://www.airlines.org/Pages/U.S.-Airline-Bankruptcies-and-Service-Cessa tions.aspx.

2.3.2   Entry and Exit, Airline Networks, and Market Structure

Entry and Exit

Expansion by existing carriers and entry by new firms dramatically altered industry structure in the immediate aftermath of deregulation. The eleven trunk and dozen local service/Alaska/Hawaii "legacy" carriers authorized to provide regulated jet service prior to 1978 were joined by forty-seven new entrants by 1984. Most of the new entrants and some of the legacy carriers left the industry through acquisition or liquidation over the subsequent decade; forty-eight carriers exited between 1984 and 1987 alone. Figure 2.8 records the number of airlines entering or exiting the industry, as well as the number of airline bankruptcy filings, each year.[35] Of the carriers who began interstate service through 1984, only seven operated in 1990, and only two

35. A common finding in many industries is that entry rates and exit rates are highly temporally correlated (see Dunne, Roberts, and Samuelson 1998).

remain in operation today.[36] This appears to reflect more than transitional uncertainty in the aftermath of deregulation. Entry peaked again in the mid-1990s, with eighteen independent new entrants between 1993 and 1995, only two of which remained in operation through 2012.[37] By the end of 2011, thirty-three years after deregulation, six of the twenty-three legacy carriers continued to serve the domestic market, with a combined domestic market share of 59 percent.[38]

Financial distress, reorganization, and exit have been as much a part of the industry as new entry since deregulation. Of the six airlines that carried at least 5 percent each of domestic US traffic in 2011, five (Continental, USAir, Delta, United, and American) have filed Chapter 11 bankruptcy at least once. Only Southwest has not gone through bankruptcy reorganization. We discuss the causes of this financial volatility in section 2.5, but emphasize here that Chapter 11 bankruptcy filings do not equate with an airline shutting down. Although some of the carriers that have entered bankruptcy have been liquidated, the majority have emerged to operate as publicly held companies or been merged into another airline, generally with operations disrupted for little or no time.

While bankruptcies are costly for the affected firms' shareholders and their workers, and are broadly disparaged by politicians and industry lobbyists, there is little evidence that they harm competitors or consumers. Borenstein and Rose (1995) found that airlines tend to lower their fares before entering bankruptcy, but healthy competitors do not follow and the fare declines are generally short lived. When bankrupt carriers do reduce service, other airlines generally are quick to jump into their abandoned markets. Borenstein and Rose (2003) find no statistically discernible effect on the service to small and large airports when a carrier with operations at the airport declares bankruptcy. Even at medium-sized airports, where they do find a statistically significant effect, total service to the airport declines by less than half the number of flights that the filing carrier offered before bankruptcy.

Airline Networks

Incumbent airlines responded to elimination of regulatory restrictions on routes they could serve by restructuring as well as expanding their networks. The almost immediate transformation from the point-to-point systems created by the CAB entry policies into hub-and-spoke networks was perhaps

36. Southwest Airlines and America West, which was renamed USAir after its purchase of that rival.

37. Those two are AirTran, which in 2013 is being merged into Southwest, and Frontier, now owned by Republic Airways Holding.

38. As of 2012, survivors included three former trunk airlines, American, Delta, and United; local service carrier USAir (though now owned by a new entrant); and former Alaskan/Hawaiian carriers Alaska and Hawaiian Airlines. The late 2013 approval of the American Airlines and USAir merger further reduces this number.

the most unanticipated result of deregulation, and fundamentally altered the economics of airline operations. The new networks served passengers traveling to and from the central hub airports with nonstop service, and passengers traveling between two points on the spokes with change-of-plane service through hub airports.

The hub-and-spoke configuration provides cost, demand, and competitive advantages. Hubs generally increase available flight options for passengers traveling to and from hubs and facilitate more convenient service on routes for which demand is not sufficient to support frequent nonstop service at relatively low prices. Operating cost economies arise from the increased density of operations, allowing the airline to offer frequent service on a segment while maintaining high load factors. At the same time, because very few airports have the logistic or economic capacity to support more than one large-scale hub operation, competition at the hub airports typically is quite limited, yielding substantial market power for airlines at their own hubs. In addition, the frequent flights and extensive destinations available on the hub airline tend to give that airline a demand advantage versus its competitors on routes out of the hub (Borenstein 1991), arising from fundamental consumer preferences and substantially enhanced by the development of airline loyalty programs subsequent to deregulation. These effects have been reflected in less competition on routes to/from hub airports compared to other markets.

Examining concentration for trips to and from the twelve major hubs that existed for a significant share of the thirty-three years since deregulation[39] reveals an interesting pattern. These routes were slightly less concentrated than the national average until the mid-1980s, but diverged markedly by 1989, with hub-route Herfindahl-Hirschman Indexes (HHIs) averaging 0.48 versus 0.40 for nonhub routes. Since then, the difference has gradually narrowed. In the most recent data, average concentration is nearly the same on hub and nonhub routes.

Market Structure

While the early entry wave substantially reduced concentration in deregulated airline markets, merger activity in the mid-1980s acted as a substantial counterweight. Mergers peaked in the mid-1980s, when antitrust policy was relatively lax and greater credence was given to the view that potential competition could discipline prices as effectively as actual competition. By 1990, as antitrust policy became stricter in general and concerns about airline competition and hub dominance increased, merger activity slowed considerably, and most subsequent successful merger proposals involved at least one airline that was in extreme financial distress. Until the spate of mergers following the 2008 financial crisis—Delta/Northwest, United/Continental,

39. These are ORD, ATL, DFW, DEN, STL, DTW, MSP, PIT, IAH, CLT, SLC, and MEM.

and Southwest/Air Tran—others, such as the USAir/United merger proposed in 1999, met with sufficient threat of antitrust opposition that they usually were withdrawn.

As mergers declined, alternative forms of linkages were introduced. In the 1980s, major US airlines had pioneered partnerships with small commuter airlines that allowed each carrier to sell tickets for trips that use the commuter airline to bring the passenger to the carrier's hub and then the large carrier to fly between major airports. These partnerships allowed coordination of schedules and "code-sharing," which presented the product as a single-airline ticket. Other carriers, most notably American, chose instead to vertically integrate into the commuter airline business, buying some commuter carriers and expanding their fleet to form American Eagle, which is wholly owned by American Airlines.[40]

Code-sharing alliances between major carriers began with agreements between US and foreign air carriers as a response to regulation of entry on international routes.[41] By the late 1990s, these were extended to relationships among many large US airlines. Northwest and Continental, for instance, formed an alliance that allowed each to sell tickets under its own brand name that included flights on the other airline. These alliances, domestic and international, now generally include cooperative arrangements for frequent flyer plans, joint marketing, facilities sharing, and scheduling, though prices are required to be set independently.

Economic analyses suggest that alliances create value for customers, by converting interairline connections to apparent online connections and by allowing airlines to coordinate schedules to improve the quality of those connections. Bamburger, Carlton, and Neumann (2004) analyze the Continental/America West and Northwest/Alaska alliances, and conclude that prices declined in markets where the alliance created an "online" code-shared flight from an interline connection across the two carriers. They find a significant increase in traffic in those markets for the Continental/America West alliance. Armantier and Richard (2006) report similar findings for code-shared connecting itineraries in the Northwest and Continental alliance, but report higher prices for nonstop flights by alliance carriers. Armantier and Richard's (2008) analysis of net consumer welfare effects suggests that surplus gains by connecting passengers were offset by surplus losses of nonstop passengers.[42] Lederman (2007) finds evidence of an additional con-

40. Some airline decisions on organizational form were undoubtedly influenced by expected operational and labor costs associated with ownership of commuter carriers. See Forbes and Lederman (2009). American Airlines twice has announced plans to sell American Eagle, but these were postponed as a result of the 2008 financial crisis and American's bankruptcy filing in 2011.

41. Frustrated by restrictions on entering international routes, major US carriers began to create "alliances" with foreign carriers that followed the same model as their partnerships with commuter airlines.

42. Bamburger, Carlton, and Neumann (2004) do not separately analyze these markets.

sumer benefit in her analysis of international alliances: an airline's domestic demand appears to increase as a result of travel opportunities created by a new international alliance. This has mixed implications for consumers in equilibrium, however. If, as seems plausible, this results from demand spillovers through a more attractive frequent flyer plan, the loyalty effect of the frequent flyer plan may provide incentives for ultimately raising prices.

The net effect of these various changes in the industry was a decline in average concentration at the route level in the immediate aftermath of deregulation. From an average route-level HHI of about 0.55 in 1980, the HHI declined on both hub and nonhub routes through the early 1980s (see figure 2.9) with the national average HHI hitting its lowest point of 0.41 in 1986. Concentration, particularly on hub routes, rose from the late 1980s through the late 1990s, before declining somewhat in the 2000s. In the 2008 to 2011 period, concentration levels for all routes averaged about 0.46. How much of the reconsolidation through the 1990s was inevitable in an unregulated market and how much was the result of ancillary government policies including liberal merger policy continues to be debated. That debate was invigorated by the post-2007 mergers among the handful of remaining large carriers. Two unanticipated developments—reconfiguration of airline route

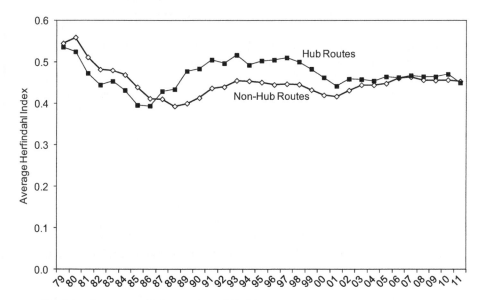

Fig. 2.9   Route-level concentration, 1979–2011

Notes: Authors' calculations are from domestic tickets in Databank 1A/1B using only tickets of 4-coupons or fewer. (See "Broadened Market Dataset," http://faculty.haas.berkeley.edu /borenste/airdata.html). The airports counted as hubs are ORD, ATL, DFW, DEN, STL, DTW, MSP, PIT, IAH, CLT, SLC, and MEM. Excludes data from the fourth quarter of 1980 (see figure 2.5 notes). Annual data are the average of quarterly calculations, weighted by revenue passenger miles.

networks into hub-and-spoke systems, and strategic innovations in loyalty programs that differentiated airlines' services and dampened competition—contributed to increases in route-level concentration. Government policies, however, particularly with respect to antitrust, exacerbated any latent tendencies toward concentration. The question of whether market power concerns require something more than antitrust attention continues to surface; we address it in section 2.5.

2.3.3   Service Quality

Once carriers were free to compete on price, the nature of competition required reevaluation. Historically, airlines have found it easier to differentiate price across passengers on a route than quality (apart from premium class service—business or first—with its own cabin), though over time there has been greater use of access to priority security lines and boarding, upgrades, and preferred seating for an airline's most valued customers. These historically were based on frequent flyer status and undiscounted fare tickets, but more recently are often available for à la carte purchase at additional fees. Some quality attributes associated with network reconfiguration and increased density, such as flight frequency and online connections, were maintained or improved following deregulation. Others, such as safety levels, which continue to be regulated, were unaffected. Many, particularly those associated with onboard amenities, have been reduced. Airport congestion and flight delays, which are among the most visible and significant declines in service quality, may be attributed more to the success of deregulation in increasing traffic and to the failure of infrastructure policy to keep pace with traffic growth than to altered carrier decisions under economic deregulation. Reduced levels of service quality overall do not imply that consumers as a group are worse off, though quality-loving, price-inelastic consumers may well be. We turn next to deregulatory impacts on service quality with respect to some of the key service quality metrics.

Flight Frequency and Connections

The reorganization of airline networks following deregulation led to increased frequency for service to and from hub airports and reduced nonstop service between smaller airports, all else equal (see Bailey, Graham, and Kaplan 1985, 83–86). There is a common view that deregulation led to a significant increase in the share of passengers that had to change planes. The change, however, was actually quite small. The dashed line in figure 2.10 presents the share of domestic passengers who changed planes from 1979 to 2011. These raw data, however, do not account for another change that was occurring at the same time: the average trip distance (nonstop origin to destination) was increasing—from 873 miles in 1979 to 1,067 in 2011—so more people were flying longer distance trips on which changing planes is more common. The solid line in figure 2.10 presents the same data adjusted

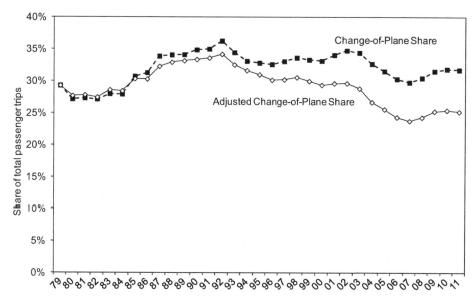

Fig. 2.10   Change-of-plane share with and without distance adjustment, 1979–2011

Notes: Author calculations from domestic tickets in Databank 1A/1B using only tickets of 4-coupons or fewer. (See "Translation of Domestic DB1A into More Usable Form," http://faculty.haas.berkeley.edu/borenste/airdata.html). Excludes 1980 data from the fourth quarter (see figure 2.5 notes). Change-of-plane (COP) share is the total number of directional trips (a round-trip is two directional trips) that include a change of planes divided by all directional trips. Adjusted change-of-plane (ACOP) share is set equal to COP share for 1979. For all successive years, ACOP share is the previous year's ACOP plus the weighted average change in COP share in all fifty-mile distance categories, where the weight is the previous year's passengers in each fifty-mile distance category.

for trip length.[43] Controlling for trip distance, a substantially smaller share of customers changed planes in 2011 than in 1979.[44]

Some studies of airline deregulation have also noted the drastic decline in interline connections—those involving a connection between two different airlines—after deregulation. Because online connecting service (change of aircraft but no change of airline) is associated with improved connections and better baggage handling, this improved the estimated net quality of service. In fact, the share of connections that were interline fell from 45 percent in 1979 to 8 percent in the early 1990s. It began to rise again in 1996, however, with the spread of code-sharing arrangements. It is more difficult to interpret interline statistics now, because some code sharing is between carriers

43. We adjust for trip length by calculating the change in change-of-plane share in 100-mile trip distance categories and then creating an overall change in change-of-plane share by taking a weighted average of the change within each category.
44. Berry and Jia (2010) argue this reflects changes in passenger demand for direct travel after 9/11.

that share some or all ownership, while others are between companies with only weak affiliations. In any case, by 2011 the share of connections reported in the DOT's Databank 1B that are interline had risen back to 44 percent.

Greater passenger volume has facilitated in many markets an increase in flight frequency, relative to the high price, low volume regulatory model. Figure 2.11 records changes in domestic service levels between 1984 and 2011. Not only has the number of flights nearly doubled in the past twenty-seven years, the number of markets with nonstop service is up more than 60 percent, even after the post-2008 service cutback.

Figure 2.11 shows a dramatic increase in the number of cities with non-stop service beginning in the late 1990s. This change corresponds to the widespread introduction of regional jets (RJs), jet aircraft with capacities of less than 100 passengers that can be efficient for routes previously served by propeller aircraft or by larger jets. RJ flights increased from 41 per day in 1997 to 8,805 per day in 2007, comprising about one-third of all domestic commercial flights. The number declined slightly in succeeding years, standing at an average of 8,182 flights per day in 2011. In 2011, the median

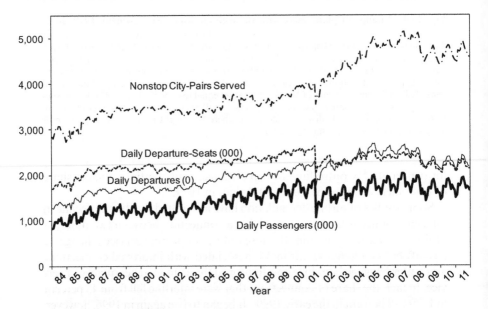

Fig. 2.11   US domestic airline service, 1984–2011 (monthly)

Notes: Authors' calculations are from the DOT T-100 service segment data set. An airport pair is defined as "served" if it averages at least one nonstop flight and ten seats per day during the month. Note that there was a change in October 2002 to the T-100 that added a number of small carriers (carrier codes added were 3C, 5C, 8C, 9E, 9J, 9K, 9L, BMJ, BSA, CHA, CMT, DH, ELL, EM, EWA, F8, FE, FI, FX, GBQ, GCH, GLA, GLF, HNA, HRZ, JX, KAH, KR, MIW, NC, NEW, NWS, PAM, PFQ, RYQ, SEA, SHA, SI, SKW, SLA, SMO, TCQ, TRI, USQ, VEE, VIQ, VPJ, WI, WP, WRD, WST, YTU, YV, ZV). These carriers are dropped in order to maintain comparability.

distance of an RJ flight was 419 miles, with 25 percent of flights less than 258 miles and 10 percent of flights over 866 miles, so these new aircraft clearly can play a variety of roles. One of those roles is introduction of nonstop service on routes that previously had none. Of the 2,053 airport pairs that gained nonstop service between July 1997 and July 2011, about 37 percent received at least some of that service with regional jets. Overall, 26 percent of RJ flights in July 2011 were on routes that had no nonstop service in July 1997.

Load Factors

Given the tendency toward inefficiently low load factors during the regulatory period (Douglas and Miller 1974a, 1974b), it is not surprising that load factors generally have increased since 1978, as shown in figure 2.3. Average load factors for domestic scheduled service climbed from lows of under 50 percent prior to deregulation, to over 60 percent in the mid-1980s, and have remained above 70 percent since the late 1990s, hitting 83 percent in 2011. While much of this increase is due to carriers' ability to compete on price in addition to flight frequency, it has been facilitated by the increasing sophistication of airline booking systems. These systems manage dynamic demand forecasts and seat allocation to the myriad fare classes, enabling airlines to fill seats that would otherwise go empty with a low-fare passenger, while reserving seats for likely last-minute high-fare passengers.

Since most costs do not vary with the number of passengers on a flight, higher load factors have contributed to lower costs per revenue passenger mile. But they have also led to lower quality flight experiences for consumers. With high load factors, late-booking travelers may not find a seat on their preferred flight, in-flight experiences are less likely to be comfortable, and rebooking to accommodate missed connections or canceled flights becomes increasingly difficult. Gone are the days of almost being assured an empty middle seat on most cross-country flights. While many travelers complain about crowded planes, it is important to recognize that airlines have the option of offering higher price, less-crowded flights. That virtually none choose to do so suggests that passenger demand is not sufficient to justify the price/cost trade-off.[45]

In-Flight Amenities

Quantifying the provision of in-flight amenities is difficult, but it seems clear that this area has experienced perhaps the greatest decline in quality

---

45. Indications of consumer dissatisfaction with the ability of airlines to recover from schedule disruptions during the summer of 2007 led some airlines to conclude that they undercut even the minimum service quality passengers are willing to pay for (see McCartney 2007). It is difficult to say whether improvements in delays and cancellation rates since then reflect intentional actions take by airlines or reduced congestion resulting from the fall in demand associated with poor macroeconomy.

since deregulation. The days of piano bars in 747s and gourmet meals are long past for most domestic travelers. More significant for many passengers has been the decrease in their space on board. Coach class seat width and pitch has decreased, even while Americans' girths have increased, and high load factors make empty middle seats less and less common. The decline in amenities has not been monotonic or universal, however. In recent years, airlines have abandoned the headset or movie charges they previously imposed for in-flight entertainment, and some, like Jet Blue and Virgin America, promote their service with in-flight entertainment options. As of 2013, most legacy airlines offer a section of the coach cabin with greater legroom, at least on longer-distance flights, allocating these seats to customers with high status in their frequent flyer programs and others who are willing to pay an extra fee. However, carriers that have differentiated themselves primarily by offering plusher onboard service for all customers have not been particularly successful, suggesting that when passengers vote with their wallets, low prices beat higher quality for many customers.

Oversales and Denied Boarding

With fixed capacity, uncertain demand, and last-minute cancellations or no-shows among passengers, airlines generally have found it optimal to offer more tickets than there are seats on a given flight. In the instances in which more passengers than anticipated show up for an oversold flight, some passengers will be denied boarding. The CAB addressed this concern in 1979 with a rulemaking on denied boarding compensation. Rather than ban oversales (one proposal that was not adopted), the Board attempted a market-based solution, which has persisted through today. Airlines are required first to seek volunteers to give up their seats, for some compensation that is at the discretion of the airline. Airlines may have some "standard offer" compensation, though many conduct informal auctions, increasing offered compensation (usually in the form of free travel, booking on the next available flight, and perhaps food or hotel vouchers) until the requisite number of volunteers are obtained. In more than 90 percent of the cases, this solves the problem.[46] In the remaining cases, passengers are to be boarded in order of check-in times, and those involuntarily denied boarding are awarded compensation determined by the regulation.[47] In 2011, the

46. The overall denied boarding rate increased from 0.15 percent in the early 1990s to a peak of 0.22 percent in 1998, and has varied within a narrow band of 0.10 to 0.13 percent since 2005. Voluntary denied boardings account for 91 to 96 percent of the total. See the US Department of Transportation, Bureau of Transportation Statistics, National Transportation Statistics 2011, table 1-64, at http://www.rita.dot.gov/bts/sites/rita.dot.gov.bts/files/publications \national_transportation_statistics/html/table_01_64.html, accessed January 14, 2013.
47. Denied boarding compensation is not mandated if the oversale is due to substitution of smaller aircraft than originally scheduled or a result of safety-related weight limits for flights operated by aircraft with sixty or fewer seats, the passenger has not complied with check-in requirements, or the delay is less than one hour.

risk a passenger faced of being involuntarily "bumped" was less than 1 in 10,000, so it appears that this is not a significant quality issue.

Travel Time and Delays

One of the most contentious issues in the deregulated airline environment has been increased travel time, particularly due to congestion and delays. Substantial increases in flight operations (see figures 2.1 and 2.11), with limited increases in infrastructure capacity and few changes in infrastructure deployment, have led to dramatic increases in congestion at key points in the aviation system. This has not only increased scheduled travel time in many markets, but increased mean delay beyond scheduled travel time and increased uncertainty around expected arrival times. The Bureau of Transportation Statistics On-Time Performance database reports that in 1988 (the first full year of statistics), roughly 20 percent of all flights arrived more than 15 minutes after their scheduled arrival (including cancellations and diversions). Despite increasingly "padded" scheduled flight times, this had increased to 27 percent in 2000,[48] when flight delays at some airports reached unprecedented levels. While there was some improvement in delays following the reduction in demand after 9/11, by 2007, delays and cancellations had once again climbed to 27 percent. It is difficult to say whether post-2008 delay and cancellation rates of roughly 20 percent reflect changes in operational procedures or are simply the byproduct of reductions in aggregate flight activity and lower congestion associated with the poor macroeconomy over recent years.

Flight delays have numerous causes. Some disruptions, such as severe weather, are beyond an airline's or airport's direct control (though the magnitude and severity may be affected by an airline's scheduling policies and availability, or lack, of redundant equipment and personnel). Incentives to set schedules based on favorable, or even average, conditions (Mayer and Sinai 2003) make some delays inevitable. The existence of delays at hub airports, where congestion *externalities* for the dominant carrier are relatively small, suggests that airlines may optimize their networks with some expected delay built in (Mayer and Sinai 2003). But a significant portion of delays appear due to inefficient infrastructure investment and utilization policies, as we discuss in section 2.5.

Safety and Security

The level of airline safety has been a focus of government policy since the infancy of the industry, when Post Office airmail contracts were shifted from military aircraft to civilian contractors after a series of fatal accidents involving military pilots. Despite economic deregulation, the Federal Avia-

48. See the discussion of LaGuardia airport's 2000 experience in section 2.5 and by Forbes (2008).

tion Administration has maintained authority over all aspects of air carrier safety, from certification of new aircraft, to airline maintenance, training, and operating procedures, to airport and air traffic control system operation. Even though safety regulation was not reduced, some opponents to the Airline Deregulation Act warned that the competitive pressures resulting from economic deregulation would reduce the level of safety provided by commercial airlines. Economic theory is not dispositive on whether such an effect would be expected (Rose 1990).

There is no evidence that airlines have reduced their provision of safety since deregulation. While research finds some evidence that carriers' safety records may be influenced by their financial condition, particularly for smaller airlines (Rose 1990; Dionne et al. 1997), and Kennet (1993) finds that engine maintenance cycles lengthened somewhat after deregulation, analyses do not suggest lower levels of safety following deregulation. This is consistent with a range of other work (e.g., Oster, Strong, and Zorn 1992; Rose 1992; Savage 1999), and with continuing declines in overall and fatal accident rates for US commercial airlines. This is not terribly surprising. Not only does safety continue to be directly regulated, but airlines also perceive strong safety reputations to be a prerequisite to attracting any passengers. The impact on carriers, such as ValuJet, who fail to maintain such reputations lends some credence to that view.[49]

Since 2001, there has been an increased emphasis on securing air travel against terrorist attack. Passenger screening that was first introduced in the 1970s in response to aircraft hijackings was shown to be inadequate, so security measures were stepped up. There have been no successful attacks since 2001, but there have been reports by the US and UK governments of interrupted plans to stage attacks. The screening raises the cost of travel, discouraging people from traveling by air. Using cross-airport variation in implementation dates of security changes, Blalock, Kadiyali, and Simon (2007) estimate that the hassle of increased passenger screening after September 11, 2001, reduced demand by about 6 percent overall and by 9 percent at the nation's fifty busiest airports.

2.4   Airline Markets outside the United States

The development of the airline industry outside the United States differed in two significant ways from the previous description. First, with relatively

---

49. Most airline accidents have modest impacts on the affected firm's capital market value and little or no measurable impact on subsequent demand (see Borenstein and Zimmerman 1988). As Borenstein and Zimmerman point out, this may be "due to very limited updating of prior beliefs [about an airline's safety] or to a low *marginal* valuation of safety" (1988, 933) at current levels of safety provision. Dillon, Johnson, and Pate-Cornell (1999) argue that some accidents may contain more information and therefore generate greater responses, such as ValuJet's loss of one-quarter of its market value in the month following its 1996 Everglades crash and its subsequent decision to rebrand as AirTran following its acquisition of that firm in 1997.

few exceptions, non-US carriers' fortunes were substantially dependent upon international routes due to their relatively small domestic markets: for example, international traffic accounted for 90 percent of major European carrier traffic in the 1970s, compared to 28 percent for comparable US carriers (Good, Röller, and Sickles 1993).The terms of competition in international markets have been governed by negotiated bilateral treaties that generally limited rivalry and often encouraged collusive behavior, as discussed in greater detail following. Second, while the US industry was characterized by privately owned firms subject to government regulation, the norm elsewhere was one or two scheduled passenger service "flag carriers," operated as entirely or majority state-owned enterprises. Many of these received significant continuing state subsidies.[50] This combination of protected markets, state ownership, and soft budget constraints created a tendency toward high costs of service and high fare levels, particularly relative to comparable US routes in the aftermath of their deregulation. Estimates of these effects suggest that they were substantial. Cost and production function-based estimates suggest relative inefficiencies of 15 to 25 percent of US carrier costs (e.g., Good, Röller, and Sickles 1993; Ng and Seabright 2001). Much of this appears linked to labor costs in a manner strongly suggestive of rent sharing. Neven, Röller, and Zhang (2006) estimate a model that explicitly endogenizes wage costs through union negotiations, and conclude that labor cost inflation ultimately led to average prices close to monopoly levels despite noncooperative markup behavior given those higher costs.

Despite these inefficiencies, the movement toward more market-based airline sectors considerably lagged US reforms. This cannot be attributed entirely to the need for international coordination. There was little progress even on actions requiring no coordination, such as privatization of airline ownership and relaxation of entry restrictions to reduce monopoly, until the mid-1980s or later. For example, Swiss Air was the only European flag carrier with no state ownership until the decision to privatize British Airways in late 1986. While entirely state-owned carriers have become less common today, many governments continue to have significant ownership shares in their national airlines. Similarly, even among countries large enough to have potentially significant domestic markets, competitive restraints remained the norm through the 1980s. In Australia—home to one of the

---

50. The focus on national "flag carriers" persists today, although private investors have replaced state ownership in most countries. Most jurisdictions, including the United States, limit foreign national ownership of airlines. Only a handful of countries—Australia, Chile, and New Zealand—have eliminated foreign ownership restrictions for domestic airlines. For airlines within the EU, nationality limits have been replaced by a 49 percent limit on foreign ownership applying only to owners outside the EU. The US statutory limit of 25 percent of voting shares in foreign ownership is now one of the most severe, and its enforcement has been aggressive. See, for example, the adjudication of Virgin America's request for certification beginning in 2006. This has been a particular source of disagreement in negotiations over international routes between the United States. and countries in the EU.

largest domestic airline markets during the industry's infancy—the tightly regulated domestic duopoly between state-owned Trans Australian Airlines (TAA) and privately owned Ansett Australian National Airlines (Davies 1971, 1977) was not relaxed until 1990. Qantas, Australia's state-owned international flag carrier and, with the purchase of TAA in 1992, domestic carrier, was not fully privatized until 1995 (see Forsyth [2003] for a discussion of the post-deregulation Australian experience).

In international markets, the need for government renegotiation of changes in air service agreements added further constraints on the pace of deregulation. The framework, but not terms, of international air service agreements was established with the 1944 International Convention on Civil Aviation, referred to as the "Chicago Convention" for its location. Despite some early pressure for multilateral agreements, the framework that was adopted focused on bilateral negotiations. The convention enunciated the possible "freedoms of the air" to be granted to commercial carriers, which were expanded over time to include nine possible "freedoms." The first two were by default granted to all signatory states, and provided for the right to fly over another country without landing and to land without picking up or discharging passengers. The third and fourth freedoms, which comprised the core of bilateral agreements, provided for rights to transport traffic between a carrier's home country and an airport in the second country. The fifth and sixth freedoms involved extensions of service to a third country through continuing or connecting service, respectively. The seventh freedom permitted international service between two countries entirely outside an airline's home country; the eighth and ninth freedoms permitted an airline to offer domestic service within a country other than its home country, either as a flight continuation from its home country (eighth) or as an independent service (ninth, also referred to as "pure cabotage.").[51]

Over the first three decades following the Chicago Convention, most air services agreements followed the traditional form set out in the US-UK 1946 "Bermuda I" agreement. These agreements generally restricted international scheduled passenger service to one designated carrier from each country providing service on a limited set of specified airport routes between the countries. Fares required approval from each government, though this approval usually was automatic for fares set by the participant airlines under the auspices of the International Air Transport Association (the international airline trade association), which also set service standards intended to limit nonprice competition across carriers. Capacity limits and revenue-sharing agreements were common, ensuring that neither country's airline had the ability or incentive to dominate passenger flows on the routes.[52] The result

51. See Doganis (2006) and Odoni (2009) for a more complete description of the convention and its freedoms.
52. Revenue-sharing agreements were not permitted in US bilaterals, as they were viewed as a violation of US antitrust policy. In addition, the CAB, on behalf of the US government, frequently protested fares set by IATA as too high.

was little or no competition and high fares on most international routes. Traffic was limited not only by high fares, but also by passenger diversion. The convention focused on regulation of scheduled passenger air service; nonscheduled charter or tour operators took advantage of the regulatory breach to expand their operations, particularly in markets with significant potential leisure traffic. This resulted in substantial passenger shifts away from scheduled passenger airlines in many markets: for example, by 1977, 29 percent of the North Atlantic market passengers flew on charter or non-scheduled services (Doganis 2006, 31).

Liberalization of international agreements began in the late 1970s (see Doganis 2006). The first major shift was toward "open market" agreements, modeled after the 1978 US–Netherlands agreement. These introduced greater flexibility into air service—the most liberal eliminated capacity and service restrictions, allowed each country to designate multiple airlines for international service, facilitated more competitive pricing, and expanded the set of airport routes flown between the two countries. They fell far short of transforming international travel in the way the 1978 US Airline Deregulation Act transformed the US domestic airline market, however. Entry and pricing flexibility were expanded, but not competitively determined. Bilateral agreements ignored the fundamental network aspect of air travel, impeding efficient network operation. Implementation for agreements that involved the United States was asymmetric: for example, while US airlines might be granted access to all airports in the foreign country, foreign carriers were restricted to a relatively small set of US gateway cities, generally defended by arguing that the large US airline market was not matched by similar opportunities abroad. The emphases tended to be more on the welfare of each country's carriers than the welfare of consumers.

A second shift, to "open skies" agreements in the 1990s, further reduced government impediments to competition in selected international markets. The US–Netherlands 1992 agreement was the first to mark the transition. This and other "open skies" agreements allowed unlimited market access on all routes between the two countries for all carriers designated by either country, as well as unlimited fifth freedom rights, competitively determined pricing, and authorization of code sharing and strategic alliances between carriers. Even open skies agreements typically were negotiated on bilateral basis, however.[53]

The most dramatic transformation in international air service took place in Europe. By the mid-1980s, the United Kingdom had begun to negotiate more flexible intra-European bilateral agreements, and several other European countries followed suit. These were similar to the agreements the United States had signed with many countries, which the United Kingdom

---

53. A few multilateral agreements eventually opened common aviation areas to competitive service, such as the Asia Pacific Economic Community agreement between the United States, Brunei, Singapore, Chile, Peru, and New Zealand.

had heretofore rejected, and continued to reject in negotiations with the United States. This, with the movement toward integration of the European Community, led to three successive airline liberalization packages in Europe in 1987, 1990, and 1992. While the early reforms were modest, the full implementation of the final package in 1997 was as revolutionary for international air travel within Europe as the 1978 Airline Deregulation Act was for domestic US air travel. This comprehensive multilateral agreement created a single, largely unregulated airline market throughout the twenty-five European Union (EU) member states, Switzerland, Norway, and Iceland, roughly commensurate with the US domestic market in passenger volume. It allows full and open access to any routes by any EU carrier (eighth and ninth freedoms), eliminates price controls, sharply constrains state subsidies, and replaces national ownership restrictions with liberal EU-wide ownership requirement (allowing up to 49 percent ownership by foreign nationals outside the EU, and any ownership patterns by EU member state nationals).

These reforms have led to a substantial increase in entry by "no frills" (primarily point-to-point) carriers, though two no-frills carriers, Ryanair and easyJet, account for more than half of their segment's total traffic. The Association of European Airlines (AEA) reported that by the summer of 2006, AEA members (primarily "full service" or network carriers) accounted for 56 percent of weekly seat capacity; no-frills carriers accounted for 18 percent, and other carriers (primarily charter and tour operators) accounted for 26 percent. This average masks much greater no-frills shares in markets with an endpoint in the United Kingdom (close to 50 percent) and lower shares (less than 15 percent) in remaining intra-EU markets. These carriers tend to operate out of satellite or regional airports, providing regional or city-pair, but not airport-pair, competition.

The EU "Third Package" goes far beyond the largely bilateral "open skies" agreements negotiated for some markets, and has placed the EU in the vanguard of the movement for more fully deregulated international aviation markets. As dramatic as these changes have been, however, their impact has been moderated by continuing constraints. Many of the largest EU airports have capacity constraints that limit or preclude entry at the airport level, protecting incumbent carriers through administrative rules for allocating access (see Odoni 2009) and constraining direct competition. Reaching the full potential of relaxed ownership restrictions was also severely impeded by the continued governance of extra-EU international service by bilateral agreements between individual countries: service between the United States and France was limited to French- and American-owned carriers, service between Japan and the United Kingdom to Japanese- and British-owned carriers, and so forth. Carriers that consolidated across national boundaries within the EU risked losing access to lucrative international markets outside the EU. This ensured that the EU carrier network remained more fragmented than might be expected in equilibrium.

Eliminating these restrictions has been a key objective of ongoing EU-wide negotiation of air service agreements with non-EU countries. At the top of the EU agenda is replacing bilateral agreements between its member states and non-EU countries with multilateral open skies agreements. Renegotiation of these agreements was effectively forced by a 2002 European Court of Justice decision invalidating substantial portions of bilateral agreements. The court objected on two key grounds: first, that the agreements concerned some terms that were in the purview of the EU, not the member states, to negotiate; and second, that they discriminated across EU airlines based on the nationality of their ownership, violating Article 43 of the European Community Treaty. Over the past several years, the EU has pushed for greater deregulation, and the United States has dragged its heels. EU negotiators have targeted relaxation of the US statutory limit of 25 percent foreign ownership of US domestic airlines, nondiscriminatory access to US–EU markets for any EU carrier, and relaxation of the US government "Fly America" policy. US negotiators insisted on greater US carrier access to London's Heathrow airport (the existing US-UK bilateral agreement restricted US carrier access to Heathrow to United and American airlines), and had been unable to deliver prospective Congressional approval of a number of EU demands—most notably relaxation of ownership restrictions.[54] A first-stage agreement that moves partway toward these goals was approved in 2007, with implementation effective in March 2008. This expanded access to Heathrow airport, allowed EU- and US-owned carriers to fly between US and EU cities regardless of national ownership, and waived nationality clauses for EU ownership of airlines in twenty-eight designated non-EU countries (primarily African). A second stage agreement was reached in 2010, with the United States promising to seek legislation to relax foreign ownership restraints; Congress has not as of this writing taken any action.

Despite liberalization of many international aviation agreements over time—incrementally with the push toward "open skies" bilateral agreements and most significantly with the transformation of European Union markets over the past ten years—competition in many international markets continues to be limited, encouraging higher prices and rent-seeking activities.[55] Protection of domestically owned carriers through ownership restrictions that preclude foreign acquisitions or mergers and continuing prohibitions on cabotage (international or domestic service that lies entirely outside a carrier's home country) preserve inefficiencies and reduce the benefits of

---

54. Congress has articulated national security, operational, safety, and labor concerns over foreign national ownership of US carriers. While most of these concerns could be addressed through less restrictive means (see the discussion of the Brattle report on these issues by Doganis [2006, chap. 3]), the political environment in the United States seems resistant to significant change.

55. See, for example, the lobbying by US carriers over the availability of new US-China routes (Torbenson 2007).

competitive markets. There continues to be a considerable distance between current policy and a competitive international aviation market.

2.5   Continuing Issues in the Deregulated Airline Industry

Airline deregulation has likely benefited consumers with lower average prices, more extensive and frequent service, and continued technological progress in both aircraft and ticketing. The industry continues to attract considerable attention from economists and policymakers, however, in part because its business practices have been so dynamic and differentiated across firms while airline earnings have been tremendously volatile. If the fundamental question of industrial organization is the degree to which unfettered markets achieve efficient production and allocation of outputs, and the extent to which government intervention can improve such efficiencies, the airline industry may illustrate those issues as well as any.

After more than three decades of experience with airline deregulation, some observers continue to call for renewed government intervention in the economic decision making of the industry. The concerns divide somewhat imperfectly into three areas. First, is the current organization of the industry economically sustainable? US airlines have lost billions of dollars during demand downturns that occurred at the beginning of the 1980s and 1990s, during 2001 to 2005, and post-2008. Also, several large carriers have exited through mergers in recent years. Do these losses indicate that fundamental change in the organization of the industry—for example, to a tight oligopoly—is necessary before the sellers will be able to sustain a competitive rate of return over the long run? Or, alternatively, are the losses the result of investor exuberance and management weakness that led to excess capital and inflated costs during high-demand periods, setting the companies up for extreme earnings downturns when demand weakens? Put differently, will firms' self-control of capacity and labor cost growth during good times be enough to reduce the cyclicality of the industry, or is the instability of this industry fundamentally different from most others?

Second, should market power be a significant public policy concern in this industry? Mergers and use of loyalty programs may raise barriers to entry by new firms and barriers to market expansion by existing firms, but how large are these effects, and can they be moderated through application of antitrust policy? Does the poor earnings record of the airlines demonstrate that market power is not a significant issue? Conversely, does the enormous apparent cost advantage of smaller airlines—which still have only about one-quarter of the US market—indicate just the opposite, that the market power of incumbents has allowed them to impede the loss of market share to much more efficient rivals. If this is the case, then the market power may create not only the usual static deadweight loss from underconsumption, but also production deadweight loss from exclusion of a more efficient firm.

Finally, much of the air travel infrastructure remains in government hands, and there remain questions about the efficiency of the interaction between government resources, including airport facilities and air traffic control, and the private air transport sector. Congestion and delays soared prior to the collapse of traffic following 9/11, and reemerged as critical issues with the return of passenger volume in 2006 and 2007 and exacerbated by the growth of smaller aircraft such as regional jets in many markets. These suggest that government-run airport and air traffic control systems may have lagged behind the industry's dramatic expansion since deregulation. While higher jet fuel prices and reduced demand may have mitigated congestion since 2008, this reprieve, like that in the early 2000s, may be temporary. Does imperfect coordination of government-controlled support activities lead to significant inefficiencies in the industry? And, would privatization of these government services be likely to improve performance?

2.5.1 Sustainability of Airline Competition

Airline nominal net profits over the post-deregulation period have fluctuated wildly, with a high of nearly $5.4 billion in net income in 1999 and a low of over $27 billion in net losses in 2005. Two different, but related, theories have been argued to show that competition in the airline industry is not sustainable. These are versions of the "destructive competition" concerns that were raised in early discussions of the need for airline regulation in the 1920s and 1930s. Their basic idea is that unconstrained competition leads to prices too low to sustain viable firms. The outcome may be evolution into a monopoly or tight oligopoly, though supranormal profits associated with this structure may then set off another round of "excessive" investment and competition.

The first theory tends to be popular with the media and with some industry lobbyists pursuing a regulatory-relief or tax-relief agenda. Proponents of this theory note that the airline industry has substantial fixed costs and very specific assets used to produce a homogeneous good, and at the same time is subject to highly cyclical demand and frequent shocks to variable cost. In such an unregulated environment, it is argued, boom/bust cycles are inevitable and will lead to underinvestment, or, in the extreme, a complete collapse of funding for the industry.

While the description of industry-specific fixed costs and cyclical demand is reasonably accurate, it should be noted these are not unique to airlines. Moreover, the conclusion of inevitable collapse is difficult to reconcile with the history of this industry, or that of other capital-intensive industries that face unpredictable demand. Like those in other industries—steel, autos, semiconductors, oil refining, and telecommunications, among others—airline earnings are likely to be volatile, which can lead to bankruptcies. With long-lived industry-specific capital, failures tend to change the identity of its owners with little effect on the overall capital stock. This can depress returns for extended periods of time, as occurred in oil refining for most of the 1980s and 1990s and in telecommunications infrastructure in the early 2000s.

These conditions present a problem in the economic or industrial organization sense only if the unpredictability results in returns insufficient to generate investment in the industry. In the airline industry, however, inadequate industry investment is virtually never mentioned as a problem. Over the last three decades, the far more frequent complaint from the airlines and industry analysts has been that there has been too much capital pouring into the industry; this complaint often is accompanied by a plea from the industry to limit entry and expansion in order to "rationalize" capacity and ensure adequate returns to investment.

The second theory appeals to the existence of scope and network economies in production of air transportation. Proponents argue that the efficient configuration of production implied by these economies suggests that the number of viable firms may be quite small in equilibrium. A nuanced version argues that there may be an "empty core" to the competitive game, if, for example, costs of producing a large set of air travel services among many cities are lowest if provided by one firm, but costs are not locally subadditive. That is, if subsets of those routes could be served at a cost below the incumbent's fares, an entrant serving just those routes could be profitable while rendering the reduced system of the incumbent unprofitable. The entrant's set of city-pair markets might, in turn, be vulnerable to further attack by entrants serving other subsets of markets, leaving groups of markets that are not break-even on a stand-alone basis.[56] Periodic upheavals in the industry might follow the breakdowns and reforming of coalitions.

There is little empirical support for either an empty core or natural monopoly characterization of the airline industry. There is widespread agreement among researchers and industry participants that economies of scale and passenger density may exist, but empirical estimates of their magnitude have found fairly modest advantages of size. Returns to density in airline networks typically have been estimated as the change in total cost of increasing passenger traffic (e.g., passenger miles) while holding constant network size (e.g., airports or routes served) and structure (e.g., average stage length). Estimated elasticities of total cost with respect to density tend to cluster around 0.85.[57] That is, doubling passenger traffic on a given network reduces average costs by roughly 15 percent. Estimated returns to scale, generally measured by the increase in expected costs from doubling output and network size, tend to be roughly constant at the scale of major

56. For a discussion of the general theory of sustainability, see Baumol, Panzar, and Willig (1982).

57. See, for example, Caves, Christensen, and Tretheway (1984); Ng and Seabright (2001); and Basso and Jara-Diaz 2005. Brueckner and Spiller (1994) estimate substantially larger returns to density, with an elasticity of marginal cost with respect to spoke density out of hub airports of −0.3 to −0.4 from their structural model of demand and profit maximization.

airlines. Moreover, across major US airlines, there seems to be little correlation between overall size of operations and unit cost, though it is quite difficult to adjust such calculations for quality and the different array of products offered. After more than twenty-five years, there is no evidence that cost advantages are giving the largest airlines increasingly dominant positions, as indicated by figures 2.6 (costs) and 2.7 (market share). Borenstein (2011) documents the airline losses on domestic service since deregulation and examines four common explanations: high taxes, high fuel costs, weak demand, and increasing competition from low-cost carriers. He finds no evidence that taxes are a significant factor, but plausible evidence that each of the other three factors has contributed significantly.

We would note, moreover, that complaints of inadequate returns on investment are not unique to the deregulated environment, nor to the airline industry. Prior to 1978, regulators faced ongoing claims of profit inadequacy, although economic analyses suggested that returns generally covered the industry's cost of capital (Caves 1962) and that attempts to increase returns through higher fares generally led to increased capacity investment rather than to increased profitability (Douglas and Miller 1974a, 1974b). While it is true that the level of profits in current dollars exhibits substantially greater fluctuations post-deregulation, this is to be expected given price inflation and the rapid increase in the overall scale of the industry. Figure 2.12 ad-

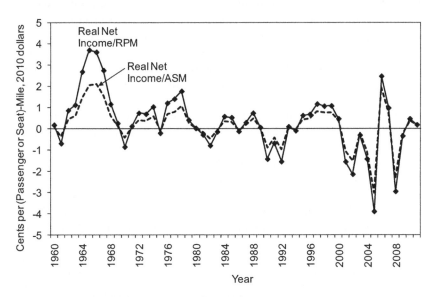

Fig. 2.12   Airline scaled net income, 1960–2011

Sources: Financial results are from Airlines for America, Inc., http://www.airlines.org/Pages /Annual-Results-U.S.-Airlines.aspx, and authors' calculations of net income deflated by urban CPI deflator, 2010 = 100. For system-wide RPM and ASM, see figure 2.1 sources.

Note: In constant 2010 cents.

justs for both of these factors, scaling industry aggregate constant dollar net income by available seat mile and by revenue passenger mile from 1960 to 2011.[58] Cyclicality in income is not new, though the losses following the demand shocks of 9/11 and the 2008 financial crisis and the fuel price shocks in 2005 make the 2000s a particularly volatile period.

Two classes of explanations go a long way toward explaining the volatility in the industry. First, the fundamental economics of the industry—volatile demand, high fixed costs, and slow supply adjustment—combine to create an environment in which profits are likely to change quickly and drastically. Second, the industry has undergone and continues to undergo a very high level of business-model experimentation, in pricing, logistics, competitive strategies, and organizational form. With companies still quite uncertain about major aspects of operations and market interactions, it would not be surprising that significant strategic errors and successes occur with negative and positive profit impacts. We consider these two areas in turn, focusing on data through 2007, prior to the most recent downturn.

Market Fundamentals

The first factor contributing to earnings volatility is volatile demand. To illustrate the demand volatility carrier's face, suppose airline demand reflected only proportional shifts in an otherwise unchanging constant elasticity demand curve. For a given elasticity, ε, we can associate observed quantities (measured by aggregate domestic revenue passenger miles) and prices (measured by real average revenue per domestic revenue passenger mile) with a demand curve of the form $ln(Q) = \alpha + \varepsilon \cdot ln(P)$. Shifts in α needed to keep observed price and quantity pairs on a demand curve can be interpreted as demand shifts. Figure 2.13 illustrates the resulting implied domestic demand shifts (changes in a normalized α) over 1960 to 2007, for assumed constant demand elasticities of -0.8, -1.0, and -1.2.[59] These are broadly within the range of industry short-run demand elasticity estimates in the literature.[60] While somewhat artificial, this captures the rapid demand changes that occurred, not just following the attacks on September 11, 2001, but also around the recessions of the early 1980s and 1990s, and at other times. Figure 2.14 presents the year-to-year changes in α for the midelasticity case of -1. The implied demand changes are quite substantial and volatile. In the early 1980s, for instance, 9 percent growth in demand one

---

58. The profit information we discuss here covers only domestic operations. U.S. carriers are required to report separate financial statements for domestic and international operations, though obviously all of the typical transfer pricing and revenue sharing issues arise in such financial breakouts. We carry out the analysis in this section only through 2007 in order to avoid concerns that the analysis is driven entirely by the extreme fuel price spike and crash in 2008 as well as the financial crisis and Great Recession that followed.

59. Many other factors may have changed over this period—most notably, demand elasticity—so the graph should not be read as literally measuring exogenous demand shifts.

60. Gillen, Morrison, and Stewart (2004) survey estimates of air travel demand elasticities.

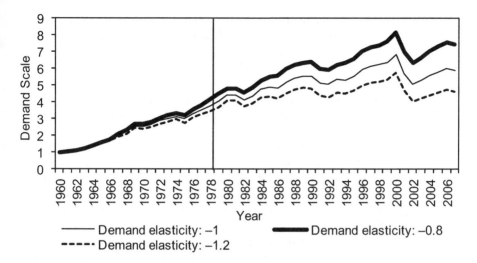

Fig. 2.13   Implied normalized demand, 1960–2007

Notes: Authors' calculations are based on domestic industry revenue passenger miles and average domestic yield (revenue per revenue passenger mile); see figures 2.1 and 2.3. Yield deflated by urban CPI deflator, 2010 = 100.

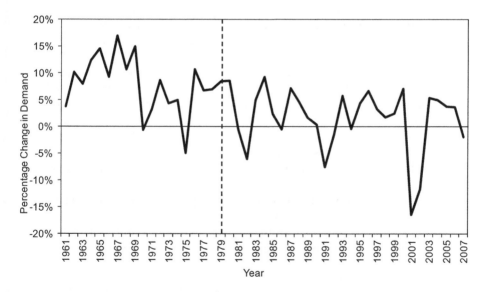

Fig. 2.14   Year-to-year changes in implied demand for air travel, 1961–2007

Note: See figure 2.13 and explanation in text.

year reverted to a 6 percent decline just two years later and back to 9 percent growth two years after that. Volatility of demand is, of course, especially challenging for producers when the good is not storable and production is characterized by strict short-run production constraints, as in the case with air travel.[61]

Volatility in demand creates even greater earnings volatility if firms are not able to resize production quickly, reducing inputs and costs when demand slackens and expanding rapidly when demand picks up. Fixed capital costs make this difficult in the airline industry, but capital costs (lease, depreciation, and amortization costs for aircraft and other capital) averaged only 15 percent of total costs from 1990 to 2007. These capital costs are actually not fixed in the usual economic sense. There are active resale markets for aircraft and other equipment, and the transaction costs are considered to be low. But their economic value fluctuates with demand and is highly correlated across firms. Moreover, financially distressed firms may be disadvantaged in "forced" asset sales (see Pulvino 1998). So, for instance, a carrier cannot generally recoup the original cost of an aircraft by selling the plane when it faces a demand downturn. In economic terms, the demand downturn creates a capital loss for the carrier because it is holding aircraft at the time the value of aircraft has declined. In accounting terms—which drive reported profits—the firm continues to recognize the financing cost and depreciation of the asset each year. Thus, for instance, a huge capital loss that carriers incurred from holding aircraft on September 11, 2001 showed up in accounting terms through depreciation of the original aircraft cost over the ensuing years.

Labor costs (wage and benefits) are a much larger cost factor for airlines, averaging 35 percent of total airline operating costs between 1990 and 2007. Figure 2.15 reproduces the implied domestic demand changes from figure 2.14 for 1989 to 2007 and adds changes in labor costs (comparable data are not available for earlier years). Changes in labor cost, total wage, and benefits bill are clearly much smoother than demand changes. This demonstrates a fundamental cause of earnings volatility in the airline industry: not just capital costs, but also labor costs, are slow to respond to demand changes.

Labor agreements in this industry generally cover both the compensation and work rules. While labor costs generally are thought of as variable costs, in the highly unionized airline industry, they are certainly not easily or quickly changed. They are not accurately characterized as fixed costs either,

61. As a point of comparison, we carried out similar exercises with gasoline, coal, and electricity demand using elasticity estimates from published demand studies. Over 1961 to 2005, the standard deviation of the growth rate of airline demand was 6.6 percent. For gasoline, coal, and electricity, the standard deviations of demand growth rates were 2.2, 3.2, and 2.8 percent, respectively. We also examined the serial correlation in demand changes, which was 0.21 for air travel demand changes over this period, while it was 0.57 for gasoline, 0.12 for coal, and 0.58 for electricity. This suggests that the demand growth for gasoline and electricity changes much less sharply than demand for air travel or coal.

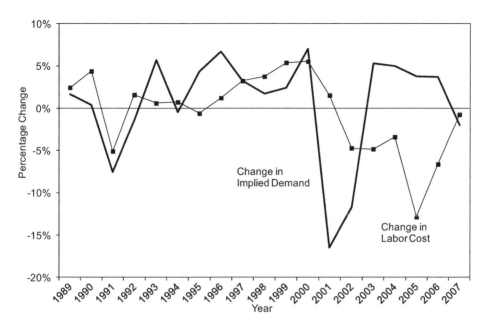

Fig. 2.15   Changes in labor cost and implied demand, 1989–2007
Note: Labor cost is total domestic salaries and benefits from DOT Form 41, Schedule P6.

however. Typically, the quantity of a fixed input can only be changed with a lag, but its purchase price is set exogenously. From statements by both airlines and labor, it is clear that wages of pilots and other high-skilled workers are endogenous to air travel demand and, it appears, to airline profits (see Hirsch 2007; Neven, Röller, and Zhang 2006). Changes in an airline's financial health affect both the quantity of the semifixed input it wants to buy and the wage it pays.

Labor relations in this industry are somewhat more complex than in most others, both because of the specialized skills and government safety certification required of some workers and because of the nonstorability of the good. The former implies that input substitutes for highly skilled workers may not be available on short notice.[62] The latter makes labor actions particularly costly to the airlines in terms of both lost business and reputation damage.

The power of the airline workforce has made it a quasi shareholder in the airlines. During high-profit periods, labor has been able to negotiate attractive compensation packages, while periods of sustained losses often

---

62. In a notable exception, Northwest Airlines trained 1,900 replacement workers in anticipation of an August 2005 mechanics strike. The strike failed and many of the mechanics were permanently replaced by workers receiving substantially lower wages.

lead to negotiated reductions. Changes in compensation packages, however, typically lag earnings changes. There is now a well-established pattern at many legacy carriers.[63] An airline's earnings decline, whether from adverse industry shocks or competitive disadvantages unique to the firm. The airline may pursue cost-saving initiatives, but labor is by far the largest cost category, and the second largest, fuel, is priced exogenously. Management therefore claims that it needs concessions from labor to remain viable. Labor unions are resistant to wage or benefit cuts, or restructuring of work rules; they express skepticism about the airline's financial difficulty and blame losses on poor management. If the financial distress of the carrier continues, labor is faced with the possibility of carrier bankruptcy—which brings the bankruptcy court into the labor negotiations with its powers to impose wage and work rule changes, merger into a stronger airline, or even possible liquidation of the company. Generally, at this point, labor representatives become more accommodating and some sort of compensation reduction is agreed to. Between 2002 and 2005, however, USAir, United, Northwest, and Delta each entered bankruptcy even after negotiating significant compensation reductions and then proceeded to negotiate for further givebacks. American Airlines, which avoided a bankruptcy filing during this period, struggled with higher labor costs than its competitors, likely setting the stage for its Chapter 11 filing in 2011.

Similarly, during strong financial periods, labor attempts to extract some of the profits. Multiyear collective bargaining agreements, however, mean that airlines can have extended periods of high earnings before the pressure to distribute some of those profits to labor alters wages. In both cases, the wage bill stickiness means that labor cost changes may be out of sync with profit changes, exacerbating the profit swings.

Among the costs that contribute to earnings volatility, fuel cost is probably the one that has received the most attention in the press and policy discussions. The exogenous price of jet fuel can been very volatile: from 1990 to 2007, fuel costs averaged 15 percent of total operating expenses, but varied from 11 to 25 percent, and was over 30 percent for the first half of 2008.[64] Airlines can make incremental operating changes to affect the amount of fuel they use for a given flight schedule—flying at slower speeds and using their most fuel-efficient aircraft—but their fuel cost per available seat mile is driven primarily by oil price fluctuations. Fuel price volatility can be large and is only somewhat correlated with the demand that the airlines face. Figure 2.16 shows the annual change in fuel cost per available seat mile (ASM). Note that the scale is different from the previous two graphs.

---

63. See Hirsch (2007) for an analysis along these lines.
64. Other than capital, labor, and fuel expenses, the largest airline cost category is service (including commissions, advertising, insurance, and nonaircraft equipment rental), which averaged 19 percent over this period, while the remaining costs include maintenance materials, food, landing fees, and other.

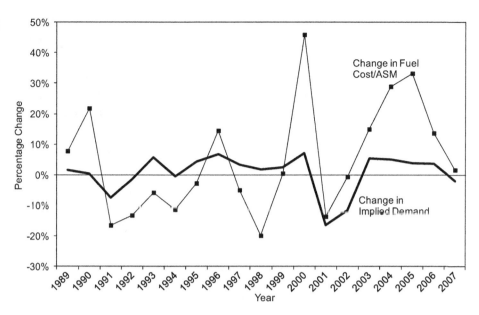

Fig. 2.16 Changes in fuel cost per ASM and implied demand, 1989–2007
Note: Fuel cost is total domestic aircraft fuel expense from DOT Form 41, Schedule P6.

As in nearly all other industries, producers complain that they are unable to pass along energy price increases as quickly as they would like. The production technology of the airline industry explains some of the difficulty in this case. For a given flight schedule, the increase in fuel consumption from carrying an additional passenger is quite small,[65] so fuel is close to a fixed cost until the carrier is willing to change the number of flights it offers. If the industry were to adjust rapidly to fuel cost changes, the number of flights would decline and load factors would likely rise whenever fuel prices increased. Airlines are reluctant to make rapid schedule reductions in response to fuel price increases, in part for logistical reasons—it requires complex rescheduling of all the carrier's aircraft and rebooking of passengers who have already bought tickets—and in part for competitive strategic reasons—concern that a reduced schedule will make them less attractive relative to competitors.[66] Empirically, it is hard to see any tendency toward adjustments in capacity flown or load factors in response to fuel price shocks during the post-deregulation data.

Figure 2.17 shows the implied demand next to the changes in output sold, measured by revenue passenger miles, and capacity, measured by available

65. On a fully loaded commercial jet, passengers and their baggage comprise about 15 percent of the takeoff weight of the aircraft.
66. This can arise from an empirical S-curve distribution of passenger share as a function of flight share on a route, discussed earlier.

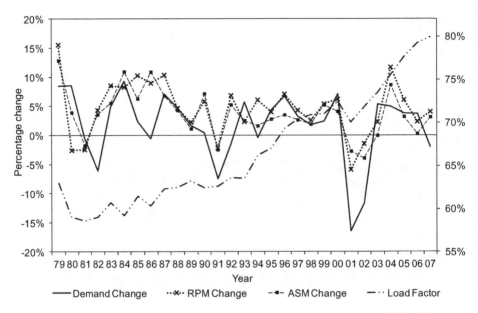

Fig. 2.17   Changes in RPMs, ASMs, load factor, and implied demand, 1979–2007
Note: See figure 2.1 sources for RPM, ASM, and load factor.

seat miles. This indicates some degree of short-run supply inelasticity; perfectly elastic supply would result in no price adjustment and quantity that would change by the full demand shift. Reductions in demand do not trigger equally large reductions in input costs; instead, price adjusts downward in the short run, so quantity falls less than the demand shift.

In addition, the common perception that planes fly very full when demand is strong and mostly empty when demand weakens is not supported by the data. The lowest line on the left side in figure 2.17 (utilizing the right-hand axis) shows the load factor, the proportion of seats filled.[67] Load factor does not seem to be affected much at all by demand shocks; even in 2002, the domestic average load factor was 70 percent, the same as in 1998 and just 1 percentage point lower than in 2000. None of the major post-deregulation demand downturns—1982, 1991, 2001 to 2002, (and 2008 to 2009, as shown in figure 2.3)—was accompanied by a significant drop in load factors. This suggests that airlines have managed their capacity and prices to keep the proportion of seats filled roughly constant in the presence of demand shocks. Fuel price shocks also do not seem to drive load factors: large fuel cost increases in 1980, 1990, 2000, and 2005 are not associated with unusual load factor increases and the plunge in fuel costs in 1986 and somewhat

67. More precisely, load factor is revenue passenger miles divided by available seat miles.

smaller drop in 1999 do not seem to have driven load factors down. Over the deregulation years, however, there has been a clear trend toward higher load factors, as shown in both figure 2.3 and figure 2.17.[68]

The demand shock following September 11, 2001 illustrates the dynamic of the interaction between demand, supply, and costs that causes earning in the industry to be so volatile. Between 2000 and 2002, demand fell 26 percent (using an assumed −1 price elasticity), real price fell 17 percent, output (RPMs) fell 6 percent, capacity (ASMs) fell 5 percent, and load factor declined from 71 to 70 percent. Real labor expenses declined only 2 percent. Yet, over the following four years, real labor expenses declined 28 percent while demand grew 13 percent.

While these data suggest that volatile demand, sticky labor and capital costs, and fluctuating fuel costs all contribute to volatile earnings, it is hard to know the magnitude of these effects from the discussion thus far. In an attempt to calibrate the effects of these factors on profits, we have created a fairly simple model of airline profits that attempts to capture these factors and roughly gauge the size of their impacts on earnings.[69]

We start from the recognition that if production were constant returns to scale even in the short run, if all cost changes were fully and immediately passed through to price, and if all demand shifts were absorbed completely by quantity changes with no price adjustment, then earnings per customer (or, more precisely, earnings per revenue passenger mile) would not vary. Then we introduce (a) some fixed component to costs, (b) the actual fuel price volatility and the assumption that it is only partially absorbed in price adjustment, and (c) short-run adjustments to demand shifts that are partially in quantity and partially in price.

We examine data for the entire domestic US airline industry for 1990 to 2007. We first calculate "low volatility" earnings, assuming airline costs per unit output, load factors, and prices are constant at their mean (in real terms) over this period. In this case, earnings fluctuations would be due entirely to shifts in demand that would shift earnings by exactly the same proportion.

The nearly flat line with hollow diamonds in figure 2.18 represents this fluctuation. The large demand fluctuations we discussed earlier are, not surprisingly, dwarfed by the actual fluctuations in industry operating profits, which are represented by the line with dark squares.

We then make a set of assumptions of incomplete industry adjustment. We assume that in any one year, as demand growth and fuel costs deviate from their average over this sixteen-year period, carriers can only adjust incompletely. In particular, only 50 percent of deviations from mean fuel

---

68. Over this time, until 2005, the real price of jet fuel has declined fairly steadily, which by itself might suggest a decline in equilibrium load factors.

69. The model is implemented in a spreadsheet that is available from the authors.

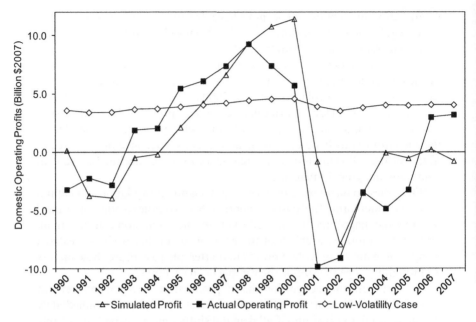

Fig. 2.18   Actual, low-volatility, and simulated domestic operating profits, 1990–2007

Note: Data sources are listed in the simulation spreadsheet, available from the authors.

cost are passed along through price changes. Similarly, when demand growth deviates from its mean level, quantity changes by only 30 percent of the horizontal demand difference between the expected and actual demand shift. The remainder of the shift is absorbed by price adjustment, as would be the case with short-run supply inelasticity, regardless of whether it is due to steep marginal costs, concerns about competitive position, or some sort of oligopoly adjustment process. We also assume that costs are not completely flexible. Of the nonfuel costs, we assume that 30 percent are fixed with respect to passengers or flights. We assume 20 percent are proportional to passengers (RPMs), and the remaining 50 percent are proportional to flights (ASMs). Finally, we assume that flight schedules adjust nearly, but not quite completely, to changes in passengers; that is, that deviations from mean quantity are associated with a 90 percent deviation from mean capacity in the same direction, so load factor exhibits minimal variation.

We do not claim that these assumptions are precisely accurate, but we would argue that they are plausible in the context of the airline industry. The model also does not capture any serial correlation due to *lagged* adjustment, as opposed to just the partial adjustment from mean levels that we model here. And the model ignores the endogeneity of input prices, such as labor. Nonetheless, even this simple model of partial adjustment to demand and cost shocks generates earnings volatility—represented by the line with hollow triangles—that is nearly the magnitude we have observed in the industry over the last decade and a half. The point is not that this is an exact model of the adjustments in the airline industry, but that demand and fuel cost fluctuations combined with sticky adjustment on the supply side can easily generate the observed magnitude of earnings volatility, without any appeal to "empty core" or destructive competition arguments.

Innovation

While the airline industry has more than three decades of experience in a deregulated environment, it would be a mistake to assume that firms have had that much time to adjust to a new but stable business environment. Technological innovation in this industry has been relatively slow compared to telecommunications, electronics, media, or a number of other industries, but the post-deregulation airline industry has been one of the leaders in experimentation with alternative production processes, pricing models, and organizational forms. It takes time to determine the success of a given experiment, and as one would expect, some of the experiments have not been successful.

Network Configuration.   The hub-and-spoke network is probably the best-known innovation attributed to airline deregulation. Though hubs existed prior to deregulation, their use expanded tremendously in the immediate aftermath of deregulation. However, while there are clear advantages of a hub system due to density economies and demand advantages, there also are costs, which have become more apparent over time. In the late 1980s, hubs were thought to be so powerful—both as an efficiency enhancement and protection from aggressive competitors—that a race to develop as many hubs as possible ensued. Many of the new hubs that airlines set up ultimately proved unprofitable and were abandoned.[70] Over the past decade, developments in the industry, including the consistent profitability of Southwest Airlines, which does not operate a formal hub system,[71] have raised further questions about the competitive advantage of hub-based airline networks.

After initial focus on cost and competitive advantages of hubs, airlines have become more cognizant of their limitations. Hubs may increase aircraft operating costs, particularly when "tightly banked," that is, when coordinated groups of flights arrive at very close intervals and then all depart 45 to

70. Former hub airports include those in Nashville, Raleigh-Durham, Kansas City, and Columbus, Ohio. Some airlines even considered opening "pure hubs," airports located in remote areas in the middle of the country with no local demand, used just for passengers to change planes, but the idea was never pursued.

71. Though Southwest does not schedule operations in a traditional hub model, as of 2011 it operated small scale hubs at Dallas Love Field, Chicago Midway, Salt Lake City, Phoenix, Las Vegas, and Baltimore, and 22 percent of its passengers traveled on connecting itineraries in 2011.

75 minutes later. These operations increase delays and congestion costs and reduce aircraft utilization (see Mayer and Sinai 2003). As delays increase, traveler inconvenience and missed connections also increase, reducing passenger demand (Forbes 2008; Bratu and Barnhart 2005). Some airlines have experimented with "de-banking" their hubs or introducing rolling hubs, in which flight operations are smoothed over the day. For example, Figure 2.19 illustrates the evolution of American Airlines' hub operations at Dallas-Fort Worth airport between 2001 and 2003, from the tightly banked hub schedule first developed during the 1980s to a rolling hub schedule with a smoother pattern of arrivals and departures. While de-banking hub operations may reduce some of the cost of hubs, rolling schedules also tend to increase passengers' expected travel time, reducing their demand for connecting flights. Further experimentation with network configuration is undoubtedly ahead.

Pricing and Distribution. Many industries have learned from the sophistication airlines have developed in peak-load pricing, price discrimination, and revenue management. But the airlines themselves remain uncertain, and often in fundamental disagreement, over how much price segmentation is optimal and precisely how to accomplish it.[72] As shown in figure 2.5, within carrier-route price dispersion peaked in 2001. A decline in business travel beginning in late 2000 and accelerating in early 2001 led to a sharp decline in unrestricted ticket sales. This, combined with the perceived slow return of high-fare passengers following September 11, 2001, led many in the industry to argue that price dispersion had exceeded profit-maximizing levels.[73] As evident in figure 2.5, price dispersion has declined sharply from that peak. The unprecedented gap between unrestricted and discount fares in the late 1990s may have significantly altered purchasing patterns. This may have been exacerbated by changes in airline distribution methods: the difference in fares is readily apparent to travelers using online travel search engines, and travelers with some flexibility in their schedules can take advantage of search tools that readily provide potential cost savings from small schedule shifts. Fare search engines may have encouraged diffusion of a wide range of ancillary fees that airlines now charge for services that may include telephone reservations, seat reservations at time of booking, checked and carry-on baggage, priority boarding, exit-row seating, in-flight food and entertainment, and more. Concern about the increasing prevalence and opacity of ancillary fees prompted the Department of Transportation to announce a rulemaking on fee disclosures, but has postponed any action in the face of ongoing industry opposition.

---

72. For example, the costly price war that erupted after American Airlines' 1992 introduction of its "simplified" value pricing plan illustrates the intense divergence of preferred price structures across airlines.

73. See Trottman (2001) and Zuckerman (2001) on the decline in unrestricted ticket sales following the tech crash in 1999 and 2000.

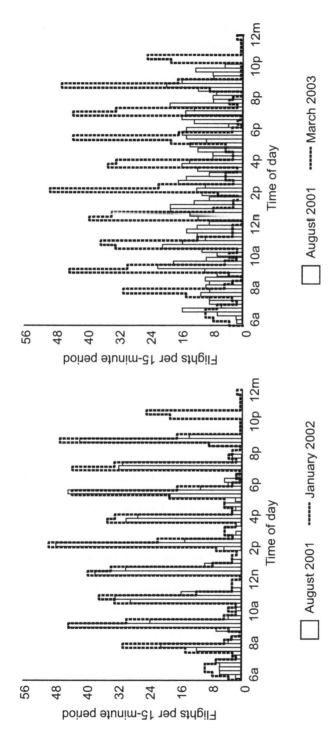

Fig. 2.19 Conversion of American Airlines DFW hub to rolling hub schedule, 2001–2003

Source: Tam and Hansman (2003), figures 4-12 and 4-13.

Legacy carriers have not only been losing formerly high-fare passengers to restricted fares on their own networks, but also appear to be losing an increasing fraction of business travelers to low-cost carriers such as Southwest and Jet Blue, contributing to the increased market shares of those carriers. This defection is ascribed in part to generally lower unrestricted walk-up fares on low-cost carriers, and in part to perceptions that their service, while no-frills, may be more reliable and consistently on time, a valuable attribute for business travelers.[74] Airlines have also experimented with changing the kinds of restrictions they impose on discount tickets. The penetration of Southwest and other low-cost airlines with simpler pricing structures and no Saturday-night stay requirements have led many legacy carriers to drop Saturday-night stay restrictions, at least on competing routes, relying instead on advanced-purchase requirements and nonrefundability for their discounted fares. Uncertainty about the optimal ticket restrictions and level of price dispersion surely contributes to the volatility of the airlines operations and financial returns.

Organizational Form.   Perhaps the most important ongoing business innovation in the airline industry is in organizational form. In the early 1980s, an airline was a stand-alone entity that sold tickets for travel on the routes it served. During the 1980s, most major airlines formed code-sharing partnerships with small commuter airlines providing feed traffic for their hubs. Though strategic alliances have since expanded greatly in number, geographic scope, and the dimensions of activities on which partners coordinate, their role remains somewhat unclear. Alliances are not mergers, and most do not have antitrust clearance to cooperate on pricing. Rather, they are a hybrid organizational form in which firms may compete in some markets, while cooperating and jointly selling their product in other markets. These agreements can be very complex, both to be beneficial to both partners and to clear antitrust scrutiny (see Brueckner and Whalen 2002; Bamberger, Carlton, and Neumann 2004; Lederman 2007, 2008; Armantier and Richard 2006, 2008; Forbes and Lederman 2009).[75]

This certainly is not an exhaustive list of the business changes the industry has seen since deregulation, but it illustrates how dynamic the airline business model has been and continues to be. The managerial skills necessary to run an airline are constantly changing. Airlines continue to experiment with alternative approaches to flight operations and scheduling, pricing, orga-

74. Southwest is frequently at or near the top in on-time performance among the major carriers and Jet Blue, until its Valentine's Day 2007 winter storm meltdown, had maintained a policy against discretionary cancellations on the theory that passengers preferred late arrivals to nonarrivals.

75. Though alliances have become a mainstay of operations among most of the large carriers, Southwest and the other low-cost airlines generally have not pursued them. Southwest's only alliance or joint-marketing agreement was with ATA (formerly known as American Trans Air), which ceased operation in April 2008.

nizational form, distribution, and many other aspects of the business. The feedback process is slow and extremely noisy, making it difficult to determine which experiments are successes and which are failures. These issues are not unique to airlines, but combined with the demand volatility and cost stickiness discussed earlier, they suggest that industry volatility in itself is unlikely to indicate a structural need for renewed government intervention.

2.5.2   Market Power Concerns

Attention to market power concerns in the airline industry has waxed and waned considerably over the post-deregulation period. It heightened during the mid- to late-1980s, as airline exits and consolidations led to dramatic increases in concentration, and again in the late 1990s, as profitability soared. Amid the recent financial distress of the industry, concerns about industry concentration and pricing power have abated. While it may be natural to worry more about market power when profits are high, the profit level tells us little about its extent. Market power does generally raise profits relative to the competitive level, though the size of this effect depends in part on the rent extraction accomplished by labor and other input suppliers. Still, given the factors discussed in the previous section—volatile demand, sticky costs, and repeated disruptions from business innovations—it is difficult to know whether airlines are making higher profits than would be the case if they were simple price takers. With the potential for inefficient production, labor rent sharing, and poor or unlucky timing of fixed investment, profit levels shed little or no light on the degree of market power that airlines present.

At the time of deregulation, it was recognized that most routes might be able to support only one or two firms and that market power could be an issue. The theory of "contestability"—that potential competition would discipline firms, forcing them to keep prices at competitive levels in order to deter new entry—was put forth in support of deregulation.[76] Through the 1980s, however, contestability theory as applied to airlines took repeated blows from studies that found the number of actual competitors significantly affected price levels on a route.[77] Potential competition in general had a modest effect disciplining pricing.[78] Fares are markedly higher on routes served by only one airline than they are on routes with more active competitors, and tend to decline significantly with entry of a second and third competitor. By the end of the 1980s, the theory was seldom raised in the context of airlines.

In the late 1980s and early 1990s, the focus of market power analysis expanded to include airport shares. The basis for this concern, first laid out by Levine (1987), was that an airline could use its dominant position at

---

76. See Bailey and Panzar (1981) and Baumol, Panzar, and Willig (1982).
77. See Borenstein (1989, 1990, 1991, 1992, 2013); Hurdle et al. (1989); and Abramowitz and Brown (1993).
78. Some studies suggest a greater effect when the potential competitor is Southwest Airlines (see Morrison 2001; Goolsbee and Syverson 2008).

an airport to deter entry. A number of economic analyses have found significantly higher fare associated with concentration at the airport level (see Borenstein 1989; Evans and Kessides 1993; Abramowitz and Brown 1993). This airport dominance effect may reflect the impact of market power exercised through loyalty rewards programs in which the value of the rewards—to travel agents, corporations, and individuals—increased more than proportionally with the points earned.[79] By inducing travelers to concentrate their business with just one or a few airlines, these programs make it difficult for a new airline to successfully enter a small subset of routes at an airport dominated by another carrier. Airport dominance could also impede entry by giving the incumbent control over scarce gates, ticket counters, and (at some airports) landing slots.

Some airlines and researchers have disputed the existence of a "hub premium," arguing that studies finding such price differences across airports fail to control for differences in the business/leisure mix of travelers (see Gordon and Jenkins 1999; Lee and Prado 2005). The argument, however, has two serious flaws. First, the critique suggests that a finding of higher prices in markets with less elastic demand—more business travelers—should not be attributed to market power. While some have suggested that there are higher costs in serving business travelers, the magnitude of these cost differentials cannot explain the price differences across airports (see Borenstein 1999). Second, in practice, most of these studies have determined the share of leisure traffic at an airport by examining the proportion of customers who purchase discount tickets. While a "leisure share" variable constructed as the proportion of passengers paying low fares goes a long way toward explaining where average prices are lower, especially in an industry with significant self-selective price discrimination, this sheds little light on the cause.

It is important to recognize that these patterns do not imply that passengers at dominated airports are necessarily worse off. Large airports with one or two dominant carriers generally are hubs and, as such, schedule a disproportionate number of flights compared to the *local* demand for air service. Improved service quality may offset part or all of the loss from higher prices resulting from airport dominance. Nor do these concerns necessarily demand regulation. Even if prices are above competitive levels, they may be no less efficient than are regulated prices. Rather, the relevant question is whether appropriately executed competition policy could enable customers to receive the benefits of greater service without having to pay higher fares associated with trips to and from the hubs.

Some of these concerns may be mooted by recent market developments. Figure 2.20 illustrates a trend toward convergence in prices across airports that is documented by Borenstein (2005, 2013). One can calculate an average fare premium at an airport in a given year by comparing the prices paid for

79. See Borenstein (1989, 1991,1996) and Lederman (2007, 2008).

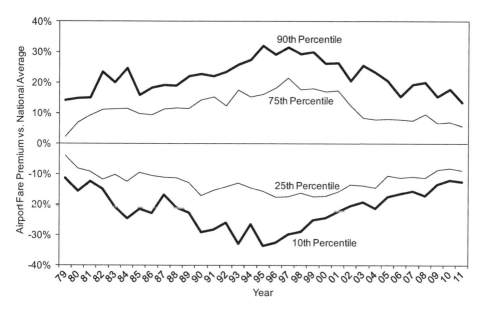

Fig. 2.20   Dispersion in airport premia across all US airports, 1979–2011

Notes: Weighted by passengers' departures at airport. Authors' calculations are from the same source and inclusion criteria as figure 2.5. See Borenstein (2013) for exact details of calculation.

trips to/from that airport to national average prices for all similar distance trips.[80] For the average fare premium across US airports (weighted by passengers at the airports), figure 2.20 presents tenth, twenty-fifth, seventy-fifth, and ninetieth percentiles during 1984 to 2011. Cross-airport price variation peaked in 1996 and has been declining since. Relative to national average, the majority of the most expensive airports have seen prices fall, and fares at most of the cheapest airports have risen. The standard deviation of the fare premium measure across US airports has fallen from 24 percent in 1996 to 13 percent in 2011, a level virtually identical to the extent of cross-airport dispersion in fare premia that existed in 1980. Borenstein (2013) examines these changes in more detail and finds mixed evidence that market power from airport dominance is declining.

The continued decline in fare disparities across airports despite recent mergers among large legacy carriers coincides with the expansion of low-cost airlines in the United States. Many low-cost or "no-frills" start-up airlines appeared in the 1980s, People Express being the most widely known, only to liquidate before the decade was over. With the exception of Southwest, they have until recently had difficulty gaining sufficient presence to ensure profitability and their continued existence. Southwest appears to

---

80. The exact method of airport premium calculation is presented by Borenstein (2013).

have avoided their fate through relentless attention to employee relations and productivity, careful control over operating costs, and judiciously paced expansion plans that until relatively recently avoided head-to-head competition at dominated airports.

There clearly is a significant "Southwest effect" in the current airline industry, in terms of its increased market share, expansion into more markets, and price impact in markets it serves or may credibly begin to serve (Morrison 2001; Goolsbee and Syverson 2008). Whether this is unique to Southwest, and hence nonreplicable, or is poised to diffuse across other airlines, may be a significant determinant of the future saliency of market power concerns in this industry.

2.5.3   Infrastructure Development and Utilization

Airport congestion was not a significant issue at most US airports during the regulated era. Most airports operated well below their technical capacity and it was rare that air traffic controllers were required to impose more than minor delays due to excess demand for ground or air space. Four airports—National (now Reagan) in Washington, DC, La Guardia and JFK in New York, and O'Hare at Chicago—were subject to significant excess demand. Under the so-called High Density Rules, the FAA imposed limits on aggregate hourly operations (takeoffs and landings) at these airports. Initially, takeoff and landing "slots" at these airports were allocated through a negotiation process among incumbent carriers. As demand grew rapidly after deregulation, the problem of congested airports worsened substantially. By 2000, fewer than three-quarters of all flights arrived at their destination airport on time, defined by the FAA as landing within 15 minutes of scheduled arrival time.[81]

Some operational delays are within the control of air carriers (see, e.g., Mayer and Sinai 2003). But an increasing share appears linked to inadequate infrastructure in the airport and air traffic control system. The airline industry in the United States and throughout the world, regardless of the degree of economic regulation, relies on an infrastructure that is largely government controlled. The US air traffic control system, which directs all aircraft flight operations, is operated by the Federal Aviation Administration. This control extends to airport runway traffic management, but not to the airport facilities. Airport terminals are managed, and usually owned, by a local government entity, which can be a city, a county, or a special government entity established purely to oversee an airport. After September 2001, security at US airports was turned over to the Transportation Security Administration, an agency within the US Department of Homeland Security.

Unfortunately, the track record of these government-controlled compo-

---

81. A significant contribution to delay in 2000 was a surge in delays at a single airport—LaGuardia—resulting from AIR21 legislation that overruled the FAA's High Density Rule constraints.

nents of the air transport system has not been particularly impressive. A preference, or in some cases, requirement, for administrative allocation of resources often has trumped any attempts to understand and employ market incentives in order to improve efficiency. Besides slow adoption of economic innovations that could improve economic welfare, technological innovation has also been slow in some areas.

Airport Access

In 1985, the federal government addressed a small part of the problem by establishing limited property rights for takeoff and landing clearance at four highly congested airports. Most of these tradeable "landing slots" were then given to incumbents based on their prior level of operations at the airports. Some were held out for allocation to new entrants at below-market prices. A market for these slots has developed and has supported thousands of trades since the beginning of the program. The slot allocation program, however, has been extended to only six US airports. Moreover, while this system has improved the allocation of scarce operational slots at these airports relative to negotiated allocations, it faces an uncertain future.

In 2000, Congress decided that small communities did not have sufficient access to service at slot-controlled airports, and it enacted legislation ("AIR 21") to suspend the High Density Rule (HDR) slot limits. LaGuardia was immediately opened to service using regional jets. The surge in scheduled service resulted in a 30 percent increase in operations, to almost 1,400 daily, at an airport that was previously ranked as the second-most delayed airport in the country. The result was predictable. In September 2000, one-third of the flights at LaGuardia were delayed, with an average delay of more than 40 minutes. LaGuardia-related delays accounted for one-fifth of all delays in the country (Maillet 2000). Forbes (2008) analyzes the effect of these delays on travelers' willingness to pay for air travel. The FAA ultimately responded with a temporary cap on total flight operations per hour and a lottery system to allocate these across carriers. In 2002, landing slots were to be abolished system wide. A similar story replayed at Chicago O'Hare airport, where both American and United substantially increased scheduled service in anticipation of the elimination of slot constraints, leading once again to egregious delays and imposition of administrative solutions. A 2008 administration proposal for landing slot auctions for LaGuardia, Kennedy, and Newark airports was met with fierce opposition by the New York Port Authority and the airlines, and amendments to ban slot auctions were introduced in Congress. In the meantime, operational caps at these most congested airports continue to be extended periodically, on a "temporary" basis. With Congress unwilling to recognize operational constraints,[82] and

---

82. While the FAA continues its "temporary" capacity caps on NYC airports, in 2012 Congress mandated sixteen additional long-distance flights to be allowed at Reagan National Airport as part of its 2012 FAA reauthorization.

airport authorities unable or unwilling to expand physical capacity to meet demand at current access prices, the future of this system remains uncertain.

The remaining (more than 300) airports that support commercial jet flights operate under a system known as "flow control," which is essentially queuing. Despite the success of market incentives in other parts of the industry, and growing interest in congestion pricing applied to some transportation segments,[83] there has been tremendous resistance to use of congestion pricing to allocate scarce runway capacity. In one case, a plan to use peak-load runway pricing at Boston's Logan airport was struck down by a federal court as being unduly discriminatory, because the system imposed higher per-passenger costs on small general aviation and commuter aircraft. Much of the opposition to runway pricing has been led by general aviation and small commuter aircraft operators who use the same airports and nearly as much scarce runway capacity as much larger commercial jets. Thus, it is not unusual for a fully loaded wide-bodied jet to be delayed in taking off by a small plane carrying just four or fewer people. Though general aviation has been discouraged at many highly congested slot-controlled airports, the slot program legislation established special categories to allocate rights to smaller commercial aircraft. The growth in corporate and private jet usage only exacerbates this problem.

Market-based airport facilities allocations are not without problems. Economists studying the possibility of pricing solutions to airport congestion have pointed out two potential concerns.[84] First, a dominant airline at a slot-constrained airport could buy excess slots in order to deter entry. It is straightforward to show that a competitive entrant could be outbid by an incumbent that intended only to withhold the slot from use. There have been some accusations of this behavior by small airlines attempting to enter a slot-controlled airport, though these arguments have been undermined somewhat by the accompanying claim that the small airline should receive the slots at no cost. Still, the incentive of a firm with market power to restrict output is real and it turns out in practice to be very difficult to monitor for such behavior.[85]

A second concern is the complexity of determining efficient congestion prices. Conventional models of congestion pricing, such as highway congestion tolls, assume atomistic users. In that case, each user imposes the same congestion externality on all other users, and symmetric tolls can enforce

83. Note, for example, the growth in private toll roads in states including California, Texas, and Virginia, and positive responses to London's congestion tolls on automobiles driving within the center city.

84. For example, see Borenstein (1988); Brueckner (2002, 2009); Brueckner and Van Dender (2008); and Morrison and Winston (2007).

85. A "use it or lose it" rule imposed at slot-constrained airports required that each slot be used on 80 percent of all days. In practice, this means that a firm could restrict output by 20 percent without being in violation of the rule, because they own many slots for each hour and can "assign" a given takeoff or landing to a different slot on different days.

efficient use of the scarce resource. For airports, such an assumption is clearly violated. Moreover, if airlines differ in their scale of operations, they will internalize the congestion externality of an additional flight to different degrees. Large carriers with many flights will internalize more of the externality; small carriers, less (see Brueckner 2002; Fan 2003; Brueckner and Van Dender 2008). For instance, if one airline has 60 percent of the flights at an airport, it will recognize that adding another flight at a peak time incrementally delays all of its existing flights. It will not fully internalize the congestion since 40 percent of the flights are operated by other airlines, but it will have more incentive to avoid further congesting peak periods than does an airline with 1 percent of all flights. This would argue for higher congestion tolls on carriers with smaller airport shares, all else equal, and apart from any market power concerns. If airlines also exercise different degrees of market power, optimal toll design becomes even more complex—it is possible that optimal tolls would be zero or negative for large carriers with considerable market power. Designing such a system would be difficult; implementing it politically would likely be impossible. It seems crucial, however, to measure the potential costs of an imperfect market-based system to the status quo, not the first-best system. Greater use of market incentives could almost surely improve economic welfare relative to the current system, which is driven by a combination of historical property rights, administrative rules of thumb, and political clout.

In addition to inefficient access to scarce infrastructure resources, the current system provides no mechanism to tie investment in that infrastructure to scarcity signals. Airport regulation typically limits fees and prices to levels that provide a fair return on historic investment costs. This may restrict landing fees to levels too low to promote efficient scheduling of scarce capacity and preclude any price signals that might guide efficient investment in future capacity. At some airports, geography or neighborhood limits may effectively preclude expansion of capacity at any reasonable cost. At others, capacity expansion may be feasible. Allocating scarce capacity through a price system and using revenue collected through that system to finance investment, may better discriminate between these two conditions.

Many of the market power concerns in congestion management of runways also arise in airport facilities management. The local authorities that operate airport terminals face the standard set of local development issues and financing concerns. They lease space to airlines and retail shops in order to finance operations. When they want to expand the facility, incumbent airlines are often the primary purchasers of the local bonds sold to finance the projects. In many cases, they have negotiated preferential access to terminal space in exchange for financing commitments. These may be necessary in order to secure financing for airport facility expansions, but they can lead to inefficient exclusion of new competitors. The airport authority must balance financial constraints against the longer-run goal of attaining competitive air service that benefits the surrounding community. Snider and Williams (forthcoming) find evidence that a change in airport financing that reduced preferential terminal space access at some airports had the effect of increasing competition at those airports.

Infrastructure Technology

A more difficult area to analyze is that of technological innovation in government-controlled infrastructure. Many industry participants have bemoaned the technology lag in the country's air traffic control system. The government has long admitted that the system is out of date and overburdened, but plans to overhaul the system and install modern technology for air traffic control have chronically failed to meet targets. The current air traffic management systems modernization effort, launched in 2004 under the umbrella "NextGen," targets completion in 2025 with significant component milestones along the way. While the FAA Modernization Act of 2012 provided longer-term FAA funding commitments than had been available in recent years, there presently is ongoing disagreement between FAA administrators and the Department of Transportation Inspector General on the likelihood of meeting near-term targets. Some critics argue that a private company would not have made the same mistakes or delayed new technology adoption so long (see Hausman and Sidak's discussion of government impediments to technological innovation in the telecomm sector in chapter 6 in this volume). The airline industry is subject to a variety of government fees and taxes. While some of these are earmarked for aviation investment, there has been no direct link between the collections and infrastructure investment, and the government has at times used the surplus in the Aviation Trust Fund to meet other budget goals. This situation has led some to call for privatization of the infrastructure system, with fees and taxes flowing to the privatized entity.[86] A privatized monopoly air traffic control system, while perhaps increasing efficiency relative to its objective function, would present a new set of concerns. We suspect that regulatory issues similar to those presented by a private monopoly electric grid operator, as discussed in Joskow's chapter, would pose considerable challenges.

2.6   Conclusion

Airline regulators attempted to assure a stable, growing industry that benefited consumers and the economy. The result was relatively high fares, inefficient operations, and airline earnings volatility. The problems with economic regulation of airlines prompted a pathbreaking shift in 1978, as the United States became the first country to deregulate its domestic airline industry. Fares have declined since deregulation and efficiency has improved,

86. See the discussion by Winston and de Rus (2008).

but it is difficult to know what counterfactual with which the current state of the industry should be compared thirty-five years after deregulation. The volatility in industry earnings has continued and average earnings have declined since deregulation.

Still, the continuing upheaval in the industry shows no signs of impeding the flow of investment in airlines or the benefits to consumers. Though the attacks of September 11, 2001 resulted in a major setback to the finances of the industry (even after the $5 billion in cash gifts the federal government bestowed upon the airlines in the following weeks), their effect on the level of air service was very short lived. More domestic routes had nonstop service in the summer of 2002 than in the summer of 2001 just prior to the attacks, and the daily number of domestic flights was nearly identical across the two years. Real fares continued to decline into 2005 and remained low through 2011. Measured by US city pairs that were connected by nonstop service or seats available on commercial flights, the level of service was better in 2007 than in any previous year, though it subsequently declined slightly, as might be expected given the 2008 financial crisis.

The post–9/11 rebound and growth in service and traffic came with a heavy price, however. As passenger volume expanded, and flight operations increased more than commensurately with the movement toward smaller aircraft and more frequent service in many markets, congestion and delay costs also reached record levels; the present reprieve may well last only until the macroeconomy strengthens. Moreover, this problem is far from unique to the United States. Efffectively managing aviation infrastructure— efficiently allocating access to current resources, investing in technology and physical capacity improvements at airports and in the air traffic control system, and ensuring efficient provision of airport security—is likely to be one of the greatest challenges facing the global aviation industry over the decades to come.

The average returns that the airlines have earned since deregulation would be insufficient to sustain the industry prospectively, although this conclusion might have been different in the late 1990s. That does not imply that competition in the industry is inherently unsustainable. The natural volatility in the demand for air travel probably will always cause earnings to be less stable than in other industries, but other factors that have depressed earnings are potentially controllable. Slow adjustment of labor costs is an institutional feature of the industry that may change either through new labor agreements at legacy carriers or through shift in market share to airlines that can adjust more nimbly. Much of the instability since deregulation has resulted from experimentation with flight scheduling, pricing, loyalty programs, distribution systems, and organization forms. Though clear, permanent answers to these management issues are unlikely to emerge, one would expect some learning to result from the experimentation and the range of both strategies and outcomes to narrow.

For most consumers, airline deregulation has been a benefit. For many airlines, it has been a costly experiment, though a few have prospered in the unregulated environment. Both the companies and economists studying the industry continue to learn from the industry dynamics.

References

Abramowitz, Amy D., and Stephen M. Brown. 1993. "Market Share and Price Determination in the Contemporary Airline Industry." *Review of Industrial Organization* 8 (4): 419–33.

Armantier, Olivier, and Oliver Richard. 2006. "Evidence on Pricing from the Continental Airlines and Northwest Airlines Code-Share Agreement." In *Advances in Airline Economics 1: Competition Policy and Antitrust*, edited by Darin Lee, 91–108. Boston: Elsevier.

———. 2008. "Domestic Airline Alliances and Consumer Welfare." *Rand Journal of Economics* 39 (3): 875–904.

Bailey, Elizabeth E. 2010. "Air-Transportation Deregulation." In *Better Living through Economics*, edited by John J. Siegfried, 188–202. Cambridge, MA: Harvard University Press.

Bailey, Elizabeth E., David R. Graham, and Daniel R. Kaplan. 1985. *Deregulating the Airlines*. Cambridge, MA: MIT Press.

Bailey, Elizabeth E., and John C. Panzar. 1981. "The Contestability of Airline Markets during the Transition to Deregulation." *Law and Contemporary Problems* 44 (1): 125–45.

Bamberger, Gustave, Dennis Carlton, and Lynette Neumann. 2004. "An Empirical Investigation of the Competitive Effects of Domestic Airline Alliances." *Journal of Law and Economics* 47 (1): 195–222.

Barnes, Brenda A. 2012. "Airline Pricing." In *The Oxford Handbook of Pricing Management*, edited by Özalp Özer and Robert Phillips. Oxford: Oxford University Press. DOI: 10.1093/oxfordhb/9780199543175.013.0003.

Barnhart, Cynthia, Peter Belobaba, and Amedeo Odoni. 2003. "Applications of Operations Research in the Air Transport Industry." *Transportation Science* 37(4): 368–91.

Basso, Leonardo J., and Sergio R. Jara-Diaz. 2005. "Calculation of Economies of Spatial Scope from Transport Cost Functions with Aggregate Output with an Application to the Airline Industry." *Journal of Transport Economics and Policy* 39 (1): 25–52.

Baumol, William J., John C. Panzar, and Robert Willig. 1982. *Contestable Markets and the Theory of Industry Structure*. New York: Harcourt College Publishing.

Belobaba, Peter. 1987. *Air Travel Demand and Airline Seat Inventory Management*. PhD diss., Massachusetts Institute of Technology.

Berry, Steven T. 1990. "Airport Presence as Product Differentiation." *American Economic Review Papers and Proceedings* 80 (2): 394–99.

———. 1992. "Estimation of a Model of Entry in the Airline Industry." *Econometrica* 60 (4): 889–917.

Berry, Steven, and Panle Jia. 2010. "Tracing the Woes: An Empirical Analysis of the Airline Industry." *American Economic Journal: Microeconomics* 2 (August): 1–43.

Blalock, Garrick, Vrinda Kadiyali, and Daniel H. Simon. 2007. "The Impact of

Post-9/11 Airport Security Measures on the Demand for Air Travel." *Journal of Law and Economics* 50 (4): 731–55.

Borenstein, Severin. 1988. "On the Efficiency of Competitive Markets for Operating Licenses." *Quarterly Journal of Economics* 103 (2): 357–85.

———. 1989. "Hubs and High Fares: Dominance and Market Power in the US Airline Industry." *Rand Journal of Economics* 20 (3): 344–65.

———. 1990. "Airline Mergers, Airport Dominance, and Market Power." *American Economic Review Papers and Proceedings* 80 (2): 400–404.

———. 1991. "The Dominant-Firm Advantage in Multi-Product Industries: Evidence from the US Airlines." *Quarterly Journal of Economics* 106 (4): 1237–66.

———. 1992. "The Evolution of US Airline Competition." *Journal of Economic Perspectives* 6 (2): 45–73.

———. 1996. "Repeat-Buyer Programs in Network Industries." In *Networks, Infrastructure, and the New Task for Regulation*, edited by Werner Sichel, 137–62. Ann Arbor: University of Michigan Press.

———. 1999. "Hub Dominance and Pricing." Testimony before the Transportation Research Board, January 21. http://faculty.haas.berkeley.edu/borenste/trb99.pdf.

———. 2005. "US Domestic Airline Pricing, 1995–2004." Competition Policy Center Working Paper CPC05-48, January, University of California, Berkeley. http://repositories.cdlib.org/iber/cpc/CPC05-048/.

———. 2011. "Why Can't US Airlines Make Money?" *American Economic Review Papers and Proceedings* 101 (5): 233–37.

———. 2013. "What Happened to Airline Market Power?" Unpublished manuscript, available at http://faculty.haas.berkeley.edu/borenste/AirMktPower2013.pdf.

Borenstein, Severin, and Nancy L. Rose. 1994. "Competition and Price Dispersion in the US Airline Industry." *Journal of Political Economy* 102 (4): 653–83.

———. 1995. "Bankruptcy and Pricing Behavior in US Airline Markets." *American Economic Review Papers and Proceedings* 85 (2): 397–402.

———. 2003. "The Impact of Bankruptcy on Airline Service Levels." *American Economic Review Papers and Proceedings* 93 (2): 415–19.

Borenstein, Severin, and Martin Zimmerman. 1988. "Market Incentives for Safe Commercial Airline Operation." *American Economic Review* 78 (5): 913–35.

Bratu, Stephane, and Cynthia Barnhart. 2005. "An Analysis of Passenger Delays Using Flight Operations and Passenger Booking Data." *Air Traffic Control Quarterly* 13 (1): 1–27.

Breyer, Stephen. 1982. *Regulation and Its Reform*. Cambridge, MA: Harvard University Press.

Brueckner, Jan K. 2002. "Airport Congestion When Carriers Have Market Power." *American Economic Review* 92 (5): 1357–75.

———. 2009. "Price vs. Quantity-Based Approaches to Airport Congestion Management." *Journal of Public Economics* 93 (5–6): 681–90.

Brueckner, Jan K., and Pablo T. Spiller. 1994. "Economies of Traffic Density in the Deregulated Airline Industry." *Journal of Law and Economics* 37 (2): 379–415.

Brueckner, Jan K., and Kurt Van Dender. 2008. "Atomistic Congestion Tolls at Concentrated Airports? Seeking a Unified View in the Internalization Debate." *Journal of Urban Economics* 64 (2): 288–95.

Brueckner, Jan K., and W. Tom Whalen. 2002. "The Price Effects of International Airline Alliances." *Journal of Law and Economics* 43 (2): 503–46.

Brunger, William G. 2009. "The Impact of the Internet on Airline Fares: The 'Internet Price Effect.'" *Journal of Revenue and Pricing Management* 9 (1–2): 66–93.

Card, David. 1997. "Deregulation and Labor Earnings in the Airline Industry." In

Regulatory Reform and Labor Markets, edited by James Peoples, 183–230. Boston: Kluwer Academic Publishers.

Caves, Douglas W., Laurits R. Christensen, and Michael W. Tretheway. 1984. "Economies of Density versus Economies of Scale: Why Trunk and Local Service Airline Costs Differ." *Rand Journal of Economics* 15 (4): 471–89.

Caves, Richard. 1962. *Air Transport and Its Regulators: An Industry Study*. Cambridge, MA: Harvard University Press.

Dana, James D., Jr. 1999a. "Equilibrium Price Dispersion under Demand Uncertainty: The Roles of Costly Capacity and Market Structure." *Rand Journal of Economics* 30 (4): 632–60.

———. 1999b. "Using Yield Management to Shift Demand When the Peak Time is Unknown." *Rand Journal of Economics* 30 (3): 456–74.

Davies, David G. 1971. "The Efficiency of Public versus Private Firms, the Case of Australia's Two Airlines." *Journal of Law and Economics* 14 (1): 149–65.

———. 1977. "Property Rights and Economic Efficiency—The Australian Airlines Revisited." *Journal of Law and Economics* 20 (1): 223–26.

Dillon, Robin L., Blake E. Johnson, and M. Elisabeth Pate-Cornell. 1999. "Risk Assessment Based on Financial Data: Market Response to Airline Accidents." *Risk Analysis* 19 (3): 473–86.

Dionne, Georges, Robert Gagnepain, Francois Gagnona, and Charles Vanassea. 1997. "Debt, Moral Hazard and Airline Safety: An Empirical Evidence." *Journal of Econometrics* 79 (2): 379–402.

Doganis, Rigas. 2006. *The Airline Business*, second edition. New York: Routledge.

Douglas, George W., and James C. Miller, III. 1974a. *Economic Regulation of Domestic Air Transport: Theory and Policy*. Washington, DC: Brookings Institution.

———. 1974b. "Quality Competition, Industry Equilibrium, and Efficiency in the Price-Constrained Airline Market." *American Economic Review* 64 (4): 657–69.

Dunne, Timothy, Mark J. Roberts, and Larry Samuelson. 1988. "Patterns of Firm Entry and Exit in US Manufacturing Industries." *Rand Journal of Economics* 19 (4): 495–515.

Eads, George. 1975. "Competition in the Domestic Trunk Airline Industry: Too Much or Too Little?" In *Promoting Competition in Regulated Markets*, edited by Almarin Phillips. Washington, DC: Brookings Institution.

Evans, William N., and Ioannis N. Kessides. 1993. "Localized Market Power in the US Airline Industry." *Review of Economics and Statistics* 75 (1): 66–75.

Fan, Terence. 2003. *Market-Based Airport Demand Management: Theory, Model and Applications*. PhD diss., Massachusetts Institute of Technology.

Forbes, Silke Januszewski. 2008. "The Effect of Air Travel Delays on Airline Prices." *International Journal of Industrial Organization* 26 (5): 1218–32.

Forbes, Silke Januszewski, and Mara Lederman. 2009. "Adaptation and Vertical Integration in the Airline Industry." *American Economic Review* 99 (5): 1831–49.

Forsyth, Peter. 2003. "Low-Cost Carriers in Australia: Experiences and Impacts." *Journal of Air Transport Management* 9:277–84.

Fruhan, W. 1972. *The Fight for Competitive Advantage: A Study of the United States Domestic Trunk Air Carriers*. Boston: Graduate School of Business Administration, Harvard University.

Gaggero, Alberto O., and Claudio A. Piga. 2011. "Airline Market Power and Intertemporal Price Discrimination." *Journal of Industrial Economics* 59 (4): 552–77.

General Accounting Office. 2003. *Airline Ticketing: Impact of Changes in the Airline Ticket Distribution Industry*. GAO-3-749.

Gerardi, Kristopher, and Adam Hale Shapiro. 2009. "Does Competition Reduce Price Dispersion? New Evidence from the Airline Industry." *Journal of Political Economy* 117 (1): 1–37.

Giaume, Stephanie, and Sarah Guillou. 2004. "Price Discrimination and Concentration in European Airline Markets." *Journal of Air Transport Management* 10 (5): 305–10.

Gillen, David W., William G. Morrison, and Christopher Stewart. 2004. "Air Travel Demand Elasticities: Concepts, Issues and Measurement." Final Report. Department of Finance. Canada. Accessed January 15, 2013. http://www.fin.gc.ca /consultresp/airtravel/airtravstdy_-eng.asp.

Good, David H., Lars-Hendrick Röller, and Robin C. Sickles. 1993. "US Airline Deregulation: Implications for European Transport." *The Economic Journal* 103 (419): 1028–41.

Goolsbee, Austan, and Chad Syverson. 2008. "How Do Incumbents Respond to the Threat of Entry? Evidence from Major Airlines." *Quarterly Journal of Economics* 123 (4): 1611–33.

Gordon, Robert J., and Darryl Jenkins. 1999. "Hub and Network Pricing in the Northwest Airlines Domestic System." Unpublished manuscript, Northwestern University, September.

Hendricks, Wallace. 1994. "Deregulation and Labor Earnings." *Journal of Labor Research* 15 (3): 207–34.

Hendricks, Wallace, Peter Feuille, and Carol Szerszen. 1980. "Regulation, Deregulation, and Collective Bargaining in Airlines." *Industrial and Labor Relations Review* 34 (1): 67–81.

Hirsch, Barry T. 2007. "Wage Determination in the US Airline Industry: Union Power under Product Market Constraints." In *Advances in Airline Economics, Vol. 2: The Economics of Airline Institutions, Operations and Marketing*, edited by Darin Lee. Amsterdam: Elsevier.

Hirsch, Barry T., and David A. Macpherson. 2000. "Earnings, Rents, and Competition in the Airline Labor Market." *Journal of Labor Economics* 18 (1): 125–55.

Hurdle, G. J., R. L. Johnson, A. S. Joskow, G. J. Werden, and M. A. Williams. 1989. "Concentration, Potential Entry, and Performance in the Airline Industry." *Journal of Industrial Economics* 38:119–39.

Jordan, William A. 1970. *Airline Regulation in America: Effects and Imperfections.* Baltimore, MD: Johns Hopkins Press.

———. 2005. "Airline Entry Following US Deregulation: The Definitive List of Startup Passenger Airlines, 1979–2003." Paper presented at the 2005 Annual Meeting of the Transportation Research Forum, George Washington University, Washington, DC, March.

Joskow, Paul L., and Roger G. Noll. 1994. "Economic Regulation." In *American Economic Policy in the 1980s*, edited by Martin Feldstein, 367–452. Chicago: University of Chicago Press.

Joskow, Paul L., and Nancy L. Rose. 1989. "The Effects of Economic Regulation." In *Handbook of Industrial Organization*, vol. 2, edited by R. Schmalensee and R. Willig, 1449–506. Amsterdam: North-Holland.

Kahn, Alfred E. 1971. *The Economics of Regulation: Principles and Institutions.* 2 vols. New York: John Wiley & Sons, Inc.

———. 1988. "Surprises of Airline Deregulation." *American Economic Review Papers and Proceedings* 72 (2): 316–22.

Kanafani, Adib, Theodore Keeler, and Shashi K. Sathisan. 1993. "Airline Safety Posture: Evidence from Service-Difficulty Reports." *Journal of Transportation Engineering* 119 (4): 655–64.

Keeler, Theodore E. 1972. "Airline Regulation and Market Performance." *Bell Journal of Economics and Management Science* 3 (2): 399–424.

Kennet, D. Mark. 1993. "Did Deregulation Affect Aircraft Engine Maintenance? An Empirical Policy Analysis." *Rand Journal of Economics* 24 (4): 542–58.

Laffont, Jean-Jacques, and Jean Tirole. 1993. *A Theory of Incentives in Procurement and Regulation.* Cambridge, MA: MIT Press.

Lederman, Mara. 2007. "Do Enhancements to Loyalty Programs Affect Demand? The Impact of International Frequent Flyer Partnerships on Domestic Demand." *Rand Journal of Economics* 38 (4): 1134–58.

———. 2008. "Are Frequent Flyer Programs a Cause of the 'Hub Premium'?" *Journal of Economics and Management Strategy* 17 (1): 35–66.

Lee, Darin, and Maria Jose Luengo Prado. 2005. "The Impact of Passenger Mix on Reported Hub Premiums in the US Airline Industry." *Southern Economic Journal* 72 (2): 372–94.

Levine, Michael E. 1965. "Is Regulation Necessary? California Air Transportation and National Regulatory Policy." *The Yale Law Journal* 74 (8): 1416–47.

———. 1987. "Airline Competition in Deregulated Markets: Theory, Firm Strategy and Public Policy." *Yale Journal on Regulation* 4 (Spring): 393–494.

Maillet, Louise E. 2000. "Statement before the House Transportation and Infrastructure Subcommittee on Aviation on AIR-21 Slot Management at LaGuardia Airport, December 5." As of September 10, 2007. http://commdocs.house.gov/committees/Trans/hpw106-114.000/hpw106-114_0f.htm.

Mayer, Christopher, and Todd Sinai. 2003. "Network Effects, Congestion Externalities, and Air Traffic Delays: Or Why Not All Delays Are Evil." *American Economic Review* 93 (4): 1194–215.

McCartney, Scott. 2007. "Airlines Apply Lessons of Bummer Summer." *Wall Street Journal*, September 4, D1.

Meyer, John R., Clinton V. Oster, Jr., Ivor P. Morgan, Benjamin Berman, and Diana L. Strassmann. 1981. *Airline Deregulation: The Early Experience.* Boston: Auburn House Publishing Co.

Morrison, Steven A. 2001. "Actual, Adjacent, and Potential Competition Estimating the Full Effect of Southwest Airlines." *Journal of Transport Economics and Policy* 35 (2): 239–56.

Morrison, Steven, and Clifford Winston. 1986. *The Economic Effects of Airline Deregulation.* Washington, DC: Brookings Institution.

———. 1995. *The Evolution of the Airline Industry.* Washington, DC: Brookings Institution.

——— 2000. "The Remaining Role for Government Policy in the Deregulated Airline Industry." In *Deregulation of Network Industries: What's Next?* edited by Sam Peltzman and Clifford Winston, 1–40. Washington, DC: AEI-Brookings Joint Center for Regulatory Studies.

———. 2007. "Another Look at Airport Congestion Pricing." *American Economic Review* 97 (5): 1970–77.

Neven, Damien J., Lars-Hendrik Röller, and Zhentang Zhang. 2006. "Endogenous Costs and Price-Cost Margins: An Application to the European Airline Industry." *The Journal of Industrial Economics* 54 (3): 351–68.

Ng, Charles K., and Paul Seabright. 2001. "Competition, Privatisation and Productive Efficiency: Evidence from the Airline Industry." *Economic Journal* 111 (July): 591–619.

Odoni, Amedeo. 2009. "The International Institutional and Regulatory Environment." In *The Global Airline Industry*, edited by Peter Belobaba et al., 19–46. Chichester: John Wiley & Sons, Ltd.

Orlov, Eugene. 2011. "How Does the Internet Influence Price Dispersion? Evidence from the Airline Industry." *Journal of Industrial Economics* 59 (1): 21–37.

Oster, Clinton V., Jr., John S. Strong, and C. Kurt Zorn. 1992. *Why Airplanes Crash: Aviation Safety in a Changing World.* Oxford: Oxford University Press.

Peltzman, Sam. 1989. "The Economic Theory of Regulation after a Decade of

Deregulation." *Brookings Papers on Economic Activity: Microeconomics* no. 3, 1–41. (Comments on 42–60.)

Peoples, James. 1998. "Deregulation and the Labor Market." *Journal of Economic Perspectives* 12 (3): 111–30.

Prescott, Edward C. 1975. "Efficiency of the Natural Rate." *Journal of Political Economy* 83 (6): 1229–36.

Pulvino, Todd. 1998. "Do Asset Fire Sales Exist? An Empirical Investigation of Commercial Aircraft Transactions." *The Journal of Finance* 53 (3): 939–78.

Richards, David B. 2007. "Did Passenger Fare Savings Occur After Airline Deregulation?" *Journal of the Transportation Research Forum* 46 (1): 73–93.

Rose, Nancy L. 1985. "The Incidence of Regulatory Rents in the Motor Carrier Industry." *Rand Journal of Economics* 16 (3): 299–318.

———. 1987. "Labor Rent-Sharing and Regulation: Evidence from the Trucking Industry." *Journal of Political Economy* 95 (6): 1146–78.

———. 1990. "Profitability and Product Quality: Economic Determinants of Airline Safety Performance." *Journal of Political Economy* 98 (5): 944–64.

———. 1992. "Fear of Flying: The Economics of Airline Safety." *Journal of Economic Perspectives* 6 (1): 75–94.

———. 2012. "After Airline Deregulation and Alfred E. Kahn." *American Economic Review Papers and Proceedings* 102 (3): 376–80.

Salop, Steven C. 1978. "Alternative Reservations Contracts." Civil Aeronautics Board Memo.

Savage, Ian. 1999. "Aviation Deregulation and Safety in the United States: The Evidence after Twenty Years." In *Taking Stock of Air Liberalization*, edited by Marc Gaudry and Robert Mayes, 93–114. Boston: Kluwer Academic Publishers.

Smith, Barry C., John F. Leimkuhler, and Ross M. Darrow. 1992. "Yield Management at American Airlines." *Interfaces* 22 (1): 8–24.

Snider, Conan, and Jonathan W. Williams. Forthcoming. "Barriers to Entry in the Airline Industry: A Regression Discontinuity Approach." *Review of Economics and Statistics*.

Stavins, Joanna. 2001. "Price Discrimination in the Airline Market: The Effect of Market Concentration." *Review of Economics and Statistics* 83 (1): 200–02.

Torbenson, Eric. 2007. "United Airlines Wins Approval for New China Service (Update7)." Bloomberg.com, January 9. Accessed February 23, 2007. http://www.bloomberg.com/apps/news?pid=newsarchive&sid=aKJGWf15jO7Q&refer=home.

Trottman, Melanie. 2001. "Several Airlines Raise Fares 5%, but That Isn't Final." *Wall Street Journal*, May 21, B6.

Unterberger, S. Herbert, and Edward C. Koziara. 1975. "Airline Strike Insurance: A Study in Escalation." *Industrial and Labor Relations Review* 29 (1): 26–45.

Whinston, Michael D., and Scott C. Collins. 1992. "Entry and Competitive Structure in Deregulated Airline Markets: An Event Study Analysis of People Express." *Rand Journal of Economics* 23 (4): 445–62.

Winston, Clifford, and Gines de Rus, eds. 2008. *Aviation Infrastructure Performance: A Study in Comparative Political Economy*. Washington, DC: Brookings Institution.

Wolfram, Catherine. 2004. "Competitive Bidding for the Early US Airmail Routes." Unpublished manuscript, University of California, Berkeley, http://faculty.haas.berkeley.edu/wolfram/Papers/Airmail1204.pdf.

Zuckerman, Laurence. 2001. "Airlines, Led by United, Show Big Losses." *New York Times*, July 19, 7.

Cable Regulation in the Internet Era

Gregory S. Crawford

3.1 Introduction

Now is a quiet time in the on-again, off-again regulation of the cable television industry. Since the 1996 Telecommunications Act eliminated price caps for the majority of cable service bundles on March 31, 1999, cable systems have been free to charge whatever they like for the services chosen by the vast majority of subscribers. That was a watershed year, as the Satellite Home Viewer Improvement Act of 1999 also relaxed regulatory restrictions limiting the ability of direct-broadcast satellite (DBS) systems to provide local television signals into major television markets.

Since then, satellite providers have added 23 million more subscribers than cable, giving them over a third of the multichannel video programming distribution (MVPD) marketplace and providing two credible competitors to incumbent cable systems in most markets (FCC 2001c; FCC 2005b). More recently, local telephone operators Verizon and AT&T have invested billions to provide video in their local service areas and, by 2010, had earned another 7 percent of the market. Online video distribution is a growing source of television viewing.

While concentration has fallen in video distribution, the last fifteen years

Gregory S. Crawford is professor of applied microeconomics in the Department of Economics at the University of Zurich.

I would like to thank Nancy Rose, Ali Yurukoglu, Tasneem Chipty, Leslie Marx, Tracy Waldon, and seminar participants at the NBER conferences on economic regulation for helpful comments. Thanks also to ESRC Grant RES-062-23-2586 for financial support for this research. An older version of this chapter circulated under the title "Cable Regulation in the Satellite Era." For acknowledgments, sources of research support, and disclosure of the author's material financial relationships, if any, please see http://www.nber.org/chapters /c12569.ack.

has also seen continued national consolidation, with the top eight firms increasing their national share of MVPD subscribers from 68.6 percent in 1997 to 84.0 percent in 2010 (FCC 1998c, 2012c). Programming markets have also become more concentrated over this period. This has raised concerns about competition and integration in the wholesale (programming) market. Horizontal concentration and channel occupancy limits enacted after the 1992 Cable Act were struck down in 2001, reinstated in 2007, and struck down again in 2009 (Make 2009). As cable prices continue to rise, lawmakers wonder about the feasibility of à la carte services to reduce cable prices (Hohmann 2012).

This chapter considers the merits of regulation in cable television markets in light of these developments. In the first part, I survey past and present cable regulations and assess their effects. I begin by surveying the reasons for and effects of the four major periods of regulation and deregulation of cable prices (1972–1984, 1984–1992, 1992–1996, 1996–present). The evidence for regulation is discouraging: unregulated periods exhibit rapid increases in quality and penetration (and prices), while regulated periods exhibit slight decreases in prices and possibly lower quality. Consumer welfare estimates, while few, suggest consumers prefer *unregulated* cable services. This highlights the difficulty regulating prices in an industry, like cable, where service quality cannot be regulated and is easily changed.

I then review the empirical record on the consequences of competition in cable markets. Evidence from duopoly ("overbuilt") cable markets is robust: an additional wireline competitor lowers cable prices, with estimates ranging from 8 percent to 34 percent. Evidence of the effect of satellite competition is less compelling: surveyed rates are often only marginally lower and sometimes higher. Empirical studies trying to measure satellite competition's effects accounting for quality changes find prices may be (somewhat) lower, that most of the consumer benefits from such competition accrues to satellite and not cable subscribers, and that significant market power remains. While telco entry has clearly been important to consumers in those markets where it has come, I know of no evidence of its effects on cable prices or quality.

Finally, I address four open issues in cable markets where conclusions are harder to come by. First, while horizontal concentration has clearly increased in the programming market, theoretical models have ambiguous predictions of its effects and empirical work is hampered by insufficient data on affiliate fees (prices). The evidence on vertical integration is more substantial: integrated systems clearly favor affiliated programming, but whether for reasons of efficiency or foreclosure remain unclear. Second, bundling impacts market outcomes in both the distribution and programming markets. In distribution, it clearly enables systems to better capture consumer surplus and offer high-quality and diverse programming, but it may do so at significant cost to consumers. Recent research by Crawford and Yurukoglu (2012) finds consumers would not be better off under à la carte.

Worse, theoretical models suggest bundling in the wholesale market may enhance market power and serve as an effective barrier to entry. Empirical evidence of this effect is critically needed. Finally, industry participants and regulators alike are keenly interested in the likely effects of growing online video consumption and what can be done about increasingly frequent bargaining breakdowns between content providers and distributors that leave consumers "in the dark."

The focus of this chapter is almost exclusively on the cable television market in the United States. I do this for several reasons. First, the evolution of the video programming industry and the regulations that apply to it differ considerably across countries. This has led to dramatic differences in the market reach of cable systems, their market share among households passed, and the relative importance of cable versus satellite versus telco operators in the retail and programming markets (OECD 2001, table 2). Second, this is a mostly empirical survey, and by virtue of a series of FCC reports both on cable industry prices and on competition in the market for video programming (e.g., FCC 2012b, 2012c) and a private data collection industry, there is surprisingly good information about cable systems in the United States, both in the aggregate and for individual systems. Adequately analyzing the experience in other countries would require a chapter in itself, a worthwhile undertaking but beyond the scope of this effort. Finally, beyond a brief description of the current regulatory treatment, I do not consider the economic and regulatory features of the market for broadband Internet access. In part, the economic issues are different and more suitable to a chapter on telecommunications, but primarily for the same reasons as aforementioned. This is a deep and substantive policy issue whose treatment would quickly exhaust the space I have here. See Jerry Hausman and Greg Sidak's chapter on telecommunications markets for further analysis of this issue.

On the whole, the future looks bright for the organization of the cable television industry. Satellite and telco competition has largely replaced price regulation as the constraining force on cable pricing quality choice. Furthermore, consumer demand for online and mobile video is driving innovation in video delivery. Several important areas of uncertainty remain, however. Issues of horizontal concentration both up- and downstream, vertical integration, bargaining breakdowns, and the potential for foreclosure in both the traditional and online video programming markets are real and significant. While there is no clear evidence of harm, more research is needed. Until then, academics and regulators would do well to analyze these issues closely in the coming years.

3.2 A Cable Television Lexicon

The essential features of cable television systems have changed little in the industry's fifty years of existence. Then, as now, cable systems choose a portfolio of television networks, bundle them into services, and offer these services to consumers in local, geographically separate, cable markets.

Cable systems purchase the rights to distribute program networks in the *programming market*. Since the mid-1990s, cable systems in the United States have had to compete for customers with direct broadcast satellite (DBS) providers. Since the mid-2000s, both have had to compete with telephone operators offering video service in their local services areas. Together, cable, satellite, and telephone company (telco) operators are said to compete in the multichannel video programming distribution (MVPD) market. This is sometimes just called the *distribution market*.

As in many media markets, the video programming industry earns most of its revenue from one of two sources: monthly fees charged by cable systems to consumers for access to programming and advertising fees charged (mostly) by networks to advertisers for access to audiences. Figure 3.1 demonstrates that advertising revenue has grown in importance to the industry and now comprises over 30 percent of cable's $97.6 billion in 2011 revenue (NCTA 2013a, 2013b). Figure 3.2 provides a graphical representation of the multichannel video programming industry.

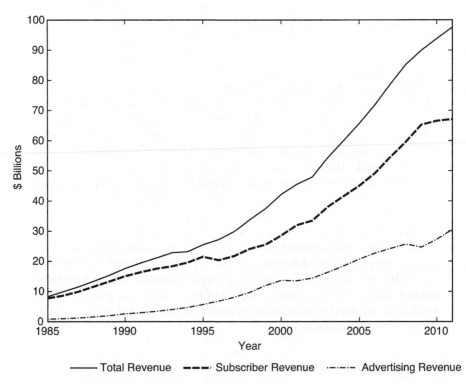

Fig. 3.1   Cable industry revenue, 1985–2011
Sources: NCTA (2013a, 2013b).

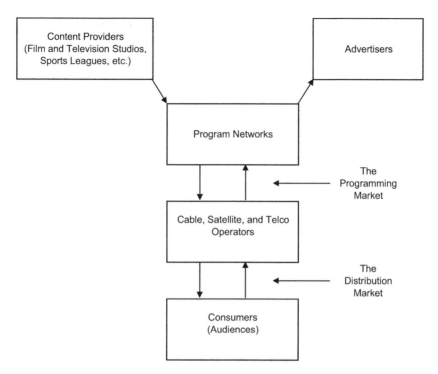

Fig. 3.2   The multichannel video programming industry

Cable systems today offer four main types of program networks. *Broadcast networks* are television signals broadcast over the air in the local cable market by television stations and then collected and retransmitted by cable systems. Examples include the major, national broadcast networks—ABC, CBS, NBC, and FOX—as well as public and independent television stations. *Cable programming networks* are fee- and advertising-supported general and special-interest networks distributed nationally to MVPDs via satellite. Examples include some of the most recognizable networks associated with pay television, including MTV, CNN, and ESPN.[1] *Premium programming networks* are advertising-free entertainment networks, typically offering full-length feature films. Examples include equally familiar networks like HBO and Showtime. *Pay-per-view networks* are specialty channels devoted to on-demand viewing of high-value programming, typically offering the most recent theatrical releases and specialty sporting events.

Systems exhibit moderate differences in how they bundle networks into services. Historically, broadcast and cable programming networks were

1. So-called cable networks earned their name by having originally been available only on cable.

bundled and offered as *basic service* while premium programming networks were unbundled and sold as *premium services*.[2] In the last twenty years, systems have diversified their offerings, often slimming down basic service to (largely) broadcast networks and offering many of the most popular cable networks in multiple bundles called *expanded basic services*. They have also taken advantage of digital compression technology to dramatically increase their effective channel capacity and offer hundreds of smaller cable networks. These networks are typically also bundled and offered as *digital services*. For basic, expanded basic, or digital services, consumers are not permitted to buy access to the individual networks offered in bundles; they must instead purchase the entire bundle.

Migration to digital technologies also allowed cable systems to offer high-speed (broadband) access to the Internet. This required significant investments in physical infrastructure, notably to accommodate digital data and allow upstream communication (compare to figure 3.3), but has proven to be a successful undertaking: despite being deployed several years after telephone systems' digital subscriber line (DSL) technology, cable systems in 2005 commanded over 63 percent of the broadband market, earning revenues of $6.7 billion in 2003, over 12 percent of cable systems' total revenue, and growing fast (FCC 2005b).[3]

MVPDs continue to innovate in delivering video programming to households. Almost all MVPDs now lease or sell digital video recorders (DVRs) with hundreds of hours of recording time.[4] Many also now offer video on demand with libraries of movies and previously aired episodes of popular television series. In June 2009, Comcast and Time Warner introduced TV Everywhere to allow authenticated cable subscribers to watch video online, on tablet computers like the iPad, or on their mobile phones.[5] While take-up has been slow due to the challenges of contracting with content providers over rights through these new distribution channels, it is only a matter of time before households will be able to consume the "four anys": any programming, on any device, in any place, and at any time.

MVPDs are not alone in these goals. It is now commonplace for consumers to rely on "over-the-top" (OTT) delivery of video programming over the Internet. According to Nielsen (via the FCC), "approximately 48% of Americans now watch video online, and 10% watch mobile video" (FCC 2012c, 111). That being said, in 2011 Nielsen also estimates the

2. In the last ten years, premium networks have begun "multiplexing" their programming; that is, offering multiple channels under a single network/brand (e.g., HBO, HBO 2, HBO Family, etc.).

3. In 2010, nonvideo services, largely Internet and telephone services, contributed 37.1 percent of cable operators revenue (FCC 2012c).

4. A digital video recorder is a device that allows households to record video to a hard drive-based digital storage medium.

5. As this chapter goes to press, Dish has introduced an "app" to rave reviews that allows access to all of their content on mobile devices (Roettgers 2013).

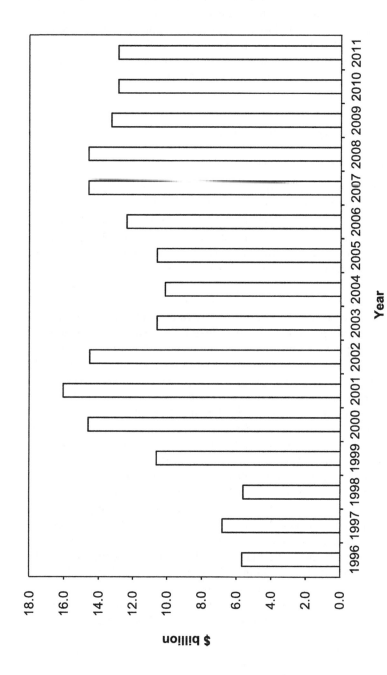

Fig. 3.3   Cable industry infrastructure investment, 1996–2011
Source: NCTA (2013c).

average American watched 27 minutes/week of video on the Internet (and 7 min/week on a mobile phone) versus over 5 hours of traditional and time-shifted television. Similarly, Screen Digest estimates that online video distributor (OVD) revenue was no more than $407 million in 2010, just 0.3 percent of the $143 billion spent by households and advertisers on traditional television. I discuss the likely effects of further growth in online video distribution in section 3.7.3.

3.3   A Brief History of Cable Regulation

3.3.1   1950–1984: The Early History

The cable television industry began in the 1950s to transmit broadcast television signals to areas that could not receive them due to interference from natural features of the local terrain.[6] In order to provide cable service, cable systems needed to reach "franchise agreements" with the appropriate regulatory body, usually local municipalities. These agreements typically included agreements on a timetable for infrastructure deployment, a franchise fee (typically a small percentage of gross revenue), channel set-asides for public interest uses (e.g., community programming), and maximum prices for each class of offered cable service in return for an exclusive franchise to use municipal rights-of-way to install the system's infrastructure.

Cable grew quickly until 1966, when the Federal Communications Commission (FCC) asserted its authority over cable operators and forbid the importation of broadcast signals into the top 100 television markets unless it was satisfied that such carriage "would be consistent with the public interest, and particularly with the establishment and healthy maintenance of UHF (ultra-high frequency) television broadcast service."[7] It also instituted content restrictions that prevented the distribution of movies less than ten years old or sporting events broadcast within the previous five years. In 1972, the FCC provided a comprehensive set of cable rules. First, it sought to balance broadcasting and cable television interests by permitting limited importation of distant broadcast signals. It also, however, imposed a host of other requirements, including must-carry, franchise standards, network program nonduplication, and cross-ownership rules (FCC 2000b).[8]

The next decade saw a gradual reversal of the 1972 regulations and a period of significant programming and subscriber growth. First, rules originally established in 1969 were affirmed in 1975 that franchise price regulation must be confined to services that included broadcast television stations (GAO 1989). As a result, premium or pay-TV stations were not nor

6. See Foster (1982, chapter 5) and Noll, Peck, and McGowan (1973) for a survey of the history of broadcast television and its regulation.
7. 2 FCC 2d at 782 as cited in Besen and Crandall (1981, 90).
8. Must-carry rules require systems to carry all local broadcast signals available in their franchise area. These rules were amended by the 1992 Cable Act.

ever have been subject to price regulation. Second, in 1972 Time introduced Home Box Office (HBO) for the purpose of providing original content on an advertising-free, fee-supported cable network. In 1975, it demonstrated the ability to distribute programming via satellite and, in 1977, fought and won in court against the FCC's content restrictions, allowing HBO and a generation of subsequent cable networks to provide whatever programming they desired.[9] Because the production of programming is a public good, the advent of low-cost satellite technology with sizable economies of scale revolutionized the distribution of programming for cable systems. WTBS, CNN, and ESPN began national distribution of general-interest, news, and sports programming, respectively, in 1979 and 1980. In all, no less than thirteen of the fifteen most widely available advertising-supported programming networks, and all of the top five most widely available fee-supported programming networks, were launched between 1977 and 1984. Cable systems grew at double-digit rates.

3.3.2   1984 to Present: Back and Forth

While the scope of federal regulations had diminished by 1979, state and local regulations remained. By the mid-1980s, however, the price terms of these contracts came under attack as cable joined the "deregulation revolution" sweeping through Congress (Kahn 1991). Convinced that three or more over-the-air broadcast television signals provided a sufficient competitive alternative to cable television service, Congress passed the 1984 Cable Act to free the vast majority of cable systems from all price regulations.[10]

By 1991, cable systems had dramatically expanded their offered services. The average system offered a basic service including a bundle of thirty-five channels as well as four to six premium services (GAO 1991). Prices also increased, however, rising 56 percent in nominal and 24 percent in real terms between November 1986 and April 1991.

Concerned that high and rising prices reflected market power by monopoly cable systems, Congress reversed course and passed the 1992 Cable Act to "provide increased consumer protection in cable television markets." Regulation differed by tiers of cable service and only applied if a system was not subject to "effective competition."[11] Basic tiers were regulated, if desired, by the local franchise authority, which was required to certify with the FCC. Cable programming (expanded basic) tiers were regulated by the FCC.[12] Both followed rules set by the FCC, reducing prices to "benchmarks" based

9. See HBO v. FCC, 567 Fd 2nd 9 (1977).
10. Other terms of franchise agreements remained in effect. See GAO (1989).
11. There are four separate tests for effective competition: (1) a cable market share under 30 percent; (2) there are at least two unaffiliated MVPDs serving 50 percent of the cable market and achieving a combined share of 15 percent; (3) the franchising authority is itself a MVPD serving 50 percent of the cable market; and (4) the local exchange carrier offers comparable video programming services (47 CFR 76.905).
12. In what follows I use expanded basic tier to refer to the FCC designation cable programming tier.

on prices charged by systems facing effective competition. In April 1993 the FCC capped per-channel cable prices that systems could charge for most types of cable service. The FCC soon found, however, that not only did cable bills fail to decline, but that for nearly one-third of cable subscribers, they had increased. Many systems had introduced new, unregulated services and moved popular programming networks to those services; others had reallocated their portfolio of programming across services (FCC 1994; Hazlett and Spitzer 1997; Crawford 2000). In February 1994 the FCC imposed an additional 7 percent price reduction.

Responding to political pressure from cable systems, the FCC almost immediately began relaxing price controls. First, "going forward" rules were established in November, 1994. As discussed by Paul Joskow in his chapter analyzing incentive regulation in electricity transmission markets, an important feature of incentive (price cap) regulation are the rules governing the maximum price over time. This is particularly important in cable markets, where both the number and cost of programming networks regularly increase over time. Instead of allowing systems to increase prices by a planned "cost + 7.5 percent" for each added network, the going forward rules permitted increases of up to $1.50 per month over two years if up to six channels were added, regardless of cost (Hazlett and Spitzer 1997). Prices controls were further relaxed by the adoption of social contracts with major cable providers in late 1995 and early 1996. These allowed systems to increase their rates for expanded basic tiers on an annual basis in return for a promise to upgrade their infrastructure.[13] The deregulatory about-face culminated with the passage of the 1996 Telecommunications Act. This eliminated all price regulation for expanded basic tiers after March 31, 1999. Regulation of basic service rates remains the only source of price regulation in the US cable television industry.

3.3.3   Must-Carry/Retransmission Consent

In addition to imposing price caps, the 1992 Cable Act introduced another set of regulations whose effects are still being felt: must-carry and retransmission consent. Since 1972, cable systems were subject to must-carry: they were required to carry all local broadcast signals available in their franchise area. Systems fought must-carry, however, arguing it interfered with their choice of content, and succeeded in having it struck down on First Amendment grounds in 1988. The 1992 Cable Act, however, not only restored it but gave local broadcast stations the option either to demand carriage on local cable systems (must-carry) or negotiate with those systems for compensa-

---

13. See, for example, FCC (1998d, 6) describing the FCC's social contract with Time Warner. In it, Time Warner was permitted to increase its expanded basic prices by $1/year for five years in return for agreeing to invest $4 billion to upgrade its system. It also dismissed over 900 rate complaints and provided small refunds to subscribers.

tion for carriage (retransmission consent). These rules were upheld by the Supreme Court in 1997.

Retransmission consent has remained a point of contention between broadcast networks and cable systems ever since. Agreements are often negotiated on repeating three-year intervals. Smaller (especially UHF) stations commonly select must-carry, but larger stations and station groups, particularly those affiliated with the major broadcast networks, have aggressively used retransmission consent to obtain compensation from cable systems. Systems initially refused to pay stations directly for carriage rights, a position that has only changed in the last few years. Instead, they signed carriage agreements for broadcaster-affiliated cable networks. ESPN2 (ABC), America's Talking (NBC), and FX (Fox) all were launched on systems this way.[14] More recently, Disney (ABC) has used retransmission consent to obtain expanded carriage agreements for SoapNet, the Disney Channel, and NBC to charge higher affiliate fees for CNBC and MSNBC (Schiesel 2001). Indeed, the power of retransmission consent to obtain carriage agreements was one stated motivation for the purchase of CBS by Viacom in 1999.

Disagreements between broadcast television stations (and their affiliated networks) and MVPDs over retransmission consent fees have become a hot-button policy issue in the last five years. Several high-profile negotiations have resulted in broadcast stations being blacked out in major media markets, and one pro-MVPD lobbying group estimates there were broadcast-station blackouts in forty television markets in 2011 and ninety-one in 2012.[15] At root have been new and growing demands by broadcasters for cash compensation for retransmission rights. An innovation as recently as 2007 to 2008, such demands are now the norm. I discuss the implications of what might be done to mitigate welfare losses from temporary blackouts in section 3.7.4.

3.3.4 Programming Market Regulations

While the focus of cable regulations has historically been on controlling prices charged by cable providers, there has been recent interest in the organization and operation of the programming (input) market. The basic features of this market are as follows.[16] Most network production costs are fixed. Rights sales generate both transfer payments ("affiliate fees") from MVPDs, typically in the form of a payment per subscriber per month, and advertising revenue. The relative importance of each varies by network, but across cable programming networks 40 percent of revenue comes from

---

14. America's Talking became MSNBC in 1996. CBS lacked any affiliated networks in the initial retransmission consent negotiations but used them to launch Eye on People in 1996.

15. See http://www.americantelevisionalliance.org/blog/ for details.

16. See Owen and Wildman (1992) for a detailed description of the market for the supply of programming.

advertising (NCTA 2005a). Programming is *nonrivalrous*: sales of programming to one MVPD does not reduce the supply available to others.

Carriage agreements are negotiated on a bilateral basis between a network (or network groups) and an individual system or system groups, also known as multiple system operators (MSOs). Comcast is the largest MSO in the United States with 22.8 million subscribers, or 22.6 percent of the MVPD market (table 3.6). Many of the largest MVPD operators either own or have ownership interests in programming networks, as do major broadcast networks. Indeed, all of the top twenty (non-CSPAN) cable networks by subscriber reach and all of the top fifteen by ratings are owned by one of eight firms, raising concerns about diversity in the media marketplace.[17]

The 1992 Cable Act introduced two important regulations regarding competition in the programming market. First, it directed the FCC to establish reasonable limits on the number of subscribers a cable operator may serve (the horizontal, or subscriber, limit) as well as the number of channels a cable operator may devote to affiliated program networks (the vertical, or channel occupancy, limit) (FCC 2005d). These were set in 1993 at 30 percent of cable subscribers for the horizontal limit and 40 percent of channel capacity (up to capacities of seventy-five) for the vertical limit.[18] In the *Time Warner II* decision in 2001, the US Court of Appeals for the DC Circuit reversed and remanded these rules, finding the FCC had not provided a sufficient rationale for their implementation. A subsequent 2007 rule that reinstated the limits was dismissed in 2009 as "arbitrary and capricious."

The 1992 Cable Act also introduced program access and carriage rules. These forbid affiliated MVPDs and networks from discriminating against unaffiliated rivals in either the programming or distribution markets and also ruled out exclusive agreements between cable operators and their affiliated networks. These rules were enforced through a complaint process at the FCC, but complaints had been relatively rare, particularly in the recent ten years.

The program access rules were required in the 1992 Cable Act to be evaluated on a rolling five-year basis. In October of 2012, the FCC permitted them to lapse, replacing them with rules giving the commission the right to review any programming agreement for anticompetitive effects on a case-by-case basis. Until 2010, the program access rules also only applied to *satellite-delivered* programming (the so-called terrestrial loophole). This was important, as for a few regional markets, including Philadelphia, San Diego, and parts of the southeastern United States, some regional networks distributed via microwave, including regional sports networks (RSNs), reached exclusive agreements with their affiliated MSO, excluding rival

17. Comcast, Time Warner, Cox, and Cablevision among cable MSOs; News Corp/Fox, Disney/ABC, Viacom/CBS, and GE/NBC among broadcasters. In 2011, Comcast purchased GE/NBC, further consolidating the market.
18. The 30 percent limit was changed in 1999 to 30 percent of MVPD subscribers.

MVPDs from access to "critical" content (FCC 2005d). The new case-by-case rules include a (rebuttable) presumption that exclusive deals with RSNs are unfair.

3.3.5   Merger Review

Under the 1934 Communications Act, the FCC's mandate is to ensure that the organization of communications and media markets serves the "public interest, convenience, and necessity." This mandate has been interpreted by the FCC to give it the power to approve or deny mergers among communications or media firms whenever it involves a transfer of licenses. Since the licenses involved are necessary to offer the firms' services,[19] in practice this gives the commission the power to approve all media or communications merger.[20] Prior to the passage of the 1996 Telecommunications Act, this power was not exercised as existing regulations on ownership (e.g., ownership limits, cross-ownership restrictions) foreclosed large communications and media mergers. Since then, however, the commission has taken an ever stronger role in approving communications and media mergers, often imposing conditions on the merged entity.

Merger conditions, while not explicit regulations, have the same effect on firms. Recent examples of conditions placed on merging parties cover a variety of alleged harms. In the Comcast-AT&T merger completed in November of 2002, the commission ordered the merged firm to divest itself of its interests in Time Warner Cable.[21] In the News Corp-DirecTV and Adelphia-Time Warner-Comcast mergers completed in December of 2003 and July of 2006, respectively, the commission imposed a number of conditions, backed by a binding arbitration process, designed to ensure nondiscriminatory access to the combined firms' regional sports and broadcast programming networks (Kirkpatrick 2003). Finally, in the recent Comcast-NBC/Universal merger approved in January 2011, the commission imposed a number of conditions over a seven-year period, including program access–like rules for newly integrated content, a nondiscrimination condition in online video (and the removal of management rights in Hulu, an OVD), and a "neighborhooding" condition for channel placement of news programming.

3.3.6   Other Cable Regulations

Cable systems are subject to a myriad of additional regulations (FCC 2000b). A few of these are briefly discussed here.

---

19. In the case of cable systems, the licenses to be transferred are the cable television relay service license that "are essential to the operation of the [firm]" (FCC 2001b).

20. Note that the FCC's merger review process is in addition to that required by competition law: any merger between firms of a given size (roughly sales or assets of $50 million) must be approved by the federal antitrust authorities, the Department of Justice, or the Federal Trade Commission, under the Clayton Act.

21. This condition had been agreed to in advance by the companies (Feder 2002).

Broadband Access Regulation

The market for high-speed (broadband) Internet access has grown con-siderably in the last ten years and is now an important source of revenue for most major cable systems. It has also caused a regulatory fight between cable systems, internet service providers (ISPs), and local telephone providers over the appropriate regulatory treatment of broadband access. As low-speed ("dial-up") access only required access to a local telephone line, ISPs like AOL and Earthlink grew in the late 1990s without regulatory oversight. As broadband access became viable, however, telephone companies were required to share access to their broadband (DSL) network with unaffili-ated rivals.

In FCC (2000c), the FCC ruled that cable broadband service was an "information service" and not a "telecommunications service" subject to common carrier (i.e., access) regulation. In June of 2005, the Supreme Court upheld this decision (Schatz, Drucker, and Searcy 2005). In August of 2005, a similar set of rules was put in place for DSL providers (Schatz 2005). Going forward, DSL and cable will compete on near-equal terms and neither will be required to share access with unaffiliated rivals. This policy is in marked contrast to wholesale broadband access policies implemented in many other developed countries.

Cable/Telco Cross-Ownership and Telephone Company Entry

The 1984 Cable Act forbid local exchange carriers (LECs) from providing cable service within their telephone service areas. The 1996 Telecommuni-cations Act relaxed this restriction, providing a number of methods under which telephone companies could provide video service, including building a wireline cable system (FCC 2000b, 17).[22] Early efforts at video entry were small in scale and often unprofitable. The largest effort was put forth by Ameritech (now owned by AT&T), which purchased and built cable systems that passed almost two million homes. They were only able to attract 225,000 subscribers, however, and exited the business in 1998 (FCC 2004b).

Each of the three extant LECs (AT&T, CenturyLink, and Verizon) now offer video programming in some form. CenturyLink largely resells DirecTV satellite services bundled with their own telephone and broadband services. Verizon and AT&T, instead, invested billions upgrading their networks to provide television service in direct competition with cable and satellite com-panies.[23] Table 3.6 shows both have been successful: they are now the seventh and ninth largest MVPDs with a total national market share of 6.5 percent.

An important determinant of the success of LEC entry is the ease with

22. Many early cable franchise agreements were exclusive within a given municipality. The 1992 Cable Act forbid exclusivity.
23. This was viewed in part as a defensive response to cable entry into local telephone service.

which they can obtain agreements to provide video service with local franchise authorities (LFAs). LECs have complained that the franchising process is an important barrier to entry in cable markets. For example, Verizon estimated it would have to obtain agreements with almost 10,000 municipalities if it wished to provide video programming throughout its service area and that LFAs (backed by incumbent cable operators) took too long and required too many concessions (FCC 2005c).[24] In September 2005, Texas passed a law introducing a simplified statewide franchising process, something CenturyLink is encouraging in a number of other states. In 2007, the FCC also adopted rules that limited cities' abilities to regulate or slow telco entry, a decision upheld by the courts in 2008.

3.3.7 Satellite Regulations

Federal regulation of the satellite television industry has also influenced the cable television industry. While satellite distribution of programming was initially intended for retransmission by cable systems, a small consumer market also developed. By the mid-1980s, approximately 3 million households had purchased C-Band (12-foot) satellite dishes, mostly in rural areas without access to cable service.

It wasn't until the mid-1990s, however, that direct satellite service to households thrived. Fueled by the complementary developments of improved compression technology, more powerful satellites, and smaller (18-inch) satellite dishes, Hughes introduced DirecTV in 1993. Subscriptions grew quickly, particularly among the estimated 20 million households without access to cable service. Wider adoption was hindered, however, by a regulatory hurdle: in an effort to protect local television stations, satellite systems were only permitted to provide broadcast network programming if the household could not receive the local broadcast signal over-the-air. This hurdle was removed, however, with the passage on November 28, 1999 of the Satellite Home Viewer Improvement Act (SHVIA). This permitted direct-broadcast satellite providers to distribute local broadcast signals within local television markets. Within a year, satellite providers were doing so in the top fifty to sixty television markets. Satellite systems now provide a set of services comparable to those offered by cable systems for the vast majority of US households.[25]

Unlike cable systems, satellite providers have never been subject to price regulations. Most other rules just described for cable service apply equally to satellite providers, however. For example, since January 1, 2002, satellite providers that distribute local signals must follow a "carry-one, carry-all" approach similar to must-carry and must negotiate carriage agreements

---

24. They particularly objected to build-out requirements, especially if they do not overlap with their service area.

25. In 2006, EchoStar (Dish Network) provided broadcast programming in about 160 television markets and DirecTV about 145.

with local television stations under retransmission consent (FCC 2005b). Furthermore, under the conditions put in place in the News Corp-DirecTV merger, the combined firm is subject to the same rules governing competition in the programming market.[26]

3.4   The Consequences of Cable Regulation and Deregulation

The cable industry has undergone several recent periods of regulation and deregulation. This has provided an ample record to evaluate the consequences of cable regulations. In this section I present broad trends in economic outcomes in the industry. In the next section I evaluate the theoretical and empirical evidence of the consequence of regulation on those outcomes.

3.4.1   The Facts to Be Explained

Prices

Figure 3.4 reports price indices from the Consumer Price Index (CPI) from December 1983 until November 2012. Reported are series for (a) MVPD (i.e., cable + satellite) services and (b) consumer nondurables.[27]

Four distinct periods are clear in the figure and are described in table 3.1. Reported in the table is the compound annual growth rate for each price index corresponding to periods of cable regulation and deregulation (first three periods) and telco entry into the video market (last period). The first period describes price increases following the passage of the 1984 Cable Act. Price deregulation from the 1984 act begins in December 1986 and continues until April 1993, when the first price caps from the 1992 Cable Act were implemented. The second period begins at that point and continues until the passage of the "going forward" rules relaxing price caps in November 1994. The third period starts at that point and continues to the end of 2005, the (effective) time of telco entry into video markets. The last period begins then and continues to the present.

From these price series, regulation (deregulation) is associated with positive (negative) relative cable price growth. Prices in the period preceding the 1992 Cable Act increased at an annual growth rate of 4.61 percent greater than that for other consumer nondurables. Similarly, prices after the relaxation of the 1992 regulation have increased at a rate 2.57 percent greater than that of nondurables, while prices during the (short) regulatory period fell 3.45 percent relative to nondurables. Telco competition also appears to matter: prices in the last period are slightly less than those for nondurables over the period.

---

26. At this time, EchoStar does not own significant programming interests and is not subject to programming rules.

27. The cable series began including satellite services in the late 1990s. In principle, it has also included satellite radio since 2003, although as of October 2005 no satellite radio data had been sampled.

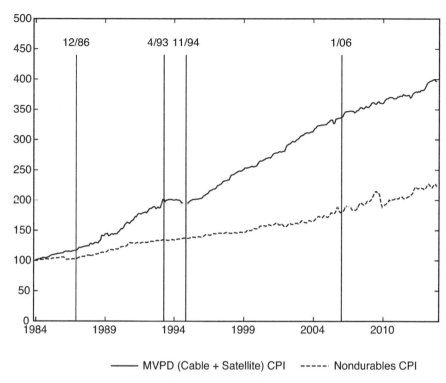

Fig. 3.4   MVPD (cable + satellite) prices, 1983–2012
Source: Bureau of Labor Statistics.
Note: December 1983 = 100.

Table 3.1   Growth rates in cable and satellite prices by period

Period	Cable and satellite CPI	Nondurable CPI	Difference
12/86–4/93	8.99	4.38	4.61
5/93–11/94	−2.34	1.11	−3.45
12/94–12/05	5.07	2.50	2.57
1/06–11/12	2.42	3.09	−0.67

Source: Bureau of Labor Statistics.

Subscriptions

Did lower prices lead to more subscriptions? Figure 3.5 reports aggregate subscribers to MVPD (cable, satellite, and telco) services by year between 1983 and 2010. Unfortunately, this data is only at the annual level, making precise predictions of the impacts of short regulatory periods difficult. Nonetheless, I duplicate the table on growth rates for prices both for cable subscribers and all MVPD subscribers and report these in table 3.2.

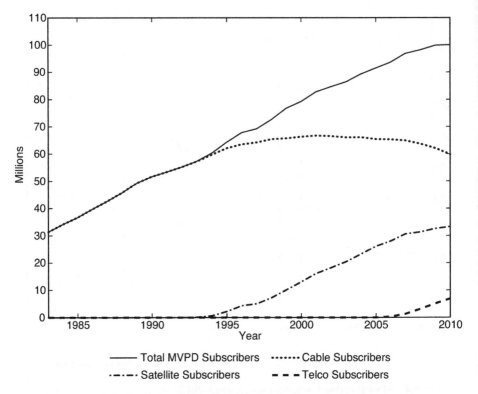

Fig. 3.5   MVPD subscribers, 1983–2010
Sources: Hazlett and Spitzer (1997); FCC (2001c, 2004b, 2005b, 2006c, 2009b, 2012c).

Table 3.2	Growth rates in MVPD subscribers by period			
Period	Cable subscriber CAGR	Satellite subscriber CAGR	Telco subscriber CAGR	Total industry CAGR
1987–1993	5.0			5.1
1994–1995	4.2			5.9
1996–2005	0.5	29.0		3.8
2006–2010	–1.7	3.5	87.2	1.3

Sources: FCC (2001c, 2002b, 2002c, 2004b, 2005b, 2006c, 2009b, 2012c).

There are three interesting features of the data in table 3.2. First, cable subscriber growth is positive throughout all periods but the last, including periods when prices were rising. While many features of the economic environment are also changing over this period, one plausible explanation for this relationship is that the quality of cable services has been increasing over time. I provide some rough measures of cable quality in what follows. Second, despite lower prices between 1993 and 1995, cable subscriber growth is *lower* than during the previous (deregulatory) period. This suggests regulation may itself have had an impact on cable quality. Third, note the dramatic reduction in cable subscriber growth after 1995. While a normal feature of a market that is reaching saturation, this also reflects the growth in satellite and telco operators as viable competitors to cable systems: total MVPD subscriber growth, while not at pre-1995 levels, is still substantial, despite reaching aggregate penetration rates of almost 90 percent of US households by 2010.

Quality

Both the price and subscription data suggest that accounting for the quality of cable service is important for understanding outcomes in cable markets. Measuring the quality of cable services can, however, be very challenging. Various approaches have been taken in the economic literature, from using simple network counts (Rubinovitz 1993; Crandall and Furchtgott-Roth 1996; Emmons and Prager 1997) to a mix of indicators for specific networks (e.g., ESPN, CNN, MTV) and network counts (Crawford 2000) to imputing it from observed prices and market shares under the assumption of optimal quality choice (Crawford and Shum 2007). Because channels are clearly very different in their value to consumers, it is perhaps best to enumerate them if the data allow it. Crawford and Yurukoglu (2012) do this for over fifty individual cable networks in their recent work analyzing the welfare effects of à la carte policies.

Figures 3.6 and 3.7 provide two rough measures of cable service quality over time. The first, figure 3.6, reports the number of programming networks available for carriage on cable systems as well as (from 1996) the average number of basic, expanded basic, and digital tier networks actually offered to households. Both the number of networks available to systems and those actually offered by systems has increased considerably over time. This is particularly true in the periods 1978 to 1988 and 1994 to present.[28]

The number of cable networks is, however, an incomplete measure of cable service quality. The value of programming on ESPN today is significantly greater than it was in 1985. This increase in the value in programming can partially be measured by the *cost* to cable systems for that programming. Figure 3.7 describes the average cost to cable systems of program networks from 1989 to 2003 (as well as duplicating the average number of networks on basic and digital tiers from figure 3.6). The top-most solid lines in the figure use the left-hand axis and report the total per-subscriber cost for networks charging affiliate fees according to Kagan World Media (Kagan World

28. These are likely supply-side phenomena, the former driven by the relaxation of FCC content restrictions and the feasibility of low-cost satellite distribution and the latter driven by significant upgrades in cable infrastructure and the (possibly anticipated) rollout of digital tiers of service.

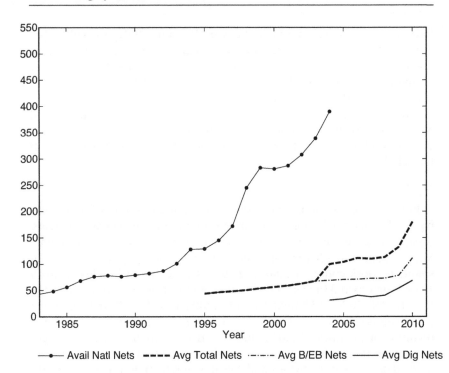

Fig. 3.6   Cable programming network availability and carriage, 1975–2004
Sources: Hazlett and Spitzer (1997, 96); FCC (1998a, 1999, 2000a, 2001a, 2002a, 2003, 2005a, 2005c).

Media 1998, 2004). The left half of this series is a list ("top-of-rate-card") price, while the right half is an average (across systems) price. One can compare the pattern of these prices with the average number networks over the same period, represented by the dashed line and using the right-hand axis. The trend in total costs roughly matches the trend in number of networks. This might be expected if network costs were constant over time. They are not, however. The bottom, dotted, lines report the total per-subscriber cost for networks charging affiliate fees *conditioning* on the networks charging positive fees in 1989. This isolates the increase in cost to cable systems from increased quality for a given set of programming networks.[29] Together, these series show that costs to cable systems have been increasing over time due both to increased costs for existing networks as well as increases in the number of offered networks.

29. Consistent with conventional wisdom, this suggests new networks charge lower average prices than established networks. Indeed, new networks often pay systems (i.e., charge negative prices) for a period of years before becoming established and negotiating positive fees.

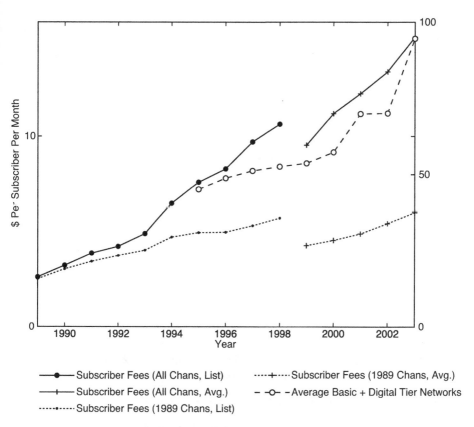

Fig. 3.7   Cable programming network cost, 1989–2003
Sources: Kagan World Media (1998, 2004); Hazlett and Spitzer (1997).

Services

A final feature of cable service that has evolved considerably over the last twenty years is the number of services from which households can choose. Cable television technology is such that all signals are transmitted to every household served by a system. As such, the least cost method of providing any cable service is to *bundle* all the programming. Early cable systems did just that. The development of premium networks in the early 1980s, however, necessitated excluding households that chose not to subscribe. This was costly, requiring a service technician go to each household and physically block programming with an electromechanical "trap." The development of scrambling (encryption) technology in the 1980s and 1990s solved that problem but instead required households interested in such programming to have an "addressable converter" (set-top box) to unscramble

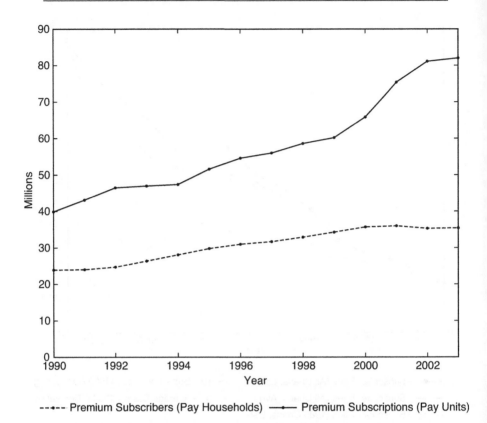

----- Premium Subscribers (Pay Households) ——— Premium Subscriptions (Pay Units)

Fig. 3.8   Premium subscribers and subscriptions, 1990–2003
Sources: FCC (1998b, 2004b, 2005b).

the video signal. Subscribers and subscriptions to premium networks grew (see figure 3.8).[30]

Addressable converters also allowed cable systems to unbundle some of their basic networks. As discussed earlier, these were called expanded basic services (or tiers). There was some concern in the late 1980s and early 1990s that cable systems were introducing tiers in order to evade rate regulation in the pre-1986 and post-1992 periods.[31] These concerns have waned since

30. Subscribers to premium networks are often called "pay households." Total subscriptions to premium networks are often called "pay units."
31. This concern was driven by differential regulatory treatment of different tiers in the various regulatory periods. The 1992 act in particular introduced a split regulatory structure, with local franchise authorities given authority to regulate rates of basic service and the FCC given authority to regulate rates of expanded basic services. Some estimates of total subscribers to expanded basic services fell after the 1984 Cable Act and increased again after the 1992 act (GAO 1989, 1991; Hazlett and Spitzer 1997).

Table 3.3   **Advanced cable services**

Year	Digital programming		Broadband access		Telephone service	
	Percent offered	Percent subscribed	Percent offered	Percent subscribed	Percent offered	Percent subscribed
1998	16.8	2.1	19.3	0.8		0.2
1999	30.0	7.3	26.6	2.2		0.4
2000	58.1	12.8	45.4	6.0		1.5
2001	77.6	21.7	70.8	10.9		2.2
2002	88.3	29.0	69.8	17.4		3.8
2003		34.1		25.0		4.5
2004	97.3	38.4	94.8	31.8		5.7
2005		43.6		38.8		9.0
2006		49.9		44.3		14.5
2007		57.2		55.0		23.0
2008		63.4		61.7		30.8
2009		68.6		67.3		35.7
2010		74.7		74.2		40.0

Sources: FCC (1999, 2000a, 2001a, 2002a, 2003, 2005a, 2006a, 2009a, 2011, 2012a, 2012b); NCTA (2005b).

the passage of the 1996 Telecommunications Act. Where offered, the vast majority of households choose at least one expanded basic service, a digital service, broadband (cable modem) access to the Internet, and/or telephone service from their cable operator. Table 3.3 describes the recent evolution of these advanced service offerings.

The growing popularity of digital tiers (and associated digital converters) has led some consumer advocates to call for cable systems to *unbundle* some or all networks and offer them to consumers on an à la carte basis (Consumers Union 2003). I discuss this important policy issue in section 3.7.2.

3.5   The Consequences of Cable Regulation

The challenge in interpreting these trends in the cable data are two. First, how much of the increase in cable prices is due to increases in cable market power and how much is due to increases in the quality of cable services? And to what extent has regulation limited the exercise of cable market power or distorted the incentives to offer quality? Second, even if systems have market power, if this gives rise to the incentives to increase product quality over time, consumers may benefit despite the welfare losses from that power. How have consumers valued changes in the portfolio of cable services? How has regulation influenced these choices? I evaluate the theoretical and empirical evidence on these questions in what follows.

3.5.1   Theoretical Models of Price and Quality Choice under Regulation

Most theory of optimal regulation focuses on products of a given quality or qualities (Braeutigam 1989; Armstrong and Sappington 2007). While there are difficult implementation issues in this case, including how best to accommodate informational asymmetries between the firm and regulator and how best to accommodate changes in the economic environment facing the regulated firm over time, the conclusions of the theory are straightforward: regulation can limit the exercise of market power by limiting the prices firms can charge.

The problem is more challenging, however, when firms can also choose product qualities. In what follows, I briefly survey the theoretical literature on price and quality choice with and without regulation for single- and multiproduct monopolists. Focusing on monopoly is in part for convenience, as that is the focus of much of the economic literature, but it is also largely appropriate for the cable television industry.[32] That being said, I provide insights from oligopoly models where possible.

Price, Quality, and Regulation for Single-Product Monopolists

Assessing the influence of regulation on price and quality choice is relatively straightforward for single-product monopolists. An unregulated single-product monopolist may under- or overprovide quality depending on the nature of consumer preferences and firm costs (Spence 1975). The key factors are two: the relationship between how much households value quality and how much they value changes in quality and the extent of quantity reduction (relative to a social planner) due to market power over price. These depend on the specific features of the market under study and empirical estimates of their relative importance are few.[33] A single-product monopolist facing price cap regulation, however, will generally underprovide quality, as it must bear the costs of any quality improvements and may not be able to increase price to recoup those costs (Brennan 1989). It is the norm, therefore, to accompany price cap regulation with mechanisms that monitor and penalize firms for adverse product quality (Benerjee 2003; Armstrong and Sappington 2007). Paul Joskow reaches the same conclusion in his chapter in this volume on incentive regulation, concluding that accounting for quality is an important practical issue facing regulators implementing incentive

---

32. Previous to 1999, the vast majority of cable systems did not face competition in their local service areas. Even after satellite entry in 1999, because satellite systems choose price and quality on a national basis, existing cable systems can be modeled as monopolists on the "residual demand" given by demand in their local market less those subscribers attracted (at each cable price and quality) to national satellite providers (Crawford, Scherbakov, and Shum 2011).

33. Crawford, Shcherbakov, and Shum (2011) attempt to estimate the relative importance of market power over quality and market power over price in cable television markets.

regulation schemes both in general and in the specific case of price cap mechanisms in electric distribution networks in the United Kingdom.

Price, Quality, and Regulation for Multiproduct Monopolists

Assessing the influence of regulation on price and quality choice is more complicated for the more realistic case of multiproduct monopolists. The seminal paper on price and quality choice without regulation is Mussa and Rosen (1978). They show that products offered by unregulated multiproduct monopolists are, under reasonable conditions, subject to *quality degradation*: offered qualities are below the efficient level for all consumers except those with the highest tastes for quality.

The intuition for multiproduct monopoly quality degradation can be understood in a simple example with a monopolist offering two goods to two types of consumers. Let the consumer that values product quality more highly be called the "high type." The monopolist would like to sell products to each consumer type at a quality and price that maximizes his profits. Because there are only two consumers, he only needs two products. In a perfect world, he would choose the quality for the high-type product at just that point where the additional revenue he could get from the high type to pay for a slightly higher quality would equal the additional cost he would have to pay to produce that slightly higher quality (and similarly for the low type). Consumers would be left with nothing (as each would be paying their maximum willingness to pay) and the monopolist would earn all the surplus that was available in the market.

Unfortunately, the monopolist's first-best price-quality portfolio is not incentive compatible: consumers will not go along with it. Under reasonable assumptions on preferences and costs, the high type would earn some surplus consuming the low-quality product (and paying less). The monopolist realizes this in advance, however, and therefore chooses a second-best pair of prices and qualities. This second best sweetens the deal for the high type in two ways. First, it keeps her quality the same, but lowers its price, making the high-quality product more attractive to the high type. Second, it degrades the quality of the low-quality product (also lowering its price), making the low-quality product less attractive to the high type. Quality degradation is costly, however: lowering quality lowers what the low type is willing to pay by more than the reduction in cost to the monopolist. Quality degradation therefore continues until the monopolist's profit losses on low types exactly matches their profit gain on high types (driven by the higher price it can charge them without causing them to switch to the low-quality product).[34]

---

34. With more types and products, there is a marginal/inframarginal trade-off in optimal price and quality choice: marginal profit losses from degrading quality for any product against inframarginal profit gains on higher prices for *all* higher qualities.

In a pair of papers, Besanko, Donnenfeld, and White (1987, 1988) extend the Mussa-Rosen model to consider a monopolist's quality choice problem in the presence of regulation. They consider three forms of regulation— minimum quality standards (MQS), maximum price (price cap) regulation, and rate-of-return regulation—the second of which is most relevant in cable markets. They show that setting a price cap has an important effect on the monopolist's offered qualities. Relative to the quality offered by an unregulated firm, the presence of a price cap lowers quality for the high-quality good. The intuition is straightforward: with a price cap, the firm cannot charge as much as it would like for a good of the efficient quality. Since it cannot raise prices, it simply reduces quality until the price cap is the optimal price to charge.[35] Do consumers benefit? Besanko, Donnenfeld, and White (1988) show that they can for small reductions in prices, but both consumer and total welfare can fall if caps are set too low.

Implications for Cable Television Markets

Are these results likely to apply in cable television markets? I argue they are, at least for basic and expanded basic services.[36] Cable price regulations before 1984 were governed by agreements negotiated between cable systems and the local franchise authority. While the theory may apply in those settings, it would depend on the specific terms of those agreements. Generalizing about the many and heterogeneous forms of local price regulation in place at that time is therefore difficult.

Price regulations implemented after the 1992 act, however, map fairly well to the theory; only a few features of the actual regulations differed from the assumptions described earlier. In particular, while the theory assumes only the high-quality good is subject to price caps, prices for *all* basic and Expanded basic (so-called cable programming) services were subject to regulation under the 1992 Act. That being said, most systems in the mid-1990s either offered a single basic service or, if offering multiple expanded basic services, earned the majority of their basic revenue from the highest-quality service(s), making the effect of the regulations on those services practically the most relevant ones.[37] Furthermore, while the theory describes price caps in levels, prices in cable markets were regulated on a per-channel basis. If anything, however, this made it easier for systems to adjust their (per-channel) product quality by allowing them to add relatively low-value

35. The effect on low types is the opposite. The firm cannot extract as much surplus from high types with a price cap. This relaxes the incentive compatibility constraint for high types, reducing the incentive to degrade quality to low types. As such, quality and prices actually rise for low-quality goods.
36. Recall that prices for premium services may not and have never been regulated (see section 3.1).
37. For example, see the sample statistics for 1995 data in Crawford and Shum (2007). Furthermore, basic services are the most important offered by cable systems, providing five times the revenue of (unregulated) premium services (NCTA 2005d).

networks rather than dropping networks, as would have been necessary to come under a fixed cap.

Why then didn't regulators also regulate product quality, as in telecommunications, electricity, and other regulated product markets? In cable markets they cannot. The primary components of product quality for cable television services are the television networks included on those services.[38] By the First Amendment, cable systems have freedom of expression and regulators cannot therefore mandate what networks to carry (or not).

What, then, can one conclude from the theory as applied to cable television markets? While the specifics of regulatory interventions matter, the theory strongly advises against the use of price caps in markets, like cable, where quality cannot be regulated and is easily changed by firms. While prices may fall, so too will quality. Furthermore, market power may be unaffected: the regulated price is likely to move toward the optimal monopoly price for the (now-lower) quality. Worse, unless caps are set well across markets and time—and how can regulators know?—consumers and firms can *both* be worse off.

3.5.2   Econometric Studies of the Effects of Regulation

Does empirical research confirm these findings? How much of the increase in cable prices is due to the exercise of cable market power and how much is due to increases in the quality of cable services? And what effect has regulation had?

Research Using Time-Series Data

A number of studies have broached these questions using time-series data. Jaffe and Kanter (1990) and Prager (1992) analyze the impact of the 1984 Cable Act on outcomes in financial markets to infer its effects on cable system market power.[39] Jaffe and Kanter (1990) analyze the impact of the 1984 Cable Act on the sales price of cable franchises exchanged between 1982 and 1987 and find important compositional effects: while sales prices appear unchanged in the top 100 television markets (where competition between cable and broadcast markets was stronger), they find large and significantly positive effects outside of these markets. This suggests that, with the relaxation of price regulations, cable systems were expected to be able to exercise market power where competition was weak and that this expectation translated into higher sales prices for franchises. Prager (1992) analyzes the impact of news events associated with the 1984 Cable Act on stock prices for ten publicly traded cable television companies between 1981 and 1988. She finds no evidence of an increase in stock prices at the time the act was

---

38. Other dimensions that matter, albeit less, include customer service, signal reliability, and advanced service offerings.

39. Such "event study" techniques were first applied to analyze the impact of regulation by Schwert (1981), Binder (1985), and Rose (1985).

passed, but does find that cable stocks outperformed the market ex post, that is, in the years after the rate deregulation was actually implemented. Such unanticipated changes are consistent either with widespread uncertainty about the likely effects of deregulation or with an actual increase in market power due to increased quality of and demand for cable services (possibly themselves influenced by deregulation).

Hazlett and Spitzer (1997) use aggregate time-series data to analyze the impacts of both the 1984 and 1992 Cable Acts. In addition to surveying the economic literature at that time, they analyze a host of outcome measures, including prices, penetration (subscriptions), cash flows, tiering, and quality (as measured by the number of networks, their expenditure on programming, and their viewing shares), and reach three main conclusions. First, price increases after the 1984 Cable Act and price decreases after the 1992 Cable Act were associated with similar changes in cable service quality. Second, (monthly) subscription data suggest that price deregulation did not decrease subscriptions and price regulation did not increase them. Finally, systems appeared to evade price regulation by introducing new expanded basic tiers and moving popular programming to those tiers.[40] Similar patterns are apparent in the aggregate data presented in the last section.

There are several difficulties drawing firm conclusions about the impact of regulation using aggregate time-series data, however. First, it is often difficult to control for all changes in the economic environment *other than* the change in regulation (e.g., aggregate sectoral, demographic, and/or macroeconomic trends). Furthermore, a lack of observations often limits the ability to draw strong statistical inferences. The majority of studies analyzing questions of cable market power and the impact of regulation have therefore used disaggregate cross-section data.

Research Using Disaggregate Cross-Section Data

Reduced-Form Approaches.   Early empirical work using cross-section data tested the joint hypothesis that cable systems had market power and that regulation reduced their ability to exercise that power. Most authors used a reduced-form approach, regressing cable prices (or other outcome variables) across markets on indicators of the presence and strength of regulatory control. The evidence from these papers is generally mixed. For example, Zupan (1989a) analyzes data on a cross-section of sixty-six cable systems in 1984 and finds prices are $3.82 per month lower in regulated markets. Prager (1990), however, analyzes a sample of 221 communities in 1984 and finds the opposite result: rate regulation is associated with both more frequent and

40. This is not surprising given the nature of the cable regulation over time. Local and state price regulations (prior to 1984) and federal price regulations (after 1994) often applied only to the lowest bundle of networks offered by the system. This introduced incentives to offer expanded basic tiers to avoid price controls. Corts (1995) and Crawford (2000) provide further theoretical and empirical support for this view.

larger rate increases. Similarly, Beutel (1990) analyzes the franchise award process in twenty-seven cities between 1979 and 1981 and finds that franchises were generally awarded to systems that promised to charge *higher* prices per channel.[41]

Possible reasons for this literature's lack of consistent results include an inability to (accurately) account for cable service quality when evaluating price effects and the likely endogeneity of the regulation decision within local cable markets. The decision to regulate prices for local cable service (when permitted) likely depends on observed and unobserved features of the cable system, market, and household tastes for cable service and regulation. Ideally, one would instrument for the decision to regulate, but finding factors that influence the presence or strength of regulation but do not influence prices can be quite challenging.[42]

A Framework for Measuring Market Power.   More recent empirical research has taken a different approach to measuring cable market power and the impact of regulation. Following Bresnahan (1987), an empirical literature within the field of industrial organization has developed that provides a set of empirical tools to measure market power using explicit models of firm behavior and observations on firms' prices and quantities (or market shares).[43] Furthermore, this framework can also measure changes in quality and the impact of regulation on firm behavior. I briefly introduce this framework and then survey existing research, applying it in cable television markets.

Consider a cross-section of markets each occupied by a single firm selling a single product of fixed quality.[44] Let aggregate demand in each market be given by $Q_n = D(p_n, y_n)$ where Q_n is quantity demanded in market n, p_n is price of the good in market n, and y_n are variables that shift demand across markets (e.g., income, other household characteristics, etc.). As each firm is a single-product monopolist, optimal prices in market n are given by:

(1)
$$p_n = c_n - \frac{Q_n}{\partial D(p_n, y_n)/\partial p_n},$$

where c_n is the marginal cost of the good in market n. This equation shows that prices in market n equal marginal costs plus a markup. Rearranging terms yields the familiar Lerner index, $(p_n - c_n)/p_n = 1/\varepsilon_n^D$, where ε_n^D is the (absolute value of the) price elasticity of demand in market n. The Lerner

41. Some authors have attributed such findings to evidence of rent seeking by local franchise authorities (Hazlett 1986b; Zupan 1989b).

42. See Crawford and Shum (2007) for a representative discussion of this issue.

43. See the citations in Bresnahan (1989) for an extensive bibliography. Berry and Pakes (1993) and Nevo (2000) are more recent applications.

44. Much of the presentation in this section follows Bresnahan (1989).

index shows that price-cost margins (equivalently, markups) are higher the lower the absolute value of the elasticity of demand facing the firm.

If we could observe marginal costs, c_n, and demand, $D(p_n, y_n)$, we could simply calculate the markup in each market. Firms facing more inelastic demand would have greater markups and thus more market power. In practice, however, we do not observe either. To infer market power, we must estimate them.

Assuming the data provides sufficient variation and good instruments for prices, estimating demand is a straightforward proposition.[45] Estimating marginal costs is more difficult. Rather than obtain hard-to-find cost data, the typical solution is to make an assumption about how marginal costs vary with observables (e.g., cost factors, quantity) and estimate them based on their influence on observed prices in (1).[46] If these issues can be overcome, it is possible to estimate the market power facing firms across markets and/or time.

Suppose now that the firm in market n is regulated. The extent to which this constrains its pricing can be parameterized as follows.

$$(2) \qquad p_n = c_n - \theta \frac{Q_n}{\partial D(p_n, y_n)/\partial p_n}.$$

Here θ measures the extent to which prices exceed marginal costs in market n. If demand and marginal costs can be estimated, one can use (exogenous) variation in demand to estimate θ by examining how much prices exceed marginal costs across markets with differing elasticities of demand.[47] If regulation is constraining firm behavior, prices will be close to marginal costs even if demand is inelastic (i.e., $\theta \approx 0$). If not, prices will be close to the monopoly markup (i.e., $\theta \approx 1$).

Quality change is also easy to accommodate, at least in principle. Let q_n measure the quality of the product in market n. If we now parameterize demand by $Q_n = D(p_n, y_n, q_n)$, prices are given by

$$(3) \qquad p_n = c_n - \theta \frac{Q_n}{\partial D(p_n, y_n, q_n)/\partial p_n}.$$

45. The last fifteen years have seen an explosion in the estimation of differentiated product demand systems in industrial organization. See, inter alia, Berry (1994); Berry, Levinsohn, and Pakes (1995); Nevo (2001); and Petrin (2003) for recent applications. Crandall and Furchtgott-Roth (1996), Crawford (2000), and Goolsbee and Petrin (2004) apply these tools in the cable industry.

46. This can introduce difficult identification issues as it may be hard to differentiate between price increases due to diseconomies of scale and those due to increased exercise of market power. Bresnahan (1989) discusses this issue in detail.

47. A similar approach underlies the method of conjectural variations. Despite lacking a sound theoretical foundation, the approach has been used to measure market power in oligopoly settings. See Bresnahan (1989) for more.

If quality is higher in some market (or time period), demand will increase and/or become more inelastic, increasing prices. Separating the influence of quality change and market power is simply then a matter of assessing the relative strength of q_n and θ on prices.[48]

Measuring Market Power and the Effects of Regulation in Cable Markets

Two papers apply the abovementioned framework to measure the impact of regulation on pricing in cable markets.[49] First, Mayo and Otsuka (1991) estimate demand and pricing equations for basic and premium services using data from a cross-section of over 1,200 cable markets in 1982. Regulation at this time was determined by terms of local (municipal or state) franchise agreements and varied across the markets in the study. Across all systems (regulated or not), θ is estimated at 0.097 (0.021). While significantly different from 0, the relatively small value suggests regulation significantly constrained system pricing.[50]

Second, Rubinovitz (1993) estimates demand, pricing, and quality (number of channels) equations for basic cable services using data from a panel of over 250 cable systems in both a regulated period (1984) and an unregulated period (1990). In the raw data, prices are 42 percent higher in the latter period, but satellite channels have more than doubled and subscriptions are more than 50 percent greater. For reasons of idiosyncratic model specification, the absolute level of θ cannot be identified in each period, but differences in θ can. This he finds to be 0.18 (0.08), implying that, controlling for increased costs due to expanded channel offerings, the increased exercise of market power increased prices by 18 percent, or $.18/.42 = 43\%$ of the observed price change. He concludes that both increased quality and increased market power were responsible for deregulated price increases.

Almost all the studies surveyed to date focus on the impact of regulation on *prices*. But what of quality? The aggregate data in section 3.4.1 suggest understanding regulation's impact on quality is critical to understanding outcomes in cable markets. Crawford and Shum (2007) extend the market power framework to assess the impact of regulation on both prices and quality in cable markets. Rather than use observed measures of service quality (e.g., number of offered networks), they use data from a cross-section of 1,042 cable markets in 1995 to estimate preferences and costs and then use the implication of the optimal price and quality choice to *infer* the level of offered quality in each cable market. An example provides the intuition for

48. Of course, this assumes there are good observable measures of product quality, q_n. This must be evaluated on a case-by-case basis.

49. While conceptually simple, implementing the framework described earlier can be quite difficult in practice. Difficult identification issues arise in each of the papers surveyed following, casting at least some doubt on their conclusions. Where possible, I note these concerns.

50. Unfortunately, the paper lacks a clear discussion of identification. Estimation is "by two-stage least squares," but the motivation for the exclusion restrictions that identify the key parameters is missing.

their procedure. Suppose the cable systems in two markets had identical market shares for each of two offered services, but the price of the high-quality service was higher in the first market. The higher price in the first market suggests households are willing to pay more for cable service quality in that market (perhaps because mean household age or household size is larger in that market).[51] By making high types more profitable, this tightens the incentive compatibility constraint for those types, increasing the incentive to degrade quality for low types. Thus even if prices are similar in the two markets, offered quality (under the theory) must be lower in the first.

After inferring the quality of each offered service in each cable market, the authors relate these quality measures to indicators of whether the cable market had certified with the FCC to regulate basic service under the terms of the 1992 Cable Act. They find that quality for high-quality goods is somewhat higher, that quality for low- and medium-quality goods is substantially higher, and that quality per dollar for all goods is higher in regulated markets (despite higher prices). Interestingly, these effects are consistent with Besanko, Donnenfeld, and White's (1987, 1988) theoretical predictions of minimum quality standards and not price cap regulation.[52]

Measuring the Consumer Benefits of Regulation

The previous studies focus on the impact of regulation on cable prices and quality. This relies on a static view of cable markets and focuses on the short-run losses from cable market power. A long-run view must acknowledge that monopoly profits provide strong incentives for systems to invest in service quality if that enhances consumer willingness to pay for cable services. Two studies estimate consumer demand for cable services and ask about the welfare effects of (i.e., benefits to consumers from) cable price regulation.[53]

Crandall and Furchtgott-Roth (1996, chapter 3) examine the welfare effects of changes arising from the 1984 Cable Act. They estimate a multinomial logit demand model on 441 households from 1992 and augment that with information about the cable service available to 279 of them in 1983. Despite the substantial increase in prices in this period (see figure 3.4), they

51. In reduced-form regressions, the level and shape of the distribution of household income, age, and size were important determinants of cable prices and quality.

52. The 1992 Cable Act, in addition to regulating prices, required systems to offer a basic service containing all offered broadcast and public, educational, and government channels. Many systems introduced "bare-bones" limited basic services as a consequence of those terms. The authors' results suggest this and not price caps had a greater effect on offered service quality in cable markets.

53. In this setting, welfare effects are measured by either the compensating or equivalent variation. The compensating and equivalent variation are measures of the amount of money required to make households in a market indifferent between facing a cable choice set (e.g., set of services, prices, and qualities for those services) before and after a change in the economic environment. The compensating variation asks how much money is required to make someone indifferent to their initial position; the equivalent variation asks how much money is required to make someone indifferent to their final position.

estimate that households would be have had to be compensated by $5.47 per month in 1992 to face the choices available to them in 1983.[54]

Crawford (2000) examines the welfare effects of changes arising from the 1992 Cable Act. He also estimates a multinomial logit demand system on 344 cable systems from 1992 and 1995.[55] Furthermore, he introduces a new approach for measuring service quality. Rather than simply counting the number of networks offered by systems, he controls for the actual identities (among the top twenty cable networks) of those networks (e.g., ESPN, CNN, and MTV). This turns out to be important not only for accurate estimation of cable demand, but in valuing household welfare from the Cable Act.[56] He finds a welfare gain of at most $0.03 per subscriber per month. The lack of effect is not due to quality reductions in response to price caps, but the simple fact that, in his data, prices increased despite the regulations.

3.5.3   Conclusion

The accumulated evidence is not encouraging for proponents of regulation in cable markets. Research based on time-series data suggest that while prices briefly declined after the 1992 Cable Act, so too may have product quality. Detailed econometric studies based on disaggregate cross-section data provide mixed evidence. Some find that regulation lowers cable prices from monopoly levels, while others find negligible effects. Evidence of the impact of regulation on quality is positive, although further research is necessary, and evidence on consumer welfare effects of changes in cable choice sets is, if anything, in favor of deregulation.

3.6   The Rise of Competition in Cable Markets and Its Effects

The rise of competition from satellite and telephone company providers has dramatically changed the cable marketplace. Whereas for forty years the vast majority of households faced a local cable monopolist, most households now have the option of three or more MVPD providers. This section addresses the impact on cable prices and services of competition in the distribution market.

---

54. This is likely an underestimate of the true welfare loss, as their quality measure is based on the number of offered broadcast and satellite channels and the latter increased significantly in quality over the period.

55. Care should be taken relying on welfare measures from logit demand systems, particularly when evaluating the introduction of new products (Petrin 2003). Crawford (2000) argues that this concern is moderated in his case because of the popularity of the newly introduced services.

56. For example, that the average number of networks increased by approximately two from 1992 to 1995 suggests limited welfare gains to households; that on average 1.5 of those two were top-twenty networks suggests the opposite conclusion. Furthermore, many systems were alleged to have moved their most popular programming to unregulated tiers of service in response to the act and he can measure that effect.

3.6.1   Duopoly ("Overbuilt") Cable Markets

There is considerable evidence that cable prices are lower when there are two wireline competitors in a market. Hazlett (1986a) finds that cable prices are $1.82 lower in duopoly relative to monopoly cable markets. Levin and Meisel (1991) analyze a cross-section of forty-seven cable systems in 1990 and find that, controlling for the number of programming networks offered, cable prices are between $2.94 and $3.33 per month less in competitive relative to noncompetitive cable markets. Emmons and Prager (1997), using data on a cross-section of 319 cable markets in 1983 and 1989, obtain similar results: prices for incumbents that face competition from another cable system are an estimated 20.1 percent lower in 1983 and 20.5 percent lower in 1989.[57]

More recent data suggests a similar pattern. Using data from the ten most recent FCC reports on cable industry prices, table 3.4 reports the average price, number of channels, and price per channel for cable systems defined by the FCC as noncompetitive, facing a wireline competitor, and facing satellite competition.[58] The upper panel of the table presents the raw data, while the lower panel presents the percentage difference between noncompetitive systems and systems facing either a wireline or satellite competitor.

The last row in the first set of columns in the table shows that, on average between 2001 and 2011, prices for systems facing wireline competition were 7.8 percent lower than for noncompetitive systems. Definitive conclusions about causality are difficult, however, due to selection problems. Entry by a competitor is not exogenous to the price charged by an incumbent cable system or the characteristics of the entertainment market. If new firms entered into markets where incumbent cable systems charged high prices, the table likely underestimates the true effect of wireline competition on prices. Similarly, as most wireline competition occurred in large urban markets and these have more substitutes to cable, the table may overestimate the true effect. Accurately controlling for differences in economic conditions across markets and the endogeneity of entry is required in order to make stronger conclusions from such data.

The last row in table 3.4 also reports the correlation between wireline competition and cable service quality, as measured by the number of basic and expanded basic channels, as well as the price per channel, a useful competitive benchmark. Keeping in mind the same concerns about selection, the data demonstrates that, on average between 2001 and 2011, wireline competitors offered 6.2 percent more basic and expanded basic channels and charged 12.9 percent less on a per-channel basis. Further analysis of recent

57. Hazlett and Spitzer (1997, table 3-3) summarize the findings of these and a number of other studies in the 1980s and early 1990s. Across a variety of data sets, duopoly cable markets are associated with prices 8 to 34 percent lower than monopoly cable markets.
58. "Price" here equals price for basic service, expanded basic service, and equipment.

Table 3.4 Noncompetitive and competitive cable systems

Year	Prices — Noncomp. systems	Prices — Facing wireline comp.	Prices — Facing DBS comp.	Basic and exp. basic channels — Noncomp. systems	Basic and exp. basic channels — Facing wireline comp.	Basic and exp. basic channels — Facing DBS comp.	Price per channel — Noncomp. systems	Price per channel — Facing wireline comp.	Price per channel — Facing DBS comp.
				Levels					
1998	$29.97	$29.46	$31.40	48.8	49.9	31.9	0.61	0.59	0.98
1999	$31.70	$30.82	$31.73	51.1	50.6	35.1	0.62	0.61	0.90
2000	$34.11	$33.74	$33.23	54.8	56.5	38.6	0.62	0.60	0.86
2001	$37.13	$34.03	$37.13	59.3	56.0	53.3	0.63	0.61	0.70
2002	$40.26	$37.61	$37.05	62.7	60.9	53.9	0.64	0.62	0.69
2003	$43.14	$37.14	$42.32	67.3	71.5	67.7	0.64	0.52	0.63
2004	$45.56	$38.67	$43.95	70.1	75.3	70.5	0.65	0.51	0.62
2005	$47.71	$40.23	$47.76	70.3	73.9	70.2	0.68	0.54	0.68
2006	$50.29	$42.91	$51.37	70.6	74.9	73.9	0.71	0.57	0.70
2007	$51.66	$47.19	$52.11	72.5	75.5	72.3	0.71	0.63	0.72
2008	$53.72	$49.40	$53.36	72.8	76.1	72.4	0.74	0.65	0.74
2009	$55.55	$56.85	$57.43	77.7	85.8	77.4	0.71	0.66	0.74
2010	$57.59	$58.54	$59.29	111.6	138.0	125.4	0.52	0.42	0.47
2011	$60.47	$61.17	$63.97	120.4	130.7	129.9	0.50	0.47	0.49
				Relative to noncompetitive systems					
1998		-1.7	4.8		2.3	-34.6		-3.9	60.3
1999		-2.8	0.1		-1.0	-31.3		-1.8	45.7
2000		-1.1	-2.6		3.1	-29.6		-4.1	38.3
2001		-8.3	0.0		-5.6	-10.1		-3.0	11.3
2002		-6.6	-8.0		-2.9	-14.0		-3.8	7.1
2003		-13.9	-1.9		6.2	0.6		-19.0	-2.5
2004		-15.1	-3.5		7.4	0.6		-21.0	-4.1
2005		-15.7	0.1		5.1	-0.1		-19.8	0.2
2006		-14.7	2.1		6.1	4.7		-19.6	-2.4
2007		-8.7	0.9		4.1	-0.3		-12.3	1.2
2008		-8.0	-0.7		4.5	-0.5		-12.0	-0.1
2009		2.3	3.4		10.4	-0.4		-7.3	3.8
2010		1.6	3.0		23.7	12.4		-17.8	-8.4
2011		1.2	5.8		8.6	7.9		-6.8	-1.9
2001–2011 Average		-7.8	0.1		6.2	0.1		-12.9	0.4

Sources: FCC (2000a, 2001a, 2002a, 2003, 2005a, 2006a, 2009a, 2011, 2012a, 2012b).

price and quality data that both analyzed the effects of recent telco entry and controlled for the potential endogeneity of this entry would be welcome.

3.6.2   Competition between Cable and Satellite

The problem with duopoly cable markets is that they are rare, accounting for only 1 to 2 percent of all cable markets before the entry of telco operators (FCC 2005b, fn. 627). From a policy perspective, it is much more important therefore to assess the impact of *satellite* competition on cable prices and quality.

Table 3.5 reports trends in cable, satellite, and telco subscribers and their respective share of the MVPD market. Satellite subscriptions grew very quickly, even before 1999 when SHVIA allowed satellite providers to distribute local broadcast channels. Telco subscriptions have also grown quickly since their entry into the market in 2006. The net effects of satellite and telco subscriber growth has been to first slow and then reverse cable industry subscriber growth. Cable systems in 2010 had fewer subscribers than at any time since 1995.

Table 3.4 also provides some evidence on the correlation between satellite competition and cable prices and service quality. Turning to the third set of columns in each group, the table reports average prices, number of channels, and price per channel for cable systems who have been granted a finding of effective competition due to facing at least two satellite competitors whose total market share exceeds 15 percent of the MVPD market.[59] The last line demonstrates that, on average between 2001 and 2011, cable markets facing DBS competition (as defined by the FCC) paid approximately the same prices, were offered approximately the same quality, and therefore had approximately the same price per channel.

Given the keen interest in the role of satellite competition, Congress commissioned the General Accounting Office to conduct several studies of satellite's impact on cable prices and product offerings (GAO 2000, 2003). The early study, using 1998 data, found a *positive* and significant impact of increased satellite market share on a cable incumbent's prices, while the latter study, using 2001 data, found a negative and significant (though economically small) impact.

So where is the benefit of satellite competition? A fundamental problem in such studies (as in table 3.4) is that the correlation between cable prices on satellite market shares may not be driven by a causal relationship, but by correlated unobservables. If tastes for video programming differ across markets, both satellite market shares and cable prices will be higher in markets with greater tastes for programming, causing an upward bias on the effect

---

59. Because of this definition, some care should be taken interpreting the results in this table too broadly. While, for example, the national satellite market share has been above 15 percent since 2001, the share of subscribers in the 2004 price survey served by cable systems that have been granted a finding of effective competition due to satellite competition was only 2.35 percent (FCC 2005a, Attachment 1).

Table 3.5   **MVPD subscribers**

Year	Subscribers (millions)				Share of MVPD subscribers		
	Cable	Satellite	Telco	Total MVPD	Cable	Satellite	Telco
1993	57.2	0.1		57.3	99.8	0.2	
1994	59.7	0.6		60.3	99.0	1.0	
1995	62.1	2.2		64.3	96.6	3.4	
1996	63.5	4.3		67.8	93.7	6.3	
1997	64.2	5.0		69.2	92.8	7.2	
1998	65.4	7.2		72.6	90.1	9.9	
1999	66.7	10.1		76.8	86.8	13.2	
2000	66.3	13.0		79.3	83.6	16.4	
2001	66.7	16.1		82.8	80.6	19.4	
2002	66.5	18.2		84.7	78.5	21.5	
2003	66.1	20.4		86.5	76.4	23.6	
2004	66.1	23.2		89.3	74.0	26.0	
2005	65.4	26.1		91.5	71.5	28.5	
2006	65.3	28.0	0.3	93.6	69.8	29.9	0.3
2007	64.9	30.6	1.3	96.8	67.0	31.6	1.3
2008	63.7	31.3	3.1	98.1	64.9	31.9	3.2
2009	62.1	32.6	5.1	99.8	62.2	32.7	5.1
2010	59.8	33.3	6.9	100.0	59.8	33.3	6.9

Sources: FCC (2001c, 2002b, 2002c, 2004b, 2005b, 2006c, 2009b, 2012c).

of satellite shares on cable prices. Similarly, if offered cable qualities are (unobservably) higher in markets with high satellite shares, as, for example, if cable systems improve service quality in the face of satellite competition, a similar effect will arise. One solution is to instrument for satellite market shares in a regression of cable prices on satellite shares, but that can be difficult if instruments are hard to find.[60]

In a widely cited study, Goolsbee and Petrin (2004) suggest a solution to this problem. First, they estimate a multinomial probit demand system for expanded basic, premium, and satellite services from a sample of roughly 30,000 households in 317 television markets in early 2001. Using a system's franchise fee as their primary price instrument, they find own-price elasticities of -1.5 for expanded basic, -3.2 for premium, and -2.4 for satellite along with quite plausible (and large) cross-price elasticities.

As in previous studies, they regress cable prices on (a nonlinear transformation) of satellite market shares.[61] Unlike previous studies, however, they

60. The GAO studies appear to use homes passed and system age as instruments for satellite share, but it is hard to see how these would be appropriate instruments. If correlated with satellite share due to differences across markets in offered cable service quality, they should also be correlated with cable prices and belong in the cable price regression.

61. Strictly speaking, they regress cable prices on the mean utility for satellite service. This can be considered a measure of the satellite market share.

also include estimates of unobserved characteristics and tastes for expanded basic and premium cable services. By including composite measures of cable service quality, this approach "takes the correlated unobservable out of the error" and allows a consistent estimate of the impact of satellite share on cable prices.[62]

They find the effect to be both statistically and economically significant. Reducing satellite penetration to the minimum observed in the data is associated with a $4.15 (15 percent) increase in the price of cable services. They also find it is associated with a slight increase in the observed quality of cable services.

In a recent paper, Chu (2010) digs more deeply into the effects of satellite competition, explicitly modeling both price and quality competition and examining the heterogeneity in cable system responses to satellite rivals. He finds that different cable operators respond differently to satellite entry. Most systems lower prices and raise quality, but in some markets they increase both (and in some markets decrease both). The total effect is consistent with widespread patterns in the industry and is similar to the effects of regulation found in Crawford and Shum (2007): prices are slightly lower (and indeed higher in some markets), but quality is substantially higher.

So, has satellite competition "worked"? On this, the evidence is mixed. Chu shows that if one does not permit cable and satellite operators to compete on quality, prices after satellite entry would indeed have been lower for both. On the other hand, estimated cable system markups and profits are only slightly (9 percent) less after satellite entry, and the consumer welfare benefits are concentrated: while estimated consumers surplus increases by 32 percent on average, most of these benefits go to the 5 percent of the market that are satellite customers. Cable customers only benefit slightly.

3.6.3   Conclusion

Are (most) cable markets competitive? The evidence for wireline competition is encouraging, but its narrow scope (pre-telco entry) has limited measured benefits to a small fraction of cable households and lack of data (post-telco entry) renders conclusions impossible. While there is some evidence of a positive impact of satellite competition on cable prices, the estimated cable price elasticities suggest cable systems still exert considerable market power.[63]

Despite this, more large-scale entry appears unlikely. Further wireline entry means paying substantial fixed costs and facing entrenched competitors.[64] Wireless broadband entry may be a solution in the long run, but

---

62. This approach, while promising, relies heavily on the assumed functional forms for demand and pricing equations.

63. For example, an own-price elasticity of −1.5 would imply a markup of 67 percent in the case of a single-product monopolist.

64. An exception, perhaps, being incumbent telco entry in their service areas not currently being provided video service.

would require both major increases in electromagnetic spectrum and strong competition from other, higher-value uses of (potentially) mobile broadband.

How then to increase consumer welfare in cable markets? My survey of the theoretical and empirical literature suggests that price regulation is not an option for raising consumer welfare in cable markets. Some have proposed mandatory à la carte cable packages and/or competition from online video providers as mechanisms to help consumers. I discuss the likely consequences of each of these, as well as other open issues in MVPD markets, in the next section.

3.7 Open Issues in MVPD Markets

In this section, I consider four open issues in cable and satellite markets: horizontal concentration and vertical integration in programming markets, bundling, online video distribution, and bargaining breakdowns.

3.7.1 The Programming Market

Horizontal Concentration and Market Power

An important economic issue in the programming market is that of market power. Cable systems have evolved from small, locally owned operations into major national corporations.

Table 3.6, drawn from FCC reports on the status of competition in the programming market, reports concentration measures for the industry for several of the past twenty years.[65]

As seen in the table, the sum of the market shares for the top four, top eight, and top twenty-five MVPD providers have all increased over time, with the top four MVPDs serving 68 percent of the market and the top eight serving 84 percent in 2010.

There are both pro- and anticompetitive effects that could arise from this increased concentration. Increased firm size may yield economies of scale, greater facility developing and launching new program networks, and lower costs for investing in and deploying new services like digital cable, broadband Internet access, telephone service, and online video services. It may also, however, increase market power in the programming market.

There have unfortunately been a number of false starts regarding the appropriate analytical framework for analyzing outcomes in the programming market. The FCC's original horizontal subscriber limits were based on an "open field" analysis that determined the minimum viable scale for a programming network and then set limits such that no two maximal-size MVPD providers could jointly exclude the network from the market

---

65. Note such measures are most relevant for the programming market. Incumbent cable systems do not strictly compete with each other.

Table 3.6   Concentration in the MVPD market

	1992		1997		2000	
Rank	Company	Market share	Company	Market share	Company	Market share
1	TCI	27.3	TCI	25.5	ATT	19.1
2	TimeWarner	15.3	TimeWarner	16.0	TimeWarner	14.9
3	Continental	7.5	MediaOne	7.0	DirecTV	10.3
4	Comcast	7.1	Comcast	5.8	Comcast	8.4
5	Cox	4.7	Cox	4.4	Charter	7.4
6	Cablevision	3.5	Cablevision	3.9	Cox	7.3
7	TimesMirror	3.3	DirecTV	3.6	Adelphia	5.9
8	Viacom	3.1	Primestar	2.4	EchoStar (Dish)	5.1
9	Century	2.5	Jones	2.0	Cablevision	4.3
10	Cablevision	2.5	Century	1.6	Insight	1.2
	Top 4	57.2	Top 4	54.3	Top 4	52.7
	Top 8	71.8	Top 8	68.6	Top 8	78.4
	Top 25	—	Top 25	84.9	Top 25	89.8

	2004		2007		2010	
	Company	Market share	Company	Market share	Company	Market share
1	Comcast	23.4	Comcast	24.7	Comcast	22.6
2	DirecTV	12.1	DirecTV	17.2	DirecTV	19.0
3	TimeWarner	11.9	EchoStar (Dish)	14.1	EchoStar (Dish)	14.0
4	EchoStar (Dish)	10.6	TimeWarner	13.6	TimeWarner	12.3
5	Cox	6.9	Cox	5.5	Cox	4.9
6	Charter	6.7	Charter	5.3	Charter	4.5
7	Adelphia	5.9	Cablevision	3.2	Verizon FiOS	3.5
8	Cablevision	3.2	Bright	2.4	Cablevision	3.3
9	Bright	2.4	Suddenlink	1.3	ATT Uverse	3.0
10	Mediacom	1.7	Mediacom	1.3	Bright	2.2
	Top 4	58.0	Top 4	69.6	Top 4	68.0
	Top 8	80.7	Top 8	86.0	Top 8	84.0
	Top 25	90.4	Top 25	—	Top 25	—

Sources: FCC (1997, 1998c, 2001c, 2005b, 2012c).

(FCC 2005d, Par 72). The *Time Warner II* decision, however, criticized this approach as lacking a connection between the horizontal limit and the ability to exercise market power. The 2007 rules dismissed by the courts used a monopsony model as an alternative framework, but that also does not appear useful as networks are differentiated and terms between programmers and cable operators are negotiated on a bilateral basis, so that if a cable operator with market power were to reduce its purchases of programming at the margin, it would have no obvious effect on the prices it pays on inframarginal programming.

A Bargaining Approach.   Given the well-documented behavior of programmers and MVPDs in the programming market, a bargaining framework clearly seems most appropriate for analyzing outcomes. Unfortunately, bargaining models are known for their wealth of predictions, often depending on subtle features of the rules of the game that are hard to verify in practice. What can bargaining theory tell us about market power and the consequences of horizontal concentration in programming markets?

The conventional wisdom is that increased concentration in the MVPD market improves the bargaining outcomes of cable systems, reducing affiliate fees to program suppliers. In a standard bargaining approach, increased size for an individual cable system reduces the viability of a program network if an agreement is not reached between the two parties. This necessarily lowers the network's "threat point," increasing the expected surplus to the cable system (with specifics determined by the particular model). These mechanisms are at play in the Nash bargaining framework used by Crawford and Yurukoglu (2012) in their analysis of the industry.[66]

What does empirical work suggest about horizontal concentration and outcomes in the programming market? Assessing the consequences of increased system size on network surplus in programming markets is conceptually simple, but a lack of data on transaction prices (affiliate fees) has prevented much empirical work. Ford and Jackson (1997) exploit rarely available programming cost data reported as part of the 1992 Cable Act regulations to assess (in part) the impact of buyer size and vertical integration on programming costs. Using data from a cross-section of 283 cable systems in 1993, they find important effects of MSO size and vertical affiliation on costs: the average/smallest MSO is estimated to pay 11 to 52 percent more than the largest MSO and vertically affiliated systems are estimated to pay 12 to 13 percent less per subscriber per month. Chipty (1995) takes a different strategy: she infers the impact of system size on bargaining power from its influence on retail prices. She also finds support for the conventional wisdom that increased buyer size reduces systems' programming costs. Finally,

---

66. Some bargaining models yield predictions contrary to this conventional wisdom. For example, Chipty and Snyder (1999) conclude that increased concentration can actually reduce an MVPDs bargaining power, as they estimate the size of the surplus to be split between a cable system and a programming network depends on the shape of the network's gross surplus function. They estimate this on 136 data points in the 1980s and early 1990s and find it is convex, implying it is better to act as two small operators than one big one. This convexity seems at odds both with the institutional relationship between network size and advertising revenue (which limits the ability of networks to obtain advertising revenue at low subscriber levels) as well as claims made by industry participants and observers of the benefits of increased size. Similarly, Raskovich (2003) builds a bargaining model with a pivotal buyer, one with whom an agreement is necessary for a seller's viability, and finds that being pivotal is *disadvantageous* since if an agreement is not reached the seller will not trade and it is only the pivotal buyer who can guarantee this outcome. This can reduce the incentives to merge if merging would make a buyer pivotal. While interesting and potentially relevant in some settings, this does not seem to accurately describe the nature of most negotiations between networks and MVPDs.

Crawford and Yurukoglu (2012) estimate the relative bargaining power of channel conglomerates like ABC Disney and Viacom relative to cable operators and satellite systems. While not the focus of their study, they find that MVPDs generally have higher bargaining power than channels for small channel conglomerates, but that the situation is reversed for large channel conglomerates, and that, among distributors, small cable operators and satellite providers have slightly less estimated bargaining power than large cable operators. While feasible, they do not estimate the effect of up- and downstream mergers within their sample on estimated bargaining power, an interesting potential avenue to directly explore the relationship between concentration and bargaining outcomes.

Vertical Integration and Foreclosure

Many MVPD operators either own or have ownership interests in programming networks. So do major broadcast networks. This has drawn considerable attention from regulators in MVPD markets. FCC (2005b) documents the status of vertical integration in MVPD markets as of 2004. In brief, of 388 national programming networks and 96 regional programming networks in 2004, 89 (24), or 23 percent (25 percent), were affiliated with a major cable operator.[67] An additional 103 (22), or 27 percent (23 percent) were affiliated with a broadcast programming provider.[68] Furthermore, in 2006 all of the top twenty networks by subscribers (save C-SPAN) and top fifteen by ratings were owned by either a cable operator or broadcast network.[69]

As in most cases of vertical integration, there are both efficiency and strategic reasons MVPDs and program networks may want to integrate. Regarding efficiency, vertical integration could eliminate double marginalization, improving productive efficiency. Similarly, it could minimize transactions costs and reduce the risk of new program development. It could also internalize important externalities between systems and networks in the areas of product choice, service quality, and brand development. Or it could eliminate inefficiencies in the bargaining process.

Unfortunately, vertical integration may also provide the integrated firm incentives to foreclose unaffiliated rivals (Rey and Tirole 2007). For example, an integrated programmer-distributor could deny access to its affiliated programming to downstream rivals or raise the costs they pay relative to that of its integrated downstream division. Similarly, the integrated programmer-distributor could deny carriage on its affiliated distributor to upstream rivals

---

67. These were Comcast with 10 affiliated national networks and 12 affiliated regional networks, Time Warner with 29 (12), Cox with 16 (5), and Cablevision with 5 (16).

68. These were News Corp/Fox with 12 affiliated national networks and 22 affiliated regional networks, Disney/ABC with 20 (0), Viacom/CBS with 39 (0), and GE/NBC with 17 (0).

69. These values have only increased since then due to the merger of Comcast with NBC/Universal in 2011.

or reduce the revenue they receive relative to its integrated upstream division. Downstream foreclosure was the primary motivator underlying the exclusivity prohibition for affiliated content in the program access rules as well as the reason for several merger conditions required by the FCC in its approval of the 2011 Comcast-NBC/Universal merger. Similarly, concerns about upstream foreclosure drove the news "neighborhooding" condition in that merger due to concerns about the incipient integration of MSNBC, the dominant network for business news, with Comcast, the largest MVPD and one with important footprints in several very large markets for business news. The latter case is instructive, as the concern addressed by the merger condition was not (necessarily) one of complete foreclosure; that is, that Comcast would no longer carry rival business news networks, but that it would disadvantage them in terms of channel placement, reducing viewership and thus rivals' advertising revenue. This highlights the subtle ways in which an integrated firm with market power in one market can disadvantage rivals in vertically related markets.

Existing empirical research has universally found that vertically integrated MVPDs are more likely to carry their affiliated program networks, but whether this is pro- or anticompetitive remains an open issue. Waterman and Weiss (1996) examine the impact of vertical relationships between pay networks and cable operators in 1989. They find that affiliated MSOs are more likely to carry their own and less likely to carry rival networks. Subscribership follows the same pattern, though they find no estimated effect on prices.[70] Chipty (2001) addresses similar questions, including whether integration influences MVPD carriage of basic cable networks. Using 1991 data, she finds integration with premium networks is associated with fewer premium nets, fewer basic movie networks (AMC), *higher* premium prices, and higher premium subscriptions. On balance she finds households in integrated markets have higher welfare than those in unintegrated markets, although the effects are not statistically significant. As in the studies analyzing the impact of regulation, however, it is difficult to assess if differences across cable systems in product offerings and prices are driven exclusively by integration or by other features of integrated systems (e.g., size, marketing, etc.). Crawford et al. (2012) have begun to analyze this issue in markets for regional sports networks, but as yet have no firm conclusions.

Conclusion

The analysis of competition in the programming market is unfortunately inconclusive. Horizontal concentration in both programming and distribution markets has clearly increased over time, but the consequences for efficiency and welfare are unclear. More research both measuring the effects

---

70. See also Waterman and Weiss (1997) for the impact of integration on carriage of basic cable networks.

of increased concentration and the appropriate public policy responses to it would be welcome.

Of more concern is the potential that this increased market power provides incentives via vertical relationships to foreclose unaffiliated rivals. While the theory clearly supports this as a possibility, so too are efficiency benefits reasonable. More empirical work is needed to assess potential foreclosure effects and to test the alternative motivations to integrate.

3.7.2   Bundling

As complaints about high and rising cable bills continue, recent regulatory and legislative focus has turned to the consequences of bundling in cable and satellite markets at both the wholesale and retail level. At the wholesale level, cable operators have long complained about programmers tying low-value programming to the ability to get high-value programming. In 2008, the FCC explored a rulemaking on the matter, but nothing was ever circulated or voted upon (Make 2008). At the retail level, both the General Accounting Office and the Federal Communications Commission have analyzed the likely effects of bundling in cable markets, finding mixed but generally negative (and extremely uncertain) effects for consumers (GAO 2003, FCC 2004a). In 2006, the FCC, under a new chairman, published a follow-up study that repudiated many of its earlier conclusions and found that unbundling could actually improve consumer welfare (FCC 2006b).

Is then bundling a market failure in cable markets? Might not à la carte sales at either the wholesale or retail level improve consumer welfare? I survey the existing theoretical and empirical evidence in what follows.

Theoretical Motivations to Bundle

In many product markets, bundling enhances economic efficiency. A variety of industries emphasize the benefits of bundling in simplifying consumer choice (as in telecommunications and financial services) or reducing costs from consolidated production of complementary products (as in health care and manufacturing). In either case, bundling promotes efficiency by reducing consumer search costs, reducing product or marketing costs, or both. Moreover, if profitable, bundling can enhance incentives to offer products by increasing the share of total surplus appropriable by firms (Crawford and Cullen 2007).

Two literatures in economics suggest that bundling can instead reduce consumer welfare in product markets. First, a long-standing and influential theoretical literature suggests bundling may arise in many contexts to sort consumers in a manner similar to second-degree price discrimination (Stigler 1963; Adams and Yellen 1976). When consumers have heterogeneous tastes for several products, a monopolist may bundle to reduce that heterogeneity, earning greater profit than would be possible with component (unbundled) prices. Bundling—like price discrimination—allows firms to design product lines to extract maximum consumer surplus. While firms clearly benefit in this case, consumer welfare may fall, often because bundling requires consumers to purchase products in which they have little interest (Bakos and Brynjolfsson 1999; Armstrong 1996).

Figure 3.9, from Crawford and Yurukoglu (2012), demonstrates the intuition of this line of argument in a simple example of a monopolist selling two goods with zero costs. In the figure, the demand curve for each good is given by the dashed lines. It is clear that if the monopolist sold the two goods à la carte, at whatever price it chose for each there would be consumers that valued each good at greater than its price who would purchase it (earning consumer surplus), as well as consumers that valued each at less than its price (but more than its cost) who would not purchase it (causing deadweight loss). Compare that to the case if the monopolist were to bundle given by the solid line in the figure. As long as valuations for the two goods are not perfectly correlated, consumers' valuation of the bundle will be less dispersed than those for the components, allowing the firm to capture more

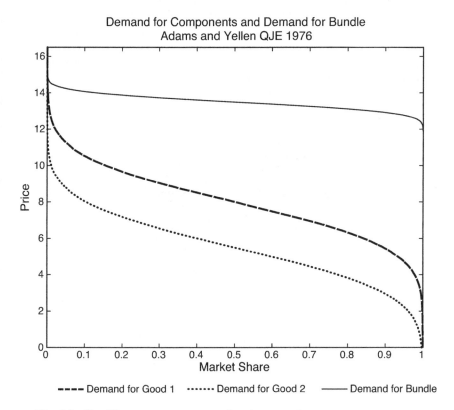

Fig. 3.9   Bundling versus component sales: An example
Source: Adapted from Adams and Yellen (1976).

of the combined surplus with a single price. While I chose valuations that are highly negatively correlated in the figure to emphasize this point, it is quite general: à la carte regulations can unlock surplus and improve consumer welfare for given input costs.

Another recent literature analyzes how bundling can also be used to extend market power or deter entry (e.g., Whinston 1990; Nalebuff 2004; Bakos and Brynjolfsson 2000). In this context, bundling reduces the market for potential entrants by implicitly providing a discount on "competitive" products for all consumers with high tastes for "noncompetitive" products. Figure 3.10, from Nalebuff (2004), demonstrates the intuition of this line of argument in another simple example, this time of a monopolist providing two goods (A and B) facing a potential entrant in the market for B. Shown in the figure are consumers' willingness to pay for each product, assumed to be distributed uniformly over a range of [0,1] for each product. As before, assume away any costs and that the monopolist must commit both to a method of sale (à la carte or bundling) as well as prices.

If the monopolist sells each good separately, the entrant will enter market B, just undercut the monopolist's price, and earn all the sales in that market. The figure demonstrates what happens if he instead chooses to bundle. If the entrant enters, all consumers that value good B at greater than its price will buy it. This is given by the shading in the southeast area of the figure. All remaining consumers that value the two goods at greater than the bundle price will buy it. This is given by the shaded area at the top of the figure. Note the effect bundling has on the *potential* market for the entrant. Because

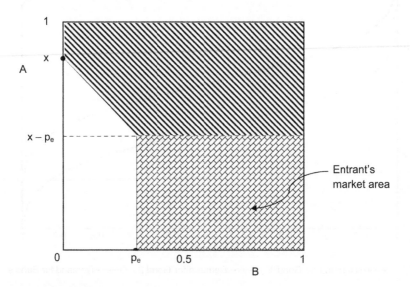

Fig. 3.10   Bundling to deter entry
Source: Nalebuff (2004).

all consumers with high willingness to pay for good A will tend to prefer the bundle, the entrant is able to only compete for half the market; that is, those with low WTP (willingness to pay) for good A. In effect, bundling A with B allows the monopolist to provide an implicit discount on good B to all consumers with high WTP for good A. The entrant cannot match that discount and is effectively foreclosed from that portion of the market. If the entrant faces fixed entry costs, bundling in this setting can foreclose the market from potential entry. Even if the entrant does enter, his profits will be lower than if the monopolist did not bundle. This can influence welfare in dynamic environments if, for example, firms have to make investment decisions based on the expected profitability of their operations.

Bundling in Cable Markets

The literature just surveyed demonstrates that there are many possible motives for bundling. Which ones are likely to apply to cable markets? And what are the implications for consumer and total welfare?

It is easy to argue that bundling reduces costs to cable systems. As described in section 3.4, it is *unbundling* networks that is costly, requiring methods to prevent consumption by nonsubscribers. While the rise of addressable converters (set-top boxes) is lowering this cost, many (especially small companies) cable subscribers still do not use them.[71] Furthermore, bundling simplifies consumer choice, reducing administrative and marketing costs, and it guarantees widespread availability, a feature viewed as essential for networks seeking advertising revenue (FCC 2004a).

It is also widely believed, however, that systems bundle to price discriminate in cable markets. Cable systems and program networks both argue that bundling allows them to capture surplus from the (possibly many) low-value consumers that would likely not choose to purchase a channel on a standalone basis (FCC 2004a).

Recent empirical work in the economics literature bears out these discriminatory effects. Using data from a cross-section of 1,159 cable markets in 1995, Crawford (2008) tests the implications of the discriminatory theory and finds qualified support for it. He estimates the profit and welfare implications of his results, finding that bundling an average top-fifteen *special-interest* cable networks is estimated to increase profits and reduce consumer welfare, with an average effect of 4.7 percent (4.0 percent). On balance, total welfare *increases*, with an average effect of 2.0 percent. In a simulation study, Crawford and Cullen (2007) confirm these effects and also find that bundling enhances industry incentives to provide networks than would à la carte sales, but may do so at significant cost to consumers. Recent work by Rennhoff

71. In 2004, Insight Communications estimates two-thirds of its one million customers did not use a converter (FCC 2004a, 39). By contrast, all satellite subscribers must have a digital receiver/converter. Many larger cable systems are migrating toward all-digital systems, particularly in large markets, but the process is ongoing.

and Serfes (2008), under somewhat restrictive assumptions, reaches similar conclusions about welfare effects of à la carte, while Byzalov (2010) finds the opposite result.

There is an important weakness in all of these papers, however: they treat the affiliate fees paid by cable systems to programmers as given. This is contrary to both the nature of programming contracts (which typically require systems to pay sometimes much higher fees if channels are offered à la carte) as well as bargaining incentives in an à la carte world (Crawford and Yurukoglu 2012, sec. 2). In an important recent paper, Crawford and Yurukoglu (2012) evaluate the welfare effects of à la carte, allowing for renegotiation between programmers and distributors in an à la carte environment. They confirm the results of the previous paragraph, that consumer surplus would rise under à la carte if programming costs to distributors were fixed, but instead estimate that renegotiation would cause these costs to rise by more than 100 percent, raising à la carte prices to households and lowering both consumer surplus and firm profits. On average, they find consumers would be no better off under à la carte (and strictly worse off under themed tiers), and that any implementation or marketing costs would likely make them worse off.[72]

Claims of bundling's potential to deter entry or enhance market power have been made in both the distribution and programming markets. In the distribution market, wireline competitors to incumbent cable systems have articulated versions of the entry deterrence argument when objecting to (a) the terrestrial exception to the program access rules and (b) the "clustering" of cable systems within localized (e.g., MSA) markets (FCC 2005b, para. 154–58). In each case, rival MVPDs may be at a significant competitive disadvantage, even if the foreclosed network is the only network by which rival bundles differ. In the programming market, MVPD buyers have complained about the bundling of affiliated program networks, both when negotiating rights to broadcast networks under retransmission consent as well as critical nonbroadcast networks (FCC 2005b, para. 162; FCC 2005d, fn 232). In this case, program networks that compete with those bundled with high-value networks may have difficulty obtaining carriage agreements, particularly if they appeal to similar niche tastes. Responding to these concerns, the FCC in late 2007 announced a new proceeding to investigate the issue, but no formal rulemaking appears to have come from it (Cauley 2007). While theoretically plausible, I know of no empirical evidence of entry deterrence in either the distribution or programming markets. Empirical studies of these topics would be welcome.

---

72. Furthermore, no paper in the literature accounts for the influence bundling may have on the quality of programming chosen by networks. It is possible to articulate scenarios where bundling encourages firms to offer program quality closer to what a social planner would offer than would be the case under à la carte and that moving to an à la carte world could have important welfare effects due to reductions in the resulting quality of programming.

Conclusion

Is bundling a market failure in the cable industry? While it would appear so at existing cable system costs, those would be sure to change in an à la carte world, casting very strong doubts about the potential welfare benefits of mandated à la carte.

More uncertainty surrounds the issue of bundling for market power or entry deterrence. While existing theoretical research does not draw explicit welfare conclusions, it is clear that bundling can have important competitive effects, particularly if, as seems to be the norm in programming markets, it is partnered with vertical integration and horizontal concentration. This could represent a substantial barrier to entry for diverse independent programming in cable markets. It is worthy of further study.

3.7.3   Online Video

In section 3.7.2, I described recent developments in the market for online distribution of video programming. In this section, I briefly discuss two implications of these developments.

The first is to address whether online video distribution (OVD) is a substitute or complement for existing pay-TV programming and whether it can plausibly provide a substantive competitive alternative to existing pay-TV bundles. Comments in the most recent FCC report on video market competition found support for both substitution and complementarity of OVD, and some mentioned that they thought it did provide a competitive threat (FCC 2012c). Before analyzing these claims, it is important to distinguish between types of video content. While there is a large amount of short-form and web-only video that will likely serve as a weak substitute for programming provided on pay-television platforms, like the FCC I will focus my analysis on video content that is similar to that professionally produced and exhibited by broadcast and cable networks and created using professional-grade equipment and talent.

While there is not yet empirical evidence on this point, economic theory suggests the effects of professionally produced online video in both the short and long run will largely be complementary. The reason is that the only entities that have the expertise and scale to produce content like that currently produced by broadcast and cable networks are those networks. While many such networks have been aggressive in exploring online video distribution, they have uniformly been doing so in ways that protect their existing revenue streams from traditional MVPDs (e.g., authentication methods like those used by TV Everywhere and/or delays in making available programming online that is also distributed via traditional channels). In practice, online-video distribution serves as a form of third-party "mixed bundling": content providers sell via an MVPD bundle to the majority of their viewers, but offer online viewing (for free) either as a way to enhance the value of the traditional bundle (TV Everywhere) or (for pay) on an à la carte basis to those few viewers who highly value online consumption and/or do not purchase an MVPD bundle. Of course, some OVDs (e.g., Netflix) are seeking to disrupt this business model by licensing *original content* in direct competition with traditional programmers, but this strategy is in its infancy and it is very uncertain if it will be successful.

The ability of OVDs to compete directly with traditional MVPDs is further complicated by foreclosure concerns. Online video distributors must necessarily rely on a high-speed broadband connection to households in order to deliver their programming, the vast majority of which are also owned by existing cable or telco MVPDs. There are legitimate concerns that MVPDs will somehow manipulate their broadband networks in ways that disadvantage rival OVDs, perhaps by offering differential download speeds for rival online content, imposing data caps that lower the value of an Internet-delivered video service, or setting usage-based prices with similar effects. Furthermore, it is hard to determine if such strategies are anticompetitive, as they can also help MVPDs efficiently manage their network traffic. Netflix has complained that AT&T, Comcast, and Time Warner have pursued strategies that disadvantage OVDs and lawmakers are concerned about this issue.

The market for online video distribution is in its infancy, so appropriate policies are difficult to determine. More empirical research establishing some basic facts about the nature of traditional and online television substitutability, measuring the incentives to foreclosure, and distinguishing between efficient and foreclosing MVPD management practices would be welcome.

3.7.4   Bargaining Breakdowns

A final topic of growing interest among policymakers is the growing number of bargaining breakdowns that result in channel blackouts on affected MVPDs. Section 3.3.3 documented blackouts arising from retransmission consent negotiations, but similar disagreements also arise for cable programming networks. Why do breakdowns happen? What are the welfare costs? Is this a market failure? And is there an appropriate public policy response? I briefly discuss each of these points in this section.

Standard bargaining theory assumes each side of a negotiation has complete information about the gains from trade and each party's threat position. In practice, of course, there can be uncertainty about these matters and this uncertainty can influence each party's demands and willingness to accede to the other party's demands. This is particularly relevant when there is a shift in the market from historical patterns of contracting, as when broadcasters began demanding cash payments for retransmission consent in the late 2000s.

It is uncertain what are the welfare costs from such breakdowns. Most are short lived (e.g., measured in days), and there are no good measures of the welfare costs of such temporary interruptions. It is also uncertain if this is a market failure. Parties on both sides of carriage negotiations have market power (hence the use of a bargaining framework) and the high costs of both developing programming and distributing that programming on a scale comparable to existing MVPDs suggest there is little policymakers can do about that market power.

Policy proposals advocated in the trade press largely focus on a binding arbitration procedure. This could work for national programming as an independent arbitrator could likely obtain access to contracts reached in settings comparable to the one being disputed. It would work less well for local or regional (broadcast and/or RSN) programming due to the lack of directly comparable settings, but is something that could be considered. Before any such policy is adopted, however, further research is needed about whether the situation demands a regulatory response and, if so, what would be the optimal such response.

3.8   Conclusion

This chapter surveys the consequences of economic regulation in the cable television industry and evaluates the impact of competition from satellite and telephone company providers on potential market failures in the industry. Prospects for efficient outcomes in the distribution market look better than ever. Satellite and telco competition has largely replaced price regulation as the constraining force on cable pricing and driving force for innovative services, a welcome outcome given the empirical record on regulation's effects in cable markets. While prices continue to rise, so too does quality and it may be that (most) consumers are better off. Mandatory à la carte, while superficially appealing, is not likely to improve average consumer welfare and could significantly decrease it.

If price and "choice" regulation is not likely to be effective at improving consumer welfare in video markets, what then should policymakers do? This is a difficult question. Owners of valuable content (sports leagues, movie studios) necessarily have market power. The media conglomerates that program this content and the cable systems that distribute it do as well. The immense time and expense required to enter any of these markets is a significant barrier to entry, as are consumer switching costs in distribution (Shcherbakov 2010).

This suggests substantial returns may arise from lowering barriers to entry wherever possible in the video supply chain. For example, the combination of national franchising standards and widespread low-cost access to public rights-of-way would lower the cost of additional wireline entry in distribution. Similarly, additional electromagnetic spectrum for fixed or mobile broadband would facilitate wireless entry and increase the capacity available for online video distribution. Standardized set-top boxes, if technically feasible, would lower consumer switching costs and increase market competitiveness.

At the same time, the competition regulators should keep a close eye on the potential anticompetitive effects of tying and bundling in the programming market as well as the risks associated with vertical integration and foreclosure in programming and both traditional and online video distribution. No one knows what the video market will look like fifteen years from now. It is important that those with the most to lose do not leverage their influence to distort that evolution.

References

Adams, W. J., and J. L. Yellen. 1976. "Commodity Bundling and the Burden of Monopoly."*Quarterly Journal of Economics* 90 (3): 475–98.

Armstrong, M. 1996. "Multiproduct Non-Linear Pricing." *Econometrica* 64 (1): 51–75.

Armstrong, M., and D. Sappington. 2007. "Recent Developments in the Theory of Regulation." In *Handbook of Industrial Organization*, vol. 3, edited by M. Armstrong, and R. Porter, chap. 1. Amsterdam: North-Holland.

Bakos, Y., and E. Brynjolfsson. 1999. "Bundling Information Goods: Pricing, Profits, and Efficiency." *Management Science* 45 (2): 1613–30.

———. 2000. "Bundling and Competition on the Internet." *Marketing Science* 19 (1): 63–82.

Benerjee, A. 2003. "Does Incentive Regulation 'Cause' Degradation of Telephone Service Quality?" *Information Economics and Policy* 15:243–69.

Berry, S. 1994. "Estimating Discrete Choice Models of Product Differentiation." *Rand Journal of Economics* 25 (2): 242–62.

Berry, S., J. Levinsohn, and A. Pakes. 1995. "Automobile Prices in Market Equilibrium." *Econometrica* 63 (4): 841–90.

Berry, S., and A. Pakes. 1993. "Some Applications and Limitations of Recent Advances in Industrial Organization: Merger Analysis." *American Economic Review* 83 (2): 247–52.

Besanko, D., S. Donnenfeld, and L. J. White. 1987. "Monopoly and Quality Distortion: Effects and Remedies." *Quarterly Journal of Economics* 102 (4): 743–67.

———. 1988. "The Multiproduct Firm, Quality Choice, and Regulation." *Journal of Industrial Economics* 36 (4): 411–29.

Besen, S., and R. Crandall. 1981. "The Deregulation of Cable Television." *Law and Contemporary Problems* 44 (1): 79–124.

Beutel, P. 1990. "City Objectives in Monopoly Franchising: The Case of Cable Television." *Applied Economics* 22 (9): 1237–47.

Binder, J. 1985. "Measuring the Effects of Regulation with Stock Price Data." *Rand Journal of Economics* 16 (2): 167–83.

Braeutigam, R. 1989. "Optimal Policies for Natural Monopolies." In *Handbook of Industrial Organization*, vol. 1, edited by R. Schmalensee and R. Willig, 1289–346. Amsterdam: North-Holland.

Brennan, T. 1989. "Regulating by Capping Prices." *Journal of Regulatory Economics* 1 (2): 133–47.

Bresnahan, T. 1987. "Competition and Collusion in the American Auto Industry: The 1955 Price War." *Journal of Industrial Economics* 35 (4): 457–82.

———. 1989. "Empirical Studies of Industries with Market Power." In *Handbook of Industrial Organization*, vol. 2, edited by R. Schmalensee and R. Willig, 1011–58. Amsterdam: North-Holland.

Byzalov, D. 2010. "Unbundling Cable Television: An Empirical Investigation." Working paper, Temple University.

Cauley, L. 2007. "FCC puts 'A La Carte' on the Menu." *USA Today*, September 11.

Chipty, T. 1995. "Horizontal Integration for Bargaining Power: Evidence from the Cable Television Industry." *Journal of Economics and Management Strategy* 4 (2): 375–97.

———. 2001. "Vertical Integration, Market Foreclosure, and Consumer Welfare in the Cable Television Industry." *American Economic Review* 91 (3): 428–53.

Chipty, T., and C. M. Snyder. 1999. "The Role of Firm Size in Bilateral Bargaining: A Study of the Cable Television Industry." *Review of Economics and Statistics* 31 (2): 326–40.

Chu, C. S. 2010. "The Effects of Satellite Entry on Cable Television Prices and Product Quality." *Rand Journal of Economics* 41 (4): 730–64.

Consumers Union. 2003. "FCC Report Shows Cable Rates Skyrocketing; Group Calls on Congress to Allow Consumers to Buy Programming on an à la Carte Basis." Consumers Union, July 8.

Corts, K. S. 1995. "Regulation of a Multi-Product Monopolist: Effects on Pricing and Bundling." *Journal of Industrial Economics* 43 (4): 377–97.

Crandall, R., and H. Furchtgott-Roth. 1996. *Cable TV: Regulation or Competition?* Washington, DC: Brookings Institution Press.

Crawford, G. S. 2000. "The Impact of the 1992 Cable Act on Household Demand and Welfare." *RAND Journal of Economics* 31 (3): 422–49.

———. 2008. "The Discriminatory Incentives to Bundle in the Cable Television Industry." *Quantitative Marketing and Economics* 6 (1): 41–78.

Crawford, G. S., and J. Cullen. 2007. "Bundling, Product Choice, and Efficiency: Should Cable Television Networks Be Offered à la Carte?" *Information Economics and Policy* 19 (3–4): 379–404.

Crawford, G. S., R. Lee, M. Whinston, and A. Yurukoglu. 2012. "The Welfare Effects of Vertical Integration in Multichannel Television Markets." Work in progress, University of Warwick.

Crawford, G. S., O. Shcherbakov, and M. Shum. 2011. "The Welfare Effects of Endogenous Quality Choice: Evidence from Cable Television Markets." Working paper, University of Warwick.

Crawford, G. S., and M. Shum. 2007. "Monopoly Quality Degradation in the Cable Television Industry." *Journal of Law and Economics* 50 (1): 181–219.

Crawford, G. S., and A. Yurukoglu. 2012. "The Welfare Effects of Bundling in Multichannel Television Markets." *American Economic Review* 102 (2): 643–85.

Emmons, W., and R. Prager. 1997. "The Effect of Market Structure and Ownership on Prices and Service Offerings in the US Cable Television Industry." *Rand Journal of Economics* 28 (4): 732–50.

Federal Communications Commission (FCC). 1994. "Changes in Cable Television Rates: Results of the FCC's Survey of September 1, 1993 Rate Changes (2nd Cable Price Survey)." Discussion Paper, Federal Communications Commission, FCC Mass Media Docket No. 92-226.

———. 1997. "Third Annual Report on the Status of Competition in the Market for the Delivery of Video Programming (1996 Report)." Discussion Paper, Federal Communications Commission, CS Docket No 96-133. Released January 2, 1997.

———. 1998a. "1997 Report on Cable Industry Prices." Discussion Paper, Federal Communications Commission, FCC 97-409. Released December 15, 1997.

———. 1998b. "Fifth Annual Report on the Status of Competition in the Market for the Delivery of Video Programming (1998 Report)." Discussion Paper, Federal Communications Commission, FCC 98-335. Released December 23, 1998.

———. 1998c. "Fourth Annual Report on the Status of Competition in the Market for the Delivery of Video Programming (1997 Report)." Discussion Paper, Federal Communications Commission, FCC 97-423. Released January 13, 1998.

———. 1998d. "Memorandum Opinion and Order in the Matter of Social Contract for Time Warner." Discussion Paper, Federal Communications Commission. http://www.fcc.gov/Bureaus/Cable/Orders/1998/fcc98316.txt.

———. 1999. "1998 Report on Cable Industry Prices." Discussion Paper, Federal Communications Commission, FCC 99-91. Released May 7, 1999.

———. 2000a. "1999 Report on Cable Industry Prices." Discussion Paper, Federal Communications Commission, FCC 00-214. Released June 15, 2000.

———. 2000b. "Cable Television Fact Sheet." Discussion Paper, Federal Communications Commission. http://www.fcc.gov/mb/facts/csgen.html.

———. 2000c. "Declaratory Ruling and Notice of Proposed Rulemaking." Discussion Paper, Federal Communications Commission, FCC 02-77.

———. 2001a. "2000 Report on Cable Industry Prices." Discussion Paper, Federal Communications Commission, FCC 01-49. Released February 14, 2001.

———. 2001b. "Memorandum Opinion and Order." Discussion Paper, Federal Communications Commission, CS Docket No. 0030, FCC 01-12.

———. 2001c. "Seventh Annual Report on the Status of Competition in the Market for the Delivery of Video Programming (2000 Report)." Discussion Paper, Federal Communications Commission, FCC 01-1. Released January 8, 2001.

———. 2002a. "2001 Report on Cable Industry Prices." Discussion Paper, FCC, FCC 02-107. Released April 4, 2002.

———. 2002b. "Eighth Annual Report on the Status of Competition in the Market for the Delivery of Video Programming (2001 Report)." Discussion Paper, Federal Communications Commission, FCC 01-389. Released January 14, 2002.

———. 2002c. "Ninth Annual Report on the Status of Competition in the Market for the Delivery of Video Programming (2002 Report)." Discussion Paper, Federal Communications Commission, FCC 02-338. Released December 31, 2002.

———. 2003. "2002 Report on Cable Industry Prices." Discussion Paper, Federal Communications Commission, FCC 03-136. Released July 8, 2003.

———. 2004a. "Report on the Packaging and Sale of Video Programming to the Public." Discussion Paper, FCC, November 18, 2004. http://www.fcc.gov/mb/csrptpg.html.

———. 2004b. "Tenth Annual Report on the Status of Competition in the Market for the Delivery of Video Programming (2003 Report)." Discussion Paper, Federal Communications Commission, FCC 04-5. Released January 28, 2004.

———. 2005a. "2004 Report on Cable Industry Prices." Discussion Paper, Federal Communications Commission, FCC 05-12. Released February 4, 2005.

———. 2005b. "Eleventh Annual Report on the Status of Competition in the Market for the Delivery of Video Programming (2004 Report)." Discussion Paper, Federal Communications Commission, FCC 05-13. Released February 4, 2005.

———. 2005c. "Notice of Proposed Rulemaking." Discussion Paper, Federal Communications Commission, MM Docket No. 05-311, FCC 05-189.

———. 2005d. "Second Further Notice of Proposed Rulemaking." Discussion Paper, Federal Communications Commission, MM Docket No. 92-264, FCC 05-96.

———. 2006a. "2005 Report on Cable Industry Prices." Discussion Paper, Federal Communications Commission, FCC 06-179. Released December 27, 2006.

———. 2006b. "Further Report on the Packaging and Sale of Video Programming to the Public." Discussion Paper, FCC, February, 2006. http://www.fcc.gov/mb /csrptpg.html.

———. 2006c. "Twelfth Annual Report on the Status of Competition in the Market for the Delivery of Video Programming (2005 Report)." Discussion Paper, Federal Communications Commission, FCC 06-11. Released March 3, 2006.

———. 2009a. "2006–2008 Report on Cable Industry Prices." Discussion Paper, Federal Communications Commission, FCC 09-53. Released January 16, 2009.

———. 2009b. "Thirteenth Annual Assessment on the Status of Competition in the Market for the Delivery of Video Programming (2006 Report)." Discussion Paper, Federal Communications Commission, FCC 07-206. Released January 16, 2009.

———. 2011. "2009 Report on Cable Industry Prices." Discussion Paper, Federal Communications Commission, DA 11-284. Released February 14, 2011.

———. 2012a. "2010 Report on Cable Industry Prices." Discussion Paper, Federal Communications Commission, DA 12-377. Released March 9, 2012.

———. 2012b. "2011 Report on Cable Industry Prices." Discussion Paper, Federal Communications Commission, DA 12-1322. Released August 13, 2012.

———. 2012c. "Fourteenth Annual Assessment on the Status of Competition in the Market for the Delivery of Video Programming (2007–2010 Report)." Discussion Paper, Federal Communications Commission, FCC 12-81. Released July 20, 2012.

Feder, B. 2002. "US Clears Cable Merger of AT&T Unit with Comcast." *New York Times*, November 14.

Ford, G., and J. Jackson. 1997. "Horizontal Concentration and Vertical Integration in the Cable Television Industry." *Review of Industrial Organization* 12 (4): 501–18.

Foster, A. 1982. *Understanding Broadcasting*, second edition. Boston: Addison-Wesley Publishing Group.

General Accounting Office (GAO). 1989. "National Survey of Cable Television Rates and Services." Discussion Paper, General Accounting Office, GAO/RCED-89-193.

———. 1991. "Telecommunications: 1991 Survey of Cable Television Rates and Services." Discussion Paper, General Accounting Office, GAO/RCED-91-195.

———. 2000. "The Effect of Competition from Satellite Providers on Cable Rates." Discussion Paper, General Accounting Office, GAO/RCED-00-164.

———. 2003. "Issues Related to Competition and Subscriber Rates in the Cable Television Industry." Discussion Paper, General Accounting Office, GAO-04-8.

Goolsbee, A., and A. Petrin. 2004. "Consumer Gains from Direct Broadcast Satellites and the Competition with Cable TV." *Econometrica* 72 (2): 351–81.

Hazlett, T. 1986a. "Competition versus Franchise Monopoly in Cable Television." *Contemporary Policy Issues* 4 (2): 80–97.

———. 1986b. "Private Monopoly and the Public Interest: An Economic Analysis of the Cable Television Franchise." *University of Pennsylvania Law Review* 134 (6): 1335–409.

Hazlett, T., and M. Spitzer. 1997. *Public Policy Towards Cable Television: The Economics of Rate Controls*. Cambridge, MA: MIT Press.

Hohmann, G. 2012. "Rockefeller Criticizes Cable TV Industry." *Charleston Daily Mail*, July 29.

Jaffe, A., and D. Kanter. 1990. "Market Power of Local Cable Television Franchises: Evidence from the Effects of Deregulation." *Rand Journal of Economics* 21 (2): 226–34.

Kagan World Media. 1998. "Economics of Basic Cable Television Networks." Discussion Paper, Kagan World Media.

———. 2004. "Cable Program Investor." Discussion Paper, Kagan World Media, March 15.

Kahn, A. E. 1991. *The Economics of Regulation: Principles and Institutions*. Cambridge, MA: MIT Press.

Kirkpatrick, D. 2003. "F.C.C. Approves Deal Giving Murdoch Control of DirecTV." *New York Times*, December 20.

Levin, S., and J. Meisel. 1991. "Cable Television and Competition: Theory, Evidence, and Policy." *Telecommunications Policy* 16 (6): 519–28.

Make, J. 2008. "Martin Weighs Wholesale Cable Unbundling, Other Video Changes." *Communications Daily*, August 1.

———. 2009. "FCC Draws Fire from Appeals Court in Cable Cap Loss." *Communications Daily*, August 31.

Mayo, J., and Y. Otsuka. 1991. "Demand, Pricing, and Regulation: Evidence from the Cable TV Industry." *Rand Journal of Economics* 22 (3): 396–410.

Mussa, M., and S. Rosen. 1978. "Monopoly and Product Quality." *Journal of Economic Theory* 18 (2): 301–17.

Nalebuff, B. 2004. "Bundling as an Entry Barrier." *Quarterly Journal of Economics* 119 (1): 159–87.

National Cable Television Association (NCTA). 2005a. "NCTA Industry Overview." Discussion Paper, National Cable Television Association. http://www.ncta.com /Docs/PageContent.cfm?pageID=86.

———. 2005b. "NCTA Industry Overview: Broadband Deployment." Discussion Paper, National Cable Television Association. http://www.ncta.com/ContentView .aspx?contentId=59.

———. 2005c. "NCTA Industry Overview: Cable Networks." Discussion Paper, National Cable Television Association. http://www.ncta.com/ContentView. aspx?contentId=63.

———. 2005d. "NCTA Industry Overview: Revenue from Customers." Discussion Paper, National Cable Television Association. http://www.ncta.com/Docs/Page Content.cfm?pageID=309.

———. 2013a. "Cable Advertising Revenue, 1999–2011." Discussion Paper, National Cable Television Association. Accessed January 10, 2013. http://www.ncta .com/Stats/AdvertisingRevenue.aspx.

———. 2013b. "Cable Industry Revenue, 1996–2011." Discussion Paper, National Cable Television Association. Accessed January 10, 2013. http://www.ncta.com /Stats/CustomerRevenue.aspx.

———. 2013c. "NCTA Industry Overview: Infrastructure Expenditures." Discussion Paper, National Cable Television Association. Accessed January 13, 2013. http://www.ncta.com/Stats/InfrastructureExpense.aspx.

Nevo, A. 2000. "Mergers with Differentiated Products: The Case of the Ready-to-Eat Cereal Industry." *RAND Journal of Economics* 31 (3): 395–421.

———. 2001. "Measuring Market Power in the Ready-to-Eat Cereal Industry." *Econometrica* 69 (2): 307–42.

Noll, R., M. Peck, and J. McGowan. 1973. *Economic Aspects of Television Regulation*. Washington, DC: Brookings Institution.

Organisation for Economic Co-operation and Development (OECD). 2001. "The Development of Broadband Access in OECD Countries." Discussion Paper, OECD, DSTI/ICCP/TISP(2001)2/FINAL. Paris: OECD.

Owen, B., and S. Wildman. 1992. *Video Economics*. Cambridge, MA: Harvard University Press.

Petrin, A. 2003. "Quantifying the Benefits of New Products: The Case of the Mini-van." *Journal of Political Economy* 110 (4): 705–29.

Prager, R. 1990. "Firm Behavior in Franchise Monopoly Markets." *Rand Journal of Economics* 21 (2): 211–25.

———. 1992. "The Effects of Deregulating Cable Television: Evidence from Financial Markets." *Journal of Regulatory Economics* 4 (4): 347–63.

Raskovich, A. 2003. "Pivotal Buyers and Bargaining Position." *Journal of Industrial Economics* 51 (4): 405–26.

Rennhoff, A. D., and K. Serfes. 2008. "Estimating the Effects of à la Carte Pricing: The Case of Cable Television." Social Science Research Network (SSRN) eLibrary.

Rey, P., and J. Tirole. 2007. "A Primer on Foreclosure." In *Handbook of Industrial Organization*, vol. 3, edited by by M. Armstrong and R. Porter, 2145–220. Amsterdam: North-Holland.

Roettgers, J. 2013. "Dish's New Second-Screen App Looks Good, Which Should Worry Its Competition." Gigaom. Accessed January 6, 2013. http://gigaom.com/2013/01/06/dish-second-screen-app/.

Rose, N. 1985. "The Incidence of Regulatory Rents in the Motor Carrier Industry." *Rand Journal of Economics* 16 (3): 299–318.

Rubinovitz, R. 1993. "Market Power and Price Increases for Basic Cable Service Since Deregulation." *Rand Journal of Economics* 24 (1): 1–18.

Schatz, A. 2005. "FCC Unanimously Approves Deregulation of DSL Service." *Wall Street Journal*, August 5.

Schatz, A., J. Drucker, and D. Searcy. 2005. "Small Internet Providers Can't Use Cable Lines; Is Wireless the Answer?" *Wall Street Journal*, June 28.

Schiesel, S. 2001. "In Cable TV, Programmers Provide a Power Balance." *New York Times*, July 16.

Schwert, G. 1981. "Using Financial Data to Measure the Effects of Regulation." *Journal of Law and Economics* 24 (1): 121–58.

Shcherbakov, A. 2010. "Measuring Consumer Switching Costs in the Television Industry." Working paper, Yale University.

Spence, A. M. 1975. "Monopoly, Quality, and Regulation." *Bell Journal of Economics* 6 (2): 417–29.

Stigler, G. J. 1963. "United States v. Loew's Inc.: A Note on Block Booking." In *The Supreme Court Review*, edited by P. Kurland, 152–57. Chicago: University of Chicago Press.

Waterman, D. H., and A. A. Weiss. 1996. "The Effects of Vertical Integration between Cable Television Systems and Pay Cable Networks." *Journal of Econometrics* 72 (1–2): 357–95.

———. 1997. *Vertical Integration in Cable Television*. Cambridge, MA: MIT Press and AEI Press.

Whinston, M. 1990. "Tying, Foreclosure, and Exclusion." *American Economic Review* 80 (4): 837–59.

Zupan, M. A. 1989a. "The Efficacy of Franchise Bidding Schemes in the Case of Cable Television: Some Systematic Evidence." *Journal of Law and Economics* 32 (1): 401–36.

———. 1989b. "Non-Price Concessions and the Effect of Franchise Bidding Schemes on Cable Company Costs." *Applied Economics* 21 (3): 305–23.

4

Regulating Competition in Wholesale Electricity Supply

Frank A. Wolak

4.1 Introduction

The technology of electricity production, transmission, distribution, and retailing together with the history of pricing to final consumers make designing a competitive wholesale electricity market extremely challenging. There have been a number of highly visible wholesale market meltdowns, most notably the California electricity crisis during the period June 2000 to June 2001, and the sustained period of exceptionally high wholesale prices in New Zealand during June to September of both 2001 and 2003. Even wholesale markets generally acknowledged to have ultimately benefitted consumers relative to the former vertically integrated monopoly regime in the United Kingdom and Australia have experienced substantial problems with the exercise of unilateral market power by large suppliers.

The experience of the past twenty years suggests that, although there are opportunities for consumers to benefit from electricity industry restructuring, realizing these benefits has proven far more challenging than realizing those from introducing competition into other network industries such as telecommunications and airlines. In addition, the probability of a costly market failure in the electricity supply industry, often due to the exercise of unilateral market power, appears to be significantly higher than in other formerly regulated industries. These facts motivate the three major questions addressed in this chapter. First, why has the experience with electric-

Frank A. Wolak is the Holbrook Working Professor of Commodity Price Studies in the Department of Economics at Stanford University and a research associate of the National Bureau of Economic Research.

For acknowledgments, sources of research support, and disclosure of the author's material financial relationships, if any, please see http://www.nber.org/chapters/c12567.ack.

ity restructuring been so disappointing, particularly in the United States? Second, what factors have led to success and limited the probability of costly market failures in other parts of the world? Third, how can these lessons be applied to improve wholesale market performance in the United States and other industrialized countries?

An important theme of this chapter is that electricity industry restructuring is an evolving process that requires market designers to choose continuously between an imperfectly competitive market and an imperfect regulatory process to provide incentives for least-cost supply at all stages of the production process. As a consequence, certain industry segments rely on market mechanisms to set prices and others rely on explicit regulatory price-setting processes. This choice depends on the technology available to produce the good or service and the legal and economic constraints facing the industry. Therefore, different segments of the industry can be subject to market mechanisms or explicit price regulation as these factors change.

Because the current technology for electricity transmission and local distribution overwhelmingly favors a single network for a given geographic area, a regulatory process is necessary to set the prices, or more generally, the revenues that transmission and distribution network owners receive for providing these services. Paul Joskow's chapter in this volume first presents the economic theory of incentive regulation—pricing mechanisms that provide strong incentives for transmission and distribution network owners to reduce costs and improve service quality and introduce new products and services in a cost-effective manner. He then provides a critical assessment of the available evidence on the performance of incentive regulation mechanisms for transmission and distribution networks.

The wholesale electricity segment of restructured electricity supply industries primarily relies on market mechanisms to set prices, although the configuration of the transmission network and regulatory rules governing its use can exert a dramatic impact on the prices electricity suppliers are paid. In addition, the planning process used to determine the location and magnitude of expansions to the transmission network has an enormous impact on the scale and location of new generation investments. Because a restructured electricity supply industry requires explicit regulation of certain segments and the regulatory mechanisms implemented significantly impact market outcomes, the entity managing the restructuring process must continually balance the need to foster vigorous competition in those segments of the industry where market mechanisms are used to set prices against the need to intervene to set prices and control firm behavior in the monopoly segments of the industry. Maintaining this delicate balance requires a much more sophisticated regulatory process relative to the one that existed under the former vertically integrated monopoly regime.

This chapter first describes the history of the electricity supply industry in the United States and the motivation for the vertically integrated monopoly industry structure and regulatory process that existed until wholesale markets were introduced in the late 1990s. This is followed by a description of the important features of the technology of supplying electricity to final consumers that any wholesale market design must take into account. These technological aspects of electricity production and delivery and the political constraints on how the industry operates make wholesale electricity markets extremely susceptible to the exercise of unilateral market power. This is the primary reason why continued regulatory oversight of the electricity supply industry is necessary and is a major motivation for the historic vertically integrated industry structure.

To provide historical context for the electricity industry restructuring process in the United States, I describe the perceived regulatory failures that led to electricity industry restructuring and outline the legal and regulatory structure currently governing the wholesale market regime in the United States. In the vertically integrated monopoly regime, the major regulatory challenge is providing incentives for the firms to produce in a least-cost manner and set prices that only recover incurred production costs. Informational asymmetries about the production process or structure of demand between the vertically integrated monopoly and the regulator make it impossible for the regulator to determine the least-cost mode of supplying retail customers.

In the wholesale market regime, the major regulatory challenge is designing market rules that provide strong incentives for least-cost production and limit the ability of firms to impact market prices through their unilateral actions. Different from the vertically integrated monopoly regime, suppliers set market prices through their own unilateral actions, which can deviate substantially from those necessary to recover production costs. To better understand this regulatory challenge, I introduce the generic wholesale market design problem as a generalization of a multilevel principal-agent problem. There are two major dimensions to the market design problem: (1) public versus private ownership, and (2) market mechanisms versus explicit regulation to set output prices. The impact of these choices on the principal-agent relationships between the firm and its owners and the firm and the regulatory body are discussed.

I then turn to the market design challenge in the wholesale market regime with privately owned firms—limiting the ability and incentive of suppliers to exercise unilateral market power in the short-term wholesale market. To organize this discussion, I introduce the concept of a residual demand curve— the demand curve an individual supplier faces after the offers to supply energy of its competitors have been taken into account. I demonstrate that limiting the ability and incentive of suppliers to exercise a unilateral market is equivalent to making the residual demand curve a supplier faces as price elastic as possible. I describe four actions by the market designer that can increase the elasticity of the residual demand curve a supplier faces. Virtually all wholesale market meltdowns and shortcomings of existing market designs can be traced to a failure to address adequately of one these dimensions of the market design process.

The final aspect of the market design process is effective and credible regulatory oversight of the industry. The regulator must engage in a process of continuous feedback and improvement in the market rules, which implies access to information and sophisticated use of the information provided. Rather than set output prices that protect consumers from the exercise of market power by the vertically integrated monopoly, the regulator must now design market rules that protect consumers from the exercise of unilateral market power by all firms in the industry, a significantly more difficult task.

The next section provides examples of common market design flaws from wholesale markets in industrialized and developing countries. These include excessive focus by the regulatory process on spot market design, inadequate divestiture of generation capacity by the incumbent firms, lack of an effective local market power mitigation mechanism, price caps and bid caps on short-term markets, and an inadequate retail market infrastructure.

The chapter concludes with a discussion of the causes of the experience with wholesale electricity markets in the United States. There are number of economic and political constraints on the electricity supply industry in the United States that have hindered the development of wholesale electricity markets that benefit consumers relative to the former vertically integrated regime. I first describe some recent developments in electricity markets in the United States that are cause for optimism about consumers realizing benefits. I then point out a number of ways to increase the likelihood that electricity industry restructuring in the United States will ultimately benefit consumers.

4.2   History of the Electricity Supply Industry and the Path to Restructuring

This section reviews the history of the electricity supply industry in the United States. I first review the origins of the vertically integrated, regulated-monopoly industry structure that existed throughout the United States until very recently. I then turn to a description of the factors that led to the recent restructuring of the electricity supply industries in many parts of the United States. In order to provide the necessary technical background to understand my analysis of the challenges facing wholesale market regime, I describe important features of the technology of electricity production and delivery. I then discuss the regulatory structure governing the electricity supply industry in the United States—how it has and has not yet evolved to deal with the wholesale market regime.

4.2.1 A Brief Industry History to the Present

The electricity supply industry is divided into four stages: (1) generation, (2) transmission, (3) distribution, and (4) retailing. Generation is the process of converting raw energy from oil, natural gas, coal, nuclear power, hydro power, and renewable sources into electrical energy. Transmission is the bulk transportation of electricity at high voltages to limit the losses between the point at which the energy is injected into the transmission network and the point it is withdrawn from the network. In general, higher transmission voltages imply less energy losses over the same distance. Distribution is the process of delivering electricity at low voltage from the transmission network to final consumers. Retailing is the act of purchasing wholesale electricity and selling it to final consumers.

Historically, electricity supply for a given geographic area was provided by the single vertically integrated monopoly that produced virtually all of the electricity it ultimately delivered to consumers. This firm owned and operated the generation assets, the transmission network, and local distribution network required to deliver electricity throughout its geographic service area. There is some debate surrounding the rationale underlying the origins of this industry structure.

The conventional view is there are economies to scale in the generation and transmission of electricity and significant economies to scope between transmission and distribution and generation at the level of demand and size of the geographic region served by most vertically integrated utilities. These economies to scale and scope create a natural monopoly, where the minimum cost industry structure to serve all consumers in a given geographic area is a vertically integrated monopoly. However, without regulatory oversight, a large vertically integrated firm could set prices substantially in excess of the average cost of production.

The prospect of a large vertically integrated firm using these economies to scale in transmission and generation and economies to scope to exercise significant unilateral market power justifies regulatory oversight to protect the public interest, set output prices, and determine the terms and conditions under which the monopoly can charge these prices. What is often called the "public interest rationale" for the vertically integrated, regulated-monopoly industry structure states that explicit output price regulation is necessary to protect consumers from the unilateral market power that could be exercised by the dominant firm in a given geographic area. Viscusi, Vernon, and Harrington (2005, chapter 11) provides an accessible discussion of this perspective on the vertically integrated, regulated-monopoly industry structure.

Jarrell (1978) proposes an alternative rationale for an industry composed of privately owned, vertically integrated monopolies subject to state-level regulation using the positive theory of regulation developed by Stigler (1971) and Peltzman (1976). He argues that this market structure arose from the early years of the industry when utilities were regulated by municipal governments through franchise agreements. A number of large municipalities issued duplicate franchise agreements and allowed firms to compete for customers. Jarrell argues that state-level regulation arose because these firms found it too difficult to maintain their monopoly status by their own actions, and instead decided to subject themselves to state-level regulatory oversight in exchange for a government-sanctioned geographic monopoly status. Jarrell demonstrates that the predictions of the traditional public interest rationale for state regulation—prices and profits should decrease and output should increase in response to state-level regulation—are contradicted by his empirical work. He finds higher output prices and profit levels and lower output levels for utilities in states that adopted state-level regulation early relative to utilities in states that adopted state-level regulation later. At a minimum, Jarrell's work suggests that the logic underlying state-level regulation of vertically integrated monopolies is more complex than the standard public interest rationale described earlier.

Until industry restructuring began in the late 1990s, the vast majority of US consumers were served by privately owned vertically integrated monopolies, although there were a number of municipally owned, vertically integrated utilities and an even larger number of customer-owned electricity cooperatives serving rural areas. As noted in Joskow (1974), customers served by privately owned, vertically integrated regulated utilities experienced continuously declining real retail electricity prices from the start of the industry until the mid-1970s. Not until the second half of the 1970s, when real electricity prices began to increase, did this structure begin to show signs of stress.

Joskow (1989) provides a perspicacious discussion of the history of the US electricity supply industry and events leading up to the perceived failure of this regulatory paradigm and the initial responses to it. He argues that particularly in regions of the countries with rapidly growing electricity demand during the late 1970s and early 1980s, new capacity investment decisions made by the vertically integrated utilities ultimately turned out to be extremely costly to consumers. This led to a general dissatisfaction with the vertically integrated regulated-monopoly paradigm.

Around this same time technical change allowed generation units to realize all available economies to scale at significantly lower levels of capacity. For example, Joskow (1987) presents empirical evidence that scale economies in electricity production at the generation unit level are exhausted at a unit size of about 500 megawatts (MW)[1]. More recent econometric work finds that the null hypothesis of constant returns to scale in the supply of electricity (the combination of generation, transmission, and distribution)

---

1. Typically there are multiple generation units at a single plant location. For example, a 1,600 MW coal-fired plant may be composed of four 400 MW generation units at that site.

by US investor-owned utilities cannot be rejected (Lee 1995), which implies that economies to scope between transmission and generation are exhausted for the geographic areas served by most vertically integrated monopolies in the United States.

During this time period a number of countries around the world were beginning the process of privatization and restructuring of their state-owned, vertically integrated electricity supply industry. In the late 1980s, England and Wales initiated this process in Europe, with Norway, Sweden, Spain, Australia, and New Zealand quickly following their lead. These international reforms demonstrated the feasibility of wholesale electricity competition and provided models for the restructuring process in the United States.

All of these factors combined to provide significant inertia in favor of the formation of formal wholesale electricity markets in the United States. Joskow and Schmalensee (1983) provide a detailed analysis of the viability of wholesale competition in electricity as of the beginning of the 1980s.

4.2.2   Key Features of Technology of Electricity Production and Delivery

This section describes the basic features of electricity production, delivery, and demand. First I summarize the cost structure of electricity generation units. I then discuss how the form of a generation unit's cost function determines when it should operate in order to meet the pattern of hourly system demand throughout the year at least cost. The validity of this logic is demonstrated with examples of the actual average daily pattern of output of specific generation units. I then explain the basic physics governing flows in electricity transmission networks, which considerably complicates the process of finding output rates for generation units to meet electricity demand at all locations in the transmission network.

Electricity production typically involves a significant up-front investment to construct a generation unit and a variable cost of producing electricity once the unit is constructed. Fossil fuel generation units using the same input fuel can be differentiated by their heat rate, the rate at which they convert heat energy into electrical energy. In the United States, heat rates are expressed in terms of British thermal units (BTUs) of heat energy necessary to produce one kilowatt hour (KWh) of electricity. For example, a natural gas-fired steam turbine unit might have a heat rate of 9,000 BTU/KWh, whereas a natural gas-fired combustion turbine generation unit might have a heat rate of 14,000 BTU/KWh. Lower heat rate technologies are typically associated with higher up-front fixed costs. Higher heat rate units are also usually less expensive to turn on and off. To convert a heat rate into the variable fuel costs of producing electricity, multiply the heat rate by the $/BTU price of the input fuel. For example, if the price of natural gas is $7 per million BTU, this implies a variable fuel cost of $63/MWh for the unit with a 9,000 BTU/KWh heat rate and a variable fuel cost of \$98/MWh for the unit with 14,000 BTU/KWh heat rate. Other variable cost factors are added to the variable fuel cost to arrive at the unit's variable cost of production.

This relationship between the fixed and variable costs of producing electricity implies a total cost function for producing electricity at the generation unit level of the form $C_i(q) = F_i + c_iq$, where F_i is the up-front fixed cost and c_i is the variable cost of production for unit i. In general, the total variable cost of producing electricity is nonlinear in the level of output.[2] Simplifying the general nonlinear variable cost function $vc_i(q)$ to the linear form c_iq makes it more straightforward to understand when during the day and year a generation unit will operate.

Suppose there are two generation units, with $F_1 > F_2$ and $c_1 < c_2$, consistent with the abovementioned logic that a lower variable cost of production is associated with a higher fixed cost of production. For the total costs of operating unit 1 during the year to be less than the total cost of operating unit 2 during the year, unit 1 must produce more than q^*, where q^* solves the following equation in q:

$$F_1 + c_1q = F_2 + c_2q, \text{ which implies } q^* = \frac{F_1 - F_2}{c_2 - c_1}.$$

At levels of annual output higher than q^*, total annual production costs for unit 1 are less than those for unit 2. Conversely, for annual output levels below q^*, total annual production costs are lower for unit 2. These facts are useful to understand the least cost mix of production from the available generation unit technologies needed to meet the annual distribution of half-hourly or hourly electricity demands.

The annual pattern of half-hourly or hourly electricity demands is usually represented as a load duration curve. Figure 4.1 plots the half-hourly load duration curve for the state of Victoria in Australia for three years: 2000, 2001, and 2002. The Victoria market operates on a half-hourly basis, so each point on an annual load duration curve gives the number of half hours during the year on the horizontal axis that demand is greater than or equal to value on the vertical axis. For example, for 8,000 half hours of the year in 2000, system demand is greater than or equal to 5,500 MW. For both 2001 and 2002, for 8,000 half hours of the year demand is greater than or equal to 6,000 MW.

The load duration curve can be used to determine how the mix of available generation units should be used to meet this distribution of half-hourly demands at least cost. Generation units with the lowest variable costs will

---

2. Wolak (2007) estimates generation unit-level daily variable cost functions implied by expected profit-maximizing offer behavior for units participating in the Australian wholesale electricity market, and finds strong evidence of economically significant nonlinearities both within and across periods of the day in the variable cost of producing electricity.

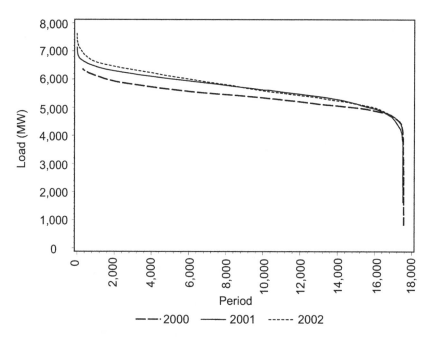

Fig. 4.1   **Load duration curves for Victoria for 2000 to 2002**

operate during all half hours of the year. This is represented on the load duration curve by a rectangle with height equal to the average half-hourly output of the unit and length equal to the number of half hours in the year. Rectangles of this form are added on top of one another from the lowest to the highest annual average cost of production until the rectangular portion of the load duration curve is filled. Additional rectangles of increasingly smaller lengths of operation are stacked up from the lowest to highest annual average cost of providing the desired amount of annual energy until the load duration curve is covered by these rectangles. This process of filling the load duration curve implies that higher variable cost units should be called upon less frequently than lower variable cost units.

This logic has implications for how the daily pattern of half-hourly demands are met. Figure 4.2 plots the annual average daily pattern of demand for Victoria for the same three years as figure 4.1. A point on the curve for each year gives the annual average demand for electricity in MW for the half-hour period during the day given on the horizontal axis. For example, during the half-hour period 20 of the year 2000, the annual average half-hourly load is 5,500 MW. This half-hourly pattern of load within the day and the process used to fill the load-duration curve just described imply different patterns of half-hourly output within the day for specific generation units depending on their cost structure. Figure 4.3 plots the average

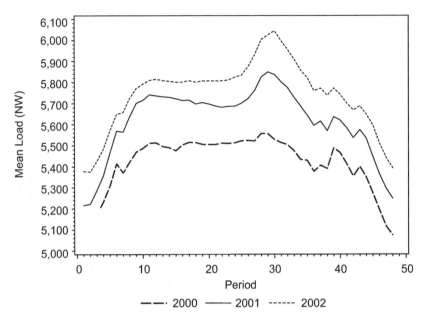

Fig. 4.2   Annual average daily pattern of system load for Victoria for 2000 to 2002

daily pattern of output from the Yallourn plant in Victoria for 2000, 2001, and 2002. This plant is composed of four brown coal units that produce output at a variable cost of approximately 5 Australian dollars ($AU) per MWh. As discussed in Wolak (2007), these units have the lowest variable cost in Australia, and by the above logic of filling the load duration curve, they should operate at the same level during all hours of the day. As predicted by this logic, figure 4.3 shows that for each of the three years, there is little difference in the average half-hourly output level across half hours of the day.

Figure 4.4 plots the average daily pattern of output from the Valley Power plant for 2002. This plant came on line in November 2001 and is composed of six generation units totaling 300 MW. Each of these units has one of the highest variable costs in Victoria, which implies that they should operate only in the highest demand periods of the day. Figure 4.2 shows that average half-hourly demand in Victoria is highest around period 30. The average half-hourly output of the Valley Power plant is highest in period 30 and slightly lower in the surrounding half hours and declines to close to zero in the remaining half hours of the day, which is consistent with the logic of filling the load duration curve.

A final aspect of the load duration curve has implications for the cost effectiveness of active demand-side participation in the wholesale market. Figure 4.5 plots the load duration curve for highest 500 half-hour periods for the same three years as figure 4.1. This figure shows that the load duration

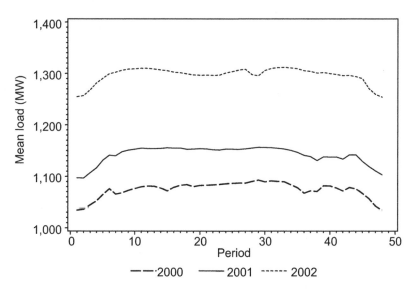

Fig. 4.3   Annual average daily pattern of output for Yallourn Electricity Generation Plant for Victoria for 2000 to 2002

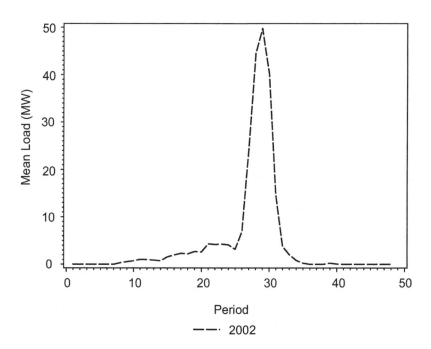

Fig. 4.4   Annual average daily pattern of output for Valley Power Electricity Generation Plant

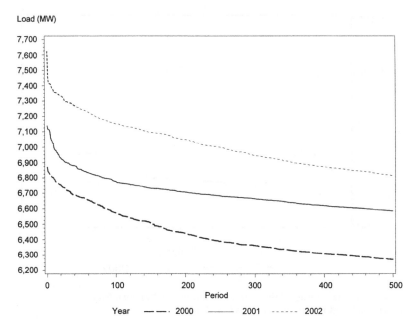

Load (MW)

Year — —· 2000   ——— 2001   ------ 2002

Fig. 4.5   Load duration curve for highest 500 half hours for Victoria from 2000 to 2002

curve for 2002 intersects the vertical axis at approximately 7,600 MW. At a value on the horizontal axis of 10 half hours, the value of the curve falls to approximately 7,400 MW, which implies that at least 200 MW of generation capacity is required to operate less than ten half-hour periods of the year. If system demand could be reduced below 7,400 MW during these ten half-hour periods through active demand-side participation, this would eliminate the need to construct and operate a peaking generation facility such as the Valley Power plant. An extremely steep load duration curve near the vertical axis implies that a substantial amount of capacity is used a very small number of hours of the year and that there is the prospect of significant saving in generation construction and operating costs by providing final consumers with incentives to reduce their demand during these hours.

Perhaps the most important feature of wholesale electricity markets is that the unilateral actions of generation unit owners to raise wholesale prices can result in a substantial divergence between the market-clearing price and variable cost of the highest cost unit operating during that half-hour period, which is the wholesale price that would arise if no supplier had the ability to exercise unilateral market power. Figure 4.6 plots the annual daily average of half-hourly prices for Victoria for 2000, 2001, and 2002. The extremely high annual average price during the half-hour period 30 for 2002 illustrates the extent to which there can be a divergence between the variable cost of

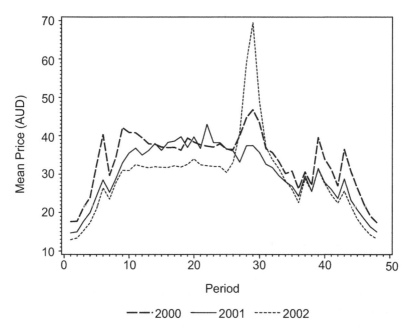

Fig. 4.6   **Annual average half-hourly prices for Victoria from 2000 to 2002**

the highest cost unit operating during a half hour and the market-clearing price. As noted before, the variable cost of producing electricity from peaking units such as the Valley Power plant depends primarily on the price of natural gas. However, the price of natural gas in Victoria changed very little from 2000 to 2002, but the annual average price of electricity for half-hour period 30 and the surrounding half-hour periods for 2002 is substantially above the annual average prices for the same half-hour periods in 2000. The annual average price for half-hour period 30 and the surrounding half hours for 2000 are significantly above the annual average prices for the same half-hour periods in 2001. These differences in annual average half-hourly prices across the years demonstrate that competitive conditions and other factors besides the variable costs of the highest cost unit operating are major drivers of the level of average electricity prices in the wholesale market regime.

A final distinguishing feature of the electricity supply industry is the requirement to deliver electricity through a potentially congested looped transmission network. Electricity flows along the path of least resistance through the transmission network according to Kirchhoff's first and second laws rather than according to the desires of buyers and sellers of electricity.[3]

3. See http://physics.about.com/od/electromagnetics/f/KirchhoffRule.htm for an accessible introduction to Kirchoff's laws.

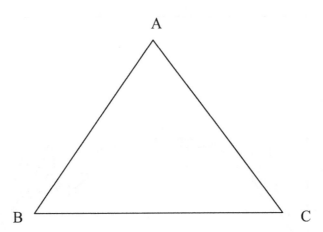

Fig. 4.7   Power flows in a three-node network

To understand the operation of looped electricity networks, consider the three-node network in figure 4.7. Assume that links AB, BC, and AC have the same resistance and that there are no losses associated with transmitting electricity in this network. Suppose a supplier located at node A injects 90 megawatts (MW) of energy for a customer at node B to consume. Kirchoff's laws imply that 60 MW of the 90 MW will travel along the link AB and 30 MW will travel along the pair of links AC and BC because the total resistance along this indirect path from A to B is twice the resistance of the direct path from A to B.

How this property of a looped transmission network impacts wholesale market outcomes becomes clear when the capacities of transmission links are taken into account. Suppose that the capacity of link AB is 40 MW, and the capacities of links AC and BC are each 100 MW. Ignoring the physics of power flows, one might think that the capacity of the AC and BC links would allow injecting 90 MW at node A and withdrawing 90 MW at node B. Kirchoff's laws imply that the maximum amount of energy that can be injected at A and withdrawn at node B is 60 MW, because 40 MW will flow along AB and 20 MW will flow along the links AC and BC. The 40 MW capacity of link AB limits the amount that can injected at node A. For this configuration of the network, the only way to allow consumers at node B to withdraw 90 MW of energy would be to inject less energy at node A and more at node C, so that the total injected at A and C is equal to 90 MW. For example, injecting 30 MW at node A and 60 MW at node C would result in a flow of 40 MW on link AB and allow total withdrawals of 90 MW at node B.

Market designs that fail to account for the fact that the electricity sold must be delivered through the existing transmission network create opportunities for suppliers to increase the prices there are paid by exploiting this divergence between the transmission network assumed to determine market prices and the one used to deliver the electricity sold to electricity consumers. As I discuss later, some progress has recently been made in the United States with correcting this source of market efficiencies.

4.2.3   Transition from Vertically Integrated Monopoly Regime

Regulatory oversight in the United States is complicated by the fact that the federal government has jurisdiction over interstate commerce and state governments have jurisdiction over intrastate commerce. This logic implies that state governments have the authority to regulate retail electricity prices and intrastate wholesale electricity transactions, and the federal government has the authority to regulate interstate wholesale electricity transactions.

The physics of electricity flows in a looped transmission network does not allow a clear distinction between interstate and intrastate sales of electricity. It is extremely difficult, if not impossible, to determine precisely how much of the electricity consumed in one state was actually produced in another state if the two states are interconnected by a looped transmission network. This has led to a number of rules of thumb to determine whether a wholesale electricity transaction is subject to federal or state jurisdiction. Clearly, trades between parties located in different states are subject to federal oversight. However, it also possible that a transaction between parties located in the same state is subject to federal oversight. One determinant of whether a transaction among parties located in the same state is classified as interstate and subject to federal oversight is the voltage of the transmission lines that the buyer withdraws from and seller injects at, because as discussed earlier, higher voltage lines usually deliver more electricity over longer distances.

The Federal Power Act of 1930 established the Federal Power Commission (which became the Federal Energy Regulatory Commission [FERC] in 1977) to regulate wholesale energy transactions using high-voltage transmission facilities. The Federal Power Act established standards for wholesale electricity prices that FERC must maintain. In particular, FERC is required to ensure that wholesale electricity prices are "just and reasonable." Prices that only recover the supplier's production costs, including a return to capital, meet the just and reasonable standard. FERC has determined that prices set by other means can also meet this standard, if this judgment is able to survive judicial review. If FERC determines that wholesale electricity prices are not just and reasonable, then the Federal Power Act gives FERC considerable discretion to take actions to make these prices just and reasonable, and requires FERC to order refunds for any payments made by consumers at prices in excess of just and reasonable levels.

It is important to emphasize that these provisions of the Federal Power Act still exist and apply to outcomes from the bid-based wholesale electricity markets in the Northeast, the Midwest, and in California. As discussed below, the requirement that wholesale electricity prices satisfy the "just and reasonable" standard of the Federal Power Act is a major challenge to introducing wholesale competition in the United States.

Under the vertically integrated monopoly regime, state-level regulation of retail electricity prices effectively controls the price utilities pay for wholesale electricity. Utilities either own all of the generation units necessary to meet their retail load obligations or supplement their generation ownership with long-term contract commitments for energy sufficient to meet their retail load obligations. The implicit regulatory contract between the state regulator and the utilities within its jurisdiction is that in exchange for being allowed to charge a retail price set by the regulator that allows the utility the opportunity to recover all prudently incurred costs, the utility has an obligation to serve all demand in its geographic service area at this regulated price. Although these vertically integrated utilities sometimes make short-term electricity purchases from neighboring utilities, virtually all of their retail energy obligations are met either from long-term contracts or generation capacity owned and operated by the utility.

The vertically integrated monopoly industry structure and state-level regulation of retail prices makes federal regulation of wholesale electricity transactions largely redundant. The state regulator does not allow utilities under its jurisdiction to enter into long-term contracts that it does not believe are in the interests of electricity consumers in the state. Therefore, under the vertically integrated state-regulated monopoly industry structure, FERC's regulatory oversight of wholesale prices often amounts to no more than approving transactions deemed just and reasonable by a state regulator. This implicit state-level regulation of wholesale prices caused FERC to have very little experience regulating wholesale electricity transactions when the first formal wholesale markets began operation in the United States in the late 1990s.

Joskow (1989) describes a number of flaws in the state-level regulation of vertically integrated monopolies that created advocates for formal wholesale markets. First, retail electricity prices are only adjusted periodically, at the request of the utility or state commission, and only after a lengthy and expensive administrative process. Because of the substantial time and expense of the review process, utilities and commissions typically wait until this time and expense can be justified by a large enough expected price change to justify this effort. Consequently, the utility's prices typically very poorly track the utility's production costs. This regulatory lag between price changes and cost changes can introduce incentives for cost minimization on the part of the utility during periods when input prices increase. As Joskow (1974) describes in detail, nominal prices remained unchanged for a number of years during the 1950s and 1960s. This is primarily explained by both gains in productive efficiency and utilities exploiting economies of scale and scope in electricity supply during a period of stable input prices.

During the late 1970s and early 1980s when input fossil fuel costs rose dramatically in response to rapidly increasing world oil prices, many utilities filed for price increases a number of times in rapid succession. Joskow (1974) emphasizes that state regulators are extremely averse to nominal price increases. They have considerable discretion to determine what costs are prudently incurred, and the utility is therefore entitled to recover in the prices it is allowed to charge. Consequently, a rational response by the regulator to nominal input cost increases is to grant output price increases lower than the utility requested. Disallowing cost recovery of some investments is one way to accomplish this. Joskow (1989) outlines the "used and useful" regulatory standard that is the basis for determining whether an investment is prudent. Specifically, if an asset is used by the utility and is useful to produce its output in a prudent manner, then this cost has been prudently incurred. Clearly there is some circularity to this argument, and that can allow regulators to disallow cost recovery for certain investments that seemed necessary at the time they were made but subsequently turned out not to be necessary to serve their customers.

Joskow (1989) states that as result of the enormous nominal input price increases faced by utilities during the mid-1970s and early 1980s, a number of generation investments at this time were subject to ex post prudence reviews by state public utilities commissions (PUCs), particularly when the forecasted future increases in fossil fuel prices used to justify these investments failed to materialize. Increasing retail electricity rates enough to pay for these investments was politically unacceptable, particularly given the reduction in fossil fuel prices that subsequently occurred in the mid-1980s. The utility's shareholders had to cover many of the losses associated with these generation unit investments that were deemed by the state PUC to be ex post imprudent. As a consequence, the utility's appetite for investing in large base load generation facilities, even in regions with significant demand growth, was substantially reduced.

Joskow concludes his discussion of these events with the following statement.

> The experience of the 1970s and early 1980s has made it clear that existing industrial and administrative arrangements are politically incompatible with rapidly rising costs of supplying electricity and uncertainty about costs and demand. The inability of the system to deal satisfactorily with these economic shocks created a latent demand for better institutional arrangements to regulate the industry, in particular to regulate investments in and operation of generation facilities. (Joskow 1989, 162)

This experience began the process of restructuring of the electricity supply industry in the United States. Joskow (2000a) describes the transition from a limited amount of competition among cogeneration facilities and small scale generation facilities to sell wholesale energy to the vertically integrated utility enabled by the Public Utilities Regulatory Policy Act (PURPA) of

1978 to the formation of formal bid-based wholesale markets, which first began operation in California in April of 1998.

Before closing this section, it is important to emphasize two key features of the regulatory process governing electricity supply in the United States that will play a significant role later. First, for the reasons just noted, FERC historically had a minor role in regulating wholesale electricity prices in the United States and was largely unprepared for many of the challenges associated with regulating wholesale electricity markets. Joskow (1989) points out that over the decade of the 1980s "FERC staff has been increasingly willing to accept mutually satisfactory negotiated coordinated contracts between integrated utilities that are de facto unencumbered by the rigid cost accounting principles used to set retail rates." (138). The fact that most of the generation capacity and the transmission and distribution assets used to serve the utility's customers were owned by the utility, combined with FERC's approach to regulating wholesale energy transactions, meant that state PUCs exerted almost complete control over retail electricity prices.

The advent of wholesale electricity markets with significant participation by pure merchant suppliers—those with no regulated retail load obligations—severely limited the ability of state regulatory commissions to control retail prices. FERC's role in controlling wholesale and retail prices was increased by the extent to which the state-regulated load-serving entities no longer own generation assets and must purchase their wholesale energy needs from short-term wholesale markets. The California restructuring process created a set of circumstances where FERC's role in regulating wholesale prices was far greater than in any of the wholesale markets in the eastern United States. The major load-serving entities were required to sell virtually all of their fossil-fuel generation assets to merchant suppliers and the vast majority of wholesale energy purchases to serve their retail load obligations were made through short-term markets. Although it was not a conscious decision, these actions resulted in California Public Utilities Commission (CPUC) giving up virtually all ability to control wholesale and retail prices in the state.

A second important feature of the regulatory process in the United States is that the Federal Power Act still requires FERC to ensure that wholesale prices are just and reasonable, even if prices are set through a bilateral negotiation or through the operation of a bid-based wholesale electricity market. FERC recognizes that markets can set prices substantially in excess of just and reasonable levels, typically because suppliers are exercising unilateral market power. FERC has also established that just and reasonable prices are set through market mechanisms when no supplier exercises unilateral market power. Wolak (2003b, 2003d) discusses the details of how FERC uses this logic to determine whether to allow a supplier to sell at market-determined prices, rather than at cost-of-service prices. If a supplier can demonstrate that it has no ability to exercise unilateral market power or there are mechanisms in place that mitigate its ability to exercise unilateral market power, the supplier can sell at market-determined prices. FERC uses a market structure-based procedure to make this assessment. Wolak (2003b) points out a number of flaws in this procedure. Bushnell (2005) discusses an alternative approach that makes use of oligopoly models and demonstrates its usefulness with an application to the California electricity market.

4.3 Wholesale Electricity Markets and
Industry-Level Regulatory Oversight

This section describes the characteristics of the technology of electricity supply and the political and economic constraints facing the industry that make it extremely difficult to design wholesale electricity markets that consistently achieve competitive outcomes—market prices close to those that would be predicted by price-taking behavior by market participants. The extreme susceptibility of wholesale electricity markets to the exercise of unilateral market power and the massive wealth transfers from consumers to producers that can occur in a very short period of time as a result make regulatory oversight beyond that provided by antitrust law essential to protecting consumers from costly market failures. The remainder of this section contrasts the major challenges facing the regulatory process in the wholesale market regime relative to the vertically integrated regulated monopoly regime.

4.3.1   Why Electricity Is Different from Other Products

It is difficult to conceive of an industry more susceptible to the exercise of unilateral market power than electricity. It possesses virtually all of the product characteristics that enhance the ability of suppliers to exercise unilateral market power.

Supply must equal demand at every instant in time and each location of the network. If this does not happen then the transmission network can become unstable and brownouts and blackouts can ensue, such as the one that occurred in the eastern United States and Canada on August 13, 2003. It is very costly to store electricity. Constructing significant storage facilities typically requires substantial up-front costs and more than 1 MWh of energy must be produced and consumed to store 1 MWh of energy. Production of electricity is subject to extreme capacity constraints in the sense that it is impossible to get more than a prespecified amount of energy from a generation unit in an hour.

As noted in section 4.2.2, delivery of the product consumed must take place through a potentially congested, looped transmission network. If a supplier owns a portfolio of generation units connected at different locations in the transmission network, how these units are operated can congest the transmission path into a given geographic area and thereby limit the number of suppliers able to compete with those located on the other side of the congested interface. The example presented in figure 4.7 with the capacity of link AB being equal to 40 MW and the capacities of links AC and BC each equal to 100 MW illustrates this point. If all of a supplier's generation units are located at node A and all load is at node B, the firm at node A can supply at most 60 MW of energy to final consumers. If demand at node A is greater than 60 MW, then the additional energy must come from a supplier at node B. For example, if the demand at node B is 100 MW, because the capacity of the transmission link AB is 40 MW, the supplier at node B is a monopolist facing a residual demand of 40 MW, if the supplier at node A is providing 60 MW.

Historically, how electricity has been priced to final consumers makes wholesale demand extremely inelastic, if not perfectly inelastic, with respect to the hourly wholesale price. In the United States, customers are typically charged a single fixed price or according to a fixed nonlinear price schedule for each kilowatt hour (KWh) they consume during the month regardless of the value of the wholesale price when each KWh is consumed. Paying according to a fixed retail price schedule implies that these customers have hourly demands with zero price elasticity with respect to the hourly wholesale price. The primary reason for this approach to retail pricing is that most electric meters are only capable of recording the total amount of KWh consumed between consecutive meter readings, which typically occur at monthly intervals. Consequently, a significant economic barrier to setting retail electricity prices that reflect real-time wholesale market conditions is the availability of a meter on the customer's premise that records hourly consumption for each hour of the month.

There is growing empirical evidence that all classes of customers can respond to short-term wholesale price signals if they have the metering technology to do so. Patrick and Wolak (1999) estimate the price responsiveness of large industrial and commercial customers in the United Kingdom to half-hourly wholesale prices and find significant differences in the average half-hourly demand elasticities across types of customers and half hours of the day. Wolak (2006) estimates the price responsiveness of residential customers in California to a form of real-time pricing that shares the risk of responding to hourly prices between the retailer and the final customer. The California Statewide Pricing Pilot (SPP) selected samples of residential, commercial, and industrial customers and subjected them to various forms of real-time pricing plans in order to estimate their price responsiveness. Charles River Associates (2004) analyzed the results of the SPP experiments and found precisely estimated price responses for all three types of customers. More recently, Wolak (2011a) reports on the results of a field experiment comparing the price responsiveness of households on a variety of dynamic pricing plans. For all of the pricing plans, Wolak found large demand reductions in response to increases in hourly retail electricity prices across all income classes.

Although all of these studies find statistically significant demand reductions in response to various forms of short-term price signals, none are able to assess the long-run impacts of requiring customers to manage short-time wholesale price risk. Wolak (2013) describes the increasing range of technologies available to increase the responsiveness of a customer to short-term price signals. However, customers have little incentive to adopt these technologies unless state regulators are willing to install hourly meters and require customers to manage short-term price risk.

For the reasons discussed in section 4.7, the vast majority of utilities that have managed to install hourly meters on the premises of some of their customers find it extremely difficult to convince state PUCs to require these customers to pay retail prices that vary with wholesale market conditions. Wolak (2013) offers an explanation for this regulatory outcome and suggests a process for overcoming the economic and political constraints on more active demand-side participation in short-term wholesale electricity markets.

A final factor enhancing the ability of suppliers to exercise unilateral market power is that the potential to realize economies of scale in electricity production historically favored large generation facilities, and in most wholesale markets the vast majority of these facilities are owned by a relatively small number of firms. This generation capacity ownership also tends to be concentrated in small geographic areas within these regional wholesale markets, which increases the potential for the exercise of unilateral market power in smaller geographic areas.

All of the abovementioned factors also make wholesale electricity markets substantially less competitive the shorter the time lag is between the date the sale is negotiated and the date delivery of the electricity occurs. In general, the longer the time lag between the agreement to sell and the actual delivery of the electricity, the larger is the number of suppliers that are able to compete to provide that electricity. For example, if the time horizon between sale and delivery is more than two years, then in virtually all parts of the United States new entrants can compete with existing firms to provide the desired energy. As the time horizon between sale and delivery shortens, more potential suppliers are excluded from providing this energy. For example, if the time lag between sale and delivery is only one month, then it is hard to imagine that a new entrant could compete to provide this electricity. It is virtually impossible to site, install, and begin operating even a small new generation unit in one month.

Although it is hard to argue that there is a strictly monotone relationship between the time horizon to delivery and the competitiveness of the forward energy market, the least competitive market is clearly the real-time energy market because so few suppliers are able to compete to provide the necessary energy. Only suppliers operating their units in real time with unloaded capacity or quick-start combustion turbines at locations in the transmission network that can actually supply the energy needed are able to compete to provide it.[4]

For this reason, real-time prices are typically far more volatile than day-ahead prices, which are far more volatile than month-ahead or year-ahead prices. An electricity retailer would be willing to pay $1,000/MWh for 10 MWh in the real-time market, or even $5,000/MWh, if that meant keeping the lights on for its customers. However, it is unlikely that this same load-serving entity would pay much above the long-run average cost of production for this same 10 MWh electricity to be delivered two years in the future, because there are many entrants as well as existing firms willing to sell this energy at close to the long-run average cost of production.

This logic illustrates that system-wide market power in wholesale electricity markets is a relatively short-lived phenomenon if the barriers to new entry are sufficiently low. If system conditions arise that allow existing suppliers to exercise unilateral market power in the short-term market, they are also able to do so to varying degrees in the forward market at time horizons to delivery up to the time it takes for significant new entry to occur. In most wholesale electricity markets, this time horizon is between eighteen months to two years. Therefore, if opportunities arise for suppliers to exercise unilateral market power in the short-term energy market, unless these system conditions change or are expected to change in the near future, suppliers can also exercise unilateral market power in the forward market for deliveries up to eighteen months to two years into the future.[5] Although these opportunities to exercise system-wide market power are transient, the experience from a number of wholesale electricity markets has demonstrated that suppliers with unilateral market power are able to raise market prices substantially during this time period, which can lead to enormous wealth transfers from electricity consumers to producers, even for periods as short as three months.

Electricity suppliers possess differing abilities to exercise system-wide and local market power. System-wide market power arises from the capacity constraints in the production and the inelasticity of the aggregate wholesale demand for electricity, ignoring the impact of the transmission network. Local market power is the direct result of the fact that all electricity must be sold through a transmission network with a finite carrying capacity. The

4. A generation unit has unloaded capacity if its instantaneous output is less than the unit's maximum instantaneous rate of output. For example, a unit with a 500 MW maximum instantaneous rate of output (capacity) operating at 400 MW has 100 MW of unloaded capacity.
5. Wolak (2003b) documents this phenomenon for the case of the California electricity market during the winter of 2001. Energy purchased at that time for delivery during the summer of 2003 sold for approximately $50/MWh, whereas energy to be delivered during the summer of 2001 sold for approximately $300/MWh, and the summer of 2002 for approximately $150/MWh.

geographic distribution of generation ownership and demand interact with the structure of the transmission network to create circumstances when a small number of suppliers or even one supplier is the only one able to meet an energy need at a given location in the transmission network.

If electricity did not need to be delivered through a potentially congested transmission network subject to line losses, then it is difficult to imagine that any supplier could possess substantial system-wide market power if the relevant geographic market was the entire United States. There are a large number of electricity suppliers in the United States, none of which controls a significant fraction of the total installed capacity in the United States. Consequently, the market power that an electricity supplier possesses fundamentally depends on the size of the geographic market it competes in, which depends on the characteristics of the transmission network and location of final demand.

Borenstein, Bushnell, and Stoft (2000) demonstrate this point in the context of a two-node model of quantity-setting competition between suppliers at each node potentially serving demand at both nodes. They find that small increases in the capacity of the transmission line between the two locations can substantially increase the competitiveness of market outcomes at the two locations. One implication of this result is that a supplier has the ability to exercise local market power regardless of the congestion management protocols used by the wholesale market. In single-price markets, zonal-pricing markets, and nodal-pricing markets, local market power arises because the existing transmission network does not provide the supplier with sufficient competition to discipline its bidding behavior into the wholesale market.[6] This is particularly the case in the United States, where the rate of investment in the transmission network has persistently lagged behind the rate of investment in new generation capacity until very recently. Hirst (2004) documents this decline in the rate of investment in transmission capacity up to the start of industry restructuring in the United States in the late 1990s.

Most of the existing transmission networks in the United States were designed to support a vertically integrated utility regime that no longer exists. Particularly around large population centers and in geographically remote areas, the vertically integrated utility used a mix of local generation units and transmission capacity to meet the annual demand for electricity in the region. Typically, the utility supplied the region's base load energy needs from distant inexpensive units using high-voltage transmission lines. It used expensive generating units located near the load centers to meet

---

6. A single price market sets one price of electricity for the entire market. A zonal-pricing market sets different prices for different geographic regions or zones when there is transmission congestion between adjacent zones. A nodal-pricing model sets a different price for each node (withdrawal or injection points in the transmission network) if there are transmission constraints between these nodes.

the periodic demand peaks throughout the year. This combination of local generation and transmission capacity to deliver distant generation was the least-cost system-wide strategy for serving the utility's total demand in the former regime.

The transmission network that resulted from this strategy by the vertically integrated monopoly for serving its retail customers creates local market power problems in the new wholesale market regime because now the owner of the generating units located close to the load center may not own, and certainly does not operate, the transmission network. The owner of the local generation units is often unaffiliated with the retailers serving customers in that geographic area. Consequently, during the hours of the year when system conditions require that some energy be supplied from these local generation units, it is profit maximizing for their owners to bid whatever the market will bear for any energy they provide.

This point deserves emphasis: the bids of the units within the local area must be taken before lower-priced bids from other firms outside this area because the configuration of the transmission network and location of demand makes these units the only ones physically capable of meeting the energy need. Without some form of regulatory intervention, these suppliers must be paid at their bid price in order to be willing to provide the needed electricity. The configuration of the existing transmission network and the geographic distribution of generation capacity ownership in all US wholesale markets and a number of wholesale markets around the world results in a frequency and magnitude of substantial local market power for certain market participants that if left unmitigated could earn the generation unit owners enormous profits and therefore cause substantial harm to consumers. Designing regulatory interventions to limit the exercise of local market power is a major market design challenge.

4.3.2   Regulatory Challenges in Wholesale Market Regime

The primary regulatory challenge of the wholesale electricity market regime is limiting the exercise of unilateral market power by market participants. The explicit exercise of unilateral market power is not possible in the vertically integrated monopoly regime because the regulator, not a market mechanism, sets the price the firm is allowed charge. This is the primary reason why a wholesale electricity market requires substantially more sophistication and economic expertise from the regulatory process at both the federal and state levels than is necessary under the vertically integrated monopoly regime.

The regulatory process for the wholesale market regime must limit the exercise of unilateral market power in the industry segments where market mechanisms are used to set prices. The regulatory process must also determine the allowed revenues and prudency of investment decisions by the transmission and distribution network owners, the two monopoly segments of the industry. However, different from the vertically integrated utility regime, these investment decisions can impact wholesale electricity market outcomes. Specifically, the capacity of the transmission link can impact the number of independent suppliers able to compete to provide electricity at a given location in the transmission network, which exerts a direct influence on wholesale electricity prices.

The major regulatory challenge in the wholesale market regime is how to design market-based mechanisms for the wholesale and retail segments of the industry that cause suppliers to produce in a least-cost manner and set prices that come as close as possible to recovering only their production costs. This is essentially the same goal as the vertically integrated utility regulatory process, but it requires far more sophistication and knowledge of economics and engineering to accomplish because firms have far greater discretion to foil the regulator's goals through their unilateral actions. They can withhold output from their generation units and offer these generation units into the market at prices that far exceed each unit's variable cost of production in order to raise the market-clearing price. Firms can also use their ownership of transmission assets and financial transmission rights to increase their revenues from participating in the wholesale market. The combined federal and state regulatory process must determine what wholesale and retail market rules will make it in the unilateral interest of market participants to set wholesale and retail prices as close as possible to those that would emerge from price-taking behavior by all market participants. This is the essence of the market design problem.

4.4 Market Design Process

This section provides a theoretical framework for describing the important features of the market design process. It is first described in general terms using a principal-agent model. The basic insight of this perspective is that once market rules are set, participants maximize their objective functions, typically expected profits for privately owned market participants, subject to the constraints imposed on their behavior by these market rules. The market designer must therefore anticipate how market participants will respond to any market rule in order to craft a design that ultimately achieves its objectives. The technology of supplying electricity described in section 4.2.2 and the regulatory structure governing the industry described in section 4.2.3 also place constraints on the market design process. This section introduces the concept of a residual demand curve to summarize the constraints imposed on each market participant by the market rules, technology of producing electricity, and regulatory structure of the industry and uses it to illustrate the important dimensions of the market design process for wholesale electricity.

For the purposes of this discussion, I assume that the goal of the market design process is to achieve the lowest possible annual average retail price of electricity consistent with the long-term financial viability of the industry. Long-term financial viability of the industry implies that these retail prices are sufficient to fund the necessary new investment to meet demand growth and replace depreciated assets into the indefinite future. Other goals for the market design process are possible, but this one seems most consistent with the goal of state-level regulatory oversight in the vertically integrated monopoly regime.

4.4.1   Dimensions of Market Design Problem

There are two primary dimensions of the market design problem. The first is the extent to which market mechanisms versus regulatory processes are used to set the prices consumers pay. The second is the extent to which market participants are government versus privately owned. Given the technologies for producing and delivering electricity to final consumers, the market designer faces two basic challenges. First is how to cause producers to supply electricity in both a technically and allocatively efficient manner. Technically efficient production obtains the maximum amount of electricity for given quantity of inputs, such as capital, labor, materials, and input energy. Allocatively efficient production uses the minimum cost mix of inputs to produce a given level of output.

The second challenge is how to set the prices for the various stages of the production process that provide strong incentives for technically and allocatively efficient production, yet only recover production costs including a return on the capital invested. This process involves choosing a point in the continuum between the market and regulation and the continuum between government and private ownership for each segment of the electricity supply industry.

Conceptually, the market designer maximizes its objective function by choosing the number and sizes of each market participant and the rules for determining the revenues received by each market participant. There are two key constraints on the market designer's optimization problem implied by the behavior of market participants. The first is that once the market designer chooses the rules for translating a market participant's actions into the revenues it receives, each market participant will choose a strategy that maximizes his payoff given the rules set by the market designer. This constraint implies that the market designer must recognize that all market participants will maximize their profits given the rules the market designer selects. The second constraint is that each market participant must expect to receive from the compensation scheme chosen by the market designer more than its opportunity cost of participating in the market. The first constraint is called the individual rationality constraint because it assumes each market participant will behave in a rational (expected payoff-maximizing) manner. The second constraint is called the participation constraint, because it implies that firms must find participation in the market more attractive than their next best alternative.

4.4.2 The Principal-Agent Problem

To make these features of the market design problem more concrete, it is useful to consider a simple special case of this process—the principal-agent model. Here a single principal designs a compensation scheme for a single agent that maximizes the principal's expected payoff subject to the agent's individual rationality constraint and participation constraint. Let $W(x, s)$ denote the payoff of the principal given the observable outcome of the interaction, x, and state of the world, s. The observable outcome, x, depends on the agent's action, a, and the true state of the world, s. Writing x as the function $x(a, s)$ denotes the fact that it depends on the both of these variables.

Let $V(a, y, s)$ equal the payoff of the agent given the action taken by the agent, a, the compensation scheme set by the principal, $y(x)$, and the state of the world, s. The principal's action is to design the compensation scheme, $y(x)$, a function that relates the outcome observed by the principal, x, to the payment made to the agent.

With this notation, it is possible to define the two constraints facing the principal in designing $y(x)$. The individual rationality constraint on the agent's behavior is that it will choose its action, a, to maximize its payoff $V(a, y, s)$ (or the expected value of this payoff) given $y(x)$ and s (or the distribution of s). The participation constraint implies that the compensation scheme $y(x)$ set by the principal must allow the agent to achieve at least its reservation level of utility or expected utility, V^*.

There are two versions of this basic model. The first assumes that the agent does not observe the true state of the world when it takes its action, and the other assumes the agent observes s before taking its action. In the first case, the agent's choice is:

$$a^* = \text{argmax}_{(a)} E_s[V(a, y(x), s)],$$

where $E_s(.)$ denotes the expectation with respect to the distribution of s. The participation constraint is $E_s(V(a^*, y(x^*), s)) > V^*$, where $x^* = x(a^*, s)$, which implies that the agent expects to receive utility greater than its reservation utility. In the second case, the agent's problem is:

$$a^*(s) = \text{argmax}_{(a)} V(a, y(x), s),$$

and the participation constraint is $V(a^*(s), y(x^*), s) > V^*$ for all s, where $x^* = x(a^*(s), s)$ in this case.

An enormous number of bilateral economic interactions fit this generic principal-agent framework. Examples include the client-lawyer, patient-doctor, lender-borrower, employer-worker, and firm owner–manager interactions. A client seeking legal services designs a compensation scheme for her lawyer that depends on the observable outcomes (such as the verdict in the case) that causes the lawyer to maximize the client's expected payoff function subject to constraint the lawyer will take actions to maximize his expected payoff given this compensation scheme and the fact that the lawyer must find the compensation scheme sufficiently attractive to take on the case. Another example is the firm owner designing a compensation scheme that causes the manager to maximize the expected value of the owner's assets subject to the constraint that the firm manager will take actions to maximize her expected payoff given the scheme is in place and the fact that it must provide a higher expected payoff to the manager than she could receive elsewhere.

4.4.3   Applying the Principal-Agent Model to the Market Design Process

The regulator-utility interaction is a principal-agent model directly relevant to electricity industry restructuring. In this case, the regulator designs a scheme for compensating the vertically integrated utility for the actions that it takes recognizing that once this regulatory mechanism is in place the utility will attempt to maximize its payoff function subject to this regulatory mechanism. In this case, $y(x)$, would be the mechanism used by the regulator to compensate the firm for its actions. For example, under a simple ex post cost-of-service regulatory mechanism, x would be the output produced by the firm, and $y(x)$ would be the firm's total cost of providing this output. Under a price cap regulatory mechanism, x would be the change in the consumer price index for the US economy and $y(x)$ would be the total revenues the firm receives, assuming it serves all demand at the price set by this regulatory mechanism. The incentives for firm behavior created by any potential regulatory mechanism can be studied within the context of this principal-agent model.

This modeling framework is also useful for understanding the incentives for firm behavior in a market environment. A competitive market is another possible way to compensate a firm for the actions that it takes. For example, the regulator could require this firm and other firms to bid their willingness to supply as a function of price and only choose the firms with bids below the lowest price necessary to meet the aggregate demand for the product. In this case x can be thought of as the firm's output and $y(x)$ the firm's total revenues from producing x and being paid this market-clearing price per unit sold. Viewed from this perspective, markets are simply another regulatory mechanism for compensating a firm for the actions that it takes.

It is well known that profit-maximizing firms that are not constrained by a regulatory price-setting process have a strong incentive to produce their output in a technically and allocatively efficient manner. However, it is also well known that profit-maximizing firms have no unilateral incentive to pass on these minimum production costs in the price they charge to consumers. Only when competition among firms is sufficiently vigorous will output prices equal the marginal cost of the highest cost unit produced.

Economic theory provides conditions under which a market will yield an optimal solution to the problem of causing the suppliers to provide their output to consumers at the lowest possible price. One of these conditions is the requirement that suppliers are atomistic, meaning that all producers believe they are so small relative to the market that they have no ability to influence the market price through their unilateral actions. Unfortunately, this condition is unlikely to hold for the case of electricity given the size of most market participants before the reform process starts. These firms recognize that if they remain large, they will have the ability to influence both market and political outcomes through their unilateral actions. Moreover, the minimum efficient scale of electricity generation, transmission, and distribution is such that it is unlikely to be least cost for the industry as a whole to separate electricity production into a large number of extremely small firms. So there is an underlying economic justification for allowing these firms to remain large, although certainly not as large as they would like to be. This is one reason why the electricity market design process is so difficult. This problem is particularly acute for small countries or regions without substantial transmission interconnections with neighboring countries or regions.

This principal-agent model is also useful for understanding why industry outcomes can differ so dramatically depending on whether the industry is government or privately owned. First, the objective function of the firm's owner differs across the two regimes. Under government ownership all of the citizens of the country are shareholders. These owners are also severely limited in the sorts of mechanisms they can design to compensate the management of the firm. For example, there is no liquid market for selling their ownership stake in this firm. It is virtually impossible for them to remove the management of this firm. In contrast, a shareholder in a privately owned firm has a clearly defined and legally enforceable property right that can be sold in a liquid market. If a shareholder owns enough of the firm or can get together with other large shareholders, they can remove the management of the company. Finally, by selling their shares, shareholders can severely limit the ability of the company to raise capital for new investment. In contrast, the government-owned firm obtains the funds necessary for new investment primarily through the political process.

This discussion illustrates the point that although government-owned and privately owned firms have access to the same technologies to generate, transmit, and distribute electricity, dramatically different industry outcomes in terms of the mix of generation capacity installed, the price consumers pay, and the amount they consume can occur because the schemes for compensating each firm's management differ and the owners of the two firms have different objective functions and different sets of feasible mechanisms for compensating their management. Applying the principal-agent model to the issue of government versus private ownership implies that different industry outcomes should occur if a government-owned vertically integrated geographic monopolist provides electricity to the same geographic area that a privately owned geographic monopolist previously served, even if both monopolists face the same regulatory mechanism for setting the prices they charge to retail consumers.

Applying the logic of the principal-agent model at the level of the regulator-firm interaction as opposed to the firm owner–management interaction implies an additional source of differences in market outcomes if, as is often the case, the government-owned monopoly faces a different regulatory process than the privately owned monopoly. Laffont and Tirole (1991) build on this basic insight to construct a theoretical framework to study the relative advantages of public versus private ownership. They formulate a principal-agent model between the management of the publicly owned firm and the government in which the cost of public ownership is "suboptimal investment by the firm's managers in those assets that can be redeployed to serve the goals pursued by the public owners" (Laffont and Tirole 1991, 84). The cost of private ownership in their model is the classical conflict between the desire of the firm's shareholders for it to maximize profits and the regulator's desire to limit these profits. Laffont and Tirole (1991) find that the existence of these two agency relationships does not allow a general prediction about the relative social efficiency of public versus private ownership, although the authors are able to characterize circumstances where one ownership form would dominate the other.

In the wholesale market regime, the extent of government participation in the industry creates an additional source of differences in industry outcomes. As Laffont and Tirole (1991) argue, the nature of the principal-agent relationship between the firm's owner and its management is different under private ownership versus government ownership. Consequently, an otherwise identical government-owned firm can be expected to behave differently in a market environment from how this firm would behave if it were privately owned. This difference in firm behavior yields different market outcomes depending on the ownership status (government versus privately owned) of the firms in the market.

Consequently, in its most general form, the market design problem is composed of multiple layers of principal-agent interactions where the same principal can often interact with a number of agents. For the case of a competitive wholesale electricity market, the same regulator interacts with all of the firms in the industry. The market designer must recognize the impact of all of these principal-agent relationships in designing an electricity supply industry to achieve his market design goals. The vast majority of electricity market design failures result from ignoring the individual rationality constraints implied by both the regulator-firm and firm owner–management principal-agent relations. The individual rationality constraint most often ignored is that privately owned firms will maximize their profits from participating in a wholesale electricity market. It is important to emphasize that this individual rationality constraint holds whether or not the privately owned profit-maximizing firm is one of a number of firms in a market environment or a single vertically integrated monopolist. The only difference between these two environments is the set of actions that the firm is legally able to take to maximize its profits.

4.4.4   Individual Rationality under a Market Mechanism versus a Regulatory Process

The set of actions available to firms subject to market pricing is different from those available to it in a price-regulated monopoly environment. For example, under market pricing, firms can increase their profits by both reducing the costs of producing a given level of output or by increasing the price they charge for this output. By contrast, under the regulated-monopoly environment, the firm does not set the price it receives for its output.

Defining the incentive constraint for a privately owned firm operating in an electricity market is relatively straightforward. If the firm would like to maximize profits, it has a strong incentive to produce its output at minimum cost. In other words, the firm will produce in a technically and allocatively efficient manner. However, the firm has little incentive to set a price that only recovers these production costs. In fact, the firm would like to take actions to raise the price it receives above both the cost of producing its output. Profit-maximizing behavior implies that the firm will choose a price or level of output such that the increase in revenue it earns from supplying one more unit equals the additional cost that it incurs from producing one more unit of output.

Figure 4.8 provides a simple model of the unilateral profit-maximizing behavior for a supplier in a bid-based electricity market. Let Q_d equal the level of market demand for a given hour and $SO(p)$ the aggregate willingness to supply as a function of the market price of all other market participants besides the firm under consideration. Part (a) of figure 4.8 plots the inelastic aggregate demand curve and the upward sloping willingness-to-supply curve of all other firms besides the one under consideration. Part (b) subtracts this aggregate supply curve for other market participants from the market demand to produce to the residual demand curve faced by this supplier, $DR(p) = Q_d - SO(p)$. This panel also plots the marginal cost curve for this supplier, as well as the marginal revenue curve associated with $DR(p)$.

The intersection of this marginal revenue curve with the supplier's marginal cost curve yields the profit-maximizing level of output and market price for this supplier given the bids submitted by all other market participants. This price-quantity pair is denoted by (P^*, Q^*) in part (b) of figure 4.8. Profit-maximizing behavior by the firm implies the following relation-

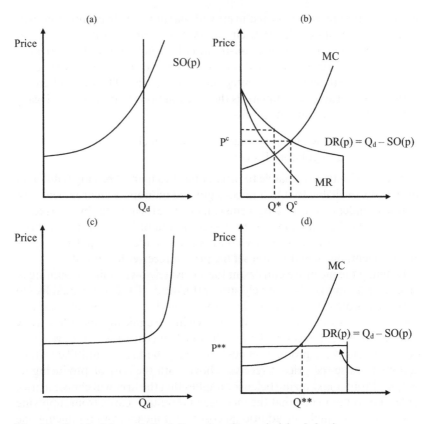

Fig. 4.8   Residual demand elasticity and profit-maximizing behavior

ship between the marginal cost at Q^*, which I denote by $MC(Q^*)$, and P^* and ε, the elasticity of the residual demand at P^*:

$$(1) \qquad \frac{P^*-MC(Q^*)}{P^*} = -\frac{1}{\varepsilon},$$

where $\varepsilon = DR'(P^*)*(P^*/DR(P^*))$. Because the slope of the firm's residual demand curve, $DR'(P^*)$, at this level of output is finite, the market price is larger than supplier's marginal cost. The price-quantity pair associated with the intersection of $DR(p)$ with the supplier's marginal cost curve is denoted (P^c, Q^c). It is important to emphasize that even though the price-quantity pair (P^c, Q^c) is often called the competitive outcome, producing at this output level is not unilateral profit maximizing for the firm if it faces a downward sloping residual demand curve. This is another way of saying that price-taking behavior—acting as if the firm had no ability to impact the market price—is never individually rational. It will only occur as an equilibrium outcome if the firm faces a flat residual demand curve.

A firm that influences market prices as shown in parts (a) and (b) of figure 4.8 is said to be exercising unilateral market power. A firm has the ability to exercise unilateral market power if it can raise the market price through its unilateral actions and profit from this price increase. We would expect all privately owned profit-maximizing firms to exercise all available unilateral market power, which is equivalent to saying that the firm satisfies its individual rationality constraint. Note that as long as a supplier faces a residual demand curve with any upward slope, it has some ability to exercise unilateral market power.

In virtually all oligopoly industries, the best information a researcher can hope to observe is the market-clearing price and quantity sold by each firm. However, in a bid-based wholesale electricity market, much more information is typically available to the analyst. The entire residual demand curve faced by a supplier, not just a single point, can be computed using bids and offers of all other market participants. The market demand Q_d is observable and the aggregate willingness to supply the curve of all other firms besides the one under consideration, $SO(p)$, can be computed from the willingness-to-supply offers of all firms. Therefore, it is possible to compute the elasticity of residual demand curve for any price level including the market-clearing price P^*. The absolute value of the inverse of the elasticity of the residual demand curve, $|1/\varepsilon|$, for $\varepsilon = DR'(P^*)*(P^*/DR(P^*))$, measures the percentage increase in the market-clearing price that would result from the firm under consideration, reducing its output by 1 percent.

Note that this measure depends on the level of market demand and the aggregate willingness-to-supply curve of the firm's competitors. Therefore, this inverse elasticity of the residual demand curve measures the firm's ability to raise market prices through its unilateral actions (given the level of market demand and the willingness to supply offers of its competitors). Parts (c) and (d) of figure 4.8 illustrate the extremely unlikely case that the supplier faces an infinitely elastic residual demand curve and therefore finds it in its unilateral profit maximizing to produce at the point that the market price is equal to its marginal cost. This point is denoted (P^{**}, Q^{**}). The supplier faces an infinitely elastic residual demand curve because the $SO(p)$ curve is infinity elastic at P^{**}, meaning that all other firms besides this supplier are able to produce all that is demanded if the price is above P^{**}.

Note that even in this extreme case the supplier is still satisfying the individual rationality constraint by producing at the point that the marginal revenue curve associated with $DR(p)$ crosses its marginal cost curve, as is required by equation (1). The only difference is that the marginal revenue curve associated with this residual demand curve also equals the supplier's average revenue curve, because $DR(p)$ is infinitely price elastic. Because the slope of the firm's residual demand curve is infinite, $1/\varepsilon$ is equal to zero, which implies that the firm has no ability to influence the market price through its unilateral actions and will therefore find unilaterally profit maximizing to produce at the point that the market-clearing price equals its marginal cost.

Figure 4.8 demonstrates that the individual rationality constraint in the context of a market mechanism is equivalent to the supplier exercising all available unilateral market power. Even in the extreme case of the infinitely elastic residual demand curve in part (d), the supplier still exercises all available unilateral market power and produces at the point that marginal revenue is equal to marginal cost. However, in this case the supplier cannot increase its profits by withholding output, because it has no ability to exercise unilateral market power.

Individual rationality in the context of explicit price regulation also implies that the firm will maximize profits given the mechanism for compensating it for its actions set by the regulator. However, in this case the firm is unable to set the price it charges consumers or the level of output it is willing to supply. The firm must therefore take more subtle approaches to maximizing its profits because the regulator sets the output price and requires the firm to supply all that is demanded at this regulated price. In this case the individual rationality constraint can imply that the firm will produce its output in a technically or allocatively inefficient manner because of how the regulatory process sets the price that the firm is able to charge.

The well-known Averch and Johnson (1962) model of cost-of-service regulation assumes that the regulated firm produces its output using capital, K, and labor, L, yet the price the regulator allows the firm to charge for capital services is greater than the actual price the regulated firm pays for capital services. This implies that a profit-maximizing firm facing the zero-profit constraint implied by this regulatory process will produce its output using capital more intensively relative to labor than would be the case if the regulatory process did not set a price for capital services different from the one the firm actually pays. The Averch and Johnson model illustrates a very general point associated with the individual rationality constraint in regulated settings: It is virtually impossible to design a regulatory mechanism that causes a privately owned profit-maximizing firm to produce in a least-cost manner if the firm's output price is set by the regulator based on its incurred production costs.

The usual reason offered for why the regulator is unable to set prices that achieve the market designer's goal of least cost production is that the regulated firm usually knows more about its production process or demand than the regulator. Although both the firm and regulator have substantial expertise in the technology of generating, transmitting, and distributing electricity to final consumers, the firm has a much better idea of precisely how these technologies are implemented to serve its demand. This informational asymmetry leads to disputes between the firm and the regulator over the minimum cost mode of production to serve the firm's demand. Consequently, the regulator can never know the minimum cost mode production to serve final demand.

Moreover, there are laws against the regulator confiscating the firm's assets through the prices it sets, and the firm is aware of this fact. This creates the potential for disputes between the firm and the regulator over the level of the regulated price that provides strong incentives for least-cost production, but does not confiscate the firm's assets. All governments recognize this fact and allow the firm an opportunity to subject a decision by the regulator about the firm's output price to judicial review. To avoid the expense and potential loss of credibility of a judicial review, the regulator may instead prefer to set a slightly higher regulated price to guarantee that the firm will not appeal its decision. This aspect of the regulatory process reduces the incentive the firm has to produce its output in a least cost manner.

Wolak (1994) performs an empirical study of the regulator-utility interaction between California water utilities and the CPUC, which specifies and estimates an econometric model of this principal-agent interaction and quantifies the magnitude of the distortions from minimum cost production induced by the informational asymmetries between firm and the regulator about the utility's production process. Even for the relatively simple technology of providing local water delivery services, where the extent of informational asymmetries between the firm and the regulator are likely to be small, Wolak (1994) finds that actual production costs are between 5 and 10 percent higher than they would be under least-cost production. Deviations from least-cost production in a vertically integrated electricity supply industry are likely to be much greater because the extent of the informational asymmetries between the firm and regulator about the firm's production process are likely to be much greater than in the water distribution industry. The substantially greater complexity of the process of generating and delivering electricity to final consumers implies more sources of informational asymmetries between the firm and regulator and therefore the potential for greater distortions from least-cost production.

The market designer does not need to worry about the impact of informational asymmetries between it and firms in a competitive market. Different from price-regulated environments, there are no laws against a competitive market setting prices that confiscate a firm's assets. Any firm that is unable to cover its costs of production at the market price must eventually exit the industry. Firms cannot file for a judicial review of the prices set by a competitive market. Competition among firms leads high-cost firms to exit the industry. There is no need to determine if a firm's incurred production costs are the result of the least-cost mode of production. If the market is sufficiently competitive and has low barriers to entry, then any firm that is able to remain in business must be producing its output at or close to minimum cost. Otherwise a more efficient firm could enter and profitably underprice this firm. The risk that firms not producing in a least-cost manner will be forced to exit creates much stronger incentives for least-cost production than would be the case under explicit price regulation, where the firm recognizes that the regulator does not know the least-cost mode of production and can exploit this fact through less technically and allocatively efficient production that may ultimately yield the firm higher profits.

The advantage of explicit price regulation is that the resulting output price should not deviate significantly from the actual average cost of producing the firm's output. However, the firm has very little incentive to make its actual mode of production equal to the least-cost mode of production. In contrast, the competitive regime provides very strong incentives for firms to produce in a least-cost manner. Unless the firm faces sufficient competition, it has little incentive to pass on only these efficiently incurred production costs in the prices charged to consumers.

This discussion shows that the potential exists for consumers to pay lower prices under either regime. Regulation may be favored if the market designer is able to implement a regulatory process that is particularly effective at causing the firm to produce in a least-cost manner and if the market designer is unable to establish a sufficiently competitive market so that prices are vastly in excess of the marginal cost of producing the last unit sold. Competition is favored if regulation is particularly ineffective at providing incentives for least-cost production or competition is particularly fierce. Nevertheless, in making the choice between a market mechanism and a regulatory mechanism, the market designer must typically make a choice between two imperfect worlds—an imperfect regulatory process or an imperfectly competitive market. Which mechanism should be selected depends on which one maximizes the market designer's objective function.

4.4.5   Individual Rationality Constraint under Government versus Private Ownership

The individual rationality constraint for a government-owned firm is difficult to characterize for two reasons. First, it is unclear what control the firm's owners are able to exercise over the firm's management and employees. Second, it is also unclear what the objective function of the firm's owners is. For the case of privately owned firms, there are well-defined answers to both of these questions. The firm's owners have clearly specified legal rights and their ownership shares can be bought and sold by incurring modest transactions costs. Because, keeping all other things equal, investors would like to earn the highest possible return on their investments, the firm's owners will attempt to devise a compensation scheme for the firm's management that causes them to maximize profits. In comparison, it is unclear if the government wants its firms to maximize profits. Earning more revenues than costs is clearly a priority, but once this is accomplished the government would most likely want to the firm to pursue other goals. This is the tension that

Laffont and Tirole (1991) introduce into their model of the behavior of publicly owned firms.

This lack of clarity in both the objective function of the government for the firms it owns and the set of feasible mechanisms the government can implement to compensate the firm's management has a number of implications. The first is that it is unlikely that the management of a government-owned firm will produce and sell its output in a profit-maximizing manner. Different from a privately owned firm, its owners are not demanding the highest possible return on their equity investments in the firm. Because a government-owned firm's management has little incentive to maximize profits, it also has little incentive to produce in a least-cost manner. This logic also implies that a government-owned firm has little incentive to attempt to raise output prices beyond the level necessary to cover its total costs of production. The second implication of this lack of clarity in objectives and feasible mechanisms is that the firm's management now has the flexibility to pursue a number of other goals besides minimizing the total cost of producing the output demanded by consumers.

Viewed from the perspective of the overall market design problem, one advantage of government ownership is that the pricing goals of the firm do not directly contradict the market designer's goal of the lowest possible prices consistent with the long-term financial viability of the industry. In the case of private ownership, the pricing incentives of the firm's management directly contradict the interests of consumers. The firm's management wants to raise prices above the marginal cost of the last unit produced, because of the desire of the firm's owner to receive the highest possible return on their investment in the company. Unless the firm faces a sufficient competition from other suppliers, which from the discussion of figure 4.8 is equivalent to saying that the firm faces a sufficiently elastic residual demand curve, this desire to maximize profits will yield market outcomes that reflect the exercise of significant unilateral market power.

However, it is important to emphasize that prices set by a government-owned firm may cause at least as much harm to consumers as prices that reflect the exercise of unilateral market power if the incentives for least-cost production by the government-owned firm are sufficiently muted and the regulator sets a price that at least recovers all of firm's incurred production costs. Although these prices may appear more benign because they only recover the actual costs incurred by the government-owned firm, they can be more harmful from a societal welfare perspective than the same level of prices set by a privately owned firm. This is because the privately owned firm has a strong incentive to produce in a technically and allocatively efficient manner and any positive difference between total revenues paid by consumers and the minimum cost of producing the output sold is economic profit or producer surplus.

Government-owned firms may produce in a technically and/or allocatively inefficient manner because of constraints imposed by its owner. For example, the government could require a publicly owned firm to hire more labor than is necessary. This is socially wasteful and therefore yields a reduced level of producer surplus relative to case of a privately owned firm producing its output in a least-cost manner. Because both outcomes, by assumption, have consumers paying the same price, the level of consumer surplus is unchanged across the two ownership structures, so that the level of total surplus is reduced as a result of government ownership because the difference between the market price and the variable cost of the highest cost unit operating under private ownership goes to the firm's shareholders in the form of higher profits.

Figure 4.9 provides a graphical illustration of this point. The step function labeled MC_p is the incurred marginal cost curve for the privately owned firm and the step function labeled MC_g is incurred marginal cost curve for the government-owned firm. I make the distinction between incurred and minimum cost to account for the fact that the management of the government-owned firm has less of an incentive to produce at minimum cost than does the privately owned firm. In this example, I assume the reason for this difference in marginal cost curves is that the government-owned firm produces in a technically inefficient manner by using more of each input to produce the

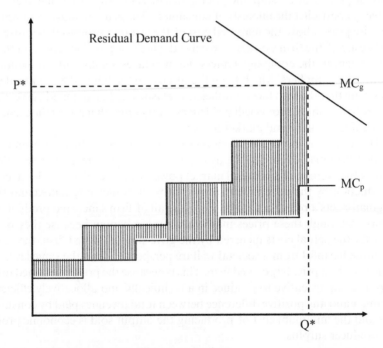

Fig. 4.9   Welfare loss from inefficient production

same level of output as the privately owned firm. Suppose that the profit-maximizing level of output for the privately owned firm given the residual demand curve plotted in figure 4.9 is Q^*, with a price of P^*. Suppose the government-owned firm behaves as if it were a price taker given its marginal cost curve and this residual demand curve, and assume that this price is also equal to the firm's average incurred cost at Q^*, $AC(Q^*)$. I have drawn the figure so that the intersection of the marginal cost curve of the government-owned firm with this residual demand curve occurs at the same price and quantity pair set by the unilateral profit-maximizing quantity offered by the privately owned firm.

Because the government-owned firm produces in a technically inefficient manner, it uses more of society's scarce resources to produce Q^* than the privately owned firm. Consequently, the additional benefit that society receives from having the privately owned firm produce the good is the shaded area between the two marginal cost curves in figure 4.9, which is the additional producer surplus earned by the privately owned firm because it produces in a technically and allocatively efficient manner but exercises significant unilateral market power.

This example demonstrates that even though the privately owned firm exercises all available unilateral market power, if the incentives for efficient production by government-owned firms are sufficiently muted, it may be preferable from the market designer's and society's perspective to tolerate some exercise of unilateral market power, rather than adopt a regime with government-owned firms setting prices equal to an extremely inefficiently incurred marginal cost or average cost of production.

If the government-owned firm is assumed to produce in an allocatively inefficient manner only, this same logic for consumers preferring private to government ownership holds. However, the societal welfare implications of government ownership versus private ownership are less clear because these higher production costs are caused by deviations from least-cost production rather than simply a failure to produce the maximum technically feasible output for a fixed set of inputs. For example, if the government-owned firm is forced to pay higher wages than private sector firms for equivalent workers because of political constraints, these workers from the government-owned firm would suffer a welfare loss if they were employed by a privately owned firm.

The example given in figure 4.9 may seem extreme, but there are number of reasons why it is reasonable to believe that a government-owned firm faces far less pressure from its owners to produce in a least cost manner relative to its privately owned counterpart. For example, poorly run privately owned companies can go bankrupt. If a firm consistently earns revenues less than its production costs, the firm's owners and creditors can force the firm to liquidate its assets and exit the industry. The experience from both industrialized and developing countries is that poorly run government-owned companies rarely go out of business. Governments can and almost always do fund unprofitable companies from general tax revenues. Even in the United States, there are a number of examples of persistently unprofitable government-owned companies receiving subsidies long after it is clear to all independent observers that these firms should liquidate their assets and exit the industry. Because government-owned companies have this additional source of funds to cover their incurred production costs, they have significantly less incentive to produce in a least-cost manner.

Megginson and Netter (2001) survey a number of empirical studies of the impact of privatization in nontransition economies and find general support for the proposition that it improves the firm's operating and financial performance. However, these authors emphasize that this improved financial performance does not always translate into increases in consumer welfare because private ownership can increase the incentive for firms to exercise unilateral market power. Shirley and Walsh (2000) also survey the empirical literature on the impact of privatization on firm performance. They conclude that the private ownership and competition are complements in the sense that the empirical evidence on private ownership improving firm performance is stronger when the private firm faces competition. They also argue that the relative performance improvements associated with private versus public ownership are greater in developing countries versus industrialized countries.

4.5 Dimensions of Wholesale Market Design Process

This section describes the five major ways that a market designer can reduce the incentive a supplier has to exercise unilateral market power in a wholesale electricity market. As discussed earlier, it is impossible to eliminate completely the ability that suppliers in a wholesale electricity market have to exercise unilateral market power. The best that a market designer can hope to do is reduce this ability to levels that yield market outcomes that come closer to achieving the market designer's goals than could be achieved with other feasible combinations of market and regulatory mechanisms. This means the market designer must recognize the individual rationality constraint that the firm will maximize profits given the rules set by the market designer and the actions taken by its competitors.

As the discussion of figure 4.8 demonstrates, the market designer reduces the ability of the firm to exercise the unilateral market by facing the firm with a residual demand curve that is as elastic as possible. As figure 4.8 itself demonstrates, the more elastic the supplier's residual curve demand is the less the firm's unilateral profit-maximizing actions are able to raise the market-clearing price. Consequently, the goal of designing a competitive electricity market is straightforward: face all suppliers with as elastic as possible residual demand curves during as many hours of the year as possible.

McRae and Wolak (2014) provide empirical evidence consistent with this goal for the four largest suppliers in the New Zealand wholesale electricity. They find that lower in absolute value half-hourly slopes of the residual demand curve faced by each supplier predict lower half-hourly offer prices by that supplier.

There are five primary mechanisms for increasing the elasticity of the residual demand curve faced by a supplier in a wholesale electricity market. The first is divestiture of capacity owned by this firm to a number of independent suppliers. Second is the magnitude and distribution across suppliers of fixed-price forward contracts to supply electricity to sold load-serving entities. Third is the extent to which final consumers are active participants in the wholesale electricity market. Fourth is the extent to which the transmission network has enough capacity to face each supplier with sufficient competition from other suppliers. The last is the extent to which regulatory oversight of the wholesale market provides strong incentives for all market participants to fulfill their contractual obligations and obey the market rules. We now discuss each of these mechanisms for increasing the elasticity of the residual demand curve facing a supplier.

4.5.1   Divestiture of Generation Capacity

To understand how the divestiture of a given amount of capacity into a larger number of independent suppliers can impact the slope of a firm's residual demand curve, consider the following simple example. Suppose there are ten equal sized firms, each of which owns 1,000 MW of capacity, and that the total demand in the hourly wholesale market is perfectly inelastic with respect to price and is equal to 9,500 MWh. Each firm knows that at least 500 MW of its capacity is needed to meet this demand, regardless of the actions of its competitors. Specifically, if the remaining nine firms bid all 1,000 MW of their capacity into the market, the tenth firm has a residual demand of at least 500 MWh at every bid price.

Mathematically, this means the value of the residual demand facing the firm, $DR(p)$, is positive at p_{max}, the highest possible bid price that a supplier can submit. When $DR(p_{max}) > 0$, the firm is said to be pivotal, meaning that at least $DR(p_{max})$ of its capacity is needed to serve demand. Figure 4.10 provides an example of this phenomenon. Let $SO_1(p)$ represent the aggregate willingness-to-supply curve of all other firms besides the firm under consideration and let Q_d represent the market demand. Part (b) of figure 4.10 shows that the firm is pivotal for $DR_1(p_{max})$ units of output, which in this example is equal to 500 MWh. In this circumstance, the firm is guaranteed total revenues of at least $DR_1(p_{max}) * p_{max}$, which it can achieve by bidding all of its capacity into the wholesale market at p_{max}.

To see the impact of requiring a firm to divest generation capacity on its residual demand curve, suppose that the firm in figure 4.10 was forced to sell off 500 MW of its capacity to a new or existing market participant.

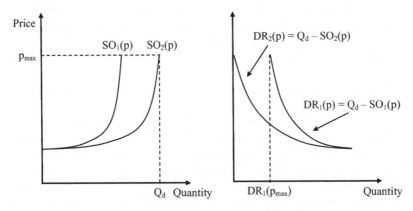

Fig. 4.10   The impact of capacity divestiture on a pivotal supplier

This implies that the maximum supply of all other firms is now equal to 9,500 MWh, the original 9,000 MWh plus the additional 500 MWh divested, which is exactly equal to the market demand. This means that the firm is no longer pivotal because its residual demand is equal to zero at p_{max}. Part (a) of figure 4.10 draws new bid supply curve of all other market participants besides the firm under consideration, $SO_2(p)$. For every price, I would expect this curve to lie to the right of $SO_1(p)$, the original bid supply curve. Part (b) plots the resulting residual demand curve for the firm using $SO_2(p)$. This residual demand curve, $DR_2(p)$, crosses the vertical axis at p_{max}, so that the elasticity of the residual demand curve facing the firm is now finite for all feasible prices. In contrast, for the case of $DR_1(p)$, the residual demand curve predivestiture, the firm faces a demand of at least $DR_1(p_{max})$ for all prices in the neighborhood of p_{max}.

This example illustrates a general phenomenon associated with structural divestiture: the firm that sells generation capacity now faces a more elastic residual demand curve, which causes it to bid more aggressively into the wholesale electricity market. This more aggressive bidding by the divested firm then faces all other suppliers with flatter residual demand curves, so they now find it optimal to submit flatter bid supply curves, which implies a flatter residual demand curve for the firm under consideration. Even in those cases when divestiture does not stop a supplier from being pivotal, the residual demand curve facing the firm that now has less capacity should still be more elastic, because more supply has been added to $SO(p)$, the aggregate bid supply function of all other firms besides the firm under consideration. This implies a smaller value for the firm's residual demand at all prices, as shown in figure 4.10.

This residual demand analysis illustrates why it is preferable to divest capacity to new entrants or small existing firms rather than to large existing firms. Applying the reverse of the logic described above to the existing supplier that purchases the divested capacity implies that this firm faces a residual demand that is likely to be larger at every price level. The acquiring firm now owns generation capacity that formerly had a willingness-to-supply curve that entered the acquiring firm's residual demand curve. The larger the amount of generation capacity owned by the acquiring firm before the divestiture occurs, the greater are the likely competition concerns associated with this acquisition.

4.5.2 Fixed-Price Forward Contracts and Vesting Contracts

In many industries wholesalers and retailers sign fixed-price forward contracts to manage the risk of spot price volatility. There are two additional reasons for wholesalers and retailers to sign fixed-price forward contracts in the electricity supply industry. First, fixed-price forward contract commitments make it unilaterally profit maximizing for a supplier to submit bids into the short-term electricity market closer to its marginal cost of production. This point is demonstrated in detail in Wolak (2000b). Second, fixed-price forward contracts can also precommit generation unit owners to a lower average cost pattern of output throughout the day. This logic implies that for the same sales price, a supplier with significant fixed-price forward contract commitments earns a higher per unit profit than one with a lower quantity of fixed-price forward contract commitments. Wolak (2007) demonstrates the empirical relevance of this point for a large supplier in the Australian electricity market.

To understand the impact of fixed-price forward contract commitments on supplier bidding behavior it is important to understand what a forward contract obligates a supplier to do. Usually fixed-price forward contracts are signed between suppliers and load-serving entities. These contracts typically give the load-serving entity the right to buy a fixed quantity of energy at a given location at a fixed price. Viewed from this perspective, a forward contract for supply of electricity obligates the seller to provide insurance against short-term price volatility at a prespecified location in the transmission network for a prespecified quantity of energy. The seller of the forward contract does not have to produce energy from its own generating facilities to provide this price insurance to the purchaser of the forward contract. However, one way for the seller of the fixed-price forward contract to limit its exposure to short-term price risk is to provide the contract quantity of energy from its own generation units.

This logic leads to another extremely important point about forward contracts that is not often fully understood by participants in a wholesale electricity market. Delivering electricity from a seller's own generation units is not always a profit-maximizing strategy given the supplier's forward contract obligations. This is also the reason why forward contracts provide strong incentives for suppliers to bid more aggressively (supply functions closer to the generation unit owner's marginal cost function) into the short-term wholesale electricity market.

To see these points, consider the following example taken from Wolak (2000b). Let $DR(p)$ equal the residual demand curve faced by the supplier with the forward contract obligation QC at a price of PC and a marginal cost of MC. For simplicity, I assume that the firm's marginal cost curve is constant, but this simplification does not impact any of the conclusions from the analysis. The firm's variable profits for this time period are:

$$(2) \qquad \pi(p) = (DR(p) - QC)(p - MC) + (PC - MC)QC.$$

The first term in (2) is equal to the profit or loss the firm earns from buying or selling energy in the short-term market at a price of p. The second term in (2) is the variable profits the firm earns from selling QC units of energy in the forward market at price PC. The firm's objective is to bid into the short-term market in order to set a market price, p, that maximizes $\pi(p)$. Because forward contracts are, by definition, signed in advance of the operation of the short-term market, from the perspective of bidding into the short-term market, the firm treats $(PC - MC)QC$ as a fixed payment it will receive regardless of the short-term price, p. Consequently, the firm can only impact the first term through its bidding behavior in the short-term market.

A supplier with a forward contract obligation of QC has a very strong incentive to submit bids that set prices below its marginal cost if it believes that $DR(p)$ will be less than QC. This is because the supplier is effectively a net buyer of $QC - DR(p)$ units of electricity, because it has already sold QC units in a forward contract. Consequently, it is profit maximizing for the firm to want to purchase this net demand at the lowest possible price. It can either do this by producing the power from its own units at a cost of MC, or purchasing the additional energy from the short-term market. If the firm can push the market price below its marginal cost, then it is profit maximizing for the firm to meet its forward contract obligations by purchasing power from the short-term market rather paying MC to produce it. Consequently, if suppliers have substantial forward contract obligations, then they have extremely strong incentives to keep market prices very low until the level of energy they actually produce is greater than their fixed-price forward contract quantity.

The competition-enhancing benefits of forward contract commitments from suppliers can be seen more easily by defining $DR_C(p) = DR(p) - QC$, the net of forward contract residual demand curve facing the firm, and $F = (PC - MC)QC$, the variable profits from forward contract sales. In terms of this notation the firm's variable profits become $\pi(p) = DR_C(p)(p - MC) + F$, which has exactly the same structure (except for F) as the firm's variable profits from selling electricity if it has no forward contract commitments. The only difference is that $DR_C(p)$ replaces $DR(p)$ in the expression for the supplier's variable profits. Consequently, profit-maximizing behavior implies that the firm will submit bids to set a price in the short-term market that satisfies equation (1) with $DR(p)$ replaced by $DR_C(p)$. This implies the following relationship between P^c, the ex post profit-maximizing price, the firm's marginal cost of production, MC, and ε^c, the elasticity of the net of forward contract quantity residual demand curve evaluated at P^c:

$$(3) \qquad \frac{P^c - MC}{P^c} = -\frac{1}{\varepsilon^c},$$

where $\varepsilon^c = DR_C{}'(P^c)*(P^c/DR_C(P^c))$.

The inverse of the elasticity of net of forward contract residual demand curve, $1/\varepsilon^c$, is a measure of the incentive (as opposed to ability) a supplier has to exercise unilateral market power. If the firm has some fixed-price forward contract obligations, then a given change in the firm's residual demand as a result of a 1 percent increase in the market price implies a much larger percentage change in the firm's net of forward contract obligations residual demand. For example, suppose that a firm is currently selling 100 MWh, but has 95 MWh of forward contract obligations. If a 1 percent increase in the market price reduces the amount that the firm sells by 0.5 MWh, then the elasticity of the firm's residual demand is $-0.5 = (0.5$ percent quantity reduction) $\div$ (1 percent price increase). The elasticity of the firm's residual demand net of its forward contract obligations is $-10 = (10$ percent net of forward contract quantity output reduction) $\div$ (1 percent price increase). Thus, the presence of fixed-price forward contract obligations implies a dramatically diminished incentive to withhold output to raise short-term wholesale prices, despite the fact that the firm has a significant ability to raise short-term wholesale prices through its unilateral actions. McRae and Wolak (2014) provide empirical evidence in support of this prediction for the four largest suppliers in the New Zealand electricity market.

In general, ε^c and ε are related by the following equation:

$$\varepsilon^c = \varepsilon\left(\frac{DR(p)}{DR(p) - QC}\right).$$

The smaller a firm's exposure to short-term prices—the difference between $DR(p)$ and QC—the more elastic ε^c is relative to ε, and the greater the divergence between the incentive versus ability the firm has to exercise unilateral market power.

Because $DR_C(p) = DR(p) - QC$, this implies that at same market price, p, and residual demand curve, $DR(p)$, the absolute value of the elasticity of the net of forward contract quantity residual demand curve is always greater than the absolute value of the elasticity of the residual demand curve. A simple proof of this result follows from the fact that $DR_C{}'(p) = DR'(p)$ for all prices and $QC > 0$, so that by rewriting the expressions for ε^c and ε, we obtain:

(4) $$\left|\varepsilon^{c}\right| = \left|DR'(p) * \frac{p}{DR(p) - QC}\right| > \left|\varepsilon\right| = \left|DR'(p) * \frac{p}{DR(p)}\right|.$$

Moreover, as long as $DR(p) - QC > 0$, the larger the value of QC, the greater is the difference between ε^{c} and ε, and the smaller is the expected profit-maximizing percentage markup of the market price above the firm's marginal cost of producing the last unit of electricity that it supplies with forward contract commitments versus no forward contract commitments. This result demonstrates that it is always unilateral profit maximizing, for the same underlying residual demand curve, for the supplier to set a lower price relative to its marginal cost if it has positive forward contract commitments.

This incentive to bid more aggressively into the short-term market if a supplier has substantial forward contracts also has implications for how a fixed quantity of forward contract commitments should be allocated among suppliers to maximize the benefits of these contracts to the competitiveness of the short-term market. Because a firm with forward contract obligations will bid more aggressively in the short-term market, this implies that all of its competitors will also face more elastic residual demand curves and therefore find it unilaterally profit maximizing to bid more aggressively in the short-term market. This more aggressive bidding will leave all other firms with more elastic residual demand curves, which should therefore make these firms bid more aggressively in the short-term market.

This virtuous cycle with respect to the benefits of forward contracting implies that a given amount of fixed-price forward contracts will have the greatest competitive benefits if it is spread out among all of the suppliers in the market roughly proportional to expected output under competitive market conditions. For example, if there are five firms and each them expects to sell 1,000 MW under competitive market conditions, then fixed-price forward contract commitments should be allocated equally across the firms to maximize the competitive benefits. If one firm expects to sell twice the output of other firms, then it should have roughly twice the forward contract commitments to load-serving entities that the other suppliers have.

Because of the short-term market efficiency benefits of substantial amounts of fixed-price forward contract commitments between suppliers and load-serving entities, most wholesale electricity markets begin operation with a large fraction of the final demand covered by fixed-price forward contracts. If a substantial amount of capacity is initially controlled by government-owned or privately owned monopolies, the regulator or market designer usually requires that most of these assets be sold to new entrants to create a more competitive wholesale market. These sales typically take place with a fixed-price forward contract commitment on the part of the new owner of the generation capacity to supply a substantial fraction of the expected output of the unit to electricity retailers at a fixed price. These contracts are typically called vesting contracts, because they are assigned to the unit as precondition for its sale. For example, if a 500 MW unit owned by the former monopolist is being sold, the regulator assigns a forward contract obligation on the new owner to supply 400 MW of energy each hour at a previously specified fixed price.

Vesting contracts accomplish several goals. The first is to provide price certainty for electricity retailers for a significant fraction of their wholesale energy needs. The second is to provide revenue certainty to the new owner of the generating facility. With a vesting contract the new owner of the generation unit in our example already has a revenue stream each hour equal to the contract price times 400 MWh. These two aspects of vesting contracts protect suppliers and loads from the volatility of short-term market prices because they only receive or pay the short-term price for production or consumption beyond the contract quantity. Finally, the existence of this fixed-price forward contract obligation has the beneficial impacts on the competitiveness of the short-term energy market described earlier.[7]

The primary causal factor in the dramatic increase in short-term electricity prices during the summer of 2000 in California is the fact that the three large retailers—Pacific Gas and Electric, Southern California Edison, and San Diego Gas and Electric—purchased virtually all of their energy and ancillary services requirements from the day-ahead, hour-ahead, and real-time markets. When the amount of imports available from the Pacific Northwest was substantially decreased as a result of reduced water availability during the late spring and summer of 2000, the fossil fuel suppliers in California found themselves facing the significantly less elastic residual demand curves for their output. This fact, documented in Wolak (2003c), made the unilateral profit-maximizing markups of price above the marginal cost of producing electricity for the five large fossil fuel suppliers in California substantially higher during the summer and autumn of 2000 than they had been during the previous two years of the market.

4.5.3   Active Participation of Final Demand in Wholesale Market

Consider an electricity market with no variation in demand and supply across all hours of the day. Under these circumstances, it would be possible to build enough generation capacity to ensure that all demand could be served at some fixed price. However, the reality of electricity consumption and generation unit and transmission network operation is that demand and supply vary over time, often in an unpredictable manner. There is always a risk that a generation unit or transmission line will fail or that a consumer will decide to increase or decrease their consumption. This implies that there is always some likelihood that available capacity will be insufficient to meet

7. The price of energy sold under a vesting contract can also be used by the seller, typically the government, to raise or lower the purchase price of a generation facility. For the same forward contract quantity, a higher fixed energy price in the vesting contract raises the purchase price of the facility.

demand. The increasing capacity share of renewable energy sources such as wind, solar, and small hydro because of ongoing efforts to reduce greenhouse gas emissions, further increases the likelihood of energy shortfalls. Electricity can only be produced from these resources when the wind is blowing, the sun is shining, or water is available behind the turbine.

There are two ways of eliminating a supply shortfall: either price must be increased to choke off demand, or demand must be randomly rationed. Random rationing is clearly an extremely inefficient way to ensure that supply equals demand. Many consumers willing to purchase electricity at the prevailing price are unable to do so. Moreover, as has been discovered by politicians in all countries where random rationing has occurred, the backlash associated with this can be devastating to those in charge. Moreover, the indirect costs of random rationing on the level of economic activity can be substantial. In particular, preparing for and dealing with rationing periods also leads to substantial losses in economic output.

A more cost-effective approach to dealing with a shortfall of available supply relative to the level of demand at the prevailing price is to allow the retail price to rise to the level necessary to cause a sufficient number of consumers to reduce their consumption to bring supply and demand back into balance. Consumers that pay the hourly price of electricity for their consumption are not fundamentally different from generation unit owners responding to hourly price signals from a system reliability perspective. Let $D(p)$ equal the consumer's hourly demand for electricity as function of the hourly price of electricity. Define $SN(p) = D(0) - D(p)$, where $D(0)$ is the consumer's demand for electricity at an hourly price equal to zero. The function $SN(p)$ is the consumer's true willingness supply curve for "negawatts," reductions in the amount of megawatts consumed. Because $D(p)$ is a downward sloping function of p, $SN(p)$ is an upward sloping function of p. A generator with a marginal cost curve equal to $SN(p)$ has the ability to provide the same hourly reliability benefits as this consumer. However, an electricity supplier has the incentive to maximize the profits it earns from selling electricity in the short-term market given its marginal cost function. By contrast, an industrial or commercial consumer with a negawatt supply curve, $SN(p)$, can be expected to bid a willingness to supply negawatts into the short-term market to maximize the profits it earns from selling its final output, which implies demand bidding to reduce the average price it pays for electricity.

Although a generation unit and consumer with an hourly meter may have the same true willingness-to-supply curve, each of them will use this curve to pursue different goals. The supplier is likely to use it to exercise unilateral market power and raise market prices, and the consumer is likely to use it to exercise unilateral market power to reduce the price it pays for electricity. Wolak (2013) describes how a load-serving entity with some consumers facing the hourly wholesale price or a large consumer facing the hourly price

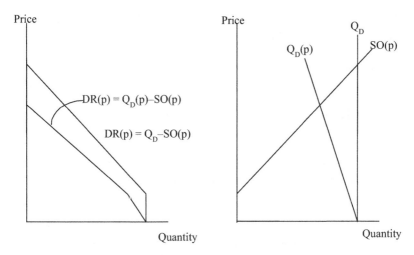

Fig. 4.11   Residual demand elasticity and price-responsive demand

could exercise market power on the demand side to reduce the average price it pays for a fixed quantity of electricity.

Besides allowing the system operator more flexibility in managing demand and supply imbalances, the presence of some consumers that alter their consumption in response to the hourly wholesale price also significantly benefits the competitiveness of the spot market. Figure 4.11 illustrates this point. The two residual demand curves are computed for the same value of $SO(p)$. For one, Q_D is perfectly inelastic. For the other, $Q_D(p)$ is price elastic. As shown in the diagram, the slope of the resulting residual demand curve using $Q_D(p)$ is always flatter than the slope of the residual demand curve using Q_D. Following the logic used for the case of forward contracts, it can be demonstrated that for the same price and same value of residual demand, the elasticity of the residual demand curve using $Q_D(p)$ is always greater than the one using Q_D, because the slope of the one using $Q_D(p)$ is equal to $DR'(p) = Q_D'(p) - SO'(p)$, which is larger in absolute value than $-SO'(p)$, the slope of the residual demand curve using Q_D. Consequently, the competitive benefit of having final consumers pay the hourly wholesale price is that all suppliers will face more elastic residual demand curves, which will cause them to bid more aggressively into the short-term market.

Politicians and policymakers often express the concern that subjecting consumers to real-time price risk will introduce too much volatility into their monthly bill. These concerns are, for the most part, unfounded as well as misplaced. Borenstein (2007) suggests a scheme for facing a consumer with a retail price that varies with the hourly wholesale price for her consumption above or below a predetermined load shape so that the consumer faces a monthly average price risk similar to a peak/off-peak time-of-use tariff.

It is important to emphasize that if a state regulatory commission sets a fixed retail price or fixed pattern of retail prices throughout the day (time-of-use prices), it must still ensure that over the course of the month or year, the retailer's total revenues less its transmission, distribution, and retailing costs, must cover its total wholesale energy costs. If the regulator sets this fixed price too low relative to the current wholesale price, then either the retailer or the government must pay the difference.

This is precisely the lesson learned by the citizens of California. When average wholesale prices rose above the average wholesale price implicit in the fixed retail price California consumers paid for electricity, retailers initially made up the difference. Eventually, these companies threatened to declare bankruptcy (in the case of Southern California Edison and San Diego Gas and Electric) and declared bankruptcy (in the case of Pacific Gas and Electric), and the state of California took over purchasing wholesale power at even higher wholesale prices. The option to purchase at a fixed price or fixed pattern of prices that does not vary with hourly system conditions is increasingly valuable to consumers and extremely costly to the government the more volatile are wholesale electricity prices.

This is nothing more than a restatement of a standard prediction from the theory of stock options that the value of a call option on a stock is increasing in the volatility of the underlying security. However, different from the case of a call option on a stock, the fact that all California consumers had this option available to them and were completely shielded from any spot price risk in their electricity purchases (but not in their tax payments) made wholesale prices more volatile. By the logic of figure 4.11, all suppliers faced a less elastic residual demand curve because all customers paid for their hourly wholesale electricity consumption at same fixed price or pattern prices rather than at the actual hourly real-time price. Therefore suppliers had a greater ability to exercise the unilateral market, which led to higher average prices and greater price volatility.

Charging final consumers the same default hourly price as generation units owners provides a strong incentive for them to become active participants in the wholesale market or purchase the appropriate short-term price hedging instruments from retailers to eliminate their exposure to short-term price risk. These purchases of short-term price hedging instruments by final consumers increases the retailer's demand for fixed-price forward contracts from generation unit owners, which reduces the amount of energy that is actually sold at the short-term wholesale price.

Perhaps the most important, but most often ignored, lesson from electricity restructuring processes in industrialized countries is the necessity of treating load and generation symmetrically. Symmetric treatment of load and generation means that unless a retail consumer signs a forward contract with an electricity retailer, the default wholesale price the consumer pays is the hourly wholesale price. This is precisely the same risk that a generation unit owner faces unless it has signed a fixed-price forward contract with a load-serving entity or some other market participant. The default price it receives for any short-term energy sales is the hourly short-term price. Just as very few suppliers are willing to risk selling all of their output in the short-term market, consumers should have similar preferences against too much reliance on the short-term market and would therefore be willing to sign a long-term contract for a large fraction of their expected hourly consumption during each hour of the month.

Consistent with Borenstein's (2007) logic, a residential consumer might purchase a right to buy a fixed load shape for each day at a fixed price for the next twelve months. This consumer would then be able to sell energy it does not consume during any hour at the hourly wholesale price or purchase any power it needs beyond this baseline level at that same price.[8] This type of pricing arrangement would result in a significantly less volatile monthly electricity bill than if the consumer made all of his purchases at the hourly wholesale price. If all customers purchased according to this sort of pricing plan then there would be no residual short-term price risk that the government needs to manage using tax revenues. All consumers manage the risk of high wholesale prices and supply shortfalls according to their preferences for taking on short-term price risk. Moreover, because all consumers have an incentive to reduce their consumption during high-priced periods, wholesale prices are likely to be less volatile. Symmetric treatment of load and generation does not mean that a consumer is prohibited from purchasing a fixed-price full requirements contract for all of the electricity they might consume in a month, only that the consumer must pay the full cost of supplying this product.

The major technological roadblock to symmetric treatment of load and generation is the necessary metering technology to allow consumption to be measured on an hourly versus monthly basis. Virtually all existing meters at the residential level and the vast majority at the commercial and industrial levels can only record total monthly consumption. Monthly meter reading means it is only possible to determine the total amount of KWh consumed between two consequence meter readings—the difference between the value on the meter at the end of the month and value at the beginning of the month is the amount consumed within the month. Without the metering technology necessary to record consumption for each hour of the month, it

---

8. Wolak (2013) draws an analogy between this pricing plan for electricity and how cell phone minutes are typically sold. Consumers purchase a fixed number of minutes per month and typically companies allow customers to rollover unused minutes to the next month or purchase additional minutes beyond these advance-purchase minutes at some penalty price. In the case of electricity, the price for unused KWhs and additional KWhs during a given hour is the real-time wholesale price.

is impossible to determine precisely how much a customer consumed during each hour of the month, which is a necessary condition for symmetric treatment and load and generation.

The economic barriers to universal hourly metering have fallen over time. The primary cost associated with universal interval metering is the up-front cost of installing the system, although there is also a small monthly operating and maintenance cost. Wolak (2013) describes the many technologies available. Many jurisdictions around the world have invested in interval meters for all customers and many others are in the process of doing so. For example, the three large retailers in California recently completed the implementation of universal interval metering as a regulated distribution network service. The economic case for interval metering is primarily based on the cost savings associated with reading conventional meters. These automated interval meter systems eliminate the need for staff of the electricity retailer to visit the customer's premises to read the meter each month. Particularly in industrialized countries, where labor is relatively expensive, these savings in labor costs cover a significant fraction of the estimated cost of the automated meter reading system.

4.5.4   Economic Reliability versus Engineering Reliability of a Transmission Network

The presence of a wholesale market changes the definition of what constitutes a reliable transmission network. In order for it to be expected profit-maximizing for generation unit owners to submit a bid curve close to their marginal cost curve, they must expect to face sufficiently elastic residual demand curves. For this to be the case, there must be enough transmission capacity into the area served by a generation unit owner so that any attempts to raise local prices will result in a large enough quantity of lost sales to make this bidding strategy unprofitable.

I define an economically reliable transmission network as one with sufficient capacity so that each location in the transmission network faces sufficient competition from distant generation to cause local generation unit owners to compete with distant generators rather than cause congestion to create a local monopoly market. In the former vertically integrated utility regime, transmission expansions were undertaken to ensure the engineering reliability of the transmission network. A transmission network was deemed to be reliable from an engineering perspective if the vertically integrated utility that controlled all of the generation units in the control area could maintain a reliable electricity supply to consumers despite unexpected generation and transmission outages.

The value of increasing the transmission capacity between two points still depends on the extent to which this expansion allows the substitution of cheap generation in one area for expensive generation in the other area. Under the vertically integrated monopoly regime, all differences across regions in wholesale energy payments were due to differences in the locational costs of production for the geographic monopolist. However, in the wholesale market regime, the extent of market power that can be exercised by firms at each location in the network can lead to much larger differences in payments for wholesale electricity across these regions.

Even if the difference in the variable cost of the highest cost units operating in the two regions is less than $15/MWh, because firms in one area are able to exercise local market power, differences in the wholesale prices that consumers must pay across the two regions can be as high as the price cap on the real-time price of energy. For example, during early 2000 in the California market when the price cap on the Independent System Operator's real-time market was $750/MWh, because of congestion between Southern California (the SP15 zone) and Northern California (the NP15 zone), prices in the two zones differed by as much as $700/MWh, despite the fact that the difference in the variable costs of the highest cost units operating in the two zones was less than $15/MWh.

This example demonstrates that a major source of benefits from transmission capacity in a wholesale market regime is that it limits the ability of generation unit owners to use transmission congestion to limit the number of competitors they face. More transmission capacity into an area implies that local generating unit owners face more competition from distant generation for a larger fraction of their capacity. Because these firms now face more competition from distant generation, they must bid more aggressively (a supply curve closer to their marginal cost curve) over a wider range of local demand realizations to sell the same amount of energy they did before the transmission upgrade.

Understanding how transmission upgrades can increase the elasticity of the residual demand curve a supplier faces requires only a slight modification of the discussion surrounding figure 4.10. Suppose that 9,500 MWh of demand is all located on the other side of a transmission line with 9,000 MW of capacity, and the supplier under consideration owns 1,000 MW of generation local to the demand. Suppose there are twelve firms, each of which own 1,000 MW of capacity located on the other side of the interface. In this case, the local supplier is pivotal for 500 MWh of energy because local demand is 9,500 MWh, but only 9,000 MWh of energy can get into the local area because of transmission constraints. Note that there is 12,000 MW of generation capacity available to serve the local demand. It just cannot get into the region because of transmission constraints. We can now reinterpret $SO_1(p)$ in figure 4.10 as the aggregate bid supply curve of the twelve firms competing to sell energy into the 9,000 MW transmission line.

Suppose the transmission line is now upgraded to 9,500 MW. From the perspective of the local firm this results in $SO_2(p)$ to serve the local demand, which means that the local supplier is no longer pivotal. Before the upgrade the local supplier faced the residual demand curve $DR_1(p)$ in figure 4.10 and after the upgrade it faces $DR_2(p)$, which is more elastic than $DR_1(p)$ at all price levels. This is the mechanism by which transmission upgrades increase the elasticity of the residual demand curve a supplier faces and the overall competitiveness of the wholesale electricity market.

The California Independent System Operator's (ISO) Transmission Expansion Assessment Methodology (TEAM) incorporates the increased wholesale competition benefits of transmission expansions. Awad et al. (2010) presents the details of this methodology and applies it to a proposed transmission expansion from Arizona into Southern California—the Palo Verde–Devers Line No. 2 upgrade. The authors find that the result of increased competition that generation unit owners in California face from generation unit owners located in Arizona is a major source of benefits from the upgrade. These benefits are much larger for system conditions with low levels of hydroelectric energy available from the Pacific Northwest and very high natural gas prices, because this transmission expansion allows more electricity imports from the Southwest, where the vast majority of electricity is produced using coal.

Wolak (2012) measures the competitiveness benefits of eliminating transmission congestion in the Alberta electricity market. This analysis quantifies how much lower wholesale prices are as a result of the change in the behavior of large suppliers in this market caused by eliminating the prospect of transmission congestion that might lead them to face steeper residual demand curves. This analysis finds that even the perception of no transmission congestion by strategic suppliers causes them to submit offer prices closer to their marginal cost of production, which results in lower short-term wholesale prices, even without any change in the configuration of the actual transmission network. This analysis suggests that failing to account for these competitiveness benefits to consumers from transmission expansions in the wholesale market regime can leave many cost-effective transmission upgrades on the drawing board.

4.6   Role of Regulatory Oversight in Market Design Process

Regulatory oversight of the wholesale market regime is perhaps the most difficult aspect of the market design process. This regulatory process focuses on the challenging task of setting market rules that yield, through the unilateral profit-maximizing actions of market participants, just and reasonable prices to final consumers. The rules that govern the operation of the generation, transmission, distribution, and retailing sectors of the industry all impact the retail prices paid by final consumers. As section 4.4 makes clear, regulatory oversight of the wholesale market regime is a considerably more difficult because of the individual rationality constraint that each firm will choose its actions to influence the revenues it receives and costs it incurs to maximize its objective function subject to these market rules.

Regulatory oversight is further complicated by the fact that actions taken by the regulator to correct a problem in one aspect of the wholesale market can impact the individual rationality constraint faced by other market participants. The change in behavior by these market participants can lead to market outcomes that create more adverse economic consequences than the problem that caused the regulator to take action in the first place. This logic implies that the regulator must examine the full implications of any proposed market rule changes or other regulatory interventions, because once they have been implemented market participants will alter the constraint set they face and maximize their objective function subject to this new constraint set, consistent with their individual rationality constraint.

Despite the significant challenges faced by the regulatory process in the wholesale market regime, the restructured electricity supply industries that have ultimately delivered the most benefits to electricity consumers are those with a credible and effective regulatory process. This section summarizes the major tasks of the regulatory process in the wholesale market regime. The first task is to provide what I call "smart sunshine regulation." This means that the regulatory process gathers a comprehensive set of information about market outcomes, analyzes it, and makes it available to the public in a manner and form that ensures compliance with all market rules and allows the regulatory and political process to detect and correct market design flaws in a timely manner. Smart sunshine regulation is the foundation for all of the tasks the regulatory process must undertake in the wholesale market regime.

For the reasons discussed in section 4.5.4, the regulatory process must also take a more active role in managing the configuration of the transmission network than it did in the former vertically integrated regime. Because the real-time wholesale market operator is a monopoly provider of this service, the regulator must also monitor its performance. The regulatory process must also oversee the performance of the retailing and energy trading sectors. Finally, the regulatory process must have the ability to take actions to prevent significant wealth transfers and deadweight losses that can result from the legal (under US antitrust law) exercise of unilateral market power in wholesale electricity markets. This is perhaps the most challenging task the regulatory process faces because knowledge that the regulator will take actions to prevent these transfers and deadweight losses can limit the incentive market participants have to take costly actions to prevent the exercise of unilateral market power.

4.6.1   Smart Sunshine Regulation

A minimal requirement of any regulatory process is to provide "smart sunshine" regulation. The fundamental goal of regulation is to cause a firm to take actions desired by the regulator that it would not otherwise do without regulatory oversight. For example, without regulatory oversight, a vertically integrated monopoly is likely to prefer to raise prices to some customers and/or refuse to serve others. One way to cause a firm to take an action desired by the regulator is to use the threat of unfavorable publicity to discipline the behavior of the firm. In the abovementioned example, if the firm is required by law to serve all customers at the regulated price, a straightforward way to increase likelihood that the firm complies is for the regulator to disclose to the public instances when the firm denies service to a customer or charges too high of a price.

In order to provide effective smart sunshine regulation, the regulator must have access to all information needed to operate the market and be able to perform analyses of this data and release the results to the public. At the most basic level, the regulator should be able to replicate market-clearing prices and quantities given the bids submitted by market participants, total demand, and other information about system conditions. This information is necessary for the regulator to verify that the market is operated in a manner consistent with what is written in the market rules.

A second aspect of smart sunshine regulation is public data release. There are market efficiency benefits to public release of all data submitted to the real-time market and produced by the system operator. As discussed in section 4.4.2, if only a small fraction of energy sales take place at the real-time price, this limits the incentive for large suppliers to exercise unilateral market power in the short-term wholesale market. With adequate hedging of short-term price risk by electricity retailers, the real-time market is primarily an imbalance market operated primarily for reliability reasons, where retailers and suppliers buy and sell small amounts of energy to manage deviations between their forward market commitments and real-time production and consumption. Because all market participants have a common interest in the reliability of the transmission network, immediate data release serves these reliability needs.

Wholesale markets that currently exist around the world differ considerably in terms of the amount of data they make publicly available and the lag between the date the data is created and the date it is released to the public. Nevertheless, among industrialized countries there appears to be a positive correlation between the extent to which data submitted or produced by the system operator is made publicly available and how well the wholesale market operates. For example, the Australian electricity market makes all data on bids and unit-level dispatch publicly available the next day. Australia's National Electricity Market Management Company (NEMMCO) posts this information by the market participant name on its website. The Australian electricity market is generally acknowledged to be one of the best performing restructured electricity markets in the world (Wolak 1999).

The former England and Wales electricity pool kept all of the unit-level bid and production data confidential. Only members of the pool could gain access to this data. It was generally acknowledged to be subject to the exercise of substantial unilateral market power by the larger suppliers, as documented by Wolak and Patrick (1997) and Wolfram (1999). The UK government's displeasure with pool prices eventually led to the New Electricity Trading Arrangements (NETA), which began operation on March 27, 2001. Although these facts do not provide definitive proof that rapid and complete data release enhances market efficiency, the best available information on this issue provides no evidence that withholding this data from the public scrutiny enhances market efficiency.

The sunshine regulation value of public data release is increased if the identity of the market participant and the specific generation unit associated with each bid, generation schedule, or output level is also made public. Masking the identity of the entity associated with a bid, generation schedule, or output level, as is done in all US wholesale markets, limits the ability of the regulator to use the threat of adverse public opinion to discipline market participant behavior. Under a system of masked data release, market participants can always deny that their bids or energy schedules are the ones exhibiting the unusual behavior. The primary value of public data release is putting all market participants at risk for explaining to the public that their actions are not in violation of the intent of the wholesale market rules. In all US markets, the very long lag between the date the data is produced and the date it is released to the public of at least six months, and the fact that the data is released without identifying the specific market participants, eliminates much of the smart sunshine regulation benefit of public data release.

Putting market participants at risk for explaining their behavior to the public is different from requiring them to behave in a manner that is inconsistent with their unilateral profit-maximizing interests. A number of markets have considered implementing "good behavior conditions" on market participants. The most well-known attempt was the United Kingdom's consideration of a market abuse license condition (MALC) as a precondition for participating in its wholesale electricity market. The fundamental conflict raised by these "good behavior" clauses is that they can prohibit behavior that is in the unilateral profit-maximizing interests of a supplier that is also in the interests of consumers. These "good behavior" clauses do not correct the underlying market design flaw or implement a change in the market structure to address the underlying cause of the harm from the unilateral exercise of market power. They simply ask that the firm be a "good citizen" and not maximize profits. In testimony to the United Kingdom Competition Commission, Wolak (2000a) made these and a number of other arguments against the MALC, which the commission eventually decided against implementing.

Another potential benefit associated with public data release is that it enables independent third parties to undertake analyses of market performance. The US policies on data release limit the benefits from this aspect of a public data release policy. Releasing data with the identities of the market participant masked makes it impossible to definitively match data from other sources to specific market participants. Virtually all market performance measures require matching data on unit-level heat rates or input fuel prices obtained from other sources to specific generation units. Strictly speaking, this is impossible to do if the unit name or market participant name is not matched with the generation unit.

A long time lag between the date the data is produced and the date it is released also greatly limits the range of questions that can be addressed with this data and regulatory problems that it can address. Taking the example of the California electricity crisis, by January 1, 2001—the date that masked data from June of 2000 was first made available to the public (because of a six-month data release lag)—the exercise of unilateral market power in California had already resulted in more than $5 billion in overpayments to suppliers in the California electricity market as measured by Borenstein, Bushnell, and Wolak (2002), hereafter BBW (2002). Consequently, a long time lag between the date the data is produced and the date it is released to the public has an enormous potential cost to consumers that should be balanced against the benefits of delaying the data release.

The usual argument against immediate data release is that suppliers could use this information to coordinate their actions to raise market prices through sophisticated tacit collusion schemes. However, there are a number of reasons why these concerns are much less relevant for the release of data from a short-term bid-based wholesale market. First, as just discussed, in a wholesale electricity market with the levels of hedging of short-term price risk necessary to leave large suppliers with little incentive to exercise unilateral market power in the short-term market, very little energy is actually sold at the short-term price. The short-term market is primarily a venue for buying and selling energy imbalances. With adequate levels of hedging of short-term price risk, both suppliers and retailers would rarely have significant positions on either side of the short-term market. Therefore, they would have little incentive to raise prices in the short-term market through their unilateral actions or through coordinated behavior.

Nevertheless, without adequate levels of hedging of short-term price risk, the immediate availability of information on bids, schedules, and actual unit-level production could allow suppliers to design more complex state-dependent strategies for enforcing collusive market outcomes. However, it is important to bear in mind that coordinated actions to raise market prices are illegal under US antitrust law and under the competition law in virtually all countries around the world. The immediate availability of this data means that the public also has access to this information and can undertake studies examining the extent to which market prices differ from the competitive benchmark levels described in BBW (2002). Keeping this data confidential or releasing it only after a long time lag prevents this potentially important form of public scrutiny of market performance from occurring.

In contrast to data associated with the operation of the short-term wholesale market, releasing information on forward market positions or transactions prices for specific market participants is likely to enhance the ability and incentive of suppliers to raise the prices retailers pay for these hedging instruments. Large volumes of energy are likely to be traded in this market. Suppliers typically sell these products, and retailers and large customers typically buy these products. Forward market position information about a market participant is unnecessary to operate the short-term market, so there is little reliability justification in releasing this data to the public.

There is a strong argument for keeping any forward contract positions the regulator might collect confidential. As noted in above, the financial forward contract holdings of a supplier are major determinants of the aggressiveness of its bids into the short-term market. Only if a supplier is confident that it will produce more than its forward contract obligations will it have an incentive to bid or schedule its units to raise the market price. Suppliers recognize this incentive created by forward contracts when they bid against competitors with forward contract holdings. Consequently, public disclosure of the forward contract holdings of market participants can convey useful information about the incentives of individual suppliers to raise market prices, with no countervailing reliability or market efficiency–enhancing benefits.

A final aspect of the data collection portion of the regulatory process is scheduled outage coordination and forced outage declarations. A major lesson from wholesale electricity markets around the world is the impossibility of determining whether a unit that is declared out of service can actually operate. Different from the former vertically integrated regime, declaring a "sick day" for a generation unit—saying that it is unable to operate when in reality it could safely operate—can be a very profitable way for a supplier to withhold capacity from the market in order to raise the wholesale price. To limit the ability of suppliers to use their planned and unplanned outage declarations in this manner, the market operator and regulator must specify clear rules for determining a unit's planned outage schedule and for determining when a unit is forced out.

To limit the incentive for "sick day" unplanned generation outages, the system operator could specify the following scheme for outage reporting. Unless a unit is declared available to operate up to its full capacity, the unit is declared fully out or partially out depending on the amount of capacity from the unit bid into the market at any price at or below the current offer price cap. This definition of a forced outage eliminates the problem of determining whether a unit that does not bid into the market is actually able to operate. A simple rule is to assume the unit is being forced out because the owner is not offering this capacity to the market. The system operator would therefore only count capacity from a unit bid in at a price at or below the price cap as available capacity. Information on unit-level forced outages according to this definition could then be publicly disclosed each day on the system operator's website.

This disclosure process cannot prevent a supplier from declaring a "sick day" to raise the price it receives for energy or operating reserves that it sells from other units it owns. However, the process can make it more costly for the market participant to engage in this behavior by registering all hours when capacity from a unit is not bid into the market as forced outage hours. For example, if a 100 MW generation unit is neither bid nor scheduled in the short-term market during an hour, then it is deemed to be forced out for that hour. If this unit only bids 40 MW of the 100 MW at or below the price or bid cap during an hour, then the remaining 60 MW is deemed to be forced out for that hour. The regulator can then periodically report forced outage rates based on this methodology and compare these outage rates to historical figures from these units before restructuring or from comparable units from different wholesale markets. The regulator could then subject the supplier to greater public scrutiny and adverse publicity for significant deviations of the forced outage rates of its units relative to those from comparable units.

A final issue associated with smart sunshine regulation is ensuring compliance with market rules. The threat of public scrutiny and adverse publicity is the regulator's first line of defense against market rule violations. However, an argument based on the logic of the individual rationality constraint implies that the regulator must make the penalties associated with any market rule violations more than the benefits that the market participant receives from violating that market rule. Otherwise market participants may find it unilaterally profit maximizing to violate the market rules. One lesson from the activities of many firms in the California market and other markets in the United States is that if the cost of a market rule violation is less than the financial benefit the firm receives from violating the market rule, the firm will violate the market rule and pay the associated penalties as a cost of doing business.

4.6.2 Detecting and Correcting Market Design Flaws

Bid-based wholesale electricity markets can have market design flaws that have little impact on market outcomes during most system conditions but result in large wealth transfers under certain system conditions. Consequently, an important role of the regulatory process is to detect and correct market design flaws before circumstances arise that cause them to produce large wealth transfers and significant deadweight losses.

The experience of the California market illustrates this point. From its start in April 1998 until April 2000, the California market set prices that were very close to those that would occur if no suppliers exercised unilateral market power, what BBW (2002) call the competitive benchmark price. BBW

(2002) compute this competitive benchmark price using daily data on input prices and the technical operating characteristics of all generation units in California and the hourly willingness to supply importers to construct a counterfactual competitive supply curve that they intersect with the hourly market demand. During the first two years of the California market, the average difference between the actual hourly market price and the hourly competitive benchmark price computed using the BBW methodology is less than or very close to equal to those computed by Mansur (2003) for the PJM market and Bushnell and Saravia (2002) for the New England market using this same methodology. Actual market prices very close to competitive benchmark prices occurred in spite of the fact that virtually all of the wholesale energy purchases by the three large California retailers were made through the day-ahead or real-time market.

This overreliance on short-term markets led to actual prices that were not substantially different from competitive benchmark prices because there was plenty of hydroelectric energy in California and the Pacific Northwest and low-cost fossil-fuel energy from the Southwest during the summers of 1998 and 1999. Any attempts by fossil fuel suppliers in California to withhold output to raise short-term prices were met with additional supply from these sources with little impact on market prices. In the language of section 4.5, these in-state fossil fuel suppliers faced very elastic residual demand curves because of the flat willingness-to-supply functions offered by hydroelectric suppliers and importers. Given these system conditions, California's fossil fuel suppliers found it unilaterally profit maximizing to offer each of their generation units into the day-ahead and real-time markets at very close to the marginal cost of production.

These unilateral incentives changed in the summer of 2000 when the amount of hydroelectric energy available from the Pacific Northwest and Southwest was significantly less than was available during the previous two summers. Wolak (2003b) shows that this event led the five largest fossil fuel electricity suppliers in California to face significantly less elastic residual demand curves because of the less aggressive supply responses from importers to California relative to the first two summers of the wholesale market. As a consequence, the five fossil fuel suppliers found it in their unilateral interest to exploit these less elastic residual demand curves and submit substantially higher offer prices into the short-term market in order to raise wholesale electricity prices in California. BBW find that the summer months of June to September of 2000, the average difference between the actual price and the BBW competitive benchmark price was more than \$70/MWh, which is more than twice the average price of wholesale electricity during the first two years of the market of \$34/MWh.

The California experience demonstrates that some market design flaws, in this case insufficient hedging of short-term price risk by electricity retailers, can be relatively benign under a range of system conditions. However, when system conditions conducive to the exercise of unilateral market power occur, this market design flaw can result in substantial wealth transfers from consumers to producers and economically significant deadweight losses. BBW (2002) present estimates of these magnitudes for the period June 1998 to October 2000.

It is important to emphasize that these wealth transfers appear to have occurred without coordinated actions among market participants that violated US antitrust law. Despite extensive multiyear investigations by almost every state-level antitrust and regulatory commission in the western United States, the US Department of Justice Antitrust Division, the Federal Energy Regulatory Commission, and numerous congressional committees, no significant evidence of coordinated actions to raise wholesale electricity prices in the Western Electricity Coordinating Council (WECC) during the period June 2000 to June 2001 has been uncovered. This outcome occurred because US antitrust law does not prohibit firms from fully exploiting their unilateral market power. This fact emphasizes the need, discussed later in this section, for the regulator to have the ability to intervene when the exercise of unilateral market power is likely to result in significant wealth transfers.

Identifying and correcting market design flaws requires a detailed knowledge of the market rules and their impact on market outcomes. This aspect of the regulatory process heavily relies on the availability of the short-term market outcome data and other information collected by the regulator to undertake smart sunshine regulation. Another important role for smart sunshine regulation is to analyze market outcomes to determine which market rules might be enhancing the ability of suppliers to exercise unilateral market power or increasing the likelihood that the attempts of suppliers to coordinate their actions to raise prices will be successful.

4.6.3   Oversight of Transmission Network and System Operation

There are also important market competitiveness benefits from regulatory oversight of the terms of conditions for new generation units to interconnect to the transmission network and determine whether transmission upgrades should take place and where they should take place. As discussed in Wolak (2003a) and demonstrated empirically for the Alberta Electricity Market in Wolak (2012), transmission capacity has an additional role as a facilitator of commerce in the wholesale market regime. As noted in section 4.5.4, expansion of the transmission network typically increases the number of independent wholesale electricity suppliers that are able to compete to supply electricity at locations in the transmission network served by the upgrade, which increases the elasticity of the residual demand curve faced by all suppliers at those locations. An industry-specific regulator armed with the data and experienced with monitoring market performance is well suited to develop the expertise necessary to determine the transmission network that maximizes the competitiveness of the wholesale electricity market.

The Independent System Operator (ISO) that operates the short-term market is a new entity requiring regulatory oversight in the wholesale market regime. The system operation function was formerly part of the vertically integrated utility. Because a wholesale market provides open access to the transmission network under equal terms and conditions for all electricity suppliers and retailers, an independent entity is needed to operate the transmission network to maintain system balance in real time. The ISO is the monopoly supplier of real-time market and system operation services and for that reason independent regulatory oversight is needed to ensure that it is operating the grid in as close as possible to a least-cost manner to benefit market participants rather than the management and staff of the ISO.

A final issue with respect to regulatory oversight of the transmission network and system operation function is the fact that the ISO has substantial expertise with operating the transmission network. Consequently, the regulator may find it beneficial to allow the ISO to play a leading role in the process of determining expansions to the transmission network.

4.6.4   Oversight of Trading and Retailing Sectors

Traders and competitive retailers are the final class of new market participants requiring regulatory oversight. Traders typically buy something they have no intention of consuming and sell something they do not or cannot produce. In this sense, energy traders are no different from derivative securities traders who buy and sell puts, calls, swaps, and futures contracts. Traders typically take bets on the direction that electricity prices are likely to move between the time the derivative contract is signed and the expiration date of the contract. Securities traders profit from buying a security at a low price and selling it later for a higher price, or selling the security at a high price and buying it back later at a lower price. Energy traders can also serve a risk management role by taking on risk that other market participants would prefer not to bear.

Competitive retailers are a specific type of energy trader. They provide short-term price hedging services for final consumers to compete with the products offered by the incumbent retailer. They purchase and sell hedging instruments with the goal of providing retail electricity at prices final consumers find attractive. The major regulatory oversight challenge for the competitive retailing sector is to ensure that retailers do not engage in excessive risk taking. For example, a retailer could agree to sell electricity to final consumers at a low fixed retail price by purchasing the necessary electricity from the short-term wholesale market. However, if short-term wholesale prices rise, this retailer might then be forced into bankruptcy because of its fixed-price commitment to sell electricity to final consumers at a price that does not recover the current price of the wholesale electricity. The regulatory process must ensure that retailers adequately hedge with generation unit owners any fixed-price forward market commitments they make to final consumers.

A trader activity that has created considerable controversy among politicians and the press is attempts to exploit potential price differences for the same product across time or locations. For the case of electricity, this could involve exploiting the difference between the day-ahead forward price for electricity for one hour of the day and the real-time price of electricity for that same hour. Locationally, this involves buying the right to inject electricity at one node and selling the right to inject electricity at another node. This is often incorrectly described as buying electricity at one node and selling it at another node. As the discussion surrounding figure 4.7 demonstrates, it is not possible to take possession of electricity and transport it from one node to another. Consequently, selling a 1 MWh injection of electricity at node A and buying a 1 MWh withdrawal at node B in the day-ahead market is taking a gamble on the difference in the direction and magnitude of congestion between these two locations in the transmission network. In the real-time market the trader can fulfill his obligation to inject at node A by purchasing electricity at the real-time price at node A and his obligation to withdraw at node B by selling energy at the real-time price at node B. In this case, the trader neither produces nor consumes electricity in real time, but its profit on these transactions is the difference between the day-ahead prices at nodes A and B less the difference of the real-time prices at nodes B and A.

Virtually all of these transactions involve a significant risk that the trader will lose money. For example, if a trader sells 1 MWh at the day-ahead price at node A and the real-time price turns out to be higher than day-ahead price at node A, then the trader must fulfill the commitment to provide 1 MWh at node A by purchasing at the higher real-time price. This transaction earns the trader a loss equal to the difference between the real-time and day-ahead prices.

Advocates of energy trading often speak of traders providing "liquidity" to a market. A liquid market is one where large volumes can be bought or sold without causing significant market price movements. Viewed from this perspective, traders can benefit market efficiency. However, there may be instances when the actions of traders degrade market efficiency by exploiting market design flaws. As Wolak (2003b) notes, virtually all of the Enron trading strategies described in the three memos released by FERC in the spring of 2002 could be classified as risky trading strategies that had the potential to enhance market efficiency. Only a few clearly appeared to degrade system reliability or market efficiency. Consequently, a final challenge for the regulatory process in the wholesale market regime is to ensure that the profit-maximizing activities of traders enhance, rather than detract, from market efficiency.

4.6.5 Protecting against Behavior Harmful to
Market Efficiency and System Reliability

The final responsibility for the regulator is to deter behavior that is harmful to system reliability and market efficiency and impose penalties for publicly observed, objective market rule violations. This is the most complex aspect of the regulatory process to implement, but it also has the potential to yield the greatest benefit. It involves a number of interrelated tasks. In a bid-based market, the regulator must design and implement a local market power mitigation mechanism, which is the most frequently invoked example of an intervention into the market to prevent behavior harmful to market efficiency and system reliability. In general, the regulator must determine when any type of market outcome causes enough harm to some market participants to merit explicit regulatory intervention. Finally, if the market outcomes become too harmful, the regulator must have the ability to temporarily suspend market operations. All of these tasks require a substantial amount of subjective judgment on the part of the regulatory process.

In all bid-based wholesale electricity markets a local market power mitigation (LMPM) mechanism is necessary to limit the bids a supplier submits when it faces insufficient competition to serve a local energy need because of a combination of the configuration of the transmission network and concentration of ownership of generation units. An LMPM mechanism is a prespecified administrative procedure (usually written into the market rules) that determines: (a) when a supplier has local market power worthy of mitigation, (b) what the mitigated supplier will be paid when mitigated, and (c) how the amount the supplier is paid will impact the payments received by other market participants. Without a prospective LMPM mechanism, system conditions are likely to arise in all wholesale markets when almost any supplier can exercise substantial unilateral market power. It is increasingly clear to regulators around the world, particularly those that operate markets with limited amounts of transmission capacity, that formal regulatory mechanisms are necessary to deal with the problem of insufficient competition to serve certain local energy needs.

The regulator is the first line of defense against harmful market outcomes. Persistent behavior by a market participant that is harmful to market efficiency or system reliability is typically subject to penalties and sanctions. In order to assess these penalties, the regulator must first determine intent on the part of the market participant. The goal of this provision is to establish a process for the regulator to intervene to prevent a market meltdown. As discussed in Wolak (2004), there are instances when actions very profitable to one or a small number of market participants can be extremely harmful to system reliability and market efficiency. A well-defined process must exist for the regulator to intervene to protect market participants and correct the market design flaw facilitating this harm. Wolak (2004) proposes such an administrative process for determining behavior harmful to system reliability and market efficiency that results from the exercise of unilateral market power by one or more market participants.

The regulator may also wish to have the ability to suspend market operations on a temporary basis when system conditions warrant it. The suspension of market operations is an extreme regulatory response that requires a prespecified administrative procedure to determine that it is the only option available to the regulator to prevent significant harm to market efficiency and system reliability. As has been demonstrated in various countries around the world, electricity markets can sometimes become wildly dysfunctional and can lead to significant wealth transfers and deadweight losses over a very short period time. Under these sorts of circumstances, the regulator should have the ability to suspend market operations temporarily until the problem can be dealt with through a longer-term regulatory intervention or market rule change. Wolak (2004) proposes a process for making such a determination.

Different from the case of the vertically integrated utility regime, the regulator must be forward looking and fast acting, because wholesale markets provide extremely high-powered incentives for firm behavior, so it does not take very long for a wholesale electricity market to produce enormous wealth transfers from consumers to producers and significant deadweight losses. The California electricity crisis is an example of this phenomenon. The Federal Energy Regulatory Commission (FERC) waited almost six months from the time it first became clear that there was substantial unilateral market power exercised in the California market before it took action. As Wolak (2003b) notes, when FERC finally did take action in December 2000, it did so with little, if any, quantitative analysis of market performance, in direct contradiction of the fundamental need for smart sunshine regulation of the wholesale market. Wolak (2003b) argues that the actions FERC took at this time increased the rate at which wealth transfers occurred. Wolak, Nordhaus, and Shapiro (2000) discuss the likely impact, which as Wolak (2003b) notes, also turned out to be the eventual impact, of the FERC's December 2000 action.

4.7 Common Market Design Flaws and Their Underlying Causes

This section describes several common market design failures and uses the framework of sections 4.4 to 4.6 to diagnose their underlying causes. These include excessive focus by the regulatory process on short-term market design, inadequate divestiture of generation capacity by the incumbent firms, lack of an effective local market power mitigation mechanism, price caps and bid caps on short-term markets, and an inadequate retail market infrastructure.

4.7.1   Excessive Emphasis on Spot Market Design

Relative to other industrialized countries, the wholesale market design process in the United States has focused much more on the details of short-term energy and operating reserves markets. This design focus sharply contrasts with the focus of the restructuring processes in many developing countries, particularly in Latin America. These countries aim to foster an active forward market for energy and many of them impose regulatory mandates for minimum percentages of forward contract coverage of final demand at various time horizons to delivery. The short-term market is operated primarily to manage system imbalances in real time, and in the majority of Latin American countries this process operates based on the ISO's estimate of the variable cost of operating each generation unit, not the unit owner's bids.

Joskow (1997) argues that the major benefits from electricity industry restructuring are likely to come from more efficient new generation investment decisions, rather than from more efficient operation of existing generation units to meet final demand. Nevertheless, there does appear to be evidence that individual generation units operating in a restructured wholesale market environment tend to be operated in a more efficient manner. Fabrizio, Rose, and Wolfram (2007) use data on annual plant-level input data to compare the relative efficiency of municipally owned plants versus those owned by investor-owned utilities in the pre- versus post-restructuring regimes. They find that the efficiency of municipally owned units was largely unaffected by restructuring, but those plants owned by investor-owned utilities, particularly in restructured states, significantly reduced nonfuel operating expenses and employment.

Bushnell and Wolfram (2005) use data on hourly fossil fuel use from the Environment Protection Agency's (EPA) Continuous Emissions Monitoring System (CEMS) to investigate changes in operating efficiency, the rate at which raw energy is translated into electricity, at generation units that have been divested from investor-owned utility to nonutility ownership. They find that fuel efficiency (or more precisely average heat rates) improved by about 2 percent following divestiture. They also find that nondivested plants that were subject to incentive regulation also realized similar magnitudes of average heat rate improvements.

The magnitude of the operating efficiency gains just described are substantially smaller than the average percentage markup of market prices over estimated competitive benchmark prices documented in the studies by BBW (2002), Joskow and Kahn (2002), Mansur (2003), and Bushnell and Saravia (2002). This implies that these operating efficiency gains are most likely being captured by generation unit owners rather than electricity consumers.

This distribution of economic benefits from restructuring is one implication of regulatory process that emphasizes short-term market design. It is extremely difficult to establish a workably competitive short-term market under moderate to high demand conditions without a substantial amount of final demand covered by fixed-priced long-term contracts. A very unconcentrated generation ownership structure, far below the levels that currently exist in all US markets, would be necessary to achieve competitive markets outcomes under these demand conditions in the absence of high levels of fixed-price forward contract coverage of final demand. By the logic of section 4.5.3, the greater is the share of total generation capacity owned by the largest firm in the market, the lower is the level of demand at which short-term market power problems are likely to show up, unless a substantial fraction of the largest supplier's expected output has been sold in a fixed-price forward contract. For virtually any number of suppliers and distribution of generation capacity ownership among these suppliers in a wholesale market without forward contracting, there is a level of demand at which significant short-term market power problems will arise.

It is important to emphasize that having adequate generation capacity installed to serve demand according to the standards of the former vertically integrated utility regime does very little to prevent the exercise of substantial unilateral market power in a wholesale market regime with inadequate fixed-price forward contracting. A simple example emphasizes this point. Suppose that there are five firms. One owns 300 MW of generation capacity, the second 200 MW, and the remaining three each own 100 MW, for a total of 800 MW. If demand is 650 MWh, then there is adequate generation capacity to serve demand, but it is extremely likely that short-term prices will be at the bid cap, because the two largest suppliers know they are pivotal—some of their generation capacity is needed to meet demand regardless of the actions of their competitors. If all suppliers have zero fixed-price forward contract commitments to retailers, even at a demand slightly above 500 MW, the largest supplier is pivotal and therefore able to exercise substantial unilateral market power.

The presence of some price-responsive demand does not alter the basic logic of this example. For example, suppose that 100 MWh of the 650 MWh of demand is willing to respond to wholesale prices, then the demand can simply be treated as an additional 100 MW negawatt supplier in the calculation of what firms are pivotal at this level of demand. In this case, the firm that owns 300 MW of generation capacity would still be pivotal because after subtracting the capacity of all other firms besides this one, including the 100 MW of negawatts, from system demand, 50 MWh is needed from this supplier or total demand will not be met. Under this scenario, unless the largest supplier has a fixed-price forward contract to supply of at least 50 MWh, consumers will be subject to substantial market power in the short-term energy market at this demand level.

One solution proposed to the problem of market power in short-term energy markets with insufficient forward contracting is to build additional generation capacity so that system conditions never arise where suppliers have the ability to exercise unilateral market power in the short-term market. In the previous example of the five suppliers with no price responsive final demand and a demand of 650 MWh, this would require constructing an additional 150 MW by new entrants or the four remaining smaller firms, with at least 50 MW being constructed by any entity but the first and second largest firms. This amount of new generation capacity distributed among new entrants and the remaining firms in the market would prevent any supplier from being pivotal in the short-term market with no forward contracting at a demand of 650 MWh.

There are several problems with this solution. First, it typically requires substantial excess capacity, particularly in markets where generation capacity ownership is concentrated. In the previous example, there would now be at least 950 MW of generation capacity in the system to serve a demand of 650 MWh. Second, there is no guarantee this new generation capacity will be built by the entities necessary for the two largest firms not to be pivotal. Finally, this excess capacity must be paid for or it will exit the industry. This excess capacity creates a set of stakeholders advocating for additional revenues to generation unit owners beyond those obtained from energy sales. Finally, this excess capacity is likely to depress short-term energy prices and dull the incentive for active demand-side participation in the wholesale energy market, which should lead to more calls for additional payments to generation owners to compensate for their energy market revenue shortfalls.

A far less costly solution to the problem of market power in short-term energy and reserve markets is for retailers to engage in fixed-priced forward contracts for a significant fraction of their final demand. This solution does not require installing additional generation capacity. In fact, it provide strong incentives for suppliers to construct the minimum amount of generation capacity needed to meet these fixed-price forward contract obligations for energy and operating reserves. To see the relationship between the level of fixed-price forward contract coverage of final demand and the level of demand at which market power problems arise in the short-term market, consider the earlier example except that all suppliers have sold 80 percent of their generation capacity in fixed-price forward contracts. This implies that the 300 MW supplier has sold 240 MWh, the 200 MW supplier has sold 160 MWh, and the remaining 100 MW suppliers have sold 80 MWh. At the 650 MWh level of demand no supplier is pivotal relative to its forward market position, because the largest supplier has forward commitment of 240 MWh, yet the minimum amount of energy it must produce to serve system demand is 150 MWh. Consequently, it has no incentive to withhold output to drive the short-term price up if in doing so it produces less than 240 MWh. If it produces less than 240 MWh, then it must purchase the difference between 240 MWh and its output from the short-term energy market at the prevailing market price to meet its forward contract obligation.

At this level of forward contracting, the largest supplier only becomes pivotal relative to its forward contract obligations if the level of demand exceeds 740 MWh, which is considerably larger than 500 MWh, the level of demand that causes it to be pivotal in a short-term market with no fixed-price forward contracts, and only slightly smaller than 800 MWh, the maximum possible energy that could be produced with 800 MW of generation capacity. In general, the higher the level of fixed-price forward contract coverage, the higher the level of demand at which one or more suppliers becomes pivotal relative to its forward contract position.

Focusing on the development of a long-term forward market has an additional dynamic benefit to the performance of short-term energy markets. If all suppliers have significant fixed-price forward contract commitments, then all suppliers share a common interest in minimizing the cost of supplying these forward contract commitments, because each supplier always has the option to purchase energy from the short-term market as opposed to supplying this energy from its generation units. The dynamic benefit comes from the fact that at high levels of forward contracting the operating efficiency gains from restructuring described earlier will be translated into short-term prices. Although the initial forward contracts signed between retailers and suppliers did not incorporate these expected efficiency gains in the prices charged to retailers, subsequent rounds of fixed-price forward contracts signed will incorporate the knowledge that these efficiency gains were achieved.

It is important to emphasize that the initial round of forward contracting cannot capture these dynamic efficiency gains in the prices that retailers must pay, because these efficiency gains will not occur unless significant fixed-price forward contracting takes place. Moreover, this required amount of fixed-price forward contracting will not take place unless suppliers receive sufficiently high fixed-price forward contract prices to compensate them for giving up the short-term market revenues they could expect to receive if they did not sign the forward contracts. This difference between expected future short-term prices with and without high levels of fixed-price contracting can be very large.

An illustration of this point comes from the California market during the winter of 2001. Forward prices for summer 2001 deliveries were approximately $300/MWh. Those for summer 2002 deliveries were approximately $150/MWh and those for summer 2003 were approximately $45/MWh. Prices in summer 2001 were that high because signing a fixed-price forward contract to supply energy during that time meant that a supplier was giving up significant opportunities to earn high prices in the short-term energy market. Forward prices for summer 2002 were half as high as those for summer 2001 because all supplies recognized that more new generation capacity and potentially more existing hydroelectric capacity could compete to supply energy to the short-term energy market in summer 2002 than in summer 2001. By the winter of 2001, hydro conditions for summer 2001 had largely been determined, whereas those for summer 2002 were still large-lyuncertain. Finally, the prices for summer 2003 were significantly lower, because suppliers recognized that a substantial amount of new generation capacity could come on line to compete in the short-term energy market by the summer of 2003. For this reason, suppliers expected that there would be few opportunities to exercise substantial unilateral market power in the short-term energy market during the summer of 2003, so they did not have to be compensated with a high energy price to sign a fixed-price forward contract to provide energy during the summer of 2003.

The second half of this story is that after the state of California signed significant fixed-price forward contracts with suppliers at prices that reflected forward market prices for the next eight to ten years, short-term market prices during the summer of 2001 reflected the exercise of low levels of unilateral market power despite the fact that hydroelectric energy conditions in the WECC were slightly worse than those during the summer of 2000. A major cause of these short-term market outcomes is the high level of fixed-price forward contract commitments many suppliers had signed to supply energy to California load serving entities (LSEs) during the summer of 2001.

The previous discussion provides strong evidence against the argument that getting the short-term market design right is the key to workably competitive short-term energy markets. Without significant coverage of final demand with fixed-price forward contracts it is virtually impossible to limit the opportunities for suppliers to exercise substantial unilateral market power in any short-term energy market during intermediate to high demand periods. In addition, those who argue that retailers should delay signing long-term forward contracts until the spot market becomes workably competitive are likely to be waiting for an extremely long time. This discussion also demonstrates why, at least for the initial rounds of forward contracting between retailers and suppliers, it is extremely difficult to capture the operating efficiencies gains from restructuring in the forward contract prices. This is another reason for beginning any restructuring process with the vesting contracts that immediately set in motion the incentive to translate operating efficiency gains into short-term wholesale prices.

4.7.2   Inadequate Amounts of Generation Capacity Divestiture

A number of restructuring processes have been plagued by inadequate amounts of divestiture or an inadequate process for divesting generation units from the incumbent vertically integrated monopoly. Typically, political constraints make it extremely difficult to separate the former state-owned companies into a sufficiently large number of suppliers. This leads to a period when existing suppliers are able to exercise substantial unilateral market power in the short-term energy market, which then leads to calls for regulatory intervention. If the period of time when these suppliers are able to exercise unilateral market power is sufficiently long, the regulator either successfully implements further divestiture or some other form of regulatory intervention takes place.

The England and Wales restructuring process followed this pattern. Initially, the fossil fuel capacity of the original state-owned vertically integrated utility, National Power, was sold off to two privately owned companies, the newly privatized National Power and PowerGen, with the nuclear capacity of original National Power initially retained in a government-owned company. This effectively created a tight duopoly market structure in the England and Wales market, which allowed substantial unilateral market power to be exercised, once a significant fraction of the initial round of vesting contracts expired. Eventually the regulator was able to implement further divestitures of generation capacity from the two fossil fuel suppliers, and the high short-term prices that reflected significant unilateral market power triggered new entry by owners of combined-cycle gas turbine (CCGT) capacity. At the same time calls for reform of the original England and Wales market design were justified based on the market power exercised by the two large fossil fuels suppliers. A strong case can be made that both the substantial amount of unilateral market power exercised from mid-1993 onwards and the subsequence expense of implementing the New Electricity Trading Arrangements (NETA) could have been avoided had more divestiture taken place at the start of the wholesale market.

New Zealand is an extreme example of insufficient divestiture at the start of the wholesale market regime. The Electricity Company of New Zealand (ECNZ), the original state monopoly, owned more than 95 percent of the generation capacity in New Zealand. Contact Energy, another state-owned entity, was given 30 percent of this generation capacity at the start of the wholesale market. However, this duopoly market structure was thought to have market power problems and the amount of generation capacity owned by the largest state-owned firm, virtually all of which was hydroelectric capacity, was thought to discourage needed private generation investment. Consequently, further divestiture of generation capacity from ECNZ was then implemented.

The poor experience of California with the divestiture process was not the result of an inadequate amount of divestiture, but how it was accomplished. First and foremost, the divested assets were sold without vesting contracts, which would have allowed the three investor-owned utilities to buy a substantial fraction of the expected output of these units for a price set by the California Public Utilities Commission. As discussed in Wolak (2003b) the lack of substantial fixed-price forward contracts between the new owners of these units and the three major California retailers created substantial opportunities for the owners of the divested assets to exercise substantial unilateral market power in California's short-term energy markets starting in June 2000 because the availability of hydroelectric energy in the WECC was significantly less than the levels in 1998 and 1999. A second problem with the divestiture of generation assets in California is that these units were typically purchased in tight geographic bundles, which significantly increased the local market power problem faced by California.

There appears to be one divestiture success story—the Victoria Electricity Supply Industry in Australia. The Victorian government decided to sell off all generation assets on a plant-by-plant basis.[9] Despite a peak demand in Victoria of approximately 7,500 MW and only three sizable suppliers, each of which owns one large coal-fired generation plant, the short-term energy market has been remarkably competitive since it began in 1994. This outcome is also due to high levels of vesting contracts associated with plants. Wolak (1999) describes the performance of the Victoria market during its first four years of operation.

Inadequate amounts of divestiture can also make achieving an economically reliable transmission network in the sense of section 4.5.4 significantly more expensive. Comparing two otherwise identical wholesale markets, except that one has substantial amounts of transmission capacity interconnecting all generation units and load centers and the other has minimal amounts of transmission capacity interconnecting generation units and load centers, the former market is likely to be able to achieve acceptable levels of wholesale market performance with less divestiture. The market with a substantial amount of transmission capacity will allow more generation units to compete supply electricity at every location in the transmission network. This logic implies the following two conclusions. First, the amount of divestiture necessary to achieve a desired level of competitiveness of wholesale market outcomes depends on the characteristics of the transmission network. Second, the economic reliability of a transmission network in the language of section 4.5.4 depends on the concentration and location of generation ownership. More concentration of generation ownership implies that a more extensive and higher-capacity transmission network is necessary to achieve the same level of competitiveness of wholesale market outcomes, as would be the case with less concentration of generation ownership. In this sense, less divestiture of generation capacity implies larger transmission network costs to attain the same level of competitiveness of wholesale market outcomes.

4.7.3   Lack of an Effective Local Market Power Mitigation Mechanism

Although the need for an effective local market power mitigation mechanism has been discussed in detail, the crucial role this mechanism plays in limiting the ability of suppliers to exercise both system-wide and local market power has not been emphasized. Once again, the experience of California is instructive about the harm that can occur as a result of a poorly

9. Recall that generation plants are typically composed of multiple generation units at the same location.

designed local market power mitigation mechanism. On the other hand, the PJM wholesale electricity market is an instructive example of how short-term market performance can be enhanced by the existence of an effective local market power mitigation mechanism.

At the start of the California market there was no explicit local market power mitigation mechanism for units not governed by what were called reliability must-run (RMR) contracts. These contracts were assigned to specific generation units thought to be needed to maintain system reliability even though short-term energy prices during the hours they were needed to run were insufficient to cover their variable costs plus a return to capital invested in the unit. All generation units without RMR contracts (non-RMR units) that were taken out of merit order, because they were needed to meet solve a local reliability need, were eligible to be paid as bid to provide this service, subject only to the bid cap on the energy market.[10]

As discussed earlier, system conditions can and do arise when virtually any generation unit owner, including a number of non-RMR unit owners, possess substantial local market power, or in engineering terms, they are the only unit able to meet a local reliability energy need. Once several non-RMR unit owners learned to predict when their units were needed to meet a local reliability need, they very quickly began to bid at or near the bid cap on the ISO's real-time market to provide this service. This method for exercising local market power became so widespread that one market participant that owned several units at the same location, two of which were RMR units, is alleged to have delayed repairs on its RMR units in order to have the remaining non-RMR units be paid as bid to provide the necessary local reliability energy. This was brought to the attention of FERC, which required the unit owner to repay the approximately $8 million in additional profits earned from this strategy, but it imposed no further penalties. For more on this case, see FERC (2001).

This exercise of substantial local market power enabled by the lack of an effective local market power mitigation mechanism in California became extremely costly. Several commentators have argued that it inappropriately led FERC to conclude that California's zonal market design was fatally flawed, despite the fact that zonal-pricing market designs are still the dominant congestion management mechanism outside of the United States. A case could be made that if California had a local market power mitigation mechanism similar to that in PJM or in several other zonal-pricing markets around the world, there would have been very few opportunities for suppliers to exercise the amount of local market power that led FERC to its conclusion.

10. A generation unit is said to be taken out of merit order if there are other lower cost units (or lower bid units) that can supply the necessary energy, but they are unable to do so because transmission constraints prevent their energy from reaching final demand.

The PJM local market power mitigation mechanism is an example of an effective local market power mitigation mechanism. It applies to all units located in the PJM control area on a prospective basis. If the PJM ISO determines that a unit possesses substantial local market power during an hour, then that unit's bid is typically mitigated to a regulated variable cost in the day-ahead and real-time price-setting process. There are two other options available that can be selected for the mitigated bid level, but this regulated variable cost is the most common choice by generation unit owners. Wolak (2002) describes the generic local market power problem in more detail and describes the details of the PJM local market power mitigation mechanism.

It is not difficult to imagine how the California market would have functioned if it had the PJM local market power mitigation mechanism from the start of the market. All suppliers taken to resolve local reliability problems would be paid a regulated variable cost, instead of as bid up to the bid cap for this additional energy. The costs to resolve local reliability constraints would have been substantially lower and very likely not have risen to a high enough level to cause alarm at FERC. This comparison of the PJM versus California experience with local market power mitigation mechanisms serves as a cautionary tale to market designers who fail to adequately address the local market power mitigation problem.

4.7.4   Lack of a Credible Offer or Price Cap on the Wholesale Market

Virtually all bid-based wholesale electricity markets have explicit or implicit offer caps. The proper level of the offer cap on the wholesale electricity market is largely a political decision, as long as it is set above the variable cost of the highest cost unit necessary to meet the annual peak demand. However, there is an important caveat associated with this statement that is often not appreciated. In order for an offer cap to be credible, the ISO must have a prespecified plan that it will implement if there is insufficient generation capacity offered into the real-time market at or below the offer cap to meet real-time demand. Without this there is an extreme temptation for suppliers that are pivotal or nearly pivotal relative to their forward market positions in the short-term energy market to test the credibility of the offer cap, and this can lead to an unraveling of the formal market mechanism.

There is an inverse relationship between the level of the offer cap on the short-term market that can be credibly maintained and the necessary amount of final demand that must be covered by fixed-price forward contracts for energy. Lower levels of the offer cap on the short-term market for energy require higher levels of coverage of final demand with fixed-price forward contracts in order to maintain the integrity of the offer cap on the energy or ancillary services market. For example, the experience of the California market has shown that even an offer cap of $250/MWh does not impose significant reliability problems or degrade the efficiency of the short-term market if virtually all of the demand is covered by fixed-price forward market arrangements.

If the offer cap is set too low for the level of forward contracts, then it is possible for system conditions to arise when one or more suppliers have an incentive to test its integrity by setting an offer price in excess of the cap. The ISO operators are then faced with the choice of blacking out certain customers in order to maintain the integrity of the transmission network, or paying suppliers their offer prices to provide the necessary energy. If the operators make the obvious choice of paying these suppliers their offer price, other market participants will quickly find this out, which encourages them to raise their offers above the cap and the formal wholesale market begins to unravel.

System conditions when suppliers had the opportunity to test the integrity of the offer cap arose frequently during the period June 2000 to June 2001 because only a very small fraction of final demand was covered by fixed-price forward contracts. Maintaining the credibility of a relatively low offer cap of, say, twice to three times variable cost of the highest cost unit in the system, requires that the regulatory process mandate fixed-price forward contract coverage of final demand at a very substantial fraction, certainly more than 90 percent, of final demand.

It is important to emphasize that this level of forward contracting must be mandated if a low offer cap is to be credible. Without this requirement, retailers have an incentive to rely on the short-term market and the protection against high short-term prices provided by the relatively low offer cap for their wholesale energy purchases, rather than voluntarily purchase sufficient fixed-priced forward contracts to maintain the credibility of the offer cap.

4.7.5   Inadequate Retail Market Infrastructure

This section describes inadequacies in the physical and regulatory retail market infrastructure in many wholesale markets that can limit the competitiveness of the wholesale market. The first is the lack of interval metering necessary for final consumers to be active participants in the wholesale market. The second is the asymmetric treatment of load and generation by the state regulatory process. The lack of interval meters and asymmetric treatment of load and generation creates circumstances where final demand has little ability or incentive to take actions to enhance the competitiveness of wholesale market outcomes.

Virtually all existing meters for small commercial and residential customers in the United States only capture total electricity consumption between consecutive meter readings. In the United States, meters for residential and small business customers are usually read on a monthly basis. This means that the only information available to an electricity retailer about these customers is their total monthly consumption of electricity. In order to determine the total monthly wholesale energy and ancillary services cost to serve this customer, this monthly consumption is usually distributed across hours of the month according to a representative load shape proposed by the retailer and approved by the state regulator. For example, let $q(i, d)$, denote the consumption of the representative consumer in hour i of day d. A customer with monthly consumption equal to $Q(\text{tot})$ is assumed to have consumption in hour i of day equal to:

$$qp(i,d) = \frac{q(i,d)Q(\text{tot})}{\sum_{d=1}^{D}\sum_{i=1}^{24} q(i,d)}.$$

This consumer's monthly wholesale energy bill is computed as

$$\text{Monthly Wholesale Energy Bill} = \sum_{d=1}^{D}\sum_{i=1}^{24} qp(i,d)p(i,d),$$

where $p(i, d)$ is the wholesale price in hour i of day d. This expression for the customer's monthly wholesale energy bill can be simplified to $P(\text{avg})Q(\text{tot})$, by defining $P(\text{avg})$ as:

$$P(\text{avg}) = \frac{\sum_{d=1}^{D}\sum_{i=1}^{24} p(i,d)qp(i,d)}{\sum_{d=1}^{D}\sum_{i=1}^{24} q(i,d)}.$$

Despite this attempt to allocate monthly consumption across the hours of the month, in the end the consumer faces the same wholesale energy price, $P(\text{avg})$, for each KWh consumed during the month. If a customer maintained the same total monthly consumption but shifted it from hours with very high wholesale prices to those with low wholesale prices, the customer's bill would be unchanged.

Without the ability to record a customer's consumption on an hourly basis it is impossible to implement a pricing scheme that allows the customer to realize the full benefits of shifting his consumption from high-priced hours to low-priced hours. In a wholesale market the divergence between $P(\text{avg})$ and the actual hourly wholesale price can be enormous. For example, during the year 2000 in California, $P(\text{avg})$ was equal to approximately 6 cents/KWh despite the fact that the price paid for electricity often exceeded 75 cents/KWh and was as high as $3.50/KWh for a few transactions. By contrast, under the vertically integrated utility regime, the utility received the same price for supplying electricity that the final customer paid for every KWh sold to that customer.

The installation of hourly meters would allow a customer to pay prices that reflect hourly wholesale market conditions for its electricity consumption during each hour. A customer facing an hourly wholesale price of $3.50/KWh for any consumption in that hour in excess of his forward market purchases would have a very strong incentive to cut back during that hour.

This incentive extends to reductions in consumption below this customer's forward market purchases, because any energy not consumed below this forward contract quantity is sold at the short-term market price of $3.50/KWh.

The importance of recording consumption on an hourly basis for all customers can be best understood by recognizing that a 1 MWh reduction in electricity consumption is equivalent to a 1 MWh increase in electricity production, assuming that both the 1 MWh demand decrease and 1 MWh supply increase are provided with the same response time and at the same location in the transmission grid. Because these two products are identical, in a world with no regulatory barriers to active demand side participation, arbitrage should force the prices paid for both products to be equal.

Virtually all customers in the United States with hourly meters still have the option to purchase all of their electricity at a retail price that does not vary with hourly system conditions. All customers without hourly meters have this same option. The supply-side analogue to this option to purchase as much electricity as the customer wants at a fixed price is not available to generation unit owners. The default price a generation unit owner faces is the real-time wholesale price. If the supplier would like to receive a different price for its output, then it must sign a hedging arrangement with another market participant. To provide incentives for final consumers to manage wholesale price risk, they must also pay a default wholesale price equal to the real-time wholesale price. No consumer needs to pay this real-time price. If the consumer would like to pay a different price then it must sign a hedging arrangement with another market participant. Wolak (2013) presents a simple model that shows if final consumers have the option to purchase as much as they want at a fixed retail price, this can destroy their incentive to manage their real-time price risk through altering their consumption in response to short-term prices.

To justify the existence of the option for consumers to purchase all of their consumption at a fixed price, state regulators will make the argument that customers must be protected from volatile short-term wholesale prices. However, this logic falls prey to the following economic reality: over the course of the year the total amount of revenues recovered from retail consumers after transmission, distribution, and retailing charges have been subtracted must be sufficient to pay total wholesale energy purchase costs over that year. If this constraint is violated the retailer will earn a loss or be forced into bankruptcy unless some other entity makes up the difference. Consequently, consumers are not shielded from paying volatile wholesale prices. They are simply prevented from reducing their annual electricity bill by reducing their consumption during the hours when wholesale prices are high and increasing their consumption when wholesale prices are low.

A number of observers complain that retail competition provides few benefits to final consumers and does little to increase the competitiveness of wholesale market outcomes. Joskow (2000b) provides an extremely persuasive argument for this position. If retail competition is introduced without hourly metering and with a fixed retail price, then it is extremely difficult to refute his argument.

The logic for this view follows. Competition among firms occurs because one firm believes that it can better serve the needs of consumers than firms currently in the industry. These firms succeed either by offering an existing product at a lower cost or by offering a new product that serves a previously unmet consumer need. Consider the case of electricity retailing without hourly meters. The only information each retailer has is the customer's monthly consumption of electricity and some demographic characteristics that might be useful for predicting its monthly load shape, the $q(i, d)$ described earlier. The dominant methodology for introducing retail competition is load-profile billing to the retailer for the hourly wholesale energy purchases necessary to serve each customer's monthly demand. This scheme implies that all competitive retailers receive the same monthly wholesale energy payment (for the wholesale electricity it allows the incumbent retailer to avoid purchasing on this customer's behalf) for each customer of a given type that they serve. Customer types are distinguished by a representative load shape and monthly consumption level.

Under this mechanism, competitors attract customers from the incumbent retailer by offering an average price for energy each month, $P(\text{avg})$ defined earlier, that is below the value offered by other retailers. The inability to measure this customer's consumption on an hourly basis implies that competition between electricity retailers takes place on a single dimension, the monthly average price they offer to the consumer. The opportunities for retailers to exploit competitive advantages relative to other retailers under this mechanism are severely limited. Moreover, this mechanism for retail competition also always requires asymmetric treatment of the incumbent retailer relative to other competitive retailers. Finally, the state PUC must also continue to have an active role in this process because it must approve the representative load shapes used to compute $P(\text{avg})$ for each customer class.

With hourly metering and a default price that passes through the hourly wholesale price, retail competition has the greatest opportunity to provide tangible economic benefits. Competition to attract customers can now take place along as many as 744 dimensions, the maximum number of hours possible in one month. A retailer can offer a customer as many as 744 different prices for a monthly period. Producers can offer an enormous variety of nonlinear pricing plans that depend on functions of the customer's consumption in these 744 hours. Retailers can now specialize in serving certain load shapes or offering certain pricing plans as their way to achieve a competitive advantage over other retailers.

Hourly meters allow retailers to use retail pricing plans to match their retail load obligations to their hourly pattern of electricity purchases.

Rather than having to buy a predetermined load shape in the wholesale market, retailers can instead buy a less expensive load shape and use their retail pricing plan to offer significantly lower prices in some hours and significantly higher prices in other hours to cause their retail customers to match this load shape yet achieve a lower average monthly retail electricity bill. This is possible because the retailer is able to pass on the lower cost of its wholesale energy purchases in the average hourly retail prices it charges the consumer.

4.8   Explaining the US Experience with Electricity Industry Restructuring

This section uses the results of the previous four sections to diagnose the underlying causes of the performance of restructured wholesale markets relative to the former vertically integrated utility regime in the United States. This experience is compared to that of a number of other industrialized countries to better understand whether improvements in market performance in the restructured regime are possible in the United States, or if industry restructuring in the United States is doomed to be an extremely expensive experiment.

4.8.1   Federal versus State Regulatory Conflict

Rather than coordinating wholesale and retail market policies to benefit wholesale market performance, almost the opposite has happened in the United States. State PUCs have designed retail market policies that attempt to maintain regulatory authority over the electricity supply industries in their state as FERC's authority grows. Retail market policies consistent with fostering a competitive wholesale market may appear to state PUCs as giving up regulatory authority. For example, making the default rate all retail customers pay equal to the real-time price appears to be giving up on the state PUC's ability to protect consumers from volatile wholesale prices. Introducing retail competition also appears to be giving up the state PUC's authority to set retail prices. The vertically integrated, regulated-monopoly regime in the United States limited opportunities for conflicts between state and federal regulators. As noted earlier, this regime involved few short-term interstate wholesale market transactions. State regulators also had a dominant role in the transmission and generation capacity planning decisions of the investor-owned utilities they regulated.

As discussed earlier, the Federal Power Act requires that FERC set "just and reasonable" wholesale electricity prices. The following passage from the Federal Power Act clarifies the wide-ranging authority FERC has to fulfill its mandate.

Whenever the Commission, after a hearing had up its own motion or upon complaint, shall find that any rate, charge, or classification, demand, observed, charged or collected by any public utility for transmission or sale subject to the jurisdiction of the Commission, or that any rule, regulation, practice, or contract affected such rate, charge, or classification is unjust, unreasonable, unduly discriminatory or preferential, the Commission shall determine the just and reasonable rate, charge, classification rule, rule, regulation, practice or contract to be thereafter observed and in force, and shall fix the same by order. (Federal Power Act, 16 USC § 824e, available at http://www.law.cornell.edu/uscode/text/16/824e)

Historically, just and reasonable prices are those that recover all prudently incurred production costs, including a return on capital invested.

For more than sixty years FERC implemented its obligations to set just and reasonable rates under the Federal Power Act by regulating wholesale market prices. During the 1990s, based on the belief that if appropriate criteria were met, "market-based rates" could produce lower prices and a more efficient electric power system, FERC changed its policy. It began to allow suppliers to sell wholesale electricity at market-based rates but, consistent with FERC's continuing responsibilities under the Federal Power Act, only if the suppliers could demonstrate that the resulting prices would be just and reasonable. Generally, FERC allowed suppliers to sell at market-based rates if they met a set of specific criteria, including a demonstration that the relevant markets would be characterized by effective competition. FERC retains this responsibility when a state decides to introduce a competitive wholesale electricity market. In particular, once FERC has granted suppliers market-based pricing authority it has an ongoing statutory responsibility to ensure that these market prices are just and reasonable.

The history of federal oversight of wholesale electricity transactions just described demonstrates that FERC has a very different perspective on the role of competitive wholesale markets than state PUCs or state policymakers. This difference is due in large part to the pressures put on FERC by the entities that it regulates versus the pressures put on state PUCs and policymakers by the entities they regulate. The merchant power producing sector has been very supportive of FERC's goal of promoting wholesale markets. These companies have taken part in a number of lawsuits and legislative efforts to expand the scope of federal jurisdiction over the electricity supply industry.

In contrast, state PUCs face a very different set of incentives and constraints. First, for more than fifty years, state PUCs have set the retail price of electricity and managed the process of determining the magnitude and fuel mix of new generation investments by the investor-owned utilities within their boundaries. This paternal relationship between the PUC and the firms that it regulates can make it extremely difficult to implement the physical and regulatory infrastructure necessary for a successful wholesale market.

Neither the state PUC nor the incumbent investor-owned utility benefits from the introduction of wholesale competition. The state PUC loses the ability to set retail electricity prices and the investor-owned utility faces the prospect of losing customers to competitive retailers. It is difficult to imagine a state regulator or policymaker voluntarily giving up the authority to set retail prices that can benefit certain customer classes and harm other customer classes. Because every citizen of a state consumes some electricity, the price-setting process can be an irresistibly tempting opportunity for regulators and state policymakers to pursue social goals in the name of industry regulation.

The introduction of wholesale competition can also limit the scope for the PUC and state policymakers to determine the magnitude and fuel mix of new generating capacity investments. Different from the former regulated regime where the PUC and state government played a major role in determining both the magnitude of new capacity investments and the input fuel for this new investment, in the wholesale market regime, this decision is typically made by independent, nonutility power producers.

For these reasons, the expansion of wholesale competition and the creation of the retail infrastructure necessary to support it directly conflict with many of the goals of the state PUCs and incumbent investor-owned utilities. Because it is a former monopolist, the incumbent investor-owned utility only stands to lose retail customers as a result of the implementation of effective retail competition. It is usually among the largest employers in the state, so it is often able to exert influence over the state-level regulatory process to protect its financial interests. Because the state PUC loses much of its ability to control the destiny of the electricity supply industry within its boundaries when wholesale and retail competition is introduced, the incumbent investor-owned utility may find a very sympathetic ear to arguments against adopting the retail market infrastructure necessary to support a wholesale market that benefits final consumers.

FERC's statutory responsibility to take actions to set just and reasonable wholesale rates provides state PUCs with the opportunity to appear to fulfill their statutory mandate to protect consumers from unjust prices, yet at the same time serve the interests of their incumbent investor-owned utilities. The state can appease the incumbent investor-owned utility's desire to delay or prohibit retail competition by relying on FERC to protect consumers from unjust and unreasonable wholesale prices though regulatory interventions such as price caps or bid caps on the wholesale market. However, as the events of May 2000 to May 2001 in California have emphasized, markets do not always set just and reasonable rates, and FERC's conception of policies that protect consumers from unjust and unreasonable prices may be very different from those the state PUC and other state policymakers would like FERC to implement.

The lesson from California is that once a state introduces a wholesale market with a significant merchant generation segment—generation owners with no regulated retail load obligations—it gives up the ability to control retail prices. As discussed earlier, California divested virtually all of its fossil-fuel generation capacity to five merchant suppliers with no vesting contracts. This is in sharp contrast to the experience of the eastern US wholesale markets in PJM, New England, and New York, which were formed from tight power pools.[11] Typically the vertically integrated utilities retained a substantial amount, if not all, of their generation capacity in the wholesale market regime. Those that were required to sell generation capacity did so with vesting contracts that allowed the selling utility to purchase energy from the new owner of the generation unit under long-duration fixed-price forward contracts. As a consequence of these decisions, the eastern ISOs began with very few generation owners with substantial net long positions in the wholesale market relative to their retail load obligations. Consequently, suppliers in these markets had less of an ability and incentive to exercise unilateral market power at all load levels, relative to California, where virtually all of the output of the nonutility generation sector was purchased in the short-term market.

4.8.2   Long History of Regulating Privately Owned Vertically Integrated Monopolies

Another reason for the different experience of the United States relative to virtually all other countries in the world is the different starting points of the restructuring process in the United States versus other industrialized countries. Before restructuring in the United States, there had been over seventy years of state-level regulatory oversight of privately owned vertically integrated monopolies. Once regulated retail prices are set, a profit-maximizing utility wants to minimize the total costs of meeting this demand. This combination of state-level regulation with significant time lags between price-setting processes for privately owned profit-maximizing utilities is likely to have squeezed out much of the productive inefficiencies in the vertically integrated utility's operations. Because the three eastern US markets started as tight power pools, it is also likely that this same mechanism operated to squeeze out many of the productive inefficiencies in the joint operation of the transmission network and generation units of the vertically integrated utilities that were members of the power pool.

By contrast, wholesale markets in other industrialized countries such as England, Wales, Australia, Spain, New Zealand, and the Nordic countries were formed from government-owned national or regional monopolies. As discussed earlier state-owned companies have significantly less incentive to minimize production costs than do privately owned, profit-maximizing companies facing output price regulation. These state-owned companies

---

11. In the former vertically integrated regime, a power pool is a collection of vertically integrated utilities that decide to "pool" their generation resources to be dispatched by a single system operator to serve their joint demand.

are often faced with political pressures to pursue other objectives besides least-cost supply of electricity to final consumers. They are often used to distribute political patronage in the form of construction projects or jobs within the company or to provide jobs in certain regions of the country. Consequently, the productive inefficiencies before restructuring were likely to be far greater in the electricity supply industries in these countries or regions than in the United States.

Consequently, one explanation for the superior performance of the restructured industries in these countries relative to the former vertically integrated utility regime in the United States is that the potential benefits from restructuring were far greater in these countries, because there were more productive inefficiencies in the industries in these countries to begin with. In this sense, the performance of restructured markets in the United States is the result of the combination of a relatively effective regulatory process and private ownership of the utilities. This logic raises the important question of whether the major source of benefits from restructuring in many of these industrialized countries is due to privatization of former state-owned utilities or the formation of a formal wholesale electricity market.

4.8.3 Increasing Amount of Intervention in Short-Term Energy Markets

Partially in response to the aftermath of the California electricity crisis, many aspects of wholesale markets in the United States have evolved to become very inefficient forms of cost-of-service regulation. One such mechanism that has become increasingly popular with FERC is the automatic mitigation procedure (AMP), which is designed to limit the ability of suppliers to exercise unilateral market power in the short-term market. Bid adders for mitigated generation units are another FERC-mandated source of market inefficiencies.

The AMP mechanism uses a two-step procedure to determine whether to mitigate a generation unit. First, all generation unit owners have a reference price, typically based on accepted bids during what are determined by FERC to be competitive market conditions. If a supplier's bids are in excess of this reference price by some preset limit—for example, $100/MWh or 100 percent of the reference level—then this supplier violates the conduct test. Second, if this supplier's bid moves the market price by some preset amount, for example, $50/MWh, then this bid is said to violate the impact test. A supplier's bid will be mitigated to its reference level if it violates the conduct and impact test. All FERC-jurisdictional ISOs except PJM have an AMP mechanism in place.

Because the reference prices in the AMP mechanism are set based on the average of past accepted bids, there is a strong incentive for what has been called "reference price creep" to occur. Accepted low bids can reduce a unit's reference price, which then limits the ability of the owner to bid high during system conditions when it is able to move the market price through its unilateral actions. Consequently, this cost to bidding low during competitive conditions implies that the AMP mechanism may introduce more market inefficiencies than it eliminates, particularly in a market with a relatively low bid cap on the short-term energy market. Off-peak prices are higher than they would be in the absence of the AMP mechanism and average on-peak prices are not reduced sufficiently by the AMP mechanism to overcome these higher than average prices during the off-peak hours.

The use of bid adders that enter into the day-ahead and real-time price-setting process have become increasingly favored by FERC as a way to ensure that generation units mitigated by an AMP mechanism or local market power mitigation mechanism earn sufficient revenues to remain financially viable. Before discussing the impact of these bid adders, it is useful to consider the goal of a market power mitigation mechanism, which is to produce locational prices that accurately reflect the incremental cost of withdrawing power at all locations in the network. Prices that satisfy this condition are produced by effective competition. An efficient price should reflect the incremental cost to the system of additional consumption at that location in the transmission network. A price that is above the short-term incremental cost of supplying electricity is inefficient because it can deter consumption with a value greater than the cost of production, but below the price. Setting price equal to the marginal willingness of demand to curtail is economically efficient only if pricing at the variable cost of the highest cost unit operating would create an excess demand for electricity. When a generation unit owner bids above the unit's incremental cost, other, more expensive units may be chosen to supply in the unit's place.

Therefore, the goal of local market power mitigation is to induce an offer price from a generation unit with local market power equal to the one that would obtain if that unit faced sufficient competition. A unit that faces substantial competition would offer a price equal to its variable cost of supplying additional energy. When the LMPM mechanism is triggered, the offer price of that unit is set to a regulated level. By the abovementioned logic, this regulated level should be equal to the ISO's best estimate of the unit's variable cost of supplying energy.

Although bid mitigation controls the extent to which offer prices deviate from incremental costs, bid adders, by adding a substantial $/MWh amount to the ISO's best estimate of the unit's minimum variable cost of operating, biases the offer price upwards to guarantee that mitigated offer prices will be noticeably higher than those from units facing substantial competition. Typically these bid adders are set at 10 percent of the unit's estimated variable cost. For units that are frequently mitigated, in terms of the fraction of their run hours, these bid adders can be extremely large, on the order of $40/MWh to $60/MWh in some ISOs, which can produce an offer price that is more than double the average wholesale price in many markets.

A bid adder known to be larger than the generation unit's minimum variable cost contradicts the primary goal of the market design process. Generation units that face sufficient competition will set an offer price close to their minimum variable cost. Combining these offers with mitigated offers set significantly above their minimum variable cost of supplying energy will result in units facing significant competition being overused. One might think that a 10 percent adder is relatively small, but it is important to emphasize that if a 100 MW generation unit is operating 2,000 hours per year with a 10 percent adder on top of a variable cost estimate of $50/MWh, this implies annual payments in excess of these variable costs of $1 million to that generation unit owner. In addition, this mitigated bid level will set higher prices for units located near this generation unit, further increasing the costs to consumers.

Frequently mitigated generation units are providing a regulated service, and for that reason should be guaranteed recovery of all prudently incurred costs. But cost recovery need not distort market prices in periods or at locations where there is no other justification for them to rise above incremental costs. Consider a mitigated unit with a $60/MWh incremental cost and a $40/MWh adder that is applied in an hour of ample supply. The market will be telling suppliers with costs less than $100/MWh that they are needed and telling demand with a value of electricity less than $100/MWh to shut down. Neither outcome is desirable. FERC has articulated the belief that it is appropriate that some portion of the fixed costs of mitigated units be allowed to set market prices. In other words, such units should not just be allowed to recover their fixed costs for themselves, but those costs should be reflected in the prices earned by other nonmitigated units.

FERC is essentially arguing that short-term prices should be set at long-run average cost. There are two problems with this view. The first is that the FERC would set prices to recover at least long-run average cost during all hours the unit operates. In a competitive market, high prices during certain periods would offset prices at incremental costs during the majority of hours with abundant supply. The average of all these resulting prices would trend toward long-run average cost. The adder approach sets the economically inefficient price all of the time, which implies higher than necessary wholesale energy costs to consumers.

4.8.4   Transmission Network Ill Suited for Wholesale Market

The legacy of state ownership in other industrialized countries versus private ownership with effective state-level regulation in the United States implies that these industrialized countries began the restructuring process with significantly more transmission capacity than did the US investor-owned utilities. In addition, the transmission assets of the former government monopoly were usually sold off as a single transmission network owner for the entire country, rather than maintained as separate but interconnected transmission networks owned by the former utilities, as is the case in the US wholesale markets. Both of these factors argue in favor of the view that initial conditions in the transmission network in these industrialized countries were significantly more likely to have an economically reliable transmission network for the wholesale market regime than the transmission networks in the United States.

4.8.5   Too Many Carrots, Too Few Sticks

There are two ways to make firms do what the regulator wants them to do: (1) pay them money for doing it, or (2) pay them less money for not doing it. Much of the regulatory oversight at FERC has used the former solution, which implies that consumers are less likely to see benefits from a wholesale market.

A potential consumer benefit from a wholesale market is that all investments, no matter how prudent they initially seem, are not guaranteed full cost recovery. Generation unit investments that turn out not to be needed to meet demand do not receive full cost recovery. As is the case in other markets, investors in these assets should bear the full cost of their "mistake," particularly if they also expect to receive all of the benefits associated with constructing new capacity when it is actually needed to meet demand. This investment "mistake" should be confined to the investor that decided to build the plant, not shared with all electricity consumers. Even if the entity that constructed the generation unit goes bankrupt, the generating facility is very unlikely to exit the market. Instead, a new owner will be able to purchase the facility at less than the initial construction cost, reflecting the fact that this new generation capacity is not needed at that time. The unit will still be available to supply electricity consumers—the original owner just will not be the entity earning those revenues. The new owner is likely to continue to operate the unit, but with a significantly lower revenue requirement than the original investor, because of the lower purchase cost. By allowing investors who invest in new generation capacity at what turns out to be the "wrong time" to bear the cost of these decisions, consumers will have a greater likelihood of benefitting from wholesale competition.

A second way that FERC implicitly ends up paying suppliers more money to do what it wants is the result of FERC's reliance on voluntary settlements among market participants. As mentioned earlier, historically wholesale price regulation at FERC largely amounted to approving terms and conditions negotiated under state-level regulatory oversight. FERC appears to have drawn the mistaken impression from this that voluntary negotiation can be used to set regulated terms and conditions. One way to characterize effective regulation is by making firms do things they are able to do, but do not want to do. For example, the firm may be able to cover its production costs at a lower output price, but it has little interest in doing so if this requires greater effort from its management. Asking parties to determine the appropriate price that suppliers can charge retailers for wholesale power through a consensus among the parties present is bound to result in the party that is excluded from this process—final consumers—paying more. In order for consumers to have a chance of benefitting from wholesale competition, FERC must recognize this basic tenet of consensus solutions, and protect consumers from unjust and unreasonable prices.

4.9   Positive Signs of Future Economic Benefits

There are three encouraging signs for the realization of future consumer benefits from restructuring in the United States. The implementation of nodal pricing and the convergence bidding appears to have produced tangible economic benefits, and the widespread deployment of interval meters opens the door to more active participation of final consumers in wholesale electricity markets.

4.9.1   Nodal Pricing

Multisettlement nodal-pricing markets have been adopted by all US jurisdictions with a formal short-term electricity market. This approach to setting short-term prices for energy and ancillary services explicitly recognizes the configuration of the transmission network and all relevant operating constraints on the transmission network and for generation units in setting locational prices. Generation unit owners and load serving entities submit their location-specific willingness to supply energy and willingness to purchase energy to the wholesale market operator, but prices and dispatch levels for generation units at each location in the transmission network are determined by minimizing the as-bid costs of meeting demand at all locations in the transmission network subject to all network operating constraints. The nodal price at each location is the increase in the optimized value of this objective function as a result of a one unit increase in the amount of energy withdrawn at that location in the transmission network. Bohn, Caramanis, and Schweppe (1984) provide an accessible discussion of this approach to electricity pricing.

A multisettlement market means that a day-ahead forward market is first run in advance of real-time system operation and this market results in firm financial schedules for all generation units and loads for all 24 hours of the following day. For example, suppose that for 1 hour during the following day a generation unit owner sells 50 MWh in the day-ahead forward market at $60/MWh. It receives a guaranteed $3,000 in revenues from this sale. However, if the generation unit owner fails to inject 50 MWh of energy into the grid during that hour of the following day, it must purchase the energy it fails to inject at the real-time price at that location. Suppose that the real-time price at that location is $70/MWh and the generator only injects 40/MWh of energy during the hour in question. In this case, the unit owner must purchase the 10 MWh shortfall at $70/MWh. Consequently, the net revenues the generation unit owner earns from selling 50 MWh in the day-ahead market and only injecting 40/MWh is $2,300, the $3,000 of revenues earned in the day-ahead market less the $700 paid for the 10 MWh real-time deviation from the unit's day-ahead schedule.

If a generation unit produces more output than its day-ahead schedule, then this incremental output is sold in the real-time market. For example, if the unit produced 55 MWh, then the additional 5 MWh beyond the unit owner's day-ahead schedule is sold at the real-time price. By the same logic, a load-serving entity that buys 100 MWh in the day-ahead market but only withdraws 90 MWh in real-time, sells the 10 MWh not consumed at the real-time price. Alternatively, if the load-serving entity consumes 110 MWh, then the additional 10 MWh not purchased in the day-ahead market must be paid at the real-time price.

A multisettlement nodal-pricing market is ideally suited to the US context because it explicitly accounts for the configuration on the actual transmission network in setting both day-ahead energy schedules and prices and real-time output levels and prices. This market design eliminates much of the need for ad hoc adjustments to generation unit output levels because of differences between the prices and schedules that the market mechanism sets and how the actual electricity network operates. Because all US markets started the restructuring process with significantly less extensive transmission networks relative to their counterparts in other industrialized countries, the market efficiency gains associated with explicitly accounting for the actual configuration of the transmission network in setting dispatch levels and prices in the day-ahead and real-time markets are likely to be the largest in the United States. The more extensive transmission networks in other industrialized countries are likely to be more forgiving of market designs that do not account for all relevant network constraints in setting generation unit output levels and prices, because the frequency and incidence that these constraints are active is much less than is typically the case in US wholesale markets.

Wolak (2011b) quantifies the magnitude of the economic benefits associated with the transition to nodal pricing from a zonal-pricing market, currently a popular market design outside of the United States. On April 1, 2009 the California market transitioned to a multisettlement nodal pricing market design from a multisettlement zonal-pricing market. Wolak (2011b) compares the hourly conditional means of the total amount of input fossil fuel energy in BTUs, the total hourly variable cost of production from fossil fuel units, and the total hourly number of starts from fossil fuel units before versus after the implementation of nodal pricing, controlling nonparametrically for the total of hourly output of the fossil fuel units in California and the daily prices of the major input fossil fuels. He finds that total hourly BTUs of energy consumed is 2.5 percent lower, the total hourly variable cost of production for fossil fuels units is 2.1 percent lower, and the total number of hourly starts is 0.17 higher after the implementation of nodal pricing. This 2.1 percent cost reduction implies that a roughly $105 million reduction in the total annual variable costs of producing fossil fuel energy in California is associated with the introduction of nodal pricing.

4.9.2   Convergence or Virtual Bidding

The introduction of nodal pricing in California has also allowed the introduction of virtual or convergence bidding at the nodal level. Virtual bidding is a purely financial transaction that is aimed at reducing the divergence between day-ahead and real-time prices and improving the efficiency of system operation. A virtual incremental energy bid (or INC bid) expresses the desire to sell 1 MWh energy in the day-ahead market, with the corresponding requirement to be a price taker at that same location for 1 MWh in the real-time market. A virtual decremental energy bid (or DEC bid) is the desire to sell 1 MWh of energy in the day-ahead market at a location, with the requirement to buy back that 1 MWh in the real-time market. A virtual bidder does not need to own any generation capacity or serve any load. Virtual bidders attempt to exploit systematic price differences between the day-ahead and real-time markets. For example, if an energy trader believes that the day-ahead price will be higher than the real-time price at a location, she should submit an INC bid at that location to sell energy at that location in the day-ahead market that is subsequently bought back at the real-time price. The profit on this transaction is the difference between the day-ahead price and real-time price. These actions by energy traders will cause the price in the day-ahead market to fall and the price in the real-time market to rise, which reduces the expected deviation between the day-ahead and real-time prices.

Besides reducing expected differences in prices for the same product sold in the day-ahead versus real-time markets, convergence bidding is expected to increase the efficiency of the dispatch of generation units, because generation unit owners and load-serving entities will have less of an incentive to delay selling or buying their energy in the day-ahead market because they expect to secure a better price in the real-time market. Because of the actions of virtual bidders, suppliers and load-serving entities should have more confidence that prices in the two markets will be equal on average, so that suppliers and load-serving entities will have no reason to deviate from their least-cost day-ahead scheduling actions to obtain a better price in the real-time market.

Jha and Wolak (2013) analyze the impact of the introduction of virtual bidding in the California ISO on February 1, 2011 on market outcomes using a similar framework to Wolak (2011b). They find that that the average deviation of between the day-ahead and real-time prices for the same hour of the day fell significantly after the introduction of convergence bidding, which is consistent with the view that the introduction of virtual bidding reduced the cost to energy traders of exploiting differences between day-ahead and real-time prices. The authors also find that tangible market efficiency benefits from the introduction of virtual bidding. Specifically, the conditional means of total hourly fossil fuel energy consumed in BTUs is 2.8 percent lower, the total hourly variable cost of fossil fuel energy production is 2.6 percent lower, and total hourly starts are 0.6 higher after the introduction of virtual bidding. These conditional means control nonparametrically for the level of total hourly fossil fuel output, total hourly renewable energy output, and the daily prices of the major input fossil fuels. It is important to control for the total hourly renewable energy output in making this pre- versus postvirtual bidding implementation comparison because of the substantial increase in the amount of renewable generation capacity in the California ISO control area over the past three years.

4.9.3   Internal Metering Deployment and Dynamic Pricing

The third recent development in the United States is the widespread deployment interval metering technology. Over the past five years, a number of state regulatory commissions have initiated processes to install interval meters for all customers under their jurisdictions. A number of municipal utilities have also implemented universal interval metering deployment plans. The widespread deployment of interval metering will allow retailers to implement dynamic pricing plans that can allow final consumers to benefit from active participation in the wholesale market.

Establishing hourly metering services as a regulated distribution service can also facilitate the development of vigorous retail competition, which should apply greater pressure for any wholesale costs reductions to be passed on the retail electricity consumers. However, as discussed in Wolak (2013), in most US states there are still considerable regulatory barriers to a vibrant retail competition and active participation of final demand in the wholesale market, but at least with increasing deployment of interval meters, the major technological barrier has been eliminated.

4.10   Conclusion

It may be practically impossible to achieve the regulatory process in the United States necessary for restructuring to benefit final consumers relative to the former vertically integrated, regulated-monopoly regime. Wholesale and retail market policies must be extremely well matched in the restructured regime. Even in countries with the same entity regulating the wholesale and retail sides of the electricity supply industry, this is an extremely challenging task. For the United States, with the historically adversarial relationship between FERC and state PUCs, presents an almost impossible challenge that has only been made more challenging by how FERC is generally perceived by state policymakers to have handled the California electricity crisis.

These relationships appear to have improved in recent years as a result of a number of changes at FERC, although there are still a number of important areas with little common ground between FERC and many state PUCs concerning the best way forward with electricity industry restructuring. The latest area of significant conflict is the role of FERC versus state PUCs in determining long-term resource adequacy policies. The specific issue is the role of formal capacity markets versus other approaches to achieving this goal. Wolak (2013) discusses some of these issues.

FERC appears to be focusing its efforts on enhancing the efficiency of the existing wholesale markets in the Northeast, the Midwest, and California, rather than attempting to increase the number of wholesale markets. As should be clear from the previous section, a significant amount of outstanding market design issues remain, and a number of them do not have clear-cut solutions, but both theoretical and empirical economic analysis can provide valuable input to crafting these solutions.

References

Averch, H., and L. Johnson. 1962. "Behavior of the Firm under Regulatory Constraint." *American Economic Review* (December):1052–69.
Awad, Mohamed, Keith E. Casey, Anna S. Geevarghese, Jeffrey C. Miller, A. Farrokh Rahimi, Anjali Y. Sheffrin, Mingxia Zhang, et al. 2010. "Using Market Simulations for Economic Assessment of Transmission Upgrades: Applications of the California ISO Approach." In *Restructured Electric Power Systems: Analysis of Electricity Markets with Equilibrium Models*, edited by Xiao-Ping Zhang, 241–70. Hoboken, NJ: Wiley.
Bohn, Roger E., Michael C. Caramanis, and Fred C. Schweppe. 1984. "Optimal Pricing in Electrical Networks over Space and Time." *RAND Journal of Economics* 15 (5): 360–76.
Borenstein, Severin. 2007. "Wealth Transfers from Implementing Real-Time Retail Electricity Pricing." *The Energy Journal* 28 (2): 131–49.
Borenstein, Severin, James Bushnell, and Steven Stoft. 2000. "The Competitive Effects of Transmission Capacity in a Deregulated Electricity Industry." *RAND Journal of Economics* 31 (2): 294–325.
Borenstein, Severin, James Bushnell, and Frank A. Wolak. 2002. "Measuring Market Inefficiencies in California's Restructured Wholesale Electricity Market." *American Economic Review* (December): 1367–405.
Bushnell, James. 2005. "Looking for Trouble: Competition Policy in the US Electricity Industry." In *Electricity Deregulation: Choices and Challenges*, edited by James Griffin and Steven Puller, 256–96. Chicago: University of Chicago Press.
Bushnell, James, and Celeste Saravia. 2002. "An Empirical Assessment of the Competitiveness of the New England Electricity Market." Center for the Study of Energy Markets Working Paper Number CSEMWP-101, May, http://www.ucei.berkeley.edu/pubs-csemwp.html.
Bushnell, James, and Catherine Wolfram. 2005. "Ownership Change, Incentives and Plant Efficiency: The Divestiture of US Electric Generation Plants." Center for

the Study of Energy Markets Working Paper Number CSEMWP-140, March, http://www.ucei.berkeley.edu/pubs-csemwp.html.

Charles River Associates. 2004. "Statewide Pricing Pilot Summer 2003 Impact Analysis." Oakland, CA: Charles River Associates.

Fabrizio, Kira M., Nancy L. Rose, and Catherine Wolfram. 2007. "Do Markets Reduce Costs? Assessing the Impact of Regulatory Restructuring on US Electric Generation Efficiency." *American Economic Review* (September): 1250–78.

Federal Energy Regulatory Commission (FERC). 2001. "Order Approving and Stipulation and Consent Agreement." AES Southland, Inc./Williams Energy Marketing & Trading Company, Docket No. IN01-3-001, United States of America, 95 FERC 61,167. Issued April 30.

Hirst, Eric. 2004. "US Transmission Capacity: Present Status and Future Prospects." Report prepared for Energy Delivery Group, Edison Electric Institute, and Office of Transmission and Distribution, US Department of Energy, June. http://electricity.doe.gov/documents/transmission_capacity.pdf.

Jarrell, Gregg A. 1978. "The Demand for State Regulation of the Electric Utility Industry." *Journal of Law and Economics* 21:269–95.

Jha, Akshaya, and Frank A. Wolak. 2013. "Testing for Market Efficiency in Arbitrage Markets with Non-Zero Transactions Costs: An Empirical Examination of California's Wholesale Electricity Market." Working paper, March, http://www.stanford.edu/~wolak.

Joskow, Paul. 1974. "Inflation and Environmental Concern: Structural Change in the Process of Public Utility Price Regulation." *Journal of Law and Economics* 17:291–327.

———. 1987. "Productivity Growth and Technical Change in the Generation of Electricity." *The Energy Journal* 8 (1): 17–38.

———. 1989. "Regulatory Failure, Regulatory Reform, and Structural Change in the Electrical Power Industry." *Brookings Papers on Economic Activity: Microeconomics*, 125–208.

———. 1997. "Restructuring, Competition and Regulatory Reform in the US Electricity Sector." *Journal of Economic Perspectives* 11 (3): 119–38.

———. 2000a. "Deregulation and Regulatory Reform in the US Electric Sector." In *Deregulation of Network Industries*, edited by Sam Peltzman and Clifford Winston, 113–88. Washington, DC: AEI-Brookings Joint Center for Regulatory Studies.

———. 2000b. "Why Do We Need Electricity Retailers? Or Can You Get It Cheaper Wholesale?" Working paper, http://econ-www.mit.edu/files/1127.

Joskow, Paul, and Edward Kahn. 2002. "A Quantitative Analysis of Pricing Behavior in California's Wholesale Electricity Market during Summer 2000: The Final Word." *The Energy Journal* 23 (December): 1–35.

Joskow, Paul, and Richard Schmalensee. 1983. *Markets for Power: An Analysis of Electric Utility Deregulation.* Cambridge, MA: MIT Press.

Laffont, Jean-Jacques, and Jean Tirole. 1991. "Privatization and Incentives." *Journal of Law, Economics, and Organization* 7:84–105.

Lee, Byung-Joo. 1995. "Separability Test for the Electricity Supply Industry." *Journal of Applied Econometrics* 10:49–60.

Mansur, Erin T. 2003. "Vertical Integration in Restructured Electricity Markets: Measuring Market Efficiency and Firm Conduct." Center for the Study of Energy Markets Working Paper Number CSEMWP-117, October, http://www.ucei.berkeley.edu/pubs-csemwp.html.

McRae, Shaun D., and Frank A. Wolak. 2014. "How Do Firms Exercise Unilateral Market Power? Evidence from a Bid-Based Wholesale Electricity Market." In

Manufacturing Markets: Legal, Political and Economic Dynamics, edited by Jean-Michel Glachant and Eric Brousseau, 390–420. Cambridge: Cambridge University Press.

Megginson, William L., and Jeffry M. Netter. 2001. "From State to Market: A Survey of Empirical Studies of Privatization." *Journal of Economic Literature* 39: 321–89.

Patrick, Robert H., and Frank A. Wolak. 1999. "Customer Response to Real-Time Prices in the England and Wales Electricity Market: Implications for Demand-Side Bidding and Pricing Options Design under Competition." In *Regulation under Increasing Competition*, edited by Michael A. Crew, 155–82. Dordrecht, the Netherlands: Kluwer Academic Publishers.

Peltzman, Sam. 1976. "Toward a More General Theory of Regulation." *Journal of Law and Economics* 19 (2): 211–40.

Stigler, George. 1971. "The Theory of Economic Regulation." *Bell Journal of Economics and Management Science* 2 (1): 3–22.

Shirley, Mary E., and Patrick Walsh. 2000. "Public versus Private Ownership: The Current State of the Debate." World Bank Policy Research Working Paper Number 2420, August, World Bank, Washington, DC.

Viscusi, W. Kip, John M. Vernon, and Joseph E. Harrington, Jr. 2001. *Economics of Regulation and Antitrust*, 3rd edition. Cambridge, MA: MIT Press.

Wolak, Frank A. 1994. "An Econometric Analysis of the Asymmetric Information Regulator-Utility Interaction." *Annales d'Economie et de Statistique* 34:13–69.

———. 1999. "Market Design and Price Behavior in Restructured Electricity Markets: An International Comparison." In *Competition Policy in the Asia Pacific Region*, edited by Takatoshi Ito and Anne Krueger, 79–134. Chicago: University of Chicago Press. http://www.stanford.edu/~wolak.

———. 2000a. "Comments on the Office of Gas and Electricity Markets (Ofgem) License Condition Prohibiting Abuse of Substantial Market Power." Submission to United Kingdom Competition Commission, July. http://www.stanford.edu/~wolak.

———. 2000b. "An Empirical Analysis of the Impact of Hedge Contracts on Bidding Behavior in a Competitive Electricity Market." *International Economic Journal* (Summer):1–40.

———. 2002. "Competition-Enhancing Local Market Power Mitigation in Wholesale Electricity Markets." November. http://www.stanford.edu/~wolak.

———. 2003a. "The Benefits of an Electron Superhighway." Stanford Institute for Economic Policy Research Policy Brief. November. http://www.stanford.edu/~wolak.

———. 2003b. "Diagnosing the California Electricity Crisis." *The Electricity Journal* (August):11–37. http://www.stanford.edu/~wolak.

———. 2003c. "Measuring Unilateral Market Power in Wholesale Electricity Markets: The California Market 1998 to 2000." *American Economic Review* (May):425–30. http://www.stanford.edu/~wolak.

———. 2003d. "Sorry, Mr. Falk: It's too Late to Implement Your Recommendations Now: Regulating Wholesale Markets in the Aftermath of the California Crisis." *The Electricity Journal* (August):50–55.

———. 2004. "Managing Unilateral Market Power in Wholesale Electricity." In *The Pros and Cons of Antitrust in Deregulated Markets*, edited by Mats Bergman, 78–102. Swedish Competition Authority.

———. 2006. "Residential Customer Response to Real-Time Pricing: The Anaheim Critical-Peak Pricing Experiment." http://www.stanford.edu/~wolak.

————. 2007. "Quantifying the Supply-Side Benefits from Forward Contracting in Wholesale Electricity Markets." *Journal of Applied Econometrics* 22:1179–209.

————. 2011a. "Do Residential Customers Respond to Hourly Prices? Evidence from a Dynamic Pricing Experiment." *American Economic Review* (May):83–87.

————. 2011b. "Measuring the Benefits of Greater Spatial Granularity in Short-Term Pricing in Wholesale Electricity Markets." *American Economic Review* (May):247–52.

————. 2012. "Measuring the Competitiveness Benefits of a Transmission Investment Policy: The Case of the Alberta Electricity Market." March. http://www.stanford.edu/~wolak.

————. 2013. "Economic and Political Constraints on the Demand-Side of Electricity Industry Re-structuring Processes." *Review of Economics and Institutions* 4 (1): Article 1.

Wolak, Frank A., Robert Nordhaus, and Carl Shapiro. 2000. "Analysis of 'Order Proposing Remedies for California Wholesale Electric Markets.'" Market Surveillance Committee of the California Independent System Operator, December. Issued November 1. http://www.caiso.com/docs/2000/12/01/2000120116120227219.pdf.

Wolak, Frank A., and Robert H. Patrick. 1997. "The Impact of Market Rules and Market Structure on the Price Determination Process in the England and Wales Electricity Market." February. http://www.stanford.edu/~wolak.

Wolfram, Catherine. 1999. "Measuring Duopoly Power in the British Electricity Spot Market." *American Economic Review* 89 (4): 805–26.

Incentive Regulation in Theory and Practice
Electricity Distribution and Transmission Networks

Paul L. Joskow

5.1 Introduction

Over the last thirty years several network industries that evolved historically as either state-owned or private regulated vertically integrated monopolies have been privatized, restructured, and some vertical segments deregulated. These industries include telecommunications, natural gas, electric power, and railroads. The reform program typically involves the vertical separation (ownership or functional) of potentially competitive segments, which are gradually deregulated, from remaining network segments that are assumed to have natural monopoly characteristics and continue to be subject to price, network access, service quality, and entry regulations. In several countries, an important part of the reform agenda has included the introduction of "incentive regulation" mechanisms for the remaining regulated segments as an alternative to traditional "cost-of-service" or "rate-of-return" regulation. The expectation was that incentive regulation mechanisms would provide more powerful incentives for regulated firms to reduce costs, improve service quality in a cost effective way, stimulate (or at least not impede) the introduction of new products and services, and

Paul L. Joskow is president of the Alfred P. Sloan Foundation and is the Elizabeth and James Killian Professor of Economics Emeritus at the Massachusetts Institute of Technology.

I have benefited from extensive comments provided by David Sappington and from discussions with Jean Tirole, Richard O'Neil, and Michael Pollitt. I am grateful to Nancy Rose for helping me to finalize this version of the chapter and for contributing to it through our joint teaching at MIT. I thank the MIT Center for Energy and Environmental Policy Research and the Cambridge-MIT Institute for research support. While the original version of this chapter was being written in 2007 I was a director of National Grid plc (2000–2007) and TransCanada Corporation (2004–2013). I am presently a director of Exelon Corporation. For acknowledgments, sources of research support, and disclosure of the author's material financial relationships, if any, please see http://www.nber.org/chapters/c12566.ack.

stimulate efficient investment in and pricing of access to regulated network infrastructure services.

Although much of the research on the "liberalization" of these sectors has focused on the evolution of the potentially competitive segments that have been deregulated (e.g., wholesale and retail electric power and natural gas markets), the performance of the remaining regulated network segments, and in particular the performance of new incentive regulation mechanisms, is also of considerable economic importance. These regulated segments often represent a significant fraction of the total price paid by consumers for retail service (prices for competitive plus regulated services). Moreover, the performance of the regulated segments can have important effects on the performance of the competitive segments when the regulated segments provide the infrastructure platform upon which the competitive segments rely (e.g., the electric transmission and distribution networks). Accordingly, the welfare consequences of these industry restructuring and deregulation initiatives depends on the performance of both the competitive and the regulated segments of these industries.

As the industry liberalization initiatives were gaining steam in Europe, Latin America, Australia, New Zealand, and North America during the late 1980s and the 1990s, theoretical research on the properties of alternative incentive regulation mechanisms developed quite rapidly as well. However, the relationship between theoretical developments and applications of incentive regulation theory in practice has not been examined extensively. In this chapter I provide an overview of the theoretical and conceptual foundations of incentive regulation theory, discuss some practical implementation issues, examine how incentive regulation mechanisms have been structured and applied to electric distribution and transmission networks (primarily in the United Kingdom where the application of these mechanisms is most advanced), review the limited available empirical analysis of the performance of incentive regulation mechanisms applied to electric distribution and transmission networks, and draw some conclusions about the relationships between incentive regulation theory and its application in practice.

As I will discuss, the implementation of incentive regulation concepts is more complex and more challenging than may first meet the eye. Even apparently simple mechanisms like price caps (e.g., so-called RPI-X regulation) are fairly complicated to implement in practice, are often imbedded in a more extensive portfolio of incentive regulation schemes, and depart in potentially important ways from the assumptions upon which related theoretical analyses have been based. Moreover, the sound implementation of incentive regulation mechanisms depends in part on information gathering, auditing, and accounting institutions that are commonly associated with traditional cost-of-service or rate-of-return regulation. These institutions are especially important for developing sound approaches to the treatment of capital expenditures, to develop benchmarks for operating costs, to implement resets ("ratchets") of prices, to take service quality attributes into account, and to deter gaming of incentive regulation mechanisms that have mechanisms for resetting prices or price adjustment formulas of one type or another over time.

5.2   Theoretical and Conceptual Foundations

5.2.1   Overview

The traditional textbook theories of optimal pricing for regulated firms characterized by subadditive costs and a budget constraint (e.g., marginal cost pricing, Ramsey-Boiteux pricing, nonlinear pricing, etc.) assume that regulators are completely informed about the technology, costs, and consumer demand attributes facing the firms they regulate and can somehow impose cost-minimization obligations on regulated firms (e.g., Boiteux 1960 [1951]; 1971 [1956]; Braeutigam 1989; Joskow 2007).[1] The focus is then on second-best pricing given defined cost functions, demand attributes, and budget balance constraints,[2] not on incentives to minimize costs or improve other dimensions of firm performance (e.g., service quality attributes).

Fully informed regulators clearly do not exist in reality. In reality, regulators have imperfect information about the cost and service quality opportunities and the attributes of the demand for services that the regulated firm faces. Moreover, the regulated firm generally has more information about these attributes than does the regulator or third parties, which have an interest in the outcome of regulatory decisions. Accordingly, the regulated firm may use its information advantage strategically in the regulatory process to increase its profits or to pursue other managerial goals, to the disadvantage of consumers (Owen and Braeutigam 1978; Laffont and Tirole 1993, chapter 1). These problems may be further exacerbated if the regulated firm can "capture" the regulatory agency and induce it to give more weight to its interests (Posner 1974; McCubbins 1985; Spiller 1990; Laffont and Tirole 1993, chapter 5). Alternatively, other interest groups may be able to "capture" the regulator and, in the presence of long-lived sunk investments, engage in "regulatory holdups" or expropriation of the regulated firm's assets. Higher levels of government, such as the courts and the legislature, also have imperfect information about both the regulator and the regulated firm and can monitor their behavior only imperfectly (McCubbins, Noll, and Weingast 1987).

---

1. This characterization is a little unfair since the development of much of this theoretical work was associated with economists in public enterprises who not only worked on optimal pricing but also developed methods for optimizing costs, reliability, and service quality in a public enterprise context.

2. In what follows I will use the terms "budget constraint," "firm viability constraint," and "firm participation constraint" interchangeably.

The evolution of "traditional" regulatory practices in the United States actually has reflected efforts to mitigate the information disadvantages that regulators confront, as well as reflecting broader issues of regulatory capture and opportunities for monitoring by other levels of government, consumers, and other interest groups. These institutions and practices are reflected in: laws and regulations that require firms to adhere to a uniform system of capital and operating cost accounts; give regulators access to the books and records of regulated firms and the right to request additional information on a case by case basis; auditing requirements, staff resources to evaluate the associated information, transparency requirements such as public hearings and written decisions, ex parte communications rules; opportunities for third parties to participate in regulatory proceedings to (in theory)[3] assist the regulatory agency in developing better information and reducing its regulatory disadvantage; and appeals court review and legislative oversight processes. In addition, since regulation is a repeated game, regulators (as well as legislators and appeals courts) can learn about the firm's attributes as they observe its responses to regulatory decisions over time and, as a result, the regulated firm naturally develops a reputation for the credibility of its claims and the information that it uses to support them.

However, although the development of US regulatory practice focused on improving the information available to regulators, the regulatory mechanisms adopted typically did not utilize this information nearly as effectively as they could have. While US regulatory practice differs significantly from the way it is often characterized, and during long periods of time provided incentives to control costs (Joskow 1974, 1989), formal incentive regulation mechanisms were historically used infrequently in the United States, Canada, Spain, Germany, and other countries with private rather than state-owned regulated network industries. Perhaps regulatory practice evolved this way due to the absence of a sound theoretical incentive regulation framework to apply in practice.

Beginning in the 1980s, theoretical research on incentive regulation rapidly evolved to confront directly imperfect and asymmetric information problems and related contracting constraints, regulatory credibility issues, dynamic considerations, regulatory capture, and other issues that regulators have been trying to respond to for decades but in the absence of a comprehensive theoretical framework to guide them. This theoretical framework is reasonably mature and can help regulators deal with these challenges much more directly and effectively (Laffont and Tirole 1993; Armstrong, Cowan, and Vickers 1994; Armstrong and Sappington 2004).

Consider the simplest characterization of the nature of the regulator's information disadvantages and its potential implications. A firm's cost opportunities may be high or low based on inherent attributes of its tech-

---

3. Of course, third parties may have an incentive to inject inaccurate information into the regulatory process as well.

nical production opportunities, exogenous input cost variations over time and space, inherent differences in the costs of serving locations with different attributes (e.g., urban or rural), and so forth. While the regulator may not know the firm's true cost opportunities, she will typically have some information about their probability distribution. The regulator's imperfect information can be summarized by a probability distribution defined over a range of possible cost opportunities between some upper and lower bound within which the regulated firm's actual cost opportunities lie. Second, the firm's actual realized costs or expenditures will not only depend on its underlying cost opportunities but also on the behavioral decisions made by managers to exploit these cost opportunities. Managers may exert varying levels of effort to get more (or less) out of the cost opportunities that the firm has available to it. The greater the managerial effort the lower will be the firm's costs, other things equal. However, exerting more managerial effort imposes costs on managers and on society. Other things equal, managers will prefer to exert less effort than more to increase their own satisfaction, but less effort will lead to higher costs and more "x-inefficiency." Unfortunately, the regulator cannot observe managerial effort directly and may be uncertain about its quality and its impacts on actual costs.

The uncertainties the regulator faces about the firm's inherent cost opportunities and managerial effort gives the regulated firm a strategic advantage. The firm would like to convince the regulator that it is a "higher cost" firm than it actually is, in the belief that the regulator will then set higher prices for the services it provides as it satisfies the firm's long-run financial viability constraint (firm participation or budget-balance constraint), increasing the regulated firm's profits, creating deadweight losses from (second-best) prices that are too high, and allowing the firm to capture surplus from consumers. Thus, the social welfare maximizing regulator faces a potential *adverse selection* problem as it seeks to distinguish between firms with high cost opportunities and firms with low cost opportunities, while adhering to a firm budget balance constraint that must be satisfied whether the firm turns out to have either high or low cost opportunities.

The uncertainties that the regulator faces about the quantity and impact of managerial effort create another potential problem. Since the regulator typically has or can obtain good information about the regulated firm's actual costs (i.e., its actual expenditures), at least in the aggregate, one approach to dealing with the adverse selection problem outlined earlier would simply be to set (or reset after a year) prices to a level equal to the firm's ex post realized costs. This would solve the adverse selection problem since the regulator's information disadvantage would be resolved by auditing the firm's costs.[4] This is the standard characterization of "cost-of-service" regulation.

---

4. Of course, the auditing of costs may not be perfect and in a multiproduct context the allocation of accounting costs between different products is likely to reflect some arbitrary joint cost allocation decisions.

However, if the loss of the opportunity for the firm and its managers to earn rents reduces managerial effort and less managerial effort increases the firm's costs, this kind of "cost plus" regulation may lead management to exert too little effort to control costs, increasing the realized costs above their efficient levels. If the "rat doesn't smell the cheese and sometimes gets a bit of it to eat" he may play golf rather than working hard to achieve efficiencies for the regulated firm. Thus, the regulator faces a potential *moral hazard* problem associated with variations in managerial effort in response to regulatory incentives (Laffont and Tirole 1986; Baron and Besanko 1987b).

Faced with these information disadvantages, the social welfare maximizing regulator will seek a regulatory mechanism that takes both the social costs of adverse selection and moral hazard into account, subject to the firm participation or budget-balance constraint that it faces, balancing the costs associated with adverse selection and the costs associated with moral hazard. The regulator may also take actions that reduce her information disadvantages by, for example, increasing the quality of the information that the regulator has about the firm's cost opportunities.

Following Laffont and Tirole (1993, 10–19), to illuminate the issues at stake, we can think of two polar case regulatory mechanisms that might be applied to a monopoly firm producing a single product. The first regulatory mechanism involves setting a fixed price ex ante that the regulated firm will be permitted to charge going forward (i.e., effectively forever). Alternatively, we can think of this as a pricing *formula* that starts with a particular price and then adjusts this price for *exogenous* changes in input price indices and other exogenous indices of cost drivers (forever). This regulatory mechanism can be characterized as a *fixed price* regulatory contract or, in a dynamic setting, a *price cap* regulatory mechanism, where prices adjust based on exogenous input price and performance benchmarks. There are two important attributes of this type of regulatory mechanism. Because prices are fixed (or vary based only on exogenous indices of cost drivers) and do not respond to changes in managerial effort or ex post cost realization, the firm and its managers are the residual claimants on production cost reductions and the costs of increases in managerial effort (and vice versa). That is, the firm and its managers have the highest powered incentives fully to exploit their cost opportunities by exerting the optimal amount of effort (Brennan 1989; Cabral and Riordan 1989; Isaac 1991; Sibley 1989; Kwoka 1993). Accordingly, this mechanism provides optimal incentives for inducing managerial effort and eliminates the costs associated with managerial moral hazard. However, because the regulator must adhere to a firm participation or financial viability constraint, when there is uncertainty about the regulated firm's cost opportunities the regulator will have to set a relatively high fixed price (or dynamic price cap) to ensure that *if* the firm is indeed inherently high cost, the prices under the fixed price contract or price cap will be high enough to cover the firm's (efficient) realized costs. Accordingly, while a fixed price mechanism may deal well with the potential moral hazard problem by providing high-powered incentives for cost reduction, it is potentially very poor at "rent extraction" for the benefit of consumers and society, potentially leaving a lot of rent to the firm due to the regulator's uncertainties about the firm's inherent costs and its need to adhere to the firm viability or participation constraint. Thus, while a fixed price type incentive mechanism solves the moral hazard problem, it incurs the full costs of adverse selection.

At the other extreme, the regulator could implement a "cost-of-service" contract or regulatory mechanism where the firm is assured that it will be compensated for all of the costs of production that it actually incurs. Assume for now that this is a credible commitment—there is no ex post renegotiation—and that audits of the expenditures the firm has incurred are accurate. When the firm produces it will then reveal whether it is a high cost or a low cost firm to the regulator. Because the regulator compensates the firm for all of its costs, there is no "rent" left to the firm or its managers in the form of excess profits. This solves the adverse selection problem. However, this kind of cost-of-service recovery mechanism does not provide any incentives for the management to exert optimal (any) effort. If the firm's profitability is not sensitive to managerial effort, the managers will exert the minimum effort that they can get away with. Even though there are no "excess profits" left on the table since revenues are equal to the actual costs the firm incurs, consumers are now paying higher prices than they would have to pay if the firm were better managed and some rent were left with the firm and its managers. Indeed, it is this kind of managerial slack and associated x-inefficiencies that most policymakers have in mind when they discuss the "inefficiencies" associated with regulated firms. Thus, while the adverse selection problem can be solved in this way, the costs associated with moral hazard are fully realized.

Accordingly, these two polar case regulatory mechanisms each have both positive and negative attributes. One is good at providing incentives for managerial efficiency and cost minimization, but it is bad at extracting the benefits of the lower costs for consumers. The other is good at rent extraction but leads to inefficiencies due to moral hazard resulting from suboptimal managerial effort. Perhaps not surprisingly, the optimal regulatory mechanism (in a second-best sense) will lie somewhere between these two extremes. In general, it will have the form of a *profit sharing* contract or a *sliding scale* regulatory mechanism, where the price that the regulated firm can charge is *partially* responsive to changes in realized costs and *partially* fixed ex ante (Schmalensee 1989b; Lyon 1996). More generally, by offering a *menu* of cost-contingent regulatory contracts with different cost-sharing provisions, the regulator can do even better than if it offers only a single profit-sharing contract (Laffont and Tirole 1993). The basic idea here is to make it profitable for a firm with low cost opportunities to choose a relatively high-powered incentive scheme and a firm with high cost opportunities a relatively low-powered scheme. Some managerial inefficiencies are incurred if the firm turns out to have high cost opportunities, but these costs are balanced by reducing the rent left to the firm if it turns out to have low cost opportunities.

Consider the following simple example that illustrates the value of offering a menu of regulatory contracts to the regulated firm.[5] Assume that there are two options, a fixed price contract or a cost-of-service contract. By offering this menu the regulator can present a more demanding fixed priced contract because the cost-of-service contract ensures that the firm's budget constraint will not be violated. If the fixed price contract is too demanding the firm will choose the cost-of-service contract. However, if the firm is potentially a very low-cost supplier and chooses the fixed price contract, more rents will be conveyed to consumers.

We can capture the nature of the range of options in the following fashion. Consider a general formulation of a regulatory process in which the firm's allowed revenues, R, are determined based on a fixed component, a, and a second component that is contingent on the firm's realized costs, C, and where b is the sharing parameter that defines the responsiveness of the firm's revenues to realized costs.

$$R = a + (1 - b)C.$$

Under a fixed price contract or price cap regulation:

$a = C^*$, where C^* is the regulator's assessment of the "efficient"
        costs of the highest cost type and
$b = 1$.

Under pure cost-of-service regulation where the regulator can observe the firm's expenditures but not evaluate their efficiency:[6]

$$a = 0$$

$$b = 0.$$

Under profit-sharing contract or sliding scale regulation (performance based regulation, or PBR)

$$0 < b < 1$$

$$0 < a < C^*.$$

The challenges then are to find the optimal performance based mechanism given the information structure faced by the regulator and for the regulator to find ways to reduce its information disadvantages vis-à-vis the regulated

5. I am grateful to David Sappington for providing this example.
6. This is not a particularly accurate characterization of cost-of-service regulation in practice in the United States, but it has become the common characterization of it, especially among those who had no experience with it (Joskow and Schmalensee 1986).

firm and to use the additional information effectively. Laffont-Tirole show that it is optimal for the regulator to offer a *menu* of contracts with different combinations of a and b that meet certain conditions driven by the firm's budget constraint and an incentive compatibility constraint that leads firms with low cost opportunities to choose a high-powered scheme (b is closer to 1 and a is closer to the efficient cost level for a firm with low cost opportunities) and firms with high cost opportunities to choose a lower powered incentive scheme (a and b are closer to zero). The lower powered scheme is offered to satisfy the firm participation constraint, sacrificing some costs resulting from managerial moral hazard, in order to reduce the rents that must be left to the low cost firm as it is induced to exert the optimal amount of managerial effort while satisfying the firm viability constraint if it turns out to be a high cost opportunity firm. (So far, this discussion has ignored quality issues. Clearly if a regulatory mechanism focuses only on reducing costs and ignores quality it will lead to firms providing too little quality. This is a classic problem with pure fixed price or price cap mechanisms and will be discussed further in the following.)

The incentive regulation literature is not a substitute for the older literature on optimal pricing for natural monopolies subject to a budget constraint, but rather a complement to it. This can be seen most clearly in the framework developed by Laffont and Tirole where the availability of government transfers creates a dichotomy or separation between optimal pricing and optimal incentives for controlling costs (Laffont and Tirole 1993, chapter 2). As a result, all of the basic second-best optimal pricing results for a natural monopoly subject to a budget constraint continue to be applied alongside the application of optimal incentive schemes (given asymmetric information) for controlling production costs. More generally, however, pricing and incentives cannot be so easily separated and their effects are likely to be interdependent. Some mechanisms can provide both good pricing and performance (cost, quality) incentives, but typically, the desire to get prices as well as performance incentives right creates another constraint that moves us further from first-best outcomes. Legal, political, bureaucratic, and other constraints may also be quite important in practice.

5.2.2   Incentive Regulation Theory Typology

The many papers that have contributed to the development of incentive regulation theory reflect a wide range of assumptions about the nature of the information possessed by the regulator and the firm about costs, cost-reducing managerial effort, demand and product quality, the attributes of the regulatory instruments available to the regulator, the risk preferences of the firm, regulatory capture by interest groups, regulatory commitment, flexibility, and other dynamic considerations. These alternative sets of assumption can be applied in both a single or multiproduct context. One strand of the literature initially focused primarily on adverse selection problems motivated by the assumption that regulators could not observe a firm's costs and ignoring the role of managerial effort (Baron and Meyerson 1982; Lewis and Sappington 1988a, 1988b). Another strand of the literature focused on both adverse selection and moral hazard problems motivated by the assumption that regulators could observe a firm's realized cost ex post, had information about the probability distribution of a firm's cost ex ante, and that managerial effort did affect costs but that this effort was not observable by the regulator (Laffont and Tirole 1986). Over time, these approaches have evolved to cover a similar range of assumptions about these basic information and behavioral conditions and lead to qualitatively similar conclusions. Armstrong and Sappington (2007) provide a comprehensive and thoughtful review and synthesis of this entire literature and I refer readers interested in a very detailed treatment of the full range of specifications of incentive regulation problems to their paper. Here I will simply lay out a "typology" of how these issues have been developed in the literature.

What are the regulator's objectives? Much of the literature assumes that the regulator seeks to maximize a social welfare function that reflects the goal of limiting the rents that are transferred from consumers and/or tax-payers to the firm's owners and managers subject to a firm participation or break-even constraint. Armstrong and Sappington (2007) articulate this by specifying an objective function $W = S + \alpha R$, where W is expected social welfare, S equals expected consumers' (including consumers as taxpayers) surplus, R equals the expected rents earned by the owners and managers of the firm (over and above what is needed to compensate them for the total costs of production and the disutility of managerial effort to satisfy the firm viability or participation constraint), and where $\alpha < 1$ implies that the regulator places more weight on consumer surplus than on rents earned by the firm. That is, the regulator seeks to extract rent from the firm for the benefit of consumers, subject as always to a firm break-even constraint. In addition, W will be reduced if excessive rents are left to the firm since this will require higher (second-best) prices and greater allocative inefficiency.

Laffont and Tirole (1986, 1993, 2000) create a social benefit from reducing the rents left to the firm in a different way. In their basic model, consumer welfare and the welfare of the owners and managers of the firm are generally weighted equally. However, one of the instruments available to the regula-tor is the provision of transfer payments from the government to the firm, which affect the rents earned by the firm. These transfer payments come out of the government's budget and carry a social cost resulting from the inefficiencies of the tax system used to raise these revenues. Thus, for every dollar of transfer payments given to the firm to increase its rent, effectively $(1 + \lambda)$ dollars of taxes must be raised, where λ reflects the inefficiency of the tax system. Accordingly, by reducing the transfers to the firm over and above what is required to compensate it for its efficient production costs and the associated managerial disutility of effort, welfare can be increased. As noted earlier, this setup also leads to a nice dichotomy between incentive mechanisms and the setting of second-best prices for the services sold by the firm. That is, regulators first establish compensation arrangements (define how the firm's budget constraint or "revenue requirements" will be determined) to deal as effectively as possible with adverse selection and moral hazard problems given the information structure assumed. The regulator separately establishes a second-best price structure to deal with allocational efficiency considerations. These prices may not yield enough revenue to cover all of the firm's costs, with the difference coming from net government transfers (or vice versa). In addition, Laffont and Tirole introduce managerial effort (e) as a variable that affects costs. Managers have a disutility of effort (U) and must be compensated for it. Accordingly, the utility of management also appears in the social welfare function.

What does the regulator know about the firm ex ante and ex post? The literature that focuses on adverse selection builds on the fundamental paper by Baron and Myerson (1982). There the regulator does not know the firm's cost opportunities ex ante but has information about the probability distribution over the firm's possible cost opportunities.[7] Nor can the regulator observe or audit the firm's costs ex post. The firm does know its own cost opportunities ex ante and ex post. The firm's demand is known by both the regulator and the regulated firm. There is no managerial effort in these early models of incentive mechanism design. Accordingly, the analysis deals with a pure adverse selection problem with no potential inefficiencies or moral hazard associated with inadequate managerial effort. The regulation in the presence of adverse selection literature then proceeds to consider asymmetric information about the firm's demand function, where the firm knows its demand but either the regulator does not observe demand ex ante or ex post or learns about demand only ex post (Lewis and Sappington 1988a; Riordan 1984).

In light of common US and Canadian regulatory practice, a natural extension of these models is to assume that the regulated firm's actual realized costs are observable ex post, at least with uncertainty. Baron and Besanko (1984) consider cases where a firm's costs are "audited" ex post, but the actual realized costs resulting from the audit are observable by the regulator with a probability less than one. The regulator can use this information to reduce the costs of adverse selection. Laffont and Tirole (1986, 1993) consider cases where the firm's realized costs are fully observable by the regulator. However, absent the simultaneous introduction of an uncertain scope for cost reductions through managerial effort, the regulatory problem then becomes trivial—just set prices equal to the firm's realized costs. Accordingly, Laffont and Tirole (1986, 1993) introduce managers of the

---

7. In models that distinguish between fixed and variable costs, the regulator may know the fixed costs but not the variable costs. See Armstrong and Sappington (2004).

firm who can choose the amount of cost reducing effort that they expend. Managerial effort is not observable by the regulator ex ante or ex post, but realized production costs are fully known to the regulator, as is the managerial "production function" that transforms managerial effort into cost reductions and the managers' utility of effort function. The regulated firm fully observes managerial effort, the cost-reducing effects of managerial effort, and demand. It also knows what managerial utility would be at different levels of effort. Armstrong and Sappington (2004) advance this analysis by considering cases where the *regulated firm* is uncertain about the operating costs that will be realized but knows that it can reduce costs by increasing managerial effort, though in a way that creates a moral hazard problem but no adverse selection problem. In the face of uncertainty over its costs, they consider cases where the firm may be either risk neutral or risk averse.

What instruments are available to the regulator, and how do the regulator and the regulated firm interact over time? Much of the incentive regulation literature is static. The regulator (or the government through the regulator) can offer a menu of prices (or fixed price contracts) with or without a fixed fee or transfer payment. The menu may contain prices that are contingent on realized costs (which can be thought of as penalties or rewards for performance) in those models where regulators observe costs ex post. Some of these instruments may be costly to utilize (e.g., transfer payments and auditing efforts). The more instruments the regulator has at its disposal and the lower the costs of using them, the closer the regulator will be able to get to the full information efficiency benchmark.

In the two-type case, the optimal regulatory mechanism involves offering the regulated firm a choice between two regulatory contract options. One is a fixed price option that leaves some rent if the firm is a low-cost type but negative rent if it is a high-cost type. The second is a cost-contingent contract that distorts the firm's effort if it is a high-cost type but leaves it no rent. The high-powered scheme is the most attractive to the low-cost type and the low-powered scheme is the most attractive to the high-cost type. The expected cost of the distortion of effort if the firm is a high-cost type is balanced against the expected cost of leaving additional rent to the firm if it is a low-cost type—*the fundamental trade-off between incentives and rent extraction.*

The two-type example can be generalized to a continuum of types (Laffont and Tirole 1993, 137ff). Assume that β indicates the firm's type ordered from low-cost to high-cost opportunities and has a continuous distribution from some lower bound β_L to some upper bound β_H with a cumulative distribution $F(\beta)$ and a strictly positive density $f(\beta)$ where F is assumed to satisfy a monotone hazard rate condition so that $F(\beta)/f(\beta)$ is nondecreasing in β.[8] The

---

8. Most commonly used distributions satisfy this assumption (e.g., uniform and normal distributions).

regulator maximizes expected social welfare subject to the firm participation and incentive compatibility constraints as before and incentive compatibility requires a mechanism that leaves more rent to the firm the lower is its type β, with the highest cost type getting no rent, the lowest cost type getting the most rent, and the intermediate type's rent defined by the difference in their marginal costs. Similarly, the effort of the lowest cost type is optimal and the effort of the highest cost type is distorted the most, with intermediate types having smaller levels of distortion (and more rents) as β declines toward β_L. In the case of a continuous distribution of types, the optimality conditions are directly analogous to those for the two-type case.

Laffont and Tirole (1993) show that these optimality conditions can be implemented by offering the firm a menu of linear contracts, which in their model are transfer or incentive payments in excess of realized costs (which are also reimbursed), of the form:

$$t(\beta, c) = a(\beta) - b(\beta)c,$$

where a is a fixed payment, b is a cost-contingent payment, and a and b are decreasing in β.

We can rewrite the transfer payment equation in terms of the gross transfer to the firm including the unit cost reimbursement:

$$R_f = a(\beta) - b(\beta)c + c = a(\beta) + (1 - b(\beta))c,$$

where $da/db > 0$

(for a given β a unit increase in the slope of the incentive payment must be compensated by an increase in the fixed payment to cover the increase in production costs),

$$\text{and } d^2a/db^2 < 0,$$

(the fixed payment is a concave function of the slope of the incentive scheme; see figure 5.1).

The lowest cost type chooses a fixed price contract with a transfer net of costs equal to U_L, and the firm is the residual claimant on cost-reducing effort ($b = 1$). As β increases, the transfer is less sensitive to the firm's realized costs (b declines), the rent is lower (a declines), and the efficiency distortion from suboptimal effort increases.

One way in which regulators can effectively reduce their information disadvantage is by using competitive benchmarks or "yardstick regulation" in the price-setting process. Shleifer (1985) shows that if there are multiple non-competing but otherwise identical firms (e.g., gas distribution companies in firms in different states), an efficient regulatory mechanism involves setting the price for each firm based on the costs of the other firms. Each individual firm has no control over the price it will be allowed to charge (unless the firms can collude) since it is based on the realized costs of $(n-1)$ other firms.

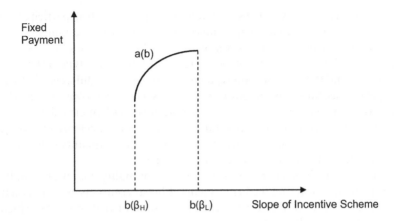

Fig. 5.1   Menu of incentive contracts
Source: Laffont and Tirole (1993, figure 1.5).

Thus, effectively each firm has a fixed price contract and the regulator can be assured that the budget balance constraint will be satisfied since if the firms are identical prices will never fall below their "efficient" realized costs. This mechanism effectively induces each firm to compete against the others. The equilibrium is a price that just covers all of the firm's efficient costs as if they competed directly with one another.

Of course, the regulator is unlikely to be able to find a large set of truly identical firms. However, hedonic regression, frontier cost function estimation, and related statistical techniques can be used to normalize cost variations for exogenous differences in firm attributes to develop normalized benchmark costs (Jamasb and Pollitt 2001, 2003; Estache, Rossi, and Ruzzier 2004). As we shall see following, these benchmark costs can then be used by the regulator in a yardstick framework or in other ways to reduce its information disadvantage, allowing it to use high-powered incentive mechanisms without incurring the cost of excessive rents that would accrue if the regulator had a greater cost disadvantage. However, data to perform this type of benchmarking analysis are not always available, a variety of benchmarking techniques can be utilized, and the failure to integrate cost and quality variables can lead to misleading results (Giannakis, Jamasb, and Pollitt 2004; Jamasb and Pollitt 2001).

Of additional practical interest are issues that arise as we consider the dynamic interactions between the regulated firm and the regulator and the availability and utilization of mechanisms that the regulator potentially has available to reduce its information disadvantage. It is inevitable that the regulator will learn more about the regulated firm as they interact over time. So, for example, if the regulator can observe a firm's realized costs ex post it will learn a lot about its true cost opportunities. Should the regulator use that information to reset the prices that the regulated firm receives (commonly known as a "ratchet"; see Weitzman 1980)? Or is it better for the regulator to commit to a particular contract ex ante, which may be contingent on realized costs, but the regulator is then not permitted to use the information gained from observing realized costs to change the terms and conditions of the regulatory contract offered to the firm? Is it credible for the regulator to commit *not* to renegotiate the contract, especially in light of US regulatory legal doctrines that have been interpreted as foreclosing the ability of a regulatory commission to bind future commissions?

Clearly, if the regulated firm knows that information about its realized costs can be used to renegotiate the terms of its contract ex post, this will affect its behavior ex ante. It may have incentives to engage in less cost reduction in period 1 or try to fool the regulator into thinking it is a high cost firm so that it can continue to earn rents in period 2. Or if the regulated firm has a choice between technologies that involve sunk cost commitments, will the possibility of ex post opportunism or regulatory expropriation, perhaps driven by the capture of the regulator by other interest groups, affect its willingness to invest in the lowest cost technologies when they involve more significant sunk cost commitments (leading to the opposite of the Averch-Johnson effect; see Averch and Johnson 1962; Baumol and Klevorick 1970). These issues are all of considerable importance when applying incentive regulation concepts in practice.

These dynamic issues have been examined theoretically more intensively over time and represent a merging of the literature on regulation with the literature on contracts and dynamic incentive mechanisms more generally (Laffont and Tirole 1988b, 1990, 1993; Baron and Besanko 1987a; Armstrong and Vickers 1991, 2000; Armstrong, Cowan, and Vickers 1994). The impacts of regulatory lag of different durations (Baumol and Klevorick 1970; Klevorick 1973; Joskow 1974) and other price adjustment procedures have been analyzed theoretically as well (Vogelsang and Finsinger 1979; Sappington and Sibley 1988, 1990).

As I will discuss further in the following, one of the regulatory mechanisms utilized extensively in the United Kingdom after its utility sectors were privatized is effectively a fixed price contract (actually a price cap that is adjusted for general movements in input prices and an assumed target rate of productivity growth—a so-called RPI-X mechanism as discussed in detail later) with a ratchet every five (or so) years when the level of the price cap is reset to reflect the current realized (or forecast) cost of service (Beesley and Littlechild 1989; Brennan 1989; Isaac 1991; Sibley 1989; Armstrong, Cowan, and Vickers 1994). It has been observed that regulated firms appear to make their greatest cost reduction efforts during the early years of the price cap period and then exert less effort at reducing costs as the date of the price review proceeding approached (OFGEM 2004a, 2004b, 2004d, 2004e). More generally, the dynamic attributes of the regulatory process and how regulators use information about costs revealed by the regulated firm's behavior over time have significant effects on the incentives the regulated firm faces and on its behavior (Gilbert and Newbery 1994).

5.3   Practical Implementation Issues

While the theoretical literature on incentive regulation is quite rich, it still provides relatively little direct guidance for empirical application in specific circumstances. Regulators need to find answers to a number of practical questions to apply the theory in practice in the design of actual incentive regulation mechanisms. Among the questions that must be answered are the following:

Where does the regulator's information about the firm's actual costs and the distribution of cost opportunities come from? If regulators are going to apply incentive regulation mechanisms that are cost contingent they must have some consistent mechanism for measuring the regulated firm's actual costs. These costs include operating costs (e.g., labor), the cost of capital investments (e.g., the cost of physical distribution network equipment), and the financial components necessary to transform this capital investment cost stock into a flow of rental or user charges for capital services (e.g., depreciation rates, the opportunity cost of capital, the appropriate debt/equity ratio, income taxes) over time.

Capital cost accounting issues have largely been ignored in the theoretical literature on incentive regulation. Although it has been of limited concern to contemporary economists, any well-functioning regulatory system needs to adopt good cost accounting rules, reporting requirements for costs, output, prices, and other dimensions of firm performance, and enforce auditing and monitoring protocols to ensure that the regulated firm applies the auditing rules and adheres to its reporting obligations. Much of the development of US regulation during the first half of the twentieth century focused on the development of these foundation components required for any good regulatory system that involves cost-contingent regulatory mechanisms. See Joskow (2007) for a more detailed discussion of capital cost accounting principles used in the United States.

Of course, cost is only one dimension of firm performance. Firm performance may also have various "quality" dimensions and there are likely to be inherent trade-offs between cost and quality. If incentives are to be extended to the quality dimension as well, as they should be, then these quality dimensions must be defined and associated performance indicia measured by the firm, reported to the regulator, and must be subject to auditing protocols. Regulators also need information to develop a view about the distribution of cost opportunities, consumer valuations of service quality, and other dimensions of firm performance to implement incentive regulation mechanisms that do not leave too much rent to regulated firms and do not lead to excessive managerial efficiency. Regulators need to have the resources to develop information about industry performance norms and the causes of variations in the performance of regulated firms. Accordingly, they need the resources to commission industry studies that give them this kind of information so that their information disadvantage can be reduced.

Should the regulator offer the regulated firm a menu of contracts or a specific contract with a single set of values for a *and* b *as discussed earlier?* The Laffont-Tirole framework implies that firms should be offered a menu of cost-contingent contracts from which they can choose. The menu forces the firm to reveal its type ex post and allows for a better balance of efficiency and rent extraction than would a single linear incentive contract designed ex ante based on the same information and subject to the same budget balance constraints. However, it appears that regulators typically offer firms only a single regulatory contract, and when the contract is cost contingent it is typically linear (Schmalensee 1989b). I am aware of two situations in which regulated firms were offered a menu of cost-contingent or sliding scale contracts. The first relates to the system operator (SO) incentive schemes that have been offered to the electric transmission system operator in England and Wales, discussed in the following. The second is the menu of sliding scale mechanisms offered to the electric distribution companies in the United Kingdom for determining future capital expenditure allowances and associated user charges for capital services pursuant to the review and resetting of electricity distribution charges issued in late 2004 for distribution charges that would be in effect from April 1, 2005 until March 31, 2010. These menus are discussed in more detail below as well. However, there may be more use of a de facto menu of contracts approach than first meets the eye when we take the attributes of the regulatory review process itself into account. The final regulatory mechanism applied to a regulated firm is often the result of formal and informal negotiations involving proposals by the regulator's staff, the regulatory firm, and interested third parties (Joskow 1973, 1974; Doucet and Littlechild 2006). This process may have similarities to the regulator's offer of a menu of contracts in the sense that the parties negotiate over the attributes of the incentive mechanism. We see only the final outcome of these negotiations.

What benchmarks are to be used to arrive at starting values for the regulated firm's costs, revenues, and other performance indicia, and how are these benchmarks adjusted over time? In some cases regulators accept the firm's current levels of costs and other dimensions of performance and focus on benchmarks for performance *improvements*, effectively benchmarking the firm against its historical performance. This approach reflects the assumption that the firm can do better than it has in the past, but still leaves open the question of performance improvement norms. Another approach is to benchmark the firm's current performance using appropriate comparisons with other similarly situated firms, properly adjusting for differences in the cost opportunities and demand patters faced by similar but not identical comparator firms. Where there is not a set of reasonable comparator firms to draw upon, regulators may rely on engineering and management "experts" to study the firm's performance and opine on cost improvement opportunities and the associated uncertainties, perhaps drawing analogies from components of firms in other industries.

What should be the power of the incentive scheme? If the regulator offers a menu of cost-contingent contracts, the height and the slope of the incentive scheme must be defined (*a* and *b* above). If the regulator applies a single incentive mechanism, both the fixed component and the "sharing" or "sliding scale" fraction must be defined. If the regulatory mechanism is a price cap, both the starting values for prices or the average price level (p_o for UK regulation of electric, gas, and water distribution and transmission networks) and the "x" intertemporal adjustment factor must be defined. In addition, an appropriate inflation index (RPI in the United Kingdom) must be identified.

In practice, incentive regulation mechanisms typically also have "resets" or "ratchets" and the period of "regulatory lag" between price reviews needs to be defined. As the review period gets longer the power of the incentive mechanism increases and vice versa. Finally, many incentive regulation mechanisms used in practice have caps and floors that effectively define a collar on the operation of the mechanism. So, for example, a cap and floor are often applied that limit the gains and the losses that the regulated firm can incur under the incentive mechanism. Once the cap or floor is hit the mechanism effectively defaults to pure cost-of-service regulation or to a renegotiation of the regulatory contract. The rationale for the use of caps and floors superimposed onto a sliding scale scheme is not immediately obvious from incentive regulation theory and is likely to have poor incentive properties around the points where the collar kicks in. The use of caps and floors is probably best thought of as a way for regulators to recognize the range of outcomes anticipated in the design of the mechanism and the associated starting values and sharing fractions that have been defined. When the caps and floors are hit this effectively triggers a renegotiation, reset, or ratchet process.

Should the incentive mechanism be comprehensive or "partial"? There are multiple dimensions of firm performance defined by cost and quality indicia and the trade-offs between them. Most regulated firms supply multiple products for which demand and cost attributes vary. There are also multiple dimensions of firm costs with different adjustment lags. Operating costs can be adjusted relatively quickly, while capital costs are often long lived and can be economically adjusted much more slowly. Moreover, both the level and adjustment opportunities for operating costs depend upon the attributes of the legacy stock of capital and investments in new facilities and can both expand the firm's capacity to supply particular products and affect its operating costs. Capital and operating costs are inherently interdependent with varying adjustment lags. As a practical matter, the line between an operating cost and a capital cost may not be well defined except by clear accounting rules. A hammer that lasts for five years may be expensed while software that has a useful life of three years may be capitalized. Under some incentive regulation mechanisms this creates opportunities for gaming by expensing capital costs or capitalizing operating costs.

Ideally, a comprehensive incentive regulation mechanism that consistently integrates all cost and quality relationships at a point of time and over time would be applied. However, as a practical matter this often places very challenging information and implementation burdens on the regulator. Partial mechanisms or a portfolio of only loosely harmonized mechanisms are often used by regulators. Operating and capital cost norms and targets are typically developed separately and the effective power of the incentive scheme applicable to operating and capital costs may vary between them. Separate incentive mechanisms may be applied to measures of quality than to measures of total operating and capital costs. This reality represents perhaps the most significant variation between received incentive regulation theory and incentive regulation in practice.

5.4   Implementation in Practice to Electricity and Gas Networks

5.4.1   Early Applications

Although the theoretical literature on incentive regulation is fairly recent, we can trace the earliest applications of incentive regulation concepts back to the early regulation of the manufactured gas distribution sector[9] (town gas) in England in the mid-nineteenth century (Joskow and Schmalensee 1986; Hammond, Johnes, and Robinson, 2002). A sliding scale mechanism in which the dividends available to shareholders were linked to increases and decreases in gas prices from some base level was first introduce in England in 1855 (Hammond, Johnes, and Robinson, 2002, 255). The mechanism established a base dividend rate of 10 percent. If gas prices increased above a base level the dividend rate was reduced according to a sharing formula. However, if gas prices fell below the base level the dividend rate did not increase (a "one-way" sliding scale). The mechanism was made symmetric in 1867. Note that the mechanism was not mandatory and it was introduced during a period of falling prices (Hammond, Johnes, and Robinson, 2002, 255–56). A related profit-sharing mechanism (what Hammond, Johnes, and Robinson call the "Basic Price System") was introduced in 1920 that pro-

---

9. This is before the development of natural gas. "City gas" was manufactured from coal by local gas distribution companies. At the time there were both private and municipal gas distribution companies in operation in England.

vided a minimum guaranteed 5 percent dividend to the firm's shareholders and shared changes in revenues from a base level between the consumers, the owners of the firm, and the firm's employees. Specifically, this mechanism established a basic price p_b to yield a 5 percent dividend rate. This dividend rate was the minimum guaranteed to the firm. At the end of each financial year the firm's actual revenues (R) were compared to its basic revenues $R_b = p_b$ times the quantity sold. The difference between R and R_b was then shared between consumers, investors, and employees, apparently subject to the constraint that the dividend rate would not fall below 5 percent.

In the early twentieth century, US economists took note of the experience with sliding scale mechanisms for local manufactured gas utilities in England, but appear to have concluded that they were not well matched to the regulation of electricity and telephone service (and other sectors) where demand and technology were changing fast and future costs were very uncertain (Clark 1913). Cost-of-service regulation (with regulatory lag, prudence reviews, and public planning processes) evolved initially as the favored alternative in the United States and other countries with private (rather than state-owned) regulated monopolies and the experience in England during the nineteenth and early twentieth centuries was largely forgotten by both regulators and students of regulation.

State public utility commissions in the United States began to experiment with formal performance based regulation mechanisms for electric utilities in the early 1980s. The early programs were targeted at specific components of an electric utility's costs or operating performance such as generation plant availability, heat rates, or construction costs (Joskow and Schmalensee 1986; Sappington et al. 2001). Formal comprehensive incentive regulation mechanism have been slow to spread in the US electric power industry (Sappington et al. 2001), though rate freezes, rate case moratoria, price cap mechanisms, and other alternative mechanisms have been adopted in many states, sometimes informally, since the mid-1990s.

5.4.2 Price Cap Mechanisms: General Considerations

Beginning in the mid-1980s a particular form of incentive regulation was introduced for the regulated segments of the privatized electric gas, telephone, and water utilities in the United Kingdom, New Zealand, Australia, and portions of Latin America as well as in the regulated segments of the telecommunications industry in the United States.[10] The primary (but not the only) mechanism chosen was the "price cap" (Beesley and Littlechild 1989; Brennan 1989; Armstrong, Cowan, and Vickers 1994; Isaac 1991). Under price cap regulation the regulator sets an initial price p_o (or a vector

10. The United States is behind many other countries in the application of incentive regulation principles to electric distribution and transmission, though their use is slowly spreading in the United States beyond telecommunications.

of prices for multiple products). This price (or a weighted average of the prices allowed for firms supplying multiple products or different types of customers) is then adjusted from one year to the next for changes in inflation (rate of input price increase or RPI) and a target productivity change factor x. Accordingly, the price in period 1 is given by:

$$p_1 = p_o (1 + \text{RPI} - x).$$

Typically, some form of cost-based regulation is used to set p_o. The price cap mechanism then operates for a preestablished time period (e.g., five years).[11] At the end of this period a new starting price p_o and a new x factor are established after another cost-of-service and prudence or efficiency review of the firm's costs. That is, there is a prescheduled regulatory ratchet built into the system.

As discussed earlier, in theory, a price cap mechanism is a high-powered "fixed price" regulatory contract that provides powerful incentives for the firm to reduce costs. Moreover, if the price cap mechanism is applied to a (properly) weighted average of the revenues the firm earns from each product it supplies, the firm has an incentive to set the second-best prices for each service (Laffont and Tirole 2000; Armstrong and Vickers 1991) given the level of the price cap. It is also fairly clear that pure "forever" price cap mechanisms are not optimal from the perspective of an appropriate trade-off between efficiency incentives and rent extraction (Schmalensee 1989b).

In practice, price cap mechanisms apply elements of cost-of-service regulation, yardstick competition, and high-powered "fixed price" incentives, plus a ratchet. Price caps on operating costs or capital plus operating costs are often one component of a larger portfolio of incentive mechanisms. As I will show presently, the details of constructing a price cap mechanism for electric distribution and transmission networks are more complicated than is often thought. Moreover, the regulated electric or gas distribution firm's ability to determine the structure of prices under an overall revenue cap is typically limited. Price caps applied to electricity and gas distribution and transmission are used primarily as an incentive mechanism, not as a mechanism to induce optimal pricing. In telecommunications, regulated firms are given more pricing freedom so that price cap mechanism affects both performance incentives and pricing incentives.

It is worth noting again that in an ongoing regulated firm context, a pure "forever" price cap without any cost sharing (i.e., without a sliding scale mechanism) is not likely to be optimal given asymmetric information and uncertainty about future productivity opportunities (Schmalensee 1989b).

11. Many implementations of price cap regulation also have "z" factors. Z factors reflect cost elements that cannot be controlled by the regulated firm and are passed through in retail prices. For example, in the United Kingdom, the charges distribution companies pay for connections to the transmission network are treated as pass-throughs. Changes in property tax rates are also often treated as pass-throughs.

Prices would have to be set too high to satisfy the firm participation constraint and too much rent would be left on the table for the firm. The application of a ratchet from time to time that resets prices to reflect observed costs is a form of cost-contingent dynamic regulatory contract. It softens cost-reducing incentives but extracts more rents for consumers in the long run.

A natural question to ask about price cap mechanisms is where does x (and perhaps p_o) come from (Bernstein and Sappington 1999)? Conceptually, assuming that RPI is a measure of a general input price inflation index, x should reflect the difference between the expected or target rate of total factor productivity growth for the regulated firm and the corresponding productivity growth rate for the economy as a whole and the difference between the rate of change in the regulated firm's input prices and input prices faced by firms generally in the economy. That is, the regulated firm's prices should rise at a rate that reflects the general rate of inflation in input prices less an offset for higher (or lower) than average productivity growth and an offset for lower (or higher) input price inflation. Unfortunately, the theory advanced by Bernstein and Sappington is rarely applied in practice.

In early applications in the United States, the computation of x was often fairly ad hoc. The initial application of the price cap mechanism by the Federal Communications Commission (FCC) to AT&T's intercity and information services used historical productivity growth and added an arbitrary "customer dividend" to choose an x that was larger than the historical rate of productivity growth. However, the expectation here was that the need for regulation would be transitory and would be phased out for AT&T's services as competition expanded. In England and Wales and some other countries, statistical benchmarking methods have come into use to help determine the relative efficiency of individual firms' operating costs and service quality compared to their peers. This information can then be used as an input to setting values for both p_o and x (Jamasb and Pollitt 2001, 2003; OFGEM 2004a) to provide incentives for those far from the efficiency frontier to move toward it and to reward the most efficient firms in order to induce them to stay on the efficiency frontier, in a fashion that is effectively an application of yardstick regulation. A variety of empirical methods have been applied to identify an operating cost efficiency frontier and to measure how far from this operating cost efficiency frontier individual regulated firms lie. The value for x is then defined in such a way as to move the firms to the frontier over a prespecified period of time (e.g., five years). These methods have recently been expanded to include quality of service considerations (Giaanakis, Jamasb, and Pollitt 2004). Benchmark rankings of relative performance may change significantly when quality attributes are introduced. Accordingly, benchmarking cost and quality as separable attributes is clearly problematic.

The extensive use of periodic "ratchets" or "resets to cost" along with price cap mechanisms reflect the difficulties of defining a fixed long-term value for p_o and x ex ante and the standard trade-offs between efficiency incentives, rent extraction, and firm viability constraints. These periodic ratchets necessarily dull incentives for cost reduction, however. Note in particular that with a predefined five-year ratchet, a dollar of cost reduction in year one is worth a lot more than a dollar of cost reduction in year four since the cost savings are retained by the firm only until the next reset anniversary (OFGEM 2004d, 2004b, 2004c).

Although it is not discussed too much in the empirical literature, the development of the parameters of price cap mechanisms using statistical benchmarking methods have typically focused primarily on operating costs only. Capital cost allowances are established through more traditional utility planning and cost-of-service regulatory accounting methods including the specification of a rate base (regulatory asset value or RAV), depreciation rates, debt and equity costs, debt/equity ratios, tax allowances, and so forth. Since operating costs for distribution networks are often a smaller fraction of total costs than are capital-related costs, the focus on operating costs (or so-called controllable costs) is potentially misleading. In addition, it is widely recognized that a pure price cap mechanism provides incentives to reduce both costs *and* the quality of service (Banerjee 2003). Accordingly, price cap mechanisms are increasingly accompanied either by specific performance standards and the threat of regulatory penalties if they are not met or formal PBR mechanisms that set performance standards and specify penalties and rewards for the firm for falling above or below these performance norms (OFGEM 2004b, 2004c; Sappington 2003; Ai and Sappington 2002; Ai, Martinez, and Sappington 2004).

5.4.3 The Basic Price Cap Mechanism for Electric Distribution Companies: The UK Implementation[12]

There are fourteen electric distribution companies in the United Kingdom, several of which are under common ownership within a holding company structure, yielding seven firms controlling fourteen electric distribution networks. These companies, which are referred to as regional electricity companies, or RECs, provide delivery services in specific geographic franchise areas to transport electricity from points of interconnection with the high voltage transmission network to points of interconnection with final consumers. Their total revenues and the associated prices for using their networks are regulated by the UK Office of Gas and Electricity Markets (OFGEM). The distribution companies themselves provide only delivery services and do not contract to buy or produce electricity for resale to final customers, a competitive function referred to as "electricity supply" in the United Kingdom,

12. After two working paper versions of this chapter (2005 and 2006) were widely distributed, Jamasb and Pollitt (2007) released a working paper that also examines aspects of the 2004 review of electric distribution network prices and incentive mechanisms in the United Kingdom. As a result, there is some overlap between portions of this chapter and their paper.

though they may have functionally separated or "ring fenced" supply affiliates that do so. The discussion that follows refers primarily to OFGEM's 2004 review of electric distribution charges, which established prices and price adjustment formulas for each REC for the period April 1, 2005, until March 31, 2010. The 2009 price review established electric distribution prices and incentive formulas for the period April 1, 2010, until March 31, 2015 (OFGEM 2009). The basic approach did not change very much from the earlier price reviews, though some changes were made to accommodate the UK's low-carbon policies. A complete review of the procedures for setting electric distribution charges, referred to as the RPI-X@20 project, is focused on integrating REC prices and incentives to align them with the UK's low-carbon policies. This review is ongoing as of this writing (OFGEM 2010).

The primary mechanism used to determine the total revenues that a regulated electricity distribution firm is permitted to recover from its prices for delivery service (the allowed revenue and associated average price level) is a price cap mechanism that sets an initial starting value for revenues (p_o), specifies an exogenous input price index (RPI) for adjusting revenues and price levels from one year to another for general inflation, and a productivity factor x, which further adjusts revenues and delivery prices over time. The value for x can be either positive or negative or zero. This regulatory framework establishes values for p_o, x, and the relevant RPI index once every five years. Thus, the basic parameters that determine distribution delivery prices and their adjustment over time are determined once every five years and then "reset" in a new regulatory hearing.

The p_o and x values are developed based on a review of the relative efficiency of each firm's operating costs, the firm's current capital stock or rate base (adjusted for depreciation and inflation since the previous price review)—referred to in the United Kingdom as the firm's regulatory asset value (RAV)—forecasts of future capital additions required to provide target levels of service quality, the application of depreciation rates to existing and new capital investments, estimates of the cost of the firm's debt and equity capital, assumptions about the firm's dept/equity ratio, tax allowances, and other variables. The allowed revenues for the firm over the five-year period are then the sum of allowed operating costs and allowed capital costs (depreciation and after-tax return on investment) determined in each year.

Variables p_o and x are chosen so that the present discounted values of revenues over the five-year period is equal to the present discounted value of the total operating and capital-related charges that have been allowed for each distribution company for the five-year price review period. The choice of the specific values for p_o and x that satisfies this present discounted value property is a matter of judgment (OFGEM 2004c). Historically, this choice was driven by the notion that the regulated firms should be given some time to achieve reductions in operating costs to the efficient benchmarked level, leading to a relatively high initial value for p_o and a value of x that brings *operating costs* to their efficient levels over the period the price cap is in effect. OFGEM abandoned this "glide path" approach in its 2004 price review for electric distribution companies, perhaps because the initial value of p_o would have otherwise increased significantly as a result of a large increase in target investment expenditures (OFGEM 2004c).

Because the overall price cap covers both capital and operating costs, the ultimate value of x depends on both the target efficiency improvements in operating costs *and* the forecast carrying charges on the existing RAV, plus the carrying charges on allowed levels for future investments over the five-year price control period. So, for example, real operating costs may be targeted to fall over time, implying a value of x in the RPI-X formula of, say, 1.5 percent per year. However, if capital-related costs are forecast to increase by 1.5 percent per year, the value of x used in the price cap mechanism over the five-year period would be negative (yielding trajectory of increasing real prices) since capital-related charges, including taxes, are typically about double the allowed operating costs for a UK electric distribution company.

To illustrate the application of these principles, I describe below the process used by OFGEM in the 2004 review of prices for electric distribution companies that established the 2005 to 2010 electric distribution prices; see OFGEM (2009) for details on the subsequent review that established electricity distribution prices for the period 2010 to 2015 and OFGEM (2010) for the RPI-X@20 project, which is developing new approaches to setting electricity distribution rates and incentives beginning in 2015. In the 2004 price review, each firm's price cap was set so that the value of x is zero, implying that prices would rise based on changes in RPI only. As can be seen from table 5.1, there was a large range in the change in p_o allowed at the beginning of the new price control period among the fourteen distribution companies (−9 percent to +9 percent) with an average increase of p_o of 1.3 percent from levels prevailing at the end of the previous price review period (OFGEM 2004a). Table 5.1 also summarizes the negotiation process that led to the final proposals. Accordingly, for each distribution company the initial level of allowed total revenues increased with the rate of inflation, with p_o set for each company so that the present discounted value of future revenues was equal to the present discounted value of the sum of target operating and capital costs over the five-year period. The choice of a zero value for x does not imply that there were no improvements in operating cost efficiency built into the mechanism. The target improvements in operating costs were built into the total allowed cost forecasts and reflected in the choice of p_o given OFGEM's decision to have a flat real price trajectory over the 2005 to 2009 price period.

Since there are fourteen distribution companies in the United Kingdom, the opportunity to perform statistical analyses of how operating costs vary with various causal factors and to estimate variations in efficiency across

Table 5.1   UK Electric distribution price caps, 2005–2010 ($x = 0$): OFGEM's initial and final proposals for p_o

DNOs	June initial proposals %	Change %	September update %	Change %	November final proposals %
CN-Midlands	–6.5	2.0	–4.5	1.6	–2.9
CN–East Midlands	–10.8	3.3	–7.5	1.8	–5.7
United Utilities	–1.8	7.4	5.6	2.4	8.0
CE-NEDL	–11.5	8.6	–2.9	–0.8	–3.7
CE-YELD	–14.7	1.8	–12.9	3.7	–9.2
WPD–South West	–0.2	1.8	1.6	–0.1	1.5
WPD–South Wales	1.7	5.6	7.3	–1.1	6.2
EDF-LPM	–2.5	–1.7	–4.2	1.8	–2.4
EDF-SPN[a]	–3.7	6.7	3.0	4.2	7.2
EDF-EPN	–4.6	2.5	–2.1	2.0	–0.1
SP Distribution	8.4	2.2	10.6	1.3	11.9
SP Manweb	4.0	–9.5	–5.5	–0.4	–5.9
SSE-Hydro	–0.1	2.8	2.7	1.2	3.9
SSE-Southern	6.1	3.1	9.2	0.1	9.3
Average	**–2.5**	**2.5**	**0.0**	**1.3**	**1.3**

Source: OFGEM (2004d).

Notes: The p_o figures for November include allowances for Innovation Funding Incentive (IFI). Those for June and September do not include IFI.

[a]For comparability, EDF – SPN is shown on the basis of $x = 0$. Actual p_o will be 3.1 percent, with RPI + 2.

firms readily presents itself. A variety of statistical analyses have been used by OFGEM to arrive at operating cost targets for each of the electric distribution companies (OFGEM 2004a). These methods are now reasonably well–developed and understood by the regulated firms and third parties. During the five-year price control period, the firms are (in principle) the full residual claimants on variations between the target and the actual operating costs.

Despite the fact that capital carrying costs are roughly twice the operating costs for electric distribution companies, the benchmarking methods for determining allowed capital expenditures have been much less well developed than are those for operating costs. Of course, during any particular review period the future stream of allowed carrying charges associated with the stock of capital investments is heavily influenced by historical investments that have been included in the RAV in the past, just like under rate of return regulation. During a new price review, the carrying charges for the historical components of the RAV are affected only by the choice of the allowed returns on debt and equity and the debt/equity ratio assumed for each firm, as well as any changes in depreciation rates. During a new price review, however, *future* capital investments are still a variable cost that can be influenced by the capital expenditure allowances approved by the regulator and built into the future allowed capital carrying charges. Accordingly, much of the focus of the price review is on the approval of a target capital expenditure schedule for the next five-year period. Future investments in capital facilities do not have an insignificant effect on future costs and prices, especially in light of the fact that in the 2004 price review, OFGEM was presented with increases in capital expenditures that averaged over 50 percent more than had been approved for the previous five-year price period (OFGEM 2004a, 2004d).

Formal statistical benchmarking studies of the type that are now applied to operating costs (so-called controllable costs) were not applied to determine allowed investment costs over the next price cap period for each electric distribution company. The appropriate investment program may vary widely depending on variables like customer growth rates, load growth rates, equipment ages and replacement expenditures, underground versus aboveground facilities, service quality improvement needs, and so forth, with little necessary relationship to recent historical trends. Indeed, the rate of investment in electricity network infrastructure has historically been quite cyclical. As a result, it has proven difficult to develop useful statistical benchmarks for future capital additions. Instead, each of the regulated firms presents a proposed capital investment budget to the regulator and the regulator retains engineering consultants to evaluate the proposals and takes evidence from third parties, which use the distribution networks as well. This has historically been a rather contentious process, sometimes yielding significant differences between what the companies claim they need and what the consultants claim they need to meet their legal responsibilities to provide safe and reliable service efficiently.

Regulatory judgments about allowances for future capital expenditures have become more sensitive issues for regulators in the United Kingdom (and the United States) as reliability considerations have become of greater political importance, as excess capacity has been squeezed out of the legacy capital stock, and as the large amount of infrastructure investment made in the 1950s and 1960s reaches the end of its useful life. In the 2004 review, OFGEM adopted an innovative "menu" of sliding scale mechanisms approach to resolve the asymmetric information problem faced by the regulator as she tries to deal with differences between the firms' claims and the consultants' claims (OFGEM 2004d) about future capital investment requirements to meet reliability targets. The sliding scale menu allows firms to choose between getting a lower capital expenditure allowance but a higher powered incentive (and a higher expected return on investment) that allows them to retain more of the cost reduction if they can beat the target expenditure levels or a higher capital expenditure allowance combined with a lower powered sliding scale mechanism and lower expected return (OFGEM

2004d). The sliding scale mechanism is based on the difference between the allowed capital expenditure target chosen by the firm from the menu and the firm's actual capital expenditures during the five-year price cap period.

The menu of sliding scale incentives adopted in 2004 is reproduced as table 5.2. The values for the sharing fractions are based on the ratio of the distribution company's (DNO) choice of capital expenditure target and that recommended by OFGEM's consultant (PB Power). These ratios vary between 100 and 140. For example, in table 5.2, if a firm agrees to accept a capital expenditure budget equal to 105 percent of the consultant's recommendation (PB Power = 100 in table 5.2) it would also be choosing the sliding scale in the first column. It would get a base bonus of 2.5 percent of its target income. If its actual expenditures turned out to be 70 percent of the target (through efficiencies) during the price control period it would get a 16.5 percent increase in its income as a reward. If the firm greatly exceeded the target and realized capital expenditures of 140 percent of the target, its income was reduced by 11.5 percent from the target.

This is the most direct and extensive application of Laffont and Tirole's menu of cost-contingent contracts result that I have seen. However, it appears to be the case that the sliding scale scheme for capital expenditures was integrated into the price cap mechanism in a way that makes the power of the incentive scheme for capital expenditures different from the power of the incentive scheme applied to operating costs.

The process is as follows: once the capital investment target for the price control period is determined, these investments are added to the starting value for the RAV or rate base as they are made. Depreciation charges for both the historical and new investments are then calculated for each future year. The depreciation charges are a current capital expense in each year and are simultaneously deducted from the RAV. An allowed rate of return equal to the firm's weighted average *real* cost of capital before tax adjustments is determined and applied to the RAV in each year. This yields a five-year cash flow profile of real capital service charges reflecting depreciation on historical and allowed future investments and the firm's real opportunity cost of capital, to which capital related taxes are added (see table 5.3). As discussed further below, the details of these computations for capital-related cost allowances are matched to the inflation-adjusted price cap mechanism, but the basic concepts are quite similar to those applied to turn capital investments into a flow of capital service costs under traditional rate-of-return regulation (Joskow 2005).

The allowed capital charges for each year are then added to the allowed operating cost expenses for that year to yield the target *total costs* for each year of the price control period. This process leads to a set of future allowed *real* operating and capital-service related costs that will automatically be adjusted in nominal terms each year by the realized rate of inflation in the RPI index chosen. A p_o and x value are chosen that together yield allowed

Table 5.2   Sliding scale matrix for capital expenditure allowance

DNO: PB Power ratio	100	105	110	115	120	125	130	135	140
Efficiency incentive	40%	38%	35%	33%	30%	28%	25%	23%	20%
Additional income	2.5	2.1	1.6	1.1	0.6	-0.1	-0.8	-1.6	-2.4
As pretax rate of return	0.200%	0.168%	0.130%	0.090%	0.046%	-0.004%	-0.062%	-0.124%	-0.192%
				Rewards and penalties					
Allowed expenditure	105	106.25	107.5	108.75	110	111.25	112.5	113.75	115
Actual exp.									
70	16.5	15.7	14.8	13.7	12.6	11.3	9.9	8.3	6.6
80	12.5	11.9	11.3	10.5	9.6	8.5	7.4	6.0	4.6
90	8.5	8.2	7.8	7.2	6.6	5.8	4.9	3.8	2.6
100	**4.5**	4.4	4.3	4.0	3.6	3.0	2.4	1.5	0.6
105	2.5	**2.6**	2.5	2.3	2.1	1.7	1.1	0.4	-0.4
110	0.5	0.7	**0.8**	0.7	0.6	0.3	-0.1	-0.7	-1.4
115	-1.5	-1.2	-1.0	**-0.9**	-0.9	-1.1	-1.4	-1.8	-2.4
120	-3.5	-3.1	-2.7	-2.5	**-2.4**	-2.5	-2.6	-3.0	-3.4
125	-5.5	-4.9	-4.5	-4.2	-3.9	**-3.8**	-3.9	-4.1	-4.4
130	-7.5	-6.8	-6.2	-5.8	-5.4	-5.2	**-5.1**	-5.2	-5.4
135	-9.5	-8.7	-8.0	-7.4	-6.9	-6.6	-6.4	**-6.3**	-6.4
140	-11.5	-10.6	-9.7	-9.0	-8.4	-8.0	-7.6	-7.5	**-7.4**

Where, for example:

$$16.5 = (105 - 70) \times 40\% + 2.5 \quad \text{(top-left corner)}$$
$$-7.4 = (115 - 140) \times 20\% - 2.4 \quad \text{(bottom-right)}$$

Source: OFGEM (2004d, 87).

Table 5.3   OFGEM cost of capital assumptions

	Midpoint (initial proposals and September update) (%)	Final proposals (%)
Cost of debt	4.1	4.1
Cost of equity	7.25	7.5
Gearing	60	57.5
Vanilla WACC	5.4	5.5
Posttax	4.6	4.8
Pretax[a]	6.6	6.9

Source: OFGEM (2004d, 109).

Notes: WACC = weighted average cost of capital.

[a] Based on a traditional tax wedge approach; compares to 6.5 percent in the previous electricity distribution price control review and 6.25 percent in the last Transco price control review; equivalent to approximately 8 percent, taking account of actual tax allowances proposed.

revenues whose present discounted value is equal to the present discounted value of allowed costs. OFGEM's decision to set x to zero has the effect of "backloading" the revenues toward the end of the price review period. An example of what the various operating and capital cost components look like for one distribution company (United Utilities) is displayed in table 5.4.

There are a number of issues that have not been fully resolved in this price-setting and incentive mechanism specification process. First, as already noted, the five-year ratchet potentially leads to differential incentives for cost reduction depending on how close the firm is to the next price review. OFGEM indicated that it was aware of this problem and committed to allowing firms to keep the benefits of "outperformance" (and presumably the costs of underperformance) for a full five years regardless of when during the five-year review period the outperformance actually occurs. For capital expenditures, OFGEM adopted a formula for rolling adjustments in the value of capital assets used for regulatory purposes (regulatory asset value or RAV) so that outperformance or underperformance incentives and penalties are reflected in prices for a five-year period. Although OFGEM made a commitment to allow operating cost (OPEX) savings to be retained for five years, it did not adopt a formal rolling OPEX adjustment mechanism in the 2004 review, due to imperfections in the operating cost accounting and reporting protocols (OFGEM 2004f). Instead, OFGEM started a process to develop a better uniform system of accounts and reporting requirements to facilitate improvements in the incentive regulation mechanisms.

A second set of issues involves potential asymmetries between the treatment of operating costs and capital costs. The power of the incentive schemes for operating costs and capital costs appears to be different for at least two reasons. First, the sliding scale mechanism applies to capital cost variations

Table 5.4   Allowed 2005 costs (year 1) for one UK distribution company

	£millions	
Operating costs	67.0	Change in p_o = +8.0%
Capital charges	103.5	$x = 0$
Tax allowances	16.0	
Capex incentives	3.4	
Opex incentives	1.4	
Pensions	16.0	
Other	1.5	
Total	212.3	

Source: OFGEM (2004d, 127).

but not operating cost variations. In addition, there is not a well-defined line between what is an operating cost that is expensed in a single year and what costs can be capitalized. The firms may have incentives to capitalize operating costs to beat the operating cost incentives during the current review period in the hope that they will be included in the RAV during the next review period. OFGEM made efforts to better define rules for capitalizing expenditures to deter this kind of gaming a priority. Second, when there is capital cost overspending the firm gets another crack to recover at least the undepreciated portion of these expenditures, beginning in the next price review. Capital expenditures have lives that are typically much longer than the five-year review period. How should capital expenditures that exceed or fall short of targets be treated in the next price review? Ordinarily these variances in capital expenditures may be handled through the incentive mechanism discussed earlier, including the impact of the rolling RAV calculation. However, firms can try to make the case that overspending was justified and get it fully included in the next price review, and OFGEM may claw back benefits of underspending that were due to reductions in service rather than efficiencies. Obviously, these adjustments may be quite subjective and need to be evaluated on a case by case basis.

A third set of issues relates to incentives to reduce both operating and capital costs today to increase profits during the current price control period, but with the result that service quality deteriorates either during the current review period or in subsequent periods. Deferred maintenance (e.g., tree trimming) and deferred capital expenditures may lead to the deterioration of service quality in either the short run or the long run or both. Regulated firms may hope that they can use adverse service quality trends to argue for higher allowances for operating and capital costs in future price reviews. The UK regulatory process tries to deal with the relationships between operating and capital cost expenditures and service quality in two ways. First, there are service quality performance norms and incentives that I will discuss presently. Second, OFGEM reserves the right to "claw back" capital cost savings if they are clearly not the result of efficiencies but rather reflect efforts to cut services in the short run or the long run. This is not an ideal approach since operating expenditures, capital expenditures, and service quality are related in complex ways over time and space. Indeed, it sounds like the "prudence reviews" that are a component of traditional cost-of-service regulation in the United States. Moreover, operating cost benchmarking studies that do not take service quality and the quality of the capital stock into account can lead to misleading conclusions (Giannakis, Jamasb, and Pollitt 2004).

There is a final issue involving capital cost accounting that has been addressed properly in the United Kingdom, but not in all countries that have implemented price cap mechanisms. When a price cap mechanism (RPI-X) is applied to capital costs, the calculation of the amortization formula for capital (depreciation, rate of return on investment) and the valuation of the capital stock (rate base or RAV) need to be done in a particular way to ensure that there is not over- or underpayment for capital services over the lives of capital investments. Specifically, at the time of a price review the RAV (original cost of capital investments less depreciation) should be adjusted for inflation that has occurred since the last price review, and the allowed rate of return on the RAV during the price review period should be based on the *real* cost of debt and equity capital net of taxes, with tax allowances then added back in. Because prices are based on both operating and capital costs, the RPI-X formula essentially yields a nominal return equal to the real cost of capital plus the rate of inflation. Capital-related charges rise with the rate of inflation in this case and this is consistent with the RAV rising with the rate of inflation, together yielding an approximation to the economic depreciation rate (depending exactly on how the depreciation rates are set; Joskow 2007; Schmalensee 1989a). Simply bolting a price cap mechanism onto the capital cost accounting formulas used in the United States (Joskow 2007) would lead to the wrong result since regulated prices in the United States are based on the nominal cost of capital and a depreciated original cost rate base (RAV) that is not adjusted for inflation.

5.4.4   Service Quality Incentives for Electric Distribution Companies in the United Kingdom and the United States[13]

Any incentive regulation mechanism that provides incentives only for cost reduction also potentially creates incentives to reduce service quality when service quality and costs are positively related to one another. The regulatory mechanisms developed for electric distribution companies in the United Kingdom have long included an additional set of incentive mechanisms to provide incentives for the regulated firms to maintain or enhance service quality. Adding quality-related incentives to cost-control incentives makes

13. The United Kingdom has also applied incentive arrangements for distribution system losses that I will not discuss here.

good sense in theory and in practice. However, integrating these incentive mechanisms into a package that gives the correct incentives on all relevant margins remains a considerable challenge for incentive regulation in practice.

By its 2004 review, OFGEM had developed several incentive mechanisms targeted at various dimensions of performance. These include: (a) two distribution service interruption incentive mechanisms targeted at the number of outages and the number of minutes per outage; (b) storm interruption payment obligations targeted at distribution company response times to outages caused by severe weather events; (c) quality of telephone responses during both ordinary weather conditions and storm conditions; and (d) a discretionary award based on surveys of customer satisfaction. Overall, about 4 percent of total revenue on the downside and an unlimited fraction of total revenue on the upside are subject to these quality of service incentive mechanisms (see table 5.5). Is this the right allocation of financial risk to variations in service quality? Nobody really knows.

OFGEM uses statistical and engineering benchmarking studies and forecasts of planned maintenance outages to develop targets for the number of customer outages and the average number of minutes per outage for each distribution company. The individual distribution companies are disaggregated into different types (e.g., voltages) of distribution circuits, and performance benchmarks and targets are developed for each based on comparative historical experience and engineering norms. Aggregate performance targets for each distribution company are then defined by reaggregating the targets for each type of circuit (OFGEM 2004a) appendix to June 2004 proposals) to match up circuits that make up each electric distribution company. Both planned (maintenance) and unplanned outages are taken into account to develop the outage targets. The targets incorporate performance improvements over time and reflect, in part, customer surveys of the value of improved service quality. There is a fairly wide range in the targets among the fourteen distribution companies in the United Kingdom, reflecting dif-

Table 5.5   **Revenue exposure to quality of service variations**

Incentive arrangement	Current	Proposal
Interruption incentive scheme	+2% to –1.75%	+/– 3%
Storm compensation arrangements	–1%	–2%
Other standards of performance	Uncapped	Uncapped
Quality of telephone response	+/– 0.125%	+0.05% to –0.25%
Quality of telephone response in storm conditions	Not applicable	0 initially +/– 0.25% for 3 yrs
Discretionary reward scheme	Not applicable	Up to + £1m
Overall cap/total	+2% to –2.875%	4% on downside No overall cap on upside

Source: OFGEM (2004d, 16).

Table 5.6   Targets for average number of customer interruptions by distribution company and year

	Actual			Target				
	2001/2	2002/3	2003/4	2005/6	2006/7	2007/8	2008/9	2009/10
CN-Midlands	120.1	99.8	113.1	109.4	107.8	106.2	104.6	103.0
CN–East Midlands	77.0	74.7	83.4	77.9	77.5	77.1	76.7	76.3
United Utilities	55.5	65.7	50.3	57.2	57.1	57.1	57.1	57.1
CE-NEDL	82.2	76.5	64.9	74.5	74.5	74.5	74.5	74.5
CE-YEDL	77.4	62.8	66.0	68.7	68.6	68.5	68.5	68.4
WPD–South West	100.7	81.8	71.0	84.5	84.5	84.5	84.5	84.5
WPD–South Wales	112.7	96.0	94.7	99.7	98.2	96.8	95.3	93.9
EDF-LPN	38.0	35.8	34.7	36.2	36.2	36.2	36.2	36.2
EDF-SPN	93.0	88.4	96.1	90.5	88.5	86.5	84.5	82.5
EDF-EPN	101.0	84.7	89.6	90.3	88.8	87.2	85.7	84.2
SP Distribution	59.0	63.4	60.2	60.9	60.8	60.8	60.8	60.8
SP Manweb	46.1	41.0	49.2	46.7	46.7	46.7	46.7	46.7
SSE-Hydro	115.4	90.0	84.1	96.2	95.8	95.5	95.2	94.9
SSE-Southern	98.3	91.5	86.1	91.0	90.1	89.2	88.3	87.4
Average	83.1	75.0	75.3	77.1	76.5	75.8	75.1	74.5

Source: OFGEM (2004d, 17).

ferences in the configurations of the networks. OFGEM also has added cost allowances into the price control (p_o) to reflect estimates of the costs of improving service quality in these dimensions. See table 5.6 as an example.

Once the performance targets are set, a financial penalty/reward structure needs to be applied to it to transform the physical targets into financial penalties and rewards. The natural approach would be to apply estimates of the value of outages and outage minutes to customers (OFGEM surveys indicated customers valued reducing the number of minutes per outage more than the number of outages) to define prices for outages and outage duration. OFGEM did not take this approach in the most recent distribution company price review. Instead it developed prices for outages and outage duration by taking the target revenue at risk and dividing it by a performance band around the target (25 percent and 30 percent, respectively). This approach seems rather arbitrary and yields a fairly wide variation in the effective price per outage and the price per minute of outage across distribution companies. See tables 5.7 and 5.8 as examples. OFGEM's 2004 review included a storm restoration compensation incentive mechanism. The distribution companies are given incentives to restore service within a specified time period and if they do not they must pay compensation to customers as defined in the incentive mechanism. The mechanism includes adjustments for exceptional events. Under normal weather conditions customers

Table 5.7 Incentive payments/penalties for interruptions by company and year

DNO	2005/6	2006/7	2007/8	2008/9	2009/10	2004/5 IIP incentive rate
CN-Midlands	0.10	0.11	0.11	0.11	0.11	0.06
CN–East Midlands	0.15	0.15	0.15	0.15	0.16	0.09
United Utilities	0.18	0.18	0.18	0.19	0.19	0.13
CE-NEDL	0.10	0.10	0.10	0.10	0.10	0.06
CE-YEDL	0.13	0.14	0.14	0.14	0.14	0.08
WPD–South West	0.10	0.10	0.10	0.10	0.11	0.07
WPD–South Wales	0.07	0.07	0.07	0.08	0.08	0.03
EDF-LPN	0.29	0.30	0.30	0.31	0.31	0.24
EDF-SPN	0.09	0.09	0.09	0.10	0.10	0.05
EDF-EPN	0.15	0.15	0.16	0.16	0.17	0.10
SP Distribution	0.23	0.23	0.23	0.23	0.23	0.13
SP Manweb	0.18	0.18	0.18	0.18	0.18	0.11
SSE-Hydro	0.08	0.08	0.08	0.09	0.09	0.04
SSE-Southern	0.18	0.18	0.18	0.19	0.19	0.11
Average	0.15 z	0.15	0.15	0.15	0.15	0.10

Source: OFGEM (2004d, 19).

Notes: IIP = International Incentive Program. Incentive rates for the number of customers interrupted per 100 customers (£m/CI – 02/03 prices).

Table 5.8 Incentive payments for minutes lost by distribution company and year

DNO	2005/6	2006/7	2007/8	2008/9	2009/10	2004/5 IIP incentive rate
CN-Midlands	0.14	0.15	0.15	0.16	0.17	0.10
CN–East Midlands	0.18	0.19	0.20	0.21	0.23	0.17
United Utilities	0.22	0.23	0.23	0.24	0.25	0.16
CE-NEDL	0.13	0.13	0.14	0.14	0.14	0.08
CE-YEDL	0.17	0.18	0.18	0.19	0.20	0.16
WPD–South West	0.17	0.17	0.17	0.18	0.18	0.13
WPD–South Wales	0.12	0.12	0.12	0.12	0.13	0.05
EDF-LPN	0.33	0.33	0.34	0.35	0.35	0.25
EDF-SPN	0.12	0.13	0.14	0.15	0.16	0.09
EDF-EPN	0.23	0.24	0.25	0.25	0.26	0.17
SP Distribution	0.27	0.28	0.30	0.33	0.35	0.14
SP Manweb	0.20	0.21	0.22	0.23	0.24	0.12
SSE-Hydro	0.10	0.11	0.11	0.11	0.11	0.04
SSE-Southern	0.24	0.25	0.26	0.27	0.28	0.15
Average	0.19	0.19	0.20	0.21	0.22	0.13

Source: OFGEM (2004f, 19).

Note: Incentive rates for the number of customer minutes lost per customer (£m/CML).

are eligible to be paid £50 pounds for an interruption that lasts more than twenty-four hours (£100 for nondomestic) and a further £25 for each subsequent twelve-hour period. It is not clear where the values for these payments come from. If a customer consumes 20 kWh per day (600 kWh per month) the implied value of lost load is £2.5 per lost kWh, or roughly $5,000/MWh of lost energy. Alternative compensation arrangements are applied when there are severe weather conditions. Both the triggers and the compensation change. The trigger periods for compensation are defined below and the amount of compensation starts at £25 when the trigger is hit with a cap of £200 per customer.

Finally, there were penalties and rewards for the quality of telephone service, based on the results of customer surveys.

In its "RIIO" (Revenue = Incentives + Innovation + Outputs) model, introduced as part of OFGEM's RPI-X@20 project, the measurement of outputs that include a number of quality metrics was emphasized, and both quantitative and subjective incentives (including the potential license revocation) are tied to performance on these dimensions (OFGEM 2010).

5.4.5   Electricity Transmission: Regulation of the National Grid Company (NGC) in England and Wales

The application of incentive regulation mechanisms to local electricity and gas distribution companies, water utilities, and local telephone companies is gaining acceptance around the world. However, these concepts have rarely been applied to the owners of electric transmission networks. The regulation of the National Grid Company (NGC) in England and Wales is one of the few examples.[14] The regulatory mechanisms used to regulate NGC are conceptually similar to those used to regulate the UK distribution companies. And, as with the UK distribution companies, the regulatory mechanisms have evolved over time as experience has been gained with them and with NGC's performance in response to them. The discussion in this section focuses on the mechanisms in place as of the 2004 review.

When the electricity sector was privatized and restructured in England and Wales in 1990, a separate transmission company—NGC—was created to own, maintain, operate, and invest in the England and Wales transmission network. It was originally owned by the distribution companies but was spun off as an independent company in 1995. NGC is subject to regulation by OFGEM. Separate but compatible incentive regulation mechanisms are applied to the transmission owner (TO) and system operating functions (SO). These regulatory mechanisms effectively yield values for the target revenues NGC is permitted to earn from charges made to generators, electricity suppliers, and distribution companies for transmission service and system operations. These mechanisms define the aggregate revenues that

---

14. Argentina has also applied incentives of various kinds to the owners of the high voltage transmission networks in the country (Pollitt 2004).

NGC is allowed to earn in each period—the incentive mechanism defines the average price *level* for transmission service.

The allowed aggregate revenues determined through the regulatory process are then recovered through a set of prices for the services provided by NGC. Transmission customers (generators and retail suppliers) pay NGC for the aggregate operating and capital costs allowed for the transmission network, defined by the basic incentive mechanism pursuant to a regulated tariff.[15] The tariff has two basic components. The first is a "shallow" connection charge that allows NGC to recover the capital (depreciation, return on investment, taxes, etc.) and operating costs associated with the facilities that support each specific interconnection (now using the "Plugs" methodology). The second component of the transmission tariff is composed of the Transmission Network Use of System Charges (TNUoS) (NGC 2004a, 2004b, 2004c). The SO revenues defined by the SO incentive mechanism are then recovered as surcharges on the price of energy delivered to each transmission customer, reflecting variations in these charges at different points in time.

Thus, the general *level* of charges is set to allow NGC to recover its cost-of-service based "revenue requirement" or "allowed revenues" as adjusted through the incentive regulation mechanism that I will discuss presently. The *structure* of the TNUoS charges provides for price variation by location on the network based upon (scaled) differences in the incremental costs of injecting or receiving electricity at different locations, as specified in the Investment Cost Related Pricing Methodology. The regulator determines the structure of the charges whose level is adjusted each year to yield NGC's allowed aggregate revenues. The objective of this pricing mechanism is described as follows:

> [E]fficient economic signals are provided to Users when services are priced to reflect the incremental costs of supplying them. Therefore charges should reflect the impact that Users of the transmission system at different locations would have on National Grid's costs, if they are to increase or decrease their use of the system. These costs are primarily defined as the investment costs in the transmission system, maintenance of the transmission system and maintaining a system capable of providing a secure bulk supply of energy. (NGC 2004a, 2004b, 2004c).

So, for example, generators pay significantly higher transmission service costs in the North of England than in the South (where the prices may be negative) because there is congestion from North to South and "deep" transmission network reinforcements are more likely to be required to accommodate new generation added at various locations in the North but not in the South.[16] Similarly, load in the South pays more than load in the North

---

15. http://www.nationalgrid.com/uk/, click on "charging."

16. "Deep" transmission network reinforcements refer to reinforcements of the core network that serves large groups of generators and demand points as opposed to facilities that connect a single generator or small group of generators to the core network.

because transmission enhancements to increase capacity from constrained generation export areas benefits customers in the South more than those in the North.

Unlike the assumption reflected in some of the theoretical work on price cap regulation, NGC is not free to adjust the price *structure* independently. Indeed, this freedom is rarely given to electric transmission and distribution companies subject to price cap regulation. Accordingly, as with the distribution companies in the United Kingdom, price caps are used primarily as mechanisms to provide incentives for cost reduction by giving the regulated firm a budget constraint that (for some time period) is exogenous, not to give the firm the freedom to set the optimal price structure.

Finally, in its role as SO, NGC has an obligation to balance the supply and demand for energy in the system in real time (energy balancing) and to meet operating reliability criteria (system balancing). These costs include the net costs NGC incurs to buy and sell power in the balancing market (or through short-term bilateral forward contracts), to balance supply and demand at each location, including to manage congestion, provide ancillary services, and other actions it must take to meet the network's operating reliability standards, and system losses. These costs are recovered from system users through an "uplift" charge based (mediated through an incentive regulatory mechanism discussed further below) on the quantities of energy supplied to or taken from the network at various points in time.

The regulatory framework for determining the revenues that NGC can recover through the use of system charges and the energy and system balancing charges is based on a set of incentive regulation mechanisms that have evolved over time.

As of the 2004 review, the primary mechanism covering NGC's TO costs and charges was a price cap developed using methods that are similar to those used for the UK electric distribution companies. This mechanism has a cost-of-service base, a performance-based incentive, and a ratchet that resets prices from time to time to reflect NGC's realized or forecast costs. A base annual aggregate "allowed revenue" for use of system charges is established at the beginning of each five-year "price review" period (though the latest period is being extended to seven years by mutual agreement on NGC and the regulator) in much the same way as for the distribution companies discussed earlier. As for the distribution companies, the accounting for operating costs and capital costs are different. For capital costs a rate base (regulatory assets value or RAV) is defined that is composed of the depreciated original cost of existing assets that make up the transmission system inflated to reflect inflation since the assets were installed. The forecast cost of incremental capital expenditures budgeted for the next five years to meet NGC's interconnection and system security criteria are added to the RAV. The final capital investment budget is determined by OFGEM through a public consultation process and reports by experts retained by OFGEM. Depreciation rates are then applied to the RAV each year to develop a depreciation component of the user charge for capital and deducted from the RAV. A real cost of debt and equity capital and a debt/equity ratio are defined and applied to the RAV to yield the allowed rate-of-return component of capital charges for each year of the price control period. The values for allowable O&M (operation and maintenance) expenditures during the future price control period are defined and added to each year's capital charges (depreciation, allowed rate-of-return on investment, and capital related taxes). A target rate of productivity improvement in operating costs—the x factor—is included in the forecast of allowable real operating costs, or alternatively, the year one allowed operating costs are adjusted by the x factor chosen by OFGEM, in addition to the RPI inflation adjustment over time.

Statistical benchmarking is very difficult for transmission networks. There is only one transmission network in England and Wales. The composition of a particular transmission network depends on many variables, including the distribution of generators and load, population density, geographic topography, the attributes and age of the legacy network's components and various environmental constraints affecting siting of new lines, transformers, and substations. Comparable cost and performance data are also not collected across transmission networks. Indeed, there is no standardization of where the transmission network ends and the distribution network begins. In the United Kingdom, the transmission network includes network elements that operate at 270kv and above. In the United States and France transmission includes network elements that operate down to 60kv or lower. Thus, "transmission" includes different types of facilities with different costs and different performance attributes in these two sets of countries. Benchmarking one against the other would not be very meaningful. In the United States there is no systematic collection of data on transmission network performance measures (US Energy Information Administration 2004). Accordingly, opportunities for relying on statistical benchmarking are not yet available in the United States because the necessary data are not collected and the value of x is determined through a regulatory consultation process rather than through statistical benchmarking studies based on NGCs forecasts of O&M requirements, wage escalation, and various engineering studies of the physical needs of the network and the costs of alternative methods to respond to them performed for OFGEM by independent consultants. Transmission service customers participate in this consultation process as well. (I suppose that the phrase "consultation process" sounds better than "rate case," but they are effectively the same animals.)

The allowed operating and capital cost values are expressed at the price levels prevailing at the time the price review is complete and then are escalated automatically during the price control period according to the RPI. Unbudgeted capital expenditures during the price review period can be considered in the next price review, though NGC may be at risk for amortization charges during the period between reviews. Underspending on capital may also be considered in the next price review and adjustments made going forward. After a five-year (or longer) period another price review is commenced, the starting price is reset to reflect then-prevailing costs, and new adjustment parameters are defined for the next review period.[17]

As outlined earlier, in its role as the E&W (England and Wales) system operator (SO),[18] NGC is also subject to a separate set of incentive regulation mechanisms. Unlike the price cap mechanism used to regulate the level of TO charges, the SO incentive mechanism was adjusted each year. Each year forward targets were established for the costs of system balancing services and system losses (OFGEM 2005). Until the 2004 SO incentive review, a sharing or sliding scale formula was specified, which places NGC at risk for a fraction (e.g., 30 percent) of deviations from this benchmark (up or down) with caps on profits and losses. There was also a cap and a floor. Table 5.9 displays the attributes of the SO incentive mechanisms in effect from 2001 to 2005 after the New Electricity Trading Arrangements (NETA) went into operation.[19] A similar incentive regulation mechanism applied to the SO during the late 1990s when the previous wholesale power pool was in operation. The choice of the SO incentive mechanism is only the second example that I am aware of where the regulated firm was offered a menu of (three) incentive arrangements with different sharing fractions and different caps and floors. The three-option menu offered to NGC for 2005 to 2006 is displayed in table 5.10. NGC chose option 2 after some adjustments to the target values.

Until the early 2000s, there was no formal incentive mechanism that applied to system reliability—network failures that lead to administrative customer outages or "unsupplied energy."[20] In response to the London blackout during the late summer of 2003, OFGEM developed and applied a new incentive regulation mechanism that applies to severe network outages that lead to customer outages and related "unsupplied energy" (OFGEM 2004f). NGC was assessed penalties or received rewards when outages fell outside of a "deadband" of +/–5 percent, defined by the distribution of historical outage experience (and with potential adjustments for extreme weather events), using a sliding scale with a cap and a floor on the rev-

17. There is also an incentive regulation mechanism that governs network losses that involves annual adjustments in the benchmark.
18. Recently expanded to include Scotland.
19. In the most recent SO incentive review, the parties could not agree on an incentive mechanism and SO compensation revered to cost of service, the default option. This suggests that the regulator failed to understand the true distribution of costs and/or to properly reflect it in the menu.
20. Transmission networks have quite a bit of redundancy built into them. When specific pieces of equipment fail, electricity is naturally rerouted over the rest of the network, and there are no customer outages that result. However, multiple transmission network equipment failures can lead to customer outages, though customer outages are most frequently the result of distribution network equipment failures.

Table 5.9   Transmission system operator incentive parameters

Parameter	2001/2 scheme	2002/3 scheme	2003/4 scheme	2004/5 scheme
Target	£484.6 million to £514.4 million	£460 million	£416 million	£415 million
Upside sharing factor	40%	60%	50%	40%
Downside sharing factor	12%	50%	50%	40%
Cap	£46.3 million	£60 million	£40 million	£40 million
Floor	–£15.4 million	–£45 million	–£40 million	–£40 million

Source: OFGEM (2005, 95).

Table 5.10   Menu of SO incentive contracts for 2005–2006

Proposed value	Option 1	Option 2	Option 3
Target	£480 million	£500 million	£515 million
Upside sharing factor	60%	40%	25%
Downside sharing factor	15%	20%	25%
Cap	£50 million	£40 million	£25 million
Floor	–£10 million	–£20 million	–£25 million

Source: OFGEM (2005, summary, page 3).

Notes: OFGEM also outlined a potential revision to the treatment of transmission losses within the SO incentive scheme, which entailed a move from a gross to a net transmission losses scheme. OFGEM considered that the introduction of a net transmission losses scheme should be considered, as it better reflects the true balancing costs to which the market is exposed.

enue impact. The incentive structure is consistent with a value of unsupplied energy of £33,000/MWh, though OFGEM indicated that it did not derive the incentive structure from an estimate of the value of lost energy, but rather to stimulate managerial attention in what was designed to be an interim incentive mechanism (OFGEM 2004f, 8, 20). OFGEM argued that it is very difficult to come up with accurate measures of the value of lost energy. Nor does the mechanism provide for compensation to customers affected by outages that trigger penalties for the SO (or charges for rewards) (OFGEM 2004f, 20). The implicit value of unsupplied energy reflected in the transmission network incentive mechanism is about an order of magnitude higher that the value reflected in the comparable distribution network mechanisms.

5.4.6 Reflections on Price-Cap Regulation versus Cost-of-Service Regulation in Practice

The basic price cap regulatory mechanism used to regulate electricity, gas, and water distribution and transmission companies in the United Kingdom is often contrasted with characterizations of cost-of-service or "cost plus" regulation that developed in the United States during the twentieth century. However, I believe that there has been less difference than may first meet the eye. The UK's implementation of a price cap based regulatory framework is best characterized as a combination of cost-of-service regulation, the application of a high-powered incentive scheme for operating costs for a fixed period of time, followed by a cost-contingent price ratchet to establish a new starting value for prices. The inter-review period is similar to "regulatory lag" in the US context (Joskow 1972, 1974; Joskow and Schmalensee 1986), except it is structured around a specific RPI-X formula that employs forward-looking productivity assessments, allows for automatic adjustments for inflation, and has a fixed duration. A considerable amount of regulatory judgment is still required by OFGEM. The regulator must agree to an appropriate level of the starting value for "allowable" O&M as well as a reasonable target for improvements in O&M productivity during the inter-review period. The regulator must also review and approve investment plans ex ante and make judgments about their reasonableness ex post, though investment programs that fall within budgeted values are unlikely to be subject to ex post review. It does this without statistical benchmarking studies, which are unavailable. An allowed rate of return must be determined as well as compatible valuations of the rate base (capital stock) and depreciation rates. Cost accounting and cost reporting protocols are required to implement sound incentive regulation mechanisms.

Thus, there are many similarities here with the way cost-of-service regulation works in practice in the United States. Indeed, perhaps the greatest difference is philosophical. OFGEM takes a view that recognizes that by providing performance-based incentives for regulated utilities to reduce costs, it can yield consumer benefits in the long run by making it profitable for the firm to make efficiency improvements. If the firm overperforms against the target, consumers eventually benefit at the next price review. It has generally (though not always) been willing to allow the regulated firms to earn significantly higher returns than their cost of capital when these returns are achieved from cost savings beyond the benchmark, knowing that the next "ratchet" will convey these benefits to consumers.[21] Under traditional US regulation, the provision of incentives through regulatory lag is more a consequence of the impracticality of frequent price reviews and changing economic conditions than by design.

5.5 Performance of Incentive Regulation Mechanisms for Electric Distribution and Transmission Network

There has been relatively little systematic analysis of the effects of the application of incentive regulation mechanisms on the performance of elec-

21. There is at least one problem with the fixed ratchet period. A dollar (or pound sterling) of cost savings in year one is worth much more to the firm than a dollar of cost savings in year five. OFGEM recently adopted policies to equalize the returns from cost saving during the inter-review period.

tric distribution and transmission companies.[22] Privatization, restructuring, and the application of high-powered regulatory mechanisms has led to improvements in labor productivity and service quality in electric distribution systems in England and Wales, Argentina, Chile, Brazil, Peru, New Zealand, and other countries (Newbery and Pollitt 1997; Rudnick and Zolezzi 2001; Bacon and Besant-Jones 2001; Estache and Rodriguez-Pardina 1998; Pollitt 2008). Sectors that had experienced physical distribution losses due to poor maintenance and antiquated equipment, as well as resulting from thefts of electric service, have generally experienced significant reductions in both types of losses. Penetration rates for the availability of electricity to the population have increased in those countries where service was not already universally available and queues for connections have been shortened. Distribution and transmission network outages have declined. Improved performance of regulated distribution (and sometimes transmission) systems has accompanied privatization and the application of high-powered PBR mechanisms almost everywhere it has been implemented. Most of these studies have focused on developing countries where the prereform levels of performance were especially poor. Moreover, it is difficult to disentangle the effects of privatization, restructuring, and incentive regulation from one another.

One of the most comprehensive studies of the postreform performance of the regional electricity distribution companies in the United Kingdom (distribution and supply functions) was done by Domah and Pollitt (2001). They find significant overall increases in productivity over the period 1990 to 2000 and lower real "controllable" distribution costs compared to a number of benchmarks. However, controllable costs and overall prices first rose in the early years of the reforms before falling dramatically after 1995. The first application of price cap mechanisms to the RECs in 1990 was too generous (average of RPI + 2.5 percent) and a lot of rent was left on the table for the REC's initial owners (who cleverly soon sold out to foreign buyers). Subsequent price cap mechanisms placed much more cost pressure on the RECs and stimulated large increases in realized productivity and falling distribution charges.

Bertram and Twaddle (2005) provide an interesting analysis of the combined effects on the prices charged for distribution service resulting from capital asset valuation decisions and the impacts of price cap-type regulation on the operating costs of distribution networks. When sector restructuring takes place, one decision that must be made is how to value the assets of the distribution and transmission companies that will be used for regulatory purposes going forward; that is, how the rate base or RAV of the

---

22. There is a much more extensive body of empirical work that examines the effects of incentive regulation mechanisms, primarily price caps, on the performance of telecommunications firms. For example, Ai and Sappington 2002; Sappington 2003; and Ai, Martinez, and Sappington 2004.

capital stock will be valued. The typical approach has been to carry forward the existing depreciated book value of historical investments in transmission and distribution into the new liberalized regime so that the base level of distribution and transmission charges associated with the recovery of capital-related charges does not change as a consequence of the transition. Incremental investments are then accounted for more or less as they were under the old regime (as in the United States and Canada) or economic/ inflation accounting methods and approximations to economic depreciation applied to incremental investments (as in the United Kingdom). These decisions are further complicated in countries where the industry was state owned and did not employ rigorous capital cost accounting protocols or where prices were kept so low as to not even cover the carrying charges on plant and equipment.

Bertram and Twaddle (2005) review the impact of decisions made in New Zealand to "write up" the value of distribution company assets to reflect their "true" economic value (something like depreciated replacement cost new) as a component of the restructuring program. These asset values were then used to set the price levels within a price cap regulatory framework. The argument for doing so was that this would allow prices to rise to their efficient level and provide consumers with appropriate price signals. The arguments against this revaluation were that (a) it would lead to significant price increases, (b) nonlinear pricing could be used to restore the correct price incentives on the margin, and (c) it created windfall profits for distribution network owners and undermined support for restructuring and competition.

Bertram and Twaddle focus on the effects of this asset revaluation program on distribution service price and profit levels in New Zealand. Prices and price-operating cost margins rose significantly. However, their work also demonstrates that *operating costs* incurred by distribution companies in New Zealand fell very significantly during the same period of time. These cost savings appear to reflect both the consolidation of many small distribution companies through mergers and the incentives for cost reduction provided by a high-powered incentive scheme (see figure 5.2).

Distribution service quality, at least as measured by supply interruptions per 100 customers and average minutes of service lost per customer, has also improved in the United Kingdom since the restructuring and privatization initiative in 1990 (OFGEM 2003a, 21). This suggests that incentive regulation has not led, as some had feared, to a degradation in these dimensions of service quality.

Let me conclude with a few observations on the performance of the incentive regulation mechanisms that were applied to NGC by OFGEM during its first decade. When the new E&W industry structure and market arrangements were implemented in 1990, the system naturally started with a legacy network and configuration of generating capacity. Substantial entry of new

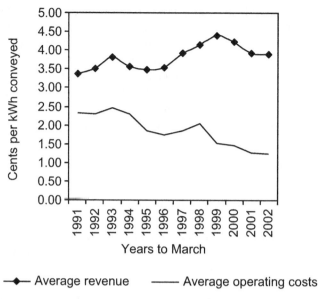

Years to March

---◆--- Average revenue   ——— Average operating costs

Fig. 5.2   Distribution network prices and costs in New Zealand
Source: Bertram and Twaddle (2005).

generating capacity and retirements of old generating capacity followed, with major changes in power flows over the legacy network. During the initial years of operation there was no incentive regulation mechanism governing system operating costs, including the costs of managing congestion and other network constraints. NGC's SO costs escalated rapidly, growing from about $75 million per year in 1990/91 to almost $400 million per year in 1993/94. After the introduction of the SO incentive scheme in 1994, these costs fell to about $25 million in 1999/2000. OFGEM estimates that NGC's system operating costs fell by about £400 million between 1994 and 2001 (OFGEM, April 2004). Overall costs of transmission service, including operating, system balancing (which includes congestion costs), use of system, and connection charges fell by about 50 percent between 1994 and 2001. NGC's loss rate has also declined over time. A new SO incentive scheme was introduced when NETA went into operation in early 2001. NGC's SO costs fell by nearly 20 percent over the three-year period since the new scheme was introduced (OFGEM, December 2003).

The organizational and regulatory arrangements that characterize the system in England and Wales are generally viewed to have been quite successful in supporting competitive wholesale and retail power markets with a transmission system that has attractive operating and investment results. During the period, demand grew, about 25,000 MW of new generating capacity entered the system, and almost an equal amount was retired (UK Department of Trade and Industry 2002). Power flows changed significantly on the network. While network investment is cyclical, following cycles of generation additions and retirements, intracontrol area investment postrestructuring has increased significantly compared to intracontrol area investment pre-restructuring, while congestion costs have declined significantly since 1994. Network losses have declined and system reliability has been maintained. A more formal assessment of performance is difficult because it is very challenging to define a counterfactual for comparison purposes.

5.6   Discussion

During the last two decades, the theoretical foundations for incentive regulation of legal monopolies have developed considerably, and now provide a reasonably mature theoretical framework for designing incentive regulatory mechanisms for practical application. However, the application of these concepts to electric distribution and transmission networks has lagged considerably behind these theoretical developments for a variety of reasons. Incentive regulation in practice is considerably more complicated than incentive regulation in theory. I offer the following observations about the relationship between theory and practice.

Incentive regulation has been promoted as a straightforward and superior alternative to traditional cost-of-service or rate-of-return regulation. In practice, incentive regulation is more a complement to than a substitute for traditional approaches to regulating legal monopolies. In some ways it is more challenging. Whether the extra effort is worth it depends on whether the performance improvements justify the additional effort. Incentive regulation in practice requires a good accounting system for capital and operating costs, cost reporting protocols, data collection, and reporting requirements for dimensions of performance other than costs. Capital cost accounting rules are necessary, a rate base for capital must still be defined, depreciation rates specified, and an allowed rate of return on capital determined. Comprehensive "rate cases" or "price reviews" are still required to implement "simple" price cap mechanisms. Planning processes for determining needed capital additions are an important part of the process of setting total allowed revenues going forward. Performance benchmarks must be defined and the power of the relevant incentive mechanisms determined. The information burden to implement incentive regulation mechanisms well is similar to that for traditional cost-of-service regulation.

What distinguishes incentive regulation in practice from traditional cost-of-service regulation is that this information is used more effectively, looking forward rather than backward, and recognizing that regulators have imperfect and asymmetric information that makes the use of regulatory mechanisms that clearly recognize the associated adverse selection and moral hazard problems and are designed to mitigate them. The proof of the pudding must ultimately lie in analyses of the performance of alternative regulatory mechanisms. More work needs to be done on the analysis of the performance of incentive regulation mechanisms applied to electric distribution and transmission system.

Incentive regulation in practice is clearly an evolutionary process. One set of mechanisms is tried, their performance assessed, additional data and reporting needs to be identified, and refined mechanisms developed and applied. This type of evolutionary process seems to me to be inevitable. However, to the extent that changes in regulatory mechanisms are contingent on past performance, this kind of evolutionary process raises credibility issues and may lead to strategic behavior of firms that are playing a repeated game with their regulators. Theoretical work that more accurately captures these adaptation properties of incentive regulation in practice would be desirable.

Price cap mechanisms are the most popular form of incentive regulation used around the world, in part because this mechanism has been heavily advertised as being a simple alternative to cost-of-service regulation. There is a lot of loose and misleading talk about the application of price caps in practice. From a theoretical perspective the infatuation with price caps as incentive devices is surprising since price caps are almost never the optimal solution to the trade-off between efficiency and rent extraction when the regulator must respect the regulated firm's budget-balance constraint (Schmalensee 1989b) and raise service quality issues. However, price caps in practice are not like "forever" price caps in theory. There are ratchets every few years that reduce the power of the incentive scheme and make it easier to deal with excessive or inadequate rents left to the firm. They are not so simple to implement because defining the relevant capital and operating costs and associated benchmarks is challenging (see also ACCC 2012). Price caps are also typically (eventually) accompanied by other incentive mechanisms to respond to concerns about service quality. Evaluating the performance of price cap mechanisms without taking account of the entire portfolio of incentive mechanisms in place can lead to misleading results. Effective implementation of a good price cap mechanism with periodic ratchets requires many of the same types of accounting, auditing, capital service, and cost of capital measurement protocols as does cost-of-service regulation. Capital cost accounting and investment issues have received embarrassingly little attention in both the theoretical literature and applied work on price caps and related incentive mechanisms, especially the work related to benchmarking applied to the construction of price cap mechanisms. Proceeding with price caps without this regulatory information infrastructure and an understanding of benchmarking and the treatment of capital costs, as has been the case in many developing countries following guidance from World Bank regulatory gurus, can lead to serious performance problems.

In practical applications to electric distribution and transmission networks there is an implicit assumption that there is a dichotomy between incentives contracts (aggregate revenue targets) and price setting (price structures). This dichotomy between the firm's budget or allowed revenues and its price structure is consistent with the historical development of regulatory practice in the United States where rate cases separate the determination of allowed revenues or *revenue requirements* from the specification of *price structures* that yield the indicated revenues (Joskow 1972; Joskow and Schmalensee 1986). A similar dichotomy has been adopted in the regulatory process in the United Kingdom. Regulated firms are given little flexibility to adjust price structures under the price cap mechanism. Accordingly, the primary role of price caps is to provide incentives for cost reduction, not to provide firms with the incentive to set optimal second-best prices given their overall budget constraints. The evaluations of the performance of price cap regulation should therefore be evaluated from the perspective of the effects on performance incentives, not on its effects on price structures since these are typically not chosen voluntarily by the regulated firm but are subject to independent regulatory determinations.

Incentive regulation theory implies that the adverse selection and moral hazard problems resulting from the regulators' information disadvantages are best handled by offering firms a *menu* of cost-contingent incentive contracts. Formal offers of menus are rare, though the give and take of regulatory negotiations may be a substitute. OFGEM's use of a menu of sliding scale schemes to deal with differences over capital investment forecasts for electric distribution companies seems to me to be an especially effective approach and, indeed, led the regulated firms to make more "reasonable" investment proposals, at least according to OFGEM. More frequent use of menus of incentive contracts in this way could improve incentive regulation in practice.

Collection of data on all relevant and significant measures of firm performance and the use of these data for benchmarking purposes and for developing performance targets is an important component of good incentive regulation in practice. To implement incentive regulation, regulators need the authority to require firms to collect performance data, to audit performance data, and to analyze these data. Absent these authorities and resources, incentive regulation mechanisms will not achieve their promise in practice.

As incentive regulation has evolved in the United Kingdom and other countries, the portfolio of incentive mechanisms that is being utilized has grown. While the initial focus was on reducing operating costs, it has now shifted to investment and various dimensions of service quality. Ideally these mechanisms should be fully integrated and differences in the power of the individual incentive schemes carefully considered. As things stand now there appear to be differences in the power of the incentives schemes as they relate to capital and operating costs. These problems are exacerbated in the United

Kingdom and many other countries new to formal regulation by the lack of uniform systems of accounts and reporting requirements. Quality of service schemes appear to have been bolted onto schemes designed to provide incentives for cost reduction and do not effectively incorporate information on consumer valuations of quality and the costs of varying quality in different dimensions. While the value of lost or unsupplied energy is uncertain, it is better to use an imperfect estimate of the right number than a very specific estimate of the wrong number. Efforts need to be made to harmonize these schemes and to guard against distortions caused by differences in the effective power of the constituent components of the overall incentive mechanisms.

Incentive regulation mechanisms often have "deadbands," caps, and floors that place limits on the performance realizations for which the regulated firm is at risk. At first blush, the use of hard caps and floors on the realizations of sliding scale mechanisms that place kinks in the incentive structure are hard to rationalize from a theoretical perspective and appear to have poor incentive properties for realizations near to the kinks in the incentive contract. Caps and floors may be justified as reflecting outcomes that were not contemplated (bounded rationality) in the level and structure of the target performance norms and the distribution of profits around these targets. They effectively trigger renegotiation. However, it is likely that a multipart sliding scale structure that softens incentives as the cap and floor approaches would have superior efficiency properties. We need to better understand the popular use of hard caps and floors and try to better understand their efficiency properties.

Our ability to use incentive regulation mechanisms effectively is dependent on the attributes of the restructuring and liberalization program of which it is a part. For example, it is much easier to develop and apply an incentive regulation program to the electric transmission system in England and Wales because there is one integrated transmission owner and system operator. The balkanized ownership structure of transmission assets in the United States, combined with the separation of system operating functions (to nonprofit independent system operators) from transmission ownership, maintenance, physical operation, and investment, makes the application of incentive regulation mechanisms (indeed, any effective regulation mechanism) a very significant challenge. The difficulties are enhanced by the peculiar mix of federal and state regulation of transmission in the United States and the failure of the federal regulator to take an active role in defining performance attributes, collecting performance data, and developing performance norms. FERC Order 2000 effectively assigns these responsibilities to RTO/ISO entities, but they have not taken up this challenge to date (Joskow 2007).

It would be worthwhile to pursue more work on the performance of incentive regulation mechanisms on electric and gas distribution and transmission companies in all relevant dimensions. The empirical research on the performance of incentive regulation in the telecommunications sector is much more extensive than is the research on electricity and gas networks. This kind of comparative institutional work is not easy, but it needs to be done, perhaps in conjunction with benchmarking studies that include firms subject to different types of regulation.

References

Ai, C., S. Martinez, and D. E. Sappington. 2004. "Incentive Regulation and Tele-communications Service Quality." *Journal of Regulatory Economics* 26 (3): 263–85.
Ai, C., and D. Sappington. 2002. "The Impact of State Incentive Regulation on the US Telecommunications Industry." *Journal of Regulatory Economics* 22 (2): 133–59.
Armstrong, M., S. Cowan, and J. Vickers. 1994. *Regulatory Reform: Economic Analysis and British Experience*. Cambridge, MA: MIT Press.
Armstrong, M., and D. M. Sappington. 2004. "Toward a Synthesis of Models of Regulatory Policy Design with Limited Information." *Journal of Regulatory Economics* 26 (1): 5–21.
———. 2007. "Recent Developments in the Theory of Regulation." In *Handbook of Industrial Organization*, vol. III, edited by M. Armstrong and R. Porter, 1557–700. Amsterdam: Elsevier Science Publishers.
Armstrong, M., and J. Vickers. 1991. "Welfare Effects of Price Discrimination by a Regulated Monopolist." *Rand Journal of Economics* 22:571–80.
Australian Competition and Consumer Commission (ACCC). 2012. "Regulatory Practices in Other Countries: Benchmarking Opex and Capex in Energy Networks." May.
Averch, H., and L. L. Johnson. 1962. "Behavior of the Firm under Regulatory Constraint." *American Economic Review* 52:1059–69.
Bacon, R. W., and J. E. Besant-Jones. 2001. "Global Electric Power Reform, Privatization and Liberalization of the Electric Power Industry in Developing Countries." *Annual Reviews of Energy and the Environment* 26:331–59.
Banerjee, A. 2003. "Does Incentive Regulation 'Cause' Degradation of Telephone Service Quality?" *Information Economics and Policy* 15:243–69.
Baron, D. 1989. "Design of Regulatory Mechanisms and Institutions." In *Handbook of Industrial Organization*, vol. II, edited by R. Schmalensee and R. Willig, 1347–447. Amsterdam: North Holland.
Baron, D., and D. Besanko. 1984. "Regulation, Asymmetric Information and Auditing." *Rand Journal of Economics* 15 (4): 447–70.
———. 1987a. "Commitment and Fairness in a Dynamic Regulatory Relationship." *Review of Economic Studies* 54 (3): 413–36.
———. 1987b. "Monitoring, Moral Hazard, Asymmetric Information and Risk Sharing in Procurement Contracting." *Rand Journal of Economics* 18 (4): 509–32.
Baron, D., and R. Myerson. 1982. "Regulating a Monopolist with Unknown Costs." *Econometrica* 50 (4): 911–30.
Baumol, W., and A. K. Klevorick. 1970. "Input Choices and Rate of Return Regu-

lation: An Overview of the Discussion." *Bell Journal of Economics and Management Science* 1 (2): 162–90.

Bertram, G., and D. Twaddle. 2005. "Price-Cost Margins and Profit Rates in New Zealand Electricity Distribution Networks: The Cost of Light Handed Regulation." *Journal of Regulatory Economics* 27 (3): 281–307.

Beesley, M., and S. Littlechild. 1989. "The Regulation of Privatized Monopolies in the United Kingdom." *Rand Journal of Economics* 20 (3): 454–72.

Bernstein, J. I., and D. M. Sappington. 1999. "Setting the X-factor in Price Cap Regulation Plans." *Journal of Regulatory Economics* 16:5–25.

Boiteux, M. 1960. "Peak Load Pricing." *Journal of Business* 33:157–79. Translated from the original in French (1951).

Boiteux, M. 1971. "On the Management of Public Monopolies Subject to Budget Constraint." *Journal of Economic Theory* 3:219–40. Translated from the original in French (*Econometrica*, 1956).

Draeutigam, R. 1989. "Optimal Prices for Natural Monopolies." In *Handbook of Industrial Organization*, vol. II, edited by R. Schmalensee and R. Willig, 1289–346. Amsterdam: Elsevier Science Publishers.

Brennan, T. 1989. "Regulating by Capping Prices." *Journal of Regulatory Economics* 1 (2): 133–47.

Cabral, L., and M. Riordan. 1989. "Incentives for Cost Reduction under Price Cap Regulation." *Journal of Regulatory Economics* 1 (2): 93–102.

Clark, J. M. 1913. "Frontiers of Regulation and What Lies Beyond." *American Economic Review* 3 (1): 114–25.

Domah, P. D., and M. G. Pollitt. 2001. "The Restructuring and Privatisation of the Regional Electricity Companies in England and Wales: A Social Cost Benefit Analysis." *Fiscal Studies* 22 (1): 107–46.

Doucet, J., and S. Littlechild. 2006. "Negotiated Settlements: The Development of Economic and Legal Thinking." Cambridge Working Papers in Economics 0622, Faculty of Economics, University of Cambridge.

Estache, A., and M. Rodriguez-Pardina. 1998. "Light and Lightening at the End of the Public Tunnel: The Reform of the Electricity Sector in the Southern Cone." World Bank Working Paper, May, World Bank, Washington, DC.

Estache, A., M. A. Rossi, and C. A. Ruzzier. 2004. "The Case for International Coordination of Electricity Regulation: Evidence from the Measurement of Efficiency in South America." *Journal of Regulatory Economics* 25 (3): 271–95.

Giannakis, D., T. Jamasb, and M. Pollitt. 2004. "Benchmarking and Incentive Regulation of Quality of Service: An Application to the UK Distribution Utilities." *Energy Policy* 33 (17): 2256–71.

Gilbert, R., and D. Newbery. 1994. "The Dynamic Efficiency of Regulatory Constitutions." *Rand Journal of Economics* 26 (2): 243–56.

Hammond, C. J., G. Johnes, and T. Robinson. 2002. "Technical Efficiency under Alternative Regulatory Regimes." *Journal of Regulatory Economics* 22 (3): 251–70.

Isaac, R. M. 1991. "Price Cap Regulation: A Case Study of Some Pitfalls of Implementation." *Journal of Regulatory Economics* 3 (2): 193–210.

Jasmsb, T., and M. Pollitt. 2001. "Benchmarking and Regulation: International Electricity Experience." *Utilities Policy* 9:107–30.

———. 2003. "International Benchmarking and Regulation: An Application to European Electricity Distribution Utilities." *Energy Policy* 31: 1609–22.

———. 2007. "Incentive Regulation of Electricity Distribution Networks: Lessons of Experience from Britain." *Energy Policy* 35 (12): 6163–87.

Joskow, P. L. 1972. "The Determination of the Allowed Rate of Return in a Formal

Regulatory Hearing." *Bell Journal of Economics and Management Science* 3: 633–44.

———. 1973. "Pricing Decisions of Regulated Firms." *Bell Journal of Economics and Management Science* 4: 118–40.

———. 1974. "Inflation and Environmental Concern: Structural Change in the Process of Public Utility Price Regulation." *Journal of Law and Economics* 17: 291–327.

———. 1989. "Regulatory Failure, Regulatory Reform and Structural Change in the Electric Power Industry." *Brookings Papers on Economic Activity: Microeconomics* 125–99.

———. 2005. "Transmission Policy in the United States." *Utilities Policy* 13: 95–115.

———. 2007. "The Regulation of Natural Monopoly." In *Handbook of Law and Economics*, vol. 2, edited by M. Polinsky and S. Shavell, 1227–348. Amsterdam: Elsevier BV.

Joskow, P. L., and R. Schmalensee. 1986. "Incentive Regulation for Electric Utilities." *Yale Journal on Regulation* 4:1–49.

Klevorick, A. K. 1973. "The Behavior of the Firm Subject to Stochastic Regulatory Review." *Bell Journal of Economics* 4:57–88.

Kwoka, J. 1993. "Implementing Price Caps in Telecommunications." *Journal of Policy Analysis and Management* 12 (4): 722–56.

Laffont, J.-J., and J. Tirole. 1986. "Using Cost Observations to Regulate Firms." *Journal of Political Economy* 94 (3): 614–41.

———. 1988a. "Auctioning Incentive Contracts." *Journal of Political Economy* 95 (5): 921–37.

———. 1988b. "The Dynamics of Incentive Contracts." *Econometrica* 56 (5): 1153–76.

———. 1990. "Adverse Selection and Renegotiation in Procurement." *Review of Economic Studies* 57 (4): 597–626.

———. 1993. *A Theory of Incentives in Regulation and Procurement*. Cambridge, MA: MIT Press.

———. 2000. *Competition in Telecommunication*. Cambridge, MA: MIT Press.

Lewis, T., and D. M. Sappington. 1988a. "Regulating a Monopolist with Unknown Demand." *American Economic Review* 78 (5): 986–98.

———. 1988b. "Regulating a Monopolist with Unknown Demand and Cost Functions." *Rand Journal of Economics* 19 (3): 438–57.

Lyon, T. 1996. "A Model of Sliding-Scale Regulation." *Journal of Regulatory Economics* 9 (3): 227–47.

McCubbins, M. D. 1985. "The Legislative Design of Regulatory Structure." *American Journal of Political Science* 29:721–48.

McCubbins, M. D., R. G. Noll, and B. R. Weingast. 1987. "Administrative Procedures as Instruments of Corporate Control." *Journal of Law, Economics and Organization* 3:243–77.

National Grid Company (NGC). 2004a. *Interim Great Britain Seven Year Statement*. November. London.

———. 2004b. *The Statement of the Use of System Charges*. Effective from November 1, 2004. London.

———. 2004c. *The Statement of the Use of System Charging Methodology*. Effective from November 1, 2004. London.

Newbery, D., and M. Pollitt. 1997. "The Restructuring and Privatization of Britain's CEGB—Was It Worth It?" *Journal of Industrial Economics* 45 (3): 269–303.

Office of Gas and Electricity Markets (OFGEM). 2003. *Annual Report 2002–03*. July 14. London.

———. 2004a. "Electricity Distribution Price Control Review." Initial Proposals, 145/04. June. London.

———. 2004b. "Electricity Distribution Price Control Review: Appendix—The Losses Incentive and Quality of Service." 145e/04. June. London.

———. 2004c. "Electricity Distribution Price Control Review: Final Proposals." 265/04. November. London.

———. 2004d. "Electricity Distribution Price Control Review: Policy Document." March. London.

———. 2004e. "Electricity Transmission Network Reliability Incentive Scheme: Final Proposals." December. London.

———. 2005. "NGC System Operator Incentive Scheme from April 2005." Final Proposals and Statutory License Consultation, 65/05, March. London.

———. 2009. "Electricity Distribution Price Control Review Final Proposals." Reference 144/09. December. London. http://www.ofgem.gov.uk/Networks/ElecDist/PriceCntrls/DPCR5/Documents1/FP_1_Core%20document%20SS%20FINAL.pdf.

———. 2010. "RIIO: A New Way to Regulate Energy Networks, Final Decision." 128/10, October. London. http://www.ofgem.gov.uk/Networks/rpix20/ConsultDocs/Documents1/Decision%20doc.pdf.

Owen, B., and R. Brauetigam. 1978. *The Regulation Game: Strategic Use of the Administrative Process.* Cambridge: Ballinger Publishing Company.

Pollitt, M. 2004. "Electricity Reform in Chile: Lessons for Developing Countries." *Journal of Network Industries* 5 (3-4): 221–62.

———. 2008. "Electricity Reform in Argentina: Lessons for Developing Countries." *Energy Economics* 30 (4): 1536–67.

Posner, R. A. 1974. "Theories of Economic Regulation." *Bell Journal of Economics* 5:335–58.

Riordan, M. 1984. "On Delegating Price Authority to a Regulated Firm." *Rand Journal of Economics* 15 (1): 108–15.

Rudnick, H., and J. Zolezzi. 2001. "Electric Sector Deregulation and Restructuring in Latin America: Lessons to be Learnt and Possible Ways Forward." *IEEE Proceedings Generation, Transmission and Distribution* 148:180–84.

Sappington, D. M. 2003. "The Effects of Incentive Regulation on Retail Telephone Service Quality in the United States." *Review of Network Economics* 2 (3): 355–75.

Sappington, D., J. P. Pfeifenberger, P. Hanser, and G. N. Basheda. 2001. "The State of Performance Based Regulation in the US Electric Utility Industry." *Electricity Journal*:71–79.

Sappington, D., and D. Sibley. 1988. "Regulating without Cost Information: The Incremental Surplus Subsidy Scheme." *International Economic Review* 31 (2): 297–306.

———. 1990. "Regulating without Cost Information: Further Observations." *International Economic Review* 31 (4): 1027–29.

Schmalensee, R. 1989a. "An Expository Note on Depreciation and Profitability under Rate-of-Return Regulation." *Journal of Regulatory Economics* 1 (3): 293–98.

———. 1989b. "Good Regulatory Regimes." *Rand Journal of Economics* 20 (3): 417–36.

Shleifer, Andrei. 1985. "A Theory of Yardstick Competition." *Rand Journal of Economics* 16 (3): 319–27.

Sibley, D. 1989. "Asymmetric Information, Incentives and Price-Cap Regulation." *Rand Journal of Economics* 20 (3): 392–404.

Spiller, P. 1990. "Politicians, Interest Groups and Regulators: A Multiple Principals

Agency Theory of Regulation, (or Let Them Be Bribed)." *Journal of Law and Economics* 33 (April): 65–101.

UK Department of Trade and Industry. 2002. *United Kingdom Digest of Energy Statistics 2002.*

US Energy Information Administration (EIA). 2004. *Electricity Transmission in a Restructured Industry: Data Needs for Public Policy Analysis.* December.

Vogelsang, I., and J. Finsinger. 1979. "A Regulatory Adjustment Process for Optimal Pricing of Multiproduct Firms." *Bell Journal of Economics* 10 (1): 151–71.

Weitzman, M. 1980. "The Ratchet Principle and Performance Incentives." *Bell Journal of Economics* 11 (1): 302–08.

Telecommunications Regulation
Current Approaches
with the End in Sight

Jerry Hausman and J. Gregory Sidak

6.1 Introduction

We consider the question in this chapter of the transition from regulated monopoly to competitive local markets in telecommunications. Technological change in terms of cellular and mobile competition has arisen over the past twenty years, where in most industrialized countries more than 80 percent of the population has cellular service. Even more important, the spread of competing fiber networks operated by cable companies that offer voice service and broadband service, in addition to pay TV, has transformed the competitive environment in the United States and has the potential to do so in many other countries. This transition will need to be managed within the framework of mandatory unbundling, first adopted in the United States in the mid-1990s, and now used by regulators in most advanced economies. We discuss the expected endpoint of competitive local markets, which should be facilities-based competition. We also discuss whether regulators will allow this process to occur or will hinder the process and end up with "regulation forever" by creating incentives for new entrants to choose a mandatory unbundling offer rather than investing in their own competing

Jerry Hausman is the John and Jennie S. MacDonald Professor of Economics at the Massachusetts Institute of Technology and a research associate of the National Bureau of Economic Research. J. Gregory Sidak is the founder and chairman of Criterion Economics LLC in Washington, DC, and the Ronald Coase Professor of Law and Economics at Tilburg University in the Netherlands.

This chapter is based on the current state of knowledge in 2007, when it was written. It has not been revised to reflect developments since 2007. For a recent analysis of developments since then, see J. Hausman and W. Taylor, "Telecommunications in the US: From Regulation to Competition (Almost)," *Review of Industrial Organization* 42 (2013). For acknowledgments, sources of research support, and disclosure of the authors' material financial relationships, if any, please see http://www.nber.org/chapters/c12568.ack.

facilities.[1] The United States is well positioned to greatly decrease regulation with the "end in sight" while the EU countries and other nations such as Australia may well be on the path to "regulation forever." Indeed, a number of US states and Canada have recently deregulated fixed-line telephone services, as we discuss in this chapter.

Economic advice to regulators regarding the correct principles to set regulated prices has often been incorrect in that it ignored the technology of the industry. Economists recognized early on that, in the situation of privately owned utilities in the United States, the first-best prescription of price set equal to marginal cost could not be used because of the substantial fixed (and common) costs that most regulated utilities needed to pay for.[2] This realization typically accompanied the claim that the economies of scale of the regulated firm were so significant that competition could not take place because the regulated firm's cost function was significantly below new entrants. Nevertheless, the most common advice from economists was that prices should be set similar to the outcome of a competitive process. Regulatory agencies largely adopted this technology worldwide. For example, the US Federal Communication Commission (FCC), when establishing the regulatory framework for setting prices under the Telecommunications Act of 1996, had the goal to adopt a pricing methodology that "best replicates, to the extent possible, the conditions in a competitive market."[3] Similar statements about using a pricing framework to replicate competition have been made by numerous regulatory agencies. Indeed, the adoption of the TELRIC model by the FCC and similar TSLRIC models by regulators elsewhere were supposed to achieve prices similar to outcomes in a competitive market.[4]

What the competitive process would be was never specified with any detail, which was to be expected since economic theory had no well-accepted model of competition with a technology exhibiting strong economies of scale, especially in the multiproduct situation. In the United States, regulators following legal principles adopted the position that the regulated firm should cover its costs.[5] However, regulators also adopted prices for certain

---

1. We do not discuss the history of telecommunications regulation and the movement from state-owned monopoly companies (in most of the world) or regulated monopolies (in the United States and Canada) prior to the 1990s. Numerous (hundreds of!) survey papers have been written that discuss this history. Excellent groups of papers with many references are contained in Cave, Majumdar, and Vogelsang (2002) and Madden (2003).

2. See, for example, Kahn (1970).

3. Federal Communications Commission, *Implementation of the Local Competition Provisions in the Telecommunications Act of 1996*, CC Docket No. 96-98, First Report and Order, September 17, 1996, ¶ 679.

4. TELRIC is "Total Element Long-Run Incremental Cost" and is explained in FCC (see note 3). TSLRIC is "Total Service Long-Run Incremental Cost." Both approaches use similar techniques but differ with respect to the level of aggregation used.

5. The Telecommunications Act of 1996 required that prices be set at cost, with the possible addition of a reasonable profit. See the Act § 252(d)(1).

services to attempt to meet social goals for these given services. For other services, regulators used arbitrary means to set prices while balancing competing claims from increasingly well-organized groups of consumers, all of whom claimed they should receive low prices with other groups paying for the fixed and common costs.

This regulatory approach arguably did not do undue damage when no actual competition existed. So long as the regulated firm was (nearly) productively efficient, the losses were essentially second-order social welfare losses. The regulated firm covered its total costs, at least approximately, although prices for individual services were often badly distorted from an economically efficient solution.

The regulatory process often failed to take sufficient notice of the importance of new product and service innovation in telecommunications. Academic research has found that much of the gains in consumer welfare occur when new services are introduced. The regulatory approach, by retarding the introduction of new telecommunications services, harmed consumers to a significant degree by retarding new product innovation, which is a first-order loss to economic efficiency. See Hausman (1997) for estimates of consumer welfare loss. Telecommunications differs in an important respect from many other regulated industries because of the rapidity of technological change. Telecommunications regulators have found it difficult to adapt to these changes and outdated regulatory policies may create perverse economic incentives for investments in new technology, as we discuss subsequently.[6]

However, when actual competition appeared and was allowed to exist by the regulators, the economists' advice of setting prices as if they were the outcome of a competitive process soon led to a regulatory morass. Regulators could no longer depend only on cost factors in setting regulated prices. The outcome of a competitive process would also need to take into account demand factors and competitive interaction (oligopoly) factors, with the first set of factors difficult to measure and the competitive interaction factors unlikely to be agreed upon. While regulators had some imperfect information about costs, they typically had little or no information about demand and no well-developed idea regarding the effects of competitive factors.

A particularly difficult problem arose when a regulated firm wanted to decrease its prices for services subject to entrant competition. Economists recognized that a price set above incremental (marginal) cost should be permitted. New entrants wanted the previously set regulator-set prices to be maintained. New entrants typically entered because regulated prices were

6. Cost-based regulation typically based consumer prices in part on depreciation lives of capital equipment. Regulators had an incentive to keep these lives at very long periods to reduce depreciation expense and hold down prices. Technological change led to much shorter economic lives of capital equipment so regulators often resisted the introduction of new equipment and new services. An example of this outcome was the delayed introduction of digital (computer driven) PBXs in the 1970s in the United States.

well above efficient levels, and the new entrants did not want these prices decreased. Furthermore, from a social welfare viewpoint the argument became first-order since inefficient new firms could be productively inefficient, causing a first-order loss of social welfare.

Regulators found it difficult to permit the regulated firm to decrease its prices, especially since under cost-of-service regulation other prices would need to increase. Even when cost-of-service regulation was replaced by incentive (price cap) regulation in the 1980s and 1990s, regulators still found it extremely difficult to allow price decreases since they believed in "regulated competition" (an oxymoron) where the regulators could better manage competition than the market.[7] Nevertheless, the regulated companies were not harmed too badly since competition did not proceed at such a rapid pace to cause extreme economic damage.

Cost-based regulation of telecommunications (e.g., rate-of-return regulation in the United States) had significant negative effects on innovation while it was claimed that it led to excessive capital investment. Most economists conclude that cost-based regulation led to significant consumer harm. In the mid-1980s when the UK government privatized British Telecom (BT), it decided not to use the historic approach of cost-of-service regulation to set regulated prices as the United States and Canada had done. The UK government instead chose price caps, a new regulatory method proposed by Littlechild.[8] Price caps regulated prices based on inflation and a productivity factor instead of regulated profits, as in the US cost-of-service based rate-of-return (ROR) regulation.

Price caps had a number of advantages over ROR regulation in terms of incentives for cost minimization (productive efficiency), innovation, and the ability of the regulated firm to rebalance its prices. In particular, the regulated firm could decrease its prices to compete. In 1989 and 1990 the Federal Communications Commission adopted price caps in the United States. Other countries such as Australia had also adopted price caps. During the 1980s and 1990s price cap regulation was implemented instead of cost-based regulation in most countries when telephone companies and other utilities were privatized. In the majority of the states of the United States, rate-of-return regulation has been replaced by price cap regulation. The battle to banish cost-based regulation appeared to be largely over.[9]

During the late 1990s and the early 2000s cost-based regulation has reappeared because of the necessity to set prices for unbundled network elements (UNEs) sold by incumbent firms to their competitors. A num-

7. See chapter 5 by P. Joskow in this volume that discusses the theory and application of using incentive-based regulation to replace traditional cost-of-service regulation.

8. See Beesley and Littlechild (1989) for a description of the economic incentives under price caps.

9. State regulatory agencies in the United States set local prices for telecommunications. California adopted the price cap in 1989 and by the mid-1990s the majority of states had adopted some form of incentive regulation.

ber of countries—including the United States, Australia, and Canada—adopted mandatory network unbundling for the incumbent local exchange carrier (ILEC). The most commonly used approach to set regulated network element prices based on costs is total service long-run incremental cost, or TSLRIC, although the United States adopted TELRIC instead of TSLRIC.[10] The adoption of TSLRIC as a cost basis to set the prices for unbundled elements has negative economic incentive effects for innovation and for new investment in telecommunications networks as we have discussed in previous academic research (Hausman 1997, 1998a, 2003; Hausman and Sidak 1999). Indeed, in the United States the two major landline telephone companies, Verizon and AT&T (previously Southwestern Bell), began construction of residential fiber optic networks soon after the FCC exempted new network investment from regulation in 2003 and began service in 2005. To the contrary, the incumbent residential telephone provider in Australia, Telstra, has so far refused to proceed with construction of a residential fiber optic network until it receives a guarantee from regulators regarding future regulatory policy toward new network construction.

How did network unbundling and a return to cost-based regulation become government policy? In 1996, the US Congress passed the Telecommunications Act of 1996. As a trade-off for being permitted to offer long-distance service, the incumbent Bell operating companies agreed to unbundle their networks.[11] The FCC adopted cost-of-service regulation to set the unbundled network element prices. Thus reappeared the well-known problems of cost-of-service regulation, with its inability to correctly treat economies of scale and economies of scope and its use of arbitrary allocations of fixed and common costs to prices. Even worse, the FCC adopted the approach of "total element long-run incremental cost" (TELRIC), which assumes that all investments in telecommunications networks are fixed, but not sunk. This assumption is, of course, directly contradicted by the actual technology of telecommunications networks. Other countries have adopted a similar approach based on total service long-run incremental costs (TSLRIC). Similar problems arise. While both TELRIC and TSLRIC regulation are supposed to be forward-looking so capital investments are not yet sunk, since networks are very long-lived investments, their sunk characteristic becomes very important in a world of uncertainty.[12] Regulators gave new entrants a "free option" to purchase either the unbundled element (TELRIC) or service (TSLRIC) on a monthly basis, which treated the investment as fixed but not sunk.

In this chapter we do not review these problems, which have been dis-

10. See fn. 4 for an explanation of the difference between TSLRIC and TELRIC.
11. The Bell Operating Companies had not been allowed to provide interLATA long distance service since the breakup of AT&T in 1984.
12. See Dixit and Pindyck (1994) for a discussion of sunk cost investment under uncertainty. Hausman (1997, 2003) and Pindyck (2004) discuss the problem in relation to telecommunications investment.

cussed in previous papers (e.g., Hausman 1997, 2003; Pindyck 2004), but instead we consider the outcomes thus far of the new regulatory approach to unbundling the incumbents' networks. We concentrate on the outcome in three countries: the United States, the United Kingdom, and New Zealand. The United States first adopted unbundling and has taken the most aggressive approach. However, in February 2005 the FCC, acting in response to a decision of the US Court of Appeals for the DC Circuit vacating the agency's unbundling rules, decided to "sunset" its most intrusive form of unbundling.[13] In response, the two most prominent local competitors, AT&T and MCI, announced they would exit the local market. Shortly thereafter, both companies announced that they would be acquired by incumbent local exchange operators, known as ILECs (SBC and Verizon). Thus, while much of the competition caused by the Telecommunications Act of 1996 was "artificial competition" (to borrow Justice Breyer's characterization), the local market in the United States will benefit from facilities-based competition as cable television networks are rapidly expanding their offering of telephone service over their networks through voice over Internet protocol (VoIP).

In the United Kingdom, the regulator initially favored facilities-based competition from the United Kingdom's cable operators, which already had a substantial share of the local telephone market. However, the regulator subsequently changed direction, in part because of directions from the European Union. We examine the effect of unbundling in the United Kingdom and its effect on the prospects for future facilities-based competition. Those prospects are all the more doubtful after the regulator (now, OFCOM) and BT announced in May 2005 that they had reached a compromise—in lieu of structural separation—that appears to "renationalize" BT insofar as governance of network unbundling is concerned.

Last, we consider New Zealand, where the regulator decided not to adopt network unbundling. New Zealand has an explicit consumer welfare test for regulation, the "long-term benefit of end-users," and bases regulatory decisions, in part, on an explicit cost-benefit analysis. Further, when the decision was made in New Zealand not to unbundle, the United States had over six years of experience of unbundling. We explore how this experience affected the regulator's decision in New Zealand.

Our general conclusion is that in both the United States and the United Kingdom unbundling may have caused an increase in competition, if one measures competition by market share of entrants. However, adverse effects occurred in terms of investments by both incumbents and new entrants. Further, the "goals" put forward by regulators in terms of unbundling have not been met.

---

13. Order on Remand, In re Unbundled Access to Network Elements, 2005 FCC LEXIS 912, WC Docket No. 04-313, CC Dkt. No. 01-338 (FCC February 4, 2005).

In the last section we consider whether, with increased facilities-based competition, especially in the United States, the "end of regulation" in telecommunications can occur. We explain that in an industry with high fixed costs and low variable costs, the incumbent will not be able to increase prices above competitive levels profitably if it loses a relatively small amount of business. Thus, the entry of cable television providers offering telephone service will serve to constrain incumbents from increasing prices above competitive levels at a quite early stage. Further, cellular telephone will also offer an additional constraining force. Thus, no economic reason exists for the incumbent's share to fall to, say, 50 percent before price deregulation can follow. Emerging facilities-based competition can allow the end of price regulation and the regulatory burden that it creates for both consumers and the economy.

6.2   The Simple Model of Cost-Based Regulation

The typical approach to cost-based regulation is to use costs of production to set prices that would be the result of a "competitive" situation.[14] These costs of production are used to set prices independent of demand factors. A very simple one-good, one-period Marshallian partial equilibrium model leads to this result, where competitive prices are independent of demand. We first describe this simple model and its inherent limitations.

6.2.1   Conditions for Prices Independent of Demand

Assume that a given regulated telecommunications service is produced by one or more input factors. No multiperiod capital goods are present. The production technology exhibits constant returns to scale. In figure 6.1 the result follows that the competitive price equals marginal cost, which in turns equals average cost, because of the assumption of constant returns to scale. As can be seen, the position and shape of the demand curve does not matter in setting the competitive price. Under these conditions, cost determines price, independent of demand. This interesting result depends very much on the assumptions of the economic model: partial equilibrium, so that demand for the product does not affect input factor prices; constant returns to scale, so there are no economies of scale; a single product, so there is no joint production and no economies of scope; and a single period, so there are no durable capital goods. We discuss later what happens when these assumptions do not hold. If any of the assumptions fail, the competitive price cannot be based on cost, independent of demand. Thus, the price-independent-of-demand result will turn out to be a very special result not applicable to the real world of telecommunications.

14. This description of regulation only holds for telecommunications regulation, not price regulation of other industries.

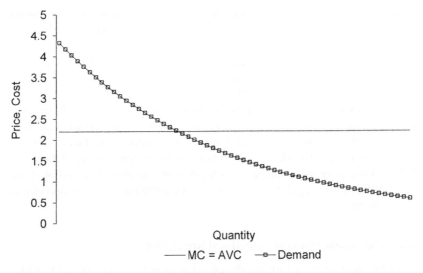

Fig. 6.1   Cost and price with constant returns to scale

6.2.2   The Role of Fixed Costs and Economies of Scale

We will now generalize this model slightly. Suppose that marginal cost remains constant but that we allow for a fixed cost of production. However, a single service is still being produced. The cost function can be written as:

$$(1) \qquad\qquad C(q,\, w) = F + wq,$$

where F is the fixed cost, q is output quantity, and w is the constant marginal cost per unit of output. A regulator might conclude that in a competitive, free-entry situation price would equal average cost, so that $p = (C/q) = (F/q) + w$. Because quantity demanded is a function of price, price is no longer independent of demand. However, setting the price equal to average cost, ATC (or average total cost), seems to be the correct outcome if the regulated utility is to recover its costs.

6.2.3   The Role of Common Costs and Economies of Scope

Now we consider common costs. A common cost arises when two (or more) services arise from a joint production process, but some of the cost is incremental to neither product. The term "fixed and common costs" arises often in discussion of regulated costs and prices because of the common occurrence of this type of cost. In terms of the cost function we will again assume constant marginal costs for each output:

$$(2) \qquad\qquad C(q_1, q_2; w_1, w_2) = G + w_1 q_1 + w_2 q_2.$$

Note that in equation (2) the fixed cost G cannot be uniquely assigned to either output. Indeed, no measure of average costs for either output exists.

Thus the statement, sometimes made, that regulators set prices equal to average cost is incorrect because no measure of "average cost" exists when a joint production process occurs.[15] Here regulators typically choose to use an allocation of the fixed cost G to each service. However, these allocations such as "fully allocated cost," "equal allocation of cost," and so on are inherently arbitrary.[16] Nevertheless, the results of the allocations have very important consequences on the regulated prices. These regulated prices in turn have important effects on competition, economic efficiency, and consumer welfare.

In competitive markets, firms set price based on cost conditions, demand conditions, and competitive conditions. Regulators attempt to base prices on only the first of these three factors. While the level of demand is used so that price times demand, across all service, is supposed to equal the cost of the regulated company, demand elasticities are almost never used. Yet in competitive markets demand elasticities are an important component of pricing decisions in a multiproduct situation. Thus, regulators do not meet their goal of setting regulated prices in a manner similar to that of a competitive market. Furthermore, they can cause billions of dollars per year of losses in economic efficiency and consumer welfare.[17] Instead of using inherently arbitrary allocation procedures, regulators could improve the outcome of the regulatory process either by taking account of demand and competitive conditions in setting regulated prices or adopting procedures such as global price caps, which will lead the regulated utility to take account of demand and competitive conditions.[18]

6.2.4   The Role of Sunk Costs

We now generalize the model one step more by considering sunk costs in addition to fixed costs. Sunk costs are costs that cannot be recovered if the economic activity ceases. Sunk costs are prevalent in telecommunications networks. Consider an investment in a (copper) loop to a residential customer. The customer has a unique loop that connects the residence to

15. A classic example in local telecommunications was how the cost of the local loop between the customer premise and the central office should be recovered. Should local service pay for it or should it be paid for by some combination of local service, long-distance service, and other services such as voice mail?

16. Indeed, the results of the allocations can depend in important ways on the units in which the outputs, q_1 and q_2, are measured. While regulators typically use arbitrary allocations (for example, the FCC used 20 percent for common costs for TELRIC), in some cases regulators used multipart tariffs, which can depend on demand conditions and are not arbitrary. However, in the large majority of situations, allocations have been used for common costs. Brown and Sibley (1986) analyze various forms of cost allocations and Laffont and Tirole (2000) consider the economic effects of allocation.

17. For an example of regulators causing losses of billions of dollars per year in economic efficiency and consumer welfare, see Hausman (1998a) and Hausman and Shelanski (1999).

18. See Laffont and Tirole (2000) for a discussion of global price caps. See P. Joskow's chapter in this volume for a further discussion.

the central office switch. If the customer decides to use a competitive service, such as local access service offered by a competitive cable company or by a wireless company for its voice (and broadband) service, the copper loop cannot be redeployed in another service. The investment in the loop is sunk. Now if a regulated telephone company faced no uncertainty over the future use of the loop and the cost and prices for the associated services provided with the loop, the distinction between a fixed cost—which arises from an asset that can be economically redeployed—and a sunk cost is not that important.

Indeed, in the "old days" of cost-based regulation for a monopoly provider, if an investment were deemed to be "used and useful" by the regulator, then the asset entered the regulatory cost base. Once the asset entered the regulatory cost base, the regulator, in principle, allowed the utility to recover the cost of the investment.[19]

However, in the current situation of competition, where the utility's competitors are allowed to use the incumbent's network at regulated prices, the distinction between fixed costs and sunk costs can be important. The competitor typically pays for the facility it uses on a monthly basis. As we explain later, regulators universally use an approach that assumes that the investment costs are fixed but not sunk. In setting the regulated prices without taking into account the interaction of sunk costs and uncertainty, regulators give competitors a "free option" to use the incumbent's network without requiring a price that takes account of the sunk cost nature of much of the investment. The regulators thus subsidize the competitors at the expense of the incumbent and create an economic disincentive for the competitors to invest in their own competing facilities.[20] Furthermore, the regulators decrease the incentive for new services offered by the incumbent. New services often fail. Yet if successful new services must be resold to competitors at cost, the incentive to undertake the required risky investment is

19. In practice, because of the interaction of incorrect depreciation schedules and inflation, utilities often did not recover the true cost of their investments. See, for example, Schmalensee (1989).

20. Regulation permits a new entrant to choose to use the new investment if it is successful, thus truncating the potential return of the incumbent who has make a risky investment in sunk costs. However, the new entrant needs to make no investment in the new project so it does not face the risk of the incumbent and thus it receives a "free option." See figure 6.2, which demonstrates that the effect of the free option is to decrease the expected return of a new investment because of truncation of the returns distribution. Justice Stephen Breyer of the US Supreme Court case AT&T Corp. v. Iowa Utilities Board, 119 S. Ct. 721 (1999), recognized how this outcome distorts and decreases the actual amount of competition. It is sometimes claimed (incorrectly) that the firm's cost of financial capital will increase to offset the increase in risk. This claim fails to recognize that a typical telecommunications firm produces many products and services (e.g., cellular, which is not price regulated). Indeed, the FCC has recognized that the cost of capital used in setting unbundled element rates may differ from the firm's overall cost of capital. See Order on Remand, In re Unbundled Access to Network Elements, 2005 FCC LEXIS 912, WC Docket No. 04-313, CC Dkt. No. 01-338 (FCC February 4, 2005).

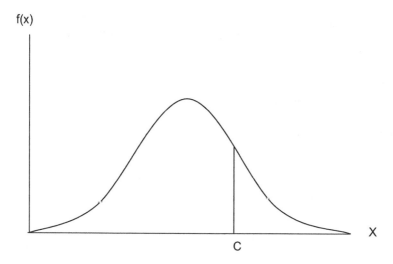

Fig. 6.2   Distribution of returns

decreased.[21] Eliminating a portion of the distribution of returns, as shown in figure 6.2, decreases the mean of the expected return of a new project. Thus, regulators are likely to decrease new services for consumers based on their approach to setting regulated prices.

6.3   Cost-Based Regulation: Economic Analysis with Cost but Not Demand

The FCC and other regulators claimed to be using a competitive model for setting regulated prices, at least for TELRIC and TSLRIC, as we stated above.[22] The FCC stated that its goal is to establish a framework that "best replicates, to the extent possible, the conditions in a competitive market." As we discussed earlier, in a simple one-period and one-good production model with constant returns to scale, a partial equilibrium Marshallian analysis demonstrates that the competitive price does not depend on demand. Marginal cost and average cost are independent of quantity produced, so the position of the demand curve does not affect the price as demonstrated in figure 6.1. However, the required description of technology does not describe accurately almost any industry in a modern industrial economy

21. For estimates of the extremely large gain to consumer welfare that can arise from new telecommunications services see Hausman (1997).

22. Federal Communications Commission, *Implementation of the Local Competition Provisions in the Telecommunications Act of 1996*, CC Docket No. 96-98, First Report and Order, August 8, 1996, ¶ 679.

and certainly not the telecommunications industry. For example, telephone and wireless networks have a very large proportion of fixed and sunk costs. We now consider whether the "price independent of demand" result holds in a broader context to see whether it is (approximately) applicable to telecommunications.

To do so we consider "nonsubstitution" theorems, which demonstrate that under certain conditions an economy will have a unique price structure determined by the costs of production, independent of the structure of final demand. We will refer to these results as Samuelson-Mirrlees nonsubstitution theorems (Mirrlees 1969).[23] We consider initially the simplest situation where labor is the only nonproduced factor in the economy. Here is a set of necessary conditions that would lead to a Samuelson-Mirrlees nonsubstitution theorem result:

Necessary Conditions for a Nonsubstitution Theorem

1. *Only one nonproduced good exists:* The good is usually assumed to be labor so that land or minerals do not exist.

2. *The technology is constant returns to scale:* A constant per unit requirement of inputs occurs regardless of the amount of output. This condition rules out economies of scale.

3. *No joint production:* A single production process cannot lead to two or more different outputs. This condition rules out economies of scope.

4. *The economy is productive:* The economy can produce a positive net vector of outputs where net output is gross output minus inputs.

With these (plus some additional technical) conditions, the product prices will be independent of final demand. The product prices will equal the cost of production, denominated in terms of the numeraire, which can be units of the nonproduced good. Thus, in a Samuelson-Mirrlees nonsubstitution model, prices of the many products in the economy are independent of demand, as in the simple partial equilibrium single-product Marshallian model.

6.3.1   Necessary Assumptions and Economic Reality: The "Regulatory Fallacy"

We now consider how realistic the necessary assumptions for the application of the nonsubstitution theorem are in the context of telecommunications. Could the regulatory goal of setting competitive prices independent of demand hold approximately true in a realistic economic situation? Because the assumptions for the Samuelson-Mirrlees nonsubstitution theorems are necessary assumptions, no weaker assumptions will do. Thus, to correctly set prices independent of demand, the four necessary assumptions must hold true. The first assumption of only a single unproduced factor cannot be cor-

---

23. See Bliss (1975, ch. 11) for a discussion of nonsubstitution theorems.

rect in a modern economy. If labor and land (minerals) are both unproduced factors, their relative prices will affect input costs and final product prices. But their relative prices will depend on the pattern of demand for products that use both labor and land (silicon, copper, and silver). Since products will use in direct and indirect form different proportions of the nonproduced products, the relative prices cannot be independent of demand. Then, neither the cost of production nor final product prices can be independent of demand. How important this departure from the necessary assumption is cannot be resolved easily. It may not be that important since, if we consider telecommunications as a separable sector of the economy (somewhat similar to partial equilibrium analysis), it might be claimed that the sector is small enough compared with a given regional economy for service and the world economy for capital goods, that it does not have a significant effect on the relative prices of the primary factors. The price of the Hicksian composite economy for the nontelecommunications sector might then be used as a numeraire without too much departure from reality. We will similarly dispose of the last assumption that the economy is productive with the remark that, as an approximation, likely departure (if any) would likely be unimportant.

We now turn to the two most important necessary assumptions for the current application: no economies of scale and no economies of scope. The presence of large economies of scale has traditionally been given as one of the primary reasons for regulation.[24] The old question of a "natural monopoly" is based on large economies of scale. Whether or not the claim of a natural monopoly is correct, modern telecommunications network regulation in the United States, United Kingdom, Australia, and Canada is based on the importance of economies of scale.[25] The idea is that a new entrant cannot duplicate the telecommunications network, so that the incumbent provider is required to sell the use of its network to the new entrant at a regulated cost. The common terminology of "fixed and common" costs in telecommunications denotes the importance of economies of scale that arise from the "fixed costs" in modern telecommunications networks. As we discuss later, the regulated price typically ignores demand factors, which is inconsistent with the whole notion of economies of scale. The higher the demand, the lower the per-unit cost, especially when fixed costs are taken into account.

The "no economies of scope" assumption of the Samuelson-Mirrlees nonsubstitution theorems is violated by all modern telecommunications networks. Economies of scope arise when it is less costly to produce two or more products jointly than by separate production processes. An example of joint production arises with modern telecommunications switches, which

24. See, for example, Kahn (1988, vol. II, 119 ff).
25. Economies of scale can often appear as economies of density in telecommunications, but the basic notion is the same.

are combinations of computers and switch blocks.[26] Switches route calls, but they also provide other services such as voice mail. The same computer is used to provide both services in a less costly manner than if switching and voice mail were provided separately. Again economies of scope are one of the stated reasons for required resale of network functions by incumbent telephone companies to their competitors. A further indication of the importance of economies of scope is the importance of "common costs" in debates over regulated prices. Common costs are typically defined to be costs that arise from two (or more) services, but the costs are not incrementally caused by either service alone. Regulatory bodies such as the Canadian Radio-television Telecommunications Commission (CRTC) and some state regulatory bodies have arbitrarily set a markup to the "direct" cost of 20 to 25 percent to account for common costs.

Yet economists know that most modern competitive companies have joint production and common costs for the production of their outputs. These competitive companies base their prices on competitive conditions for their products. Competitive conditions take account of demand conditions that arise from overall market demand for the product as well as firm demand conditions that arise as a result of competition. Although regulators often say they want to replicate the outcome of a competitive process, they miss the obvious point that a competitive process involves cost factors as well as demand factors. Regulators, to the contrary, often ignore the effect of demand factors on competitive outcomes. Instead, regulators use arbitrary markups over some measure of incremental (or variable) cost to account for economies of scale and economies of scope.

An additional necessary assumption for a nonsubstitution theorem to hold is that the economy is on a steady state growth path. This assumption allows for durable capital goods to enter the model. This assumption for an economy may be a reasonable approximation in certain circumstances, but for the telecommunications sector it departs from any approximation to economic reality. Economists agree that the telecommunications sectors are among the most dynamic in the economy. And since a substantial portion of the durable capital goods used in the telecommunications sector are closely connected to semiconductors and optical transmission, innovations in these sectors will directly affect investment in capital goods in telecommunications. Thus, the steady-state growth assumption is not a good assumption for telecommunications.

Thus, our evaluation is that modern telecommunications differ in many significant and quantitatively important ways from the necessary conditions for price to be independent of demand. Economies of scale and economies of scope are universally recognized to be important economic characteris-

---

26. For a further discussion of economies of scope with switches, see Hausman and Kohlberg (1989).

tics of modern telecommunications networks. The regulatory attempt to set prices as if they were the outcome of a competitive process but to ignore the importance of demand factors and competitive conditions leads to what we call the *regulatory fallacy*.

No serious student of economics would claim that the necessary conditions for the nonsubstitution theorem hold in a telecommunication network environment. Yet the regulatory assumption that price would be based on cost alone in a competitive market is wrong. Economic theory has developed precise conditions when price is independent of demand, and they do not hold, even as an approximation, in telecommunications. Thus regulators are acting on an erroneous belief that, with competition, price equals cost, independent of demand. This erroneous belief leads directly to the resulting regulatory fallacy. The consequent use of arbitrary allocations and markups to regulated prices to take account of fixed and common costs—which are *exactly the costs that arise from economies of scale and scope*—leads to significant consumers' harm. If regulators instead took account of demand factors in setting regulated prices, economic efficiency and consumer welfare could be increased significantly. For example, Hausman (1998a) estimated that the FCC caused a deadweight loss to the economy exceeding $10 billion per year when it levied a "tax" to fund broadband connections in schools, when an alternative method of raising the same amount of funds would have led to a deadweight loss of approximately zero.

6.3.2   Distortions to Competition

Why does incorrect regulation harm consumers more when competition exists? Let us consider an incumbent fixed line provider who decides to explore the economic potential of upgrading its network by increasing fiber penetration. This upgrade would likely cost in the billions of dollars and would be largely a sunk cost investment. The company would have an economic incentive to invest in the upgrade so it could provide higher speed DSL (broadband Internet) service to compete better with cable providers who until recently had a 67 percent market share of broadband Internet connections through cable modems, although DSL has now increased its share from about 33 percent to 40 percent. Cable modems typically provide both faster download speeds and faster upload speeds than current telephone DSL service.[27] Cable companies typically charge a significant premium for their service, so incumbent investment would likely lead to increased competition and lower prices for consumers.

A potential larger benefit to consumers would arise if the incumbent decided to provide pay television service in competition with cable.[28] Thus,

---

27. DSL speeds depend in part on the distance of the premise from the central office, but typically cable modems provide two to three times faster download speeds.
28. These developments are currently ongoing in both Canada and New Zealand.

economies of scope would exist in the provision of two services, DSL and pay TV over the same network. Cable companies have exercised market power for many years. The FCC has reported that monthly cable rates in January 2004 were 15.7 percent lower in areas where incumbent cable operators face competition from a wireline overbuilder.[29] Almost all of the cable competitors have suffered financial difficulties that have limited their ability to expand (for example, RCN in the United States), but an incumbent telecommunications company would have much greater financial resources. Thus, phone company entry into the pay TV market could lead to significant gains for consumers.

However, under the initial implementation of the 1996 act incumbents would be required to allow competitors to utilize these new investments at TELRIC-based prices, which did not recognize the sunk cost character of the investments.[30] Further, because of economies of scope that exist in the provision of DSL, some state regulators who set actual TELRIC rates (as did California), set the TELRIC rate for DSL elements at essentially zero. Unsurprisingly, incumbent companies made little investment in next-generation networks in the United States. Since 2003, the FCC has begun to recognize the errors in its approach, in part at the direction of the DC Circuit, which by then had ruled three times that the FCC regulations on unbundling were inconsistent with the Telecommunications Act of 1996. In August 2005, the FCC finally exempted DSL from all unbundling requirements because of competition from cable networks (subject to a one-year phaseout).[31] However, by refusing for nearly a decade to recognize the role of competition and instead using cost-based regulation that did not take account of the risks of sunk cost investment in new technologies, the FCC has severely distorted competition and harmed consumers. First-order losses to social welfare occur in these types of situations when new products are not introduced to consumers.[32]

6.4   Has Unbundling the Network Achieved Its Goals?

In the 1990s, mandatory unbundling became the proposed remedy of choice in telecommunications regulatory proceedings. In the United States,

29. Statistical Report on Average Rates for Basic Service, Cable Programming Service, and Equipment, MM Dkt. No. 92-266, 4 ¶ 12 (2005).

30. In the United States, state regulatory commissions set TELRIC price based on the FCC framework. Quite different results occurred because of the state implementation of TELRIC prices. Indeed, regulators almost always set TELRIC prices using the overall company cost of capital, rather than taking account of the much higher risk that arises with sunk cost investments. See Hausman (1997, 1998b, 2003) and Pindyck (2004).

31. Report and Order and Notice of Proposed Rule Making, CC Dkt. No. 05-150, 5 August 2005.

32. For a further explanation of the first-order effects, see Hausman (1997, 2003).

the Telecommunications Act of 1996 rests on the hypothesis that requiring a firm to share the use of its facilities with its competitors will enable the competitors eventually to build their own facilities, presumably to the eventual benefit of consumers. The mandatory sharing of facilities is thus the prelude to eventual competition between rival infrastructures or platforms. The corollary of this assumption is that, but for this exact form of regulatory intervention, natural market forces cannot be counted on to produce facilities-based competition.

Any firm may choose to unbundle or lease components of its network with a third party *at a voluntarily negotiated rate*. The firm is also able to decide the scope of unbundling it wants to undertake—that is, how much of its network to resell. The term mandatory unbundling describes an involuntary exchange between an incumbent network operator and a rival *at a regulated rate* where the scope of unbundling is determined by regulators. Determination of the access rate thus becomes the major bone of contention between incumbent and entrant, as a regulatory access rate that is equal to the voluntarily agreed-upon access rate cannot really be said to constitute "mandatory" unbundling. When formulating that access rate, regulators have generally opted in favor of a measure of total element long-run incremental cost (TELRIC) or total service long-run incremental cost (TSLRIC) and against a measure of opportunity cost or option value.[33]

Mandatory unbundling at a regulated rate may apply to various network elements, which are defined by the US Telecommunications Act of 1996 as "a facility or equipment used in the provision of a telecommunications service."[34] The act instructs the FCC to consider whether "the failure to provide access to such network elements would impair the ability of the telecommunications carrier seeking access to provide the services that it seeks to offer."[35] Under the act, prices for unbundled network elements (UNEs) are based on the cost of providing the interconnection or network element.[36] The FCC interpreted that pricing rule as "forward-looking, long-run, incremental cost."[37] In practice, prices are "based on the TSLRIC [total service long-run incremental cost] of the network element . . . and will include a reasonable allocation of forward-looking joint and common costs."

As part of its *Triennial Review Order* of its unbundling regulations, the FCC explained that ILECs were required to provide access to network ele-

---

33. For a detailed analysis of the scope of the unbundling decision and the access pricing decision by a telecommunications regulator, see Hausman and Sidak (1999).

34. 47 U.S.C. § 153(29).

35. 47 U.S.C. § 251(d)(2)(B).

36. 47 U.S.C. § 252(d)(1).

37. *Implementation of the Local Competition Provisions in the Telecommunications Act of 1996; Interconnection between Local Exchange Carriers and Commercial Mobile Radio Service Providers*, CC Docket Nos. 96-98, 95-185, First Report and Order, 11 F.C.C. Rcd. 15499, ¶ 620 (1996).

ments "to the extent that those elements are capable of being used by the requesting carrier in the provision of a telecommunications service."[38] The FCC ordered all ILECs to make available at regulated rates the following UNEs:

(1) stand-alone copper loops and subloops for the provision of narrowband and broadband services;

(2) fiber loops for narrowband service in fiber loop overbuild situations where the incumbent LEC elects to retire existing copper loops;

(3) subloops necessary to access wiring at or near a multiunit customer premises;

(4) network interface devices (NID), which are defined as any means of interconnecting the ILEC's loop distribution plant to wiring at a customer premises location;

(5) dark fiber, DS3, and DS1 transport, subject to a route-specific review by the states to identify available wholesale facilities;

(6) local circuit switching serving the mass market;

(7) shared transport only to the extent that carriers are impaired without access to unbundled switching;

(8) signaling network when a carrier is purchasing unbundled switching;

(9) call-related databases when a requesting carrier purchases unbundled access to the incumbent LEC's switching;

(10) operations support systems (OSS) for qualifying services, which consists of preordering, ordering, provisioning, maintenance and repair, and billing functions supported by an ILEC's databases and information; and

(11) combinations of UNEs, including the loop-transport combination (enhanced extended link, or EEL).

Based on this exhaustive list, it is reasonable to conclude that, at least in the United States, virtually no component of an incumbent's network was immune from unbundling obligations eight years after the passage of the Telecommunications Act.

6.4.1   Line Sharing versus Bitstream Access of Data Services

Bitstream access provides service-level (resale) entry to digital subscriber line (DSL) data provision. Under the bitstream approach, the entrant buys the complete service for a high-speed link to the consumer, and the service includes delivery to the first data switch in the incumbent's network. Unbundled network line sharing, by contrast, allows the entrant to acquire the high-frequency portion of the copper connection but requires it to make some investments in infrastructure.

38. Review of the Section 251 Unbundling Obligations of Incumbent Local Exchange Carriers, Report and Order and Order on Remand and Further Notice of Proposed Rulemaking, CC Dkt. No. 01-338, 20 August 2003, p. 42 ¶ 59 [*Triennial Review*], rev'd, U.S. Telecom Ass'n v. FCC, 290 F.3d 415, 428-29 (D.C. Cir. 2002).

Mandatory line sharing was attempted and then abandoned in the United States. In the FCC's *Line Sharing Order* released in 1999, the FCC directed ILECs to provide the high-frequency portion of the local loop (HFPL) to requesting carriers as a UNE.[39] The commission found in the *Line Sharing Order* that "[t]he record shows that lack of access would materially raise the cost for competitive LECs to provide advanced services [such as DSL] to residential and small business users, delay broad facilities-based market entry and materially limit the scope and quality of competitor service offerings." In May 2002, however, the US Court of Appeals for the DC Circuit vacated the *Line Sharing Order*, finding that the commission had failed to give adequate consideration to existing facilities-based competition in the provision of broadband services, especially by cable systems.[40] In its August 2003 *Triennial Review Order*, the FCC decided not to reinstate the vacated line-sharing rules because it determined that "continued unbundled access to stand-alone copper loops and subloops enables a requesting carrier to offer and recover its costs from all of the services that the loop supports, including broadband service."[41]

The FCC rejected its prior finding that lack of separate access to the high-frequency portion would cause impairment for four reasons. The two most important reasons from our viewpoint is that the FCC noted that the difficulties of cost allocation for different portions of a single loop had led most states to price the high frequency portion of the loop at approximately zero, which distorted competitive incentives. Also, the FCC recognized the substantial intermodal competition from cable companies, which lessened any competitive benefits associated with line sharing. In its March 2004 opinion, the DC Circuit upheld the FCC's decision to eliminate line sharing, concluding that the FCC "reasonably found that other considerations outweighed any impairment."[42] The court added that "intermodal competition from cable ensures the persistence of substantial competition in broadband."

Regulators in other nations have chosen bitstream access over line sharing. For example, in December 2003, the New Zealand Commerce Commission recommended the designation of an "asymmetric DSL bitstream access service."[43] The agency defined ADSL bitstream access service as "a

39. Deployment of Wireline Services Offering Advanced Telecommunications Capability and Implementation of the Local Competition Provisions of the Telecommunications Act of 1996, CC Dkt. Nos. 98-147, 96-98, Third Report and Order in CC Dkt. No. 98-147, and Fourth Report and Order in CC Dkt. No. 96-98, 15 F.C.C. Rcd. 3,696 (1999).
40. U.S. Telecom Ass'n v. FCC, 290 F.3d 415, 428-29 (D.C. Cir. 2003).
41. See Triennial Review, p. 125 ¶ 199.
42. United States Telecom Association v. FCC, 359 F.3d 554, 585 (D.C. Cir. 2004).
43. New Zealand Commerce Commission, Section 64 Review and Schedule 3 Investigation into Unbundling the Local Loop Network and the Fixed Public Data Network, Final Report, December 2003 (available at http://www.comcom.govt.nz/telecommunications/llu/finalreport .PDF).

high speed IP access service which provides good performance, but could not typically support extensive use of mission critical applications which require excellent real-time network performance or availability." The commission defined bitstream access as a situation in which the incumbent's access link "is made available to other operators, which are then able to provide high-speed services to end-consumers." The agency concluded the net social benefits from bitstream access exceeded the net social benefits of line sharing due to the lower total cost of providing the unbundled service (collocation costs are avoided in bitstream access). The commission reasoned that, under bitstream access, entrants face a lower risk of investing in network components such as DSLAMs (digital subscriber line access multipliers) that might not be fully utilized. We discuss the New Zealand experience in greater detail in a later section.

In February 2005, the FCC released a new unbundling order that, most significantly, eliminated UNE-P as a separate network element entitled to mandatory unbundling.[44] The commission found that the ability of CLECs (competitive local exchange carriers) to compete would not be impaired if they did not have access to unbundled switching at TELRIC prices. The FCC also established new unbundling rules for mass market local circuit switching, high-capacity loops, and dedicated interoffice transport. With switching removed from the list of UNEs, it followed that UNE-P could no longer be mandated at regulated TELRIC prices—although ILECs obviously could still offer UNE-P to CLECs at commercially negotiated rates. The FCC also found that the Telecommunications Act of 1996 did not require that the agency mandate ILECs to offer UNE-P.

Despite the reasonable prospect that it could eventually be thrown out by the DC Circuit, mandatory UNE-P at TELRIC rates had become the cornerstone of the business plan for AT&T and MCI in the local market. In the case of AT&T, the company had abandoned its facilities-based strategy for local markets by selling off its cable television assets at an enormous loss of approximately $40 to 50 billion, and it spun off AT&T Wireless, which soon merged with Cingular, the joint venture of SBC and BellSouth. With the commercial and regulatory demise of mandatory UNE-P, and with its long-distance revenues under increasing pressure from Bell company entry following the completion of the section 271 approval process for the RBOCs (Regional Bell Operating Companies) in all states and the District of Columbia, AT&T was rapidly becoming a brand name in search of a product. Although AT&T embarked on yet another nonfacilities-based strategy by negotiating with Sprint PCS to rebrand wholesale wireless minutes as an AT&T cell phone product, the highest priority for AT&T's management (and, similarly, the prize for the managers who took MCI through chapter

---

44. Order on Remand, In re Unbundled Access to Network Elements, 2005 FCC LEXIS 912, WC Docket No. 04-313, CC Dkt. No. 01-338 (FCC February 4, 2005).

11 reorganization) was to concentrate on readying the company for sale to one of the three financially stable RBOCs. Thus, AT&T, with its symbol "T" (telephone) on the NYSE and its long history as the primary company in US telecommunications, lacked an economic rationale for its continued existence.

6.4.2 Rationales for Network Unbundling

We examine the theoretical underpinnings of mandatory unbundling. We also survey the rationales offered by regulatory agencies in support of mandatory unbundling. In general, mandatory unbundling was believed to, among other items, (a) generate competition in retail markets through greater innovation and investment and lower prices, (b) generate greater competition in wholesale markets, and (c) encourage entrants to migrate from unbundling to a facilities-based approach. Because our focus is on the benefits of mandatory unbundling, we do not consider its regulatory costs, such as the difficulties in implementation or compliance costs for operators. When considering unbundling, a regulator also should take account of a full range of efficiency considerations, including allocative (consumer welfare gains associated with greater penetration at lower prices), productive efficiency (producer surplus associated with reductions in marginal costs), and dynamic efficiency (how welfare is generated and distributed over time).

Rationale 1: Competition in Retail Markets Is Desirable

In a static model that does not consider investment in future periods, consumers benefit from mandatory unbundling to the extent that such regulation lowers retail prices. In a dynamic model, mandatory unbundling at regulated rates runs the risk of decreasing investment by both incumbent ILECs (by truncating returns by granting a free option to new entrant CLECs)[45] and CLECs (by increasing the relative return of UNE-based entry). Despite these factors, proponents argued that the net effect of mandatory unbundling was to increase investment by both ILECs and CLECs.

Innovation and Investment. According to its proponents, mandatory unbundling at regulated rates encourages innovation and investment on behalf of both incumbents and entrants. In its *Third Order* implementing the Telecommunications Act, the FCC explained that a positive by-product of mandatory unbundling at TELRIC was greater innovation on behalf of entrants and incumbents:

> Unbundling rules that encourage competitors to deploy their own facilities in the long run will provide incentives for both incumbents and competitors to invest and innovate, and will allow the Commission and the

45. See Hausman (1997).

states to reduce regulation once effective facilities-based competition develops.[46]

The more competitors in the market, the FCC reasoned, the greater the incentive to introduce a new technology to gain a technological edge. With the correct incentives in place, the need for wholesale regulation would disappear:

> The unbundling standards we adopt in this Order . . . seeks [sic] to create incentives for both incumbents and requesting carriers to invest and innovate in new technologies by establishing a mechanism by which regulatory obligations to provide access to network elements will be reduced as alternatives to the incumbent LECs' network elements become available in the future.

With greater facilities-based investment, the FCC reasoned, the market could one day be relied upon to discipline ILEC prices for local services.

Although it was aware of arguments that mandatory unbundling at regulated rates might discourage ILEC investment, the FCC believed that other factors in the marketplace would mitigate these negative effects:

> We acknowledge that the incumbent LEC argument that unbundling may adversely affect innovation is consistent with economic theory, but events in the marketplace suggest that other factors may be driving incumbent LECs to invest in xDSL technologies, notwithstanding the economic theory.

For example, investment by cable companies in cable modem service was believed to be sufficient motivation for ILECs to invest in DSL facilities. Although the negative investment effects might not overcome these other factors, it is not clear how mandatory unbundling at regulated rates actually *increases* investment by ILECs. One theory is that an ILEC would have to respond to greater competition from CLECs by investing in new facilities. But to the extent that those new investments would be subject to unbundling rules, those investments might not be undertaken.[47] Another theory is that the ILEC will invest in new access technologies that potentially will not be subject to unbundling rules.

Prices and Retail Margins.   When a CLEC obtains an access line at incremental cost, it is free to charge the end user an amount anywhere between the incremental cost and the retail price. A CLEC can charge below incremental cost if it can bundle the access line with other services such as vertical ser-

---

46. See Third Order, ¶ 7.

47. See AT&T Corp. v. Iowa Utilities Bd., 525 U.S. 366 (1999). Justice Breyer, concurring in part and dissenting in part, stated "a sharing requirement may diminish the original owner's incentive to keep up or to improve the property by depriving the owner of the fruits of value-creating investment, research, or labor."

vices or long distance. Competition among CLECs is predicted in theory to discipline CLECs in their pricing behavior. If competition among CLECs is intense, then the retail price offered by CLECs should equal the access price for the unbundled loop plus the incremental cost of other inputs. Finally, ILECs must respond to price cuts by CLECs with their own price cuts. The equilibrium outcome of that game is lower prices.

The FCC believed that the Telecommunications Act encouraged the agency to promote retail price competition through mandatory unbundling:

> [T]he 1996 Act set the stage for a new competitive paradigm in which carriers in previously segregated markets are able to compete in a dynamic and integrated telecommunications market that promises lower prices and more innovative services to consumers.[48]

Even if the mandatory unbundling at TELRIC never led to facilities-based competition, the FCC reasoned, consumers would be better off to the extent that prices for local services declined:

> National requirements for unbundling allow [sic] requesting carriers, including small entities, to take advantage of economies of scale in network. Requesting carriers, which may include small entities, should have access to the same technologies and economies of scale and scope available to incumbent LECs. Having such access will facilitate competition and help lower prices for all consumers, including individuals and small entities.

Because ILECs enjoyed a cost advantage vis-à-vis CLECs, the FCC argued, it was preferable from a social welfare perspective for retail prices to be based on the ILECs' costs and not on the CLECs' costs. Because ILECs are subject to state-sponsored price regulation, it was not clear that prices would decrease absent subsidized UNE rates. Although the FCC was concerned about stimulating retail competition for local telephone and broadband access services, most European regulators focused exclusively on stimulating retail competition in broadband markets.

Rationale 2: Competition in Retail Markets
Cannot Be Achieved without Mandatory Unbundling

Even if competition in retail markets is desirable, it is still necessary to show that competition would not occur in the absence of mandatory unbundling. In this part, we explain the reasoning articulated by unbundling proponents as to why natural market forces cannot deliver the benefits of competition in local services.

A Vertically Integrated Firm Generally Prefers Its Own Downstream Affiliate. In general, a vertically integrated firm prefers retail sales by its af-

---

48. See Third Order, ¶ 2.

filiated retail division to sales by an unaffiliated retailer. This preference can be reversed, however, if the access price exceeds the retail margin. Much academic work has been dedicated to analyzing the incentives of vertically integrated firms to deny access to key inputs to unaffiliated downstream rivals.[49] If a vertically integrated firm can solidify its market power in future periods by refusing to deal with rivals in a downstream market, then that firm has an anticompetitive reason for such a refusal to deal.[50] A vertically integrated firm might also refuse to deal with other unaffiliated firms in the downstream market as a means to acquire market power in that market.

Although no ILEC prefers unbundling its network elements *at a regulated rate* to selling its services through its own retail division, some ILECs have voluntarily unbundled their network elements to rivals at a commercially negotiated rate. For example, in January 1995, Rochester Telephone implemented its own Open Market Plan for unbundling network services in New York.[51] Under the Open Market Plan, Rochester restructured itself into a network services company, which retained the Rochester name, and a competitive company, Frontier Communications of Rochester, which the New York Public Service Commission regulated as a nondominant carrier. Rochester provided on an unbundled, nondiscriminatory basis the local loop, switching, and transport functions as a wholesaler, at discounted (yet voluntary) prices lower than its standard retail rates.

Entry Barriers Prevent Natural Competition.   In the United States, a CLEC is considered impaired when lack of access to an incumbent LEC network element poses a barrier to entry that is likely to make entry into a market uneconomic.[52] In its *Triennial Review Order*, the FCC offered the following factors that contribute to entry barriers in the provision of local telephone service: (a) scale economies, (b) sunk costs, (c) first-mover advantages, (d) absolute cost advantages, and (e) barriers within the control of ILECs. The FCC's explanation of sunk costs provides some insight as to the regulator's decision making:

> Sunk costs increase a new entrant's cost of failure. Potential new entrants may also fear that an incumbent LEC that has incurred substantial sunk costs will drop prices to protect its investment in the face of new entry. In addition, sunk costs can give significant first-mover advantages to the incumbent LEC, which has incurred these costs over many years and has already had the opportunity to recoup many of these costs through its rates.

49. See, for example, Riordan and Salop (1995) and Sidak and Crandall (2002).
50. Carlton (2001).
51. FCC News Release, *Rochester Telephone Corporation Granted Rule Waivers to Implement Its Open Market Plan*, March 7, 1995, available at http://www.fcc.gov/Bureaus/Common_Carrier/ News_Releases/1995/nrcc5030.txt.
52. See Triennial Review, p. 9.

According to its proponents, mandatory unbundling is necessary to overcome such barriers. The corollary of this proposition is that, without mandatory unbundling, facilities-based investment cannot occur. In its May 2002 decision vacating certain portions of the *UNE Remand Order*, the DC Circuit concluded that the commission had failed to adequately explain how a uniform national rule for assessing impairment would help to achieve the goals of the act, including the promotion of facilities-based competition.[53]

Opponents of mandatory unbundling also cite the large sunk cost of the ILEC's network, but for different reasons. They argue that sunk costs imply that regulators should abstain from appropriating the quasi rents of ILECs, which undermines the incentive of ILECs to invest in new technologies.[54] They also argue that, to the extent that network investment cannot be directed toward other uses in the event of low market demand, large sunk costs require that access prices are set higher than what would otherwise be necessary to induce investment under a standard present discounted value calculation.

Rationale 3: Mandatory Unbundling Enables Future Facilities-Based Investment

Access-based competition is supposedly the stepping stone to facilities-based competition. This proposition, or hypothesis, lies at the heart of regulatory decisions on unbundling and access pricing that the FCC and its counterparts in other nations have made since the mid-1990s. In the telecommunications industry, the examples of the *stepping-stone hypothesis* are numerous. For example, MCI successfully made the transition from reseller of long-distance services to facilities-based carrier. The leasing of selected unbundled elements at regulated prices is vigorously defended by CLECs and regulators as a complement to subsequent facilities-based entry, not a substitute for it. Within the strata of regulated access-based entry options, regulators may consider UNE-P to be a stepping stone to a CLEC's subsequent investment in its own switches and its more limited reliance on unbundled local loops.[55]

In implementing the unbundling rules, the FCC sought to follow the intent of Congress by creating an intermediate phase of competition, during which some new companies would deploy their own facilities to compete directly with the incumbents:

---

53. See USTA, p. 427 (emphasis in original).

54. For a description of the role of sunk costs in access pricing and unbundling, see generally Hausman and Sidak (1999).

55. Similarly, regulators may consider mandatory roaming at regulated prices to be a stepping stone to a wireless carrier's eventual investment in base stations and spectrum in another geographic region. However, a component of the relevant infrastructure is radio spectrum, the allocation of which is controlled by the government (at least in the primary market). Consequently, it is not clear where the stepping stone of mandated access leads in wireless.

> Although Congress did not express explicitly a preference for one par-
> ticular competitive arrangement, it recognized implicitly that the pur-
> chase of unbundled network elements would, at least in some situations,
> serve as a *transitional arrangement* until fledgling competitors could
> develop a customer base and complete the construction of their own net-
> works.[56]

The FCC thus sought to force the incumbents to allow others to access their
systems, in the hope that mandatory unbundling would create competitors
who would later invest in their own facilities.

In the long run, the FCC expected that entrants would build their own
facilities because doing so would enhance the entrants' ability to compete
more effectively with incumbents:

> We fully expect that over time competitors will prefer to deploy their own
> facilities in markets where it is economically feasible to do so, because it
> is only through owning and operating their own facilities that competitors
> have control over the competitive and operational characteristics of their
> service, and have the incentive to invest and innovate in new technologies
> that will distinguish their services from those of the incumbent.

Thus, mandatory unbundling would allow entrants to derive revenue from
offering services over the unbundled network elements, and then use that
revenue to construct their own networks once the technology shifted. Of
course, if the access rate were set too low, the transition to a facilities-based
competitor would not occur, as CLECs would never find it in their interests to invest in their own facilities. If access rates were set just right, this
transition to facilities-based competition would generate additional social
benefits, which are described in the next section.

Rationale 4: Competition in Wholesale Access Markets Is Desirable

Competition in the input markets was, by itself, desirable. In this part, we
review how input-level competition can, in theory, generate technological
innovation and incentives for gains in productive efficiency and can eventually lead to regulatory withdrawal.

A Network of Networks.   Facilities-based entry by CLECs in the current
period meant that future entrants would not have to depend exclusively
on ILECs to obtain network elements. The FCC believed that mandatory
unbundling would expedite this process:

> Moreover, in some areas, we believe that the greatest benefits may be
> achieved through facilities-based competition, and that the ability of
> requesting carriers to use unbundled network elements, including various

---

56. See Third Order, note 39, ¶ 6 (emphasis added).

combinations of unbundled network elements, is a necessary precondition to the subsequent deployment of self-provisioned network facilities.[57]

In theory, facilities-based entry generates greater benefits than UNE-based entry because the former signals a credible commitment to stay in the market. If an entrant has not made sunk investments in infrastructure, it cannot use sunk costs to make that signal. Nor will the incumbent face the prospect of durable capacity that survives the demise of the company that invested to create it. Moreover, facilities-based competition leads to technological diversity, which increases choice and may provide newer and better services because the CLEC does not depend on a legacy network.

The FCC envisioned that facilities-based entrants would spawn a new generation of UNE based entrants, who in subsequent periods would become facilities-based entrants:

> In order for competitive networks to develop, the incumbent LECs' bottleneck control over interconnection must dissipate. As the market matures and the carriers providing services in competition with the incumbent LECs' local exchange offerings grow, we believe these carriers may establish direct routing arrangements with one another, forming a network of networks around the current system.

Thus, the FCC believed that mandatory unbundling at TELRIC would evolve into voluntary access arrangements. Under this scenario, some facilities-based entrants might choose to become a pure wholesaler of network elements, leaving the retail component to other CLECs.

Regulatory Withdrawal.   Competition among facilities-based providers to supply network elements to future generations of CLECs would decrease the price of those network elements. The next generation of CLECs would, in turn, pass those savings along to end users in the form of lower retail prices. At some point in the process, the regulator could, in theory, withdraw and allow a competitive market for inputs to discipline the price of retail service.

In practice, however, regulators are reluctant to relinquish their power to control entry and allocate rents in a given market. This vision of mandatory unbundling also ignores the strategic use of regulation by competitors. Given the large rents at stake, it is not realistic to believe that the regulatory machinery could be dismantled very easily. Indeed, in the United States, the degree of regulation has increased since the passage of the Telecommunications Act of 1996.

In summary, mandatory unbundling was based on the following rationales: (a) competition in retail markets is desirable; (b) competition in retail markets cannot be achieved without mandatory unbundling; (c) mandatory

57. See http://transition.fcc.gov/Bureaus/Common_Carrier/Orders/1999/fcc99238.txt.

unbundling promotes future facilities-based investment, the *stepping-stone hypothesis*; and (d) competition in wholesale access markets is desirable. Fortunately, there is testable hypothesis associated with each rationale.

6.5   The Unbundling Experience in the United States, United Kingdom, and New Zealand

The previous section considered how mandatory unbundling should work *in theory*. With the benefit of several years of experience, we turn now to an evaluation of the extent to which the rationales for mandatory unbundling were substantiated *in practice*. We note that many of the studies we refer to are necessarily confounded by the effects of the telecom boom and bust of the late 1990s and early 2000s. Further, many of the studies cannot be claimed to be necessarily causal in nature; nevertheless, the data presented in them are often suggestive of the economic effects. In addition, due to the small sample nature of the outcomes differing interpretations can exist (and do exist) regarding the economic reasons for a particular outcome. We discuss what we consider the primary interpretation with differing interpretations also noted.

We focus on the unbundling experience in the United States, the United Kingdom, and New Zealand. For each country, we examine whether any of the four primary rationales for mandatory unbundling at TELRIC was substantiated in practice. We rely on data from the relevant regulatory agency that implemented the unbundling regime. For example, we discuss why regulators in New Zealand did not adopt mandatory unbundling.

In compiling the country surveys, we observed a large variation in the degree to which economic analysis informed the regulator's decision-making process. In the United States, for example, the process was informed by legal interpretation of specific language (such as the meaning of "impaired") or by engineering measures of hypothetical operating costs. In New Zealand, by contrast, the process was informed largely by economic analysis and by international experience with mandatory unbundling. Using economic methods, the New Zealand regulator literally assigned net welfare gains to each regulatory option and selected the path with the greatest net welfare gain. New Zealand had the benefit of studying the experience of other nations before it decided on the optimal regulatory approach. The FCC still has not used economic analysis when modifying its rules, despite the fact that the United States now has more than six years of unbundling experience.

6.5.1   United States

The Telecommunications Act of 1996 ordered the FCC to introduce competition into the local services market by forcing ILECs to provide entrants access to the ILECs' existing facilities at regulated rates. In 1999, the FCC explained that Congress did not provide the agency much flexibility in the exact form of managed competition: "Congress directed the Commission to implement the provisions of section 251, and to specifically determine which network elements should be unbundled pursuant to section 251(c)(3).7." Hence, the FCC did not have the discretion to reject or embrace any of the rationales for mandatory unbundling. The only decisions left to the FCC concerned the *extent* of mandatory unbundling—namely, which elements would be included in the list of UNEs and the appropriate pricing of those elements.

Retail Competition

In this part, we review the unbundling experience in the United States with respect to retail pricing and investment.

Pricing. Retail competition triggered by mandatory unbundling should manifest itself in terms of lower retail prices. Even if price regulation of local services by state PUCs were binding, the introduction of UNE-based competition could still reduce price. In the United States, however, mandatory unbundling does not appear to have decreased local service prices measurably—despite the fact that CLECs had more than 13 percent of the nation's access lines by 2003. Figure 6.3 shows the Bureau of Labor Statistics' (BLS) Consumer Price Index for local telephone services from 1993 through 2003.

As figure 6.3 shows, prices of local telephone services offered by *all carriers* in urban areas grew at a slower annual rate on average before passage of the act (1.21 percent versus 2.96 percent).

It bears emphasis that such price comparisons do not control for other changes in the price of local service. For example, since the passage of the Telecommunications Act, the subscriber line charge (SLC) was increased and long-distance access prices were decreased. Hence, a small part of the BLS CPI price increase might be attributable to regulatory tax shifting. According to the FCC, the average residential rate for local service provided by ILECs in urban areas *before taxes, fees, and miscellaneous charges* increased from $13.71 in 1996 to $14.55 in 2002.[58] Hence, mandatory unbundling does not appear to have decreased retail prices in the way the FCC intended. This experience is in marked contrast to the prices of other telecommunications services, which uniformly decreased over the same period.[59] An alternative interpretation of figure 6.3 is that the increased prices are the result of rebalancing of the relative price differences between residential and business rates; however, the basic fact we emphasize is that price increases

58. Trends in Telephone Service, FCC Industry Analysis Division, 2003 Report, p. 13-1 (rel. August 2003), available at http://www.fcc.gov/Bureaus/Common_Carrier/Reports/FCC-State_Link/IAD/trend803.pdf.
59. The prices of telecommunication equipment were decreasing over this period at the rate of approximately 8 to 10 percent per year.

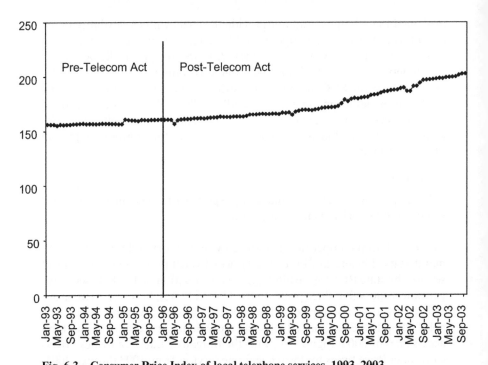

Fig. 6.3   Consumer Price Index of local telephone services, 1993–2003

Source: Bureau of Labor Statistics, Consumer Price Index, All Urban Consumers, Telephone Services, Local Charges (available at http://data.bls.gov/labjava/outside.jsp?survey=cu).
Note: Prices normalized to 1984 dollars.

were greater after the Telecom Act was implemented, when most other telecommunications prices were falling rapidly in real terms.

Investment.   Many scholars have examined the effect of mandatory unbundling on ILEC investment. For example, in work performed for AT&T (the largest CLEC) and submitted to the FCC, Robert D. Willig, William H. Lehr, John P. Bigelow, and Stephen B. Levinson examined the relationship between UNE-P wholesale rates and Bell companies' capital expenditures.[60] They attempted to distinguish between the "competitive stimulus hypothesis" that UNE-P creates competition that induces increased ILEC network investment, and the "investment deterrence hypothesis" that UNE-P diminishes the return on network investment by ILECs and causes them to invest less. Willig et al. hypothesized that TELRIC-based UNE-P rates encourage entry by CLECs, which forces Bell companies to invest more in their net-

60. Willig et al. (2002).

works to protect market share. They therefore expected to find that ILEC capital expenditures are inversely related to UNE-P prices. They calculated that the elasticity of ILEC investment to UNE-P prices was between –2.1 and –2.9, meaning that a 1 percent decrease in the UNE-P rate generated between a 2.1 and 2.9 percent increase in ILEC investment.

In a book published by the Brookings Institution, Robert W. Crandall explained that the loss of end-user subscribers to CLECs reduces ILECs' revenues by more than their costs.[61] Crandall found that, whereas ILECs lose roughly 60 percent of the revenues associated with a given line when provisioned on an unbundled, rather than retail, basis, the avoided costs of customer service and marketing are only about 10 percent of the Bell companies' total costs.

Crandall also examined the relationship between the FCC's state-by-state capital expenditure data and the various measures of state UNE-P rates found in various studies. Crandall hypothesized that the UNE-P rate should not have a significant negative effect on capital expenditures because it is not logical to invest more if the ILEC receives less revenue under mandatory unbundling. Crandall concluded that none of the previous studies provided support for the theory that UNE-P rates have influenced capital spending by Bell companies. Crandall further demonstrated that Bell companies scaled back their capital expenditures in 2002 and 2003, and that the decline in capital expenditures was greatest in those states that reduced their UNE-P rates. However, as discussed earlier, these results may well be confounded with the effects of the telecom boom and bust period. The fact that RBOC revenue and investment has been reduced relative to historic averages implies that mandatory unbundling in the United States did not achieve its intended effect if these effects arose from the effects of mandatory unbundling.

We turn to the question of CLEC investment in the next sections on entry barriers and the stepping stone hypothesis. Investment activities during the late 1990s were undoubtedly affected by exceptional capital market conditions during the telecom boom period when access to capital markets by technology companies (and especially telecommunications companies) was extremely cheap. But capital expenditure by CLECs was modest even when considered in terms of the way in which the CLECs have applied their resources. For example, an analysis of financial statements of EarthLink and Covad, two data CLECs, suggests that the ratio of capital expenditure to sales was 5 to 6 percent in 2001 and 2002, compared with a ratio of 20 to 25 percent for ILECs such as Verizon, SBC, and BellSouth.[62] Similar results are found for other ILECs.

61. Crandall (2004).
62. Sales and capital expenditure data were taken from company annual reports. See also Hausman (2002a) who discusses Covad and other CLECs' competitive strategies.

Entry Barriers

The second rationale for mandatory unbundling is that, without that particular form of regulatory intervention, market forces cannot deliver facilities-based competition. In the United States, cable telephony appears to disprove that proposition. According to the National Cable Television Association (NCTA), the number of cable telephony subscribers in the United States increased from 180,000 in the first quarter of 2000 to 2.5 million by September 2003.[63] In addition to the deployment of circuit-switched telephony, many companies have begun trials or are launching voice over Internet protocol (VoIP) service. For example, in 2003 Cablevision launched Optimum Voice VoIP throughout its New York City service area of four million homes. As of December 2006 all of the major cable companies are now offering cable-based voice services in competition with the ILECs. The service typically combines local and unlimited long-distance services. Further, the service is often also offered as a bundled service with broadband Internet cable modem service and cable TV service in the so-called triple play. The discounts of the bundled package are typically quite substantial (for example, Comcast offers a discount of approximately 33 percent).

In its *Third Report* in 1999, however, the FCC dismissed the emergence of cable telephony as a substitute for the ILECs' fixed-line networks:

> We also disagree with the incumbent LECs' argument that cable television service offers a viable alternative to the incumbent's unbundled loop. Cable service is largely restricted to residential subscribers, and generally supports only one-way service, not the two-way communications telephony requires. Moreover, we conclude that declining to unbundle loops in areas where cable telephony is available would be inconsistent with the Act's goal of encouraging entry by multiple providers. Given that neither mobile nor fixed wireless can yet replace wireline service, if we were to take the incumbents' approach, consumers might be left to a choose [*sic*] between only the cable company and the incumbent LEC.[64]

The FCC's reasoning is unpersuasive. If two facilities-based carriers offer a similar service, and if the first carrier is not compelled to share its network with rivals, then consumers would no longer be subject to monopoly prices for local services. Moreover, the FCC's suggestion that cable infrastructure supports only one-way service is outdated given that, as of June 2003, cable modems accounted for nearly two-thirds of all residential broadband subscriptions,[65] which is a two-way service. Cable networks are now rapidly upgrading their service offerings to provide telephone service using VoIP technology.

---

63. National Cable Television Association, Statistics & Resources, available at http://www.ncta.com/Docs/PageContent.cfm?pageID=86.

64. See Third Order, ¶ 189.

65. See FCC High-Speed Services, p. 10 (tbl. 3).

When the availability of cable telephony was on the verge of ubiquity in late 2003, the FCC was forced to offer a different explanation for why the threat of cable telephony should be discounted:

> As a general matter, while these [cable] systems are increasingly being used for the delivery of retail narrowband and broadband services (e.g., telephony and high-speed Internet access services), the record indicates that such systems are not being used currently to provide wholesale local loop offerings that might substitute for access to incumbent LECs' loop facilities. Some cable companies also have augmented their networks to enable the provision of two-way voice telephony services. For such services, the cable infrastructure serves as a replacement for loops. At this time, however, deployment of voice telephony by cable companies has been substantially exceeded by the deployment of cable modem service.[66]

Hence, the FCC argued that unbundling of the ILECs' network is necessary because cable operators were not inclined to share their own network with rivals at marginal cost. It bears emphasis that the DC Circuit rejected this very rationale for mandatory sharing of broadband in its May 2002 decision, explaining that competition removes the reason for mandatory sharing.[67] To date, the FCC has refused to recognize the effect of interplatform competition to fixed line telephony despite the DC Circuit's repeated admonitions that such competition cannot be ignored.

In May 2004, Comcast, the nation's largest cable company, announced that it planned to offer phone service to half of the households reached by the company's cable systems by the end of 2005 and to all 40 million of them by the end of 2006.[68] Verizon perceived the threat posed by cable telephony to be significant. Verizon began selling video over fiber optic lines to homes and businesses in 2005, which was "part of a long-term strategy to fight cable companies on their own turf before they erode too much of Verizon's traditional telephone business."[69] Verizon has already applied for licenses for cable franchises in several states. AT&T (formerly SBC) has also begun to construct fiber networks that will provide pay-TV services. Both Verizon and AT&T have decided that they need to offer a "triple play" bundle in competition with the cable companies. Both ILECs are investing in the tens of billions of dollars in these upgraded networks.

Wireless phone service also constrains the ability of ILECs to raise the

66. Review of the Section 251 Unbundling Obligations of Incumbent Local Exchange Carriers, Implementation of the Local Competition Provisions of the Telecommunications Act of 1996, Deployment of Wireline Services Offering Advanced Telecommunications Capability, CC Dkt. Nos. 01-338, 96-98, 98-147, Report and Order and Order on Remand and Further Notice of Proposed Rulemaking, 18 F.C.C. Rcd. 16,978, 16,979 ¶ 229 (2003).

67. See USTA, p. 428.

68. Peter Grant, *Wall St. J.*, 26 May 2004, p. A3.

69. Justin Hyde, *Reuters News*, 19 May 2004, *1.

price of voice services. There is a growing evidence of "wireless substitution" in the United States, which documents the degree to which consumers perceive wireless phones to be substitutes for fixed-line connections. The California Public Utilities Commission in August 2006 found that wireless substitution accounts for approximately half of ILEC primary residential wireline losses.[70] The combined number of wireless and cable telephony subscribers as of 2004 exceeded the number of end-user switched access lines and has continued to increase rapidly since that time. Wireless substitution is not unique to the United States. A J. D. Power and Associates survey in May 2004 revealed that 53 percent of UK contract customers "use mobile as main method of communication."[71] The emergence of facilities-based competition for voice customers implies that the rationale for mandatory unbundling based on insurmountable barriers to entry is not substantiated in the United States.

Stepping-Stone Hypothesis

The stepping-stone hypothesis implies that CLECs will migrate toward facilities-based entry over time as they gain market share. One way to measure the effect of mandatory unbundling on the method of CLEC entry is through time-series analysis. Figure 6.4 demonstrates that, contrary to the stepping-stone hypothesis, CLECs are, in the aggregate, increasingly relying on UNE-P as their preferred mode of entry.

The vertical axis is the share of total CLEC switched access lines: the sum of the shares across all types is 100 percent.[72] Whereas CLECs relied on UNEs for 23.9 percent of their lines in December 1999, by June 2003, UNE lines accounted for 58.5 percent of all CLEC lines.[73] Of all UNE lines in December 2002, 70.5 percent were acquired in combination with the ILEC's switch.[74] The availability of wholesale access appears to have discouraged CLECs from investing in their own facilities (including switches) over time.

The increasing share of UNEs might be attributable to entry by new CLECs, which rely on UNEs extensively in their early stages. Stated differently, it is possible that mature CLECs have, in fact, made the transition to

70. Most of the other half of residential wireline losses went to cable telephone providers. See Public Utilities Commission of the State of California, "Order Instituting Rulemaking on the Commission's Own Motion to Assess and Revise the Regulation of Telecommunications Utilities," Proposed Decision, August 25, 2006. The CPUC found "Finding of Fact No. 39. Wireless service is a substitute for wireline service."

71. J. D. Power and Associates, Consumer Survey, May 2004.

72. Since the total number of switched access lines was approximately constant over this period (although it has decreased more recently), we believe that discussing the share of CLEC Switch Access lines is easier than considering the total number of CLEC access lines. In addition, most regulatory analysis of CLECs has been in terms of their share of access lines.

73. See FCC, Local Telephone Competition: Status as of June 30, 2003, tbl. 3 (rel. 22 December 2003), available at http://www.fcc.gov/Bureaus/Common_Carrier/Reports/FCC -State_Link/IAD/lcom1203.pdf.

74. Ibid., tbl. 4.

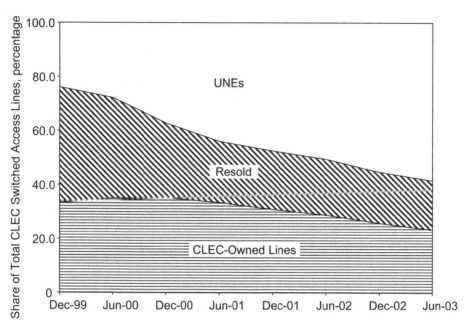

Fig. 6.4   CLEC lines by type, 1999–2003

Source: FCC, Local Telephone Competition: Status as of June 30, 2003, p. 6 (tbl. 3) (rel. December 22, 2003).

Note: UNEs include UNE-loops and UNE-platform.

facilities-based lines, but entry by new UNE-based CLECs is artificially inflating the share of CLEC lines that are UNEs. To examine this hypothesis, we analyzed the progress of seventeen specific CLECs from the first quarter 2000 through the fourth quarter 2004. If the stepping-stone hypothesis were valid, then one would expect to observe the share of facilities-based lines *for a given CLEC* to increase over time. We found that a very small share of CLECs increased their share of facilities-based lines before the telecommunications meltdown of 2001. Roughly one-quarter of the firms in the sample increased their share of facilities-based lines in 2000. The majority of the CLECs continued to rely on UNEs to the same extent during that time period. Thus, we do not find evidence in support of the stepping-stone hypothesis. Other empirical analyses support the position that mandatory unbundling does not provide a stepping-stone to facilities-based investment. For example, Crandall, Ingraham, and Singer find that the share of CLEC lines that are facilities-based is lower in states where the UNE rental rates are lower, which suggests that unbundling decreases facilities-based competition in the short term.[75]

75. Crandall, Ingraham, and Singer (2004).

Wholesale Competition

The FCC's vision of a network of networks does not appear to have materialized in the US residential market. For certain sectors of the US enterprise market, however, several CLECs have established themselves as pure wholesale providers of local access. In its *Triennial Review Order*, the FCC reported that "[t]o a smaller degree, some competitive LECs began to provide selected transport services to other competitive LECs on a wholesale basis."[76] Since 1998, CLEC-owned fiber has increased from 100,000 to 184,000 route miles. In addition, wholesale suppliers of fiber continue to invest in facilities that are being used by all carriers.[77] The FCC noted that much of this interoffice transport is long-haul intercity, rather than local. In summary, an operating wholesale market appears to have emerged in enterprise switching, transport, and high-speed (DS3) loops only according to the FCC analysis.

Other Observations about the Process

The Telecommunications Act retained the BOCs' (Bell Operating Company) interLATA (interstate long-distance) prohibition while establishing, in section 271,[78] a process—involving each state public utilities commission, the FCC, and the Department of Justice (DOJ), acting on a state-by-state basis—by which the BOCs could earn regulatory approval to enter the interLATA market within the regions in which they provide local exchange service. By 2004, the BOCs had received section 271 authorizations to provide in-region interLATA service in forty-eight states (long-distance customers in Alaska and Hawaii are not yet served by BOCs) and the District of Columbia.[79] For the FCC, BOC entry into the in-region interLATA market has been "an incentive or reward for opening the local exchange market."[80] That view implicitly subordinates the possible harm to consumers (in the form of delayed price reductions) from the restrictions on the BOCs while they seek that carrot.[81]

In an article with Gregory Leonard published in the *Antitrust Law Journal*, we found that the average US consumer received a savings of 8 to 11 percent on the monthly interLATA bill in the states where BOC entry occurred as compared with "control" states where BOC entry had not occurred. We also found that CLECs gained a substantial increase in cumulative share of the local exchange market in states where BOC entry occurred as compared

76. See Triennial Review, p. 31 ¶ 37.
77. BOC UNE Fact Report 2002, pp. III-8 to III-14.
78. 47 U.S.C. § 271.
79. See FCC, *RBOC Applications to Provide In-region, InterLATA Services Under § 271*, available at http://www.fcc.gov/Bureaus/Common_Carrier/in-region_applications/.
80. 1997 Michigan Section 271 Order, 12 F.C.C. Rcd. Pp. 20,746 ¶ 388.
81. Hausman, Leonard, and Sidak (2002).

with control states without BOC entry. Finally, we found that that there was no significant change in the local bill of the average consumer in states where BOC entry into interLATA service occurred as compared with those bills in the control states. Thus, the failure of the FCC and the DOJ to consider the trade-off between consumer harm from entry restriction of the BOCs into long distance and the marginal gains from further delaying BOC entry by requiring greater regulatory adherence led to significant consumer harm in the billions of dollars per year. We return to the question of how consumer interests should enter regulatory deliberation when we examine the regulatory experience in New Zealand.

6.5.2 United Kingdom

Mandatory unbundling in the United Kingdom was first considered by the former telecommunications regulator, the Office of Telecommunications (Oftel), in 1996. Oftel stated that three facilities-based service providers would be *sufficient* to provide effective competition in the telecommunications market of the United Kingdom.[82] Oftel acknowledged that at least three facilities-based service providers (including British Telecom [BT], a cable operator, and a radio access operator) already competed in many UK geographic markets. Because of the strong level of existing and expected future facilities-based competition in the United Kingdom in July 1996, Oftel decided that:

> Any move to allow operators to take over BT exchange lines would undermine past investments and jeopardize future plans. Our conclusion, therefore, is that direct connection to the BT Access Network would adversely affect the development of competition and would not be in the interests of the UK consumer.[83]

In short, Oftel recognized that mandatory unbundling would undermine the goals of dynamic efficiency.

From 1994 through 1997, regulation shifted in favor of infrastructure competition over service competition.[84] In 1996, Oftel became convinced that "the key to achieving a vibrant market for services provided over telecommunication networks is the promotion of fair, efficient and sustainable network competition."[85] This emphasis of infrastructure competition

---

82. Oftel, Oftel's Policy on Indirect Access, Equal Access and Direct Connection to the Access Network, ¶ 46, July 1996, available at http://www.ofcom.org.uk/static/archive/oftel/publications/1995_98/competition/ access96.htm.
83. Ibid., ¶¶ 46–47. Facilities-based investment by BT's competitors existed even in the early 1990s. In particular, ILECs in the United States and Canada invested in UK cable companies. Those cable companies then began to offer telephone services to their customers. Consequently, by January 2004, over 400,000 homes in the United Kingdom were offered telephone service by a cable operator.
84. See, for example, Geradin and Kerf (2003, 163).
85. Oftel (1996).

affected Oftel's treatment of issues such as number portability and equal access. The regulatory emphasis shifted back to service competition in 1998 with the issuance of several EU directives, which encouraged national regulators not to discriminate between firms that were building networks and those that were not.

In December 1998, Oftel released a consultation document that called for mandatory unbundling as a *necessary* condition for bringing higher bandwidth services to consumers.[86] Oftel cited four reasons why mandatory unbundling was needed in the United Kingdom. First, BT, which supplied service to 85 percent of UK consumers, was not equipped in 1998 to provide DSL service. Second, the forthcoming 1999 European Union review on telecommunications markets was anticipated to place local loop unbundling high on its agenda. Third, the UK government had stressed the importance of the deployment of new technologies to all consumers. Fourth, other countries, such as the United States, had already implemented mandatory unbundling. Although UK consumers already benefited from platform competition, Oftel felt that mandatory unbundling was important for the United Kingdom to maintain its "competitive advantage" vis-à-vis the rest of the world.

In November 1999, Oftel announced that unbundled loops and collocation would become available to competitive providers.[87] BT was required by July 2001 to allow unbundling and collocation within its network.[88] In its *Access to Bandwidth Report*, Oftel provided the following rationale for pursuing mandatory unbundling:

> The best way to achieve the variety of services that consumers want at reasonable prices is to promote effective competition in the provision of access to and delivery of these services. In examining the case for action, Oftel has considered the level of demand in various segments of the market, the supply of products available and whether there are barriers to the competitive delivery of higher bandwidth access and services. The conclusion is that regulatory action is needed to introduce competition into the upgrade of the local loop.[89]

---

86. Oftel, Access to Bandwidth: Bringing Higher Bandwidth Services to the Consumer, December 1998 (available at http://www.ofcom.org.uk/static/archive/oftel/publications/1995_98/competition/llu1298.htm) [*Oftel Access to Bandwidth December 1998*].

87. Oftel, Access to Bandwidth: Delivering Competition for the Information Age, November 1999 (available at http://www.ofcom.org.uk/static/archive/oftel/publications/1999/consumer/a2b1199.htm) [*Oftel Access to Bandwidth 1999*].

88. For a thorough discussion of the regulatory requirements under mandatory unbundling in the United Kingdom, see Geradin and Kerf (2003, 172–74). Along with the requirement of mandatory unbundling, the Director General of Telecommunications (DGT) permitted that rates for mandatory unbundling should (1) permit the recovery of an appropriate share of common cost, (2) permit the recovery of reasonably incurred long-run incremental cost, (3) may differ across BT's service area according to varying economic circumstances, and (4) should include a reasonable return on capital employed (Geradin and Kerf 2003, 173).

89. See Oftel (1999,¶ 2.4).

Oftel intended that mandatory unbundling would lead to enhanced competition in broadband services. Thus, the primary intent of mandatory local loop unbundling in the United Kingdom was to expedite the delivery of advanced services to consumers, even though regulators conceded that natural market forces might provide competitive offerings within a reasonable period of time.

Retail Competition

Pricing.   One rationale for mandatory unbundling is increased competition in retail services, which is characterized by lower retail prices.[90] Pricing data from Oftel indicate that mandatory unbundling, which was implemented in the United Kingdom in the middle of 2001, has not measurably decreased prices of telecommunications service. According to Oftel, from 1996 through the middle of 2001, the time at which BT was required to begin unbundling, prices for residential service decreased by approximately 20 percent.[91] In contrast, prices for residential service slightly increased after BT was required to unbundle.[92] Similarly, the price of telecommunications service for businesses decreased by 40 percent between 1996 and mid-2001, but it has not declined measurably since mandatory unbundling was implemented. Only a few carriers have actually provided or were attempting to provide local telephone service via unbundled access.

Although UNE-based competition for residential voice customers has not flourished in the United Kingdom, CLECs have provided broadband Internet service extensively through unbundled access. As of July 2003, entrants providing broadband service through unbundled access increased their DSL lines to over 536,000, which nearly equaled the total DSL customers of BT.[93] Almost all of these new entrants provided high-speed Internet service, as only 3,500 of the new entrants' 536,000 unbundled lines were used to provide *both* voice and data service.

Retail competition in broadband services is intense and prices have been decreasing. Mandatory unbundling may not be the cause of the price decline. Facilities-based cable operator NTL launched the first UK broadband offering in April 1999, followed by Telewest in March 2000. Although BT did not launch its first DSL offering until mid-2000, owing to technical prob-

90. Oftel has stated that "competitive markets are most likely to promote innovation and increased productivity with resulting benefits in terms of lower prices and better quality and choice for consumers." See Oftel (1998, ¶ 4.2). Oftel has also maintained that regulatory intervention "should be limited to situations where competition is either not possible or is not working effectively or where costs and benefits accruing to third parties are not taken into account by market participants." By pursuing a policy of mandatory unbundling, Oftel believed that it could correct a market failure which, once eliminated or reduced, would result in lower retail prices.

91. Oftel (2003, 7).

92. Residential access lines in the United Kingdom were not subsidized to the extent found in the United States. Thus, this change in prices is not due to rebalancing.

93. Commission of the European Communities (2003, 59).

lems, lines were not widely available until May 2001. The launch of retail DSL products by BT and various third parties (via BT's wholesale offer) began a period of intense price competition among broadband providers. By the middle of 2003, price reductions had transformed the UK broadband market from one of the most expensive in the OECD (Organisation for Economic Co-operation and Development) to the cheapest, as observed in Oftel's survey of the broadband market.[94] Hence, price decreases in the UK market can be directly linked to competition between DSL and cable providers.[95] In the months after the launch of BT's DSL service, NTL and Telewest responded with significant price reductions such that by mid-2001, prices were around 50 percent of their launch levels. BT responded in March 2003 with a 25 percent price reduction, which provided the trigger for a series of price cuts by other ISPs using BT's resale service.

Investment.   Another rationale for mandatory unbundling is the expectation that it will increase the ILEC's incentive to upgrade its network. Table 6.1 lists BT's investment in fixed capital assets for its fiscal years ending in March between 1996 and 2003.

The data in table 6.1 indicate that in its fiscal year 1999, BT spent £1.8 billion on fixed-capital investment. During 2000, BT spent £5.8 billon on fixed capital investment,[96] and in 2001 BT spent £5.2 billion on fixed capital investment. In fiscal year 2002, BT reduced its investment to £1.2 billion, and in fiscal year 2003, BT spent only £555 million on fixed capital investment. Hence, BT's investment in fixed capital assets reached its apex at the end of fiscal year 2001, which ended in March 2001, before mandatory unbundling was introduced in the United Kingdom. Of course, the end of BT's fiscal year 2001 coincided almost perfectly with the bursting of the telecommunications bubble, which likely contributed, at least in part, to the decrease in BT's investment.

BT's pattern of investment corresponds closely with the pattern of investment by the entire UK telecommunications industry. From 1994 through 2000, telecommunications investment in the United Kingdom increased substantially. Approximately £4 billion was invested by the telecommunications industry in 1994, accounting for 4 percent of total investment in the United Kingdom that year.[97] By 2000, nearly £12 billion was invested by the telecommunications industry. Between 2000 and 2001, telecommunications investment in the United Kingdom fell by approximately £4 billion.

94. Oftel's Internet and Broadband Brief, 12 October 2003, available at http://www.ofcom .org.uk/legacy_regulators/oftel/oftel_internet_broadband_brief/?a=87101#10.

95. *OECD 2001 Broadband Study*, p. 42.

96. BT, Annual Report & Form 20-F 2003, p. 27, available at http://www.btplc.com/report /report03/index.htm.

97. OFCOM, Strategic Review of Telecommunications: Phase I Annex F-J 35 (Spring 2004), available at http://www.ofcom.org.uk/codes_guidelines/telecoms/strategic_ review_telecoms /?a=87101#remit.

Table 6.1   **BT investment in fixed capital assets: Fiscal years 1996–2003**

Fiscal year	Fixed capital investment (£ billion)
1993	0.74
1994	1.31
1995	1.08
1996	1.06
1997	1.27
1998	1.71
1999	1.83
2000	5.88
2001	5.20
2002	1.22
2003	0.56

Sources: BT, Annual Report and Form 20-F 2003, p. 27 (released 2003), available at http://www.btplc.com/report/report03/index.htm; BT, Annual Report and Form 20-F 2000, p. 26 (released March 2000), available at http://www.btplc.com/Sharesandperformance/Howwe havedone/Financialreports/Annualreports/Annualreportsarchive.htm.

Entry Barriers

Mandatory unbundling is considered necessary whenever market forces cannot be relied upon to produce facilities-based competition. An analysis of platform competition for broadband services in the United Kingdom, however, reveals that entry unrelated to unbundling currently exists. As of July 2003, BT operated over 563,000 DSL lines in the United Kingdom,[98] while cable operators served nearly 1.1 million customers. Given the nearly two-to-one advantage of cable modem service to BT's DSL service in the United Kingdom, it is not reasonable to presume that BT has market power in the broadband Internet services market, especially in those geographic markets passed by cable networks.

Cable operators NTL and Telewest also compete vigorously with BT for residential and business voice customers.[99] UK cable companies have offered residential telephone service for nearly a decade. When the cable companies first deployed coaxial cable for television services, they simultaneously laid regular copper phone lines in the same trenches.

Cable telephony's share of fixed voice connections has steadily increased over time. In March 1998, cable operators NTL and Telewest provided telephone service to 9.1 percent of residential customers.[100] By December

98. See Commission of the European Communities (2003).

99. NTL and Telewest had geographically separate networks that have now merged into a single company, Virgin Media. Also, in the United Kingdom, cable companies compete again with an extremely competitive satellite provider (BSkyB), which controls football (soccer) telecasts in the United Kingdom, which provides a significant competitive advantage.

100. Oftel, The UK Telecommunications Industry Market Information: 2001/02, March 2003, p. 27 (tbl. 8a) (available at http://www.ofcom.org.uk/static/archive/oftel/publications/market _info/2003/ami0303.pdf) [*2003 UK Telecommunications Information Report*].

2003, their combined share of the residential voice market had increased to 16.6 percent.[101] Hence, in households passed by cable networks, cable operators have roughly 33 percent of fixed-line voice connections.[102] The increase in the cable companies' share of residential voice services in the United Kingdom came largely at the expense of BT, whose share fell from 86.2 percent to 82.7 percent between March 1998 and December 2003.[103]

Cable companies' share of business voice service revenues in the United Kingdom has also increased. Between 1996 and 1997, NTL and Telewest controlled only 2.6 percent of business voice revenues, but by December 2003 those companies had acquired a 4.8 percent share.[104] Cable's share of business voice revenues is smaller than its share of residential voice revenues because cable operators must compete with several other facilities-based CLECs, including Colt Telecom Group (COLT), in the business sector.

COLT, which has operations in thirty-two cities in thirteen European countries, competes directly with BT and cable operators for business customers. COLT established its metropolitan area network in London in 1993.[105] It expanded its network to include Birmingham in December 2000 and Manchester in February 2002. The COLT network is largely deployed on COLT's fully owned fiber, which when supplemented with current hardware, can reach multigigabit speeds on a single circuit. COLT targets its services to business users (COLT interAccess) and resellers of Internet access (COLT InterTransit). COLT also offers its business customers a full range of voice services. Fidelity Investments owns 56 percent of COLT. COLT expected to spend between £150 million and £200 million in capital expenditure in 2004, depending on customer demand.[106] As of March 2004, COLT reported having over 17,000 business customers across Europe.[107]

BT's share of both residential and business voice revenues has decreased significantly since 1993. BT's share of residential voice revenues, which was nearly 100 percent in 1993, declined steadily to just below 70 percent in 2001.[108] Since 2001, when BT was required to unbundle the local loop, BT's share of residential revenues has remained constant at 70 percent. In 1993, BT controlled approximately 85 percent of the voice revenues in the busi-

101. Ofcom, Ofcom Fixed Telecoms Market Information Update, May 2004, at tbl. 7, available at http://www.ofcom.org.uk/research/industry_market_research/m_i_index/telecoms_providers/fix_t_mkt_info/.

102. Ibid.; Ofcom, ITC Multichannel Quarterly, July 2003, available at http://www.ofcom.org.uk/research/industry_market_research/m_i_index/tv_radio_region/itc_market_info/cable_sat_stats/multichannel_q2_2003.doc. Cable companies pass approximately 50 percent of UK residences.

103. Ibid., 2003 UK Telecommunications Information Report, p. 27 (tbl. 8a).

104. See 2003 UK Telecommunications Information Report, p. 32 (tbl. 13); Ofcom FTMI Update, tbl. 11.

105. COLT, About Us (available at www.colt.net).

106. Nic Fildes, Dow Jones Newswire, 22 April 2004,*1

107. COLT Telecom expands metro optical services offering, M2 Presswire, 9 March 2004, *1.

108. OFCOM, Strategic Review of Telecommunications: Phase I Annex F-J 35 (Spring 2004), available at http://www.ofcom.org.uk/codes_guidelines/telecoms/strategic_review_telecoms/.

ness sector. That share, however, had steadily declined to below 60 percent by 2001. By 2003, BT's share of business voice revenues had decreased to approximately 52 percent.

Stepping-Stone Hypothesis

As of 2005, it was not apparent that new entrants in the United Kingdom had used unbundled loops to evolve into facilities-based competitors. A lack of conversion from unbundled access to facilities-based service is likely due to the high level of facilities-based investment that already occurred *before* unbundling was mandated. In particular, entrants controlled 24.0 percent of the revenues for residential voice services by March 2001, and 39.5 percent of the business revenues from voice services by March 2001.[109] The high level of facilities-based competition that predated the decision-making process for local loop unbundling raises serious issues as to whether mandatory unbundling was even needed for voice or broadband services in the United Kingdom by the time that Oftel mandated it in November 1999.

Wholesale Competition

A final rationale for mandatory unbundling is increased competition in the wholesale market, which is typically characterized by supply of alternative networks by CLECs for new entrants. The size of the wholesale market in the United Kingdom has grown considerably since the mid-1990s. Between 1996 and 2002, the wholesale market for voice services in the United Kingdom increased from £1.9 billion to £4.5 billion—a 130 percent increase. By March 2002, the largest share of the wholesale voice market, approximately 49.1 percent, was controlled by BT. Cable operators NTL, Telewest, and Cable & Wireless controlled approximately 19.9 percent of the wholesale voice revenues in the United Kingdom. The remaining 31 percent of the market was controlled by other operators. Business districts in most major cities and towns in the United Kingdom are served by facilities-based CLECs. These CLECs typically offer service to both business customers and CLECs for resale.

Other Observations about the Process

The industry structure facing UK regulators was unique in the sense that competition from cable telephony emerged *before* mandatory local loop unbundling was ordered, let alone implemented. Cable operators have opposed mandatory unbundling on the grounds that it would not encourage facilities-based competitors to expand into rural areas. For example, Telewest stated in February 2000:

> [W]e do not believe that local loop unbundling will deliver the necessary universal broadband upgrades that Government policies require. It may

109. *2003 UK Telecommunications Information Report.*

purely delay the dominant player from full broadband upgrade of its local infrastructure (assuming that ADSL over twisted copper pair is only an interim solution) and deter alternative local loop investors from further substantial build, particularly to the lower density areas.[110]

Telewest argued, correctly, that CLECs that rely on unbundled access were likely to focus their activities in densely populated markets.

Although the cable companies in the United Kingdom have begun to offer broadband Internet and voice service to their existing base of customers, only 50 percent of the homes in the United Kingdom were passed by the cable network as of July 2003.[111] This lack of coverage explains in part why cable television accounted for only 26.4 percent of the multichannel television market in the United Kingdom as of 2003. Satellite television is much stronger in the United Kingdom than in the United States, as British Sky Broadcasting (BSkyB) controls much of the sports content that cable operators cannot provide. It might be tempting for regulators to consider the cable industry's investment in broadband and telephony *in cables' existing footprint* as a sunk investment that cannot be reversed through mandatory unbundling of BT's local loops. But mandatory unbundling of BT's network in rural areas might indirectly decrease the incentive of the cable operators to expand into rural areas, as UNE-based CLECs could enter those rural areas through unbundling *at a lower cost*. Cable operator Telewest succinctly explained the fallacy of the regulator's decision making when it declared: "[I]f demand [for unbundled access] really exists, the market will deliver access products for new broadband services without regulatory intervention."[112] Figure 6.5 shows the percent of homes passed by a cable operator in the United Kingdom between 1990 and 2003.

The deployment of any new technology typically follows an S-curve. Initially, technology penetration increases at an increasing rate. After some critical point, the technology is deployed at a diminishing rate until the entire market is saturated. Until 1999, cable penetration in the United Kingdom followed a deployment schedule similar to that suggested by the S-curve. In particular, cable penetration rapidly increased from only 6.2 percent in 1990 to 50 percent by 1999. Since 1999, however, cable penetration has increased by only 1.8 percent. The slow deployment of cable services to new markets in the United Kingdom could be explained, in part, by the introduction of mandatory unbundling of BT's network. If this effect is present, consumers have been injured by the decrease in competition to BSkyB. Hence, Ofcom's

110. Response of Telewest Communications, Toward a New Framework for Electronic Communications Infrastructure and Associated Services—The 1999 Communications Review, February 2000, §E ¶ 2.3, available at http://europa.eu.int/ISPO/infosoc/telecompolicy/review99/comments/telewest28b.htm.

111. See ITC Multichannel Quarterly.

112. See Response of Telewest Communications, § E ¶ 2.5.

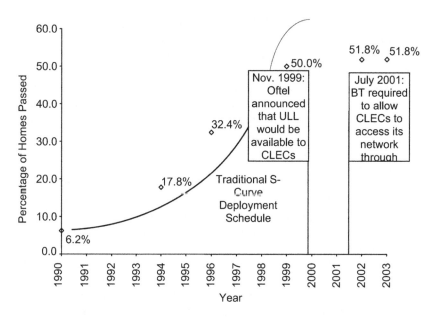

Fig. 6.5   Percent of UK homes passed by cable, 1990–2003

Sources: Peter Humphreys, Radio and Television Systems in Great Britain, Spring 1999 (available at http://www.obs.coe.int/oea_publ/hbi/HBI2K_GB.html); Teldok, Teldok Yearbook 1997, July 24, 1997, p. 245; Martyn Williams, TS News-UK Market Roundup, December 4, 1996; OFCOM, ITC Multi-Channel Quarterly-Q3 2002, December 17, 2002, p. 7; OFCOM, ITC Multi-Channel Quarterly-Q2 2003, June 2003, p. 7.

policy has led to greater market power for a company that Ofcom recognizes is exercising market power.[113] Again, the regulator in the United Kingdom, as in the United States, did not do an analysis of the effect of its regulatory policy on consumer welfare.

As late as mid-2005, Ofcom believed that it was necessary to resort to greater levels of regulatory intervention to make unbundling work. In June 2005, Ofcom stated that "years of intrusive regulation have not created the conditions for the sustainable competition necessary for long-term consumer benefit and which, in other countries, has spurred investment in next generation core and access networks."[114] Ofcom's fundamental concern was that some assets were supposedly economically impossible to replicate, which created an "enduring bottleneck," especially in the access part of

113. See, for example, OFCOM, The Regulation of Electronic Programme Guides, March 2003, ¶ 16, available at http://www.ofcom.org.uk/consultations/past/epg/stat_provisions/?a =87101; Oftel, Beyond the Telephone, the Television and the PC, August 1995, ¶ 4.4.12, available at http://www.ofcom.org.uk/ static/archive/oftel/publications/1995_98/info_super/multi.htm.

114. OFCOM Telecommunications Statement, June 23, 2005, p. 1, available at http://www .ofcom.org.uk/consult/condocs/telecoms_p2/statement/main.pdf.

the network. Ofcom rejected the option of recommending a Competition Commission investigation, which could have led to the breakup of BT, and it instead opened a public consultation on the proposal to accept a series of solutions offered by BT.[115]

In November 2004, Ofcom opened the Phase 2 consultation of its Strategic Review of Telecommunications.[116] The review noted that the fixed line market in the United Kingdom has remained fragmented and that BT was larger than most of its competitors combined, in terms of revenues, market capitalization, and investment. The review argued that the economies of scale and sunk costs for fixed networks are especially difficult for entrants to overcome, which made them reliant on BT to provide wholesale access to the network. Ofcom stated that the result of this reliance on BT was slow product development, inferior wholesale products, poor transactional processes, and a general lack of transparency, which combined to create an unattractive market for competition.

Ofcom offered three potential courses of action in its November 2004 review. The first option involved across-the-board deregulation and complete reliance on competition law to constrain BT's purported market power. The second option was to make a reference to the Competition Commission under the Enterprise Act of 2002, which would actively consider the structural separation of BT. The third option was to seek from BT "real equality of access," which consisted of two parts.[117] The first part would require "BT's own downstream operations use the same products, processes, and prices as those used by their retail rivals." The second part would require "operational separation within BT that would ensure that those responsible for overseeing BT's bottleneck assets had real incentives to wish to serve other operators in practice and on the ground with the same zeal, efficiency and enthusiasm as they served the remainder of BT's downstream activities." BT chose Ofcom's third option.

BT responded to Ofcom's November 2004 review in February 2005 by announcing a "comprehensive set of proposals to stimulate the UK telecoms industry."[118] The proposals announced in February 2005 formed the basis for the proposed regulatory settlement with Ofcom, which was formally pro-

115. Notice under Section 155(1) of the Enterprise Act 2002: Consultation on undertakings offered by British Telecommunications plc in lieu of a reference under Part 4 of the Enterprise Act, OFCOM, June 30, 2005, ¶ 1.1, available at http://www.ofcom.org.uk/consult/condocs/sec155/sec155.pdf.

116. Strategic Review of Telecommunications: Phase 2 consultation document, OFCOM, November 18, 2004, available at http://www.ofcom.org.uk/consult/condocs/telecoms_p2/tsrphase2/maincondoc.pdf.

117. OFCOM Telecommunications Statement, p. 2.

118. *BT Unveils Proposals to Stimulate the UK Telecoms Industry*, BT Press Release DC05-057, February 3, 2005, available at http://www.btplc.com/News/Articles/Showarticle.cfm?ArticleID=a13fbce7-157c-4220-bc38-c4c482026d50.

posed by BT in June 2005.[119] In response to BT's proposal, Ofcom opened a public consultation to elicit comments on BT's solutions.[120]

The most significant of BT's proposed undertakings was the creation of a new business unit within BT, provisionally named the Access Services Division (ASD), which would provide equal access to its nationwide network. The ASD would provide, on behalf of BT, wholesale line rental, local loop unbundling, wholesale extension service, partial private circuits, backhaul extension service, and various other products. The ASD would not provide any service to BT unless it also offered that product to BT's competitors on an "equivalence of input" basis, which would include the same time frames, terms, conditions, and prices. The ASD would have its own staff of approximately 30,000 employees, and it would have a distinct brand name.[121]

A significant part of the agreement between BT and Ofcom was the creation of an internal, five-member Equality of Access Board, supported by an Equality of Access Office, to monitor the company's compliance with its "Undertakings" agreement and to recommend remedial action to BT's management. Three members of the board would be independent, meaning that BT would select them with Ofcom's advice and consent. Ofcom would receive minutes of the proceedings of the Equality of Access Board, as well as regular reports. The Equality of Access Board "may suggest to BT remedial action to ensure compliance with these Undertakings," and "BT shall take due account of any suggestions or comments the [Equality of Access Board] may have." The Equality of Access Board "shall inform Ofcom, within ten working days, when it comes to its attention that there has been a non-trivial breach of these Undertakings." BT is required to fund and staff this internal oversight activity satisfactorily: "BT shall ensure that the [Equality of Access Office] is resourced commensurate with the demands placed upon it and is able to operate with the level of independence required." The Equality of Access Board would have access to information held anywhere in or by BT that the board deemed that "it needs to fulfil its role," and, in a curiously worded provision, the board "shall determine how best to engage with representatives of industry in order to understand their issues and concerns."[122]

This arrangement underscores that decisions concerning network access implicate both ownership and control of the incumbent firm. One way to view BT's undertaking with Ofcom is that the regulator's indirect majority participation in the governance of the ASD eliminates detailed ex ante regu-

---

119. *BT Commits to Support New Era of Regulation*, BT Press Release DC05-405, June 23, 2005, available at http://www.btplc.com/News/Articles/Showarticle.cfm?ArticleID=e89ed523 -12a0-45a1-bc2b-321f127e83be.

120. OFCOM Consultation, p. 4.

121. BT Press Release DC05-405.

122. Annex E: The Undertakings offered by BT, § 10.

lation of wholesale services. Nonetheless, the risks of ownership (including the financial risk inherent in making sunk investments in network infrastructure) would remain with BT's shareholders. Perhaps this hybrid renationalization of BT's access network will purchase regulatory relief for its retail business. But there is reason for skepticism, given the familiar tendency of regulators to perpetuate (and even initiate) intervention in markets that have become demonstrably competitive. Further, the UK government's previous record with a somewhat similar plan for the railroads ended in financial disaster in 2001 because the regulator would not permit the network provider to set rates high enough for continued investment and modernization of the rail network.[123]

As of 2006 it appears that the United Kindgom's insistence on "equality of access" may lead BT to invest neither in a "fiber to the home network," as Verizon is currently doing in the United States, nor in a "fiber to the node" network, as AT&T (SBC) is currently doing. Given the current technology both of these forms of fiber networks do not permit "equality of access" to competitors. While the US ILEC investments are risky and may not succeed economically, the UK regulatory policy may well lead to a significant distortion in technology choice and future competition among pay-TV providers compared with likely outcomes in the United States, Australia, Canada, and a number of other advanced economies.

6.5.3   New Zealand

Deregulation of the telecommunications industry in New Zealand began in April 1989 with the separation of Telecom Corporation (Telecom) from New Zealand Post Office.[124] Telecom became fully privatized in 1990. In accordance with New Zealand's Commerce Act of 1986 and the Fair Trading Act of 1986, Telecom was declared dominant in the telecommunications market. As a result, the regulator placed certain constraints on Telecom, but "reaffirmed its reliance on general competition law to achieve its objective in telecommunications."

Unlike many other countries, New Zealand did not adopt any sector-specific regulation.[125] Section 64 of the Telecommunications Act of 2001 required the Commerce Commission (CC) to determine the necessity of regulating access to the unbundled elements of Telecom's local loop network and fixed public data network.[126] The CC initially set resale discounts as specified in the Telecom Act of 2001. In December 2003, the CC recom-

123. Hausman and Myers (2002) discuss the railroad network financial disaster in the United Kingdom.
124. New Zealand Telecommunications 1987–2001, Publication No. 8, ¶¶ 8–9 (August 2001).
125. See, for example, Geradin and Kerf (2003, 119), explaining how New Zealand adopted the opposite approach of the United States, where sector-specific regulation was pervasive.
126. Telecommunications Act 2001, Section 64 Review and Schedule 3 Investigation into Unbundling the Local Loop Network and the Fixed Public Data Network, Final Report, 9 December 2003, p. i.

mended in its *Final Report* against unbundling local loops, line sharing, and unbundling "elements of Telecom's fixed Public Data Network beyond those supporting the Asymmetric Digital Subscriber Line (ADSL) bitstream services."

To measure the efficacy of full local loop unbundling, the CC used a cost-benefit analysis that measured the changes in total surplus (consumer and producer surplus) relative to the status quo of no regulation. The New Zealand CC uses the Long-Term Benefits to End-Users (LTBE) criteria in determining its regulatory policies. This determination usually involves an explicit cost-benefit analysis.[127] To the extent that mandatory unbundling reduces prices in the short term, consumer welfare increases. The increase in consumer welfare due to an expansion in output is referred to as an "allocative efficiency" gain. The CC also considered the "wealth transfer" from producers to consumers when prices decline, which occurs independent of output expansion. Although the CC found short-run gains in welfare, the calculations were subject to considerable uncertainty and criticism, and did not take account of effects on investment by the incumbent. Although it recognized the potential importance of dynamic efficiency, the CC believed that there was no robust method of quantifying dynamic efficiency gains that were applicable to its decision.

The CC ultimately elected not to adopt local loop unbundling and listed several reasons in support of its decision. First, the CC noted that platform competition, especially in the form of fixed wireless networks, was likely to "evolve and reduce the extent of [Telecom's] bottleneck over time." Second, the CC explained that the potential for dynamic efficiency gains from local loop unbundling was tempered by international experience, noting that "in a significant number of countries, the gains from local loop unbundling have been disappointing." Third, the CC revealed that responses to its draft report indicated "fairly limited demand for local loops" as the preferred means of competitive entry. Fourth, the CC explained that mandatory unbundling was "a resource intensive activity," which generated "a significant level of controversy in determining terms of access to unbundled loops in overseas jurisdictions." Most importantly, the CC determined the economic incentives for the incumbent to invest in new services would be significantly decreased and that these new services could lead to very large welfare gains to consumers.

Instead of mandatory unbundling, the CC recommended access to Telecom's ADSL service for residential and small and medium size enterprises (SMEs), along with the associated backhaul transmission services and operational support systems (OSSs). With the exception of updating the

127. Australia uses a similar approach. The ACCC calls its test the "Long-Term Interest of End-Users" (LTIE) approach. Australia and New Zealand are the two regulatory bodies that use an explicit economic approach to determination of regulation.

Kiwi Share, which imposes universal service obligations on Telecom and establishes a price ceiling for its residential calls,[128] the result of the CC's recommendations was a largely unregulated telecommunications market relative to most European countries and the United States.

Retail Competition

In this section, we examine the recent trends in investment and pricing in New Zealand. The New Zealand survey provides a potential counterfactual to the unbundling experience in other countries.

Pricing. Despite the fact that the CC has abstained from mandatory unbundling, prices for telecommunications services in New Zealand have not increased substantially. Figure 6.6 shows the prices for telephone rental and connection and telephone call charges in New Zealand since June 1999. However, to a large extent this outcome is influenced by the Kiwi Share Obligation, which permits New Zealand Telecom only to increase residential monthly access charges at the rate of inflation, although no regulatory restriction is placed on business access charges.

As figure 6.6 shows, telephone rental and connection charges offered by all carriers in New Zealand consistently decreased from June 1999 to December 2001. From March 2003 through March 2004, telephone rental and connection charges have increased by a modest 2.5 percent. Similarly, the price for telephone call charges has remained flat over the past few years. According to Statistics New Zealand, prices for residential telephone service decreased by an average of 3.5 percent per year between 1991 and 2001.[129] One possible explanation for the decline in prices in the absence of mandatory unbundling is that TelstraClear and other facilities-based rivals compete with Telecom in urban areas.[130]

Investment. As of June 2003, Telecom had decreased its capital expenditure by over 60 percent since 2001.[131] The decline in Telecom's investment may be attributable to the rapid decline in telecommunications prices and the general decline of the global telecommunications market. The decline

128. Government Announces Updated Kiwi Share Obligation, available at http://www.med .govt.nz/pbt/telecom/minister20011218b.html; Determination for TSO Instrument for Local Residential Service for Period between 20 December 2001 and 30 June 2002, p. 11, available at http://www.comcom.govt.nz/telecommunications/obligations/FinalDetermination17Dec2002. PDF. Among other requirements, Telecom is required to provide (1) a monthly line rental no higher than the CPI-adjusted price of the residential line rental charged on 1 November 1989, and (2) free local calling.

129. See New Zealand Pub. No. 8, pp. 22–23.

130. TelstraClear's network was established before TelstraSaturn bought Clear Communications in 2001. TelstraSaturn and Clear separately invested in fiber optic networks in New Zealand.

131. Telecom New Zealand Annual Report for the Year Ended 30 June 2003, p. 4, available at http://www.telecom.co.nz/binarys/annual_report_2003.pdf.

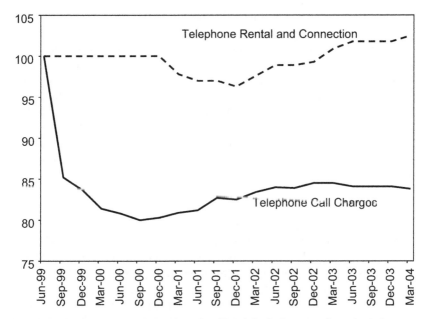

Fig. 6.6   Statistics New Zealand's real residential telephone service price index: Percent change from June 1999 index

Source: Statistics New Zealand (available by request at http://www.stats.govt.nz/).

in Telecom's *rate* of investment is potentially misleading, however, because Telecom increased its investment in the late 1990s. In particular, Telecom introduced high-speed Internet access in 1999 with the rollout of Jetstream, which is based on ADSL technology.[132] In 2000, following the development of Jetstream, Telecom connected New Zealand's North and South Islands using a submarine cable, with an estimated investment of NZ$38 million. The submarine cable allows 98 percent of New Zealand's population to access Telecom's wireless network. Telecom also introduced VoIP in 2000.[133] Telecom offers VoIP to business customers, which is a fully managed service that includes extensive IP services and is the base for their next generation network (NGN), which is currently being developed and will gradually be rolled out over the next ten years.[134] Telecom's NGN is composed of "a single network that delivers multiple applications (voice, data, video) to multiple

132. TelstraClear Company Information, available at http://www.telecom.co.nz/content /0,3900,200633-1548,00.html.

133. NetIQ Case Study, *Telecom New Zealand Prepares for IP Telephony with NetIQ's Vivinet Manager*, 2003, available at http://www.netiq.com/products/vm/whitepapers.asp.

134. See Telecom New Zealand's website, http://www.telecom.co.nz/content /0,3900,202900-201383,00.html; TelstraClear, *Telecom NZ Next Generation Network Regulatory Issues Raised by NGN Deployment*, Conference on Commerce Commission Draft Report, 10–14 November 2003, p. 5, available at http://www.comcom.govt.nz/telecommunications/llu /Conf/tclngn.PDF.

devices, whether fixed or mobile."[135] In addition to the development of the NGN, Telecom has begun to roll out its 3G wireless services.

Perhaps more importantly, Telecom is rolling out video services over ADSL, which will lead to large benefits to New Zealand consumers.[136] Fearing Telecom would slow its investment in video capabilities, the CC gave TelstraClear low grade (128K) bitstream in lieu of full loop unbundling. The main competition for Telecom's video service is satellite television, as cable television penetration in New Zealand is lacking (except in Wellington). Soon, Telecom will have the "triple play" of voice, broadband, and television over a single network. It is noteworthy that New Zealand is in the forefront of video over the fixed-access network.

Entry Barriers

As of early 2004, facilities-based competition was well underway in New Zealand. TelstraClear represents the most significant facilities-based competitor to Telecom. TelstraClear invested over $1 billion in New Zealand through 2002, with an additional investment of approximately $200 million in 2003.[137] By June 2002, TelstraClear had acquired a 7 percent share of all fixed-access voice connections.[138] TelstraClear, which owns Clear Net and Paradise.net, and other entrants had acquired 28 percent of the residential broadband market by June 2003.

Before the purchase of Clear Communications by TelstraSaturn and Austar in December 2001 (which formed TelstraClear), both Clear and TelstraSaturn independently invested millions of dollars to establish their own fiber-optic networks.[139] Since the acquisition, TelstraClear has been developing a nationwide network in New Zealand to provide telephone, data, Internet, mobile, and cable television services.[140] TelstraClear plans to spend NZ$14 million to roll out its network in nine cities.[141] In January 2002, TelstraClear proposed the construction of an overhead network with underground connections in Auckland, which will provide direct competition to Telecom's network.[142] During the Section 64 Review proceeding in 2003, TelstraClear claimed that it had determined not to continue rolling out its network because it was too expensive.[143] Such claims seem implausible in

135. Milner and Pizzica (2003).
136. See Hausman (2003a, 5).
137. New Zealand Commerce Commission, *4th Annual New Zealand Telecommunications & ICT Summit*, 25 June 2003, pp. 2–3.
138. See New Zealand Profile, p. 27.
139. See 4th Summit, p. 14.
140. See TelstraClear Information.
141. See New Zealand Profile, p. 19.
142. *TelstraClear Application: Area 3 Rollout Assessment of Environmental Effects*, January 2002, p. 3, available at http://www.telstraclear.co.nz/network_proposal.pdf.
143. See New Zealand Profile, p. 14: "Over a year ago [TelstraClear] basically abandoned the roll out of any new fixed infrastructure themselves and their future now depends on utilising TNZ's national network wherever it can."

light of the fact that Telstra is the largest Australian company and paid its shareholders an interim dividend of A\$1.6 billion in April 2004.[144] Thus, our hypothesis that mandatory unbundling undermines the incentive of CLECs to invest in their own facilities seems to hold. While the CC did not mandate unbundling it did mandate bitstream sharing for DSL and TelstraClear has not increased its network coverage (except marginally) in the last three years. Another significant facilities-based rival in New Zealand is Countries Power, which rolled out a fiber optic and radio network on May 8, 2003.[145] The project, called Wired Country, provides high-speed Internet and telephone services to business and residential customers in the Franklin and Papakura regions of New Zealand.[146]

Fixed wireless access (FWA) providers represent yet another source of facilities-based competition. In its decision not to require unbundling, the CC noted the potential for fixed wireless to constrain Telecom's local telephone prices:

> The Commission notes the potential for Fixed Wireless Access (FWA) to evolve and reduce the extent of this bottleneck over time, although the Commission has reservations over the technical capacity of FWA to be a substitute for services that can run over the local loop network. FWA is likely to evolve over time in terms of its capacity and its ability to substitute for services that run over the local loop network, although the timing and nature of this evolution is uncertain.[147]

The CC's inclusion of fixed wireless in the relevant product market is notably at odds with the position of the US FCC, which has argued that FWA is not a suitable substitute for the fixed copper network.[148]

Beginning in 1999, Woosh Wireless (formerly Walker Wireless) began rolling out a national FWA network to compete with Telecom's fixed-access network.[149] Woosh competes with Telecom in voice and data services by targeting residential and business customers. As of May 2004, deployment of Woosh's network was underway in Auckland and Southland, and was expected to continue in Wairarapa, Northland, Canterbury, and other major markets in late 2004.[150] In addition to Woosh, other FWA providers, such as Broadcast Communications Limited (BCL), are investing in FWA tech-

144. Telstra Press Release, *Telstra Pays Shareholders Interim Dividend of \$1.6 Billion*, 29 April 2004, available at http://www.telstra.com.au/communications/shareholder/docs /tls225_interimdividend.pdf. Telstra has announced a total expected payout of over A\$4 billion over the next few years.

145. See 4th Summit, pp. 2–3.

146. *Counties Power Gets Totally Wired*, Axon, October 2003, available at http://www.axon .co.nz/info/Counties%20Power%20gets%20totally%20wired.htm.

147. See CC Final Report, p. 196 ¶ 788.

148. See Triennial Review, p. 141 ¶ 231.

149. See CC Final Report, p. 91 ¶¶ 368–370.

150. Whoosh Wireless, About Us, available at http://www.woosh.com/UserInterface/Woosh / Static/WhoisWoosh/WhoisWoosh.aspx.

nology intended to compete with Telecom. For example, BCL is rolling out an FWA network that covers rural and provincial areas in New Zealand.[151]

Telecom regards Woosh and other FWA providers as competitors in the local telephone services market. According to a Telecom study, if Woosh were able to capture 10 percent of the local market covered by its rollout, then Woosh would be able to undercut Telecom's prices by 22 percent.[152] As Woosh and other CLECs increase their geographic scope, they will be able to exert further pricing pressure on Telecom.[153]

Facilities-based entrants argue that mandatory unbundling would hinder the introduction and development of new technologies that compete with Telecom's local loops. In particular, those CLECs explain that mandatory unbundling will make raising investment capital increasingly difficult. They also point out that mandatory unbundling would reduce the price at which competitive fixed-line services could be offered, thereby undermining the return on their investment.

Stepping-Stone Hypothesis

The stepping-stone hypothesis implies that after initial entry into the market through the use of a competitor's lines, CLECs will eventually invest in construction of their own network. The New Zealand government accepted the CC's recommendation on mandatory unbundling.[154] Hence, the stepping-stone hypothesis was never put to the test in New Zealand.

Wholesale Competition

We are not aware of any evidence that facilities-based entrants are providing wholesale access to new entrants in New Zealand. As of December 2003, the CC characterized the wholesale markets for local loops, bitstream access, fixed public data network (PDN) services, and backhaul services as "limited," with the exception of wholesale competition in certain central business districts. Given the nature of the supply of and demand for switching, transport, and high-capacity loops serving business customers, however, we expect that the development of a wholesale market in New Zealand should be no different from the US experience.

Other Observations about the Process

New Zealand is unique among the countries we discuss in that the CC used the appropriate *social welfare* framework—namely, the sum of consumer

---

151. See CC Final Report, p. 95, ¶ 392.
152. Telecom's Response to the Commission's Draft Report, 29 October 2003, p. 55.
153. See CC Final Report, p. 96, ¶ 399.
154. Honorable Paul Swain, Decision on Telecom Network Recommendations, 19 May 2004, available at http://www.beehive.govt.nz/ViewDocument.cfm?DocumentID=19750. He explains that his "decision that has the potential to quickly promote more competition in the long term interests of consumers."

and producer surplus—to assess various regulatory policies. Most regulators, including the US FCC, have embraced a *competitor welfare* framework when formulating telecommunications policy. Perhaps more remarkable, the CC considered dynamic efficiency in addition to static efficiency when evaluating alternatives, and defined the former as "how well the competitive process works: how well the market ultimately responds to the demands of end users over time, by changes to what is produced and how it is produced." The CC concluded that (negative) dynamic efficiency effects of unbundling could potentially exceed (positive) static effects:

> The general point, though, is that regulation imposes risks on investors and can potentially hamper investment and, as a consequence, innovation. Regulation may mean that firms with access to Telecom's local loop network or fixed PDN may have access to the benefits of an upgraded network without taking associated risks, which are borne by the owner of the network. Regulated firms may be reluctant to invest when competing firms have access to some of the rents provided by their assets. A risk for the regulated firm is that entrants may "cherry pick" markets, without committing to the market in the same way as the incumbent has. The importance of these possibilities would depend on the extent of unbundling and the behaviour of access-seekers.

As other countries are considering whether to mandate unbundling, the CC's framework for analysis provides a different point of view in that it was more explicitly economic in focus.

However, in 2006 the majority party in New Zealand decided to overrule the CC and require mandatory local loop unbundling of Telecom's copper network using TSLRIC pricing principles in New Zealand.[155] While the final outcome of the process is not definite, it currently appears that the government will not require telecom to be structurally separated into wholesale and retail segments. However, it does appear likely that the regulatory basis for the wholesale price of bitstream access will change from retail minus to a cost-based approach, as with mandatory unbundling.[156]

155. Since New Zealand has a parliamentary form of government, this new policy direction will be adopted. The major reason for the change in policy is the relatively low level of broadband penetration in New Zealand compared to other countries with comparable income levels. However, New Zealand is the only country outside of North America and Hong Kong with free residential calling, which makes narrowband Internet access "free" on a per call basis and that makes broadband Internet access relatively more expensive than in other countries that have telephone charge on either a per call (e.g., Australia) or per minute (e.g., most EU countries) basis. Thus, the effect on broadband access of this relative price difference would need to be analyzed to determine what amount of the New Zealand broadband "shortfall" arises from this feature of telecom regulation that requires free residential calls in New Zealand.

156. The relevant government websites as of November 2006 are: http://www.med.govt.nz/templates/ContentTopicSummary____20266.aspx and http://www.parliament.nz/en-NZ/PB/Legislation/Bills/7/2/1/72144abd2b5c4524b0792c1f7295640c.htm.

6.6   The End of Regulation?

The public pronouncements of most regulators suggest that the end point of the current regulatory process should be facilities-based competition. As we discussed in the beginning of this chapter, regulation sets prices based only on costs, which cannot be the correct approach when competition exists together with technologies that exhibit important fixed costs (economies of scale) and economies of scope, and that require large sunk cost investments. Further, we believe that the former "natural monopoly" justification for a single network has been demonstrated to no longer hold given the success of cable networks in providing both broadband Internet and residential voice service in both the United States and the United Kingdom. Also, the increasing use of cellular telephony and other wireless technology such as fixed wireless, WiFi, and in the future WiMax, provides additional competition to the landline network.[157] While regulators such as the FCC have been very slow to take account of competition, scrutiny by the US Court of Appeals for the DC Circuit has forced the FCC to moderate its approach. Indeed, in August 2005 the FCC voted to deregulate ILEC provision of broadband Internet service, DSL, so that it need no longer be unbundled after a one-year transition period. Thus, the FCC has retreated from its mandatory sharing approach and recognized the competitive reality that cable networks have approximately a 60 percent share of broadband Internet demand.

We first consider the question: Will landline service in the United States continue to be regulated, or will we see "the End of Regulation"? Telecommunications regulators, along with many antitrust authorities, are sometimes fixated by market share calculations. Given past experience, we might expect them to require the incumbent landline providers' share to fall below a particular threshold (say, 50 percent) before substantial deregulation would occur.[158] However, this approach would be incorrect because in a high fixed cost business such as telecommunications, only a small loss in market share is sufficient to constrain a large firm from increasing price above competitive levels.

Suppose prices under regulation are set at approximately "competitive levels." Consider the decision of an incumbent to increase prices 5 percent above the competitive level in a given market.[159] Because competition takes place at the margin, only a small proportion of the ILEC's customers need to defect to defeat its attempted price increase. In a simple example, it is possible

---

157. For a discussion of wireless technology as a competitive factor for landline networks, see Hausman (2002b).

158. This approach was used by the FCC in its decision to deregulate prices for AT&T in the long-distance markets in the 1990s.

159. A 5 percent price increase above the competitive level is often used in antitrust analysis. Regulation sometimes leads to prices below the competitive level, so this analysis would need to be modified in those situations.

to calculate that necessary proportion. Suppose that an ILEC attempted to increase prices on end-user access by 5 percent. How much traffic would that ILEC need to lose before the increase would be unprofitable? The formula to calculate that "critical share" is:

$$(3) \qquad \left(1-\frac{MC}{P}\right)Q_1 < \left(1.05-\frac{MC}{P}\right)Q_2.$$

An important empirical fact for network elements is that fixed costs are a very large component of the overall cost, so marginal cost is a relatively small component. Assume, for example, that the ratio of marginal cost to price, MC/P, is 0.2. Then Q_2 would be $0.94Q_1$, so that the critical share is 6 percent. Thus, if the ILEC were to attempt to raise its price by 5 percent, and if, as a result, it were to lose more than 6 percent of its traffic, the attempted price increase would be unprofitable and thus unilaterally rescinded.[160] This calculation demonstrates that only quite small competitors' shares are needed to defeat supracompetitive pricing by an incumbent.[161] This calculation would imply a minimum (in magnitude) own price elasticity of -1.2, which seems quite likely to exist where ILEC voice telephony competes with cable-based telephony. Econometric investigation of this elasticity will require a few years of data since the competition is quite recent in most geographic areas.

Two further considerations operate in opposite directions. First, we have assumed no price discrimination. If price discrimination occurs, the calculation of equation (3) operates in only narrower markets. However, although historically price discrimination was often required by regulators for monopoly providers, with competition it is more difficult to undertake price discrimination profitably, especially in a business with large fixed costs and low marginal costs.[162] Further, in the United States section 202 of the Communications Act of 1934 forbids price discrimination.[163] So long as price discrimination does not occur, our calculation of a share below 10 percent continues to hold.

This relatively low share will decrease when we further consider the fact that many customers buy bundles of services. If they stop their landline subscription, they are very likely to stop subscription for voice mail, broadband Internet, call forwarding, and other services provided as bundles. In this situation the required percentage loss to constrain prices can be signifi-

160. For a more extensive discussion of critical share, see Hausman, Leonard, and Vellturo (1996).
161. We do not consider coordinated interaction among the incumbent and its competitors. Given the technologies involved and services offered, such coordination would be extremely unlikely to occur or be successful.
162. See Hausman, Leonard, and Vellturo (1996). The calculations in the paper demonstrate that the firm would have to be able to successfully target customers in approximately 95 percent of the cases to be profitable. Firms are unlikely to have the requisite information to be correct 95 percent of the time.
163. 47 U.S.C. § 202.

cantly below 5 percent.[164] Thus, we conclude in the quite near future, or even at present, where the incumbents have lost greater than 5 percent of their landline subscription to cable and wireless competition, regulators could safely decree the end of regulation. Incumbents could then provide new services and compete better against the cable networks, which currently exercise market power, without the possibility that they will be required to share their successful new services with competitors at regulatory decreed prices.

Indeed, in August 2006 (eleven months after the conference at which this chapter was presented), the California Public Utility Commission (CPUC) decided to deregulate fixed-line telecommunications services in California.[165] The CPUC found significant competition from cable telephone providers and from VoIP offered over broadband, which is available in 100 percent of the zip codes within California. The CPUC noted that Cox Communications had a 40 percent penetration of cable telephony in Orange County, a very populous county in between Los Angeles and San Diego. The CPUC determined: "VoIP provided by cable telephone companies is a direct substitute for circuit-switched wireline service." They also recognized the competition that mobile (cellular) networks provide to fixed-line networks: "Verizon's survey data regarding customers who have 'cut the cord' indicate that many customers consider mobile telephones and landline telephones to be close substitutes. . . . Verizon demonstrated that wireless substitution accounts for approximately half of ILEC primary residential wireline losses." Lastly, the CPUC found, "[w]ireless service is a substitute for wireline service." In terms of competition, the CPUC recognized that competition occurs at the margin (as in our previous calculation) and that market shares could not be used to infer market power: "The calculation of HHI [Herfindahl-Hirschman Index] values provides no information relevant to our assessment of ILEC market power, because rapidly changing technological and market conditions undercut our ability to use HHI as a measure of market power." California has thus decided the correct policy is the "End of Regulation" for fixed line telecommunications. A number of other large states are currently holding regulatory proceedings to determine whether they should also end regulation of fixed-lined telephone service. Both Illinois and New York state have also decided to deregulate fixed-line telephone services. The Canadian government also voted recently to deregulate fixed-line telephone services in geographic areas where cable TV competition and cellular competition exist.[166]

A potentially important economic question is whether two competing platforms, operated by the ILECs and the cable TV companies, are sufficient

164. See Weisman (2006).

165. Public Utilities Commission of the State of California, "Order Instituting Rulemaking on the Commission's Own Motion to Assess and Revise the Regulation of Telecommunications Utilities," Proposed Decision, August 25, 2006.

166. Canada adopted deregulation in April 2007.

to insure a competitive outcome.[167] Alternatively, would the two platform operators coordinate their actions to maintain high prices? Our view is that coordination is very unlikely. The two sets of firms begin at opposite ends of the "Hotelling product space" since cable beings with a near zero amount of telephone customers and the ILECs begin with a near zero amount of pay-TV customers. Further, given the high fixed costs and relatively low marginal costs of new customers (especially for telephone service) the economic incentives to coordinate pricing is low and the economic incentives to cheat are high. More importantly, evidence to date demonstrates that the cable companies and ILECs have been highly competitive with each other. Cable companies are now establishing cellular service to expand from a "triple play" to the "quadruple play" to allow them to compete better with Verizon and AT&T, both of whom are adding pay-TV and will have a "quadruple play" since they both own cellular companies. Thus, we conclude that deregulation and competition will likely work well with facilities-based competition, but other economists might not agree with this conclusion. In addition, the growing importance of cellular networks almost makes coordination between telephone platform operators and cable platform operators even less likely to occur.

The alternative to wireline facilities-based competition and deregulation is "regulation forever." Our reading of the regulatory experience in the United Kingdom and New Zealand is that the onset of regulation coincided with the end of competitor-based expansion of wireline networks. As we discussed, the cable television networks stopped their expansion in the United Kingdom and Telstra-Clear stopped its network expansion in New Zealand. Similar experiences occurred in other countries such as Australia. Although we can advance other reasons for this observed end to geographic expansion, a leading cause would seem to be that competitors need not make significant sunk investments in regulatory access to incumbents' networks. Instead, they acquire access at below competitive prices without the risk of sunk network investments. We find it interesting that the United States and Canada will now have deregulation while the United Kingdom, Australia, and New Zealand are heading toward "regulation forever."[168]

Without facilities-based competition, the regulator will be in charge of the future direction of telecommunications in these countries. Indeed, this future role for regulators seems to have been made explicit in the proposed restructuring of BT, since Ofcom would assume corporate governance of BT's access network, even though ownership (and, hence, financial risk) would remain with private shareholders. Similarly, in Australia where the government sold off its controlling (51 percent) interest in the incumbent

167. To the extent that other technologies such as cellular and WiMax increase in competitive importance, this potential concern would not be important.
168. We apologize for our English language bias in country selection. However, the EU is also headed toward "regulation forever."

ILEC Telstra in November 2006, it could have divested the fiber optic cable network that Telstra operates in the large cities in Australia. Facilities-based competition might then have replaced the mandatory local unbundling regulatory framework used by the ACCC (Australian Competition and Consumer Commission), which has been the topic of intense controversy between Telstra and the ACCC. However, Telstra was divested with its control of both the copper loop network and the largest fiber-based cable network intact so that the prospect for facilities-based competition in Australia has decreased.[169]

Experience has demonstrated that markets do considerably better than regulators in creating consumers' welfare gains. Although international benchmark comparisons will provide some useful information, the natural regulatory tendency is toward a competitor welfare standard rather than a consumer welfare standard. Thus, our two closing comments are that regulation might be improved if regulators adopt an explicit consumer welfare goal, as in New Zealand and Australia, and that a viable regulatory plan is adopted where the endpoint is facilities-based competition and deregulation. The technology and economics exist for such an endpoint, as recent action in the United States has demonstrated. The regulatory framework in a given country will determine the speed at which this endpoint of the "End of Regulation" is approached.

References

Beesley, M., and S. Littlechild. 1989. "The Regulation of Privatized Monopolies in the United Kingdom." *Rand Journal of Economics* 20 (3): 454–72.

Bliss, C. 1975. *Capital Theory and the Distribution of Income.* Amsterdam: North Holland.

Brown, S., and D. Sibley. 1986. *The Theory of Public Utility Pricing.* Cambridge: Cambridge University Press.

Carlton, D. W. 2001. "A General Analysis of Exclusionary Conduct and Refusal to Deal: Why Aspen and Kodak Are Misguided." *Antitrust Law Journal* 68:659–74.

Cave, M., S. K. Majumdar, and I. Vogelsang, eds. 2002. *Handbook of Telecommunications Economics.* Amsterdam: North Holland.

Commission of the European Communities. 2003. *Ninth Report from the Commission on the Implementation of the Telecommunications Regulatory Package: European Telecoms Regulation and Markets 2003.* Annex 1, November 11. Brussels: European Commission.

Crandall, R. W. 2004. *Competition and Chaos: The US Telecommunications Sector Since 1996.* Washington, DC: Brookings Press.

169. A group of CLECs in Australia has proposed to build its own fiber-based network, which could lead to facilities-based competition. However, the economic feasibility of such a network investment has not yet been demonstrated and no current plans exist to begin construction of the network.

Crandall, R. W., A. T. Ingraham, and H. J. Singer. 2004. "Do Unbundling Policies Discourage CLEC Facilities-Based Investment?" *B. E. Journals in Economic Analysis and Policy* 4:1–25.

Dixit, A., and R. Pindyck. 1994. *Investment under Uncertainty.* Princeton, NJ: Princeton University Press.

Geradin, D., and M. Kerf. 2003. *Controlling Market Power in Telecommunications: Antitrust vs. Sector Specific Regulation.* New York: Oxford University Press.

Hausman, J., 1997. "Valuation and the Effect of Regulation on New Services in Telecommunications." *Brookings Papers on Economic Activity: Microeconomics* 28:1–54.

———. 1998. "Taxation by Telecommunications Regulation." In *Tax Policy and the Economy*, vol. 12, edited by James M. Poterba, 29–48. Cambridge, MA: MIT Press.

Hausman, J. 1998b. "Telecommunications: Building the Infrastructure for Value Creation." In *Sense and Respond*, edited by S. Bradley and R. Nolan. Boston: Harvard Business School Press.

———. 2002a. "Competition and Regulation for Internet-Related Services: Results of Asymmetric Regulation." In *Broadband*, edited by R. Crandall and J. Alleman, 129–56.

———. 2002b. "From 2G to 3G: Wireless Competition for Internet-Related Services." In *Broadband*, edited by R. Crandall and J. Alleman.

———. 2003a. "Analysis of OXERA Cost Benefit Analysis." Paper presented at the Local Loop Unbundling conference. November 11, Wellington.

———. 2003b. "Regulated Costs and Prices in Telecommunications." In *International Handbook of Telecommunications*, edited by G. Madden, 199–233. Northampton, MA: Edward Elgar.

Hausman, J., and W. E. Kohlberg. 1989. "The Evolution of the Central Office Switch Industry." In *Future Competition in Telecommunications*, edited by S. Bradley and J. Hausman. Boston: Harvard Business School Press.

Hausman, J., G. Leonard, and J. G. Sidak. 2002. "Does Bell Company Entry into Long-Distance Telecommunications Benefit Consumers?" *Antitrust Law Journal* 70 (2): 463–84.

Hausman, J., G. K. Leonard, and C. A. Velluro. 1996. "Market Definition under Price Discrimination." *Antitrust Law Journal* 64 (2): 367–86.

Hausman, J., and S. Myers. 2002. "Regulating the United States Railroads: The Effects of Sunk Costs and Asymmetric Risk." *Journal of Regulatory Economics* 22 (3): 287–310.

Hausman, J., and H. Shelanski. 1999. "Economic Welfare and Telecommunications Welfare: The E-Rate Policy for Universal Service Subsidies." *Yale Journal on Regulation* 16 (1): 19–51.

Hausman, J., and J. G. Sidak. 1999. "A Consumer-Welfare Approach to the Mandatory Unbundling of Telecommunications Networks." *Yale Law Journal* 109 (3): 417–505.

Hausman, J., and W. Taylor. 2013. "Telecommunications in the US: From Regulation to Competition (Almost)." *Review of Industrial Organization* 42 (2): 203–30.

Hyde, Justin. 2004. *Reuters News*, May 19.

Kahn, A. 1970. *The Economics of Regulation*, vol. 1. New York: J. Wiley.

———. 1988. *The Economics of Regulation.* Cambridge, MA: MIT Press.

Laffont, J. J., and J. Tirole. 2000. *Competition in Telecommunications.* Cambridge, MA: MIT Press.

Madden, G., ed. 2003. *World Telecommunications Markets* (International Handbook of Telecommunications, vol. III). Cheltenham: Edward Elgar Publishing Limited.

Milner, Murray, and Vince Pizzica. 2003. "Telecom New Zealand: Pragmatic Evolution to Next Generation Networks." Alcatel, April 22.

Mirrlees, J. 1969. "The Dynamic Nonsubstitution Theorem." *Review of Economic Studies* 36:67–76.

Oftel. 1996. "Promoting Competition in Services over Telecommunication Networks." London: Oftel, June.

Pindyck, R. S. 2004. "Mandatory Unbundling and Irreversible Investment in Telecom Networks." NBER Working Paper no. 10287, Cambridge, MA.

Riordan, M., and S. Salop. 1995. "Evaluating Vertical Mergers: A Post-Chicago Approach." *Antitrust Law Journal* 63:513–68.

Schmalensee, R. 1989. "An Expository Note on Depreciation and Profitability under Rate-of-Return Regulation." *Journal of Regulatory Economics* 1:293–98.

Sidak, J. G., and R. W. Crandall. 2002. "Is Structural Separation of Incumbent Local Exchange Carriers Necessary for Competition?" *Yale Journal on Regulation* 19:335–411.

Weisman, D. 2006. "When Can Regulation Defer to Competition for Constraining Market Power? Complements and Critical Elasticities." *Journal of Competition Law and Economics* 2:101–12.

Willig, R. D., W. H. Lehr, J. P. Bigelow, and S. B. Levinson. 2002. "Stimulating Investment and the Telecommunications Act of 1996." Paper filed by AT&T in FCC Docket 01-338, October 11.

Regulation of the Pharmaceutical-Biotechnology Industry

Patricia M. Danzon and Eric L. Keuffel

7.1 Introduction

Pharmaceuticals and human biologic products are regulated in virtually all aspects of the product life cycle: safety, efficacy, and manufacturing quality as a condition for market access; promotion; and pricing. Since the regulatory structure developed for pharmaceuticals has largely been extended to human biologic medicines, we hereafter use "pharmaceuticals" to include biologics, and we note explicitly where biologics are treated differently. The rationale for heavy regulation of pharmaceuticals is not intrinsic natural monopoly, since any market power enjoyed by individual products derives ultimately from government-granted patents (see Paul Joskow's chapter in this volume for more on natural monopoly). Rather, regulation of market access, manufacturing, and promotion arise because product efficacy and safety can be critical to patient health but are not immediately observable. Evaluating safety and efficacy as a condition of market access and monitoring manufacturing quality and promotion accuracy over the product life cycle are public goods that can in theory be efficiently provided by an expert agency such as the Food and Drug Administration (FDA). By contrast, price regulation is best understood as a response by public insurers to the fact that insurance makes consumers price insensitive. When consumers are heavily insured, producers of patented products face highly inelastic demand and hence can charge higher prices than they would in the absence of insur-

Patricia M. Danzon is the Celia Moh Professor of Health Care Management at the Wharton School, University of Pennsylvania, and a research associate of the National Bureau of Economic Research. Eric L. Keuffel is assistant professor in the Risk, Insurance, and Healthcare Management Department at the Fox School of Business, Temple University.

For acknowledgments, sources of research support, and disclosure of the authors' material financial relationships, if any, please see http://www.nber.org/chapters/c12572.ack.

ance. Price regulation and other reimbursement controls are a response of government payers to this interaction of insurance and patents.

Although these considerations suggest that regulation of the pharmaceutical industry is potentially welfare enhancing, designing the optimal structure of such regulation is not simple. Market access regulation entails both resource costs and foregone patient benefits in terms of fewer drugs and delay of those that do launch. Measuring these costs, designing the optimal regulatory structure, and finding the best balance between costs and benefits has been the subject of both academic research and policy debate and experimentation. Optimal regulation of promotion and the expansion of post-marketing regulatory control are relatively recent extensions of this debate. On the pricing side, regulation should ideally constrain pricing moral hazard while preserving insurance coverage for patients and sufficient patent power to assure incentives for appropriate research and development (R&D). Much has been learned from the experience with different price regulatory regimes, mostly in countries with national health insurance systems. But designing regulatory structures that are both theoretically sound and empirically practical remains an important theoretical and policy challenge.

In this chapter, section 7.2 describes the technological characteristics of the pharmaceutical sector and the primary objectives of regulation. Section 7.3 provides an overview of safety and efficacy regulation in the United States and abroad. Section 7.4 reviews the empirical evidence, lessons learned, and proposals for change in safety and efficacy regulation.

Section 7.5 discusses patents, focusing on those aspects of pharmaceutical patenting that interact with regulation, which include patent extension policy and regulatory exclusivities, regulation of generic entry, the extension of patents to developing countries, and affordability concerns. Section 7.6 describes regulation of pricing, reimbursement, and profit; the evidence on effects of this regulation; and evidence on industry structure and competition. Section 7.7 summarizes evidence on pharmaceutical promotion, focusing mainly on direct-to-consumer advertising (DTCA) in the United States, which has become far more important over the last fifteen years, following changes in regulatory oversight that remain contentious and unsettled. The final section concludes on lessons learned and areas for future research.

7.2   Technological Background and Objectives of Regulation

The pharmaceutical industry is characterized by unusually high costs of R&D. Historically, the research-based industry has invested between 15 to 20 percent of sales in R&D (CBO 2006; EFPIA 2011) and the R&D cost of bringing a new compound to market was estimated at $1.3 billion in 2005 (an update from the commonly cited $802 million estimated in 2001), an increase from $138 million in the 1970s and $318 million in the 1990s. (Adams and Brantner 2006; DiMasi and Grabowski 2007; DiMasi, Hansen, and Grabowski 2003; DiMasi et al. 1991; Hansen 1979). Variation in the expected cost exists across therapeutic categories and depends on a range of factors (DiMasi, Grabowski, and Vernon 2004). Generally, the high cost per new drug approved reflects high costs of preclinical testing and human clinical trials, high failure rates, and the opportunity cost of capital tied up during the eight to twelve years of development. To some extent, this high and rising cost of R&D reflects regulations that exist in all industrialized countries, requiring that new compounds meet standards of safety, efficacy, and manufacturing quality as a condition of market access. The main initial focus of regulation since the 1930s was safety, and this has reemerged recently as a critical issue. Since the 1960s most countries also require preapproval evidence of efficacy, monitor manufacturing quality throughout the product life, and regulate promotion and advertising to physicians and consumers.

The economic rationale for these requirements derives from the fact that the risks and benefits of pharmaceuticals are nonobvious, can differ across patients, and can only be known from controlled studies in large patient populations. Gathering and evaluating such information is a public good, and a regulatory agency that has both medical and statistical expertise can more accurately and efficiently monitor and evaluate the evidence from clinical trials than can individual physicians or patients. However, regulation that requires extensive prelaunch clinical trial data on safety and efficacy increases the R&D costs incurred by firms, increases delay in launch of new medicines, and may reduce the number of drugs developed and the extent of competition. The size and duration of clinical trials required to detect remote risks or cumulative risks from long-term therapies can be large. The rising costs of R&D, combined with new technologies for evaluating information, have prompted recent initiatives to accelerate approvals and optimally integrate evidence from preapproval clinical trials with postapproval observational experience. In the United States, the statutory regulation of pharmaceuticals through the FDA is in addition to—and uncoordinated with—the increasing level of indirect regulation through tort liability. Critical unresolved issues in market access regulation are: (1) how much information on risks and benefits should be required prior to launch; (2) what is the appropriate trade-off between benefits and risks, given that some risks are inevitable; and (3) what is the appropriate mix of pre- and postlaunch monitoring of risks, what methods should be used, and what is the appropriate mix of regulation by an expert agency (such as the FDA or an independent agency) and tort liability?

A second important characteristic of the pharmaceutical industry is the critical role of patents, which results from its research intensity. Given the cost structure with high, globally joint fixed costs of R&D and low marginal costs of production, patents are essential to enable innovator firms to recoup their R&D investments. However, patents work by enabling innovator firms to charge prices above marginal cost, which raises issues of appropriate levels of prices and profits and appropriate structure and duration of patents. Concern that prices may be excessive is one rationale for price regulation in many countries (although, as discussed following, insurance coverage is probably an equally important determinant of price levels). Defining regulatory criteria for admitting postpatent generic entrants remains a contentious issue, even for traditional chemical compounds. More complex and yet to be fully resolved by regulatory agencies are the conditions for approving biosimilars, that is, alternative versions of large molecule, biotechnology products such as proteins, monoclonal antibodies, and so forth. As the number and utilization of these expensive biologics expand, so does concern to establish a low-cost regulatory path for approval of generic biologics without full-scale clinical trials, in order to stimulate postpatent price competition.

The global nature of pharmaceutical products has also raised contentious questions over optimal patent regimes in developing countries and cross-nationally. The World Trade Organization's (WTO) Agreement on Trade-Related Aspects of Intellectual Property Rights (TRIPS) requires all member countries to recognize twenty-year product patents by 2015. However, in response to concern that patents would make drugs unaffordable in low-income countries, TRIPS permits member states to issue compulsory licenses under certain conditions, including a "national emergency." TRIPS also leaves decisions on allowing parallel imports to the discretion of individual member states. In most industrialized countries, including the United States, the traditional rule has been national exhaustion of patent rights, which means that patent holders can bar the unauthorized importation of the patented product (parallel trade) from other countries. Proposals in the United States to legalize parallel trade, including commercial drug importation by wholesalers, would undermine the traditional rule of national exhaustion of patent rights. If enacted, this would undermine manufacturers' ability to price discriminate between countries, which could have serious welfare consequences, as discussed below.

A third characteristic of the pharmaceutical industry is the dominant role of third-party payment through social and private health insurance. Like any insurance, third-party payment for drugs creates moral hazard, with incentives for consumers to overuse and/or use unnecessarily expensive drugs. In addition, by making demand less elastic, insurance creates incentives for firms to charge higher prices than they would in the absence of insurance. In response to these insurance-induced distortions, since the 1980s government-run health systems in most countries have adopted elaborate regulatory systems to control pharmaceutical expenditures through regulation of manufacturer prices and/or reimbursement and limits on total drug spending and on company revenues. Private insurers in the United States also use formularies of covered drugs, copayments, and negotiated prices;

however, because these private insurers must compete for market share, their controls lack the leverage of public payer controls. The controls adopted by both public and private insurers have significant effects on demand for pharmaceuticals, on the nature of competition (and hence on profitability), incentives for R&D, and the supply of new medicines.

Because pharmaceuticals are potentially global products and R&D incentives depend on expected global revenues, national regulators face free rider incentives. Each country faces a short-run incentive to adopt regulatory policies that drive its domestic prices to country-specific marginal cost, free riding on others to pay for the joint costs of R&D. But if all countries pay only their country-specific marginal cost, R&D cannot be sustained. The global nature of pharmaceuticals and the long R&D lead times—roughly twelve years from drug discovery to product approval, on average—make the incentives for short-run free riding by individual countries particularly acute. While there is widespread consensus in support of differential pricing between the richest and poorest nations, no consensus exists on appropriate price levels for these countries or between high- and middle-income countries. In practice, the ability of pharmaceutical firms to price discriminate is diminishing as more countries adopt national price regulatory policies that reference prices in other countries and/or legalize drug importation (also called parallel trade or international exhaustion of patent rights). These cross-national price spillovers in turn create incentives for firms to delay or not launch new drugs in low price markets, if these low prices would undermine potentially higher prices in other markets. Thus the design of each country's price regulatory system can affect not only their domestic availability of drugs but also availability in other countries through price spillovers in the short run, and through R&D incentives in the long run.

Unlike some other industries, regulation of the pharmaceutical industry has not diminished or undergone fundamental changes over recent decades, although focus of market access regulation has shifted between concerns for safety versus cost and delays, and the structure of price/reimbursement regulation has become more complex. The motivations for regulation of pharmaceuticals—imperfect and/or asymmetric information for market access regulation, patents, and insurance-related moral hazard for price/reimbursement regulation—remain and have, if anything, increased over time. These are summarized in table 7.1.

Regulatory trends over time within the United States and cross-national differences provide a wealth of useful experience from which some lessons can be learned. This review will focus primarily on US issues and evidence, reflecting the dominance of US-based literature. Moreover, US regulatory policy has a disproportionately large effect on the industry, because the US market accounts for almost 50 percent of global pharmaceutical revenues. However, we draw extensively on experience from other countries for

Table 7.1   Objectives and examples of regulation of the pharmaceutical industry

Rationale for regulation	Examples of regulation
Imperfect information about drug safety and efficacy	Market access requirements of safety, efficacy, and quality Regulation of promotion Tort liability
High fixed costs of R&D	Patents and regulation of generic entry Orphan Drug Act Accelerated approval measures
Insurance-induced moral hazard	Regulation of prices, reimbursement, profits, expenditure/revenues

evidence on price and reimbursement regulation, cross-national spillover effects, and access to pharmaceuticals in developing countries.

The appropriate economic model of the pharmaceutical industry is either monopolistic competition or oligopoly with product differentiation. However, both positive and normative analysis must also take into account the roles of physician prescribing and third-party payment as key determinants of demand elasticities and cross-price elasticities. Moreover, models of optimal pricing must recognize the importance of R&D and fixed costs. In this context, welfare conclusions about optimal levels of R&D, product variety, or drug use are problematic. Most analysis to date and most of our discussion are therefore positive rather than normative. Although the industry is characterized by high fixed costs, models in which firms endogenously choose sunk costs—in the form of either R&D or promotion to retain competitive advantage and deter competition/entry (Sutton 1991)—do not seem appropriate and appear to be clearly refuted by the evidence of entry over the last two decades by thousands of small firms. We return to this later.

7.3   Overview of Safety and Efficacy Regulation

7.3.1   The United States

The first comprehensive federal legislation regulating food and drugs in the United States was the Pure Food and Drug Act of 1906 (the Wiley Act), which required that product labels and packaging not contain false statements about curative effects, but stopped short of requiring manufacturers to provide evidence to prove safety or efficacy (Palumbo and Mullins 2002). The 1938 Food, Drug, and Cosmetics Act (FDCA), which replaced the Wiley Act, required any firm seeking to market a new chemical entity (NCE) to file a new drug application (NDA) to demonstrate that the drug was safe for use as suggested by the proposed labeling. The FDA had 180 days to reject the NDA. As new forms of print and radio advertising had emerged since the Wiley Act, the FDCA established jurisdiction over drug advertising, but policing was left to the Federal Trade Commission (FTC) rather than the FDA. This Act also established the requirement that patients obtain a prescription from a physician in order to obtain retail drugs.

The 1962 Kefauver-Harris Amendments to the 1938 FDCA were the outcome of hearings that were initiated due to concern over the proliferation, pricing, and advertising of drugs of dubious efficacy. The final legislation also reflected concern to strengthen safety requirements, following the thalidomide tragedy that caused hundreds of birth defects in Europe whereas the drug was still under review in the United States. The 1962 Amendments define the regulations that largely still operate today. They strengthened safety requirements; added the requirement that drugs show proof of efficacy, usually by double blind, randomized controlled trials of the drug relative to placebo; removed the time limit (previously 180 days) within which the FDA could reject an NDA; extended FDA regulation to cover clinical testing and manufacturing; and restricted manufacturers' promotion to approved indications. Basic requirements for promotional materials were defined, including that such materials cannot be false or misleading; they must provide a fair balance of risks and benefits; and they must provide a "brief summary" of contraindications, side effects, and effectiveness. Regulatory oversight of promotional material was ceded back to the FDA from the FTC.

The presumption underlying the requirement for proof of efficacy was that imperfect and possibly asymmetric information prevented physicians and consumers from making accurate evaluations, leading to wasted expenditures on ineffective drugs and other associated costs, and excessive product differentiation that undermined price competition. Although Phase III trials, involving double-blinded, randomized, placebo-controlled trials in large patient populations, were initially intended to establish efficacy, over time these trial requirements have been expanded to detect remote risks and/or cumulative treatment risks of chronic medications. The size and duration of clinical trials, together with increased regulatory review time, added to delay in the launch of new drugs, leading to foregone benefits for consumers, shorter effective patent life, and foregone revenue for firms, albeit with the intent of avoiding potentially larger costs for consumers.[1] Moreover, since

1. In theory, firms may submit for OTC (over-the-counter or nonprescription) status, but the new product would have to be proven safe and effective under self-medication, which could be a higher bar since some consumers may not use the product appropriately (Mahinka and Bierman 1995). In contrast to medicines, dietary supplements are regulated under the Dietary Supplement Health and Education Act of 1994. Manufacturers of dietary supplements are responsible for assuring that their products are safe but they are not required to get FDA approval before marketing. However, they cannot make explicit health claims unless these claims have been demonstrated by clinical trials. The ability to make health claims and, most important, to be eligible for health insurance coverage probably makes prescription status the most attractive status, for any drug that (a) can potentially meet FDA standards for safety and efficacy, and (b) is patentable and hence can expect to recoup the costs of clinical trials.

some regulatory costs are fixed, independent of potential market size, such regulation raises the expected revenue threshold required to break even on a new drug, leading to higher break-even prices, ceteris paribus, and fewer drugs, particularly drugs to treat rare diseases with small potential market size.

Subsequent legislation has addressed several of these cost-increasing effects of the 1962 Amendments. The Orphan Drug Act of 1983 (ODA) significantly increased incentives to invest in orphan diseases (defined as conditions that affect less than 200,000 individuals in the United States) by increasing revenues and decreasing costs. Specifically, drugs that receive orphan status are granted market exclusivity for seven years (i.e., similar compounds will not be approved to treat the same condition) and receive a 50 percent tax credit for expenses accrued through clinical testing. Orphan drugs may also benefit from research grants from the National Institute of Health (NIH) and accelerated or Fast Track FDA approval (see below). Following the ODA, the number of orphan drug approvals has increased significantly (see figure 7.1). Between 1979 and 1983, orphan drug approvals increased at approximately the same rate as other drugs. By 1998, there were more than five times as many orphan drugs as in 1979, but fewer than twice as many nonorphan drugs (Lichtenberg and Waldfogel 2003). However, these numbers may overstate the growth of true orphan compounds because some orphan drug filings represent small indications of drugs that have large overall markets and that would probably have been developed without

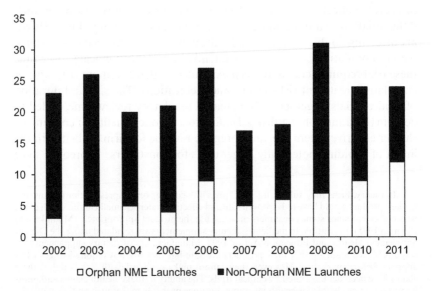

Fig. 7.1   Orphan drug launches in United States, 2002–2011
Source: IMS (2012).

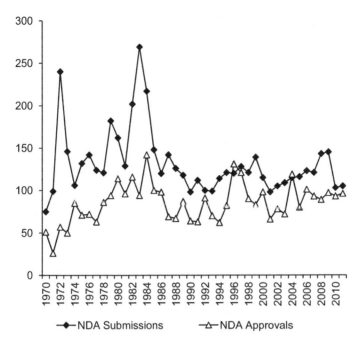

Fig. 7.2 New drug applications and approvals, 1970–2011
Source: FDA.

the ODA, including many specific cancer types for cancer drugs. Overall, the annual number of New Drug Applications (NDAs) and approvals has increased modestly since 1970 (figure 7.2) but the number of new molecular entities (NMEs) has remained fairly flat (figure 7.3), despite steadily increasingly R&D spending (figure 7.4).

An important initiative to reduce delay in the FDA review of regulatory filings was the Prescription Drug User Fee Act (PDUFA) of 1993.[2] Under PDUFA, pharmaceutical firms agree to pay substantial user fees to enable the FDA to hire more reviewers and hence expedite drug review.[3] In fiscal year 2010, the $573 million in fees accounted for 62 percent of total processing costs at the FDA (FDA 2011). In addition to user fees, the PDUFA created a system that classifies new drug applications that target unmet medical needs as "priority review," as opposed to "standard review," with target duration of ten months for standard review and six months for priority

2. This has subsequently been renewed twice as part of the Food and Drug Modernization Act (1997) and the Bioterrorism and Preparedness and Response Act (2002).

3. The fee for review of data related to product approval for fiscal year 2013 is $1,958,800 for applications with new clinical data, $979,400 for supplemental applications or those with no new clinical data. There is also a fee for each manufacturing facility ($526,500) and an annual fee for the right to market products ($98,500).

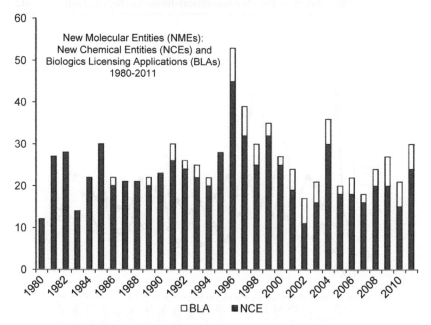

Fig. 7.3   New molecular entities, 1980–2011
Source: FDA, Dechert LLP (BioLawGics.com).

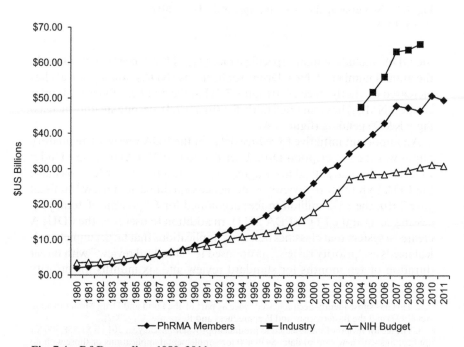

Fig. 7.4   R&D spending, 1980–2011
Sources: PhRMA Industry Profile (2012); NIH.

review drugs. Prior to 1992, the FDA classified drugs into either A, B, or C categories, and an AA category was developed to speed the review of AIDS products. PDUFA significantly increased the review staff of the FDA and reduced review times for drugs. On net, the implementation of PDUFA has increased social welfare with benefits accruing to both manufacturers (who effectively extend their patent window) and the public (who receive drugs faster). The main criticisms of the system are the potential for "regulatory capture" (although clearly the FDA continues to reject many applications) and concern that speedier approvals may impinge on safety—although welfare analyses that make conservative assumptions of the effects of PDUFA on drug withdrawal rates (and consumer harm associated with such withdrawals) suggest that the negative impact is relatively small in relation to the benefits of the legislation (Berndt et al. 2005; Philipson et al. 2008). The most recent iterations of PDUFA (PDUFA IV and V, 2007 and 2012) established and strengthened the FDA's ability to grant conditional approval, subject to Risk Evaluation and Mitigation Strategies (REMS), and strengthened the Sentinal Program, which enables the FDA to monitor postlaunch safety by querying large patient claims databases to detect rare adverse events. These programs enable the FDA to approve drugs for restricted usage and improve postlaunch detection of remote risks, which should increase the net welfare gains from market access regulation.

The 1997 FDA Modernization Act (FDAMA) renewed the priority review system and created Fast Track status to potentially expedite the entire clinical trial process for novel drugs (FDA, n.d.) by additional meetings, correspondence, and review programs with the FDA. Products may receive fast track designation if they are "intended for the treatment of a serious or life-threatening condition" and "demonstrate the potential to address unmet medical needs for the condition" (FDA 1997, n.d.). In addition, "Accelerated Approval" status refers to FDA acceptance of approval on the basis of a surrogate endpoint that "is reasonably likely to predict clinical benefit" rather than a clinical benefit. Accelerated approval is one of the potential review processes for which fast track drugs may qualify. Fast track has reduced overall development times by approximately 2.5 years (TCSDD 2003), but some have argued that fast track and priority review are associated with increased prevalence of postapproval adverse events (see below).

The increased time taken by clinical trials and regulatory review not only increases the out-of-pocket cost of R&D but also reduces effective patent life. To address this, the 1984 Patent Term Restoration and Competition Act (hereafter the Hatch-Waxman Act) granted innovator firms an extension of patent term for up to five years.[4] However, as a quid pro quo, the 1984 Act expedited postpatent entry by generic manufacturers. Specifically, generic

---

4. The patent term restoration is 0.5 years per year spent in clinical trials and one-for-one for years spent in regulatory review.

manufacturers are permitted to work on the active ingredient before the patent expiry (the Bolar exemption) and generics can be approved with an Accelerated New Drug Application (ANDA), which requires only that the generic prove bioequivalence and chemical equivalence to the originator product, without new safety and efficacy trials. Hatch-Waxman conferred a five-year maximum data exclusivity period after the innovator's NDA approval (three years for other data not submitted in support of an NCE approval), after which generic firms are free to use innovator clinical trial data to prepare their ANDA (the EU allows ten years of data exclusivity) (Kuhlik 2004). Moreover, Hatch-Waxman grants to the first generic firm to successfully challenge a patent (a paragraph IV filing) 180 days as the exclusive ANDA-approved generic in the market (Kuhlik 2004). In the 1990s, some originator firms were accused of "evergreening" their drugs by late filing of follow-on patents on minor aspects of the compound, excessively litigating challenges to patents, entering collusive agreements with generic manufacturers, and developing follow-on products that resemble the original product except for minor changes that nevertheless may suffice for a new patent (e.g., single isomer versions). The FTC has taken antitrust enforcement action against agreements between originator and generic firms to delay the launch of generics (FTC 2002). The 2003 Medicare Modernization Act includes changes to deter these practices, but this remains an unsettled area.

The Hatch-Waxman Act laid the necessary foundation for fast and cheap generic entry immediately after patent expiry in the United States. As of 2011, generics accounted for 80 percent of prescriptions filled in the United States, compared to 19 percent in 1984 when Hatch-Waxman was enacted; but generics accounted for only 27 percent of national drug expenditures, reflecting their low prices (IMS 2012). In addition to Hatch-Waxman provisions, the rapid and comprehensive generic erosion of originator sales post patent expiry also reflects state-level legislation authorizing pharmacists to substitute generics for originator drugs (unless the physician notes "brand required") and insurance reimbursement incentives to pharmacies and patients to accept generic substitution (see section 7.6). The speed of generic entry, generic market shares, and prices differ significantly across countries, reflecting regulatory differences in market access and in reimbursement incentives for pharmacists and patients (Danzon and Furukawa 2003). Empirical evidence related to Hatch-Waxman as well as cross-national differences are discussed later.

The FDAMA also initiated significant change in promotion regulation, by permitting companies to inform physicians of potential unapproved ("off-label") uses of drugs through the distribution of peer-reviewed journals, provided that the company commits to "file, within a specified time frame, a supplemental application based on appropriate research to establish the safety and efficacy of the proposed use." The law also permits companies to issue economic analyses based on dependable facts to payers and formulary committees, but "it does not permit dissemination of economic information that could affect prescribing choices to individual medical practitioners" (FDA 1997).

The regulations governing direct-to-consumer advertising (DTCA) were subject to revised interpretation in an FDA draft guidance issued in 1997. Previously, product claim advertisements that named both the drug and the condition it treated were required to disclose all the risks and contraindications within the content of the advertisement (Wilkes, Bell, and Kravitz 2000). The 1997 FDA guidance still required firms to present a "fair balance" between risks and benefits and not mislead with false advertising; however, broadcast ads could meet the requirement for disclosure by providing several other sources to obtain the full label, including a toll-free number, an Internet site, a print ad, or "see your physician" advice (GAO 2002b). The 1997 draft guidance (formalized in 1999) stimulated the growth of DTCA, especially broadcast ads. Total annual DTCA spending grew from $266 million in 1994 (prior to FDA relaxation in advertising policy) to $5.4 billion in 2006, but has subsequently moderated to $4.5 billion as of 2009 (Donohue, Cevasco, and Rosenthal 2007; Ventola 2011) Much of the growth is attributable to expansion of spending for television advertising.

7.3.2 Other Industrialized Countries

Each country has its own drug approval process, although in practice smaller countries frequently review and reference approvals granted by other major agencies such as the US FDA or the European Medicines Agency (EMA). Following the thalidomide tragedy and the strengthening of safety and efficacy requirements in the United States in 1962, the United Kingdom tightened safety regulations in 1964 and added efficacy requirements in 1971. Other industrialized countries adopted similar regulations, although some, such as France and Japan, have had less stringent efficacy requirements (Thomas 1996).

In 1995 the European Union established the European Medicines Agency (EMA) as a centralized approach to drug approval for EU member states. The EMA offers two tracks to drug approval. The centralized procedure involves review by the EMA and provides simultaneous approval of the drug in all countries of the EU. Alternatively, a firm can use the mutual recognition approach, seeking approval by one rapporteur country with reciprocity in other EU countries, subject to their review and objection. The EMA is the required approval route for biotech products and is optional for other new drugs. National systems remain for products that seek approval in only a few countries. The EMA also has made more progress than the FDA in establishing approval pathways for biosimilars—although both regulatory bodies likely will continue to modify these guidelines as experience with biosimilars accumulates.

Since the 1990s the regulatory authorities and the industry in the three major pharmaceutical markets—the United States, the EU, and Japan—have worked through the International Commission on Harmonization (ICH) to harmonize their evidence requirements for safety, efficacy, and manufacturing quality. As a result of the harmonization measures, companies can, to a significant degree, compile a single dossier for submission to the EMA, the US FDA, and Japan. However, some important differences in regulatory requirements remain and each agency still makes its own evaluation based on its own risk-benefit trade-off. For example, the EMA often requires trials of new drugs relative to current treatment whereas the FDA more often uses a placebo comparator, except where use of placebo would imply unethical treatment of patients. Japan requires some trials on Japanese nationals.

The EMA and the UK Medicines Agency have adopted user fee programs to expedite review, and the EMA has adopted an Orphan Drug Law. As a result of harmonization and other measures, differences in market approval requirements are no longer a major source of difference in timing of drug launch between the United States and "free pricing" countries in the EU, notably the United Kingdom and Germany (until 2004). Larger differences remain in the approval process for generics. Measures similar to the US Hatch-Waxman provisions have been proposed for the EU but so far have not been adopted by the EMA or by all EU countries' national regulatory agencies.

7.3.3   Developing Countries

More problematic is the appropriate regulatory agency and standards for drugs intended primarily for use in developing countries. Since disease incidence, competing risks, and costs and benefits of treatment may be vastly different in these countries, decisions based on FDA or EMA risk-benefit trade-offs may be inappropriate. For example, in 1999 Wyeth withdrew its rotavirus vaccine, Rotashield, from the US market due to concern that the risk of severe (but infrequent) intussuception would be unacceptable relative to the vaccine's benefit, given the relatively low risks from rotavirus in the United States. The vaccine became unavailable in developing countries, which expressed no interest in using it, although their benefit-risk ratio would have been very different, given their much higher incidence and higher death rates from rotavirus (Hausdorff 2002).

More generally, if willingness to pay high R&D and delay costs in order to reduce drug risks is income elastic, then requiring that drugs targeted at developing countries meet the standards of the FDA/EMA may impose inappropriately high regulatory costs in developing countries. On the other hand, anecdotal evidence indicates that the developing countries themselves are unwilling to accept drugs that are not approved for marketing in the

United States or the EU. There is some potential for reducing regulatory burden in order to accelerate approvals important for addressing health in developing countries. One example is the "Tentative Approval" designation introduced by the FDA specific to the PEPFAR (President's Emergency Plan for AIDS Relief) program, which has enabled generic and innovator firms to introduce new combinations and speed generic approvals for distribution of AIDS products primarily in sub-Saharan Africa. Through 2009, over 100 generic formulations had been approved under the program (PEPFAR 2012).

But for many drugs, especially those for diseases specific to developing countries, inappropriately high costs of regulatory compliance are probably less important than low potential revenues in discouraging R&D for drugs to treat diseases prevalent only or predominantly in less developed countries, such as malaria, TB, or leischmaniasis. Various "push" and "pull" subsidy mechanisms have been proposed and some have been implemented, to increase financial incentives for investment in these drugs for less-developed countries (LDC) (see, e.g., Kremer 2002; Mahmoud et al. 2006; Towse et al. 2012; Towse and Kettler 2005). In order to encourage greater R&D efforts on "developing country" diseases, the US Congress also approved a priority review legislation (2009) in which the FDA grants a transferable priority review voucher that allows for accelerated review by the FDA for any product in return for an approval of a product that treats a "neglected disease" (Grabowski, Ridley, and Moe 2009; Moe et al. 2009; Ridley, Grabowski, and Moe 2006). While this approach has proven more politically feasible than a subsidy financed by a broader tax, the efficiency and distributional consequences are uncertain. To date, one voucher has been granted for an approval of an antimalarial (Novartis-Coartem: voucher used for priority review for Ilaris sBLA, which was ultimately denied). Overall, recent evidence indicates an increase in R&D activity on "neglected diseases," although the absolute level of activity is still quite limited and it is not clear which push or pull incentives have been most influential in helping to accelerate development activity (Moran et al. 2009).

7.4   Effects of Safety and Efficacy Regulations: Evidence and Issues

7.4.1   Costs of Regulation

Much of the early economic analysis of pharmaceutical regulation focused on effects of the 1962 Kefauver-Harris Amendments on R&D costs, delays in launch of new drugs, decline in the number of new drug introductions, and changes in industry structure that occurred in the 1960s and 1970s, raising questions of causation (Baily 1972; Grabowski, Vernon, and Thomas 1978; Peltzman 1973; Wiggins 1981).

Number of New Drug Launches

Grabowski, Vernon, and Thomas (1978) report that the number of NCEs fell from 233 in the five-year period 1957–1961 to 93 in 1962–1966 and 76 in 1967–1971. Some decline would be consistent with the intent of the legislation, if some of the prior introductions were ineffective. However, the percentage of total ethical drug sales accounted for by new NCEs declined roughly in proportion to the number of drugs, from 20.0 percent in 1957–1961 to 5.5 percent in 1967–1971. The authors contend that this finding is inconsistent with the argument that only the most insignificant drugs were eliminated.[5]

Grabowski et al. also attempt to measure the marginal reduction plausibly attributed to the 1962 Amendments after controlling for other possible contributing factors, including the depletion of new product opportunities; the thalidomide tragedy that may have made manufacturers and physicians more risk averse, hence reduced demand for new drugs; and pharmacological advances that may have raised R&D costs independent of regulation. They compared trends in NCE discoveries in the United States relative to the United Kingdom, an appropriate comparator country because of its strong and successful research-based pharmaceutical industry. This is a quasi-natural experiment since the United Kingdom did not adopt efficacy requirements until 1971 and its 1963 safety requirements were statistically unrelated to the flow of new discoveries. Grabowski et al. find that research productivity, defined as number of NCEs per (lagged) R&D expenditure, declined sixfold between 1960 and 1961 and 1966 and 1970 in the United States, compared to a threefold decline in the United Kingdom, and that the 1962 Amendments increased the cost per new NCE in the United States by a factor of 2.3. They conclude that these differentials are plausibly attributable to regulation, since the United Kingdom would have been equally affected by exogenous changes in scientific opportunities and testing norms and by any thalidomide-related change in demand. In fact, these estimates based on using the United Kingdom as a benchmark are probably conservative estimates because regulatory changes in the United States, as the largest single pharmaceutical market, would influence incentives for innovative R&D for all firms, regardless of country of domicile, and hence could have contributed to the decline in NCE discoveries in the United Kingdom.

R&D Cost per NCE

There is little doubt that regulation has contributed to the increase in R&D cost per new drug approved, but the relative contribution of regu-

5. Assuming that more important drugs typically have atypically high price or quantity, and therefore revenues, the percentage decline in revenue share of new drugs should be less than the percentage decline in number of new drugs, if the Amendments only eliminated minor drugs of dubious efficacy.

lation versus other factors is uncertain. Baily (1972) and Wiggins (1981) concluded that the 1962 Amendments led to a large increase in the R&D cost per new drug approved, but with significant variation across therapeutic categories. More recent evidence shows that the cost of developing new drugs has continued to outpace the Consumer Price Index (CPI), despite no major change in explicit regulatory requirements, although undocumented changes in regulatory requirements may have occurred. DiMasi et al. have found that capitalized cost per approved NCE, measured in present value at launch, grew from $138 million in the 1970s to $318 million in the 1980s to $802 million in the 1990s, and is currently estimated to be in the $1.2–$1.3 billion range for both traditional and biotech products (see figure 7.5; DiMasi and Grabowski 2007; DiMasi, Hansen, and Grabowski 2003; DiMasi et al. 1991). Although critics contest the estimate, in part, due to the confidential nature of the firm and product-specific panel data required for appropriate calculation of costs over time, other recent attempts have found similar cost levels (Adams and Brantner 2006). Roughly half of the total cost is out-of-pocket expense, including spending on drugs that ultimately fail; the remainder is foregone interest or opportunity cost of capital. Updating the cost of capital calculation with the Fama-French three factor model rather than the traditional capital asset pricing model (CAPM) approach also suggests greater risk and, therefore, a larger opportunity cost component (Vernon, Golec, and Dimasi 2010). The inflation-adjusted rate of growth of out-of-pocket costs has remained relatively constant (7.0 percent 1970–1980, 7.6 percent 1980–1990). Interestingly, despite—or because of—

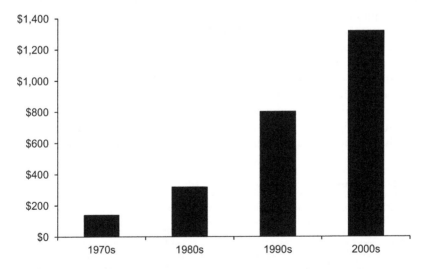

Fig. 7.5   Estimated cost per NCE over time (average)
Sources: Hansen (1979); DiMasi et al. (1991); DiMasi, Hansen, and Grabowski (2003); DiMasi and Grabowski (2007).

the major advances and investments in microbiology, combinatorial chemistry, high-throughput screening, robotics, bioinformatics, and genomics, that revolutionized drug discovery in the 1980s and 1990s, preclinical costs related to drug discovery have grown at a slower annual rate (2.3 percent in the 1990s) than the costs of clinical trials (11.8 percent), which reflect shifts in medical care technologies rather than drug discovery technologies. The clinical cost growth rate in the 1990s includes an increase in number of trial participants, more procedures, and higher cost per participant, the latter partly reflecting new medical care technologies.[6] Besides changing regulatory requirements, other contributing factors include: change in types of drugs and diseases pursued, as R&D effort shifts toward more difficult diseases once the "low hanging" diseases have been addressed; increased focus on chronic diseases, which require longer trials to detect cumulative effects; collection of economic as well as clinical data, to satisfy growing payer demands for evidence of cost-effectiveness; and possibly growing public demand for safety that might lead firms to invest voluntarily in larger/longer trials in order to detect rare effects.

For certain types of drugs, particularly those used by large populations of relatively healthy subjects, such as vaccines, reluctance to tolerate even remote risks is increasing the size and duration of trials in order to detect very rare adverse events. For example, recent trials for the rotovirus vaccine involve 70,000 patients. In a qualitative survey Coleman et al. (2005) report that vaccine manufacturers attribute vaccine shortages and reduced incentives for discovery, in part, to the high safety standards that are required by the FDA (Coleman et al. 2005).[7] Danzon et al. (2005) show that both regulatory requirements and competition have contributed to exit of vaccine manufacturers (Danzon and Pereira 2005; Danzon, Pereira, and Tejwani 2005).

On the other hand, regulatory changes (such as use of biomarkers rather than survival as the endpoints, Fast Track status, etc.) that expedite drugs that treat life-threatening diseases for which no effective therapies exist have no doubt reduced costs and delay, contributing to the growth in number of drugs approved and in development for cancer, inflammatory diseases, and so forth in recent years. Other factors, such as advances in science and relatively generous reimbursement under Medicare Part B, have also con-

6. Boston Consulting Group (BCG 1993) reports that the mean number of subjects included in NDAs increased from 1,576 for 1977–1980; to 1,321 for 1981–1984; and 3,233 for 1985–1988. DiMasi, Hansen, and Grabowski (2003) report a mean number of subjects per NDA of 5,303 for trials completed in the late 1990s. DiMasi (2002) reports that total cumulative time from drug synthesis to approval increased from 8.1 years for 1963–1969 to 14.2 by 1990–1999.
7. Finkelstein (2004) examines the effects on vaccine R&D of three plausibly exogenous shifts in policy (the 1991 CDC recommendation to vaccinate infants against Hepatitis B, the 1993 expansion of Medicare to cover influenza vaccines, and the 1986 introduction of the Vaccine Injury Compensation Fund) that plausibly increased expected revenues. She finds a lagged increase in vaccine clinical trials after these events, but no increase in early stage patent activity or preclinical trials.

tributed to the proliferation of R&D, particularly biologics for these high-priority conditions, making it hard to identify the net effect of regulatory changes on R&D. However, it seems safe to conclude that, given PDUFA, FDAMA, and other measures that have been adopted to expedite trials and review for high-priority drugs, the balance has shifted and there is now less concern over undue costs and delay (at least for these high-priority drugs), and perhaps more concern over adequate proof of safety and efficacy. As indicated earlier, the 2012 reauthorization of PDUFA (2012) enhances the tools available to the FDA to address postlaunch safety.

Lags in Launch

Several analyses find that the 1962 Amendments increased delay in launch of new drugs in the United States relative to other countries (Grabowski 1976; Wardell 1973; Wardell and Lasagna 1975; Wiggins 1981). Grabowski and Vernon (1976) compare introduction dates in the United States and the United Kingdom for drugs discovered in the United States between 1960 and 1974. The proportion of drugs introduced first in the United States declined significantly between 1960 and 1962 and 1972 and 1974, while the proportion introduced later in the United States increased significantly. The authors conclude that increased regulatory scrutiny in the United States caused multinational companies to introduce new products abroad before their US launch. Similarly, Grabowski (1976) finds that many more drugs were introduced first in Europe despite most being discovered in the United States or by US-based firms. Dranove and Meltzer (1994) estimate that the average time from a drug's first worldwide patent application to its approval by the FDA rose from 3.5 years in the 1950s to almost 6 years in the 1960s and 14 years in the mid-1980s (Dranove and Meltzer 1994). They also found that, beginning in the 1950s, more important drugs—especially drugs that proved to be successful in the marketplace—have been developed and approved more rapidly than less important drugs. They attribute this differential to actions of drug companies as much as to regulatory priority setting.[8]

However, evidence since the 1990s (see figure 7.6) indicates that the United States no longer lags and may lead the major EU markets in number and timing of major new drug launches (Danzon, Wang, and Wang 2005).

Given the coordination of standards and similarity of regulatory requirements in the European EMA and the FDA, differences in launch timing between the United States and the EU appear to be driven less by differences in market approval requirements and more by price and reimbursement regulation in the EU, including the fact that price spillovers create incentives

8. Dranove and Meltzer (1994) used several measures of drug importance, including citations in medical textbooks, medical journals, and subsequent patent applications; the extent of worldwide introduction; and US sales. To the extent that these ex post measures of importance are noisy measures of ex ante forecasts of importance, their estimates of differential delay may be understated.

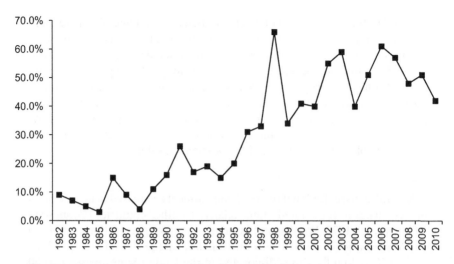

Fig. 7.6   Drug launches—share of first launch in the United States
Sources: Woodcock (2012); FDA.

for manufacturers to intentionally delay launch in low-price markets. One exception is Japan, which has relatively high launch prices and unusually long launch lags due to its unique market approval requirements, including country-specific trials.

7.4.2   Benefits of Safety and Efficacy Regulation

Compared to costs, there are many fewer studies of the benefits to consumers from regulation. The only significant attempt to weigh both the benefits and costs of the 1962 Amendments is Peltzman's (1973) study. He attempts to measure the benefit associated with the new efficacy standards by comparing the growth of market shares of drugs launched prior to 1962 to those launched after 1962. The assumption was that new products would capture greater initial market share after 1962 if the Amendments increased the average efficacy of new drugs relative to drugs already on the market (Peltzman 1973). He concludes that the benefits were minimal and were far outweighed by the costs of regulation, which he estimates as foregone consumer surplus due to the reduced flow of NCEs. These conclusions depend critically on the methods for estimating costs and benefits, which have been questioned (e.g., Temin 1979). In particular, benefits may be understated and costs may be overstated by ascribing the decline in NCEs solely to the regulation. Nevertheless, this is an important study because it offers a theoretical and empirical framework for evaluating the net benefits of the 1962 efficacy requirements.

Several recent studies have examined the benefits and costs of the priority review policy introduced by PDUFA in 1992. Undoubtedly, PDUFA expedited the time to market for "priority" drugs. Between 1993 and 2003 the median time to approval declined from 14.9 to 6.7 months, while review times for "standard" products only decreased from 27.2 to 23.1 months (Okie 2005). Olson (2000) uses data from 1990 to 1992 and 1992 to 1995 to examine the difference in the effects of firm characteristics on review times before and after the 1992 PDUFA. She finds that firm characteristics were not associated with review times after 1992, suggesting that the regulatory change helped eliminate firm advantages that existed prior to 1992 (Olson 2000). PDUFA was also subsequently amended to reduce filing fees for smaller firms.

Olson (2004) also attempts to quantify the safety impact of PDUFA and compare the costs of faster approvals to the benefits. She finds that postlaunch reports of adverse drug reactions (ADRs) are more likely for drugs that the FDA rates as "priority," after controlling for drug utilization, disease characteristics, patient characteristics, drug review time, and year-specific effects (Olson 2004). Controlling for these factors, she concludes that there are 60–84 percent more serious ADRs, 45–72 percent more ADRs that result in hospitalization, and 61–83 percent more ADRs that result in death due to PDUFA. In order to calculate benefits from reduced delay, Olson uses Lichtenberg's estimate of how the increase in the stock of priority review drugs for particular therapeutic categories increased life expectancy for persons with those conditions (Lichtenberg 2005). She finds that under the most conservative assumptions (biasing against safety) the safety impact reduces net benefit by just 8 percent (measured in expected gain in life years). A large share of the benefit is attributed to the faster launch of new drugs with priority review status. This figure increases to 11 percent if ADRs are underreported by 30 percent. Subsequent research has found that ADRs gathered through the FDA postmarketing surveillance mechanisms generally underreport ADRs, but the degree is not well established (Bennett et al. 2005; Brewer and Colditz 1999). Whereas Olson finds significant negative safety effects of accelerated review, the General Accounting Office found that drug withdrawals rates differed insignificantly between the period before and after the PDUFA; however, this study did not control for other factors that may have influenced drug withdrawals rates (GAO 2002a).

None of these studies estimate the savings to firms from accelerating the R&D process, including lower capitalized costs of R&D and increased effective patent life. DiMasi (2002) estimates that a 25 percent reduction in phase length for all phases of clinical trials would reduce the average cost per NCE by $129 million, or by 16.1 percent, assuming a base cost of $802 million (DiMasi 2002). Since this estimate is based on a random sample of sixty-eight drugs that entered clinical trials between 1983 and 1994, it probably overstates the dollar savings for the types of drugs that receive fast track status; however, the percentage effect may be valid.

7.4.3   Discussion and Proposals for Change in Regulation of Safety and Efficacy

Despite the reduction in regulatory review times under PDUFA, total R&D time remains high primarily due to duration of Phase III trials.[9] Concern to reduce launch delay without sacrificing risk information has led to growing interest in supplementing prelaunch randomized controlled trials (RCTs) with postlaunch observational evidence, from either controlled or uncontrolled studies. Advances in data collection from routine care and in statistical methods for analyzing such data to adjust for possible nonrandom assignment of patients to different treatments offer a potentially rich and relatively cheap source of information that could supplement clinical trial data, providing larger sample sizes, detail on subpopulations, and evidence on long-term effects. The Center for Medicare and Medicaid (CMS) is undertaking such studies in order to evaluate effectiveness of alternative treatment regimens for the Medicare Drug Benefit. Integrating such findings with FDA's prelaunch data from RCTs could significantly enhance the information base available for postlaunch decisions—for example, on labeling changes by the FDA and/or reimbursement decisions by CMS—and could potentially affect the relative role of the FDA versus CMS.

The net benefit to consumers from a shift toward earlier approval of drugs based on biomarkers (such as tumor shrinkage) depends in part on whether postlaunch studies are in fact completed, in order to validate that biomarker results are predictive of longer term efficacy in clinical outcomes (such as survival) and safety. As of March 2012, 1,500 postapproval studies assigned to industry for both NDA/ANDAs or BLA (biologics) were in process, and in the majority of cases these were on schedule (17 percent were off schedule) (FDA 2012). This represents an improvement over prior periods and suggests that the political will for enforcement as well as statistical feasibility for these studies are improving.

Although models of producer versus consumer capture are no doubt relevant to understanding the regulation of pharmaceuticals, current events and crisis also play a major role in the shifting emphasis between safety and speed to market. For example, public and congressional concerns focused on speeding up access to new drugs in the 1980s and 1990s, partly in response to the AIDS crisis. Subsequently, postlaunch evidence on risks of some widely used drugs, including the COX-2 inhibitors for arthritis and pain, notably rofecoxib (Vioxx) and valdecoxib (Bextra), and the SNRI antidepressants, led to a range of proposals to enhance regulatory protection of safety. The

---

9. DiMasi, Hansen, and Grabowski (2003, 164–65) report that total time from start of human testing to approval for a representative drug was 90.3 months in the 1990s, down from 98.9 in the 1980s.

FDA's expanded MedWatch program reports adverse events on an FDA website as soon as reported (Longman 2005; FDA, n.d.), enabling consumers to draw their own conclusions. In February 2005 the FDA created a Drug Safety Oversight Board (DSOB) to review safety issues on approved drugs. Critics argue that such an effective oversight board should be independent of the FDA as the approving agency, and/or that the FDA is captured by industry (Okie 2005). Counter arguments are that coordination within the FDA of prelaunch review and postlaunch monitoring permits greater consistency in decision making and takes advantage of expertise and economies of scale in reviewing data. Others have called for requiring public disclosure of results from all industry supported clinical trials—although this concept is increasingly becoming a reality, particularly for later phase trials, as many firms are registering key data elements, basic results, and adverse events for the majority of trials on the FDA's portal (clinicaltrials.gov) since the Food and Drug Administration Amendments Act (FDAAA) effectively mandated registration of non–Phase I trials and the International Committee of Medical Journal Editors (ICMJE) required registration as a precondition for publication in 2004 (Califf et al. 2012; Longman 2005). These policies should increase the information available to physicians and patients. While one may surmise that increasing prelaunch information would lead to gains in social welfare, increased risk of postlaunch regulatory review, possibly by an agency using different risk-benefit criteria than the FDA, would increase postlaunch risk for firms and could reduce incentives to invest in drugs with novel mechanisms or for new targets.

Some argue that drugs should be available for prescription after successful completion of Phase II trials with the stipulation that firms are mandated to continue with Phase III trials. In such a system, patients and physicians would make their own evaluations as to whether expected benefits outweigh risks (Madden 2004).[10] The counterargument is that the limited safety and efficacy data available after Phase II trials are seriously inadequate for informed decision making, which requires the more comprehensive data collected in Phase III trials that are powered to provide statistically meaningful results. Moreover, the FDA has specialized expertise and provides a public good in evaluating the evidence on safety and efficacy, including imposing minimum standards with respect to each of these factors, before launch. Such information would be underprovided in a free market regime and costly to assimilate for individual physicians and patients. Although health plans can—and do—serve as intermediaries who assess the relative merits of individual drugs, consumers may view health plans as imperfect agents, given their financial stake in controlling drug spending. Independent review-

---

10. Postlaunch efficacy trials would be required with results posted on the Internet, for consumers to make their own evaluations (Madden 2004).

ers such as Consumer Reports lack access to the full clinical information, which is essential to identify drug effects, controlling for patient condition and other treatments.

Moreover, the social benefit of a regulatory review process that establishes minimum standards for marketed drugs has plausibly increased with the growth in number of drugs and with insurance coverage. At the time of the 1962 Amendments, there were far fewer drugs on the market and virtually all consumers paid out of pocket. Hence the main potential benefit from a regulatory requirement for efficacy was to protect consumers from wasteful spending on useless drugs, including delayed recovery and other medical costs. At that time, the drugs available were few and mostly well known, hence the information burden on physicians or consumers was relatively modest. Since then, there has been a vast expansion in number, complexity, and potency of drugs available, and many consumers, especially seniors, take multiple prescriptions. Consequently, the potential frequency and severity of adverse drug reactions and interactions has increased, as has the burden of staying informed and the potential cost of being misinformed. Moreover, the growth of insurance coverage has undermined individual consumers' financial incentives to avoid ineffective drugs that could exacerbate wasteful spending on drugs that are of low or only minor benefit. Thus in our view, the case remains strong for a regulatory agency such as the FDA to establish minimum standards of safety, efficacy, and quality as a condition of market access. However, the optimal integration of postlaunch data with the prelaunch RCT data remains an important issue to be resolved.

A second critical regulatory issue is the optimal mix and coordination of agency regulation and tort liability. The theory of optimal policy to control safety when markets suffer from imperfect information generally views regulation and tort liability as alternatives. In theory, since the FDA is an expert agency that employs specialists in the design and evaluation of clinical trials and is guided by advisory panels comprised of external medical and statistical experts that review and evaluate comprehensive data on risks and benefits, their decisions should be better informed and more consistent across drugs than decisions of lay juries, made in the context of an adverse outcome to an individual patient who may have had many competing medical and lifestyle risk factors in addition to taking the drug at issue. The FDA approves drugs on the basis of population risks and benefits, which by definition are average effects, but it is intrinsically difficult to apply such trade-offs to individual patients in tort cases. For example, if the FDA decided that a 1 percent risk of an adverse outcome from a drug was acceptable in view of its benefits, how does a jury decide whether an individual patient's adverse event is within this 1 percent, in which case the producer should not be found liable, or lies outside the 1 percent, in which case the drug may be less safe than expected and the firm should be liable? More generally, the concept of a "defective product," which is the basis of product liability, is problematic when applied to drugs that necessarily entail risks and/or are ineffective for some patients. Unclear standards lead to erratic and unpredictable liability rulings, in which case incentives for safety are likely to be excessive (Craswell and Calfee 1986). Moreover, tort decisions made ex post, after a drug has been on the market, are at risk of applying current information retroactively; that is, holding a firm liable for rare or cumulative adverse events that only emerge after widespread or long-term use, which the firm could not reasonably have foreseen and for which the FDA did not require testing. Given the extensive premarket regulation of drugs, one proposal is that if a drug is in full compliance with FDA requirements, including full information disclosure by the company to the FDA, then FDA compliance should be a bar to tort claims except on grounds of gross negligence, or at least a bar to punitive damages.

A more extreme proposal would replace tort liability for negligence or product defect with a no-fault compensation fund, to provide compensation to patients injured by drugs without regard to producer negligence or product defect, funded by a tax on drugs. The model for this proposal is the workers' compensation system or the Vaccine Compensation Fund (VCF), which was established in 1984 to provide compensation on a no-fault basis for injuries caused by vaccines, replacing tort liability on manufacturers, and funded by a tax on vaccines. However, the VCF model is relatively simple to administer because vaccine injuries are rare, they occur in otherwise healthy individuals, and causation is usually clear. By contrast, patients take therapeutic drugs because they are sick; these drugs claim to increase the probability of cure but with no guarantees and with some risk of side effects. In these circumstances, if an individual patient is not cured by the drug or suffers an adverse effect, determining whether their condition is inappropriately caused by the drug or is simply the inevitable progression of their disease is problematic, both conceptually and empirically. Thus, implementing a no-fault compensation system that accurately assigns liability if and only if an adverse outcome is caused by a drug, which is a necessary condition for appropriate deterrence signals to producers, is far more problematic for therapeutic drugs than for vaccines or workplace injuries.

7.5   Patents

Given the high cost of pharmaceutical R&D, patents are essential to induce sustained investment and few, if any, industries rely on patents to the extent that the pharmaceutical industry does. The pharmaceutical industry benefits from the same patent provisions (twenty years from filing) available to firms in any industry, except for the special patent term restoration granted for pharmaceuticals under the 1984 Hatch-Waxman Act, to restore time lost in clinical trials (see section 7.3). However, pharmaceutical product patents are more readily enforceable and harder to circumvent than patents in many other industries, including medical devices. Consequently, many originator pharmaceuticals enjoy an economic life until the patent expires and generic entry occurs. By contrast, the economic life of a medical device is at most a few years, because imitative entry occurs long before patent expiry, leading to continual incremental product improvement. Because of the necessity and value of pharmaceutical patents, the pharmaceutical industry has been at the forefront of international negotiations over WTO patent provisions.

There is an extensive general economics literature examining the trade-off between the duration/scope of patents and optimal incentives for innovation (Gilbert and Shapiro 1990; Klemperer 1990; Lerner 1994; Levy 1999). Early research attempted to quantify the impact of patents by surveying pharmaceutical managers. Based on a survey of 100 R&D managers, Mansfield (1986) reported that between 1981 and 1983 60 percent of pharmaceutical products would not have been developed and 65 percent would not have entered competitive markets without the benefit of patent protection (Mansfield 1986). Similar research among R&D directors in the United Kingdom reported that pharmaceutical investment in R&D would be 65 percent lower without patents (Silberson 1987; Taylor and Silberston 1973). While these survey estimates may be useful benchmarks, they do not necessarily provide an accurate estimate of the counterfactual level of R&D effort in a world without patents. Although a full review of pharmaceutical patents is beyond the scope of this chapter, issues that intersect with regulation are briefly reviewed here.

7.5.1   Patent Length and Conditions for Generic Entry

The effective patent life of pharmaceuticals is less than the statutory twenty years because patents are usually filed early in the discovery process, but drug development and approval takes many years. Analysis of 126 products introduced in the 1990 to 1995 period shows average patent life of 11.7 years, with a right skewed tail (Grabowski and Vernon 2000; Grabowski, Vernon, and Di Masi 2002; Kuhlik 2004). The Hatch-Waxman Act provides for patent term restoration on a 1:1 basis for NDA review time and a 0.5:1 basis for clinical testing time, up to a maximum of five years restored and total effective patent length of fourteen years.

The Hatch-Waxman compromise counterbalanced these patent extensions with an Abbreviated New Drug Application (ANDA) process for generics, which requires that generics show chemical and bio-equivalence to the originator drug, but permits them to reference the safety and efficacy data of the originator product. Moreover, the Bolar Amendment permitted companies to start work on generics before the originator patent has expired, thereby enabling prompt generic entry as soon as patents expire. By reducing the cost of regulatory approval, these measures increased the number of generic entrants, which in turn increases competitive pressure on prices.

In addition, during the 1970s and 1980s, all states repealed antisubstitution dispensing laws and established default rules that allow pharmacists to substitute an AB-rated (FDA-approved bioequivalent) generic for a brand drug unless the physician specifies that the brand is required. By 1984, generic substitution had already expanded from 7.3 percent of eligible prescriptions in 1980 to 16 percent in 1984 (Levy 1999). In the 1980s and 1990s the reimbursement strategies used by pharmacy benefit managers (PBMs), HMOs, and Medicaid established strong financial incentives for pharmacists to substitute generics, where available. These third-party payers treat generics and brands as fully substitutable. They use a form of generic reference pricing (see below) in reimbursing pharmacies for multisource drugs. Specifically, they typically pay pharmacies a maximum allowable cost (MAC), which is based on the acquisition price of a low-cost generic, regardless of which generically equivalent product is dispensed. Since pharmacies capture the margin between the MAC and their acquisition cost, they have strong incentives to substitute the cheapest generics, and this in turn creates incentives for generic suppliers to compete on price. If patients want the brand, they must pay the difference between the MAC and the cost of the brand (plus any other copayment). Thus the main customers of generic firms are the large pharmacy chains, including mass merchandisers such as Walmart, and the wholesalers that supply the independent pharmacies; these customers are highly concentrated and highly price sensitive, and generics compete on price, not brand image. In contrast to this pharmacy-driven generics market model in the United States, generics markets in many other countries, including the EU and Latin America, have been physician-driven, with higher-priced, branded generics. For example, until recently countries such as France, Spain, and Italy paid pharmacists a percentage of the price of the drug and/or did not permit generic substitution by pharmacies unless the physician prescribes by generic name. In this environment, generic producers market to physicians, competing on brand rather than price, and generic market shares are smaller and generic prices are higher than in the United States (Danzon and Furukawa 2003). Several EU countries have recently changed their regulation of generics in order to encourage lower prices and larger generic shares.

In the United States, the generic share of total prescriptions dispensed grew from 38.3 percent in 1999 to over 70 percent in 2011 (see figure 7.7), while the generic share of sales grew from 7.4 to over 25 percent in 2011.[11] The higher generic share of prescriptions than sales reflects the low generic prices, relative to brands. This generic share of total scripts understates the share of eligible, off-patent scripts that are filled generically, which can

11. Data from IMS Health, unpublished presentation. Note that these figures include only unbranded generics, which compete on price rather than brand image. Branded generics, which include some old single source drugs, account for an additional 9.8 percent of prescriptions and sales.

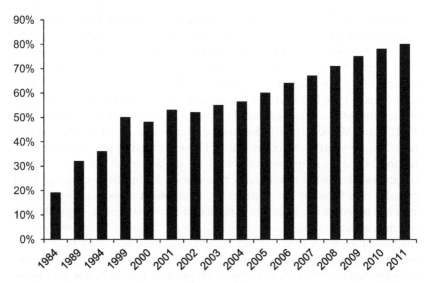

Fig. 7.7   Generic share of total prescriptions after the Hatch-Waxman Act (US)
Sources: Berndt and Aitken (2011); Aitken, Berndt, and Cutler (2009); IMS (2012).

exceed 80 percent within three months of patent expiry in the United States. The growth of generic share of scripts reflects not only increased generic penetration of compounds that are off patent but also the growing number of major drugs that are off patent.

Several research-based pharmaceutical firms attempted to enter the generics market in the 1990s, but most have divested their generic activities. Since generic firms compete for the business of large pharmacy chains and wholesalers by their breadth of product line, prompt availability of new generics inventory management, and low prices, it is hardly surprising that originator firms were unable to compete simply by offering generic versions of their own drugs. Most originator firms now focus on other postpatent strategies, except that some originator firms do produce "authorized generic" versions of their own drugs (see below). One major exception is Novartis, whose Sandoz generic division is a broad scale and global generic producer, particularly after the purchase in 2005 of Eon and Hexal. The Israel-based generics company Teva produces the largest volume of US prescriptions, with 639 million retail prescriptions filled in 2010, compared to 265 million for Novartis (Cacciotti and Clinton 2011). Teva also has entered the branded market with select, limited novel product efforts and acquisitions, but for the most part there is limited crossover between branded and generic firms (Cartwright 2011; Tsao 2003). With respect to the emerging biosimilar market, early indications suggest that branded, generic, and even nontraditional entrants (such as Samsung) will compete in these more potentially lucrative markets (IMS 2011).

Originator brands respond to the rapid generic erosion of brand share after patent expiry by a range of strategies, including: raising price to maximize profit from the shrinking, relatively price-inelastic brand-loyal segment (Frank and Salkever 1992); shifting patients to a follow-on product, such as a delayed release version of the original drug (Procardia XL vs. Procardia) or a single isomer version (Nexium vs. Prilosec), which requires heavy marketing, sampling, and discounting before the patent expires on the original drug; switching the drug to over-the-counter status, which may require clinical trials to show that it is safe and effective under patient self-medication; or filing additional patents, challenging generic entrants, and/or producing an "authorized generic." The growth in litigation around patent expiry was fueled by several provisions of the Hatch-Waxman Act that have been partly amended in the 2003 Medicare Modernization Act (MMA). Specifically, Hatch-Waxman provided that if a generic challenged an originator patent, the originator could file for a thirty-month stay that blocked generic entry for thirty months or until the case was resolved, whichever came first. Originator firms could thus delay generic entry indefinitely by filing for additional patents on ancilliary features of the drug, and then file successive thirty-month stays when generics challenged these patents. The MMA limited the number of thirty-month stays to one per ANDA. FTC and class action suits against firms that have allegedly filed frivolous patents have also reduced incentives for such behavior.

In addition, Hatch-Waxman provides for 180 days of market exclusivity for the first generic firm to successfully challenge a patent and show that it is invalid (a Paragraph IV ANDA filing). Paragraph IV filings have increased over time—from just 2 percent of expirations in the 1980s to 20 percent in the late 1990s, and more recently approximately a 65 percent challenge rate for more recent studies (see figure 7.8; Grabowski et al. 2011; Hemphill and Sampat 2012). Unsurprisingly, patent challenges are more likely for high-revenue products (Kuhlik 2004). Debate continues as to whether the increased Paragraph IV challenges reflect increased aggressiveness by generic companies "prospecting" for payoffs in settlement or increased filing of frivolous patents (also known as "evergreening") by originators— although the issuance of "weaker" patents unrelated to the core active ingredient (non-AI patents) has also increased over this period (Hemphill and Sampat 2012; Kesselheim 2011). While the intent of the 180-day exclusivity was to reward and therefore encourage costly challenges to dubious patents, the competitive effects are unclear. In some cases, originator firms colluded with the generic manufacturers that received the 180-day generic exclusivity period, paying them to delay launch of the generic, which effectively stayed entry by other potential generic producers of the compound (FTC 2002). The incentive for such collusion has been greatly reduced both by FTC challenges and by the MMA reforms, which provide that the 180-day exclusivity period is forfeited if not used in a timely manner. However, the

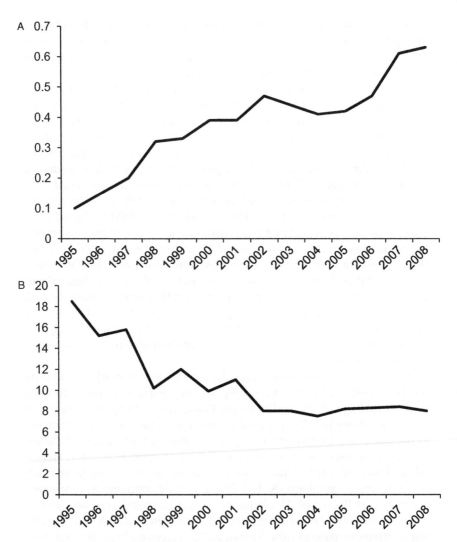

Fig. 7.8   *A*, **Paragraph IV patent challenges by generic firms;** *B*, **average time from brand name launch to Paragraph IV challenge**
Source: Grabowski et al. (2011).

circumstances in which originators can legally settle with generic challengers remains unresolved and there are valid arguments on both sides: some originator and generic firms argue that settling patent disputes is a legitimate and efficient means to resolve uncertainty as to ultimate court decision on patent challenges, and that settlement reduces litigation expenditures and enables both sides to pursue long-term investment strategies; on the other hand, the FTC tends to view such settlements as anticompetitive, which would be correct if the challenged patents are clearly invalid and settlement were solely a means to delay competitive entry.

A final area of litigation is over the originator strategy of marketing an authorized (i.e., licensed) generic version of the brand product during the Paragraph IV 180-day exclusivity period. Absent an authorized generic, the sole generic during a 180-day exclusivity period generally captures significant market share at a price only slightly below the brand price. Competition from an "authorized generic" generally reduces the price, quantity, and profit earned by the generic owner of the 180-day exclusivity, and hence may reduce incentives of generic firms to challenge patents. Clearly, if the US Patent Office could rule instantly and accurately on all patent filings, originator firms would have no incentive to file dubious patents and there would be no social value in patent challenges by generics. But since patent filings are reviewed only with delay, and higher courts may overturn decisions by lower courts, incentives for frivolous filings remain and hence there may be some social value in encouraging generic patent challenges. Whether generic incentives to challenge patents are closer to optimal with or without authorized generics is an unresolved empirical question.

As costs of generic entry and hence the number of generic entrants depend, in part, on the ability to reference data from studies conducted by originator firms, data exclusivity policies are an important determinant of effective patent protection. Hatch-Waxman granted data exclusivity for five years from the NDA approval (and three years for data not used in clinical trial), and these exclusivity provisions have been relaxed by subsequent rulings (Kuhlik 2004). By contrast, the 2010 PPACA provides for data exclusivity of twelve years for biologics, potentially creating a bias in favor of biologics over chemical drugs. Differences across countries in effective patent life in part reflect differences in these data exclusivity provisions, as well as differences in regulatory requirements for generic approval and substitution by pharmacies, and reimbursement incentives for pharmacists and patients to prefer generics (Danzon and Furukawa 2011).

Empirical studies of generic entry have shown that generic prices are inversely related to number of generic competitors in the United States (Grabowski and Vernon 1992); generic entry is more likely for compounds with large markets (measured by preexpiry brand revenue), chronic disease markets, and oral-solid (pill) form (Scott Morton 1999, 2000). Caves, Whinston, and Hurwitz (1991) find that total volume does not increase after patent expiration, despite the significant drop in price due to generic entry, indicating that the price effect is offset by the negative promotion effect, because incentives for promotion cease at patent expiration. Similarly, Scott Morton (2000) finds no significant generic deterrent effect of incumbent advertising via detailing or journal advertising from two to three years prior to generic entry. This is unsurprising, given that the generic switching decision is made mainly by pharmacists and patients, in response to their financial incentives, not by physicians who are the target of detailing and journal advertising. Danzon and Furukawa (2011) show that generic markets that are physician driven rather than pharmacy driven (due to weak authorization and/or incentives for pharmacy substitution) are less price competitive.

Originator firms can seek FDA regulatory permission to switch a prescription (Rx) branded product to over-the-counter (OTC) status (which makes it available to patients without prescription) at any time, but this is usually done around patent expiry, to avoid cannibalization of the Rx version and possibly to preempt generic erosion. If the OTC switch involves a change of formulation, strength, or indication, the FDA requires additional clinical trials to show safety and efficacy under patient self-medication. To encourage these costly investments, the FDA grants three years of market exclusivity to a successful OTC switch, which delays entry of generic (private label) versions of the OTC formulation, but not of the Rx version. OTC approval is more likely for drugs to treat conditions that are easily self-diagnosed, the potential for abuse or misuse is low, labeling can reasonably communicate any risks, and medical oversight is not required for effective and safe use of the product. Prices of OTC products are lower than Rx medicines, possibly reflecting lack of insurance coverage for OTC products. Social welfare is likely to increase, unless the OTC entails significant patient risk or preempts a potentially cheaper generic Rx version (Temin 1983). Keeler et al. (2002) estimate a demand function for nicotine replacement drugs and combine this with epidemiological evidence of medical and quality of life benefits to determine a net social benefit of approximately $2 billion per year for OTC conversion of these drugs (Keeler et al. 2002).

7.5.2 Patents, "Access," and Static Efficiency: Industrialized versus Developing Countries

Pharmaceutical patents raise the standard issue of static efficiency loss, if prices to consumers exceed marginal cost and result in suboptimal consumption. However, for most industrialized countries that have comprehensive health insurance coverage for drugs with at most modest patient copayments, this patent-induced tendency for underconsumption is mitigated by an insurance-induced tendency for overconsumption. Probably a greater concern in these contexts is that health insurance reduces the demand elasticity facing the firm and hence creates incentives to charge prices that are significantly higher than would occur due solely to patents. Public insurers' response to this by price regulation is discussed later.

However, the potential for significant static inefficiency and welfare loss due to patent-induced underconsumption remains a serious concern for developing countries, where insurance is limited and most consumers pay out of pocket for drugs. Under the WTO TRIPS requirements, all WTO members must adopt a patent regime with twenty-year product patents (from date of filing) by 2015, with the proviso that governments may grant a compulsory license to generic producers in the event of a "national emergency."[12] The scope of this compulsory licensing provision remains disputed, both with respect to the health conditions and the countries to which it applies, and whether it is de facto being undermined by bilateral trade agreements initiated particularly by the United States, which stipulate stricter patent provisions.

It is an empirical question whether product patents in developing countries result in a significant welfare loss due to high prices and undercon-sumption (Chaudhuri, Goldberg, and Jia 2006; Fink 2001; Watal 2000). If demand facing a patent holder is highly price elastic due to low willingness or ability to pay, then a firm's profit-maximizing strategy may be to charge prices closer to marginal cost, despite the patent. In fact, some companies have not bothered to file patents in several African countries that (in theory at least) would enforce them (Attaran 2004), suggesting that they perceived little value in patents due to some mix of highly elastic demand, costs of fil-ing, and weak enforcement. If demand is highly elastic such that, even with enforceable patents, profit-maximizing prices in low-income countries would be close to marginal cost, then the welfare loss due to patents is small, but so is the incentive to invest in R&D to treat diseases endemic to these coun-tries. Chaudhuri, Goldberg, and Jia (2006) estimate demand elasticities and supply parameters in the anti-infective market for quinolones and conclude that patents would result in a welfare loss to consumers of $305 million per year, compared to a gain to patent holders of only $20 million, and a reduc-tion of "generic" firm profits of $35 million. The welfare loss estimates are obviously sensitive to demand elasticities and might be reduced by price discrimination within country, but in practice such within-country price dis-crimination is difficult to sustain. Consequently, prices are on average higher, relative to average per capita income, in lower income countries (Danzon, Mulcahy, and Towse 2013).

In designing an optimal regulatory framework for pharmaceuticals for developing countries, it is important to distinguish between two classes of drugs, global versus LDC-only drug. For global drugs that treat diseases such as diabetes, cardiovascular conditions, or ulcers, which are common in both developed and developing countries, market segmentation and dif-ferential pricing can in principle reconcile affordability in LDCs with incen-tives for R&D: firms can recoup their R&D investments by pricing above marginal cost in high-income countries while pricing close to marginal cost in LDCs. In this context, price discrimination across countries is likely to increase output and static efficiency, while also enhancing dynamic efficiency, through quasi-Ramsey pricing of the R&D joint assets.[13] In practice, actual

12. See Article 31, http://www.wto.org/english/tratop_e/trips_e/t_agm3_e.htm.
13. For a discussion of these issues, see, for example, Danzon (1997); Jack and Lanjouw (2003); Malueg and Schwartz (1994); Danzon and Towse (2003, 2005).

cross-national price differences diverge from ideal Ramsey differentials for several reasons, including the risks of external referencing and parallel trade (Danzon and Towse 2003, 2005); rational targeting of the quality- and price-inelastic market segment in the face of competition from branded generics (Danzon, Mulcahy, and Towse 2013); and possibly incentives for regulatory free riding by large purchasers in regulated markets (see following).

The theoretical case is strong for establishing regulatory frameworks that support price discrimination and limit cross-national price spillovers through external referencing and parallel trade, and institutions to enable within-country differential pricing. Under these conditions, patent regimes could function to stimulate R&D for drugs with a significant industrialized market potential, without significant welfare loss in developing countries if firms choose to set low prices to countries/segments with elastic demand.[14] Other policy levers may be necessary to address incentives to price high on account of the skewed income distributions common in middle- and low-income countries (MLICs) (Flynn, Hollis, and Palmedo 2009). Enforcement of bioequivalence requirements for generics could help reduce quality uncertainty, which contributes to competition on brand and weakens price competition (Danzon, Mulcahy, and Towse 2013).

As a modification to improved regulatory oversight and patent enforcement, Lanjouw (2002) proposes a regime in which firms could opt for patents in either developed or developing countries. Assuming that most firms would opt for developing country patents, the main benefit of such a system would be to reduce uncertainty with respect to patent enforcement and prices in developing countries. A number of firms have effectively followed policies toward this end by offering low-cost licensing rights specific for developing countries (CFR 2010; Gilead 2010).

However, for drugs to treat diseases that are endemic only in developing countries, patents are likely to be an ineffective mechanism to achieve the dynamic efficiency goal of stimulating investment in R&D, because consumers cannot pay prices sufficient to recoup R&D investments. In that case the question of static efficiency loss is moot. The low level of private sector R&D for LDC-only diseases, despite patent regimes in most low-income countries, tends to confirm that patents are ineffective in inducing R&D for LDC-only drugs.

In response to the great need but low levels of private sector investments in drugs to treat LDC-only diseases, there has been a recent spate of "push" and "pull" subsidy proposals and some initiatives to find new institutional solutions. In particular, a highly diverse set of public private partnerships

14. Institutional arrangements that facilitate differential pricing between the low and high income subgroups within developing countries may also be necessary. Without such segmentation, manufacturers may rationally choose a single price for a low-income country that is profit maximizing given demand of the affluent minority of the population, but is unaffordable for the lower income majority.

(PPPs) and product development partnerships (PDPs) have developed that combine government and philanthropic funds with private industry expertise and resources, to address diseases such as malaria (Medicines for Malaria Venture), tuberculosis (the Global Alliance for TB), an AIDS vaccine (the International AIDs Vaccine Initiative, IAVI), and many others. The basic issues are outlined in Kremer (2002); for a review of PDP initiatives see the G-Finder database (G-Finder 2012). The G8 countries also committed to fund an advance market commitment (AMC) that commits to paying a prespecified price to purchasing vaccines that meet specified conditions, and have applied it purchasing the pneumococcal vaccine. The Advance Medicines Facility for Malaria (AMFm) offers subsidies at the manufacturer level for first-line antimalarials in select countries in order to promote appropriate use of antimalarials, although poor information about disease status, antibiotic resistance, and distribution-related markups bring into question whether the program will ultimately prove successful.(Arrow, Panosian, and Gelband 2004; Laxminarayan and Gelband 2009; Laxminarayan, Over, and Smith 2006; Laxminarayan et al. 2010). The aforementioned FDA priority review vouchers, in theory, should also serve an additional "pull" mechanism. While the optimal mix of push and pull mechanisms will continue to evolve, the extent of donor funding and range of current initiatives is very encouraging, with several promising candidates in late stage development (Moran et al. 2009). LDC governments and international agencies such as the Global Fund are appropriately reluctant to pay for drugs that have not passed regulatory review of safety and efficacy. Thus as more of these drugs reach clinical trials, the case for developing a regulatory review agency or pathway that is appropriate for LDC drugs (see section 7.3) will become more pressing. The aforementioned FDA "tentative approval" program, which focuses on accelerating ANDA and NDA applications for production of existing AIDS medicines for the PEPFAR program, represents a step in this direction—although the chemical entities in these applications typically have already been approved for distribution in the United States.

7.6   Regulation of Prices, Insurance Reimbursement, Profits, and So Forth

7.6.1   The Rationale for Price and Profit Regulation

Regulation of pharmaceutical prices is a priori anomalous because the pharmaceutical industry is structurally competitive, with relatively low concentration overall. Although concentration within specific therapeutic categories is greater, the market is contestable, as evidenced by the growing share of new products discovered by relatively new biotechnology firms. Patents grant exclusivity on a specific compound for the term of the patent. But a patent on one compound does not prevent competition from other compounds to treat the same condition. Competitive entry is initiated long before the first compound in a new class reaches the market. Competitor firms can obtain information on each others' drugs in development from patent filings, scientific conferences, and other sources that are collated in publicly available databases, while techniques of rational drug design facilitate the development of close substitute compounds in new therapeutic classes.

Acemoglu and Linn (2004) show that entry of new drugs responds to expected demographic market size. Specifically, they find that a 1 percent increase in expected demographic demand results in a 4 percent increase in entry of NMEs/nongeneric drugs and a 6 percent increase in total number of drugs, including generics (Acemoglu and Linn 2004). DiMasi and Paquette (2004) find that entry of follow-on compounds has reduced the period of market exclusivity of first entrants to a new therapeutic class from 10.2 years in the 1970s to 1.2 years in the late 1990s (DiMasi and Paquette 2004). Lichtenberg and Philipson (2002) compare the effect on a drug's net present value at launch of within molecule (generic) competition versus between molecule (therapeutic) competition. They conclude that the reduction in discounted drug lifetime value from therapeutic competition (most of which occurs while the drug is on patent) is at least as large as the effect due to postpatent generic entry (Lichtenberg and Philipson 2002). Of course, a much higher discount factor is applied to generic erosion because the net present value (NPV) is measured at launch; still, this study provides an interesting measure of therapeutic competition.

The limited market power that results from patents is reinforced by two other institutional characteristics of pharmaceuticals. First, in industrialized countries patients must obtain a physician's prescription in order to get most drugs. If physicians are uninformed about drug prices and/or are imperfect agents for patients and are not themselves at risk for drug spending, the separation of prescribing from consumption reduces demand elasticity.

Second, insurance coverage for pharmaceuticals makes patients less price sensitive, hence makes the demand facing manufacturers less elastic, which would lead them to charge higher prices, in the absence of controls. Copayments can mitigate the insurance effect, but because copayments also reduce financial protection, in practice most public insurance plans include only very modest copayments. To counteract this price-increasing tendency of insurance, both private and public insurers set limits on the prices that they pay for all insured services including drugs and physician and hospital visits. In the United States, private insurers negotiate drug prices with manufacturers as a condition of formulary placement and insurance coverage; although large private payers such as Kaiser have significant bargaining power, none have monopsony power, and suppliers can and do choose not to supply a particular plan if its offered prices are unacceptably low.

Most industrialized countries other than the United States have either a universal national insurance scheme, with the government as sole insurer, or a system of mandatory quasi-private social insurance funds that are regulated by the government. Controlling prices as a way to control supplier moral hazard applies to all services, including pharmaceuticals. For example, Japan has a single fee schedule that sets fees for all medical services, including drugs. Consistent with this view of pharmaceutical price regulation as fundamentally an insurance strategy to control supplier moral hazard, price controls in most countries apply only if drugs are reimbursed by the public health plan. A firm is free to market a drug at unregulated prices once registration requirements are met. It is only if the firm seeks to have its product reimbursed by the public insurance that the price must be approved by the price regulatory body.

In the United States, the Medicare program for seniors and the disabled did not cover outpatient prescription drugs until the new Medicare Part D drug benefit—authorized in the 2003 Medicare Prescription Drug, Improvement, and Modernization Act (MMA)—was implemented in January 2006. Following intense debate over the design of the program, the 2003 MMA stipulated that the Medicare drug benefit was to be delivered through private prescription drug plans (PDPs) using negotiated formularies similar to those negotiated by private sector pharmacy benefit managers (PBMs). The federal government is specifically barred from negotiating drug prices. However, if expenditures under this program exceed original projections, future legislation could renounce this noninterference clause and establish a government-run plan, making the US government the purchaser for roughly 50 percent of US drug spending, although evidence to date suggests that the spending for Part D is less than anticipated—a result that some attribute to the competition between PDPs.

Other government drug purchasing programs in the United States include the federal-state Medicaid program and several smaller federal programs. The 1990 Omnibus and Reconciliation Act requires originator drugs to give Medicaid the lower of (a) the "best price" offered to any nonfederal purchaser, or (b) a 15.1 percent discount off AMP (average manufacturer price). This has subsequently increased to 23 percent under the 2010 PPACA. To deter incentives to increase private price in response to the best price provision, an "excess inflation" rebate is also required for price increases that exceed the CPI. For 2003, the combined effect of these mandatory discounts resulted in a 31.4 percent discount for Medicaid, relative to AMP (CBO 2005). Similarly, for the "Big Four" federal programs (the Department of Defense, the Department of Veterans Affairs, the Public Health Service, and the Coast Guard) the federal ceiling price mandates a discount of 24 percent off nonfederal average manufacturing price, plus an excess inflation rebate. Thus public purchasers in the United States have regulated prices by mandatory discounts off private sector prices. This has resulted in relatively low prices for public programs, but has also reduced the discounts firms grant to private plans and possibly increased list prices. This inflationary effect on private prices of best price requirements by public payers declined in 2006 since the MMA transferred seniors who were eligible for both Medicaid and Medicare ("dual eligibles") from the Medicaid program to the privately administered Medicare Part D program. This reduced the effective Medicaid best price "tax" on discounts granted to private purchasers.

Empirical evidence confirms that these rules tying Medicaid rebates to "best" private sector prices lead to a decline in discounts to private payers. GAO (1993) found that median best price discounts to HMOs declined from 24.4 percent before the law went into effect in 1991, to 14.2 percent in 1993 (GAO, 1993); CBO (1996) found similar evidence. Because discounts are confidential, academic studies have focused on the effects of the Medicaid best price provision on available measures of prices, which are gross of buyer-specific discounts (CBO 1996). Using transactions prices from IMS, Scott Morton (1997) found no effect for drugs that did not have generic competition, but modest price increases in product categories with generic competition after the enactment of the Medicaid best price policy in 1991(Scott Morton 1997). In a similar study, Duggan and Scott Morton exploit the variation in the Medicaid market share for the top 200 selling products in the United States to estimate the effect of the Medicaid legislation on average prices. They conclude that a 10 percent increase in Medicaid market share resulted in a 7 to 10 percent increase in their measure of average price.[15] Widespread awareness that tying public prices to private prices leads to increases in private prices is one reason this approach was not adopted for Medicare Part D.

7.6.2   Pricing and Competition in Unregulated Markets

On-Patent Brands

The early literature provides some evidence on competition in pharmaceutical markets before the advent of widespread insurance coverage and associated price controls. Opinion in the economic and policy literature was divided on extent and welfare effects of competition. Some viewed closely substitutable, patented products as wasteful "me-toos," arguing that patent protection leads to excessive product differentiation and higher prices (e.g., Comanor 1986; Temin 1979). Under this view, the 1962 Amendments, by requiring proof of efficacy and restricting drug advertising, may have restricted "excessive differentiation." The alternative view is that the availability of more substitute products prior to 1962 increased price competition and benefited consumers. To assess the impact of the 1962 Amendments on prices, Peltzman (1973) examined average price changes from 1952 to 1962

---

15. As a proxy for price to private payers, they use the average price paid by Medicaid, which is a percent of a list price. They report that, in a limited sample of drugs, the log of this price is highly correlated with the log of a better measure of transactions price to private payers.

and a cross-sectional analysis for 1958 to 1961, prior to the 1962 regulations. He found no evidence that the number of NCEs had any net impact on drug price inflation and concluded that, if anything, drug price growth increased after the 1962 Amendments, contrary to the "wasteful competition" hypothesis.

Other studies have examined launch prices and price trends over a drug's life cycle. In a study of launch prices of drugs introduced between 1958 and 1975, Reekie (1978) found that new drugs that offer significant therapeutic advance were priced above existing drugs but tended to lower price over time, whereas imitators were priced lower initially but tended to increase prices. Similarly, Lu and Comanor (1998), using data for 144 new drugs launched in the United States between 1978 and 1987, found evidence of a skimming strategy for innovative drugs and a penetration strategy by imitators (Lu and Comanor 1998). This evidence is consistent with some degree of competition but imperfectly informed buyers, such that sellers offer a low initial price to encourage use and build reputation or loyalty, then raise prices over time (Schmalensee 1982).

In the United States, the nature and extent of competition in pharmaceutical markets has changed with the growth of managed drug coverage in the 1980s and 1990s, as practiced by HMOs, pharmacy benefit managers (PBMs), and the prescription drug plans (PDPs) that manage the Medicare drug benefit.[16] PBMs typically establish formularies of preferred drugs that are selected on the basis of price and effectiveness. Tiered copayments and other strategies are used to encourage patients and their physicians to the use "preferred" drugs in the class. Such strategies are designed to increase the cross-price elasticity of demand between therapeutic substitutes and between generic equivalents. By using formularies to shift market share between therapeutically similar on-patent drugs and hence increase the demand elasticity facing manufacturers, PBMs are able to negotiate discounts in return for preferred formulary status. These discounts are confidential, hence detailed analysis is not available. However, anecdotal evidence confirms the theoretical prediction that discounts are larger to purchasers that have tight control over drug use, such as Kaiser, and in classes with several close substitute products. Evidence that new drugs are launched at list prices below the price of established drugs in the same product class and that the discount is greater the larger the number of existing drugs in the product class (BCG 1993) indicates that competition does reduce prices even for unmanaged consumers.

Although discounting through confidential, electronic rebates to PBMs,

16. Some insurers contract with PBMs as specialized intermediaries to manage their drug benefit, while other larger plans manage their own benefit using similar techniques. Thus although PBMs are estimated to manage approximately 57 percent of the US population's drug benefit (Health Strategies, 2005) the share of the population that has managed drug benefits, including HMOs and seniors under Medicare Part D, is probably over 70 percent.

as agents of payers and consumers, has no doubt stimulated price competition, it has been attacked on several grounds. First, because it is essentially a system of price discrimination, those who pay higher prices feel aggrieved and indeed the results would strike many as inequitable. Specifically, the largest discounts go to plans with tightly controlled formularies that tend to attract relatively healthy, privately insured nonseniors, whereas uninsured and other cash-paying customers face the highest prices. This differential in manufacturer prices is amplified for retail prices because PBMs also negotiate discounts in pharmacy dispensing margins, relative to unmanaged dispensing fees pharmacies charge to cash-paying customers. Combining the manufacturer and pharmacy discounts, consumers with managed drug benefits face approximately 20 percent lower drug costs compared to uninsured patients, including many seniors before the 2006 implementation of Medicare Part D (GAO 1997, 2003). Recent evidence also suggests that health insurers and PBMs extracted larger price reduction from manufacturers after the passage of Part D. Moreover, the expansion of market power effectively conferred to insurers under Part D allowed for "spillover" price reductions to non-Medicare beneficiaries (Duggan and Morton 2012; Lakdawalla and Yin 2010).

Second, discounting has been challenged by retail pharmacists in antitrust litigation alleging collusive pricing and price discrimination by drug manufacturers (Danzon 1997; Scherer 1997). Dispensing pharmacies do not receive the same discounts given to PBMs because pharmacies cannot—and arguably should not—independently influence a physician/patient's choice between therapeutic substitutes. This litigation conspicuously excluded off-patent, multisource drugs, because for these drugs the discounts go to the pharmacies, because they are the decision makers in choosing between generically equivalent versions of a prescribed compound. Under the settlement of this litigation, manufacturer discounts were to be made available on the same terms to all purchasers; however, because PBMs design the formularies that drive therapeutic substitution, they remain the main recipients of discounts on on-patent drugs, although wholesalers do receive modest prompt payment and volume-related discounts.

Third, as noted earlier, incentives for discounts to private payers have been reduced by the matching requirement, that manufacturers of brand drugs give to Medicaid the "best price" given to private payers, or a 23 percent discount off average manufacturer price, whichever is lower. This best price provision effectively imposes a significant tax on discounts to private payers, because Medicaid demand is totally inelastic with respect to this discount. Theory suggests that this best price provision would reduce best price discounts to private payers and this is confirmed by evidence from several studies (CBO 1996; GAO 1994).

Finally, because the discounts are confidential, payers who contract with PBMs as agents accuse the PBMs of pocketing rather than passing on the discounts. Since the Medicare drug benefit will be delivered by competing, private "prescription drug plans" similar to PBMs, both Medicare (that will heavily subsidize the benefit) and seniors (who contribute to premiums, pay significant copayments, and must choose between competing plans) have demanded "price transparency." However, CBO (2004) estimated a significantly higher cost for a variant of the Medicare drug benefit that required price transparency, under the assumption that transparency would erode drug manufacturers' competitive incentives to discount and hence would lead to higher drug prices (CBO 2004). The final MMA legislation required PDPs to reveal discounts in aggregate but not drug-specific prices.

Generics

In most US health plans, reimbursement for multisource drugs (off patent drugs with at least one generic, in addition to the originator) is designed to create strong incentives for decision makers to prefer generics over their brand equivalents. These regulatory and reimbursement structures in turn generate intense generic price competition and large generic market shares. Specifically, most HMOs, PBMs, and Medicaid plans cap pharmacy reimbursement for multisource drugs at the price of a low priced generic, the MAC or maximum allowable charge for that compound. If the patient wants the originator brand, he or she must pay the difference between the brand price and the MAC (or a third-tier copay, in some tiered formularies). Since the 1980s, most states have overturned traditional antisubstitution laws and now authorize pharmacists to dispense any bioequivalent generic, unless the physician explicitly requires the brand.

Since pharmacists capture any margin between the MAC and their acquisition cost, pharmacists have strong incentives to seek out cheap generics. For generic drug manufacturers, the primary customers are large pharmacy chains and group purchasers for independent pharmacies. This highly concentrated and price-sensitive pharmacy demand creates incentives for generics to compete on price. If the 1984 Hatch-Waxman Act opened the door to cheap and prompt generic entry in the United States, generic substitution programs adopted by PBMs, HMOs, and Medicaid in the late 1980s and 1990s stimulated generic market shares while MAC reimbursement drives generic price competition. Masson and Steiner (1985) show that for a sample of thirty-seven multisource drugs in 1980, pharmacists obtained the generic at an average price of 45 percent lower than the brand, but the difference at retail was only 24.3 percent, because the pharmacist retained a higher average absolute margin on the generics (Masson and Steiner 1985). Similarly, Grabowski and Vernon (1996) show that for fifteen drugs whose patents expired between 1984 and 1987, the average absolute margin was roughly 40 percent higher on the generic. More recent anecdotal reports confirm that pharmacy margins are higher on generics than on on-patent brands.

Most studies of generic drug markets focus on the effects of the 1984 Hatch-Waxman Act on generic entry and on the effect of generics on prices, promotional activity, and market shares of brand drugs. Since market conditions have evolved in the 1990s with the growth of managed drug benefits, the findings of these studies should be viewed as context dependent. Grabowski and Vernon (1992), using data on patent expirations that spanned the 1984 Act, find that generic prices were significantly inversely related to number of generic competitors, but some brand prices increased after generic entry (Grabowski and Vernon 1992). Frank and Salkever (1992) show that a brand manufacturer may rationally increase the brand price following generic entry, as a response to market segmentation in which generics attract the price elastic consumers, leaving the brand with the price-inelastic, brand-loyal consumers (Frank and Salkever 1992). Brand advertising may decrease, since much of the benefit accrues to generics due to substitution; conversely, generics have no incentive to advertise if they are viewed as substitutable.

Caves, Whinston, and Hurwitz (1991) analyze postpatent pricing and promotion for thirty drugs whose patents expired between 1976 and 1987 (Caves et al. 1991). They find significant reduction in brand promotion even before patent expiration. The net effect of less promotion and lower generic prices is that quantity sold does not increase significantly after patent expiration, despite a lower weighted average price for the molecule. All of these studies underestimate generic penetration since the growth of managed drug benefits in the 1990s. Whereas Caves, Whinston, and Hurwitz (1991) find that pharmacists were quite conservative in exercising their right to substitute a generic, for recent patent expirations the originator may lose over 80 percent of the market within several weeks of patent expiry in the United States.

In summary, conclusions on competition in the brand and generic pharmaceutical industries depend on the context, in particular, of the insurance arrangements, reimbursement and price regulatory structure and resulting incentives for physicians, pharmacies, and patients, which interact to determine manufacturer demand elasticities, and hence optimal manufacturer pricing strategies. Similarly, estimates of demand elasticities depend on the context, including such factors as whether the drug is on patent or generic, whether the measure of price is the copayment to the patient, the full transaction price to the payer, or a list price, and on relevant pharmacy and physician incentives.

7.6.3 Forms of Price and Reimbursement Regulation

Design of the optimal structure of price regulation or other controls on pharmaceutical spending is a complex problem. The one clear conclusion is that no country has an ideal solution. As noted earlier, market power of pharmaceuticals derives from patents and from comprehensive insurance coverage, hence standard regulatory models of price regulation for natural monopolies are inappropriate. Standard models of optimal insurance contracts are also inadequate. These tend to focus on the design of consumer copayments to constrain moral hazard (Ma and Riordan 2002; Pauly 1968; Zeckhauser 1970). Because higher copayments reduce financial protection, optimal copayments for drugs may be too low to provide much constraint on pricing, especially for chronic and expensive drugs, given the concentration of spending by patients with multiple prescriptions. Optimal provider cost sharing has been analyzed for physician and hospital services but not for pharmaceuticals (Ellis and McGuire 1993). Moreover, the optimal insurance/reimbursement contract for drugs must deter not only insurance-induced overuse by patients/physicians, but also excessive prices by manufacturers, while paying prices sufficient to reward appropriate R&D, taking into account the global scope of pharmaceutical sales. Recent papers have developed pricing models that in theory simultaneously achieve static and dynamic efficiency (Lackdawalla and Sood 2009; Danzon, Towse, and Ferrandiz 2013).

In practice, the structure of pharmaceutical price and reimbursement regulation differs across countries and continually evolves (Kanavos et al. 2011). This review focuses on the main prototypes and evidence of their effects. As noted earlier, regulation usually applies only if the drug is reimbursed. Effectively, the regulated price is the maximum reimbursement; it may also (but need not) be the maximum price that the firm may charge to insured patients.

Direct Price Limits

Under direct price regulation, as used in France, Italy, Spain, Japan, and so forth, the initial launch price and any price increases must be approved as a condition of reimbursement, and price decreases may be mandated. Most countries use one or both of two criteria in setting prices: (1) comparison with other, established drugs in the same class, with potential markups for improved efficacy, better side-effect profile or convenience, and sometimes for local production (hereafter "internal benchmarking"); and (2) comparison with the price of the identical product in other countries (hereafter "external benchmarking").[17]

Internal Benchmarking.   Effects of regulation through internal benchmarking differ depending on the details of each country's system, including markups for innovation and other factors. Hypothesized effects of price regulation on supply decisions include: adjustments to the price profile (Anis and

---

17. Although some countries, including Italy, have attempted to base prices on costs, this approach is not widely used because of the difficulty of obtaining accurate measurement of costs. Measuring R&D cost is particularly problematic, because it occurs over many years, includes the cost of failures and foregone interest, and is largely a joint cost that must be allocated across global markets. In practice, price regulation based on costs has relied on transfer pricing rules that were designed for tax purposes, not price regulation.

Wen 1998); distortions of R&D level and focus; and distortions of location of R&D and/or manufacturing plants, if prices are related to investment in the local economy.

If postlaunch price increases are not permitted, a drug's real price declines over its life cycle. Consequently, if follow-on products are benchmarked to an old drug, the real launch price declines for successive entrants in a class. This downward trend of prices over the life cycle is most extreme in Japan, where physicians traditionally dispense drugs and capture any margin between a drug's reimbursement and its acquisition cost. In such contexts, manufacturers have an incentive to discount the acquisition price in order to increase the physician's margin and hence gain market share.[18] The Japanese government audits acquisition prices biannually and reduces the reimbursement price to leave only a 1 to 2 percent margin, until the next rounds of competitive price cuts. This system of declining postlaunch prices allegedly traditionally created incentives for Japanese pharmaceutical firms to focus their R&D on frequent, minor improvements of existing products in order to obtain higher prices, rather than invest in the major innovations necessary to achieve global competitiveness.[19]

Such price regulatory systems are also widely alleged to be used to promote industrial policy, by rewarding locally produced products with higher prices, despite the 1989 EU Transparency Directive, which requires that regulations be "transparent" and neutral with respect to country of origin. Such biased regulation creates incentives for nonoptimal location and/or an excessive number of manufacturing plants, if these excessive production costs are "offset" by higher prices (Danzon and Percy 1999).

Although secondary (processing and packaging) manufacturing facilities may plausibly be located disproportionately in countries that reward domestic manufacturing through their regulated prices, the opposite charge is made with respect to R&D. Specifically, the pharmaceutical industry sometimes argues that price regulation discourages investment in R&D, due to low and uncertain prices in countries that regulate prices. In theory, price regulation could reduce R&D due to both the incentive effect of lower expected profits and the financing effect of lower retained earnings. It is empirically true that most R&D is located in countries with relatively free pricing, mainly the United States and the United Kingdom. However, the causal relationship is unclear. In theory, given the potentially global market for innovative drugs, and extensive in- and out-licensing networks that enable small firms

18. Similar incentives existed in the United States under Medicare B, which, until 2005, paid for physician-dispensed drugs based on a percent of average wholesale price (AWP). Since physicians captured the margin between AWP and their acquisition cost, manufacturers could increase physicians' financial incentives by discounting the acquisition price.

19. Thomas (1996) discusses other factors, including weak efficacy requirements for drug approval, that may have contributed to the relatively weak international competitiveness of Japan's pharmaceutical industry, compared to its prowess in other high technology industries.

to reach global markets regardless of their location, there is no necessary connection between domestic price regulation and firms' location of R&D. Access to world-class scientific research and a large pool of human capital may be more critical. As governments in many countries are establishing tax subsidies to try to attract pharmaceutical and biotechnology R&D, more may be learned about the relative importance of financial versus other factors in R&D location.

External Benchmarking.   Whereas internal benchmarking compares the price of the new drug to the prices of competitor products in the domestics, external benchmarking uses as the comparator the mean, median, or minimum price of the same drug in a designated set of countries. For example, Italy uses an average European price, Canada uses the median of seven countries (five European countries plus the United States and Japan), and so forth.

External benchmarking limits the manufacturer's ability to price discriminate across countries. Predicted effects include convergence in the manufacturer's target launch prices across linked markets, with launch delays and nonlaunch becoming an optimal strategy in low-price countries, particularly those with small markets. Parallel trade, which is legal in the EU, has similar effects to external referencing, except that it generally only affects a fraction of a product's sales. Several studies provide evidence consistent with these predictions (Danzon and Epstein 2012; Danzon, Wang, and Wang 2005; Kyle 2007; Lanjouw 2005).

Welfare effects of regulatory pressures for price convergence across countries are theoretically ambiguous but likely to be negative. Analyses of price discrimination versus uniform pricing show that price discrimination increases static efficiency if output increases. That differential pricing increases drug use seems plausible, given the evidence of delays and nonlaunch of new drugs in low price countries. Moreover, Ramsey pricing principles suggest that differential pricing also contributes to dynamic efficiency (Baumol and Bradford 1970; Ramsey 1927).[20] So far, external referencing and parallel trade apply mostly between countries at fairly similar levels of income, notably within Europe. Welfare losses would likely be much larger if referencing or importation were authorized directly between high-and low-income countries, or indirectly via middle-income countries. The proposed US Health Security Act of 1994 would have limited drug prices in the United States to the lowest prices in a group of twenty-two other countries, including several with much lower incomes than the United States. More recently, the United States has enacted a proposal to legalize drug importation from a broad group of countries, but implementation is stalled because

20. For analysis of differential pricing in the context of developing countries, see Danzon and Towse (2003, 2005); Jack and Lanjouw (2003).

required safety and savings conditions have not been met. Aside from the safety issues raised by drug importation, linking the dominant US market to other smaller, lower income markets could have serious negative effects on price and availability of drugs in those countries. From a global welfare perspective, forms of price regulation that are country specific are likely to yield lower welfare loss than regulatory systems that attempt to control one country's prices by referencing prices or importing drugs from other countries.

Reference Price Reimbursement Limits

Some countries, including Germany, the Netherlands, and New Zealand, have established reference price (RP) reimbursement systems that limit the reimbursement for drugs in designated groups but leave prices uncontrolled. Under RP, products are clustered for reimbursement based on either the same compound (generic referencing) or different compounds with similar mode of action and/or same indication (therapeutic referencing). All products in a group are reimbursed the same price per daily dose—the reference price (RP). The RP is usually set at the price of, say the cheapest (or the median, the thirtieth percentile, etc.) of drugs in the group. Manufacturers may charge prices above the RP, but patients must pay any excess. In practice, manufacturers typically drop their prices to the reference price, suggesting that demand is highly elastic when patients must pay.

Reference price reimbursement resembles price regulation with internal benchmarking to similar products, but with critical differences that make RP potentially more constraining. First, whereas informal benchmarking may permit higher reimbursement for drugs with superior efficacy or fewer side effects, under RP the reimbursement is the same per daily dose, for all products in a group, and obtaining higher reimbursement for a more effective drug requires establishing a separate class within the same therapeutic category. The RP classification system is therefore critical, and assignment of individual drugs is often litigated. Second, therapeutic RP systems typically cluster compounds without regard to patent status. Consequently, if the RP is based on the cheapest product in the cluster, once one patent expires and generic entry occurs, reimbursement for all products in the group drops to the generic price, thereby effectively truncating patent life for the newer products in the group, unless patients are willing to pay surcharges. The greater the magnitude of this patent-truncating effect, the broader the definition of reimbursement clusters and the more price competitive the generic market. Therapeutic RP is predicted to reduce incentives for R&D in general, if the patent-truncating effect is large. Negative effects on R&D incentives are likely to be greatest for follow-on products or line extensions of existing drugs. Whether any such reduction would be welfare enhancing, by eliminating wasteful R&D, or welfare reducing, by eliminating potentially cost-effective new drugs and reducing competition in a class, is obviously context specific and cannot be predicted a priori. More generally, because incentives for R&D depend on global expected revenues, the effects of RP so far are not expected to be large because so far no major market has long experience with therapeutic RP. Thus the experience to date is insufficient to predict the likely effects on R&D if the United States, with its large share of global revenues and highly price-competitive generic market, were to adopt therapeutic RP (Danzon and Ketcham 2003).

Although Germany adopted RP for some classes starting in 1989, new patented drugs were exempt from 1996 to 2004. Moreover, in interpreting the German experience with RP and extrapolating to other countries such as the United States, it is important to note that generic prices are lower, both absolutely and relative to brand prices, in the United States than in Germany.[21] Moreover, Germany—like all other countries with RP or price regulation—adopted multiple price and spending controls simultaneously. Identifying the separate effects of RP and other constraints is therefore problematic.

The early literature on RP is summarized in Lopez-Casasnovas and Puig-Junoy (2000). Early evidence from Germany confirmed that brand drugs generally dropped their prices when RP was introduced, as theory predicts. However, both theory and evidence suggest that dynamic price competition over time is weak under RP, because firms have no incentive to reduce prices below the RP, unless other provisions make pharmacists price sensitive. Zweifel and Crivelli (1996) analyze firms' response to RP using a duopoly model; however, since RP generally applies to classes with multiple products, oligopoly or monopolistic competition models may be more relevant (Zweifel and Crivelli 1996). Danzon and Ketcham (2003) provide empirical evidence on effects of RP in Germany, the Netherlands, and New Zealand, the three most comprehensive RP systems (Danzon and Ketcham 2003). This evidence suggests that RP had little effect on average drug prices or drug availability in Germany or the Netherlands, but that effects on prices and availability were significant in New Zealand, which used broader classes and where the regulatory agency explicitly required RP-reducing price cuts as a condition of admitting new drugs to reimbursement.

In theory, since RP limits only the insurer's reimbursement, patients may be willing to pay a surcharge if a drug truly offers greater therapeutic benefits. But patients may be imperfectly informed about the risks and benefits of individual drugs, and physicians may be reluctant to spend the

21. In Germany, pharmacies were required to dispense the brand prescribed by the physician and could substitute a generic only if the script was written by generic name. Until 2004, German pharmacies were paid a percentage of the price of the drug they dispensed, hence they had neither legal authority nor financial incentive to seek out cheaper generics. Not surprisingly, in this system generics competed on brand rather than price, and generic prices were relatively high, compared to US generic prices (Danzon and Furukawa 2003). In 2006 German sick funds began contracting directly with generic suppliers in order to obtain lower generic prices.

time required to inform patients, since such time is unreimbursed and may have a significant opportunity cost. Some manufacturers may choose to charge prices above the RP, despite high demand elasticities, to avoid price spillovers to other markets. For example, when British Columbia adopted RP, some manufacturers retained prices above the RP, plausibly to avoid undermining potentially higher prices in other Canadian provinces. If manufacturers do charge surcharges, patients may face significant copayments, with possible effects on drug choice and health outcomes. The evidence on patient health outcomes under RP is mixed: some studies find no evidence of adverse effects, while others find an increase in adverse outcomes, possibly because patients switched to less appropriate drugs to avoid surcharges. The risks of such adverse effects depend on the degree of substitutability between drugs, which varies across therapeutic classes. For this reason, Australia and British Columbia only apply RP to a select set of therapeutic classes in which drugs are considered highly substitutable for most patients. PBMs in the United States rarely use therapeutic RP, preferring the more flexible tiered formularies.

Drug Budgets and Expenditure Controls

Price or reimbursement controls alone do not control the growth of drug spending, which is also driven by prescription volume and "mix"; that is, switching from older, cheaper drugs to newer, higher priced drugs. Most countries that initially controlled only price or reimbursement have added other measures to limit total drug spending. Specifically, from 1993 to 2003, Germany had a drug budget (limit on aggregate spending), with physicians and the pharmaceutical industry nominally at risk for successive tiers of any overrun. Physicians responded initially by reducing the number of prescriptions and switching to cheaper drugs, leading to a 16 percent reduction in drug spending in the first year of the budget (Münnich and Sullivan 1994). Schulenburg and Schöffski (1994) report that referrals to specialists and hospitals increased, because the drug budget excluded inpatient drugs (Schulenburg and Schöffski 1993; Schulenburg and Schöffski 1994). Thus the overall budget saving was less than the saving in outpatient drug costs. Germany's aggregate drug budget was abolished in 2003, because enforcing the repayment of overruns was practically and politically problematic. Some regions have adopted physician-specific budgets. Whether payers have sufficient information to achieve appropriate risk adjustment of physician-specific budgets based on each physician's patient population remains to be seen—if not, such controls could create incentives for physicians to avoid high-risk patients and/or constrain their drug choices. France has a limit on total drug spending that is enforced by limits on each company's revenues. Overruns are recouped by price cuts or mandatory rebates on companies and therapeutic classes that exceed allowed targets, and on companies that exceed promotion guidelines. Similarly, since 2001 Italy limits drug spending to 13 percent of health spending; overruns have been recouped by price cuts in major therapeutic classes.

Since expenditure caps that are enforced by price cuts imply a price-volume trade-off for manufacturers, one potential—and intended—effect is to reduce manufacturers' incentives to expand volume through promotion. However, penalties that apply collectively to all firms have only weak effects on firm-specific incentives in the absence of collusion. Company-specific revenue limits, as in France, create more powerful incentives to constrain promotion but also undermine incentives for R&D. As with price and reimbursement controls, these R&D incentive effects are negligible as long as controls apply in markets that are a small share of global revenue. Such effects would be more significant if drug spending caps enforced by price-volume offsets were adopted in the United States or EU-wide.

Profit or Rate-of-Return Controls

The United Kingdom is unique among industrialized countries in regulating the rate of return on capital, leaving manufacturers (relatively) free to set the price of individual drugs. The UK Prescription Price Regulation Scheme (PPRS) is renegotiated every five years between the patented pharmaceutical industry and the government. The PPRS limits each company's revenues from sales to the UK National Health Service as a percentage of their capital invested in the United Kingdom, with specified limits on deductible expenses to preempt incentives for expense padding. The allowed rate of return is around 17 to 21 percent; excesses can be repaid directly or through lower prices the following year. Companies with minimal capital in the United Kingdom can substitute a return-on-sales formula.

One simple theory predicts that pure rate-of-return regulation induces excessive capital investments relative to labor and hence reduces productivity, although these predictions only hold under restrictive assumptions (Averch and Johnson 1962; Joskow 1974). For multinational companies, the costs of distortions may be small if capital in manufacturing plants can be allocated across countries at a relatively low cost in order to maximize revenues. Such flexibility may become more constrained as more regulatory systems link their prices or reimbursement to local investment. In a study of the effects of such biased regulatory schemes in the United Kingdom, France, and Italy on labor productivity and total factor productivity, Danzon and Percy (1999) found that although the rate of growth of capital and labor in the UK pharmaceutical industry has been high, relative to other UK industry and relative to pharmaceuticals in other countries, it has not been biased toward capital relative to labor, possibly because the permitted company-specific rate of return on capital may partly depend on employment levels (Danzon and Percy 1999). Overall, the United Kingdom experienced relatively high total factor productivity growth, compared to other regulated and unregulated countries.

With respect to effects on drug prices, the United Kingdom is generally considered to have higher brand prices than those in the regulated markets of France, Italy, and Spain. Consistent with this, the United Kingdom has a relatively large parallel import share, whereas the price regulated markets of France, Italy, and Spain are parallel exporters. However, precise price differentials are sensitive to the sample of drugs, the time period, and the exchange rate (Danzon and Chao 2000b; Danzon and Furukawa 2003, 2008). The United Kingdom's overall spending on drugs, either as a share of health spending or per capita, is not out of line with other EU countries, plausibly reflecting other characteristics of their health care system, including strong pharmacy incentives for generic substitution and physician reimbursement that creates incentives for cost-conscious prescribing.[22] The UK pharmaceutical industry has also contributed more significantly to the flow of new medicines than most other countries of comparable size. Nevertheless, following a recent review of the PPRS the UK Office of Fair Trade recommended that the United Kingdom move to a system of "value-based pricing" regulation, in place of profit regulation (Office of Fair Trade 2007). Details of this approach remain to be determined.

Cost-Effectiveness Requirements

Australia, Canada, New Zealand, and the United Kingdom require a formal review of the cost-effectiveness of a new drug as a condition of reimbursement by national health systems; in other countries, such data are used as input to price negotiations. For example, in 1999 the United Kingdom established the National Institute for Clinical Excellence (NICE) to review the efficacy and cost of technologies expected to have major health or budgetary impact, including drugs, relative to current treatment, using standard metrics of the cost per quality-adjusted life year (QALY). Cost reflects not only the price of the drug but also associated medical costs, such as reduced inpatient days or doctor visits. A similar expert body to review clinical effectiveness and now cost-effectiveness was established in Germany in 2004 and made part of a formal price approval system in 2010. Many other countries in the EU and elsewhere are adopting some review of outcomes evidence as part of price and reimbursement regulation. Regulating prices indirectly through a review of cost-effectiveness is in theory more consistent with principles of efficient resource allocation than the other criteria for regulating drug prices reviewed here (Danzon, Towse, and Ferrandiz 2013). In practice, such approaches are only as sound as the data and judgment used in implementation, of course. Still, the rapidly growing body of methodological and

22. Primary care physicians in the United Kingdom are organized into primary care groups, by locality. Each group must serve all residents in its area and receives a global budget for their costs. Thus, spending more on drugs means less money for other services. Physicians are trained to prescribe generically and pharmacists in the United Kingdom can profit from substituting generics for brands, if the script is generically written.

empirical literature on the measurement of cost-effectiveness offers some hope that this approach could provide one cornerstone to a more theoretically sound framework for drug price regulation.

7.6.4 Effects of Regulation on Prices

Cross-national comparisons of drug prices vary significantly, depending on the time period, sample of drugs used, the price index methodology used—including unit for measuring price (grams, units, daily doses), consumption weights, and exchange rates. Most price comparisons have been biased by use of very small, nonrandom samples including only branded drugs, and have not adhered to standard index number methods (GAO 1992; GAO 1994). The exclusive focus on branded drugs tends to bias comparisons in favor of countries with strict price regulation. Regulation and competition are to some degree substitutes: less regulated markets tend to have higher brand prices but larger generic market shares and lower priced generics. Overall, countries that use direct price controls do not consistently have lower prices than countries that use other indirect means to constrain prices (Danzon and Chao 2000a, 2000b; Danzon and Furukawa 2003, 2006). However, comparisons are very sensitive to the sample of drugs, weights, exchange rate, and prices used.

7.6.5 Price Regulation: Lessons Learned and Future Research

The research of the 1960s, 1970s, and early 1980s focused on effects of regulation of market access, focusing more on measuring the costs of launch delay, with less success in measuring any benefits from reduced risks or more appropriate drug use. In the 1990s regulatory change has focused on the design of price regulatory systems, first to control prices and subsequently to control total drug spending, while preserving access for patients and incentives for R&D. In theory, optimal design of insurance and price regulatory systems would ideally achieve appropriate use of existing drugs prices that strike a reasonable balance between short-run spending control and incentives for R&D for the future (Garber, Jones, and Romer 2006, Lackdawalla and Sood 2009; Danzon, Towse, and Ferrandiz 2013). The evidence in practice focuses on specific short-run impacts of particular regulatory regimes.

In theory, reimbursement limits that are based on cost-effectiveness offer more efficient incentives for R&D and for drug choices than price regulation using ad hoc internal benchmarking or reference price reimbursement. Under CE, more effective/safer drugs can charge higher prices and still be cost-effective relative to less effective/less safe drugs. Moreover, if costs and effects are measured using appropriate guidelines, decisions can in theory reflect all relevant social costs and benefits and be more consistent across drugs than is likely with ad hoc price regulation. More appropriate regulatory mechanisms for reviewing prices could provide better incentives for both R&D and for prescribing.

Although CE offers a more appropriate criterion for drug price review than other widely used criteria, important details remain unresolved. One concern is that the data available for evaluating cost-effectiveness at launch are based on controlled, prelaunch clinical trials, which may not accurately reflect the costs or effects of a drug in actual usage in broad patient populations. Updating the CE analysis with postlaunch data from actual use is increasingly feasible, as databases become more comprehensive and statistical methods improve for dealing with potential nonrandom treatment assignments. A second controversial issue with use of cost-effectiveness analysis arises if the manufacturer is permitted to charge the maximum price at which a drug is cost-effective for a given, payer-specific CE threshold. This enables the manufacturer to capture the full social surplus from the innovation, at least for the period of the patent, which is consistent with dynamic efficiency but may be politically unacceptable. Third, the methodology for measuring effectiveness (QALYs or some other measure) and the threshold value for incremental cost-effectiveness remain contentious. Nevertheless, review of cost-effectiveness is becoming a necessary condition for reimbursement in an increasing number of countries, often supplementing rather than replacing other price and expenditure controls.

7.6.6   Profitability and Rates of Return

The pharmaceutical industry is widely perceived to earn excessive profits. Accurate measurement of profits using standard accounting data is problematic for pharmaceuticals because capital investments are primarily intangible R&D investments made over twelve years prior to drug launch, with value over a product life of ten to fifteen years in global markets. Several methods have been used to measure profitability. One approach attempts to adjust accounting rates of return to better account for investments in intangible capital of R&D and promotion. Standard accounting practices treat R&D and promotion spending as current expenses rather than as investments in intangible capital. This leads to upward bias in accounting rates of return for industries with relatively high intangible investments. Clarkson (1996) illustrates the effects of these adjustments for firms in fourteen industries for the period 1980 to 1993 (Clarkson 1996). Before adjustment, the average accounting rate of return on equity for the fourteen industries is 12.3 percent; the pharmaceutical industry has the highest return of 24.4 percent. After adjustment for intangible capital, the average is 10.2 percent, compared to 13.3 percent for pharmaceuticals, which is less than the adjusted return for petroleum, computer software, and foods.

A second approach uses the Lerner index of price relative to marginal production cost. Caves, Whinston, and Hurwitz (1991) estimate the ratio of the price of originator drugs relative to generic price several years after patent (a proxy for marginal cost) at roughly 5. However, this price ratio at patent expiry overstates the average Lerner index over the life cycle in the United

States because prices of originator drugs rise and marginal costs decline with time since launch. More fundamentally, a one-year Lerner index based on short-run marginal production cost in one country is both theoretically and empirically inadequate as a measure of profit for global products with high and long-lived R&D investments.

A third—and conceptually more correct approach—measures the rate of return on investment in a cohort of drugs, using discounted cash flow estimates of costs and returns. Grabowski and Vernon (1990, 1996, 2002) estimate the return on R&D for new drugs introduced in the 1970s, early 1980s, and 1990s, respectively (Grabowski, Vernon, and DiMasi 2002; Grabowski and Vernon 1996). Market sales data for the United States are used to estimate a twenty-year sales profile, with extrapolation to global sales using a foreign sales multiplier. Applying a contribution margin to net out other, non-R&D costs yields a life cycle profile for net revenue, which is discounted to present value at launch using the estimated real cost of capital (10 to 11 percent). This NPV of net revenues is compared to the estimated average capitalized cost of R&D per NCE, at launch. Grabowski and Vernon conclude that the 1970s drug cohort on average earned a return roughly equal to their cost of capital; the 1980s cohort on average yielded a positive net present value of $22.2 million, or an internal rate of return of 11.1 percent, compared to the 10.5 percent cost of capital. Similarly, results for the 1990s cohort show a small, positive excess return. Given the large number of assumption, confidence intervals are not reported. In all three time periods, the returns distribution is highly skewed, such that only the top 30 percent of drugs cover the average R&D cost. This extreme result would be mitigated if the distribution of revenues were compared to the distribution of R&D costs, rather than to a single mean R&D cost per NCE, but the overall result would remain. An important implication of this skewed distribution of returns is that regulatory strategies that target these "blockbuster" drugs while on patent could significantly reduce expected average returns and hence reduce incentives for R&D. By contrast, a competitive regulatory environment that permits high prices for patented drugs but then promotes generic competition after patent expiry has a much less negative effect on incentives for R&D, because loss in sales revenue that occurs late in the product life is more heavily discounted.

Although this cohort rate-of-return approach in theory provides the most accurate measure of returns to R&D, it is arguably of limited relevance for policy in an industry with low barriers but long lead times for entry and high unpredictability of science and market risk. In the absence of significant barriers to entry to R&D for new firms, if the expected return on R&D exceeded the cost of capital, competitive entry would occur until the excess expected profit is eliminated. Such competitive adjustments may not be instantaneous, due to risks and time lags in R&D, and the actual realization of returns may differ radically from that anticipated due to changes in market and regulatory conditions. But if the assumption of dynamic competition with free entry is correct—and all the evidence suggests that it is—then if analysts were to estimate that returns either exceeded or fell short of the cost of capital over a particular time period, this would either reflect measurement error or market disequilibrium that will be corrected by competitive entry, rendering the analyst's estimate obsolete.

Since the evidence indicates extensive competitive entry to exploit R&D opportunities and hence that dynamic competition should reduce expected profits to competitive levels, the more important policy question is whether the resulting rate of R&D yields a level and mix of new drugs that is socially optimal. In this model, changes in the regulatory and reimbursement environment may affect profitability in the short run. But in the long run, the rate and mix of R&D readjusts such that normal returns are realized on average. Whether the resulting R&D expenditures entail significant duplicative investment is an important issue. Henderson and Cockburn (1996) provide some evidence against this hypothesis, but not a definitive rejection. The current trend of payers to demand evidence of cost-effectiveness relative to existing drugs as a condition for reimbursement reinforces incentives for manufacturers to target R&D toward innovative therapies and away from imitative drugs (Henderson and Cockburn 1996). The great ex ante uncertainty as to the ultimate therapeutic value and timing of new drugs implies that ex post realizations will still yield some "me-too" drugs. Even the optimal number of me-toos is uncertain, given their value as a competitive constraint and in improving therapies for some subsets of patients. Although product differentiation can be excessive in models of monopolistic competition or oligopoly, in the pharmaceutical industry any such excess more likely results from generous insurance coverage and high reimbursed prices, rather than firm strategies to use endogenous investments in R&D or marketing as an (unsuccessful) entry barrier.

7.6.7   Industry Structure and Productivity: Regulation or Technology?

Several studies have examined the effects of regulation and other factors on industry structure. Grabowski (1976) and Grabowski and Vernon (1978) suggest that regulation-induced increases in R&D cost and risk created scale economies that resulted in the concentration of innovation in large firms. Temin (1979) analyzed the impact of regulatory and technological change on the structure of the US pharmaceutical industry from 1948 to 1973. He concludes that the size of drug firms increased dramatically during this period with much of the growth concentrated in large firms. Thomas (1990) shows that the decline in NCE introductions around 1962 was concentrated in the smallest firms, many of which ceased R&D. Thomas (1996) extends the argument that strict safety and efficacy regulation in the United States and United Kingdom led to a shakeout of smaller, less innovative firms and concentration of innovative effort in larger firms (Thomas 1996).

However, since the late 1980s and 1990s the biotechnology and genomics revolutions appear to have eliminated the advantages of size, at least for drug discovery. Over the last decade innovation has occurred increasingly in small firms, despite increasing R&D cost and risk. These trends have dramatically changed the structure of the pharmaceutical-biotechnology industry. Previously, the chemistry basis of drug discovery implied an advantage for large firms that had large proprietary libraries of compounds, often created by their in-house chemists. Now, the basis for drug discovery has shifted to microbiology and associated sciences, with comparative advantage in smaller firms that are often spun out from academic research centers. Large firms have continued to grow larger, mostly by acquiring other large firms in horizontal mergers or acquiring biotechnology companies or in-licensing their compounds, in quasi-vertical acquisitions. However, even the largest manufacturer (Pfizer, by global revenues in 2011) accounted for less than 10 percent of total sales (across both generic and branded manufacturers). The FTC monitors the effect of mergers on competition within therapeutic categories, requiring merging firms to divest overlapping products if concentration would be unacceptably high.

Although firms have often rationalized their horizontal mergers on grounds of economies of scale and scope in R&D, the empirical evidence does not support the claims and in fact R&D productivity of large firms has declined relative to smaller firms (Danzon, Epstein, and Nicholson 2004). A growing share of new drug approvals is originated by smaller firms, including not only biologics but also some chemistry-based drugs. Conversely, large firms rely increasingly on in-licensing—both research tools and target compounds—from smaller firms. Initially these start-up small firms specialize in discovery research, sometimes forming alliances with larger firms that provide funding and expertise for late-stage clinical trials and marketing, where experience and size play a greater role (Danzon, Nicholson, and Pereira 2005b). The growth of contract research, sales, and manufacturing organizations has increased the outsourcing opportunities for small firms and hence reduced their need to rely on larger, more experienced partners. Many small firms also purchase human capital expertise, by hiring experienced personnel from larger firms. A growing number of biotechnology firms have fully integrated capabilities, with Genentech and Amgen being the most successful. Thus if, as earlier studies suggest, the 1962 regulatory changes did contribute to increased industry concentration and disadvantage small firms, the regulatory changes of the 1990s do not appear to have harmed small firms, and technological change has certainly benefited them. Moreover, competition for promising products developed by smaller discovery firms is strong and prices paid for such products have risen over the last decade, reflecting the shifting of bargaining power from large to smaller firms (Longman 2004, 2006).

It might be argued that the high rate of new start-ups in this industry reflects excessive entry as firms compete for profits in a differentiated products oligopoly, that such entry is welfare reducing due to the repeated initial costs associated with achieving reasonable scale. However, the great majority of new start-ups are formed around new technologies, which face great scientific uncertainty that can only be resolved by preclinical and clinical testing, which takes time. The rate of discovery of new technologies is driven in part by NIH funding of basic research and the incentives under the Bayh Dole Act (1980) to commercialize such research, and possibly by favorable tax treatment of R&D, especially for orphan drugs. Whether or not NIH funding to basic research is excessive or suboptimal is an important subject for research. Thus in the current environment it does not appear that regulation of market access or endogenous investments in sunk R&D costs are major contributors to excessive product differentiation or monopoly power, with the possible exception of orphan drugs that by design receive five years of market exclusivity.

However, it is plausible that health insurance coverage for modestly differentiated on-patent drugs, when cheap generics are available for off-patent, therapeutic substitutes, contributes to product differentiation through slightly differentiated molecules and new formulations. Whether insurance creates incentives for excessive product differentiation, including extensions and new formulations, and/or reduces cross-price demand elasticities is an important subject for future research.

7.7   Promotion

7.7.1   Trends in Promotion

Promotion by manufacturers is an important mechanism whereby physicians, consumers, and payers learn about drugs. In 2008 the industry spent $20.5 billion on US promotion, or 10.8 percent of US sales—similar to several other experience-good industries with significant product differentiation such as toys and cosmetics (Frank et al. 2002; Berndt 2005, 2007; CBO 2009).[23] This estimate of total promotion spending omits the promotion-related components of pre- and postlaunch clinical trials and also excludes free samples distributed to physicians for patient use. Other, higher estimates of promotion spending include samples valued at either a list price or a retail price that significantly exceeds the economic cost to manufacturers (Berndt 2007).[24] In 2008, physician detailing accounted for $12.5 billion,

23. For 2003, the reported promotion spending in the United States is less than the spending on R&D of $34.5 billion (PhRMA 2005); however, this country-specific measure of R&D-to-sales is imprecise for multinational firms with global sales, but R&D concentrated in at most a few countries.

24. A more accurate measure of the true cost of samples to firms lies somewhere between the marginal production cost and the actual price the manufacturer might have received, had the patient filled the prescription and paid for the drug.

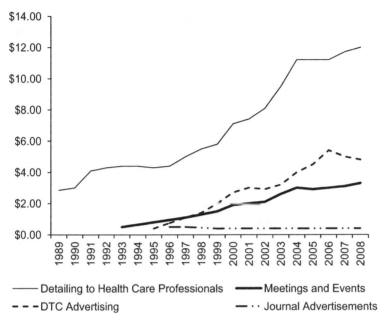

Fig. 7.9   Promotional spending, 1989–2008
Sources: Congressional Budget Office (2009); SDI; author estimates.

direct-to-consumer advertising accounted for $4.2 billion, industry/medical meetings $3.4 billion, and medical journal advertising approximately totaled $400 million (see figure 7.9; CBO 2009).

Direct-to-consumer advertising (DTCA) grew most rapidly, from just $12 million in 1989 and $791 million in 1996—prior to the 1997 FDA reinterpretation of the guidelines for broadcast DTCA—to a peak of $5.2 billion in 2006. DTC expenditure decreased, in part as many of the blockbuster drugs that it supported lost patent protection, and declined to $4.3 billion as of 2008 (Berndt 2005; CBO 2009; Palumbo and Mullins 2002). DTCA is concentrated on the leading drugs in therapeutic categories that are particularly amenable to patient awareness and choice. For example, in 2008 spending for the top ten drugs accounted for 30 percent of all DTCA, but detail spending on the top ten drugs comprised just 16 percent of all detail spent. According to CBO data, the top ten therapeutic categories for DTCA in 2008 were for erectile disfunction, bone resorption inhibitors, sleep aids (nonbarbitutes), autoimmune treatments, statins, SNRI antidepressents, antiplatelet agents, seizure disorders, atypical antipsychotics, and CNS stimulants.

7.7.2   Regulation of Promotion: Background and Issues

As discussed in section 7.3, promotion of prescription drugs in the United States has been regulated by the FDA since the 1962 Amendments, which remains the statutory base guiding the FDA's regulation of promotion to both physicians and consumers. This statute restricts promotional claims to facts established in clinical trials, requires that risks as well as benefits be described in brief summary, and excludes promotion of unapproved indications. The FDA's 1997 guidance relaxed the requirement that the full product label, which includes all known risks, be displayed in broadcast ads. Rather, the requirement for a brief summary of risks and benefits could be provided by giving a website, a toll-free number, or reference to a print ad with the full label, in addition to advice to "see your physician." These changes were deemed to reflect the ways in which consumers currently get information.

The US constitutional right to freedom of speech has been interpreted to include commercial speech and hence to support limits on regulation of promotion by the FDA. The FDA cannot require preclearance of ads; however, once they appear the FDA can require changes, removal, and even dissemination of corrective information. Promotion of information about off-label (unapproved) uses of drugs was not permitted until 1997, when companies were permitted to disseminate peer reviewed publications discussing off-label use. In its oversight of promotion, as for its other activities, the FDA is required by statute to consider risks and benefits; costs are not mentioned. Thus the FDA is concerned with the effects of promotion on patients and physicians; whether or not it results in unnecessary costs is beyond its purview.

In addition to the FDA, regulations at the state, local, health plan, or hospital level affect promotion policy. Within the United States, recent legal challenges and regulations set at the state level seek to increase transparency in provider promotion activities by either limiting the total value of gifts and/or posting all financial transactions on the Internet and restricting the use of pharmaceutical audit data to market drugs as is done in Maine, Vermont, and New Hampshire (Grande 2010; Mello and Messing 2011; Tsai 2003). Proponents of these efforts claim that marketing in its current form leads to excess (static) costs, conflict of interest, and potentially inappropriate use (Grande and Asch 2009). Detractors of the policies emphasize that limitations on interactions with providers can be deleterious to knowledge transfer and potentially lead to suboptimal treatment (Chressanthis et al. 2012). In addition to state laws, numerous academic institutions have restricted or banned promotion within their facilities. As with other industries (e.g., smoking), restrictions in particular forms of advertising over time may simply lead to greater efforts in less-regulated forms of advertising. The recent increase in Internet promotion for both providers and consumers (still a small share of overall spending) likely is partially due to the saturation or increasing regulatory cost associated with more traditional forms of pharmaceutical promotion.

7.7.3   Evidence on Effects of Pharmaceutical Promotion

The pharmaceutical industry's large expenditure on advertising is controversial, with policy concern over both magnitude and form. The economic literature outlines the issues and provides some evidence, but basic questions remain unresolved. The growth of DTCA since 1997, in particular, has prompted research to better understand its effects. The economic rationale for promotion is that it provides information to physicians and consumers about the benefits and risks of drugs, which is necessary for appropriate prescribing and to encourage appropriate patient compliance. Critics contend that much promotional expenditure is in fact designed to persuade rather than inform; that it increases product differentiation, brand loyalty, market power and prices, and that it leads to inappropriate use, including use of high-price, on-patent drugs when cheap generics would be equally effective.

Promotion Studies Pre-1997

An early proponent of the anticompetitive hypothesis, Walker (1971) argues that large promotion expenditures raise entry barriers and increase market power by requiring new entrants to make large outlays in order to attract attention to new products. The alternative view is that advertising may enhance competition by facilitating the introduction of new products and new firms. Schwartzman (1975) finds that more innovative firms spend larger sums on promotion. Telser et al. (1975) finds that the extent of new entry into a therapeutic class is positively related to promotional intensity. However, it is unclear whether this positive correlation indicates that promotion enhances competitive entry or whether both are simply related to unobservable factors such as technological advancement and market potential.

Leffler (1981) estimates a model across therapeutic categories, with selling effort as the dependent variable and the number of new products introduced as the primary explanatory variable. He finds a significant positive effect, which he interprets as suggesting that pharmaceutical advertising is at least partly informative. He also finds evidence, however, that advertising of established pharmaceutical products accomplishes "reminder" and "habit-formation" purposes. These results suggest that the impact of advertising is multidimensional and that the net effect on competition may differ, depending on the circumstances. The distinction drawn by Leffler between the "persuasion" and "information" roles of pharmaceutical promotion is extended and supported by Hurwitz and Caves (1988). Berndt et al. (1995) find that promotional stocks of detailing, journal advertising, and DTCA (pre-1997) significantly affect industry-level demand for antiulcerants, but with diminishing returns, again suggesting the importance of reminder or loyalty-building promotion (Berndt et al. 1995).

Beales (1996) uses the FDA policy restricting manufacturer advertising of unapproved indications as a natural experiment to test the importance of pharmaceutical marketing as a source of information for physicians. He analyzes the impact of promotional activity following FDA approval of second indications for existing drugs on the share of patients treated with the newly approved product, the total fraction of patients treated with drug therapy, and the average price level. He finds some evidence that seller provided information after approval results in increased market share for the new indication as well as lower average price per prescription of other products in the market, suggesting an increase in consumer benefits from increased manufacturer-provided information. However, identifying the impact of FDA approval itself versus promotional expenditures is problematic.

Effects of Direct-to-Consumer Advertising Post-1997

Much of the analysis of DTCA has focused on its effects on drug sales in aggregate and on share of the individual brand. Although some of these studies use state-of-the-art methods applied to the best data available and provide valuable evidence, important issues remain unresolved. This reflects both data and empirical challenges and the difficulty of weighing costs and benefits to drawing overall welfare conclusions.

One major empirical challenge is that DTCA is endogenously determined and just one of several types of a promotion a firm may use. Ignoring the endogeneity of DTCA and its correlation with other (often unobserved) forms of promotion can potentially lead to serious biases in results. For example, both theory and evidence suggest that DTCA is likely to have a higher payoff for best-in-class drugs. This assumes that physicians, as good agents, are more likely to write the prescription for the best-in-class product, even if the patient requests another advertised brand. In that case, an observed positive correlation between promotion and market share may reflect in part these incentives for market leaders to invest more in promotion, leading to upward biased estimates of the reverse effect of promotion on market share. Second, estimates of promotional effects must take into account lagged and future impact on information stocks, as physicians form prescribing habits and patients tend to stay with a particular brand for chronic medications, once they have found a drug that works for them. Third, the net effect of one firm's promotion depends on competitors' strategic responses.

Finally, drawing welfare conclusions from the empirical evidence is particularly problematic. The economic/marketing literature generally views advertising that expands aggregate category sales as more likely to be informative, and hence welfare enhancing, whereas advertising that simply changes market shares without affecting aggregate use is more likely to be wasteful (Berndt 2005; Kravitz 2005). However, in the case of heavily insured pharmaceuticals, for which consumers pay only a small fraction of the cost out of pocket, it is possible that even category-expanding effects could reflect unnecessary use (and/or unnecessarily costly use), even though such purchases are well informed and rational for individual consumers, given their insurance coverage. With these caveats, the main findings from the recent literature are reviewed here (for a more detailed review, see Berndt 2005).

The study of promotional effects in the antihistamine and antiviral categories by Narayanan, Desiraju, and Chintagunta (2004) is unusual in including data on DTCA, detailing, pricing, and other medical spending as alternative marketing mechanisms to influence sales; measuring both the short-and long-run effects of promotion; and estimating cross-firm elasticities. All marketing mix variables are modeled as endogenous. This study finds that, of the four marketing variables, only DTCA has a positive but small effect on aggregate category sales. Each product's own DTCA also positively affects its own brand sales, but interaction effects with other brands' DTCA are negative. Own DTCA and detailing appear to be complements rather than substitutes. The estimated return on investment is lower for DTCA than for detailing, suggesting that firms might gain by reallocating marketing budgets away from DTCA and toward detailing. Although it would be a mistake to generalize the findings of this study, which focused on only two therapeutic categories, it does illustrate the importance of including the full marketing mix and controlling for endogeneity of the marketing variables when estimating the effects of DTCA.[25]

In general, with the important exception of the Narayanan et al. (2004) paper cited earlier, findings from other studies suggest that DTCA has a greater effect on category sales than on individual brand sales (Narayanan et al. 2004). Rosenthal et al. (2003) use data for five large therapeutic categories to estimate effects of DTCA, controlling for sampling and detailing (Rosenthal et al. 2003). They conclude that DTCA has a significant positive impact on class sales, with an average elasticity of roughly .1, but they find no evidence that detailing or DTCA has a significant effect on product-specific market shares.[26] The authors emphasize that failure to find brand-specific effects could reflect learning or unmeasured longer term effects. Wosinska (2002) finds that DTCA for the cholesterol reducing medications (statins) positively affects brand share only if the brand had preferred formulary status (Wosinska 2002). Similarly, Iizuka and Jin (2005b) find that DTCA increases total category sales, but brand-specific share is only significantly shifted by physician promotion such as detailing and journal publications.

25. Narayanan et al. rely on three sets of instruments for price, DTCA, and detailing. Price is instrumented with the pharmaceutical PPI interacted with product dummy variables as well as lagged (three years total) PPI interacted with product dummies (thirty-six instruments for twelve product categories). DTCA is instrumented with the PPI for television, radio, and print advertising. Detailing was instrumented with employment data.
26. Instruments include a quadratic of the drug's remaining patent life, a post-1997 time trend, and the monthly cost of TV advertising.

The authors conclude that a product should hold at least 58 percent market share of its therapeutic category sales in order to recoup DTCA investment (Iizuka and Jin 2005a). In fact, they find that 69 percent of DTCA spending is on drugs with at least a 60 percent market share. They also find that DTCA increases the number of doctor visits at which a drug is prescribed (Iizuka and Jin 2005b), with some differences between patient types in their responsiveness to DTCA (young versus elderly; private versus public insurance). Donohue and Berndt (2004) find that DTCA has no significant effect on choice of product, but that it does motivate individuals to visit the physician. An analysis by Dave and Saffer (2012) focusing on four major therapeutic categories suggests there are positive own-product elasticities for both price and volume, with respect to the DTCA spending, after accounting for physician promotion (Dave and Saffer 2012). On net, early evidence indicated that the stronger effects on expenditures occurred at the category level, but more recent empirical work is suggestive of significant own-product effects.

A randomized control trial by Kravitz (2005) supports the ambiguous conclusions reached in other studies that use observational data on medical care. Standardized patients (who were not sick, but were scripted with dialog to feign depression or adjustment disorder) asked unsuspecting blinded physicians for either A) no medication, B) a generic drug, or C) a specific brand. For both disorders, those who requested were significantly more likely to receive a drug (31% vs. 76% vs. 53% for depression, 10% vs. 39% vs. 55% for adjustment disorder), but not necessarily the suggested drug (in the case of those who requested one). Various conclusions can be drawn from these data, including that there is both over- and undertreatment of depression, and that responses to patient requests differ across physicians. Policy implications for DTCA regulation are therefore very unclear. Moreover, welfare conclusions would also require data on costs and medical outcomes.

The effects of DTCA on quality of care and patients' compliance with prescribed regimens are examined by Donohue (2003) and Wosinska (2004). Donohue (2003) finds that patients in the top quartile of exposure to DTCA had 32 percent higher odds of initiating therapy. Conditional on any therapy, those in the top quartile of DTCA spending also had a 30 percent ($p < .05$) greater probability of adherence (measured as filling at least four prescriptions over the first six months of therapy). Wosinska's examination of the Blue Cross and Blue Shield of California data for adherence to statin regimes finds a minor impact for total DTCA spending, but current and lagged own DTCA has no affect on product adherence (Wosinska 2004). With respect to the potential for inappropriate use stemming from DTC, David, Markowitz, and Richards (2009) find that DTC stock in select therapeutic categories leads to increased adverse event reports (AERs) in select categories (e.g., depression), but appears to have a benign or even positive effect in other therapy areas (e.g., allergy and arthritis). As such, therapy-specific regulation with respect to DTC and safety is likely warranted to ensure that the patient-physician interaction is not disrupted adversely by DTC (David et al. 2009).

Iizuka (2004) finds that high-quality drugs, as defined by whether a drug had "priority" status for FDA approval, have significantly more DTCA spending. The interaction term between the quality dummy variable and a dummy variable indicating that the drug was either first or second to market within a particular class also had positive significance. He also finds that DTCA spending decisions are significantly related to the potential market size but not the currently treated market size—a result that supports the hypothesis that DTCA has positive social value in that it targets consumers who might potentially benefit from medicines rather than those who already take medicines.

7.7.4   International Regulation of Promotion

Several countries include in their price regulation systems features that are designed to discourage promotion. The UK PPRS limits the promotional expenditure that can be deducted as a cost in calculating the net rate of return. Germany's 1993 German global drug budget legislation placed the pharmaceutical industry at financial risk for budget overruns, second in line after physicians, in order to discourage promotion. Similarly, France penalizes "excessive" promotion, both directly through fines for exceeding allowed promotion limits and indirectly through penalties for overshooting target sales limits. Some countries prohibit samples; even where there is no prohibition, there may be little incentive to give free samples in countries where patient copayments are low. Most countries restrict DTCA to so-called help-seeking ads, which inform consumers about a specific health condition and the availability of treatment for that condition. The only other country that permits DTCA to name a specific product to treat a condition is New Zealand. New Zealand has a strict freedom of commercial speech commitment and it has no constraining statute that requires DTCA to present a "fair balance" between risks and benefits. Survey results indicate that between 82 and 90 percent of individuals recall benefits information in DTCA in both the United States and New Zealand, but only 20 to 27 percent recall risk information in New Zealand, compared to 81 to 89 percent recall for risks in the United States (Hoek, Gendall, and Calfee 2004).

Studies of regulatory systems and their effects are more limited for promotion than for prices, in part because data on promotion spending is more limited and less informative across countries. For example, the content of a visit by a detail representative to a physician can be very different, depending on time spent, messaging allowed, whether sampling is permitted, and so forth. Berndt, Danzon, and Kruse (2007) provide some evidence on cross-national differences in promotion and in diffusion of new drugs.

7.7.5   Promotion to Managed Care

The growth of managed care has fundamentally changed the nature of marketing of pharmaceuticals. The autonomy of the physician has been reduced, with power shifting to payers or their pharmaceutical and therapeutics committees that make formulary decisions, in addition to consumers. This shift in the primary "customer" from the physician to more cost-conscious decision makers has been accompanied by a dramatic increase in the importance of cost-effectiveness analysis, to demonstrate that a particular drug is more cost-effective than the alternatives. Use of cost-effectiveness analysis by managed care organizations is summarized in Elixhauser, Luce, and Steiner (1995) and Neumann (2004). In response to the wide use of cost-effectiveness, the FDA proposed regulations that would require that a pharmaceutical firm's cost-effectiveness claims be supported by "sound" analysis. A debate ensued as to whether this requirement requires a double blind, randomized clinical trial (RCT) between the two drugs under comparison. Such a requirement would raise the same issues that were debated at the time of the 1962 Amendments: are the gains from reducing the risk of misleading claims outweighed by the costs of additional clinical trials? The social value of head-to-head RCTs as a requirement for cost-effectiveness claims is weaker than the case for RCTs for efficacy prior to launch, in part because the information on both costs and effects produced in RCTs is not necessarily an accurate measure of cost-effectiveness in actual use, because trials do not mirror actual practice. Moreover, for firms considering investing in such trials, the payoff diminishes as patent expiry approaches and the risks could be significant, if negative findings must be publicized. So far the FDA regulations fall short of requiring RCTs to support economic claims. Some managed care firms require that studies submitted to support marketing claims follow specified guidelines, including comparison of any new treatment with the standard of care for their patient population. If CMS develops guidelines for effectiveness studies for the Medicare Drug Benefit, the private sector may choose to free ride, in which case the government guidelines may de facto acquire the status of regulation for the conduct of cost-effectiveness studies and, potentially, for decisions on reimbursement. The PPACA (2010) Health Reform legislation in the United States leaves open the possibility for Medicare to evaluate costs and effects centrally (but does not require it). While some form of centralized evaluation may appear an increasingly possible scenario in the wake of the expanded funding for comparative effectiveness research of $1.1 billion from the ARRA (2009), such a policy development seems unlikely in the near term, given political opposition.

7.7.6 Discussion of Promotion

Some of the effects of DTCA appear consistent with social welfare, while other evidence suggests some inappropriate effects. Given other evidence that there is both under- and overuse of pharmaceuticals, relative to medical guidelines, it is not surprising that drawing welfare conclusions on effects of DTCA and of DTCA regulation is problematic. Moreover, the real policy decisions in the United States are less about whether DTCA should be permitted but about the specific details of appropriate regulatory rules that may be too nuanced for empirical analysis.

Moreover, the effects of regulation depend not only on the rules but on enforcement. The staffing levels at the FDA's division of drug advertising, marketing, and communications (DDMAC) are reportedly inadequate for the amount of material they must review, including television and print advertising (GAO 2002b). The HHS policy since 2001 to review warning letters from the DDMAC has further inhibited enforcement (Gahart et al. 2003). While firms have generally complied with warning letters for infractions and no major disciplinary action has been required, in some instances multiple letters have been sent and the delay in enforcement may have effectively allowed commercials to influence public opinion before modification or withdrawal.

The recent withdrawals of a few widely advertised products and of some widely disseminated ads have prompted both the FDA and the industry to address their policies related to DTCA (Dubois 2003). Industry has issued voluntary guidelines for DTCA that reinforce the "fair balance" standard and stipulate that firms provide copy of advertisements prior to, rather than concurrent with, planned public release (PhRMA 2005). The guidelines also call for firms to abstain from DTCA for several months after launch of a new drug, in part to enable education of physicians about new products in advance of DTCA release.

7.8 Conclusion

Regulation of pharmaceuticals derives from intrinsic product characteristics, in particular, significant but uncertain risks and benefits to health, rather than to structural features of the industry, such as natural monopoly. Information about a drug's risks and benefits in humans can only be obtained from careful study in large numbers of patients with appropriate controls for patient characteristics and comorbidities. There is a strong argument that structuring and interpreting such data analysis is a public good that is best delivered by an expert regulatory agency. The existence of regulatory systems to perform these functions and control market access in all industrialized and most developing countries is strong evidence for consensus opinion on this basic proposition. However, the regulatory details of what information to gather, whether relative to placebo or current treatment, from prelaunch or postlaunch sources, and under what conditions to make a drug available to the public, raise questions of effects of different regulatory regimes and optimal regulatory structure. Economic analysis has shed considerable light on these issues, but many fundamental questions remain. Moreover, since the fundamental problem is imperfect information, the optimal regulatory structure may change over time, as technologies for data gathering and analysis change and consumers' willingness to bear risk and demand for information change with technology, income, and other factors.

Early research on the 1962 Keffauver-Harris Amendments strongly suggests that it was one—but not the only—factor contributing to rising costs of R&D, reduction in number of new drugs, and probably reduced market share for small firms. However, the evidence from the 1990s and 2000s suggest that, while some regulatory changes accelerated the review process and stimulated R&D for diseases with smaller market size, rising concern over drug risks contributed to rising R&D costs. At the same time, the biotechnology and genomics revolutions have transformed drug discovery and transformed industry structure, with biologics accounting for an increasing share of sales and a rapidly growing share of new drugs in the pipeline. Thus regulation no longer appears to play a significant role in the size distribution of firms.

In contrast to the evidence on costs and delay, the debate over appropriate minimum standards for safety and efficacy and the optimal trade-off between them has generated more heat than light. Important topics for future research include the political economy questions, to shed light on economic reasons for the changes over time in FDA policy, and standard economic analysis of effects of various alternatives. Some advocate greater disclosure of all clinical trial results and stricter requirements for safety and efficacy relative to current standard of care, via larger trials and mandated registration of both preapproval and postmarketing trials in publicly available registries, while others assert that greater autonomy of patients and physicians to select drugs that meet minimal safety standards would offer expanded choice and potentially increase net welfare. While the methodology of cost-effectiveness analysis has become increasingly sophisticated for use in reimbursement decisions, little progress has been made on the application of such concepts or other formal decision analytic tools to weighing risks and benefits in drug approval decisions, or determining optimal thresholds for safety and efficacy.

Another important topic for future research involves identifying best practices and best data sources for integrating postlaunch observational data with prelaunch clinical trial data, to evaluate safety and efficacy decisions on an ongoing basis as information accumulates. An important related question will be the effect of postlaunch drug evaluation on costs and ex ante risks and returns to firms, and hence on firm R&D investment decisions. Optimal integration of postlaunch regulatory review with tort liability is a related issue.

The interface between patents and regulation is another important topic on which economic research has shed some light, but many interesting questions remain. Although pharmaceuticals are subject to the same twenty-year patent life as other products, effective patent life depends on regulation. FDA requirements for proof of safety and efficacy truncate early product life, but regulation also restores patent term and grants additional market exclusivities for new formulations, pediatric indications and so forth. Most important, regulatory requirements for market access of generics effectively define the end of patent life for originator products. Litigation between generic and originator firms has proliferated in recent years, indicating considerable uncertainty about patent validity and/or perverse incentives for strategic patent filing and patent challenges. More research is needed on how far new formulations and new indications for established drugs add to consumer welfare versus serve as mechanisms for "evergreening" the original patent. Such research could be useful input into regulation and patent provisions for these follow-on products and could inform antitrust activity toward settlements between originator and generics firms. Clearer standards for patents could in turn help reduce wasteful litigation.

Defining appropriate regulatory provisions for approval of generic biologics is partly a scientific question, but with important potential for economic impact. The regulatory details must consider safety and efficacy and the need to avoid biasing R&D incentives for or against biologics versus chemical drugs. Moreover, the extent to which price competition occurs between similar biologic products will depend on reimbursement provisions and incentives for physicians who typically dispense these drugs. Reimbursement for physician-dispensed drugs is in flux and current models have perverse incentives (Danzon, Wilensky, and Means 2005). Resolving these issues is essential if consumers and payers are to realize the potential for savings from generic biologics.

Regulation of price and reimbursement for pharmaceuticals differs from price regulation in other industries in that the rationale for regulation arises out of insurance and its effects on demand elasticity. Both private and public insurers adopt supply side policies, including limits on reimbursed prices, in order to control supplier pricing moral hazard, in addition to patient copayments to control consumer moral hazard. Price regulatory systems are generally an ad hoc mix of historical policies that have evolved over time as a trade-off between controlling drug spending and assuring access for patients. Because the details of each country's system differ, attempts to measure effects of regulatory prototypes, such as "price controls" or "reference pricing" are fraught with confounding from other unmeasured country-specific details and nonregulatory factors. Moreover, effects on R&D are confounded by the fact that incentives for pharmaceutical R&D depend on global revenues. Nevertheless, understanding effects of different systems for controlling drug prices, reimbursement, and expenditures is clearly an important subject for future research, including effects on prices, utilization, patient outcomes, and firm R&D incentives. Such research is particularly important as some form of regulation becomes more likely in the United States, as the federal government becomes a much larger purchaser of pharmaceuticals through the Medicare drug benefit, albeit thus far through private administration.

Finally, regulation of promotion remains a relatively uncharted territory, with some useful studies but many remaining questions, particularly related to DTCA. Empirical issues are particularly challenging, given the number of promotional channels that are simultaneously determined, and interdependence between firm strategies. The existing evidence on effects of DTCA is mixed, with quite strong evidence for category expansion and weaker evidence for improved compliance and product-specific benefits. Effects on patient outcomes and on competition and overall costs have not been measured. Thus, several of the components of a full welfare analysis remain to be developed.

In summary, although there is a large and growing literature on regulation of the pharmaceutical industry that has produced valuable information and useful lessons learned, large and important issues remain for future research. Models of regulation in other industries are either not relevant or require significant adaptation and extension, in order to fit this industry's peculiar characteristics—in particular, high rates of R&D and technical change, with life-or-death effects, patents, insurance, and physicians, consumers, payers, and pharmacists as potential customers. This industry remains a fertile area for future research.

References

Acemoglu, D., and J. Linn. 2004. "Market Size in Innovation: Theory and Evidence from the Pharmaceutical Industry." *Quarterly Journal of Economics* 119:1049–90.

Adams, C. P., and V. V. Brantner. 2006. "Estimating the Cost of New Drug Development: Is It Really $802 Million?" *Health Affairs* 25:420–28.

Aitken M., E. Berndt, and D. M. Cutler. 2009. "Prescription Drug Spending Trends in the United States: Looking Beyond the Turning Point." *Health Affairs* 28 (1): w151–w160

Anis, A. H., and Q. Wen. 1998. "Price Regulation of Pharmaceuticals in Canada." *Journal of Health Economics* 17:21–38.

Arrow, K. J., C. Panosian, and H. Gelband. 2004. *Saving Lives, Buying Time: Economics of Malaria Drugs in an Age of Resistances.* Washington, DC: National Academies Press.

Attaran, A. 2004. "How Do Patents and Economic Policies Affect Access to Essential Medicines in Developing Countries?" *Health Affairs* 23:155–66.

Averch, H., and L. L. Johnson. 1962. "Behavior of the Firm under Regulatory Constraint." *American Economic Review* 52:1052–69.

Baily, M. N. 1972. "Research and Development Costs and Returns: The US Pharmaceutical Industry." *Journal of Political Economy* 80:70–85.

Baumol, W. J., and D. F. Bradford. 1970. "Optimal Departures from Marginal Cost Pricing." *American Economic Review* 60:265–83.

Beales, J. H. 1996. "New Uses for Old Drugs." In *Competitive Strategies in the Pharmaceutical Industry*, edited by R. B. Helms, 281–305. Washington, DC: The American Enterprise Institute Press.

Bennett, C. L., J. R. Nebeker, E. A. Lyons, M. H. Samore, M. D. Feldman, J. M. McKoy, K. R. Carson, et al. 2005. "The Research on Adverse Drug Events and Reports (RADAR) project." *JAMA: Journal of the American Medical Association* 293:2131–40.

Berndt, E. R. 2005. "The United States' Experience with Direct-to-Consumer Advertising of Prescription Drugs: What Have We Learned?" Presented at the International Conference on Pharmaceutical Innovation, Taipei, Taiwan.

———. 2007. "The United States Experience with Direct-to-Consumer Advertising of Prescription Drugs: What Have We Learned?" Unpublished Manuscript, Massachusetts Institute of Technology.

Berndt, E. R., and M. Aitken. 2011. "Brand Loyalty, Generic Entry, and Price Competition in Pharmaceuticals in the Quarter Century after the 1984 Waxman-Hatch Legislation." *International Journal of the Economics of Business* 18 (2): 161–76.

Berndt, E. R., L. Bui, D. R. Reiley, and G. L. Urban. 1995. "Information, Marketing, and Pricing in the US Antiulcer Drug Market." *American Economic Review* 85:100–05.

Berndt, E. R., P. M. Danzon, and G. B. Kruse. 2007. "Dynamic Competition in Pharmaceuticals: Cross-National Evidence from New Drug Diffusion." *Managerial and Decision Economics* 28:231–50.

Berndt, E. R., A. H. B. Gottschalk, T. J. Philipson, and M. W. Strobeck. 2005. "Industry Funding of the FDA: Effects of PDUFA on Approval Times and Withdrawal Rates." *Nature Reviews Drug Discovery* 4:545–54.

Boston Consulting Group (BCG). 1993. *The Contribution of Pharmaceutical Companies: What's at Stake for America*. Boston: BCG.

Brewer, T., and G. A. Colditz. 1999. "Postmarketing Surveillance and Adverse Drug Reactions: Current Perspectives and Future Needs." *JAMA: Journal of the American Medical Association* 281:824–29.

Cacciotti, J., and P. Clinton. 2011. "The Lull between Two Storms." *Pharmaceutical Executive* 31:3–13.

Califf, R. M., D. A. Zarin, J. M. Kramer, R. E. Sherman, L. H. Aberle, and A. Tasneem. 2012. "Characteristics of Clinical Trials Registered in ClinicalTrials.gov, 2007–2010." *JAMA: Journal of the American Medical Association* 307:1838–47.

Cartwright, H. 2011. "Teva Looks to Diversify Its Branded Drugs Portfolio with US $6.8 B Cephalon Acquisition." *PharmaDeals Review 2011*.

Caves, R. E., M. D. Whinston, and M. A. Hurwitz. 1991. "Patent Expiration, Entry, and Competition in the United-States Pharmaceutical-Industry." *Brookings Papers on Economic Activity: Microeconomics* no. 3, 1–66.

Chaudhuri, S., P. Goldberg, and P. Jia. 2006. "Estimating the Effects of Global Patent Protection in Pharmaceuticals: A Case Study of Quinolones in India." *American Economic Review* 96:1477–514.

Chressanthis, G. A., P. Khedkar, N. Jain, P. Poddar, and M. G. Seiders. 2012. "Can

Access Limits on Sales Representatives to Physicians Affect Clinical Prescription Decisions? A Study of Recent Events with Diabetes and Lipid Drugs." *Journal of Clinical Hypertension* 14:435–46.

Clarkson, K. W. 1996. "The Effects of Research and Promotion on Rates of Return." In *Competitive Strategies in the Pharmaceutical Industry*, edited by R. B. Helms, 238–68. Washington, DC: The American Enterprise Institute Press.

Coleman, M. S., N. Sangrujee, F. J. Zhou, and S. Chu. 2005. "Factors Affecting US Manufacturers' Decisions to Produce Vaccines." *Health Affairs* 24:635–42.

Comanor, W. S. 1986. "The Political Economy of the Pharmaceutical Industry." *Journal of Economic Literature* 24 (3): 1178–1217.

Congressional Budget Office (CBO). 1996. "How the Medicaid Rebate on Prescription Drugs Affects Pricing in the Pharmaceutical Industry." Washington, DC: CBO.

———. 2004. "A Detailed Description of CBO's Cost Estimate for the Medicare Prescription Drug Benefit." Washington, DC: CBO.

———. 2005. "The Rebate Medicaid Receives on Brand-Name Prescription Drugs." Congressional Budget Office of the United States.

———. 2006. "Research and Development in the Pharmaceutical Industry." Washington, DC.

———. 2009. "Promotional Spending for Prescription Drugs." Washington, DC: CBO.

Council of Foreign Relations. 2010. "Open Labs, Open Minds: Breaking Down the Barriers to Innovation and Access to Medicines in the Developing World." Interview with Andrew Witty, CEO GSK.

Craswell, R., and J. E. Calfee. 1986. "Deterrence and Uncertain Legal Standards." *Journal of Law, Economics, and Organization* 2:279–303.

Danzon, P. M. 1997. *Pharmaceutical Price Regulation: National Policies versus Global Interests*. Washington, DC: American Enterprise Institute Press.

Danzon, P. M., and L. W. Chao. 2000a. "Cross-National Price Differences for Pharmaceuticals: How Large, and Why?" *Journal of Health Economics* 19:159–95.

———. 2000b. "Does Regulation Drive out Competition in Pharmaceutical Markets?" *Journal of Law and Economics* 43:311–58.

Danzon, P. M., and A. J. Epstein. 2012. "Effects of Regulation on Drug Launch and Pricing in Interdependent Markets." In *The Economics of Medical Technology*, edited by Kristian Bolin and Robert Kaestner, Advances in Health Economics and Health Services Research 23, 33–69. Bingley, UK: Emerald Group Publishing Limited.

Danzon, P. M., A. Epstein, and S. Nicholson. 2004. "Mergers and Acquisitions in the Pharmaceutical and Biotech Industries." NBER Working Paper no. 10536, Cambridge, MA.

Danzon, P. M., and M. F. Furukawa. 2003. "Prices and Availability of Pharmaceuticals: Evidence from Nine Countries." *Health Affairs*: 3–521.

———. 2006. "Prices and Availability of Biopharmaceuticals: An International Comparison." *Health Affairs* 25:1353–62.

———. 2008. "International Prices and Availability of Pharmaceuticals in 2005." *Health Affairs* 27:221–33.

———. 2011. "Cross-National Evidence on Generic Pharmaceuticals: Pharmacy vs. Physician-Driven Markets." NBER Working Paper 17226, Cambridge, MA.

Danzon, P. M., and J. D. Ketcham. 2003. "Reference Pricing of Pharmaceuticals for Medicare: Evidence from Germany, the Netherlands and New Zealand." NBER Working Paper no. 10007, Cambridge, MA.

Danzon, P. M., A. W. Mulcahy, and A. K. Towse. 2013. "Pharmaceutical Pricing in

Emerging Markets: Effects of Income, Competition and Procurement." *Health Economics*, doi:10.1002/hec.3013.

Danzon, P. M., S. Nicholson, and N. S. Pereira. 2005. "Productivity in Pharmaceutical-Biotechnology R&D: The Role of Experience and Alliances." *Journal of Health Economics* 24:317–39.

Danzon, P. M., and A. Percy. 1999. "The Effects of Price Regulation on Productivity in Pharmaceuticals." In *International and Interarea Comparisons of Income, Output, and Prices*, edited by Alan Heston and Robert Lipsey, 371–418. Chicago: University of Chicago Press.

Danzon, P. M., and N. S. Pereira. 2005. "Why Sole-Supplier Vaccine Markets May Be Here to Stay." *Health Affairs* 24:694–96.

Danzon, P. M., N. S. Pereira, and S. S. Tejwani. 2005. "Vaccine Supply: A Cross-National Perspective." *Health Affairs* 24:706–17.

Danzon, P. M., and A. Towse. 2003. "Differential Pricing for Pharmaceuticals: Reconciling Access, R&D and Patents." *International Journal of Health Care Finance and Economics* 3:183–205.

———. 2005. "Theory and Implementation of Differential Pricing for Pharmaceutical." In *International Public Goods and Transfer of Technology under a Globalized Intellectual Property Regime*, edited by K. E. Maskus and J. H. Reichman, 425–56. Cambridge: Cambridge University Press.

Danzon, P. M., A. Towse, and J. Ferrandiz. 2013. "Value-Based Differential Pricing: Efficient Prices for Drugs in a Global Context." *Health Economics*, doi:10.1002/hec.3021.

Danzon, P. M., Y. R. Wang, and L. Wang. 2005. "The Impact of Price Regulation on the Launch Delay of New Drugs—Evidence from Twenty-Five Major Markets in the 1990s." *Health Economics* 14:269–92.

Danzon, P. M., G. Wilensky, and K. Means. 2005. "Alternative Strategies for Medicare Payment of Outpatient Prescription Drugs: Part B and Beyond." *American Journal of Managed Care* 11:173–80.

Dave, D., and H. Saffer. 2012. "Impact of Direct-to-Consumer Advertising on Pharmaceutical Prices and Demand." *Southern Economic Journal* 79:97–126.

David, G., S. Markowitz, and S. Richards. 2009. "The Effects of Pharmaceutical Marketing and Promotion on Adverse Drug Events and Regulation." NBER Working Paper no. 14634, Cambridge, MA.

DiMasi, J. A. 2002. "The Value of Improving the Productivity of the Drug Development Process—Faster Times and Better Decisions." *Pharmacoeconomics* 20:1–10.

DiMasi, J. A., and H. G. Grabowski. 2007. "The Cost of Biopharmaceutical R&D: Is Biotech Different?" *Managerial and Decision Economics* 28:469–79.

DiMasi, J. A., H. G. Grabowski, and J. Vernon. 2004. "R&D Costs and Returns by Therapeutic Category." *Drug Information Journal* 38:211–23.

DiMasi, J. A., R. W. Hansen, H. G. Grabowski. 2003. "The Price of Innovation: New Estimates of Drug Development Costs." *Journal of Health Economics* 22:151–85.

DiMasi, J. A., R. W. Hansen, H. G. Grabowski, and L. Lasagna. 1991. "Cost of Innovation in the Pharmaceutical Industry." *Journal of Health Economics* 10:107–42.

DiMasi, J. A., and C. Paquette. 2004. "The Economics of Follow-on Drug Research and Development—Trends in Entry Rates and the Timing of Development." *Pharmacoeconomics* 22:1–14.

Donohue, J. M. 2003. "The Evolving Roles of Consumer and Consumer Protection: The History of Prescription Drug Advertising." Working paper, Department of Ambulatory Care and Prevention, Havard Medical School, Cambridge, MA.

Donohue, J. M., and E. R. Berndt. 2004. "Effects of Direct-to-Consumer Advertising on Medication Choice: The Case of Antidepressants." *Journal of Public Policy & Marketing* 23 (2): 115–27.

Donohue, J. M., M. Cevasco, and M. B. Rosenthal. 2007. "A Decade of Direct-to-Consumer Advertising of Prescription Drugs." *New England Journal of Medicine* 357:673–81.

Dranove, D., and D. Meltzer. 1994. "Do Important Drugs Reach the Market Sooner?" *RAND Journal of Economics* 25:402–23.

Dubois, R.W. 2003. "Pharmaceutical Promotion: Don't Throw the Baby out with the Bathwater." *Health Aff* (Millwood) Suppl Web Exclusives, W3-96-103.

Duggan, M. G., and F. S. Morton. 2012. "The Medium-Term Impact of Medicare Part D on Pharmaceutical Prices." *American Economic Review* 101:387–92.

Elixhauser, A., B. R. Luce, and C. A. Steiner. 1995. *Cost Effectiveness Analysis, Medical Technology Assessment, and Managed Care Organizations*. Bethesda, MD: MEDTAP International Inc.

Ellis, R. P., and T. G. McGuire. 1993. "Supply-Side and Demand-Side Cost Sharing in Health Care." *Journal of Economic Perspectives* 7:135–51.

European Federation of Pharmaceutical Industries and Associations (EFPIA). 2011. *2011 EU Industrial R&D Investment Scoreboard*. European Commission (JRC/DG Research and Innovation).

Federal Trade Commission (FTC). 2002. *Generic Drug Entry Prior to Patent Expiration*. Washington, DC: Federal Trade Commission.

Fink, C. 2001. "Patent Protection, Transnational Corporations, and Market Structure: A Simulation Study of the Indian Pharmaceutical Industry." *Journal of Industry, Competition and Trade* 1:101–21.

Finkelstein, A. 2004. "Static and Dynamic Effects of Health Policy: Evidence from the Vaccine Industry." *Quarterly Journal of Economics* 119 (2): 527–64.

Flynn, S., A. Hollis, and M. Palmedo. 2009. "An Economic Justification for Open Access to Essential Medicine Patents in Developing Countries." *Journal of Law, Medicine & Ethics* 37:184–208.

Food and Drug Admisistration (FDA). 1997. FDA Backgrounder on FDAMA. November 21. http://www.fda.gov/RegulatoryInformation/Legislation/Federal FoodDrugandCosmeticActFDCAct/SignificantAmendmentstotheFDCAct /FDAMA/ucm089179.htm.

———. 2011. *FY 2010 PDUFA Financial Report*. Washington, DC: FDA.

———. 2012. "Report on the Performance of Drug and Biologics Firms in Conducting Postmarketing Requirements and Commitments." *Federal Register* 77, no. 44 (March 6).

———. n.d. Medwatch Safety Alerts for Human Medical Products. Accessed November 4, 2013. http://www.fda.gov/SAFETY/MEDWATCH/SAFETY INFORMATION/SAFETYALERTSFORHUMANMEDICALPRODUCTS /DEFAULT.HTM.

Frank, R. G., E. Berndt, J. Donohue, A. Epstein, and M. Rosenthal. 2002. *Trends in Direct-to-Consumer Advertising of Prescription Drugs*. The Kaiser Famly Foundation.

Frank, R. G., and D. S. Salkever. 1992. "Pricing, Patent Loss and the Market for Pharmaceuticals." *Southern Economic Journal* :165–79.

G-Finder. 2012. *G-Finder: Global Funding of Innovation for Neglected Diseases*. The George Institute.

Gahart, M. T., L. M. Duhamel, A. Dievler, and R. Price. 2003. "Examining the FDA's Oversight of Direct-to-Consumer Advertising." *Health Aff* (Millwood), Suppl Web Exclusives, W3-120-123.

Garber, A. M., C. I. Jones, and P. M. Romer. 2006. "Insurance and Incentives for Medical Innovation." NBER Working Paper no. 12080, Cambridge, MA.

Gilbert, R., and C. Shapiro. 1990. "Optimal Patent Length and Breadth." *Rand Journal of Economics* 21:106–12.

Gilead. 2010. *Expanding Antiretroviral Treatment Coverage in the Developing World.* Foster City, CA.

Government Accountability Office (GAO). 1992. "Prescription Drugs: Companies Typically Charge More in the United States Than in Canada. (GAO-HRD-92-110)." Washington, DC: GAO.

———. 1993. "Medicaid: Changes in Drug Prices Paid by HMOs and Hospitals Since Enactment of Rebate Provisions." Washington, DC: GAO.

———. 1994. "Prescription Drugs: Companies Typically Charge More in the United States Than in the United Kingdom. (GAO/HEHS-94-29)." Washington, DC: GAO.

———. 1997. "Pharmacy Benefit Managers, FFHRP Plans Satisfied with Savings and Services, but Retail Pharmacies Have Concerns." Washington, DC: GAO.

———. 2002a. "Effect of User Fees on Drug Approval Times, Withdrawals, and Other Agency Activities." Washington, DC: GAO.

———. 2002b. "Prescription Drugs: FDA Oversight of Direct-to-Consumer Advertising Has Limitations." Washington, DC: GAO.

———. 2003. federal employees' health benefits: Effects of Using Pharmacy Benefit Managers on Health Plans, Enrollees, and Pharmacies.

Grabowski, H. G. 1976. *Drug Regulation and Innovation: Empirical Evidence and Policy Options.* Washington, DC: American Enterprise Institute.

Grabowski, H. G., M. Kyle, R. Mortimer, G. Long, and N. Kirson. 2011. "Evolving Brand-Name and Generic Drug Competition May Warrant a Revision of the Hatch-Waxman Act." *Health Affairs* 30:2157–66.

Grabowski, H. G., D. B. Ridley, and J. L. Moe. 2009. *Priority Review Vouchers to Encourage Innovation for Neglected Diseases. Prescribing Cultures and Pharmaceutical Policy in the Asia-Pacific.* Washington, DC: Brookings Institution Press.

Grabowski, H. G., and J. M. Vernon. 1976. "Structural Effects of Regulation on Innovation in the Ethical Drug Industry." In *Essays on Industrial Organization in Honor of Joe S. Bain,* edited by R. T. Masson and P. D. Qualls. Cambridge: Lippincott, Ballinger.

———. 1990. "A New Look at the Returns and Risks to Pharmaceutical R&D." *Management Science* 36:804–21.

———. 1992. "Brand Loyalty, Entry and Price Competition in Pharmaceuticals After the 1984 Drug Act." *Journal of Law and Economics* 35:331–50.

———. 1996. "Prospects for Returns to Pharmaceutical R&D under Health Care Reform." In *Competitive Strategies in the Pharmaceutical Industry,* edited by R. B. Helms. Washington, DC: The American Enterprise Institute Press.

———. 2000. "The Determinants of Pharmaceutical Research and Development Expenditures." *Journal of Evolutionary Economics* 10:201–15.

Grabowski, H. G., J. Vernon, and J. A. DiMasi. 2002. "Returns on Research and Development for 1990s New Drug Introductions." *Pharmacoeconomics* 20:11–29.

Grabowski, H. G., J. M. Vernon, and L. G. Thomas. 1978. "Estimating the Effects of Regulation on Innovation: An International Comparative Analysis of the Pharmaceutical Industry." *Journal of Law and Economics* 21:133–63.

Grande, D. 2010. "Limiting the Influence of Pharmaceutical Industry Gifts on Physicians: Self-Regulation or Government Intervention?" *Journal of General Internal Medicine* 25: 79–83.

Grande, D., and D. A. Asch. 2009. "Commercial versus Social Goals of Tracking What Doctors Do." *New England Journal of Medicine* 360:747–49.

Hansen R. 1979. "The Pharmaceutical Development Process: Estimates of Current Development Costs and Times and the Effects of Regulatory Changes." In *Issues in Pharmaceutical Economics*, edited by R. Chen. Lexington: Lexington Books.

Hausdorff, W. 2002. "Challenges to Globalizing the Benefits of Rotavirus Vaccination." Wharton Impact Conference: Pharmaceutical Innovation in the Global Economy, Philadelphia, Pennsylvania.

Hemphill, C. S., and B. N. Sampat. 2012. "Evergreening, Patent Challenges, and Effective Market Life in Pharmaceuticals." *Journal of Health Economics* 31:327–39.

Henderson, R., and I. Cockburn. 1996. "Scale, Scope and Spillovers: Determinants of Research Productivity in the Pharmaceutical Industry." *RAND Journal of Economics* 27 (1): 32–59.

Hoek, J., P. Gendall, and J. Calfee. 2004. "Direct-to-Consumer Advertising of Prescription Medicines in the United States and New Zealand: An Analysis of Regulatory Approaches and Consumer Responses." *International Journal of Advertising* 23:197–227.

Hurwitz, M. A., and R. E. Caves. 1988. "Persuasion or Information: Promotion and the Shares of Brand Name and Generic Pharmaceuticals." *Journal of Law & Economics* 31 (2): 299–320.

Iizuka, T. 2004. "What Explains the Use of Direct-to-Consumer Advertising of Prescription Drugs?" *Journal of Industrial Economics* 52 (3): 349–79.

Iizuka, T., and G. Jin. 2005a. "Direct to Consumer Advertising and Prescription Choices." Working paper, Owen Graduate School of Management, Vanderbilt University, Nashville.

———. 2005b. "The Effect of Prescription Drug Advertising on Doctor Visits." Working paper, Owen Graduate School of Management, Vanderbilt University, Nashville.

IMS Health. 2011. *Shaping the Biosimilar Opportunity: A Global Perspective on the Evolving Biosimilars Landscape*. London: IMS Health.

———. 2012. *The Use of Medicines in the United States: Review of 2011*. IMS Health–IMS Institute for Healthcare Informatics.

Jack, W. L., and J. O. Lanjouw. 2003. "Financing Pharmaceutical Innovation: How Much Should Poor Countries Contribute? Working paper no. 28, Centre for Global Development, Washington, DC.

Joskow, P. L. 1974. "Inflation and Environmental Concern: Structural Change in the Process of Public Utility Price Regulation." *Journal of Law and Economics* 17: 291–327.

Kanavos, P., S. Vandoros, R. Irwin, E. Nicod, and M. Casson. 2011. *Differences in Costs of and Access to Pharmaceutical Products in the EU*. London: London School of Economics.

Keeler, T., T.-w. Hu, A. Keith, R. Manning, M. D. Marciniak, M. Ong, and H.-Y. Sung. 2002. "The Benefits of Switching Smoking Cessation Drugs to Over-the-Counter Status." *Health Economics* 11:389–402.

Kesselheim, A. S. 2011. "An Empirical Review of Major Legislation Affecting Drug Development: Past Experiences, Effects, and Unintended Consequences." *Milbank Quarterly* 89:450–502.

Klemperer, P. 1990. "How Broad Should the Scope of Patent Protection Be." *Rand Journal of Economics* 21:113–30.

Kravitz, R. L. 2005. "Influence of Patients' Requests for Direct-to-Consumer Advertised Antidepressants." *Journal of the American Medical Association* 293:1995–2002.

Kremer, M. 2002. "Pharmaceuticals and the Developing World." *Journal of Economic Perspectives* 16:67–90.

Kuhlik, B. N. 2004. "The Assault on Pharmaceutical Intellectual Property." *The University of Chicago Law Review* 71:93–109.

Kyle, M. K. 2007. "Pharmaceutical Price Controls and Entry Strategies." *The Review of Economics and Statistics* 89:88–99.

Lakdawalla, D. N., and N. Sood. 2009. "Innovation and the Welfare Effects of Public Drug Insurance." *Journal of Public Economics* 93:541–48.

Lakdawalla, D. N., and W. Yin. 2010. "Insurers' Negotiating Leverage and the External Effects of Medicare Part D." NBER Working Paper no. 16251, Cambridge, MA.

Lanjouw, J. O. 2002. "A New Global Patent Regime for Diseases: U.S. and International Legal Issues." *Harvard Journal of Law and Technology* 16 (1): 85–124.

———. 2005. "Patents, Price Controls and Access to New Drugs: How Policy Affects Global Market Entry." NBER Working Paper no. 11321, Cambridge, MA.

Laxminarayan, R., and H. Gelband. 2009. "A Global Subsidy: Key to Affordable Drugs for Malaria?" *Health Aff* 28:949–61.

Laxminarayan, R., M. Over, and D. L. Smith. 2006. "Will a Global Subsidy of New Antimalarials Delay the Emergence of Resistance and Save Lives?" *Health Affairs* 25:325.

Laxminarayan, R., I. W. H. Parry, D. L. Smith, and E. Y. Klein. 2010. "Should New Antimalarial Drugs Be Subsidized?" *Journal of Health Economics* 29:445–56.

Leffler, K. 1981. "Persuasion or Information? The Economics of Prescription Drug Advertising." *Journal of Law and Economics* 24:45–74.

Lerner, J. 1994. "The Importance of Patent Scope: An Empirical Analysis." *Rand Journal of Economics* 25:319–33.

Levy, R. 1999. *The Pharmaceutical Industry: A Discussion of Competitive and Anti-Trust Issues in an Environment of Change.* Washington, DC: Federal Trade Commission.

Lichtenberg, F. 2005. "Pharmaceutical Knowledge-Capital Accumulation and Longevity." In *Measuring Capital in the New Economy*, edited by C. Corrado, J. Haltiwanger, and D. Sichel, 237–74. Chicago: University of Chicago Press.

Lichtenberg, F. R., and T. J. Philipson. 2002. "The Dual Effects of Intellectual Property Regulations: Within- and between-Patent Competition in the US Pharmaceuticals Industry." *Journal of Law & Economics* 45:643–72.

Lichtenberg, F. R., and J. Waldfogel. 2003. "Does Misery Love Company? Evidence from Pharmaceutical Markets before and after the Orphan Drug Acts." NBER Working Paper no. 9750, Cambridge, MA.

Longman, R. 2004. "Why Early-Stage Dealmaking Is Hot." *IN VIVO: The Business & Medicine Report* 28.

———. 2005. "A Little Knowledge: The FDA's Public Approach to Safety." *IN VIVO: The Business and Medicine Report.* May.

———. 2006. "The Large Molecule Future." *IN VIVO: The Business & Medicine Report.* June.

López-Casasnovas, G., and J. Puig-Junoy. 2000. "Review of the Literature on Reference Pricing." *Health Policy* 54:87–123.

Lu, Z. J., and W. S. Comanor. 1998. "Strategic Pricing of New Pharmaceuticals." *Review of Economics and Statistics* 80:108–18.

Ma, A., and M. Riordan. 2002. "Health Insurance, Moral Hazard and Managed Care." *Journal of Economics and Management Strategy* 11:81–107.

Madden, B. J. 2004. "Breaking the FDA Monopoly." *Regulation* 27:64–66.

Mahinka, S. P., and M. E. Bierman. 1995. "Direct-to-OTC Marketing of Drugs—Possible Approaches." *Food And Drug Law Journal* 50:49–63.

Mahmoud, A., P. M. Danzon, J. H. Barton, and R. D. Mugerwa. 2006. "Product Development Priorities." *Disease Control Priorities in Developing Countries* 2006:139.

Malueg, D. A., and M. Schwartz. 1994. "Parallel Imports, Demand Dispersion, and International Price Discrimination." *Journal of International Economics* 37: 167–95.

Mansfield, E. 1986. "Patents and Innovation—An Empirical Study." *Management Science* 32:173–81.

Masson, A., and R. L. Steiner. 1985. "Generic Substitution and Prescription Drug Prices: Economic Effects of State Drug Product Selection Laws." Bureau of Economics, Federal Trade Commission.

Mello, M. M., and N. A. Messing. 2011. "Restrictions on the Use of Prescribing Data for Drug Promotion." *New England Journal of Medicine* 365:1248–54.

Moe, J., H. Grabowski, D. Ridley, and A. S. Kesselheim. 2009. "FDA Review Vouchers." *New England Journal of Medicine* 360:837–38.

Moran, M., J. Guzman, A.-L. Ropars, A. McDonald, N. Jameson, B. Omune, S. Ryan, and L. Wu. 2009. "Neglected Disease Research and Development: How Much Are We Really Spending?" *PLoS Med* 6.

Münnich, F. E., and K. Sullivan. 1994. "The Impact of Recent Legislative Change in Germany." *Pharmacoeconomics* 6:22–27.

Narayanan, S., R. Desiraju, and P. K. Chintagunta. 2004. "Return on Investment Implications for Pharmaceutical Promotional Expenditures: The Role of Marketing-Mix Interactions." *Journal of Marketing* 68:90–105.

Neumann, P. J. 2004. "Evidence-Based and Value-Based Formulary Guidelines." *Health Affairs* 23:124–34.

Office of Fair Trading (OFT). 3007. *The Pharmaceutical Price Regulation Scheme: An OFT Market Study*. London: OFT.

Okie, S. 2005. "What Ails the FDA?" *New England Journal of Medicine* 352:1063–66.

Olson, M. K. 2000. "Regulatory Reform and Bureaucratic Responsiveness to Firms: The Impact of User Fees in the FDA." *Journal of Economics & Management Strategy* 9:363–95.

———. 2004. "Managing Delegation in the FDA: Reducing Delay in New-Drug Review." *Journal of Health Politics Policy and Law* 29:397–430.

Palumbo, F. B., and C. Mullins. 2002. "The Development of Direct-to-Consumer Prescription Drug Advertising Regulation." *Food and Drug Law Journal* 57: 423–43.

Pauly, M. V. 1968. "The Economics of Moral Hazard: Comment." *The American Economic Review* 58:531–37.

Peltzman, S. 1973. "An Evaluation of Consumer Protection Legislation: The 1962 Drug Amendments." *The Journal of Political Economy* 81:1049–91.

PEPFAR (President's Emergency Plan for AIDS Relief). 2012. "Increasing the Availability of Safe, Effective, Low-Cost Generic Medicines." http://www.pepfar.gov/documents/organization/115245.pdf.

Pharmaceutical Research and Manufacturers of America (PhRMA). 2005. *PhRMA Guiding Principles: Direct to Consumer Advertisements about Prescription Medicines*. PhRMA.

Philipson, T., E. R. Berndt, A. H. B. Gottschalk, and E. Sun. 2008. "Cost-Benefit Analysis of the FDA: The Case of the Prescription Drug User Fee Acts." *Journal of Public Economics* 92:1306–25.

Ramsey, F. P. 1927. "A Contribution to the Theory of Taxation." *The Economic Journal* 37:47–61.

Reekie, W. D. 1978. "Price and Quality Competition in the United States Drug Industry." *Journal of Industrial Economics* 26:223–37.

Ridley, D. B., H. G. Grabowski, and J. L. Moe. 2006. "Developing Drugs for Developing Countries." *Health Affairs* 25:313–24.

Rosenthal, M. B., E. Berndt, J. M. Donohue, A. M. Epstein, and R. G. Frank. 2003. *Demand Effects of Recent Changes in Prescription Drug Promotion.* The Kaiser Family Foundation.

Scherer, F. M. 1997. "How US Antitrust Can Go Astray: The Brand Name Prescription Drug Litigation." *International Journal of the Economics of Business* 4: 239–56.

Schmalensee, R. 1982. "Product Differentiation Advantages of Pioneering Brands." *The American Economic Review* 72:349–65.

Schulenburg, J.-M. Graf v. d., and O. Schöffski. 1993. *Implications of the Structural Reform of Healthcare Act on the Referral and Hospital Admission Practices of Primary Care Physicians.* Hanover: University of Hanover.

———. 1994. "Transformation des Gesundheitswesens im Spannungsfeld zwischen Kostendämpfung und Freiheit, Eine ökonomische Analyse des veränderten Überweisungs- und Einweisungsverhaltens nach den Arzneimittelregulierungen des GSG" ("Transformation of the Health Care System, An Economic Analysis of the Changes in Referrals and Hospital Admissions after the Drug Budget of the Health Care Reform Act of 1992"). In *Probleme der Transformation im Gesundheitswesen (Issues in the Transformation of Health Care Systems)*, edited by P. Oberender, 45–81. Baden, Ger.: Nomos.

Schwartzman, D. 1975. *The Expected Return from Pharmaceutical Research.* Washington, DC: The American Enterprise Institute Press.

Scott Morton, F. 1997. "The Strategic Response by Pharamceutical Firms to the Medicaid Most-Favored Customer Rules." *RAND Journal of Economics* 28: 269–90.

———. 1999. "Entry Decisions in the Generic Pharmaceutical Industry." *RAND Journal of Economics* 30:421–40.

———. 2000. "Barriers to Entry, Brand Advertising, and Generic Entry in the US Pharmaceutical Industry." *International Journal of Industrial Organization* 18:1085–104.

Silberson, Z. 1987. *The Economic Importance of Patents.* London: Common Law Institute of Intellectual Property.

Sutton, J. 1991. *Sunk Costs and Market Structures.* Cambridge, MA: MIT Press.

Taylor, C. T., and Z. Silberston. 1973. *The Economic Impact of the Patent Systems.* Cambridge: Cambridge University Press.

Telser, L. G., W. Best, J. W. Egan, and H. N. Higinbotham. 1975. "The Theory of Supply with Applications to the Ethical Pharmaceutical Industry." *Journal of Law and Economics* 18:449–78.

Temin, P. 1979. "Technology, Regulation, and Market Structure in the Modern Pharmaceutical Industry." *Bell Journal of Economics* 10 (2): 429–46.

———. 1983. "Costs and Benefits in Switching Drugs from Rx to OTC." *Journal of Health Economics* 2 (3): 187–205.

Thomas, L. G. 1990. "Regulation and Firm Size: FDA Impacts on Innovation." *RAND Journal of Economics* 21 (4): 497–517.

———. 1996. "Industrial Policy and International Competitiveness in the Pharmaceutical Industry." In *Competitive Strategies in the Pharmaceutical Industry*, R. B. Helms, 107–29. Washington, DC: The American Enterprise Institute.

Towse, A., and H. Kettler. 2005. "Advance Price or Purchase Commitments to Create

Markets for Treatments for Diseases of Poverty: Lessons from Three Policies." *Bulletin of the World Health Organization* 83:301–17.

Towse, A., E. Keuffel, H. Kettler, and D. Ridley. 2012. "Drugs and Vaccines for Developing Countries." In *The Oxford Handbook of the Economics of the Biopharmaceutical Industry*, edited by P. Danzon and S. Nicholson, 302–35. Oxford: Oxford Univerity Press.

Tsai, A. C. 2003. "Policies to Regulate Gifts to Physicians from Industry." *JAMA: Journal of the American Medical Association* 290:1776.

Tsao, A. 2003. "Seeking a Prescription for Biogenerics." *Business Week Online*, October 24.

Tufts Center for Drug Discovery (TCSDD). 2003. "FDA's Fast Track Initiative Cut Total Drug Development Time by Three Years, According to Tufts CSDD, Vol. 2005." Tufts Center for the Study of Drug Development; 2003.

Ventola, C. L. 2011. "Direct-to-Consumer Pharmaceutical Advertising: Therapeutic or Toxic?" *Pharmacy and Therapeutics* 36:669.

Vernon, J. A., J. H. Golec, and J. A. Dimasi. 2010. "Drug Development Costs When Financial Risk Is Measured Using the Fama-French Three-Factor Model." *Health Economics* 19:1002–05.

Walker, H. 1971. *Market Power and Price Levels in the Ethical Drug Industry*. Bloomington: University of Indiana Press.

Wardell, W. M. 1973. "Introduction of New Therapeutic Drugs in the United States and Great Britain: An International Comparison." *Clinical Pharmacology and Therapeutics* 14 (5): 773–90.

Wardell, W. M., and L. Lasagna. 1975. *Regulation and Drug Developments*. Washington, DC: American Enterprise Institute for Public Policy Research.

Watal, J. 2000. "Pharmaceutical Patents, Prices and Welfare Losses: Policy Options for India under the WTO TRIPS Agreement." *World Economy* 23:733–52.

Wiggins, S. N. 1981. "Product Quality Regulation and New Drug Introductions— Some New Evidence from the 1970s." *Review of Economics and Statistics* 63: 615–19.

Wilkes, M. S., R. A. Bell, and R. L. Kravitz. 2000. "Direct-to-Consumer Prescription Drug Advertising: Trends, Impact, and Implications." *Health Affairs* 19:110–28.

Woodcock, J. 2012. "FDA User Fees 2012: How Innovation Helps Patients and Jobs." http://www.fda.gov/NewsEvents/Testimony/ucm300568.htm.

Wosinska, M. 2002. "Just What the Patient Ordered? Direct-to-Consumer Advertising and the Demand for Pharmaceutical Products." Marketing Research Paper Series. Harvard Business School, Boston.

———. 2004. "Directo-to-Consumer Advertising and Drug Therapy Compliance." Working paper, Harvard Business School, Cambridge, MA.

Zeckhauser, R. 1970. "Medical Insurance: A Case Study of the Tradeoff between Risk Spreading and Appropriate Incentives." *Journal of Economic Theory* 2:10–26.

Zweifel, P., and L. Crivelli. 1996. "Price Regulation of Drugs: Lessons from Germany." *Journal of Regulatory Economics* 10:257–73.

Regulation and Deregulation of the US Banking Industry
Causes, Consequences, and Implications for the Future

Randall S. Kroszner and Philip E. Strahan

8.1 Introduction

The banking industry has been subject to extensive government regulation covering what prices (that is, interest rates) banks can charge, what activities they can engage in, what risks they can and cannot take, what capital they must hold, and what locations they can operate in. Banks are subject to regulation by multiple regulators at both the state and federal level. Each state has its own regulatory commission. At the federal level the primary bank regulators are the Office of the Comptroller of the Currency (OCC), the Federal Deposit Insurance Corporation (FDIC), and the Federal Reserve Board. Even banks that operate at a single location are likely to be regulated by at least one state and two federal bodies.

The banking industry also plays a significant part in both the financial system and the economy as a whole. The importance of the banking industry goes beyond its mere size; numerous studies (as we describe later) have shown that the health of this sector has significant effects on overall economic activity, as well as the size and persistence of economic cycles. Banks (along

Randall S. Kroszner is the Norman R. Bobins Professor of Economics at the Booth School of Business and was formerly a governor of the Federal Reserve System; he is also a research associate of the National Bureau of Economic Research. Philip E. Strahan is the John L. Collins Professor of Finance at Boston College and a research associate of the National Bureau of Economic Research.

We would like to thank participants in the NBER regulation conference for helpful comments, particularly the discussant Charles Calomiris, Jonathan Macey, and Nancy Rose. Thanks also to William Melick and seminar participants in the Bundesbank. Randall S. Kroszner is grateful for support from the Stigler Center for the Study of the Economy and the State at the Graduate School of Business of the University of Chicago. For acknowledgments, sources of research support, and disclosure of the authors' material financial relationships, if any, please see http://www.nber.org/chapters/c12571.ack.

with other financial institutions) encourage and collect savings that finance economic growth. By allocating that savings and monitoring the use of those funds, banks play an integral role in assuring the productivity of resource use throughout the economy. Banks are also a crucial provider of liquidity to both individuals and firms, and this role becomes particularly important in times of economic stress and crisis. The quality of bank regulation, which affects the stability, efficiency, and size of the sector, thus has an important effect on the level and volatility of economic growth.

Regulation of banking has undergone tremendous change over time, with extensive regulations put into place in the 1930s, and later removed in the last quarter of the twentieth century. This deregulation has been accompanied by a dramatic reduction in the number of banking institutions in the United States, but not an increase in banking concentration at the local level. Regulatory change has been driven by both macroeconomic shocks as well as competition among interest groups within banking and between banks and other financial services providers. As we show, the role of both private interests and public interests play a key part in the analysis.

This chapter was completed and presented at an NBER conference in 2005, prior to the financial crisis of 2008. One of the themes that we developed was the importance of "market adaptation" to regulatory constraints. By "market adaptation," we mean actions and innovations undertaken by banks and their competitors to circumvent or reduce the costs of regulation. One of the consequences of market adaptation was to provide incentives for the creation of alternative institutions and markets competing with but also connected to the banking system. This web of alternative institutions and markets is now loosely referred to as the "shadow banking" sector. While we will keep the bulk of the chapter as it was, we have added an epilogue to show how "market adaptation" may have contributed to fragilities that set the conditions for the financial crisis. We also touch briefly on postcrisis regulatory responses, such as Dodd-Frank and Basel III. Since many, if not most, of the postcrisis responses are yet to be implemented or will be phased in over many years, we will not be able to undertake the same detailed empirical analysis of the post-2008 regulatory responses that we do for the regulation from the financial crisis of the 1930s until the early 2000s.

This chapter has four main goals. First, we provide an overview of the major regulations that have affected the structure and efficiency of the banking industry. In section 8.2 we explain the origins of state and federal banking regulation and briefly describe how the laws and regulations have evolved. We focus on five areas: restrictions on entry and geographic expansion; deposit insurance; product-line and activity restrictions; pricing restrictions; and capital regulation.

Second, we evaluate the consequences of these regulations for the banking industry as well as for the financial system more broadly. Glass-Steagall regulation, to take one example, prevented commercial bank involvement in the corporate bond and equity underwriting businesses until its recent repeal. Glass-Steagall not only kept commercial banks from competing with investment banks, but also spawned a variety of innovations and institutions such as venture capital to substitute where banks could not go. As noted earlier, "market adaptation" to regulatory constraints has generated change in the banking and financial services industry, as banks and their competitors attempt to circumvent the costs of regulations. Moreover, a regulation that at one point helped the industry may later become a burden and hence sow the seeds of its own demise. Interest rate restrictions that eliminated price competition among banks, for example, lost the support of the industry when new financial institutions and markets emerged to provide market rates of interest on checking-like accounts (e.g., the Merrill Lynch Cash Management Account from the 1970s). The first half of section 8.3 provides a brief overview of such consequences, adaptations, and regulatory responses.

Third, we investigate some of the real effects of bank regulatory change, on both the industry and the economy. The elimination of geographic restrictions on bank expansion that limited competition, for example, had positive consequences on the industry (by reducing the riskiness of banks and increasing their efficiency), on credit supply (by providing lower pricing of loans), and on the economy (by increasing economic growth and reducing economic fluctuations). Deregulation of restrictions on geographical expansion and product lines also led to a more consolidated but generally less locally concentrated banking system dominated by large and diversified banking organizations that compete in multiple markets.

Fourth, we provide a positive explanation for regulatory change (section 8.4). A variety of technological, legal, and economic shocks have altered the relative strengths, effectiveness, and interests of different groups competing for support or reform of banking regulation. The development of the automated teller machine (ATM) in the early 1970s, for example, reduced the value of geographic protections to smaller local banks, thereby reducing their willingness to fight to maintain restrictions on branching. A number of court decisions also changed the impact of long-standing regulations in areas such as usury ceilings. Economic crises, either system wide, as in the 1930s, or to parts of the financial system, as in the savings and loan crisis of the 1980s, have also had important distributional impacts that led to regulatory change. We provide some explanations for both the timing of regulatory changes broadly, and for the patterns of change across states.

Finally, in the epilogue, we describe briefly how many of the themes we saw develop in the seven decades following the Great Depression, such as market adaptation to regulation, accelerated during the 2000s and set the stage for the 2007–2008 crisis. To take one prominent example, more than $500 billion in loan pools moved from bank balance sheets to asset-backed commercial paper conduits between 2004 and 2007 (Acharya, Schnabl, and Suarez 2013). These assets were financed with short-term commercial paper, rather than bank deposits as in traditional intermediation, motivated in least in part by an attempt to escape the original Basel capital regulations. The consequence was to create opaque interconnections and made the entire system vulnerable to losses of confidence in the underlying assets, such as mortgages.

8.2   Evolution of Key Dimensions of Bank Regulations

We begin by describing the historical origins and evolution of the most important dimensions of banking regulation in the United States: restrictions on bank entry and geographic expansion, deposit insurance, regulation of bank products, pricing restrictions, and capital requirements. Table 8.1 summarizes this history with the origins and evolution of the key legislative and regulatory decisions.[1]

8.2.1   Historical Background: States and the Federal Government

As we discuss in more detail in the next section, the origin of the power of states in the United States to regulate banking goes back to 1789. The Constitution gave states the right to charter banks as well as to regulate their activities. Alexander Hamilton, however, advocated the creation of a federally chartered bank to deal with debt from the Revolutionary War and to unify the currency. The First Bank of the United States was created in 1791 and operated until 1811. The accumulation of federal debt due to the War of 1812 then revived interest in a federal bank and the Second Bank of the United States was chartered in 1816. Farm interests and generally interests outside of the Northeast strongly opposed the Second Bank, arguing that it involved excessive centralized control of the financial system, usurped states' rights to charter banks, inappropriately drew resources from around the country into the hands of wealthy members of the Northeast elite, and unfairly competed with state-chartered banks (see Hammond 1957). Andrew Jackson built a coalition of antibank forces to win reelection in 1832 and vetoed the rechartering of the Second Bank. During the 1830s and 1840s, a number of states passed "free banking" statutes that encouraged entry of more banks.

This veto took the federal government out of banking and its regulation until the Civil War, when a variety of acts, including the National Banking Act of 1863, created a federal charter for banks and initiated the so-called dual banking system of competing state and federal regulation (see White

---

1. Another important and growing area of regulation are fair lending laws that attempt to expand credit to low-income areas and to reduce lending discrimination (e.g., the Community Reinvestment Act and the Home Mortgage Disclosure Act). We are not going to discuss these laws because this dimension of banking regulation, while very important, has not had major effects on the structure of the banking industry. For a comprehensive review of these laws, see Thomas (1993).

Table 8.1   **Evolution of banking regulations**

	Origin of regulation	History of deregulation
Restrictions on entry and expansion	Nineteenth century: States and comptroller of the currency limit access to bank charters and restrict branching. 1927: McFadden Act permits states to restrict branching of national banks. 1956: Bank Holding Company Act give states authority to restrict entry by out-of-state banks and holding companies.	1970s–1980s: States gradually relax restrictions on in-state branching and cross-state ownership; OCC and states relax chartering restrictions. 1982: Garn St Germain Act permits banks to purchase failing banks or thrifts across state lines. 1994: Interstate Banking and Branching Efficiency Act permits banks and holding companies to purchase banks across state lines and permits national banks to branch across state lines.
Deposit insurance	Early twentieth century: Some states introduce mutual-guarantee deposit insurance systems. 1933: Federal deposit insurance adopted ("temporary" then permanent in 1934). 1950–1980: Deposit insurance limit periodically raised, reaching $250,000 in 2008.	1987: Competitive Equality in Banking Act allocates $10.8 billion to recapitalize the FSLIC. 1989: Financial Institutions Reform, Recovery, and Enforcement Act adds additional funds to deposit insurance and restricts activities of thrifts. 1991: FDIC Improvement Act imposes risk-based deposit insurance and requires "prompt corrective action" of poorly capitalized depository institutions. 2006: Federal Deposit Insurance Reform Act merges bank and thrift funds, allows greater flexibility in setting risk-based premiums, and indexes coverage to inflation beginning in 2010. 2008: Deposit insurance increased to $250,000 overall and the limit is temporarily removed for all transactions deposits in response to the global financial crisis.

(continued)

Table 8.1 (*continued*)

	Origin of regulation	History of deregulation
Product restrictions	1933: Glass-Steagall Act separates commercial lending and underwriting. 1956: Bank Holding Company Act prevents holding companies from owning insurance or securities affiliates.	1987: Federal Reserve allows banks to underwrite corporate debt and equity. 1989–1996: Federal Reserve relaxes revenue restrictions on bank securities affiliates. 1999: Financial Modernization Act allows banks to underwrite insurance and securities through affiliates.
Limits on pricing	Nineteenth century and earlier: State usury laws limit interest on loans. 1933: Banking Act of 1933 (Glass-Steagall) limits interest on deposits (Regulation Q).	1978: *Marquette* decision allows banks to lend anywhere under the usury laws of the bank's home state. 1980: Depository Institutions Deregulation and Monetary Control Act (DIDMCA) phases out interest rate ceilings on deposits. 1980s: Credit card business flocks to South Dakota and Delaware to take advantage of elimination of usury laws.
Capital requirements	Nineteenth century and earlier: State and national banks are required to invest a minimum amount of equity to attain a bank charter.	1980s: Minimum capital-asset ratios required for banks. 1988 (effective 1992): Basel Accord mandates minimum ratio of capital to risk-weighted assets, which accounts crudely for differences in credit risk across loans and for bank off-balance sheet exposures. 1996: Market risk amendment to the Basel Accord introduces model-based capital requirement for trading positions. 2005 (with phased implementation): Consensus between international regulators achieved on Basel II Accord, which moves toward a comprehensive risk-based capital adequacy standard incorporating market, credit, and operational risk and encourages banks to use internal models to measure risk, but still subject to revision. 2009: International regulators begin negotiating to increase bank capital buffers and introducing liquidity ratio tests under the Basel III process.

1983). These newly created "national" banks were enticed to hold federal government debt to back their issuance of bank notes, thereby helping to finance the Civil War. The act also taxed the issuance of bank notes by state-chartered institutions, thereby giving an incentive for banks to switch from state to federal charters.

In the nineteenth century, private clearinghouse systems developed to provide some forms of private sector monitoring and "regulation" of bank activities. Although there is much controversy concerning the efficacy of the private clearinghouse system, the Panic of 1907 and the inability of the New York clearinghouses to prevent the collapse of important parts of the banking system again revived interest in federal involvement in banking.[2] The Federal Reserve Act of 1913 created a federally chartered central bank with important federal bank regulatory powers and a system of regional Federal Reserve Banks. This decentralized structure reflected the continuing struggle between the financial elites in the Northeast and interests in the rest of the country.

8.2.2   Chartering Restrictions and Restrictions on Geographic Expansion

After the United States Constitution prevented the states from issuing fiat money and from taxing interstate commerce, states used their powers over banks to generate a substantial part of their revenues (Sylla, Legler, and Wallis 1987). States received fees for granting bank charters, and state governments often owned or purchased shares in banks and levied taxes on banks. During the first third of the nineteenth century, for example, the bank-related share of total state revenues exceeded 10 percent in a dozen states. In Massachusetts and Delaware, a majority of total state revenue was bank related.

States used their regulatory authority over banks to enhance revenues coming from this source.[3] In particular, each state had an interest in restricting competition among banks, and many of the restrictions on the geographical expansion of banks originate in this period. To enter the banking business, one had to obtain a charter from the state legislature. States received no charter fees from banks incorporated in other states, so the states prohibited out-of-state banks from operating in their territories—hence the origin of the prohibition on interstate banking.

In addition to excluding banks from other states, the legislatures often restricted intrastate expansion. States would grant a charter for a specific location or limit bank branches to that city or county, but these restrictions would also typically protect the bank from intrusion by branches of another

2. See, for example, Calomiris and Kahn (1991) and Kroszner (2000).
3. Noll (1989) has characterized conceiving of governments as distinct interest groups concerned about financing their expenditures as the Leviathan approach; see Buchanan and Tullock (1962), and Niskanen (1971).

bank.[4] By adopting branching restrictions, the states were able to create a series of local monopolies from which they could extract at least part of the rents. Some state legislatures even passed "unit banking" laws that prevented a bank from having any branches. Such regulations, naturally, produce beneficiaries who are loathe to give up their protections and privileges. Benefits tend to be concentrated, while costs to consumers of a less efficient and competitive financial sector tend to be diffuse, as we describe more fully in the political economy section below (e.g., Stigler 1971; Peltzman 1976).

The 1927 McFadden Act clarified the authority of the states over the regulation of national bank's branching activities within their borders.[5] Although there was some deregulation of branching restrictions in the 1930s, most states continued to enforce these policies into the 1970s. For example, only twelve states allowed unrestricted statewide branching in 1970. Between 1970 and 1994, however, thirty-eight states deregulated their restrictions on branching. Reform of restrictions on intrastate branching typically occurred in a two-step process. First, states permitted multibank holding companies (MBHCs) to convert subsidiary banks (existing or acquired) into branches. MBHCs could then expand geographically by acquiring banks and converting them into branches. Second, states began permitting *de novo* branching, whereby banks could open new branches anywhere within state borders. Figure 8.1 describes the timing of intrastate branching deregulation across the states.

In addition to branching limitations within a state, until the 1980s states prohibited cross-state ownership of banks. Following passage of the McFadden Act, banks had begun circumventing state branching restrictions by building multibank holding companies with operations in many states. The Douglas Amendment to the 1956 Bank Holding Company (BHC) Act ended this practice by prohibiting a BHC from acquiring banks outside the state where it was headquartered unless the target bank's state permitted such acquisitions. Since all states chose to bar such transactions, the amendment effectively prevented interstate banking.

The first step toward change began in 1978, when Maine passed a law allowing entry by out-of-state BHCs if, in return, banks from Maine were allowed to enter those states. (Entry in this case means the ability to purchase existing banks, not to enter de novo.) No state reciprocated, however, so the interstate deregulation process remained stalled until 1982, when Alaska and New York passed laws similar to Maine's. State deregulation

---

4. Until the early 1990s, for example, the Illinois Banking Commission would grant "home office protection," which prohibited a bank from opening a branch within a certain number of feet of another bank's main office.

5. Hubbard, Palia, and Economides (1996) examine the political economy of the passage of the McFadden Act and find results consistent with a triumph of the numerous small and poorly capitalized banks over the large and well-capitalized banks. See also White (1983) and Abrams and Settle (1993).

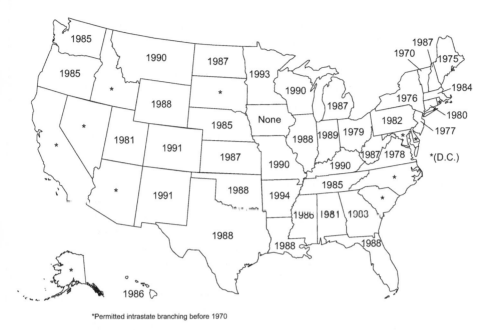

*Permitted intrastate branching before 1970

Fig. 8.1   Timing of deregulation of restrictions on intrastate branching
Source: Kroszner and Strahan (1999).

of interstate banking was nearly complete by 1992, by which time all states but Hawaii had passed similar laws. The transition to full interstate banking was completed with passage of the Reigle-Neal Interstate Banking and Branching Efficiency Act of 1994, which effectively permitted banks and holding companies to enter another state without permission (see Kroszner and Strahan 2001b).

8.2.3   Deposit Insurance

Federal deposit insurance in the United States dates back to 1933, when Congress passed a series of laws designed to restore confidence in the financial and banking systems. Early debate over deposit insurance illustrates a clear understanding of the idea that while insurance could reduce bank runs and the associated disruptions to bank-loan supply, the cost of deposit insurance could be greater risk taking by banks (see, e.g., Kroszner and Melick 2008). This understanding reflected the experiences of earlier state-sponsored insurance and guarantee regimes during the nineteenth and early twentieth century. Half of the state-run bank note insurance systems set up before the Civil War were at times unable to meet their obligations. Later, eight states created deposit insurance systems between 1907 and 1917, and all eight systems failed during the 1920s due to excessive risk taking by banks in those states (Calomiris and White 2000). The legislation creating the federal deposit insurance in the Great Depression itself was initially opposed by the Roosevelt administration and many of the major congressional leaders. Calomiris and White argue that federal insurance was ultimately adopted only because the general public, concerned about bank safety following the banking collapse in the early 1930s, became aligned with small and rural banks, the traditional supporters and main beneficiaries of deposit insurance.

Historical evidence suggests an important interaction between branching restrictions just described and the riskiness of banks, namely that branch banking lowered risk and increased stability, thereby reducing the call for deposit insurance. Gorton (1996) offers some unique evidence that markets understood the stabilizing effect of branch banking. He shows that during the nineteenth century when private banks issued currency, notes in circulation that were issued by new banks from branch banking states were discounted substantially less than notes issued by banks from unit banking states. Calomiris (1993) shows that both bank reserves and bank capital were lower in states with branch banking. He also studies bank failure rates in three states allowing branching but affected by the agricultural bust of the 1920s—Arizona, Mississippi, and South Carolina. Failure rates in these three states were much lower for banks with branches than those without. Comparing states that allowed branching with those that limited it, Calomiris (1992) also finds faster asset growth during the agricultural recession of the 1920s in states that allowed branching. And, as is widely recognized, the Canadian banking system, which contained a small number of large banks with nationwide branching, experienced no bank failures during the 1930s.[6]

Both political debate as well as some limited evidence from roll call voting patterns leading up to deposit insurance passage indicate that small and rural banks supported both restrictions on bank branching (to reduce competitive pressure from large banks) and deposit insurance (to increase deposit supply). By contrast, large and urban banks pushed for branch banking to allow them to compete with small banks directly, and generally opposed deposit insurance as a subsidy to small, poorly diversified banks. Calomiris and White (2000) compare bank characteristics in states with relatively high support for a federal insurance bill brought to a vote in 1913 (H.R. 7837). They show that banks were smaller (particularly state banks) and branching was less prevalent in states with high support.

Small banks won the political battle in the 1930s, and continued to win subsequent battles over the next several decades. Deposit insurance cover-

6. Dehejia and Lleras-Muney (2007) analyze the political economy of deposit insurance adoption from 1900 to 1940. After controlling for the endogeneity of the deposit insurance regime, they provide evidence of a negative relationship between the adoption of deposit insurance and growth, suggesting that such regimes may have impaired the efficiency of the banking system and capital allocation in these states.

age was increased in 1950 (from $5,000 to $10,000); in 1966 (to $15,000); in 1969 (to $20,000); in 1974 (to $40,000); and in 1980 with passage of DIDMCA (to $100,000). White (1998) argues that small banks supported each of these increases, while large banks opposed them. As a result, the real value of deposit insurance rose from $5,000 (in 1934 dollars) initially to $10,000 to $15,000 during the 1970s. Since 1980, deposit insurance coverage has remained flat, with inflation eroding its real value by about 50 percent over the past twenty-five years. Deposit insurance has also been expanding globally (Demirguc-Kunt and Kane 2002). Similar political forces seem to explain coverage levels across countries. For example, Laeven (2004) shows that coverage levels are higher in countries with weaker and riskier banking systems.

The large number of bank and thrift failures during the 1980s and early 1990s halted the increasing coverage of deposit insurance in the United States (see figure 8.2). During the 1980s, to take the most extreme example, the federal insurer of thrift deposits (the Federal Savings and Loan Insurance Association, or FSLIC) itself became insolvent. The S&L crisis had its roots in the basic lack of diversification of thrift assets (long-term mortgages financed with short-term deposits), coupled with regulators' failure to close market-value insolvent thrifts after the run-up of interest rates in the early 1980s. FSLIC was dismantled in 1989 when the Financial Institutions Reform, Recovery, and Enforcement Act (FIRREA) both recapitalized the

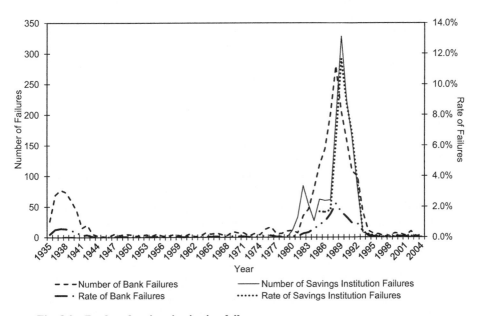

Fig. 8.2   Bank and savings institution failures
Source: FDIC.

Savings Association Insurance Fund (SAIF) and gave the FDIC responsibility for overseeing deposit insurance for thrifts.[7]

This very costly experience with deposit insurance led to reform in the early 1990s. The FDIC Improvement Act (FDICIA) of 1991 attempts to reduce the risk-taking incentives inherent in deposit insurance by introducing risk-based premiums and by directing the FDIC to resolve failed banks in the least costly way to the deposit insurance fund. The deposit insurance premia were required to generate sufficient revenue to reach a target ratio of 1.25 percent of deposits insured by the fund. The motivation behind the least-cost resolution provisions were the failure of large banks such as Continental Illinois and Bank of New England during the 1980s in which *all* creditors had been bailed out to avoid "systemic" disruptions. The comptroller of the currency even announced publicly after Continental Illinois that some large banks were "too big to fail."[8] This public announcement was quickly seen as unwise, and the 1991 law attempted to correct market perceptions that some banks were too big to fail and thereby reign in excessive risk taking incentives. Importantly, FDICIA also introduced "prompt corrective action" whereby regulators are required to respond swiftly and not exercise "forbearance" as institutions fall into trouble.[9]

In recent years, the tide has turned again, toward expansion of deposit insurance. In 2002, small banks began issuing fully insured certificates of deposit through the Certificates of Deposit Account Registry Service (CDARS). CDARS works through a network of banks whereby a customer's large deposits are split up and placed as accounts under the $100,000 deposit insurance limit at bank members of the system. Thus, large depositors can effectively get around deposit insurance limits. At the same time, pressure for extended *de jure* coverage seems to be coming from small banks. For example, the Independent Community Bankers Association "has been in the forefront of the campaign for comprehensive Federal deposit insurance reform including automatic inflation adjustments of coverage levels. In the 24 years since FDIC coverage was last adjusted, inflation has eroded away more than half its value. The stability of our financial system depends on consumer confidence that their funds will be protected. We are working with key Members of Congress to make comprehensive deposit insurance reform with automatic inflation adjustments a reality."[10]

At the same time, bank deposit growth has pushed the Bank Insurance Fund to near the 1.25 percent reserve threshold, potentially triggering assess-

7. Much has been written about the S&L crisis of the 1980s, and we will not review that very large literature here. See, for example, Kane (1989), Kroszner and Strahan (1996), White (1991).
8. Stock prices of those banks listed in the *Wall Street Journal* as "too big to fail" rose upon hearing the comptroller's unwillingness to close them (O'Hara and Shaw 1990).
9. Mitchener (2007) analyzes different state regulatory regimes during the Great Depression and finds that states allowing supervisors to liquidate troubled banks quickly had less bank instability than other states.
10. See http://www.ibaa.org/advocacy/.

ments for deposit insurance for even highly rated institutions. The prospect of these assessments, along with small-bank advocacy of increasing deposit insurance coverage, led to the passage of the Federal Deposit Insurance Reform Act of 2005. The act is part of the Deficit Reduction Act of 2005 (S 1932) that was signed into law on February 8, 2006. The act creates a new Deposit Insurance Fund (DIF) that merges the old Bank Insurance Fund with the Savings Institution Insurance Fund, increases deposit insurance for retirement accounts to $250,000, provides for the adjustment of deposit insurance limits for inflation beginning in April 2010, and, perhaps most importantly, increases the FDIC's flexibility in setting risk-based premiums. Constraints on risk-based premiums remain, however, because once the new DIF reserve fund reaches 1.35 percent of total insured deposits, dividends must be paid to member institutions so that the reserve ratio does not exceed this threshold.

8.2.4 Product-Line Restrictions

Explicit restrictions prohibiting bank involvement in underwriting, insurance, and other "nonbank" financial activities began with the passage of the Banking Act of 1933. The four sections of the act that separate banking and nonbanking activity—16, 20, 21, 32—are collectively known as the Glass-Steagall Act (Mester 1996). The Bank Holding Company Act of 1956 (and the amendment to the act in 1970) further strengthened the demarcation between banks, insurance, and securities firms. It was not until the mid-1980s that the Federal Reserve and the Office of the Comptroller of Currency (OCC) began loosening restrictions on bank participation in investment banking and insurance.

Even though concerns about the stability of the banking system would be a rationale for the continuation of the Glass-Steagall separations subsequently, such considerations did not form an important part of the debate in 1933. Banks that were involved in underwriting securities tended to be larger and better diversified than other banks and were less likely to fail during the 1930s (see White 1986). Instead, the main focus of the debate on bank powers concerned conflicts of interest. With their close relationships with firms, bankers might have an information advantage relative to the market about the prospects for a firm. If a bank knows that a firm may be heading for distress before the market does, a bank that succumbs to conflicts would issue a security to the public and have the firm use the proceeds to repay its loans to the bank. A number studies of bank underwriting behavior during the 1920s and 1930s, however, have found little evidence to suggest that such conflicts were important in practice (see Kroszner and Rajan 1994 and 1997; Ang and Richardson 1994; Puri 1996).[11]

11. On the political economy of the origins of Glass-Steagall, see Macey (1984) and Shughart (1988).

Although Glass-Steagall and the subsequent Banking Acts of 1956 and 1970 disallowed underwriting by banks and bank holding company (BHC) affiliates, certain securities, deemed "eligible" securities by regulators, were exempted from the original act, and were therefore never in question by regulators. These eligible securities included municipal general obligation bonds, US government bonds, and real estate bonds (Kwan 1998).

The Federal Reserve began the expansion of BHC powers with a decision in 1987 to allow subsidiaries of three BHCs to underwrite certain previously prohibited securities on a limited basis.[12] The Federal Reserve derived legal authority for the decision from a clause in Section 20 of the 1933 Banking Act that prohibits banks from affiliating with a company "engaged principally" in underwriting or dealing securities (Mester 1996). On April 30, 1987, the Federal Reserve argued that the "engaged principally" clause allowed BHC subsidiaries to underwrite certain "ineligible securities" such as municipal revenue bonds, commercial paper, and mortgage-related securities as long as the revenue from such underwriting did not exceed 5 percent of the subsidiary's gross revenue (Bhargava and Fraser 1998).

On January 18, 1989, the Federal Reserve allowed the "Section 20 subsidiaries" to underwrite corporate debt and equity securities contingent on the 5 percent revenue limitation. The Federal Reserve continued its incremental lifting of restrictions by increasing the revenue limit on Section 20 subsidiaries to 10 percent on September 13, 1989 and to 25 percent on December 20, 1996 (Bhargava and Fraser 1998; Ely and Robinson 1998). To relax this revenue restriction further, banks also placed other activities, such as those related to government securities, in these subsidiaries.

Throughout the debate on BHC involvement in nonbank financial operations, the Federal Reserve enforced firewalls between banking and nonbanking activity within the subsidiary structure of the BHC. These firewalls were instituted to prevent financial and information flows between securities and banking subsidiaries, and to insulate banking activity from unforeseen shocks to nonbank activity (Shull and White 1998). For example, bank lending to nonbank subsidiaries was limited, and restrictions were placed on payments from banks to the holding company (Boyd and Graham 1986). Beginning in July of 1996, the Federal Reserve began loosening the barriers between banking and nonbanking activities. Interestingly, similar firewalls had emerged endogenously during the 1920s as investment companies affiliated with banks sought to commit credibly to markets not to abuse private information from lending relationships (Kroszner and Rajan 1997).

While the Federal Reserve oversaw BHC expansion into securities, OCC rulings backed by the federal courts simultaneously loosened restrictions on national banks' insurance activity. These regulatory changes allowed

---

12. See Kroszner and Stratmann (1998, 2000) and Stratmann (2001) on the politics behind legislation aimed at removing restrictions on Glass-Steagall.

BHCs to make some inroads into nonbanking financial services. Lown et al. (2000) show, for example, that BHCs' percentage of the securities industry's aggregate revenue went from 9 percent in 1993 to over 25 percent in 1999. Bhargava and Fraser (1998) report similar findings, and show that bank underwriting activities broadened considerably and included a full range of debt and equity issues. Lown et al. (2000) also show that BHCs greatly expanded annuity sales after the 1995 Supreme Court decision (*Nationsbank v. VALIC*) ruling that states could not prohibit the sales of annuities by national banks (which we describe in more detail in section 8.4). Although BHCs were exploring the insurance sales sector, the authors show that BHC involvement in the insurance market remained small, in part because strict barriers between insurance underwriting remained a significant impediment to the joint production of cross-sector financial services.

Congress finally completed the dismantling of Glass-Steagall altogether by passing the Financial Modernization Act in 1999, which allows financial holding companies (FHCs) to own affiliates engaged in banking, insurance underwriting, and securities activities. The act, known also the Gramm-Leach-Bliley Act or GLBA, was passed a little more than six months following the merger of Citicorp and Travelers, which formed the first full-service financial conglomerate in the United States since the 1920s.

While the newly formed Citigroup has subsequently divested much of its insurance holdings, the lines between commercial and investment banking have become increasingly blurred during the past five years. As figure 8.3 shows, for example, financial conglomerates have come to dominate the

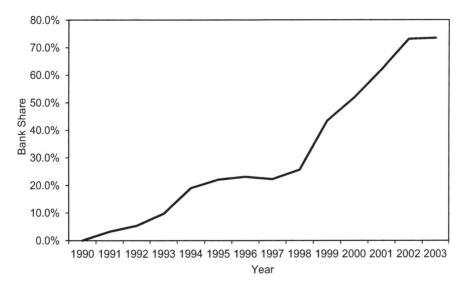

Fig. 8.3 Share of corporate debt underwritten by commercial banks
Source: Sufi (2005).

market for debt underwriting (see Sufi 2005). In 1996, the top five debt underwriters were all stand-alone investment banks (Morgan Stanley, Salomon Brothers, Goldman Sachs, Merrill Lynch, and First Boston). By 2003, however, four of the top five underwriters were owned by full-service financial conglomerates (Citigroup, JPMorgan Chase, Bank of America, Merrill Lynch, and Credit Suisse). At the same time, traditional investment banks have made inroads into commercial lending. According to Loan Pricing Corporation, for example, Goldman Sachs ranked seventh and Lehman Brothers ranked ninth in arranging syndicated loans during the first half of 2005.[13]

This convergence offers a striking parallel between recent times and the 1920s, particularly with respect to pressures on commercial banks to become more involved in the corporate securities markets (Kroszner 1997). One of the most notable developments then was the increasing frequency with which firms accessed the public equity and debt markets. The volume of new equity issues grew during the 1920s, skyrocketing in late 1928 and 1929. The 1980s also was a period that witnessed a dramatic increase in the number of initial public offerings (IPOs). The number of IPOs nearly tripled from the 1970s to the 1980s, from an average of 120 per year to an average of 350 per year (Loughran and Ritter 1995).

More firms also were beginning to use bond financing in both periods. Smaller and lesser known firms were enjoying new access to the bond markets in both the 1920s and 1980s. With the entrance of a new class of firms, the average rating of corporate bonds declined. The proportion of bonds that were initially rated below investment grade rose steadily during the 1920s, from 12 percent in 1921 to 43 percent by 1929 (Kroszner and Rajan 1994). The same phenomenon occurs during the 1980s with the growth of original issue high-yield debt (so-called junk bond) market. The number of initially rated below investment grade bonds grew from 24 in 1981 to 200 by 1986, and the amount issued rose from $1.2 billion to $30.9 billion during this period (Asquith, Mullins, and Wolff 1989).[14]

With the growth of the public markets as a source of funds for firms came a corresponding decline in reliance on commercial bank borrowing. In addition, banks were facing greater competition from other financial institutions. As table 8.2 illustrates, commercial bank share of the total assets of US financial institutions had held steady at 60 to 65 percent from 1880 to 1922. Commercial banks then experienced a sharp decline in share between 1922 and 1929 to 54 percent, while investment companies (i.e., mutual funds), securities brokers and dealers, finance companies, and insurance companies

---

13. See http://www.loanpricing.com/.
14. The "junk bonds" of the 1980s often had equity-like characteristics, so it is possible to interpret the turning toward equity and away from debt in the late 1920s as a form of this type of financing.

Table 8.2 Percentage shares of assets of financial institutions in the United States, 1860–2004

	1860	1880	1900	1912	1922	1929	1939	1948	1960	1970	1980	1993	2004
Commercial banks	71.4	60.6	62.9	64.5	63.3	53.7	51.2	55.9	38.2	37.9	34.8	25.4	24.4
Thrift institutions	17.8	22.8	18.2	14.8	13.9	14.0	13.6	12.3	19.7	20.4	21.4	9.4	6.7
Insurance companies	10.7	13.9	13.8	16.6	16.7	18.6	27.2	24.3	23.8	18.9	16.1	17.4	15.2
Investment companies	—	—	—	0.0	0.0	2.4	1.9	1.3	2.9	3.5	3.6	14.9	21.7
Pension funds	—	—	0.0	0.0	0.0	0.7	2.1	3.1	9.7	13.0	17.4	24.4	21.7
Finance companies	—	0.0	0.0	0.0	0.0	2.0	2.2	2.0	4.6	4.8	5.1	4.7	4.2
Securities brokers and dealers	0.0	0.0	3.8	3.0	5.3	8.1	1.5	1.0	1.1	1.2	1.1	3.3	5.3
Mortgage companies	0.0	0.0	1.3	1.2	0.8	0.6	0.3	0.1	a	a	0.4	0.2	0.1
Real estate investment trusts	—	—	—	—	—	—	—	—	0.0	0.3	0.1	0.1	0.7
Total (*percent*)	100	100	100	100	100	100	100	100	100	100	100	100	100
Total (*trillion dollars*)	.001	.005	.016	.034	.075	.123	.129	.281	.596	1.33	4.0	13.9	34.9

Sources: Data for 1860–1948 (except 1922) from Goldsmith (1969, table D-33, pp. 548–49); data for 1922 from Goldsmith (1958, table 10, pp. 73–74); and data for 1960–1993 from Board of Governors of the Federal Reserve System, "Flow of Funds Accounts," various years.

Notes: The table is expanded from Kaufman and Mote (1994). Assets held by government-sponsored enterprises and asset-backed securities issuers are not included.

aData not available.

grew in share.[15] Between 1980 and 2004, commercial banks again saw a sharp drop in their share, which had held relatively steady between 1960 and 1980 at between 35 and 38 percent, to 24 percent by 2004.

One additional comparison and contrast between the economic and financial conditions of the 1920s and 1980s is of note (see Kroszner 1997).[16] Both decades began and ended with recessions and had a lengthy period of economic growth in between. The recession at the beginning of the 1920s, like the one at the beginning of the 1980s, was sharp and short lived. Both periods witnessed a major stock market crash (October 1929 and October 1987) toward the end of each period. The economic downturns that ended each decade were decidedly different—one was the start of the Great Depression whereas the other was quite mild. Both cases, however, were accompanied by a major wave of depository institution failure and closure. The banking problems in the Great Depression were system wide and led to a near collapse of the entire financial system (see e.g., Friedman and Schwartz 1963; Calomiris and Mason 2003), whereas the troubles in the thrift and banking industries in the 1980s and early 1990s, while considerable, did not have the same consequences (see, e.g., Barth 1991; Kane 1989; Kroszner and Strahan 1996; and White 1991).

The difference in the severity of the end-of-decade downturns and banking problems can account for at least part of the sharp contrast in the bank regulatory response in 1933 compared to the opposing deregulatory response that began in the 1990s (discussed in section 8.4). In the early period, Congress began seriously to debate the restriction of bank powers soon after the stock market crash. Three years later, these restrictions were enacted in the first hundred-day wave of New Deal legislation as part of a broad bill to reform the banking system, including the creation of federal deposit insurance.

8.2.5   Restrictions on Pricing

Regulations have historically constrained pricing of both bank deposits and bank loans. Ceilings on bank deposit interest rates, for example, were in effect into the early 1980s under the Federal Reserve's Regulation Q. During periods when market interest rates rose above these ceilings, banks and other depositories faced reduced deposit supply, forcing them to cut back on lend-

15. As Boyd and Gertler (1994) and Kaufman and Mote (1994) note, a reduction in the share of assets of all financial institutions itself does not address the broader issue of whether the banking industry is in decline.

16. One significant factor today that was not operative in the 1920s is the Basel Bank Capital Accord, which provides an incentive for banks to hold relatively more (government) securities than loans on their books. Unlike the early period, during the late 1980s and early 1990s, the increase in securities holdings was primarily in terms of government rather than corporate issues. By raising and risk adjusting the minimum capital requirements and giving government securities a zero "risk weight," the Basel Accord has given banks a strong incentive to increase their holdings of government securities.

ing. This disintermediation became acute during the 1970s as market rates soared in response to high inflation and loose monetary policy. Moreover, the costs of holding noninterest bearing required reserves at bank members of the Federal Reserve System rose sharply with inflation. In response to the plight of banks (as described more in the political economy section below), Congress passed the Depository Institutions Deregulation and Monetary Control Act (DIDMCA) in 1980, which lowered reserve requirements and gradually phased out most deposit rate ceilings. DIDMCA substantially leveled the competitive playing field across depository institutions by imposing uniform reserve requirements and access to Federal Reserve services, and by allowing banks to pay interest on NOW accounts nationwide (checkable deposits).

On the lending side, usury laws restricting the rates banks may charge date back to the colonial period in the United States and have a very long history before that (e.g., Ellis 1998; Glaeser and Scheinkmann 1998). Conventional interpretation of these laws is that they exist to protect politically powerful borrowers. Consistent with this view, Benmelech and Moskowitz (2007) find that states with more powerful incumbent elites tended to have tighter usury restrictions and responded less to external pressure for repeal. In contrast, Glaeser and Scheinkmann (1998) argue that the pervasiveness of usury restrictions across the world, as well as their persistence over time, implies that such laws exist to reduce the impact of incomplete credit markets. In their model, agents borrow to smooth consumption in the face of negative income shocks, and usury laws transfer wealth to such low-income states, thus moving toward optimal risk sharing.

The importance of state usury laws was permanently reduced in 1978 when the Supreme Court undermined states' ability to enforce them in the *Marquette National Bank v. First Omaha Service* case. The court ruled that Section 85 of the National Banking Act allowed a lender to charge up to the maximum amount allowed in its home state, *regardless of the location of the borrower*. Because credit card lending is not geographically based (in contrast to small business lending), this decision created an incentive for states to raise their usury limits to compete for banks. In fact, Delaware and South Dakota eliminated them entirely, leading to rapid entry of credit card banks in those two states. By 1988, eighteen states had removed interest rate ceilings, and the supply of credit card loans expanded rapidly over the subsequent twenty years. This increase in supply was concentrated most among high-risk borrowers because the interest rate ceilings restrict credit most among that segment of the market. As a consequence, personal bankruptcy rates began a long and steady increase, starting in 1978 with the *Marquette* decision (see figure in Ellis 1998).[17]

---

17. Recent tightening of the personal bankruptcy code has occurred in part to reduce personal bankruptcy rates.

DIDMCA of 1980 also relaxed some constraints on usury ceilings. Although state usury ceilings continue to be in place in most states, they are generally not indexed to inflation, so in the recent low inflation environment they have not been binding on traditional bank lending. For "subprime" borrowers who may be riskier, however, the ceilings may still bind in some circumstances. Credit to subprime borrowers from alternative financial institutions, such as pawn shops and payday loan companies, also are subject to interest rate ceilings. Payday lenders, which provide small-value short-term loans (typically under $300 for roughly two weeks), typically charge annualized interest rates that are at the state level maximum (see Flannery and Samolyk 2005).

8.2.6   Regulation of Bank Capital

Regulations designed to ensure sufficient capital in the banking industry date to the nineteenth century. The grant of a bank charter typically came with a requirement for a minimum absolute amount of capital. Regulations of bank capital-asset ratios did not emerge until the 1980s, however, after capital ratios in the banking industry had reached historical lows. In fact, leverage ratios in the US banking system increased gradually but consistently, starting in the nineteenth century until the early 1980s. Part of the increase in leverage is due to the introduction of deposit insurance during the Great Depression, but part is likely due to increased bank size and diversification, as well as better risk management practices that evolved over time (see Peltzman 1970).

In the past two decades, regulations dictating minimum capital-asset ratios (maximum leverage ratios) have become increasingly complex and comprehensive. Banks first faced minimum requirements based on the raw ratio of equity capital to total assets. These regulations, however, were quickly seen as inadequate as a greater share of bank business was associated with off-balance sheet activities such as credit guarantees and unfunded loan commitments (Boyd and Gertler 1994). These off-balance sheet activities came with a sharp increase in bank revenues from noninterest sources (Mishkin and Strahan 1999), and also represented an important component of bank risk that was not measured at all by total assets or loans. The 1988 Basel Capital Accord addresses this changing nature of banking (or bank accounting) by including off-balance sheet exposures and by accounting for credit risk in constructing risk-based assets. Under the simple scheme, loans with different risks face different marginal capital requirements. For example, banks had to fund business loans with at least 8 percent capital, whereas residential mortgages could be funded with only 4 percent capital. The 1988 accord also addressed perceived inequities in capital requirements across countries, and attempted to level the competitive playing field for internationally active banks.

During the past decade, banks have adopted increasingly sophisticated risk management models, and these new financial technologies have spurred changes to capital requirements. For example, new capital requirements for market risks were adopted using banks' internal risk measurement models in 1996. The key innovation leading to the regulatory change was the introduction of value-at-risk models (e.g., JP Morgan's *RiskMetrics* model), which estimate quantiles of profit and loss distributions for bank trading positions. These models are useful because they quantify the likely magnitude of bank losses during "normal" market conditions, such as conditions covering 99 percent of trading days, and sophisticated versions of such models can avoid making strong distributional assumptions (Jorion 2000).

Following the successful introduction of market risk capital requirements, international bank regulators began to negotiate a more complex and comprehensive capital regime. Referred to as Basel II, this new accord has three "pillars" that focus on trying to update capital requirements, ensure effective regulatory supervision, and enhance the role of market discipline (see Bank for International Settlements 2005). The simple risk adjustment approach in the original accord was seen as no longer adequate to deal with market developments.

As with both the 1988 accord and the 1996 Market Risk Amendment, the move to update the capital requirements has been driven by advances in financial technology. For example, innovations such as securitization and credit derivatives in the late 1990s have made it easier for banks to trade risk, but such trading allows banks to undermine the simple measurement of asset risk behind the 1988 accord (e.g., Calomiris and Mason 2004). At the same time, credit risk measurement tools similar to those used for market risk have become increasingly available. Thus, the capital required under Basel II will depend on model-based construction of the main dimensions of risk (market, operational, and credit risks), and the system is designed to encourage banks to develop internal models rather than rely on externally imposed supervisory models. In the United States, the new accord is likely to apply to only the largest banks that compete internationally, and the minimum leverage ratio (which does not involve risk adjustment of the assets) from the original accord will still apply.

It is important to recognize that capital regulations not only respond to changes in financial technology but may also spur such innovations. For example, efforts to avoid capital may in part explain the rise in off-balance sheet banking during the 1980s. Similarly, the 1988 accord may have encouraged banks to securitize loans in order to reduce required capital ratios, and to trade risks via products such as credit default swaps.

8.3 Consequences of Regulation and Deregulation

This section describes the consequences of banking regulations for the financial industry and for the economy. Much of our understanding of these effects comes from research examining how the banking system evolves following regulatory changes, which are concentrated in the period of regulatory tightening during the early 1930s, and the deregulatory period of the 1980s and 1990s. As we describe, the increased regulations of banking and the securities markets in the 1930s was followed by a decline in securities markets. Later, "market adaptation" generated alternative and less tightly regulated financial institutions to get around regulatory constraints and provide services to investors that had previously been rendered by banks.

The experience of the last two decades has reversed the process. Regulations on banks and markets have eased, and this deregulation has occurred in part in response to the emergence of competing financial institutions during the earlier period. Despite market adaption that likely mitigated the costs of the 1930s regulations, the recent wave of deregulation was followed by substantial restructuring of banking leading to greater efficiency, improved credit access, and better economic performance in some areas, but the development of shadow banking and opaque interconnections increased the fragility of the system.

8.3.1   Consequences of "Market Adaption" after Glass-Steagall: Rise of Alternative Institutions

Decline of Securities Markets

The Glass-Steagall Act of 1933 effectively precluded banks from underwriting corporate securities (see Macey and Miller 1992), but for almost two decades after its enactment, the securities markets saw much less activity than in the 1920s. Almost no corporate securities were issued between 1932 and 1935, even though the industrial production was rebounding strongly from the depths of 1932. Although the economy was recovering, output was still below its 1928 peak so there may not have been much desire on the part of firms to issue securities to finance operations. Alternatively, the removal of the commercial banks from underwriting and the new federal regulation of securities market through the Securities Acts of the 1930s could have increased the cost of securities issuances to prohibitive levels.

Even after the public issuance market revives a bit by the late 1930s, total issuance remained below the levels following World War I. During the 1930s and much of the 1940s, however, there was an enormous increase in government bond issuance. The growth of this market was favorable to commercial banks because they played a major role in this market. As shown in table 8.2, from the late 1930s to the late 1940s, commercial banks actually increased their share of total assets held by financial institutions. By the early 1950s, the corporate securities markets were once again reviving and beginning to pose more of a challenge to bank lending. This situation led some bankers to attempt to avoid the Glass-Steagall prohibitions and reenter the securities markets through a holding company structure. The Bank Holding Company Act of 1956, and its subsequent amendments in 1966 and 1970, thwarted this movement by effectively extending the Glass-Steagall restrictions on banks to holding companies that had banking subsidiaries (see Blair 1994).

Market Adaptation: The Growth of Alternative Financial Institutions and "Shadow Banking"

Until the 1980s, as noted earlier, US commercial banks were effectively prohibited from universal banking following the 1930s legislation. This situation contrasts sharply with Germany, and to some extent Japan, where banks are able to play a much more central role in the financing of private enterprise (see Edwards and Fischer 1994; Aoki and Patrick 1994). Interestingly, a variety of other financial organizations have arisen in the United States that can be interpreted as a means of filling the gap that is the legacy of Glass-Steagall. The organizations discussed following are much more developed in the United States than in other countries, perhaps stimulated by Glass-Steagall. If we are to look for the silver lining in the cloud of Glass-Steagall, the richer variety of alternative sources of funds for enterprise that the United States has relative to other countries could be it.

As table 8.2 illustrates, there are a number of important financial actors in the United States besides commercial banks.[18] Pension funds, insurance companies, and investment companies (i.e., open- and closed-end mutual funds), for example, have come to control large shares of the total assets in financial institutions in the United States. Firms therefore have a rich variety of funding sources. Each set of financial institutions has a distinct set of regulations and a distinct set of interests. These institutions compete to influence financial legislation and regulation (see Kroszner and Stratmann 1998 and 2000), and the regulatory agencies themselves may compete to increase their domains of influence (see Kane 1989). Expanding banking powers in such an environment is unlikely to cause one group to capture all of the financial regulators and use them to impede competition.

In the post–World War II era, a variety of alternative organizations and contractual structures have arisen in the United States that, at least in part, substitute for a universal bank.[19] Perhaps the alternative that has been able to come closest is the venture capital (VC) organization. The first modern VC organization dates back to 1946 when a group of Boston investors formed American Research and Development to invest in firms adapting

---

18. Kaufman and Mote (1994) note that ignoring the trust services of banks, as the table does, may significantly understate the actual overall share of commercial banks.

19. Jensen (1989) has argued that these alternatives arose directly in response to restrictions like Glass-Steagall. Also note that this now broadens the definition of universal banking to include ownership and active monitoring roles by the banks rather than simply corporate securities dealing and underwriting.

war-related technological innovations for commercial use (Gompers 1994; Gompers and Lerner 1996).

The VC industry, however, did not begin to grow rapidly until the late 1970s. In 1979, the "prudent expert" standard that governs permissible investments for pension funds was broadened to allow pension funds to invest in VC funds.[20] This change was extremely important since the regulations associated with ERISA (Employee Retirement Income Security Act) discourage pension funds from directly becoming "active investors," that is, investors who participate in both the financing and management of an enterprise (see Roe 1994). Following the change in the "prudent expert" standard, annual investment in VC funds grew substantially.

The VC form has been a method for pension fund managers and other fund managers to pool their resources in VC funds and act indirectly as active investors. VC funds typically provide not only equity and debt financing but also management expertise and strategic consulting, activities that regulations and tax incentives strongly discourage the pension funds and investment companies themselves from doing (Roe 1994). The VC industry has helped to finance numerous start-up firms that then go public so it has an important effect on the growth of the IPO market.

Another closely related form, the leveraged-buyout organization (LBO), also has had a large impact on corporation finance and restructuring, especially during the 1980s (see Jensen 1989). Much like VC, LBO organizations take debt and equity stakes in firms and become active in the management of the firm. Unlike VC, they purchase existing firms or divisions of firms, typically by using debt to purchase equity, thereby increasing the financial leverage of the enterprise. LBOs involving the purchase of public companies rose from 16 in 1979 to a peak of 125 in 1988, and the annual dollar volume grew from $65 million to nearly $500 million (see Jensen 1989). Jensen (1989) has argued that LBOs are effectively a form of universal banking that is an "end-run" around Glass-Steagall. Starting in the late 1990s, hedge funds have also emerged as an important pool of (unregulated) capital invested in private equity.

This process of market adaptation accelerated in the 2000s with the rapid growth of what has come to be called the "shadow banking" sector, constituting a variety of nonbank institutions and markets that compete with and are connected to the banking system. Much of this market adaptation involved regulatory arbitrage to create vehicles, institutions, and products that would avoid or reduce regulatory capital burdens and oversight, setting the stage for fragilities of the financial crisis of the late 2000s, which we discuss in the epilogue.

---

20. In addition, in 1978 the tax rate on capital gains was reduced from 49.5 percent to 28 percent, thereby making VC more attractive for taxable investors also.

8.3.2   Real Impact of Recent Financial Deregulation

The Structure of the Banking Industry

Deregulation of restrictions on geographical expansion and product lines has led to a more consolidated but less locally concentrated banking system dominated by larger and better diversified banking organizations that compete in multiple markets. Relaxation of restrictions on bank expansion during the 1980s (removal of branching and interstate banking restrictions) led to larger banks operating across wider geographical areas. The effects of this deregulation on industry structure can be seen graphically in the next few figures.

The number of institutions, which remained almost constant for half a century, begins to fall dramatically starting in the early 1980s, just as states began to dismantle restrictions on geographic expansion (figure 8.4). The reduction in the number of banks occurs primarily through mergers. As figure 8.5 shows, the rate of bank mergers rises consistently from roughly 1980 until the end of the 1990s. This decline of more than 40 percent in the number of banks reflects an industry restructuring made possible by deregulation, rather than removal of "excess" banking capacity. In fact, as figure 8.4 illustrates, the number of bank offices increases steadily throughout the 1980s and 1990s—rising by more than one-third—despite the consolidation. Moreover, the rate of *de novo* banking (new charters) is high on average during the 1980s and 1990s (figure 8.5).

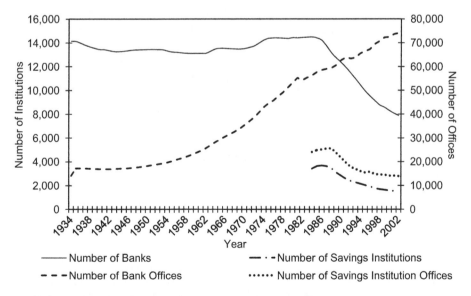

Fig. 8.4   Number of bank and savings institutions and offices
Source: FDIC.

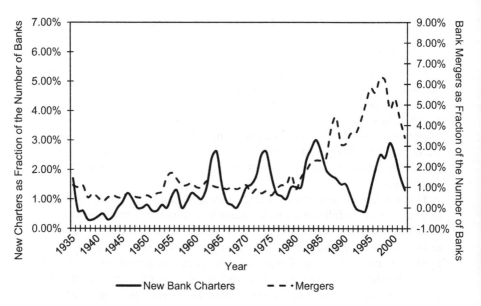

Fig. 8.5   Entry and consolidation of banking
Source: Five-year moving average, from FDIC data.

The number of savings institutions also shrank over this period (see figure 8.4), but the decline occurs mainly in response to the S&L crisis. During the second half of the 1980s the annual failure rate for savings institutions reached almost 10 percent of institutions per year (recall figure 8.2). Following this decline, the banking industry began purchasing large numbers of branches from failed savings institutions and began holding more residential mortgages. Moreover, during the 1990s, the government-sponsored enterprises (GSEs)—the Federal National Mortgage Association (Fannie Mae) and the Federal Home Loan Mortgage Corporation (Freddie Mac)—began to play an increasingly important role in holding and securitizing mortgages, as shown in figure 8.6. In 1985, for example, about 25 percent of the outstanding mortgages were either purchased and held or purchased and securitized by the GSEs. By 2003, this market share had increased to about 50 percent.[21]

Following passage of the Riegle-Neal Interstate Banking and Branching Act in 1994, the US banking system has been transformed from a "balkan-

21. Policymakers have voiced concerns about the resulting expansion of interest rate risk at the GSEs (Greenspan 2004). Passmore, Sherlund, and Burgess (2005) argue that most (but not all) of the benefits of GSE-subsidized borrowing benefits their shareholders rather than mortgage borrowers. Loutskina (2011) and Loutskina and Strahan (2009) show, however, that securitization fostered by GSE activities helps banks manage their liquidity risk and reduces the impact of financial constraints on bank-loan supply.

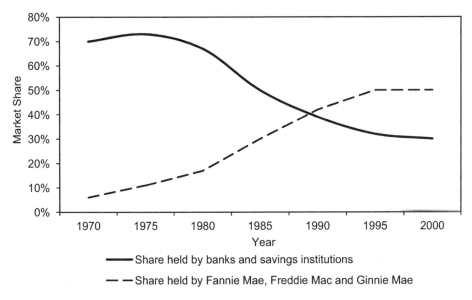

Fig. 8.6   Mortgage holdings by depository institutions and government-sponsored enterprises
Source: Frame and White (2005).

ized" one in which institutions operated locally or within a state to a system that is nationally integrated. This integration is primarily a result of the emergence of multistate banking organizations that can take advantage of operating branches across state lines. Figure 8.7 illustrates this transformation. The number of multistate banks rises from only 10 in 1994 to 387 in 2005. Over this period, the number of branches in interstate organizations rises from 328 to more than 28,000, which now comprise almost 40 percent of all banking offices.

Because the consolidation of the system involved national integration, the dramatic reduction in the number of banks did *not* increase local banking-market concentration or market power. Restrictions on branching and interstate banking generally did not constrain banks' ability to expand *within* local markets, with the exception of the unit banking states. Thus, deregulation allowed banks to enter *new* local markets by buying banks or branches, but it did not spur banks to consolidate within markets. Banks could do that all along in most states.

Figure 8.8 illustrates the trend in banking concentration starting in 1975. We measure concentration with the Herfindahl-Hirschmann Index (HHI), based on deposits. The HHI equals the sum of squared market shares (times 10,000), where shares are based on branch-level deposit data from the Federal Deposit Insurance Corporation's *Summary of Deposits.* We define

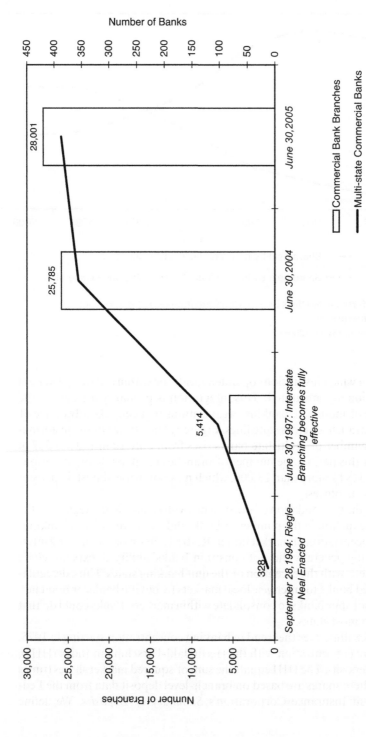

Fig. 8.7 Number of interstate branches operated by FDIC-insured commercial banks and number of multistate banking organizations, 1994–2005

Source: FDIC Summary of Deposits (2005).

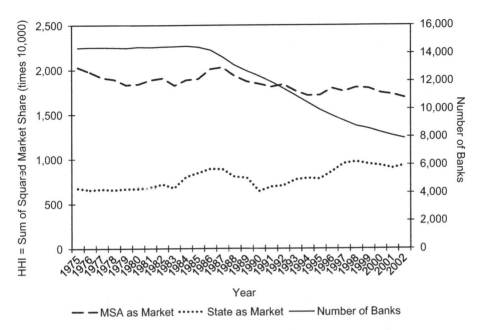

Fig. 8.8   State and local banking market concentration
Source: Authors' calculations and Dick (2006) based on data from FDIC.

"market" either locally (metropolitan statistical area) or at the state level. As the figure shows, while the number of banks falls off sharply, local concentration remains flat or even falls. Concentration measured over states rises only slightly during the 1980s and 1990s.[22] Thus, the net effects of these structural changes has been fewer, but larger and better diversified banks are operating across more local markets with more branches.

These broad trends suggest but do not demonstrate definitively that deregulation altered the structure of banking markets; concurrent macroeconomic and/or technological factors could explain these changes to some degree. Most of the deregulation during the 1980s and 1990s occurred through state-level actions. Because this deregulation occurred at different times in different states, we can study how both within-state branching and interstate banking affected banking structure, as well as the real economy, after controlling for time trends. To explore systematically how these reforms affected banking and the economy, we report a set of regressions using the following unified framework:

(1) $\qquad y_{st} = \alpha_t + \beta_s + \gamma^1 \textit{Within-state branch deregulation}_{st}$
$\qquad\qquad + \gamma^2 \textit{Interstate-banking deregulation}_{st} + \varepsilon_{st} ,$

---

22. Concentration at the national level, however, has increased substantially.

where s indexes states; t indexes time; y_{st} is a set of dependent variables (measures of banking market structure and economic performance); α_t is a year-specific fixed effect (estimated by including year indicator variables); β_s is a state-specific fixed effect (estimated by including state indicator variables); *Within-state branch deregulation*$_{st}$ is an indicator set to one after a state permits a bank or bank holding company to buy branches throughout the state; and, *Interstate-banking deregulation*$_{st}$ is an indicator set to one after a state permits banks from other states to enter that state.[23]

Due to the cross-state and over-time variation in the regulatory status of different states, both unobserved state differences and aggregate shocks (and any trends) can be fully absorbed with the inclusion of state and year fixed effects, while leaving sufficient variation in the regulatory variables to estimate their effects on state-level structural and economic performance variables (y_{st}). Moreover, by using the state rather than the firm as the relevant unit of observation, the resulting panel data set is balanced because states do not enter or exit the sample. Thus, there is no need to worry about (or attempt to correct for) survivorship biases that can plague attempts to draw inferences from bank-level or firm-level data.[24] The coefficients on the deregulation indicators reflect state-specific *changes* in the dependent variable following deregulation.

As we describe below, aggregate trends in technology affected all financial services firms and created increasingly strong pressures for regulatory regime change; interest group factors within financial services can account for differences in the *timing* of state-level deregulation. Hence, a cross-sectional comparison of banking structure or state growth performance might be misleading, or at least difficult to interpret. For example, consider comparing states in a single year, say 1987. If states permitting interstate banking had more large banks than states that did not yet permit interstate banking in 1987, it could be that regulation led to structural changes favoring large banks (i.e., regulation caused the structural change). Or it could be that states with more large banks deregulated before states with fewer large banks (i.e., regulation was caused by the cross-state differences in structure).

The estimators reported here are not likely to be affected by the political economy factors. By including the state fixed effects in the model, all of the cross-sectional variation (such as when a state deregulates) gets removed; coefficients are driven by *changes* in variables after a state alters its regulations. Persistent differences across states (e.g., those dominated by large

---

23. Most states first permitted banks and bank holding companies to branch through mergers or acquisitions of existing banks or bank branches, and later allowed banks to open new branches throughout the state.

24. These issues are especially important for studies of entry regulations because the competitive shakeout that occurs after regulatory change increases the odds that some banks will not survive. Nevertheless, firm-level studies of banking efficiency generally suggest that during the 1990s, the consolidation in banking led to larger and more efficient organizations. For a review of this literature, see Berger, Demsetz, and Strahan (1999).

versus small banks) do not affect the results. Moreover, there is no evidence that changes in bank structure or economic conditions lead (or predict) deregulation, as might occur if states deregulated to try to jump-start a stalled economy by improving credit supply. Instead, all of the changes occur *after* reform.[25]

Panel A of table 8.3 documents how the structure of states' banking systems change following removal of restrictions on geographic expansion using the regression framework in equation (1). The regressions use data for forty-eight states plus the District of Columbia between 1976 and 1994, the period of rapid state-level regulatory change.[26] In column (1), the dependent variable equals the degree to which banking within a state is integrated with bank operations in other states. The extent of *integration* is defined as the share of the state's banks that are owned by a banking organization that also owns banking assets in other states. The results suggest that, on average, 17 percent of a state's banking assets become integrated with banks in other states after interstate banking deregulation. This increase is both statistically and economically large, equal to about 50 percent of the overall mean level of integration in the sample. Hence, state banking systems become better diversified following interstate deregulation as ownership ties between banks operating in many states become established.

While integration, and therefore bank diversification, increases, the second column of table 8.3 shows that local market concentration does *not* increase following deregulation; if anything, there is a slight drop following interstate banking reform, consistent with the trend toward lower local-market concentration (figure 8.8). The third column of table 8.3 shows that the market share of small banks declines, particularly after within-state branching reform. The share of assets held by banks with under $100 million (1994 dollars) in assets falls by 3.1 percentage points after branching is permitted and about 1.2 percentage points after interstate banking reform. Together, these two state-level regulatory changes account for about half of the trend decline in small-bank share between 1976 and 1994. So, the trends in bank structure can be accounted for in large part from removal of regulatory constraints on bank expansion.

Bank Risk

As noted earlier, geographic deregulation in the 1980s led to larger and better diversified banks. Theoretically, it is ambiguous whether the increase in competition that led to the diversification benefits of branch banking would be offset by costs of greater risk taking as monopoly rents in banking are competed away. Keeley (1990) and Hellman, Murdock, and Stiglitz

25. For detailed evidence on the timing of the effects of regulatory changes, see Jayaratne and Strahan (1996); Kroszner and Strahan (1999); and Morgan, Rime, and Strahan (2004).
26. We drop the states of South Dakota and Delaware because the entry of credit card banks into these two states makes their historical evolution during the 1980s unique.

Table 8.3   Panel regression of bank structural and economic performance on deregulation indicators

	Panel A: Banking market structure			Panel B: State economic performance		
	Share of assets held by out-of-state BHCs	Local-market deposit HHI	Share of assets held by banks with under $100 million in assets (1994 dollars)	Employment growth	Growth in new incorporations	Absolute value of unexpected employment growth
Postbranching	−0.007	−18.9	−0.031***	0.0083***	0.032**	0.0005
	(0.035)	(61.3)	(0.011)	(0.0028)	(0.012)	(0.0028)
Postinterstate banking	0.171***	−78.8	−0.012	0.0047*	−0.011	−0.0077**
	(0.035)	(55.9)	(0.007)	(0.0028)	(0.016)	(0.0030)
Dependent variable statistics						
Mean	0.34	1,909	0.196	0.021	0.039	0.010
(Standard deviation)	(0.28)	(665)	(0.170)	(0.022)	(0.119)	(0.009)
N	931	905	931	931	931	931
R^2	0.13	0.86	0.95	0.55	0.23	0.26

Notes: Standard errors in parentheses. All models include both year and state fixed effects. The local deposit HHI is the sum of squared market shares for all banking organizations operating within a local market, defined as an MSA. For states with multiple MSAs, we average the HHI across MSAs within the state, weighted by the amount of deposits in the MSA. The model is estimated using a fixed-effects model with both year and state effects. These regressions are estimated using a fixed-effects model with both year and state effects. Sample includes forty-nine states (DC included, South Dakota and Delaware dropped) and nineteen years (1976–1994). Standard errors are constructed assuming that residual is clustered across states.

*** Significant at the 1 percent level.

** Significant at the 5 percent level.

* Significant at the 10 percent level.

(2000) emphasize that risk-taking incentives from deposit insurance are mitigated by access to monopoly rents fostered by regulatory barriers to aggressive competition. Thus, bank stability during the period between 1940 and 1970 may be explained by the absence of competition in the face of pricing restrictions and restrictions on branching and interstate banking. Keeley (1990) and Demsetz, Saidenberg, and Strahan (1996) show that high stock market valuation of banks relative to book values ("franchise value") is associated with banks holding lower risk loans and more capital.

Removal of restrictions on bank underwriting activities also has the potential to enhance bank diversification.[27] Whether such diversification leads to less risk depends on how bank operating and financial policies adapt to the deregulation. Demsetz and Strahan (1997) find, for example, that large banks, while better diversified, are no less risky than small banks because they tend to hold riskier loans and less capital. Given this fact, it is perhaps not surprising that the evidence on the effects of cross-sector expansion of banks into securities and underwriting is mixed. Certainly, this issue has become an important point of controversy following the 2007 to 2008 financial crisis, as we describe in the epilogue.

Deposit insurance also of course played a role in shaping the risk of banking. Deposit insurance creates incentive for banks to maximize asset risk and minimize capital because bank shareholders capture all upside gains but do not face the full costs of bank risks (Peltzman 1970; Merton 1978). As noted, the US banking system was stable throughout the first thirty-five years after federal deposit insurance, and much of that stability occurred because banks enjoyed limited competition. With limits on both price competition and entry, banks had access to high profits and thus low failure rates. Moreover, the incentive to take advantage of deposit insurance by increasing asset risk and reducing capital were offset by monopoly rents. During the 1980s, however, increased competition both within the financial industry and from the development of securities markets reduced profitability in banking and came with dramatically increased failures.

The experiences of the savings and loan (S&L) industry in particular indicate that badly structured deposit insurance can encourage excessive risk taking. Kroszner and Strahan (1996) show, for example, that S&Ls

27. Kwast (1989) examines banks' balance sheets and compares returns on trading account and nontrading account assets. He finds only limited potential diversification benefits from securities underwriting by banks. Boyd and Graham (1988) and Boyd, Graham, and Hewitt (1993) use a combination of merger simulations and portfolio weighting to find that bank involvement in life and property/casualty insurance could, ceteris paribus, reduce the risk of bank failure. Involvement in securities or real estate, however, would likely increase the risk of failure. Lown et al. (2000) simulate mergers between financial companies over a more recent time period and find a potential reduction in the risk of failure as a result of hypothetical mergers between life insurance firms and BHCs. Kwan (1998) finds that BHC securities activity is associated with greater risk, but provides potential diversification benefits due to the low correlation between returns on banking and securities activities. For a review, see Kwan and Laderman (1999).

that converted from mutual to stock ownership grew faster, expanded their holdings of risky assets (e.g., junk bonds), and disgorged cash in the form of dividend payments. In fact, there were even instances of insolvent S&Ls paying dividends. Thus, those firms that explicitly altered their ownership form to be able to profit from deposit insurance tended to increase risk most dramatically to exploit the government subsidy. More broadly, Kane (1989) emphasizes the failure of regulators to close institutions despite the costs to the deposit insurance regime, thus increasing the problem of excessive risk taking.

On balance, US banking was stable from the initiation of deposit insurance in the 1930s until the early 1980s. This stability occurred despite the latent incentive toward high-risk strategies embedded in government-subsidized deposit insurance, in part because regulatory barriers to competition fostered high rents in the industry. This protection allowed inefficient institutions to dominate, thus harming bank customers facing higher cost and lower quality than they would under a more competitive regime. The landscape began to change in the 1970s and 1980s as small and inefficient banks lost capital in the face of macro instability and high interest rates. With less wealth on the line, these generally small banks lost both the ability and incentive to battle larger banks in the political arena. At the same time, large banks, which historically favored unrestricted expansion, began to use new technologies such as ATMs to compete in new markets (even without explicit deregulation). These changes tipped the political balance toward advocates of regulatory openness (see Kroszner and Strahan 1999 and 2001b, and section 8.4). With deposit insurance still firmly in place but access to rents rapidly diminishing (for both technological and regulatory reasons), many banks and thrifts "gambled for resurrection" by raising insured deposits and investing the proceeds in high-return but high-risk strategies. The result was the high rate of failures at both banks and savings institutions during the 1980s.

More recently, the 2007 to 2008 financial crisis raises the issue of bank risk more broadly. As we touch on in the epilogue (and describe in more detail in Kroszner and Strahan 2011), the increasing development, depth, and efficiency (see below) can enhance growth but can also increase the volatility of the financial sector and growth. Market adaptation also contributed to the development of a web of interconnections through over-the-counter derivative markets that increased the fragilities of both individual banks and the system as a whole.

Efficiency and Pricing

Do regulatory changes lead to meaningful improvements in the efficiency of banks, reductions in costs, and reductions in the price of bank services? As noted earlier, interest rate regulation—maximum lending and deposit rates—had effects on prices during periods when market interest rates made these constraints binding. For deposit markets, the effects were relatively homogeneous because there are limited differences in risk due to government guarantees. Banks facing binding Regulation Q interest rate ceilings did face disintermediation, which became acute in the 1970s both because market rates soared and because nonbank financial firms began to offer close substitutes for checkable deposits. Banks attempted to compete for funds by providing higher quality service (more branches), and by offering gifts and other inducements for deposit, thereby dissipating much of the potential rents generated by the absence of price competition. Usury limits on loan interest rates also restricted credit supply overall, but probably restricted credit most among high-risk borrowers. As noted before, the *Marquette* decision, which effectively undermined states' ability to limit credit card interest rates, was followed by a steady increase in bankruptcy as higher risk households gained access to unsecured credit.

Removal of restrictions on geographic expansion also came with better efficiency and pricing. Jayaratne and Strahan (1998) and Black and Strahan (2001) report that noninterest costs, wages, and loan losses all fell following branching reform. These cost reductions led, in turn, to lower prices on loans (although not on deposits). The mechanism for this better performance seems to be changes in the market shares of banks following deregulation (Stiroh and Strahan 2003). Prior to regulatory reform, well-run banks faced binding constraints on the markets in which they could operate. When these constraints were lifted, however, assets were reallocated toward the better-run banks as they gained the opportunity to acquire market share.[28]

Figure 8.9 shows the consequences of these healthy competitive dynamics by plotting the market share of banks with above-median profits for states that have permitted branching since the 1930s or before (twelve states) compared with the unit banking states that did not permit any form of branching (sixteen states). The figure illustrates the detrimental effects of these constraining regulations. For example, in 1980, before deregulation, the higher-profit banks held slightly under 50 percent of the banking assets in the average unit-banking state; in contrast, the higher-profit banks held about 70 percent of assets in states where banks were never constrained by branching restrictions. This difference disappears completely by 1994. By then the unit banking states had permitted within-state branching, thus allowing the better-run banks to dominate the industry.[29]

---

28. Hubbard and Palia (1995) also show that management compensation became more sensitive to performance after deregulation.

29. Sorting banks in a given regulatory regime by profits is designed to separate well-run from poorly run banks. To the extent that regulations generate rents, all banks in a given regime may tend to have high profits. What matters for this comparison is the relative ranking across banks. A similar result can be seen by sorting banks on cost-based measures of performance. Studies that examine efficiency gains for within-sector consolidation include Berger (1998), Hughes et al. (1999); Goldberg et al. (1991).

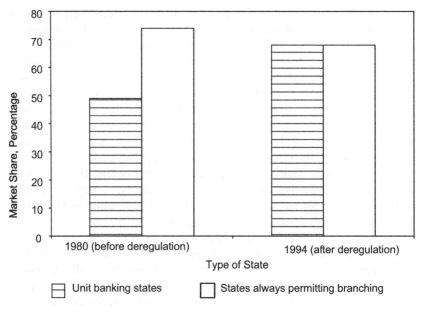

Fig. 8.9   Market share of high-profit banks
Source: Stiroh and Strahan (2003).

Expansion of Activities and Potential for Conflicts of Interest

A separate category of research examines the production advantages of financial conglomeration across business lines. Once again, there are many studies of efficiency and profitability *within* banking, securities, and insurance, but research on advantages of *cross-sector* consolidation is limited. Existing research concentrates on bank underwriting of corporate debt and equity securities, and emphasizes information scope economies in the joint production of commercial lending and underwriting. Through their lending activities, banks may gain more knowledge about a firm's prospects than other market participants. This informational advantage can be a double-edged sword. On the positive side, banks may be able to identify firms with good opportunities earlier and at lower cost than other financial institutions. On the negative side, a commercial bank might use its superior information to its own advantage, for example, not revealing potential problems and issuing securities to the public that are riskier than the market believes (see Kroszner 1997 for a summary).

The empirical research suggests that banks are not succumbing to conflicts of interest and abusing their information to mislead the market. Indeed, research on commercial bank underwriting prior to Glass-Steagall (Kroszner and Rajan 1994, 1997; Ang and Richardson 1994; Puri 1996) suggests that debt securities underwritten by banks had a *better* default record than those underwritten by investment banks. Kroszner and Rajan (1997) show that throughout the 1920s, commercial banks increasingly underwrote their securities through separately incorporated and capitalized affiliates rather than through internal departments of the commercial bank itself. Otherwise similar securities received higher prices (lower risk premia) when underwritten by a commercial bank affiliate than those underwritten directly by the bank, suggesting that the "firewall" structure enhanced the credibility of the underwriting bank. In particular, the greater the proportion of independent directors on the affiliate's board, the greater was the reduction in the risk premium on the securities underwritten by the affiliate. Thus, the increasing use of the affiliates could at least in part be explained by commercial banks adapting their organizational structure to address public concerns about the potential for conflicts of interest.

After the repeal of Glass-Steagall with the Financial Modernization Act of 1999, underwriter fees are lower for bank-underwritten debt securities relative to similar securities issued by stand-alone investment banks (Sufi 2005). Drucker and Puri (2005) find that evidence that banks bundling lending and equity underwriting services reduce costs to customers. Schenone (2004) finds lower underpricing during initial public offerings at firms that have established a lending relationship with a commercial bank capable of underwriting the IPO, consistent with the idea that informed banks can certify the value of securities. Gande et al. (1997) argue that banks' unique information advantage with respect to firms with lower credit ratings results in relatively higher prices (lower yields) on underwritten debt securities for these types of firms. Yasuda (2005) reaches the same conclusion; she finds that client-specific relationship capital is a unique bank advantage in underwriting when banks have strong prior lending relationships with the issuing company.

Another potential source of conflicts occurs when commercial bankers serve as board members of client firms, or when executives of client firms serve on the boards of their banks. Kroszner and Strahan (2001a, 2001c) investigate the frequency of connections between banks and nonfinancial firms through board linkages, and examine whether those connections affect lending. We document that banks are heavily involved in the corporate governance network through frequent board linkages. Banks tend to have larger boards with a higher proportion of outside directors than nonfinancial firms, and bank officer-directors tend to have more external board directorships than executives of nonfinancial firms. We then show that low-information cost firms—large firms with a high proportion of tangible assets and relatively stable stock returns—are most likely to have board connections to banks. These same low-information cost firms are also more likely to borrow from their connected bank, and when they do so the terms of the loan appear similar to loans to unconnected firms. In contrast to this last finding, Guner, Malmendier, and Tate (2008) do find evidence that firms with financial experts on board appear to have better access to financial resources, although this increase is concentrated among large and relatively unconstrained firms.

Given the lack of data, it is not surprising that there is little research on either bank production advantages in insurance or on the joint production of insurance and securities services in the United States. Lown et al. (2000) argue that Europe provides a convenient model for how the US financial system could be affected by GLBA because most European countries permit financial conglomerates. They show that banks have become increasingly involved in insurance activities and argue that economies of scope in market and distributing both banking and insurance products through the branch network can explain their success. In fact, about 10 percent of all financial M&A activity in Europe occurred between banks and life insurance companies over the past fifteen years.

In the financial crisis of 2007 to 2008, questions have been raised about whether market forces were able to deal with the potential for conflicts of interest related to mortgages and mortgage-backed securities. For example, Keys et al. (2010) provide evidence that credit evaluation for mortgages expected to be securitized was less careful than for those expected to be held by originating lenders and that such loans defaulted more frequently. As we discuss further in the epilogue, conflicts related to securitization can help explain the expansion of credit that fueled the housing boom in the 2000s (Mian and Sufi 2009).

Growth and Entrepreneurship

Did the beneficial changes in banking have quantitatively important effects on the real economy? Schumpeter (1969) argued in the early part of the twentieth century that efficient financial systems promote innovations; hence, better finance leads to faster growth. Robinson (1952) countered that the causality was reversed; economies with good growth prospects develop institutions to provide the funds necessary to support those good prospects. In other words, the economy leads and finance follows. Recent theoretical developments have fleshed out two potential causal links from financial systems to growth, even in the long run. Financial markets can matter either by affecting the volume of savings available to finance investment or by increasing the productivity (or quality) of that investment. These theories show that an improvement in financial market efficiency can act as a lubricant to the engine of economic growth, allowing that engine to run faster.

Empirical research has increasingly provided support for the Schumpterian view that financial market development can play an important causal role in driving long-run growth. For example, King and Levine (1993) demonstrated that the size and depth of an economy's financial system is positively correlated with its future growth in per capita real income.

While this evidence is appealing, it cannot rule out the possibility that financial development and growth are simultaneously driven by a common factor not controlled in the empirical analysis. Rajan and Zingales (1998) and Cetorelli and Gambera (2001) attempt to answer this criticism by exploiting cross-industry differences in financial dependence. They show that in countries with well-developed financial markets, industries that require more external finance grow faster than "cash cow" industries that can finance investment with internally generated funds.[30] Kroszner, Laeven, and Klingebiel (2007) examine the impact of bank crises on cross-industry differences in financial dependence. Consistent with an important "credit channel" role of banking, they find that bank crises have a disproportionately negative impact on financially dependent firms in countries with well-developed financial systems: in such systems, the financially dependent firms grow faster in normal times but are hit harder in crisis times. Levine, Loayza, and Beck (2000) attempt to establish a causal link from finance to growth by using preexisting legal differences across countries as instruments for the development of the banking system; they show that the exogenous component of banking development is positively related to growth performance.[31]

Another way to establish that better finance (or, specifically, better banking) can lead to faster growth is to find policy changes that lead to more efficient finance (banking) and see how the economy responds.[32] Bekaert, Harvey, and Lundblad (2003) do this for equity market liberalization across countries and find that economic growth sped up after reform. Jayaratne and Strahan (1996) study state-level branching deregulation and find that this improvement in banking market openness spurred faster economic growth.[33] Using data from 1972 to 1992, they estimate the change in economic performance before and after deregulation and found that annual growth rates accelerated by 1/2 to 1 percentage point. In that study, they worked hard to rule out other interpretations of the finding. For example, they showed that states did *not* deregulate their economies in *anticipation* of future good growth prospects. They also found no other concomitant policy changes that could account for the result and no consistent political changes, such as a change in the party controlling the state government, around the time of deregulation.

In panel B of table 8.3, we reestimate a growth model similar to the one

---

30. Cetorelli (2001, 2003) attempts to gain a better understanding of the channels through which better finance can affect economic performance. He shows that countries with concentrated banking sectors tend to have more concentrated industrial sectors, particularly in those sectors where external finance is important. On the other hand, Bonacorrsi di Patti and Dell'Ariccia (2004) find that banking concentration in Italy helps foster creation of new firms.

31. Bertrand, Schoar, and Thesmar (2007) find important improvements in allocative efficiency across firms in France following deregulation of French banking that began in the mid-1980s.

32. For a comprehensive review, see Levine (2005).

33. More recently, Collender and Shaffer (2003) explore how other aspects of banking structure affect economic growth.

in Jayaratne and Strahan using a slightly different sample period (1976 to 1994). The table reports the results of the growth regressions based on overall state-level employment. The result (column 4) suggests that average per capita income growth accelerated following both branching and interstate banking reform.[34]

If more competitive banking really spurs growth, we would expect particularly large benefits among relatively bank dependent sectors of the economy, such as small firms or entrepreneurs. To test this idea, panel B of table 8.3 reports how growth in new business incorporations—a measure of firm entry and thus entrepreneurial activity—changes following banking reform (column 5).[35] We find that the growth of entrepreneurial activity increased significantly following banking deregulation. Annual growth of new incorporations per capita increased by 3.2 percentage points after branching deregulation, while the coefficient on interstate banking deregulation is not statistically significant. Thus, the effects of geographic banking reform on entrepreneurial activity are substantially larger than their effects on overall growth of employment. This makes sense because bank credit is most important in financing small businesses without access to public securities markets, and suggest that the reason why growth accelerates after geographic deregulation is that credit supply to the entrepreneurial sector expands.[36]

Stability and Business Cycles

The evidence so far points to substantial benefits of opening up banking markets to potential entry and greater competition through deregulation. Entrepreneurs are able to start businesses and, perhaps through their efforts, economic growth accelerates. Cross-country evidence is beginning to emerge, suggesting that opening up financial markets to foreign entry can also create benefits associated with macroeconomic stability (Barth, Caprio, and Levine 2004). As noted earlier, however, there is also evidence from studies at the bank level that risk taking may increase with the reductions in franchise value that come following banking deregulation.

Morgan, Rime, and Strahan (2004) test how state-level volatility changed as the US banking system integrated across state lines following interstate

34. Jayaratne and Strahan (1996) also show that gross state product grows faster after branching reform. Moreover, they are careful to rule out the possibility that the growth increases were driven by just a few states; that growth accelerated because reform occurred during business cycle troughs or around banking crises (note that this is not the case following interstate banking reform, making it harder to draw causal inferences from this result); and that growth accelerated because other policies changed at the same time as banking reform.

35. We use new business incorporations as a measure of entrepreneurial activity in each state, again from 1976 to 1996, because it offers the best proxy available that is compiled on a consistent basis over a relatively long period. Black and Strahan (2002) provide evidence that this measure is a reliable indicator of business formations.

36. Consistent with a greater rate of creation of new firms, Cetorelli and Strahan (2006) also find that the number and share of small firms increases with measures of banking market competition, especially in sectors dependent on external finance.

banking reform. The expected effect of banking integration on business cycles, however, is theoretically ambiguous. Shocks to the value of local collateral can actually become more destabilizing after integration because, for example, multistate banks can move capital elsewhere. In contrast, local shocks to the banking system itself become much less destabilizing when banks operate across many markets. Overall, Morgan et al. find that economic volatility declines with interstate banking deregulation but not with in-state branching reform.[37]

The last column of table 8.3 reports the bottom-line finding in Morgan et al. In this regression, the dependent variable equals the absolute value of the employment growth residual from the model reported in column (4). The dependent variable thus measures the magnitude of each state's business cycle shock. These shocks become smaller on average after interstate banking reform and the associated integration of the banking system.[38] The coefficient suggests that the average shock size falls by 0.8 percentage points, relative to an unconditional mean shock size of 1.0 percentage points. In other words, prior to deregulation and banking integration, the typical state's deviation from expected growth is about 1.4 percentage points, while after deregulation the typical deviation falls to about 0.6 percentage points.

The theoretical analysis in Morgan et al. suggests better macroeconomic stability following deregulation because state economies become insulated from shocks to their own banks. In a disintegrated banking system, such as the one we had in the 1970s and early 1980s, shocks to bank capital lead to reductions in lending, thereby worsening downturns. In contrast, with integration a state can import bank capital from abroad (i.e., from other states) when its banks are down, thus continuing to fund positive NPV (net present value) projects. If this explanation really holds, then the correlation between local measures of economic performance or loan availability with the financial capital of local banks ought to weaken with deregulation and integration.

We put this notion to the test by regressing state-level loan growth and employment growth on the growth rate of total bank capital in the state, along with interactions between bank capital growth and the deregulation indicator variables. The structure of the model follows:

$$(2)\ Growth_{st} = \alpha_t + \beta_s + \gamma^1 Within\text{-}state\ Branch\ Deregulation_{st}$$
$$+ \gamma^2 Interstate\ Banking\ Deregulation_{st} + \gamma^3 CapitalGrowth_{st}$$
$$+ \gamma^4 (Within\text{-}state\ Branching\ Deregulation_{st} * CapitalGrowth_{st})$$
$$+ \gamma^5 (Interstate\ Banking\ Deregulation_{st} * CapitalGrowth_{st})$$
$$+ \varepsilon_{st}.$$

37. In addition, Gatev and Strahan (2006) and Gatev, Schuermann, and Strahan (2006) show how banks help provide liquidity during periods of market pullbacks such as the one following the Russian default during the fall of 1998, thereby helping stabilize the financial system.

38. Morgan et al. measure banking integration in more detail—for example, by taking account of transition following interstate reform—and find larger and more robust declines in volatility than those reported here.

Table 8.4   **Panel regression of state-level real loan growth on banking deregulation indicators and bank capital**

	Loan growth		
	Total loans	Commercial and industrial loans	Employment growth
Postbranching	0.029**	0.039***	0.007**
	(0.011)	(0.014)	(0.003)
Postinterstate banking	0.021	0.028*	0.004*
	(0.013)	(0.016)	(0.002)
Growth in bank capital	0.833***	0.580***	0.154***
	(0.089)	(0.160)	(0.037)
Growth in bank capital *	−0.043	0.061	−0.055
Postbranching	(0.113)	(0.181)	(0.036)
Growth in bank capital *	−0.332***	−0.300**	−0.061
Postinterstate banking	(0.094)	(0.130)	(0.040)
P-value for F-Test:			
Interactions jointly equal zero	0.001	0.08	0.02
Dependent variable statistics			
Mean	0.024	0.008	0.021
(Standard deviation)	(0.092)	(0.109)	(0.022)
N	882	882	882
R^2	0.56	0.62	0.60

Notes: Standard errors in parentheses. These regressions are estimated using a fixed-effects model with both year and state effects. Sample includes forty-nine states (DC included, South Dakota and Delaware dropped) and nineteen years (1977–1994). Standard errors are constructed assuming that residual is clustered across states.
*** Significant at the 1 percent level.
** Significant at the 5 percent level.
* Significant at the 10 percent level.

If interstate banking insulates the economy from local shocks to bank capital, we would expect $\gamma^5 < 0$. We also include an interaction between state-level capital growth and branching reform, although branching only permits integration within states, so there is less reason to expect this interaction effect (γ^4) to be economically and statistically significant.[39]

The results reported in table 8.4 suggest that interstate banking deregulation reduces the link between local lending and local bank performance.[40] According to the estimated coefficients, prior to banking deregulation there is nearly a one-to-one correspondence between state-level loan growth and capital growth (i.e., the coefficient on capital growth equals 0.83). By contrast, this link falls by about 40 percent after interstate deregulation.

39. In contrast, branching may weaken the link between local banking resources and lending at the city or county level. This channel merits further research.
40. Local banks here means banks headquartered within the state.

Similarly, the correlation between local employment growth and local bank capital growth weakens, although less dramatically than the effects on loan growth. Integration thus has salutary effects on business cycles by insulating the local economy from the ups and downs of its local banking system (and vice versa).

In contrast to the earlier period of geographical deregulation, financial integration during the 2000s, fostered by the growth of securitization, may have worsened the boom/bust cycle by facilitating huge capital flows into local markets (Loutskina and Strahan 2012). Theoretically, greater financial depth and development could either increase or decrease stability (see Kroszner and Strahan 2011). On the one hand, a larger and more developed financial sector could improve risk sharing and diversification and thereby reduce volatility. On the other, a larger and more developed financial sector could allow greater concentrations of risk and generate interconnections, thereby potentially making the entire system more fragile and vulnerable to shocks. In the epilogue, we touch on how postcrisis regulatory reform attempts to deal with these opposing forces in the financial system.

8.4   Deregulation: Why So Long in Coming?

As we have explained, the early part of the twentieth century was characterized by financial deepening, particularly in the 1920s. This process came to a halt with the Depression and much regulation of banking and securities markets passed during the first half of the 1930s. Markets adapted to regulatory constraints, but the beneficial changes following deregulation suggest that restrictions on competition in particular reduced the quality and availability of financial resources and hampered economic performance. Given the costs of these regulations, why was deregulation so long in coming?

8.4.2   The Politics of Deregulation

As we described in section 8.2, understanding interest group competition can be helpful in understanding the development of some Depression-era regulations, and it can be helpful in understanding more recent deregulation. In two earlier papers, we offer systematic evidence consistent with the importance of interest group politics in shaping regulatory change (Kroszner and Strahan 1999, 2001b). We use information in the timing of state deregulation of branching as well as congressional voting patterns on several legislative amendments to allow nationwide branching and to limit deposit insurance coverage. The first study shows that measures of interest group, public interest, and political-institutional factors can explain the timing of state-level branching deregulation during the last thirty years (Kroszner and Strahan 1999).

In particular, we employ a hazard model technique to estimate how cross-state differences in these factors influence the timing of deregulation relative to the average.[41] Private interest factors receive both economically and statistically significant support in the data. As the share of small banks in the state increases, for example, branching deregulation is delayed. In particular, a one standard deviation increase in the small bank share results in a 30 percent increase in the time until deregulation, or about 4.7 years. (The average time until branching deregulation from 1970 is sixteen years.) This result is consistent with an intraindustry rivalry hypothesis of small banks preferring branching restrictions and large banks preferring deregulation.

Interindustry competition also helps explain the timing of deregulation. In states where banks can sell insurance, a relatively large insurance sector is associated with an increase in the expected time to deregulation. A one standard deviation increase in the relative size of the insurance sector in those states that permit banks to sell insurance leads to a 22 percent increase in the time until deregulation, or about 3.5 years. This result is difficult to explain on purely public interest grounds.

Deregulation also occurs earlier in states where small, bank-dependent firms are relatively numerous. A one standard deviation increase in the share of small firms reduces the time until deregulation by 18 percent, or about three years. This result concerning the interests of users of banking services is consistent with both the private and public interest theories.

Finally, the partisan structure of the state government also influences when states deregulate. As expected, a higher proportion of Democrats in the government tends to delay deregulation. A one standard deviation rise in the share of the government controlled by Democrats slows the deregulation by about two years. Whether the state is dominated by one party, however, does not appear to affect the timing of the deregulation.

Private interests thus appear to play an important role in the deregulatory process. Although private interests and public interests do sometimes coincide, the results on the relative share of small banks and large banks and on the relative size of insurance where banks compete are consistent with a private interest approach but are difficult to explain on public interest grounds.

To check the plausibility of the results, we also consider whether the ex post consequences of deregulation are consistent with the ex ante positions attributed to each interest group (see Kroszner and Strahan 1999 for details). Small banks lose market share following deregulation and, in states where banks can enter the insurance business, the insurance sector shrinks relative to the banking sector following deregulation. Borrowers also benefit because the average interest rates on loans tends to fall following branching deregulation. These findings support the private interest interpretation of the results

41. We estimate a Weibull hazard function with time-varying covariates. The same results are obtained in simple ordinary least squares regressions. We also control for a variety of other factors that might affect the likelihood of deregulation, such as the frequency and size of bank failures in the state and regional clustering of deregulation.

described earlier: groups that will benefit push to speed deregulation and those that will be harmed push to delay it.

Do the forces driving intrastate branching deregulation also drive interstate deregulation at the federal level? Financial services interests are active contributors and lobbyists. Their political action committees constitute the largest group of contributors to legislators, providing nearly 20 percent of total congressional campaign contributions (Makinson 1992), and much of their lobbying effort involves competition among rival interests within financial services (see Kroszner and Stratmann 1998, 2000, and 2005).

After virtually all states adopted intra- and interstate branching deregulation, the 1994 Riegle-Neal Act repealed the 1927 McFadden Act to phase out all barriers to interstate banking and branching by 1997. The key votes concerning the Riegle-Neal Act were either voice votes or extremely lop sided, so it is not possible to estimate a voting model for them. A number of bills and amendments related to interstate branching had been debated in Congress during the years prior to the passage of the Riegle-Neal Act, but a search of the weekly *BNA Banking Reporter* and the *Congressional Record* produced only one roll-call vote related to interstate branching that was not lopsided. This vote occurred in the House of Representatives on November 14, 1991 on an amendment sponsored by Wylie (R-OH) and Neal (D-NC) to introduce interstate banking and branching deregulation to a financial services reform package.[42] Although the amendment passed by 210 to 208, the bill to which it was attached subsequently was defeated.

To check for the impact of the factors that were found to be influential in the state-level reforms, we also consider both the sponsorship of interstate banking legislation and voting on the amendment. The sponsors of the Wylie-Neal amendment are from states with low small bank shares—0.04 in Ohio (Wylie) and 0.02 in North Carolina (Neal). In contrast, the sample mean in 1991 is 0.08 (median = 0.07). Michigan, home state of the Senate's sponsor of the 1994 Riegle-Neal Act, also had relatively low small bank strength (small bank share of 0.05).

Consistent with the state-level deregulation process, the second study uses a probit model to analyze voting patterns and shows that legislators are more likely to support the amendment if their states have a relatively low share of small banks (see Kroszner and Strahan 1999). As in the analysis of the timing of intrastate deregulation, the fraction of small banks is the most important interest group influence on a legislator's voting decision. The impact of rival interests outside of banking is also consistent with intrastate deregulation results. Where banks can sell insurance, legislators from states with larger insurance sectors relative to banking are less likely to vote in favor of interstate branching. Overall, the analysis of the vote on federal

---

42. The Wylie-Neal amendment also included provisions limiting certain insurance and real estate powers of national banks (*Congressional Record*, November 14, 1991, pp. 10239–42).

branching deregulation provides a consistency check that the importance of interests operating on the state legislatures are very similar to those operating at the federal level.

8.4.3   Why Did Deregulation Take So Long?

An important question remains in order to understand the broad timing of deregulation: Why begin in the 1980s rather than the 1950s or some earlier period? The market for financial regulation, like all regulation, involves competition among groups with competing interests with significant campaign contributions at both the state and national levels (see Makinson 1992; Kroszner and Stratmann 1998, 2000, and 2005; and Kroszner 2000). Financial services interests, for example, rarely comprise a unified block, with much of their lobbying effort involving competition among themselves. The beneficiaries were able to support an equilibrium coalition in favor of geographical restrictions from the 1930s through the early 1980s despite their costs to (unorganized) consumers of financial services long after the value of them to governments as a key source of revenue had faded.

While political economists have often had success in identifying the group that receives concentrated benefits of a particular regulation in order to explain the persistence of that regulation, deregulation has been more difficult to explain. Many factors affect the highly complex process of regulatory change. Nonetheless, to understand the broad timing of deregulation, it can be helpful to try to identify technological, legal, and economic shocks that would alter the old equilibrium. We now consider some of these shocks in detail to see whether they can help explain why regulatory change occurred when it did.

Beginning in the 1970s, three major innovations reduced the value to the protected banks of local geographic monopolies by increasing the elasticity of depositors' funds. First, the invention of the automatic teller machine (ATM) helped to erode the geographic ties between customers and banks. After some legal challenges, ATM networks were determined not to constitute branches, thereby permitting ATM networks to spread throughout the United States and the world. Table 8.5 shows the rapid proliferations of ATMs, which did not exist before 1970. Second, consumer-oriented money market mutual funds also originated in the 1970s. Checkable money market mutual funds and the Merrill Lynch Cash Management Account demonstrated that banking by mail and telephone provided a convenient alternative to local banks.[43] From zero in 1970, table 8.5 shows that money market mutual funds are roughly one-third the size of deposits held at banks. Third, technological innovation and deregulation have reduced transportation and

---

43. Regulation Q, which limited the interest rates that banks could pay on deposits, may have helped to drive depositors away from banks when the gap between market rates and deposit ceilings grew during the 1970s.

Table 8.5   Broad trends in commercial banking, 1950–2000

Year	Number of ATMs	Domestic bank deposits (billions)	Money market mutual fund (billions)	Percentage of deposits + money funds held by banks	Small banks' percentage of banking assets
1950	0	$154	$0	100	n/a
1955	0	191	0	100	n/a
1960	0	228	0	100	24
1965	0	330	0	100	20
1970	0	479	0	100	18
1975	9,750	775	4	99	18
1980	18,500	1,182	76	94	17
1985	61,117	1,787	242	88	14
1990	80,156	2,339	493	83	11
1995	122,706	2,552	530	82	8
2000	273,000	3,146	1,134	74	4

Notes: For column (1), ATM figures are from *Bank Network News, The EFT Network Data Book* (New York: Faulkner and Gray, Inc.). The 1975 figure was unavailable. The number of ATMs in 1978, the first year for which complete data are available, is 9,750. For columns (2)–(4), banks' domestic deposits are from the Reports of Income and Condition; money market mutual funds are from the Flow of Funds. Data on all bank deposits, foreign plus domestic, are only available beginning in 1970. The trend in banks' share (column 4) is the same using total deposits instead of domestic deposits. For column (5), percentage of banking assets held by small banks, where a small bank is defined as a commercial bank less than $100 million in assets in 1994 dollars. These data are based on the Reports of Income and Condition. Data on small banks are not available before 1960.

communication costs, particularly since the 1970s. Customers thus now have lower costs of using banks located farther away from them than in the past (Petersen and Rajan 2002).

Because the increasing elasticity of deposits supplied to banks reduces the value of geographical restrictions to their traditional beneficiaries, we argue that these beneficiaries had less incentive to fight strenuously to maintain them. While any deregulation that eliminates inefficient regulation is broadly consistent with the public interest theory, the timing of the deregulation is difficult to explain by that approach. The deregulation occurs precisely when the branching restrictions are becoming less burdensome for the public, due to the elasticity-increasing innovations discussed earlier (see Peltzman 1976). If deregulation were motivated by public interest concerns, the lifting of branching restrictions would have happened much earlier when depositors were more dependent on local banks for both asset management and payments services.

On the lending side, increasing sophistication of credit-scoring techniques, following innovations in information processing technology, financial theory, and the development of large credit databases, have begun to change the relationship character of bank lending toward less personal and more standardized evaluation. As a result of these innovations, a national market developed for residential mortgages in the late 1970s. In the 1980s, consumer lending relied increasingly on automated information processing, leading to the development of credit card securitization. In recent years even banks' lending to small businesses has become increasingly automated, relying on standardized credit scoring programs rather than the judgment of loan officers.

Technological change thus has diminished the value of specialized local knowledge that long-established local bankers might have about the risks of borrowers in the community. Such changes have increased the feasibility and potential profitability for large banks to enter what had traditionally been the core of small bank activities. The large banks have therefore had an incentive to increase their lobbying pressure to attain the freedom to expand into these markets. In addition, as the value of a local banking relationship declined, small firms (borrowers) also would be more likely to favor the entry of large banks into local markets. These factors combined to start undermining the economic performance of the small banks that had benefitted most from the geographic restrictions. Table 8.5 shows the relative decline in small banks' market share even prior to the branching deregulation that began in the early 1970s.

One can also point to "exogenous" forces outside the development of new technologies in the financial sector. For example, Kane (1996) argues that a major shock to the old equilibrium is an increase in the public's awareness of the costliness of having government-insured but (geographically) undiversified financial institutions. In the late 1970s the failure rate of banks begins to rise (recall figure 8.2). In the 1980s, the savings and loan crisis and taxpayer bailout further heighten the awareness by the public of the costs of restrictions that make depository institutions more fragile and more likely to require infusions of taxpayer funds. The failures thus may have heightened public awareness of and support for branching deregulation. For example, West Virginia's state legislature passed a bill lifting most branching restrictions to help an ailing economy. The legislature's actions were "inspired by the state's need for industrial expansion and a greater job base. West Virginia leads the nation in unemployment" (*American Banker*, 04/17/84).

Consistent with Kane's argument, economic conditions also played a part in relaxing restrictions on interstate banking. The Garn St Germain Act of 1982 amended the Bank Holding Company Act by permitting the acquisition of *failed* thrifts and banks by out-of-state banks or holding companies. Banks and thrifts failed by the hundreds in some states in the early 1980s after the recessions of 1980 and 1981 to 1982 and the "third-world debt" crises. Surviving institutions in hard-hit states were often not fit to recapitalize the failed ones, so Congress acted to let in healthy banks from out of state.[44] Some states then allowed out-of-state banks to buy their banks,

---

44. While some states did relax restrictions on bank expansion in response to macroeconomic downturns, there is no correlation between rates of bank failures or the state-level business

but typically these moves were done on a reciprocal basis. For example, when Maine first allowed entry by out-of-state BHCs, the law stipulated that banks from Maine must be allowed to enter those states. Over time, state reciprocal agreements to allow interstate banking grew, and the transition to full interstate banking was completed with passage of the Reigle-Neal Interstate Banking and Branching Efficiency Act of 1994. Reigle-Neal made interstate banking a bank right, rather than a state right; banks or holding companies could now enter another state without permission. This act also permits banks to operate branches across state lines for the first time, allowing multibank holding companies to consolidate their operations.

Certainly, the major economic and financial shocks surrounding the 2007 to 2008 financial crisis led to important political economy changes, resulting in the most sweeping financial regulatory reforms since the 1930s, and we now turn to that in the epilogue.

8.5   Epilogue: Lessons from the 2008 Crisis

We have described the causes and consequences of banking deregulation prior to the financial crisis of 2008–2009. The reforms removed many of the constraints binding since the 1930s or before, thus reshaping the financial industry and, in turn, the economy. Reform came with many benefits, but many of the preconditions for the 2008 financial crisis came, at least in part, from efforts to avoid or reduce the costs of regulation; that is, what we call market adaptation. In this epilogue, we discuss some of the causes of the financial crisis and consider whether recent reforms may prevent the next one.

During the years leading up to the financial crisis, the long-term trends that we document transforming both the liability and asset sides of bank balance sheets accelerated, creating greater interlinkages among institutions, increasing the relative importance of securities markets, facilitating financial integration, and speeding up capital mobility. On the liability side, banks and other financial institutions rely more on market-based sources of short-term funding, such as commercial paper, asset-backed commercial paper (ABCP), and repurchase agreements. As we have seen, money market mutual funds have grown to nearly the size of bank deposits and have become key sources of funding. On the asset side, intermediaries securitize many of the assets they originate (e.g., loans and mortgages). This "originate to distribute" model of intermediation thus relies on the operation of securitization markets, thereby connecting intermediaries to these markets.

As we have discussed, the evolution to a more complex and intercon-

---

cycle conditions and the timing of branching reform (see Jayaratne and Strahan 1996; Kroszner and Strahan 1999). Similarly, Morgan, Rime, and Strahan (2004) show that the timing of interstate banking deregulation *cannot* account for the decline in state-level economic volatility that follows reform.

nected system came about, in part, by market adaptation to, and sometimes avoidance of, regulations. Some changes occurred in response to financial institutions' attempts to lower the burden of regulations. Securitization, which fosters the benefits of both diversification and liquidity, expanded too far in part due to government subsidies and in part because it lowered the burden of required capital. During the 2000s, Fannie Mae and Freddie Mac subsidized securitization by offering low-priced credit enhancements to mortgage pools and by purchasing securitized subprime mortgages in the secondary market. Moreover, the Basel capital framework encouraged securitization of low-risk loans because it treated all loans to businesses equally for the purposes of required capital. Thus, it became attractive to securitize loans to highly rated creditors and hold on-balance sheet loans to lower-rated creditors.

As a consequence, in the 2000s, the ABCP market grew dramatically, with outstandings rising by more than $500 billion between 2004 and mid-2007. These instruments created off-balance sheet conduits with similar asset transformation characteristics of banks (long-term loan pools financed with short-term liabilities). Issuers could reap the same upside as if those assets had stayed on-balance sheet—because they were residual claimants in the conduits—but with no required regulatory capital (Acharya, Schnabl, and Suarez 2010). Thus, much of the explosive growth of this market may be due to regulatory arbitrage, one form of market adaptation. The dramatic expansion of mortgage credit fueled by securitization likely played a role in driving home prices to unsustainable levels. Moreover, the collapse of the ABCP market in August of 2007 marked the beginning of the financial crisis.

Transformations in the financial system away from traditional intermediaries and toward securities markets have also come with more opaque distribution of risks across the system. Derivatives have grown in parallel with the expansion of the securities markets, and these markets have faced little regulatory analysis of their potential systemic consequences. In the 1970s, options markets grew in response to better understanding of pricing and hedging of nonlinear instruments (Black and Scholes 1973). Interest rate swaps grew in popularity in the 1980s, and, in the 1990s, credit default swaps emerged and grew rapidly. Today's system involves long chains, with many links being market-based intermediaries that do not rely on deposits for funding (see Adrian and Shin 2009; Kroszner and Shiller 2011). The many links in the modern financial system allow shocks to propagate rapidly across the system. With the explosive growth of derivatives, the distribution of risks becomes harder to assess, particularly without a central clearinghouse to monitor and to aggregate information. Misjudgments about risks, rather than being self-correcting, can thus cascade through the system as major players reduce credit due to uncertainty about the distribution of risk exposures (Kroszner 2011). Contraction of wholesale, short-term credit markets was a key mechanism that propagated and amplified fundamental shocks from housing during the financial crisis (Gorton and Metrick 2012).

Thus, the welfare calculation for assessing both past deregulation and potential future regulatory reform is complex. As we have seen, deregulation led to faster growth and lower volatility during the 1970s and 1980s. Moreover, international evidence suggests that financial liberalization has come with greater credit availability and faster growth, and much evidence suggests that this link is causal (e.g., Levine 2005; Kroszner, Laeven, and Klingebiel 2007). That evidence has generally been used to support reduced restrictions on the financial sector. Yet financial liberalization and integration, by allowing financial capital to flow away from low-growth areas and into booming ones, can also amplify local cycles. During the 2000s, for example, capital mobility fostered by securitization allowed funds collected from global capital markets to pay for housing booms in areas like Florida, Arizona, Nevada, and southern California. Had such areas been forced to rely on local pools of savings, the boom-bust cycle likely would have been smaller (Loutskina and Strahan 2012).

Regulatory reform thus faces a fundamental tension: How do we allow continued innovation that fosters financial deepening, cheaper credit, and faster growth, while mitigating the potential for instability inherent in the interconnections that come with financial development? In some cases, such as removal of geographical restrictions on bank expansion, financial sector reform has not involved a trade-off and has resulted in both higher growth and lower volatility. Obviously, this is not the case in all circumstances. In Kroszner and Strahan (2011), we offer two key principles to guide thinking about future reform. First, we discuss avoiding the next round of regulatory arbitrage in which financial activity moves "into the shadows," where risks may accumulate like dead wood ready to ignite the next wildfire. Second, we argue that reforms that improve market transparency can reduce the uncertainty of counterparty exposures and interlinkages between major players, thereby lowering contagion risk.

Looking ahead, regulatory change over the next decade will likely be shaped by the gradual implementation of the Dodd-Frank Wall Street Reform and Consumer Protection Act, passed into law on July 21, 2010, and new Basel III capital and liquidity regulations. As in previous episodes of financial downturns, such as those in the 1930s and 1980s, the passage of Dodd-Frank comes in response to perceived weaknesses and excesses in the system following the 2008 crisis. Dodd-Frank included the so-called Volcker rule, which requires commercial banks and bank holding companies to almost completely divest their activities in hedge funds, private equity, and proprietary trading. This is an echo of the Glass-Steagall separation of commercial from investment banking activities passed in the 1930s. In both cases, however, the evidence does not seem to be consistent with these activities at major banks being a key source of fragility in the crises. Difficulty defining exactly what constitutes proprietary trading and concerns about regulatory avoidance also have slowed the implementation of the Volcker rule.

Dodd-Frank eliminated one regulatory agency, the Office of Thrift Supervision, which arose from a reorganization of the oversight of thrift institutions following the savings and loan crisis in the late 1980s. Other regulatory agencies, such as the Fed, FDIC, and OCC will now oversee thrifts. The legislation attempts to deal with concerns about predatory lending that emerged as credit flowed to new and unsophisticated borrowers in the 2000s by setting up a separate consumer protection bureau. The legislation, however, does not address Freddie Mac and Fannie Mae, the federal housing government-sponsored enterprises that fueled the rapid growth of mortgage securitization.

The new law creates the Financial Stability Oversight Counsel, a consortium of regulators chaired by the Treasury Department, that is to have new authority to search out and address sources of system-wide risks both within and beyond the banking sector, and encourages the migration of over-the-counter derivatives onto centrally cleared platforms.

Dodd-Frank also attempts to mitigate the "too big to fail" (TBTF) problem by creating new resolution authority. Under the law, the FDIC may close and liquidate distressed financial institutions in ways that avoid costs associated with bankruptcy. Dodd-Frank's new resolution approach allows the FDIC to impose losses on uninsured creditors, shareholders, and managers. In principle, such authority ought to help mitigate TBTF by increasing the ex ante belief that creditors would bear losses in default, but few specifics on the circumstances in which this authority would be exercised have been put out, raising questions about its effectiveness. The Dodd-Frank Act also requires large institutions to develop a resolution plan, which may help reduce uncertainty about failure resolution (Kashyap 2009; Kroszner and Shiller 2011).

Despite reasonable concern about large financial institutions, since the crisis markets appear to be more, rather than less, attentive to risk. There is thus little evidence that risk taking incentives have become more distorted; if anything, just the opposite is true. Strahan (2013) shows that credit default swap (CDS) spreads reflect risk more after the crisis than before, even for the largest financial firms. The postcrisis patterns suggest that risk takers now face (at least some) costs of their actions in the form of higher borrowing rates. What is harder to assess is why do markets price risk more postcrisis? One possibility is that government bailouts have become less likely for political reasons. Another possibility is that Dodd-Frank is working as intended—by constructing mechanisms to soften the blowback of a large failure, perhaps markets now believe that losses are more likely to be imposed on creditors in the event of distress. Or, perhaps some very large banks have become "too big to save," at least in relation to resources available to governments and central banks facing long-run fiscal imbalances.

With the wide-ranging but partially implemented regulatory changes embodied in Dodd-Frank and the new Basel III capital and liquidity rules, it is too early to assess the consequences for market adaptation, the real economy, and stability of the system going forward. Concerns about issues we have analyzed here, including the potential for conflicts, the incentive consequences of the safety net, and maintaining a competitive, efficient, and stable banking system will play key roles in the debates over future regulatory change.

References

Abrams, Burton A., and Russell F. Settle. 1993. "Pressure-Group Influence and Institutional Change: Branch-Banking Legislation during the Great Depression." *Public Choice* 77:687–705.

Acharya, Viral, Philipp Schnabl, and Gustavo Suarez. 2013. "Securitization without Risk Transfer." *Journal of Financial Economics* 107:515–36.

Adrian, Tobias, and Hyun Song Shin. 2009. "Money, Liquidity, and Monetary Policy." *American Economic Review* 99 (2): 600–605.

Ang, James S., and Terry Richardson. 1994. "The Underwriting Experience of Commercial Bank Affiliates Prior to the Glass Steagall Act: A Re-examination of Evidence for Passage of the Act." *Journal of Banking and Finance* 18 (2): 351–95.

Aoki, Masahiko, and Hugh Patrick, eds. 1994. *The Japanese Main Bank System.* Oxford: Clarendon Press.

Asquith, Paul, David Mullins, and Eric Wolff. 1989. "Original Issue High Yield Bonds: Aging Analyses of Defaults, Exchanges, and Calls." *Journal of Finance* 44:923–52.

Bank for International Settlements. 2005. "Basel II: International Convergence of Capital Measurement and Capital Standards: A Revised Framework." Basel, Switzerland, November.

Barth, James. 1991. *The Great Savings and Loan Debacle.* Washington, DC: AEI Press.

Barth, James R., Gerald Caprio, and Ross Levine. 2004. "Bank Regulation and Supervision: What Works Best?" *Journal of Financial Intermediation* 13:205–48.

Bekaert, Geert, Campbell Harvey, and Christian T. Lundblad. 2003. "Equity Market Liberalization in Emerging Markets." *Federal Reserve Bank of St. Louis Review* 85 (4): 53–74.

Benmelech, Efraim, and Tobias Moskowitz. 2007. "The Political Economy of Financial Regulation: Evidence from the US Usury Laws in the 19th Century." NBER Working Paper no. 12851, Cambridge, MA.

Berger, A. N. 1998. "The Efficiency Effects of Bank Mergers and Acquisition: A Preliminary Look at the 1990s Data." In *Bank Mergers and Acquisitions*, edited by Y. Amihud and G. Miller, 79–111. Boston: Kluwer Academic.

Bertrand, Marianne, Antoinette Schoar, and David Thesmar. 2007. "Banking Deregulation and Industry Structure: Evidence from the French Banking Reforms of 1985." *Journal of Finance* 62 (2): 597–628.

Bhargava, Rahul, and Donald R. Fraser. 1998. "On the Wealth and Risk Effects of Commercial Bank Expansion into Securities Underwriting: An Analysis of Section 20 Subsidiaries." *Journal of Banking and Finance* 22:447–65.

Black, Sandra E., and Philip E. Strahan. 2001. "The Division of Spoils: Rent Sharing and Discrimination in a Regulated Industry." *American Economic Review* 91 (4): 814–31.

———. 2002. "Entrepreneurship and Bank Credit Availability." *Journal of Finance* 57 (6): 2807–33.

Blair, Christine E. 1994. "Bank Powers and the Separation of Banking and Commerce: An Historical Perspective." *FDIC Banking Review* 7 (1): 28–38.

Bonaccorsi di Patti, Emilia, and Giovanni Dell'Ariccia. 2004. "Bank Competition and Firm Creation." *Journal of Money, Credit and Banking* 36:225–51.

Boyd, John, and Mark Gertler. 1994. "Are Banks Dead? Or Are the Reports Greatly Exaggerated?" *Federal Reserve Bank of Minneapolis Quarterly Review* 18 (3): 2–23.

Boyd, John H., and Stanley L. Graham. 1986. "Risk, Regulation, and Bank Holding Company Expansion into Nonbanking." *Federal Reserve Bank of Minneapolis Quarterly Review* 10 (2): 2–17.

———. 1988. "The Profitability and Risk Effects of Allowing Bank Holding Companies to Merge with Other Financial Firms: A Simulation Study." *Federal Reserve Bank of Minneapolis Quarterly Review* 12 (2): 3–20.

Boyd, John H., Stanley L. Graham, and Shawn Hewitt. 1993. "Bank Holding Company Mergers with Nonbank Financial Firms: Effects on the Risk of Failure." *Journal of Banking and Finance* 17:43–63.

Buchanan, James, and Gordon Tullock. 1962. *The Calculus of Consent: Logical Foundations of Constitutional Democracy*. Ann Arbor: University of Michigan Press.

Calomiris, Charles W. 1992. "Do Vulnerable Economies Need Deposit Insurance? Lessons from US Agriculture in the 1920s." In *If Texas Were Chile: A Primer on Banking Reform*, edited by Philip L. Brock, 237–349, 450–458. San Francisco: Sequoia Institute.

———. 1993. "Regulation, Industrial Structure and Instability in US Banking: An Historical Perspective." In *Structural Change in Banking*, edited by Michael Klausner and Lawrence J. White, 19–116. New York: New York University.

Calomiris, Charles, and Charles Kahn. 1991. "The Role of Demandable Debt in Structuring Optimal Banking Arrangements." *American Economic Review* 81:497–513.

Calomiris, Charles W., and Joseph Mason. 2003. "Consequences of US Bank Distress during the Great Depression." *American Economic Review* 93:937–47.

———. 2004. "Credit Card Securitization and Regulatory Arbitrage." *Journal of Financial Services Research* 26 (1): 5–27.

Calomiris, Charles W., and Eugene N. White. 2000. "The Origins of Federal Deposit Insurance." In *US Bank Deregulation in Historical Perspective*, Charles W. Calomiris, 164–211. New York: Cambridge University Press.

Cetorelli, Nicola. 2001. "Does Bank Concentration Lead to Concentration in Industrial Sectors?" Federal Reserve Bank of Chicago, Working Paper 01-01.

———. 2003. "Life-Cycle Dynamics in Industrial Sectors: The Role of Banking Market Structure." *Federal Reserve Bank of St. Louis Quarterly Review* 85:135–47.

Cetorelli, Nicola, and Michele Gambera. 2001. "Banking Market Structure, Financial Dependence and Growth: International Evidence from Industry Data." *Journal of Finance* 56 (2): 617–48.

Cetorelli, Nicola, and Philip E. Strahan. 2006. "Finance as a Barrier to Entry: Bank Competition and Industry Structure in Local US Markets." *Journal of Finance* 61 (1): 437–61.

Collender, Robert N., and Sherrill L. Shaffer. 2003. "Local Bank Office Ownership,

Deposit Control, Market Structure, and Economic Growth." *Journal of Banking and Finance* 27 (1): 27–57.

Dehejia, Rajeev, and Adriana Lleras-Muney. 2007. "Financial Development and Pathways of Growth: State Branching and Deposit Insurance Laws in the United States from 1900 to 1940." *Journal of Law and Economics* 50:239–72.

Demirgüç-Kunt, Asli, and Edward J. Kane. 2002. "Deposit Insurance around the Globe: Where Does It Work?" *Journal of Economic Perspectives* 16 (2): 175–95.

Demsetz, Rebecca S., Marc R. Saidenberg, and Philip E. Strahan. 1996. "Banks with Something to Lose: The Disciplinary Role of Franchise Value." *Federal Reserve Bank of New York Economic Policy Review* 2 (2): 1–14.

Demsetz, Rebecca S., and Philip E. Strahan. 1997. "Diversification, Size, and Risk at Bank Holding Companies." *Journal of Money, Credit, and Banking* 29:300–13.

Dick, Astrid. 2006. "Nationwide Branching and Its Impact on Market Structure, Quality and Bank Performance." *Journal of Business* 79 (2): 567–92.

Drucker, Steven, and Manju Puri. 2005. "On the Benefits of Concurrent Lending and Underwriting." *Journal of Finance* 60:2763–99.

Edwards, Jeremy, and Klaus Fischer. 1994. *Banks, Finance, and Investment in Germany*. Cambridge: Cambridge University Press.

Ellis, Diane. 1998. "The Effect of Consumer Interest Rate Deregulation on Credit Card Volumes, Charge Offs, and the Personal Bankruptcy Rates." FDIC Working Paper no. 98–05.

Ely, David P., and Kenneth J. Robinson. 1998. "How Might Financial Institutions React to Glass-Steagall Repeal? Evidence from the Stock Market." *Federal Reserve Bank of Dallas Financial Industry Studies*: 1–11.

Flannery, Mark, and Katherine Samolyk. 2005. "Payday Lending: Do the Costs Justify the Price?" FDIC Working Paper no. 2005-09, June.

Frame, W. Scott, and Lawrence J. White. 2005. "Fussing and Fuming about Fannie and Freddie: How Much Smoke, How Much Fire?" *Journal of Economic Perspectives* 19 (2): 159–84.

Friedman, Milton, and Anna Jacobson Schwartz. 1963. *A Monetary History of the United States, 1867–1960*. Princeton, NJ: Princeton University Press.

Gande, Amar, Manju Puri, Anthony Saunders, and Ingo Walter. 1997. "Bank Underwriting of Debt Securities: Modern Evidence." *The Review of Financial Studies* 10 (4): 1175–202.

Gatev, Evan, Til Schuermann, and Philip E. Strahan. 2006. "How Do Banks Manage Liquidity Risk? Evidence from the Equity and Deposit Markets in the Fall of 1998." In *The Risks of Financial Institutions*, edited by Mark Carey and René Stulz, 105–27. Chicago: University of Chicago Press.

Gatev, Evan, and Philip E. Strahan. 2006. "Banks Advantage in Hedging Liquidity Risk: Theory and Evidence from the Commercial Paper Market." *Journal of Finance* 61 (2): 867–92.

Glaeser, Edward, and José Scheinkmann. 1998. "Neither a Borrower nor a Lender Be: An Economic Analysis of Interest Restrictions and Usury Laws." *Journal of Law and Economics* 41:1–36.

Goldberg, Lawrence G., Gerald A. Hanweck, Michael Keenan, and Allan Young. 1991. "Economies of Scale and Scope in the Securities Industry." *Journal of Banking and Finance* 15:91–107.

Gompers, Paul A. 1994. "The Rise and Fall of Venture Capital." *Business and Economic History* Winter: 1–25.

Gompers, Paul A., and Josh Lerner. 1996. "The Use of Covenants: An Empirical Analysis of Venture Partnership Agreements." *Journal of Law and Economics* 39:463–98.

Gorton, Gary. 1996. "Reputation Formation in Early Bank Note Markets." *Journal of Political Economy* 104 (2): 346–97.

Gorton, Gary, and Andrew Metrick. 2012. "Securitized Banking and the Run on the Repo." *Journal of Financial Economics* 104 (3): 425–51.

Greenspan, Alan. 2004. "Testimony before the Committee on Banking, Housing, and Urban Affairs." US Senate, February 24.

Guner, A. Barak, Ulrike Malmendier, and Geoffrey Tate. 2008. "The Impact of Boards with Financial Expertise on Corporate Policies." *Journal of Financial Economics* 88 (2): 323–54.

Hammond, Bray. 1957. *Banks and Politics in America from the Revolution to the Civil War*. Princeton, NJ: Princeton University Press.

Hellman, Thomas, Kevin Murdock, and Joseph Stiglitz. 2000. "Liberalization, Moral Hazard in Banking, and Prudential Regulation: Are Capital Requirements Enough?" *American Economic Review* 90 (1): 147–65.

Hubbard, Glenn R., and Darius Palia. 1995. "Executive Pay and Performance: Evidence from the US Banking Industry." *Journal of Financial Economics* 39:105–30.

Hubbard, R. Glenn, Darius Palia, and Nicolas Economides. 1996. "The Political Economy of Branching Restrictions and Deposit Insurance." *Journal of Law and Economics* 39 (2): 667–704.

Hughes, J. P., W. W. Lang, L. J. Mester, and C.-G. Moon. 1999. "The Dollars and Sense of Bank Consolidation." *Journal of Banking and Finance* 23:291–324.

Jayaratne, Jith, and Philip E. Strahan. 1996. "The Finance-Growth Nexus: Evidence from Bank Branch Deregulation." *Quarterly Journal of Economics* 111:639–70.

———. 1998. "Entry Restrictions, Industry Evolution and Dynamic Efficiency: Evidence from Commercial Banking." *Journal of Law and Economics* 41 (1): 239–74.

Jensen, Michael C. 1989. "Eclipse of the Public Corporation." *Harvard Business Review* September: 61–74.

Jorion, Philippe. 2000. *Value at Risk: The New Benchmark for Controlling Market Risk*. New York: McGraw-Hill.

Kane, Edward. 1989. *The S&L Insurance Mess: How Did It Happen?* Washington, DC: The Urban Institute.

———. 1996. "De Jure Interstate Banking: Why Only Now?" *Journal of Money, Credit, and Banking* 28 (2): 141–61.

Kashyap, Anil. 2009. "A Sound Funeral Plan Can Prolong a Bank's Life." *Financial Times*, June 29.

Kaufman, George, and Larry Mote. 1994. "Is Banking a Declining Industry? A Historical Perspective." *Federal Reserve Bank of Chicago Economic Perspectives* 2–21.

Keeley, Michael. 1990. "Deposit Insurance, Risk and Market Power in Banking." *American Economic Review* 80:1183–200.

Keys, Benjamin J., T. K. Mukerjee, Amit Seru, and Vikrant Vig. 2010. "Did Securitization Lead to Lax Screening? Evidence from Sub-Prime Loans." *Quarterly Journal of Economics* 125 (1): .307–62

King, Robert, and Ross Levine. 1993. "Finance and Growth: Schumpeter Might Be Right." *Quarterly Journal of Economics* 108:717–38.

Kroszner, Randall S. 1997. "The Political Economy of Banking and Financial Regulation in the United States." In *The Banking and Financial Structure in the NAFTA Countries and Chile*, edited by George M. von Furstenberg, 200–13. Boston: Kluwer Academic Publishers.

———. 2000. "The Economics and Politics of Financial Modernization." *Federal Reserve Bank of New York Economic Policy Review* 6 (4): 25–37.

Kroszner, Randall S., Luc Laeven, and Daniela Klingebiel. 2007. "Banking Crises, Financial Dependence, and Growth." *Journal of Financial Economics* 84 (1): 187–228.

Kroszner, Randall S., and William Melick. 2008. "Lessons from the U.S. Experience with Deposit Insurance." In *Deposit Insurance around the World: Issues of Design and Implementation*, edited by Asli Demirgüç-Kunt, Edward J. Kane, and Luc Laeven, 181–218. Cambridge, MA: MIT Press.

Kroszner, Randall S., and Raghuram G. Rajan. 1994. "Is the Glass-Steagall Act Justified? A Study of the US Experience with Universal Banking before 1933." *American Economic Review* 84:810–32.

———. 1997. "Organization Structure and Credibility: Evidence from Commercial Bank Securities Activities before the Glass-Steagall Act." *Journal of Monetary Economics* 39:475–516.

Kroszner, Randall S., and Robert Shiller. 2011. *Reforming U.S. Financial Regulation: Before and Beyond Dodd-Frank*. Cambridge, MA: MIT Press

Kroszner, Randall S., and Philip E. Strahan. 1996. "Regulatory Incentives and the Thrift Crisis: Dividends, Mutual-to-Stock Conversions, and Financial Distress." *Journal of Finance* 51:1285–320.

———. 1999. "What Drives Deregulation? Economics and Politics of the Relaxation of Bank Branching Restrictions." *Quarterly Journal of Economics* 114 (4): 1437–67.

———. 2001a. "Bankers on Boards: Monitoring, Conflicts of Interest, and Lender Liability." *Journal of Financial Economics* 62 (3): 415–52.

———. 2001b. "Obstacles to Optimal Policy: The Interplay of Politics and Economics in Shaping Bank Supervision and Regulation Reforms." In *Prudential Supervision: What Works and What Doesn't*, edited by Frederic S. Mishkin, 233–72. Chicago: University of Chicago Press.

———. 2001c. "Throwing Good Money after Bad? Board Connections and Conflicts in Bank Lending." NBER Working Paper no. 8694, Cambridge, MA.

———. 2011. "Financial Regulatory Reform: Challenges Ahead." *American Economic Review* 101 (3): 242–46.

Kroszner, Randall S., and Thomas Stratmann. 1998. "Interest Group Competition and the Organization of Congress: Theory and Evidence from Financial Services Political Action Committees." *American Economic Review* 88:1163–87.

———. 2000. "Congressional Committees as Reputation-Building Mechanisms: Repeat PAC Giving and Seniority on the House Banking Committee." *Business and Politics* April: 35–52.

———. 2005. "Corporate Campaign Contributions, Repeat Giving, and the Rewards to Legislator Reputation." *Journal of Law and Economics* 48 (1): 41–72.

Kwan, Simon. 1998. "Securities Activities by Commercial Banking Firms' Section 20 Subsidiaries: Risk, Return, and Diversification Benefits." Federal Reserve Bank of San Francisco Working Paper, May.

Kwan, Simon, and Elizabeth Laderman. 1999. "On the Portfolio Effects of Financial Convergence—A Review of the Literature." *Federal Reserve Bank of San Francisco Economic Review* 2:18–31.

Kwast, Myron L. 1989. "The Impact of Underwriting and Dealing on Bank Returns and Risks." *Journal of Banking and Finance* 13:101–25.

Laeven, Luc. 2004. "The Political Economy of Deposit Insurance." *Journal of Financial Services Research* 26 (3): 201–24.

Levine, Ross. 2005. "Finance and Growth: Theory and Empirics." In *Handbook of Economic Growth*, edited by Philippe Aghion and Steven N. Durlauf, 865–934. Amsterdam: North Holland.

Levine, Ross, Norman Loayza, and Thorsten Beck. 2000. "Financial Intermediation and Growth: Causality and Causes." *Journal of Monetary Economics* 46 (1): 31–77.
Lopez, Jose. 2005. "Recent Policy Issues Regarding Credit Risk Transfer." FRBSF Economic Letter, 2005-34, December.
Loughran, Tim, and Jay Ritter. 1995. "The New Issues Puzzle." *Journal of Finance* 50:23–51.
Loutskina, Elena. 2011. "The Role of Securitization in Bank Liquidity and Funding Management." *Journal of Financial Economics* 100:663–84.
Loutskina, Elena, and Philip E. Strahan. 2009. "Securitization and the Declining Impact of Bank Financial Condition on Loan Supply: Evidence from Mortgage Acceptance Rates." *Journal of Finance* 64:861–89.
———. 2012. "Financial Integration, Housing and Economic Volatility." Working paper, Boston College, http://papers.ssrn.com/sol3/papers.cfm?abstract _id=1991430.
Lown, Cara, Carol L. Osler, Philip E. Strahan, and Amir Sufi. 2000. "The Changing Landscape of the Financial Services Industry: What Lies Ahead?" *Federal Reserve Bank of New York Economic Policy Review* 6 (4): 39–55.
Macey, Jonathan. 1984. "Special Interest Groups Legislation and the Judicial Function: The Dilemma of Glass-Steagall." *Emory Law Journal* 33 (Winter): 1–40.
Macey, Jonathan, and Geoffrey Miller. 1992. *Banking Law and Regulation.* Boston: Little, Brown and Company.
Makinson, Larry. 1992. *Open Secrets: The Encyclopedia of Congressional Money and Politics* Washington, DC: Congressional Quarterly.
Merton, Robert. 1978. "On the Cost of Deposit Insurance When There Are Surveillance Costs." *Journal of Business* 51:439–51.
Mester, Loretta J. 1996. "Repealing Glass Steagall: The Past Points the Way to the Future." *Federal Reserve Bank of Philadelphia Business Review* (July/August): 3–18.
Mian, Atif, and Amir Sufi. 2009. "The Consequences of Mortgage Credit Expansion: Evidence from the 2007 Mortgage Crisis." *Quarterly Journal of Economics* 124 (4): 1449–96.
Mishkin, Frederic S., and Philip E. Strahan. 1999. "What Will Technology Do to Financial Structure?" In *The Effect of Technology on the Financial Sector*, Brookings-Wharton Papers on Financial Services, edited by Robert Litan and Anthony Santomero, 249–87. Washington, DC: Brookings Institution.
Mitchener, Kris. 2007. "Are Prudential Supervision and Regulation Pillars of Financial Stability? Evidence from the Great Depression." *Journal of Law and Economics* 50:273–302.
Morgan, Donald P., Bertrand Rime, and Philip E. Strahan. 2004. "Bank Integration and State Business Cycles." *Quarterly Journal of Economics* 119 (4): 1555–85.
Niskanen, William. 1971. *Bureaucracy and Representative Government.* Chicago: Aldine-Atherton.
Noll, Roger. 1989. "Comment on Peltzman, 'The Economic Theory of Regulation After a Decade of Deregulation.'" *Brookings Papers on Economic Activity: Microeconomics 1989*: 48–58.
O'Hara, Maureen, and Wayne Shaw. 1990. "Deposit Insurance and Wealth Effects: The Value of Being Too Big to Fail." *Journal of Finance* 45:1587–600.
Passmore, Wayne, Shane M. Sherlund, and Gillian Burgess. 2005. "The Effect of Housing Government-Sponsored Enterprises on Mortgage Rates." *Real Estate Economics* 33 (3): 427–63.
Peltzman, Sam. 1970. "Capital Investment in Commercial Banking and Its Relationship to Portfolio Regulation." *The Journal of Political Economy* 78 (1): 1–26.

———. 1976. "Toward a More General Theory of Regulation." *Journal of Law and Economics* 19:211–40.

Petersen, Mitchell, and Raghuram G. Rajan. 2002. "Does Distance Still Matter? The Information Revolution in Small Business Lending." *Journal of Finance* 57 (6): 2533–70.

Puri, Manju. 1996. "Commercial Banks in Investment Banking: Conflict of Interest or Certification Role?" *Journal of Financial Economics* 40:373–401.

Rajan, Raghuram, and Luigi Zingales. 1998. "Financial Dependence and Growth." *American Economic Review* 88:559–86.

Robinson, Joan. 1952. *The Rate of Interest and Other Essays.* London: Macmillan.

Roe, M. J. 1994. *Strong Managers, Weak Owners: The Political Roots of American Corporate Finance.* Princeton, NJ: Princeton University Press.

Schenone, Carola. 2004. "The Effect of Banking Relationships on the Firm's IPO Underpricing." *Journal of Finance* 59 (6): 2903–58.

Schumpeter, Joseph. 1969. *The Theory of Economic Development.* Oxford: Oxford University Press.

Shughart, William F., II. 1988. "A Public Choice Perspective on the Banking Act of 1933." *Cato Journal* 7 (3): 595–613.

Shull, Bernard, and Lawrence J. White. 1998. "Of Firewalls and Subsidiaries: The Right Stuff for Expanded Bank Activities." *Journal of Banking Law* May: 508–30.

Stigler, George J. 1971. "The Theory of Economic Regulation." *Bell Journal of Economics and Management Science* 2 (1): 3–21.

Stiroh, Kevin, and Philip E. Strahan. 2003. "Competitive Dynamics of Deregulation: Evidence from US Banking." *Journal of Money, Credit and Banking* 35 (5): 801–28.

Strahan, Philip E. 2013. "Too Big to Fail: Causes, Consequences, and Policy Responses." *Annual Review of Financial Economics* 5, forthcoming.

Stratmann, Thomas. 2001. "Can Special Interests Buy Congressional Votes? Evidence from Financial Services Legislation." *Journal of Law and Economics* 45:345–73.

Sufi, Amir. 2005. "The Joint Production of Lending and Debt Underwriting: The Effect of Deregulation on Firms." Working paper, University of Chicago, May.

Sylla, Richard, John Legler, and John Wallis. 1987. "Banks and State Public Finance in the New Republic: The United States, 1790–1860." *Journal of Economic History* 47 (2): 391–403.

Thomas, Kenneth. 1993. *Community Reinvestment Performance: Making CRA Work for Banks, Communities, and Regulators.* Chicago: Probus Professional Publishers.

White, Eugene. 1983. *The Regulation and Reform of the American Banking System, 1900–1929.* Princeton, NJ: Princeton University Press.

———. 1986. "Before the Glass-Steagall Act: An Analysis of the Investment Banking Activities of National Banks." *Explorations in Economic History* 23:33–55.

White, Lawrence J. 1991. *The S&L Debacle: Public Policy Lessons for Bank and Thrift Regulation.* New York: Oxford University Press.

Yasuda, Ayako. 2005. "Do Bank Relationships Affect the Firm's Underwriter Choice in the Corporate-Bond Underwriting Market?" *Journal of Finance* 60 (3): 1259–92.

Retail Securities Regulation in the Aftermath of the Bubble

Eric Zitzewitz

9.1 Introduction

The stock market bubble of the 1920s was accompanied by questionable conduct by security issuers, underwriters, brokers, and investment companies. Stock in sham companies was issued and pushed on novice investors by aggressive stockbrokers, and the prospects of established firms were knowingly exaggerated.[1] Shareholders in investment companies had their assets diluted by self-dealing managers.[2] The subsequent crash motivated the creation of the institutions and laws that form the core of modern US financial regulation.

During the late 1990s and early 2000s, history repeated itself on a smaller scale. A set of abuses by accountants, equity analysts, brokers, and investment companies motivated a major new law (the Sarbanes-Oxley Act of 2002), new rulemaking by the Securities and Exchange Commission (SEC), and newly vigorous enforcement of existing laws and rules by the SEC and other regulators. It also led to a surge in interest in further refining finan-

Eric Zitzewitz is associate professor of economics at Dartmouth College and a research associate of the National Bureau of Economic Research.

Thanks to Severin Borenstein, Charles Calomiris, Randall Kroszner, Jonathan Macey, Jonathan Reuter, Nancy Rose, an anonymous group of reviewers, and participants at the NBER conference for helpful suggestions. For acknowledgments, sources of research support, and disclosure of the author's material financial relationships, if any, please see http://www.nber.org/chapters/c12573.ack.

1. For example, in the conference report accompanying the 1933 Securities Act, the House of Representatives (1933, 2) claims that "fully half or $25,000,000 worth of securities floated during this period [the decade following World War I] have been proved to be worthless." While this is a claim about the ex post value of these securities after the 1929–1933 market decline, it clearly reflects a belief that many of these securities were of questionable value ex ante.

2. See Baumol et al. (1990) and Securities and Exchange Commission (1992) for more details.

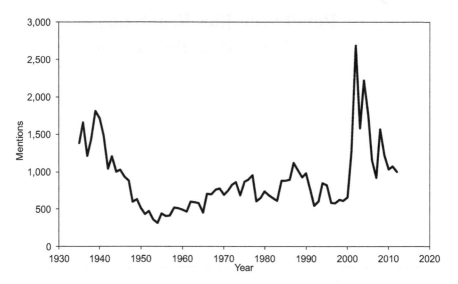

Fig. 9.1   Mentions of "Securities and Exchange Commission" in the *New York Times*

cial regulation, especially among generalists. As a crude proxy of generalist interest, figure 9.1 plots mentions of the phrase "Securities and Exchange Commission" in the *New York Times*. Mentions spiked with the collapse of Enron in late 2001 to levels not seen since the 1930s, and they remained at high levels for about four years.

The first draft of this chapter was written and presented at an NBER conference in 2005, as this peak of interest was receding. Interest in financial regulatory reform was revived after the financial crisis of 2008. While the specifics of the policy discussions of 2002 to 2005 and 2008 to 2012 have differed, the underlying market failures that provide a rationale for regulation are surprisingly consistent.

To illustrate this point, I have left the main body of the chapter largely as it was written in 2005, but will conclude by relating this discussion to issues that emerged after 2008. The chapter provides an overview of the regulation of the US retail securities and investments industry from the perspective of an industrial organization economist. It discusses the economic rationale for regulation, the institutions and laws that emerged after the 1929 crash, and then turns to a discussion of more current issues. Given the vastness of the field, this discussion is focused on three issues with parallels in other industries: the regulation of pricing, antitrust, and firm boundaries and their implications for conflicts of interest.[3] With the benefit of postfinancial

3. Readers interested in a more comprehensive survey of the field are referred to Seligman (2003) or the legal textbook Coffee and Seligman (2002). Baumol et al. (1990) and Securities

crisis hindsight, I have added a discussion of a fourth issue: the potentially perverse effects of competition when important aspects of product quality, such as the safety of investments, are unobserved by most consumers. This issue emerged in the literature before the financial crisis, but has become more widely discussed since.

The remainder of the chapter is outlined as follows. Section 9.2 discusses the scope and economic size of the retail securities and investments industry, while section 9.3 discusses the underlying reasons why it might require regulation. Section 9.4 provides a brief overview of the main institutions and laws, while sections 9.5 through 9.7 discuss the three current issues just outlined. A conclusion follows.

9.2 Size and Scope of the Retail Securities Industry

Financial services, broadly construed, are a larger piece of the economy than many economically literate Americans realize. Most regular newspaper readers are aware that US health care expenditures are about 15 percent of GDP and that this ratio is about 1.5 times higher than in other advanced countries (OECD 2005). This figure is the centerpiece of an active debate about the extent to which it reflects high quantity and quality, high prices and economic rents, or waste.

Fewer are aware that the corresponding figures for financial services are about as high.[4] Because financial services are an intermediate good as well as a final good, a direct comparison of expenditure data is not meaningful. Table 9.1 reports that gross value added of the financial intermediation sector (which includes banking, insurance, and securities) is 8.1 percent of GDP for the United States and an average of 5.1 percent in the rest of the G7. For comparison, gross value added figures for "health and social work" are provided. Gross value added excludes purchases of materials, services, and capital equipment, and so these figures are not directly comparable to the more commonly quoted expenditure data, but they do suggest that finance and health care are roughly comparable in size.

An alternative measure of the sector's size is provided by revenue data from the 2002 Economic Census. The total revenue of the financial intermediation sector in 2002 is $2.7 trillion, or about 25 percent of GDP (table 9.2). This figure includes both revenue from interest on loans and double counts revenue from intermediate goods and services, so it overstates the size of the sector. The Economic Census data show that the sector accounts for

and Exchange Commission (1992) also provide histories of investment management regulation. Kitch (2001) and Goshen and Parchomovsky (2006) provide complementary reviews of current issues in financial regulation.

4. After the financial crisis of 2008, the size of the financial services sector has received more discussion (e.g., Philippon and Reshef 2009; Gennaioli, Shleifer, and Vishny 2012; Greenwood and Scharfstein 2013).

Table 9.1   Relative sizes of financial services and health care, 2003 (percent of GDP)

	Gross value added in financial intermediation (%)	Gross value added in health and social work (%)	Total national expenditure on health care (%)
United States	8.1	6.9	15.0
Equal-weighted average of rest of G7	5.1	5.9	9.2
Canada	5.9	5.4	9.9
France	4.3	7.6	10.1
Germany	3.8	6.1	11.1
Italy	5.4	4.5	8.4
Japan	7.0	n/a	7.9
United Kingdom	4.4	5.9	7.7

Sources: OECD National Accounts for value added; OECD Health Data for total health care expenditures. National accounts data is from 2001 for Canada and the United Kingdom; health expenditure data is from 2002 for Japan and the United Kingdom.

12.8 percent of revenue, 10 percent of payroll, and 6 percent of employment reported in all industries. The last two ratios do not suffer from double counting and the first includes it in both numerator and denominator, so these are better indicators of its share in the economy. The conclusion that the sector is about as large as health care still seems at least roughly valid.

Of the $2.7 trillion in revenue reported in the census, about $400 billion falls into the scope of this chapter: securities and investment products purchased by (but not necessarily exclusively by) retail investors. The activities of this industry can be roughly thought of as a value chain with four steps (figure 9.2). First, securities are underwritten and distributed to their initial owners, for example, through an initial public offering (IPO). Second, securities are traded on secondary markets by both proprietary traders and brokers acting as agents for either individual investors or portfolio managers. Third, many securities are purchased and held by investment products such as mutual funds or variable annuities. Fourth, the investment products are sold to retail investors by financial advisors, brokers, banks, insurance agents, or mutual fund companies. In some cases, stages of the process are bypassed. For example, some investors bypass stages 3 and 4 by purchasing securities directly through discount brokers, or bypass stage 3 but not 4 by purchasing securities on the advice of a full-service broker. Likewise, some investors bypass stage 4 by buying investment products such as mutual funds directly from the fund's manager. Investors and investment funds also often bypass stage 2 by investing directly and holding new issues, especially for bonds with illiquid secondary markets. Even given these exceptions, the four-stage value chain is a useful organizing framework, particularly given that, as discussed later, laws, rulemaking, and regulatory bodies are organized around this delineation of activities.

Table 9.3 provides a product level breakdown of revenue accounted for by

Table 9.2   Size of US financial intermediation industries, 2002

NAICS code		Revenue ($ millions)	Payroll ($ millions)	Employees (thousands)
52	Finance and insurance	2,732,546	377,236	6,534
521	Monetary authorities—central bank	28,909	1,234	22
522	Credit intermediation and related activities	1,061,126	148,211	3,229
5221	Depository credit intermediation	598,871	97,143	2,220
52211	Commercial banking	481,231	79,924	1,748
52212	Savings institutions	78,840	10,311	255
52213	Credit unions	37,397	6,503	211
52219	Other depository credit intermediation	1,404	404	5
5222	Nondepository credit intermediation (credit card issuers, leasing, etc.)	403,513	36,617	690
5223	Activities related to credit intermediation (loan brokerage, transaction processing, etc.)	58,742	14,451	319
523	Securities intermediation and related activities	325,184	105,549	869
52311	Investment banking and securities dealing	104,011	31,486	143
52312	Securities brokerage	104,812	36,428	361
52313	Commodity contracts dealing	3,905	835	10
52314	Commodity contracts brokerage	2,381	1,045	12
5232	Securities and commodity exchanges	3,213	721	7
5239	Other financial investment activities	106,363	35,034	336
52391	Miscellaneous intermediation	10,359	3,054	29
52392	Portfolio management	65,483	22,244	181
52393	Investment advice	15,098	5,473	67
52399	All other financial investment activities	15,423	4,263	59
524	Insurance carriers and related activities	1,294,941	120,683	2,387
52593	Real Estate Investment Trusts—REITs	22,386	1,559	26

Source: 2002 Economic Census.
Note: The economic census includes only REITs from NAICS (North American Industry Classification System) code 525, excluding, for example, pension funds.

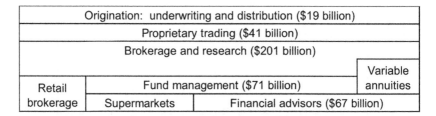

Origination: underwriting and distribution ($19 billion)		
Proprietary trading ($41 billion)		
Brokerage and research ($201 billion)		

			Variable
Retail	Fund management ($71 billion)		annuities
brokerage	Supermarkets	Financial advisors ($67 billion)	

Fig. 9.2   The retail securities and investments value chain

Notes: Figures are annual revenue by product line for commercial banks (NAICS 5221) and securities firms (NAICS 523) taken from table 9.3. Product codes are assigned to the categories above as follows: origination = product code 533; proprietary trading = 565 – 569; brokerage and research = 554 to 564; and the other product categories (575, 576, and 578 for securities firms only), fund management, and financial advisors = 574 + 577. The revenue from product code 577 (investment management and advice giving) is allocated according to the industry classification of the establishment; revenue from portfolio management and investment banking establishments is called "fund management" and revenue from other industries (largely commercial banking, brokerage, and investment advising establishments) is classified as financial advice.

commercial banks and securities firms in 2002.[5] The origination of securities accounted for $18.8 billion in revenue, which is primarily divided among investment banking ($11.7 billion), commercial banking ($4.4 billion), and brokerage ($2.4 billion) establishments.[6] Proprietary trading yielded $40.9 billion, with commercial and investment banking establishments each accounting for about $17.5 billion. The profitability of proprietary trading, particularly by entities engaged in other client business, is a recent source of concern for regulators, for reasons discussed more following. Brokerage and related products such as investment research accounted for $201 billion in revenue, although less than half of this was earned by brokerage establishments, with commercial and investment banking establishments

5. Insurance companies also offer products with investment characteristics. A variable annuity is an investment product in its accumulation stage, while fixed annuities and whole life insurance also have investment aspects to them. Total annuity revenue for insurance establishments in 2002 was approximately $200 billion, but since this could not be separated into variable and fixed annuities, I exclude it from the revenue figures in this section.

6. As in other industries, an establishment refers to all the activities of a particular firm at a particular location. So, for example, if the small asset management arm of a large commercial bank was housed in its own location, it would be classified as a fund management establishment, while if it were housed in that bank's headquarters building, it would usually appear as asset management activities of a commercial banking establishment. In some cases, however, the Census Bureau separates the activities of a common owner into multiple establishments even when they are collocated. The decision to do so appears related to the ease with which the activities can be cleanly separated. "When two or more activities were carried on at a single location under a single ownership, all activities generally were grouped together as a single establishment. The entire establishment was classified on the basis of its major activity and all data for it were included in that classification. However, when distinct and separate economic activities (for which different industry classification codes were appropriate) were conducted at a single location under a single ownership, separate establishment reports for each of the different activities were obtained in the census" (US Census Bureau 2005, A-1).

Table 9.3   Revenue of US commercial banks and securities firms by product, 2002 ($ millions)

Product line code	Product	Commercial banking (5221)	Investment banking (52311)	Securities brokerage (52312)	Investment management and advice (5239)	Total
Banking products						
550	Loan income	419,611	1,081	113	1,771	422,576
552	Nonloan credit products	324,557	1,081	113	1,771	327,522
570	Deposit accounts	32,571				32,571
571	Cash management	38,456				38,456
572,573	Document payment products (i.e., cashier's checks, money orders) and retail forex	21,783				21,783
		2,244				2,244
Securities products		88,021	89,880	100,472	100,428	378,800
Securities origination		4,353	11,680	2,362	357	18,754
5531	Public equity	3,400	5,256	1,556	177	10,389
5532	Public debt	849	5,085	584	109	6,627
5533	Private placement equity	13	630	84	69	796
5534	Private placement debt	92	709	138	2	942
Brokering and dealing		42,415	48,618	78,480	7,071	176,584
554	Debt instruments	29,429	8,932	12,199	1,427	51,988
556	Equity	1,723	27,948	51,474	3,502	84,647
557	Derivatives	6,324	3,758	2,615	543	13,241
559	Mutual funds	1,298	200	8,004	585	10,087
558, 560, 561	Other products (currency, commodity pools, correspondent products)	400	126	797	238	1,560
562 to 564	Financing related to securities (securities lending, repurchase agreements)	3,241	7,654	3,392	775	15,061

(continued)

Table 9.3   (*continued*)

Product line code	Product	Commercial banking (5221)	Investment banking (52311)	Securities brokerage (52312)	Investment management and advice (5239)	Total
Proprietary trading		**17,715**	**17,299**	**3,438**	**2,463**	**40,915**
565	Debt instruments	**12,675**	**11,950**	**552**	**556**	**25,733**
566	Equities	**905**	**2,104**	**658**	**850**	**4,518**
567	Derivatives	**2,739**	**2,636**	**2,112**	**313**	**7,800**
568,569	Other	**1,397**	**610**	**115**	**743**	**2,864**
Trust, asset management, and financial planning		**21,727**	**12,215**	**15,699**	**88,659**	**138,300**
574	Trust fiduciary fees	14,098	135	116	10,559	24,909
577	Financial planning and investment management	7,629	12,080	15,583	78,100	113,391
5771	Businesses and governments	4,691	7,652	3,446	26,164	41,954
5772	Individuals	2,937	4,428	12,137	51,935	71,437
Other products		93,049	13,175	4,719	6,042	116,986
575,576	Financial market clearing products and ACH	1,810	125	493	1,878	4,305
578	Other products	91,239	13,050	4,227	4,164	112,681
Total		598,871	104,011	104,812	106,363	914,057

Source: 2002 Economic Census.
Note: Bold type denotes the scope of this chapter.

dividing the other half roughly evenly. Asset management and financial planning accounted for $138 billion. Both managing a collective investment vehicle such as a mutual fund and providing investment advice to an individual investor are regarded "investment advice," and revenues from the two sources are not distinguished in the Economic Census. Of the $138 billion, $71 billion is earned by establishments engaged in portfolio management or investment banking establishments, while the remaining $67 billion is earned by investment advising, commercial banking, brokerage, and investment banking establishments. The former is presumably largely portfolio management, while the latter is presumably largely financial advising to retail customers.

The $400 billion in total revenue represents about 3.6 percent of GDP and 2 percent of the stock of financial market assets held by households.[7] As with health care, it is impossible to infer over- or underspending from the $400 billion number alone, but these figures are useful in roughly sizing the economic importance of the sector. Financial services play a special role in capital formation in an economy, and inefficiency in financial services can have disproportionate effects on welfare. For example, suppose that this 3.6 percent of GDP either includes 1 percent of GDP in pure waste or, alternatively, reflects an underinvestment in intermediation services that leads to a misallocation of capital that leads to a net waste of 1 percent of GDP.[8] Recall from the Solow (1956) growth model that the steady state capital-output ratio is equal to $s/(d + n + g)$, where s is savings as a percent of GDP, d is the depreciation rate, n is population growth, and g is total factor productivity growth. Taking reasonable values for the last three parameters of $d = 5\%$, $n = 1\%$, and $g = 2\%$ implies that waste or misallocation that lowers the savings rate by 1 percent of GDP reduces the steady state capital-output ratio by 12.5 percent. Assuming Cobb-Douglas production with a capital share of 0.3, this lowers steady state output per capita by about 6 percent.[9] This 6 percent reduction, which occurs over time as a lower net savings rate leads to slower accumulation of capital, is in addition to the direct waste

7. The census year 2002 was a trough year for the securities industry. Data from the Service Annual Survey for 2000 to 2004 reveal that revenue for securities firms with employment (about 90 percent of the total by revenue) fell from $385 billion in 2000 to $293 billion in 2002 and then recovered to $349 billion in 2004. Product-level data suggests that the declines and recoveries in underwriting, proprietary trading, brokerage, and asset management/advice were roughly proportional. The stock of financial market assets held by households is calculated as $19.6 trillion for 2002 by taking total financial assets ($29.7 trillion) less bank deposits ($4.0 trillion), equity in noncorporate business ($5.2 trillion), and insurance reserves ($0.9 trillion). Source: Federal Reserve, *Flow of Funds Accounts for the United States*, table L100.

8. For comparison, French (2008, 1537) estimates that "the fees and expenses paid for mutual funds, the investment management costs paid by institutions, the fees paid to hedge funds and funds of funds, and the transaction costs paid by traders" account for about 0.75 percent of the value of equity outstanding. The difference between this and the 0.09 percent that French estimates would be that the cost of passive investing corresponds to just over 1 percent of GDP.

9. If the Cobb-Douglas production function is $Y = A * K \wedge a * L \wedge (1 - a)$, then $(Y/L) = (Y/K) \wedge [a/(1 - a)] * A \wedge [1/(1 - a)]$.

of the 1 percent of GDP.[10] In short, the most common argument made in favor of lower taxation of capital, that it leads to more capital accumulation and thus higher returns to labor, can also be made in favor of an efficient financial sector.[11] The desirability of an efficient financial sector is usually uncontroversial, however. The key questions are where are the inefficiencies and whether better designed regulation can address them?

9.3   The Economic Rationale for Securities Regulation

A necessary, but not always sufficient, condition for regulation to be useful is for the unregulated competitive equilibrium to not be socially optimal. The standard conditions for a competitive equilibrium to be optimal are full and symmetric information, rational agents, the absence of externalities, and competitive behavior. Each of these conditions is arguably unmet in at least part of the securities industry, giving rise to potential rationales for regulation.

9.3.1   Imperfect Information

Gathering value-relevant information about securities is costly, leading even rational investors to choose to be not fully informed in equilibrium (Grossman and Stiglitz 1980). Delegation to expert agents is often the response, and as discussed earlier, a typical investor invests via multiple layers of agents: a financial advisor to select investment managers, investment managers to select securities and exercise any voting rights, brokers to trade those securities, and managers of the securities' issuers to produce returns.

As alignment of incentives in these agency relationships is often imperfect, delegation and imperfect information can give rise to moral hazard problems. Financial advisors may prioritize recommending the investment products of their employer (Christofferson, Evans, and Musto 2005).[12] They may also make recommendations based on sales commissions or other considerations provided by the fund family.[13] Managers of investment products

10. This simple Solow model exercise actually understates the importance of an efficient and effective financial sector in several ways. Savings is exogenous in the Solow model; if savers react to financial-sector inefficiencies by reducing their saving, the effects could be greater. In addition, the Solow model assumes that capital accumulation and technological progress are independent. It thus ignores the fact that new firms and new vintages of capital equipment are a primary means through which new technologies are developed and deployed, respectively.

11. For an example of the former, see Council of Economic Advisers (2003, chap. 5).

12. This prioritization is sometimes less straightforward to detect than one might assume, given the practice of using investment product brands that differ from the brand under which the adviser conducts business but are nonetheless owned by the same firm (e.g., an advisor in a First Union bank branch selling an Evergreen mutual fund).

13. Generally, doing so is legal so long as the payments are disclosed. Recent regulatory cases illustrate the boundaries of what is permitted. Some advisors sold higher commission "B share" versions of a mutual fund to investors without disclosing that lower commission "A share" versions were available (e.g., SEC administrative case 3-11179 against IFG Network Securities). Others sold funds from an approved list that mutual funds made undisclosed payments to

may engage in activities that lower the returns of their portfolios but benefit them privately, such as tolerating arbitrage trading in exchange for investments in other high-fee funds (Zitzewitz 2003). They may also reallocate returns into portfolios with higher incentive-based compensation (Cici, Gibson, and Moussawi 2006) or more return-sensitive investors (Gaspar, Massa, and Matos 2006) through a variety of techniques. Brokers may place trades in a manner that reduces clients' execution quality but provides them with a private benefit.[14] And, of course, issuing firms' managers may manage in a way that places their own interests ahead of their shareholders.

Regulation can seek to limit agency problems in several ways. Merit regulation proscribes certain practices, investment products, or fee levels. Examples include laws prohibiting front running (trading in advance of one's clients to profit from the impact their trades have on prices) or Ponzi schemes. Antifraud regulation can help make voluntary disclosure about agents' performance and practices credible by prosecuting agents who lie. Mandatory disclosure regulation can both require disclosure of performance and practices and impose standards to make such disclosures more comparable.

Imperfect information can also give rise to adverse selection problems. In the absence of regulation, agents who engage in behavior that benefits themselves at the expense of their clients may be more profitable and if so will have more incentive to market their products aggressively. This can create a lemons problem (Akerlof 1971) in which bad agents and products drive out good ones. Regulation can potentially help, again by either mandating disclosure or prohibiting practices.

9.3.2   Investor Behavior

The question of whether efforts to protect consumers should focus on disclosure requirements or on merit regulation that restricts products and behavior is a central debate in financial regulation. As discussed later, the SEC generally favors the former, while the state regulators who enforce antifraud statues tend to take the latter approach. As Zingales (2004) emphasizes, an advantage of disclosure regulation is that its costs are usually smaller than those of merit regulation, which risks limiting innovation.

A problem, though, is that for the unsophisticated investors most in need of protection, the benefits of additional disclosure may be small too. Whether regulation requiring disclosure is effective depends on whether

---

be included on (e.g., SEC administrative case 3-11780 against Edward Jones). Others recommended funds in exchange for the funds' having directed brokerage business to the advisor's firm (e.g., SEC administrative case 3-11868 against Putnam Investment Management, LLC).

14. Examples include internally matching client orders with proprietary or favored-client trades at disadvantageous prices, bundling orders with informed order flow from hedge fund clients or proprietary traders, routing orders to lower volume exchanges in exchange for payments for order flow, and illegally front running clients' transactions.

investors can make use of the information. When buying securities or investments, many consumers are unaware of the most basic information that is disclosed. In addition, they exhibit behavioral biases, particularly naïveté about the incentives of experts.

For many financial products, the majority of customers do not understand the rather central concept of a "price." For example, in a 2002 survey by Vanguard and *Money* magazine, only 25 percent of investors correctly identified the expense ratio as the annual fee they pay for a mutual fund (on a multiple choice question with no guessing penalty). Likewise, an OCC/SEC survey reported on by Alexander, Jones, and Nigro (2001, 164) found that only 19 percent of mutual fund investors reported knowing the (approximate) expense ratio of their largest fund investment.[15] Hortascu and Syverson (2004) find that a large proportion of investors choose S&P index funds as if they had very high search costs. An alternative interpretation of their results would be that investors observe price imperfectly when choosing their funds (Busse, Elton, and Gruber 2004), or misunderstand the strong negative relationship between fees and after-fee performance (Carhart 1997 and others).[16] Barber, Odean, and Zheng (2004) find that investors react more to fees that are salient, such as front-end sales commissions that are deducted from their investment at time of purchase, than to fees that are less salient, such as expenses or deferred commissions that are deducted over time. Choi, Laibson, and Madrian (2010) find that undergraduate and MBA students at top schools fail to choose the lowest expense ratio index fund even when furnished with information on fees, in part because of a belief that past returns are informative about future returns.

One might think that investors do not need to understand expense ratios, since expense ratios are deducted from net returns, and investors should care primarily about net returns. The problem with this logic is that past net returns are almost uncorrelated with future net returns, and a low expense ratio is by the far the best single predictor of high future returns. Mutual funds are unlike many other products in that future "quality" (at least as measured by before-expense returns) is close to uncorrelated with past quality, but quality is *negatively* related to price. Studies of investor demand for funds (Chevalier and Ellison 1997 and others) suggest that many investors appear to invest as if they expect quality (returns) to be positively serially

15. In contrast, a recent Investment Company Institute (2006) survey found that 74 percent of investors claimed to have reviewed the expense ratio before making their most recent mutual fund investment. Possible reconciliations of these results include: (a) investors may have become more sensitive to fees since 2002; (b) the ICI sample was more sophisticated than the Vanguard-*Money* or OCC-SEC samples; or (c) the ICI survey asked whether investors had review the fund's fees, but did not test this knowledge.

16. Mutual funds are unlike many other products in that quality (at least as measured by after-expense returns) is close to uncorrelated with past quality, but quality is strongly *negatively* related to price. Studies of investor demand for funds (Chevalier and Ellison 1997 and others) suggest that many investors appear to invest as if they expect quality (returns) to be positively serially correlated and to get more when they pay more, as one might expect if these investors were applying their experience from other products to mutual funds.

correlated and to get more when they pay more, as one might expect if these investors were applying their experience from other products to mutual funds (Mullainathan, Schwartzstein, and Shleifer 2008).

A similar percentage in the Vanguard-*Money* survey misunderstood loads (sales commissions paid to the broker who sells a fund). Along with the salience issue discussed by Barber, Odean, and Zheng, this might help explain the recent popularity of "B" shares, in which the broker's commission is deducted gradually from shareholder's assets as opposed to being deducted from their investment upfront. As mentioned earlier, it is alleged that brokers misrepresent "B" shares as being no-load funds or steer investors into "B" shares where there are lower commission alternatives.

Among investment products, however, mutual fund fees are perhaps the most transparent. Variable annuities carry a variety of fees that are in many cases collectively large enough to pay sales commissions of 5 to 10 percent of the amount invested.[17] In July 2004, the *New York Times* reported on the sales of a set of extremely disadvantageous contractual mutual fund and life insurance products on military bases (Henriques 2004). In both types of products, the fees that finance sales commissions are not deducted from an investor's investment upfront in a transparent manner, but instead are spread across various administration fees, expenses charged to the underlying investments, and fees for death benefits that are well above the cost of a comparable amount of term life insurance.

In brokerage accounts, many investors understand commissions, and are less likely to understand other trading costs such as the bid-ask spread and how it is affected by order handling rules. When investors buy bonds from a brokerage at no commission, many do not realize that the brokerage is charging a markup that usually exceeds the commission on comparably sized stock transactions (see, e.g., Harris and Piwowar 2006). Likewise, when investors buy shares in public offerings, some are unaware that the company is paying an underwriting commission on the proceeds, creating a wedge between the amount they pay and the funds that management is able to invest on their behalf. Some have argued (e.g., Lee, Shleifer, and Thaler 1991) that the fact that investors buy closed-end fund IPOs at a premium to net asset value despite the fact that these funds typically trade at a discount several months later provides an example of investors misunderstanding these issues.

Apart from difficulty understanding prices, the field of behavioral finance has documented a variety of psychological biases that affect consumers when making financial decisions.[18] Investors, especially males, trade too

---

17. See, for example, Securities and Exchange Commission (2004, 2).
18. A full review of the field is well beyond the scope of this chapter—Shefrin (2002), Barberis and Thaler (2003), and Shiller (2003) provide excellent summaries. The findings of behavioral finance about consumer behavior in this industry has motivated some to consider the implications of boundedly rational consumer behavior in other industries, see, for example Gabaix and Laibson (2006).

frequently (Shefrin and Statman 1994; Odean 1998). Investors also react to news inefficiently. At short-to-medium time horizons (e.g., one year) investors suffer from the disposition effect, holding on to losing investments too long and selling winners too quickly (Shefrin and Statman 1985). This is the reverse of what would be optimal given the tax treatment of capital gains and the long-standing findings of momentum in stock prices at the one-year time horizon (Jegadeesh and Titman 1993). Investors also display the disposition effect in their mutual fund investments, holding on to underperforming mutual funds despite the fact that these funds tend to repeat their underperformance (Carhart 1997; Kacperczyk, Sialm, and Zheng 2008). A psychological reason for avoiding selling a losing investment is that it creates cognitive dissonance—booking a loss is an acknowledgement that the initial investment was a mistake.[19] Firing a financial advisor that one once trusted requires a similar acknowledgement and creates a stickiness that some advisors may exploit.

Many investors also appear to be excessively influenced by and naïve about the incentives of financial advisors, equity analysts, and the financial media. Across a variety of metrics, financial advisors choose funds for their clients that are no better than the funds no-load investors choose for themselves (Bergstresser, Chalmers, and Tufano 2009), and advisors are particularly unlikely to advise a client to sell a persistently underperforming fund offered by their employer (Christofferson, Evans, and Musto 2005). Alexander, Jones, and Nigro (2001) report that many investors have misconceptions about the sign of the correlation between expenses and future returns, the degree of persistence in mutual fund returns, and whether money market funds are FDIC insured, and that in some cases they acquire these misconceptions from their financial advisors.[20] One of the strongest predictors of mutual fund inflows is high 12b1 fees; 12b1 fees are collected from investors and mostly used to finance payments to the brokerage or advisor that recommended the fund (Reid and Rea 2003).[21] Mutual fund recommenda-

19. Investors overreact to positive news at longer time horizons (e.g., three to five years), buying stocks that have performed well in the last three to five years and pushing up their prices to the point where they underperform in the future (De Bondt and Thaler 1985 and 1989). This can also be rationalized as being due to cognitive dissonance if investors window dress their own portfolios, removing long-term losing stocks and buying stocks they wish they had bought earlier.

20. For example, 35 percent of investors in money market mutual funds who used a broker believe that these funds are insured, and 23 percent of those report being told this by their broker (180). The number of investors who believe in a positive relationship between expenses and returns outnumbers those who believe in a negative relationship (19.9 percent to 15.7 percent); the margin widens to 21.0 to 14.0 for investors who invest only through intermediaries (banks, brokers, insurance companies, or retirement plans) (165). Twenty-four percent of investors expect a fund with a good performance in the previous year to have above average performance in the next year (166).

21. A 12b1 fee refers to a fee that a fund can charge its shareholders to pay for the marketing and distribution of fund, authorized under rule 12b1 promulgated by the SEC under the Investment Company Act of 1940. The fund's trustees must conclude that doing so is in the

tions in personal finance magazines are associated with significant future inflows, despite the fact that positively mentioned funds perform no better than average in the future and that mentions are correlated with a fund family's past advertising (Reuter and Zitzewitz 2006). Investors in stocks react to media reports, even when they contain no new information. One of the most famous examples is the fourfold increase in the stock price of EntreMed that followed a front-page *New York Times* story, despite the fact that the potential breakthrough in cancer research highlighted in the article had been published in *Nature* and written up in other newspapers (including the *Times*) over the prior five months (Huberman and Regev 2001). CEO interviews on CNBC from 1999 to 2001 were accompanied by a 1.65 percent stock price appreciation that mean reverted over the next day (Kim and Meschke 2011; see also Busse and Green 2002). The discounts of foreign closed-end funds (the difference between the price of a fund and the value of its underlying assets) react to whether and how extensively foreign news is reported in the US press (Klibanoff, Lamont, and Wizman 1998). Media-savvy issuers appear to exploit these biases, by directing media attention to the most favorable earnings metric (Dyck and Zingales 2005) and by announcing bad news on Friday afternoons (Bagnoli, Clement, and Watts 2004; DellaVigna and Pollet 2009). Investors' reliance on the media has also been exploited to include trading in advance of media coverage and the use of the media to manipulate asset prices.[22]

There are limits to the extent to which regulation can protect investors from their own biases or a lack of sophistication. As with regulation designed to address information problems, regulatory responses to investor behavior have generally taken two different approaches. First, merit and antifraud regulations protect the least sophisticated investors by restricting the availability of certain types of securities or financial services that are viewed as particularly abusive (e.g., Ponzi schemes) and limiting others to sophisticated investors (e.g., hedge funds). Both the SEC and self-regulatory bodies such as the National Association of Securities Dealers (NASD) regulate the behavior of investment professionals such as stockbrokers and investment advisors, particularly the exploitation of investors' naïveté and biases. Second, regulations force the disclosure of certain characteristics of issuers and investments to ensure that sophisticated investors have access to a certain

---

interests of shareholders, for example, by generating enough asset growth to allow a management fee reduction that more than offsets the fee. While there is strong evidence that 12b1 fees are correlated with inflows, some have questioned whether this growth leads to reduction in management fees sufficient to provide a net benefit to shareholders (e.g., Walsh 2004). As a result, more recent justifications of 12b1 fees have argued that they benefit shareholders because they are used to pay brokers for services provided to shareholders.

22. Examples include the insiders who provided tips on the content of the *Wall Street Journal*'s Heard on the Street and *Business Week*'s Inside Wall Street columns and financial columnists who have allegedly recommended stocks they hold positions in.

minimum level of information and in some cases mandate certain standard-ized formats to increase the salience of the information to investors.[23]

9.3.3   Externalities

Two example of externalities that potentially provide a rationale for regu-lation are free riding in monitoring and so-called preference externalities. Monitoring corporate or investment managers generates benefits that are shared by other investors. It therefore suffers from a potential free rider problem. This free rider problem is partially addressed through three mecha-nisms. First, the pricing of securities or investments in the secondary market can create an incentive for a shareholder to acquire a large stake and then monitor management, internalizing the benefits of their monitoring in pro-portion to their stake. As an example, investors have recently purchased stakes in underperforming closed-end mutual funds at a discount and then forced management to redeem all or some of their shares at net asset value. Some of the benefits of this form of monitoring spill over to the other share-holders of the fund, suggesting that it will be underprovided by the market.

Second, shareholders exert monitoring through boards of directors. Cor-porate security issuers have boards of directors that monitor management. Investments such as mutual funds are formally organized as companies, and they are required to have a board of directors whose responsibilities include hiring, monitoring, and negotiating fees with the investment manager. The desired level of independence of both corporate and investment company board members is a matter of active debate. Tufano and Sevick (1997), Del Guercio, Dann, and Partch (2003), and Zitzewitz (2003) provide evi-dence that investment company board independence is correlated with shareholder-friendly fee and valuation policies. The SEC recently issued a rule requiring that 75 percent of investment company board members and the board chair be independent of employment or other business relation-ships with the investment manager, although this rule has been challenged in court. On the other hand, some question whether boards are necessary for investments (Tkac 2004), invoking the fact that investment companies in other countries do not have boards (Damato, Reilly, and Richardson 2004). Khorana, Servaes, and Tufano (2005 and 2009) compare mutual fund industries across countries, finding that the industry is larger and fees are lower in countries with stronger investor protections, including boards of directors.

Third, the media and other third-party experts can potentially play a monitoring role. Media publications motivated by subscription revenue or analysts interested in building followership in the markets have an incen-

---

23. For example, the SEC requires that mutual fund prospectuses contain at their beginning a "Risk-Return Summary" that includes information on fees and past performance. It also regulates the reporting of past performance to limit the extent to which fund companies can distort their track records by manipulating the time period reported.

tive to provide high-quality information to their clients. At the same time, these experts may have other, conflicting motivations. As mentioned earlier, Reuter and Zitzewitz (2006) find a correlation between the mutual fund recommendations of personal finance magazines and past advertising.[24] They also find that the publications overweight past returns and underweight fees when determining which fund to recommend, which might be regarded as a form of proindustry bias.[25] Lin and McNichols (1998) and Michaely and Womack (1999) find a correlation between analysts' security recommendations and their employer's underwriting business, and this relationship has been extensively probed by regulators in recent years.

Investor's preferences can also impose externalities on other investors. George and Waldfogel (2003) argue that when newspaper readers are homogeneous they create positive externalities for one another by enlarging the market and generating scale economies. When they are heterogeneous, however, they can generate negative externalities. George and Waldfogel (2006) provide an example, arguing that the entrance of the *New York Times* to a newspaper market "spreads ignorance and apathy" by attracting educated readers away from the local paper, making it optimal for the local paper to reduce national coverage and appeal to less-educated readers. Both externalities are present in securities and investment markets. In investments, Vanguard arguably plays the role of the *New York Times*, attracting expense ratio–sensitive investors and lowering the average fee sensitivity of other firms' clients.

Regulation can and does address these externalities in several ways. On some issues regulators play the role of monitor themselves, by enforcing rules against certain behavior. By mandating boards and regulating the independence and election of their members, regulators can make the collective action problem cheaper for investors to solve. By mandating disclosure, regulators can facilitate the monitoring roles of both boards and outsiders such as analysts and the media. Regulators can also address externalities arising from the bifurcation of markets into products targeting sophisticated and unsophisticated investors, either by aiding investors who seek to become sophisticated or by limiting the exploitation of the unsophisticated.

24. In contrast, Miller (2006) finds that the media's coverage of accounting fraud in an industry is not related to the industry's propensity to advertise.

25. Arguably another potential example of proindustry bias in the financial media is that fact that academic studies documenting the extent of stale price arbitrage in mutual funds (e.g., Goetzmann, Ivkovic, and Rouwenhorst 2001; Greene and Hodges 2002; Zitzewitz 2003) were known to reporters at major publications, and yet they were discussed extremely rarely until the announcement of New York attorney general (NYAG) Eliot Spitzer's investigation in September 2003. Two notable exceptions were Stone (2002) and Carnahan (2003), although it should be noted that even these articles appeared only in the online editions of *Business Week* and *Forbes*, respectively. Other articles discussed the issue, but framed it in a way that buried the lead (e.g., "Monitoring Trades for the Good of the Fund," *New York Times*, April 9, 2000). After the announcement of the NYAG's investigation, the financial media did report on the issues thoroughly.

9.3.4   Competitive Behavior

Most financial industries have free entry and large numbers of competitors, and so there is a temptation to assume that they are close to perfectly competitive. At the same time, some of the institutional features that industrial economists normally associate with soft competition are present in these industries. Especially following the relaxation and ultimately the repeal of the separations between commercial banking, insurance, and securities in the Glass-Steagall Act, many financial services firms compete against each other in multiple markets, which can facilitate soft competition (Bernheim and Whinston 1990). In addition, agency relationships (e.g., steering financial advisory clients toward or away from a competitor's offerings) may provide an inexpensive means of rewarding or punishing a firm for behavior in another market. In many settings, prices or fees are readily observable to one's competitors, making secret discounting more difficult to implement. For example, underwriting fees are disclosed in offering documents, investment fees are disclosed in prospectuses, and spreads charged market makers are readily observable by other market makers. One should not necessarily expect free entry to lead to tough competition; as Hsieh and Moretti (2003) illustrate in their study of residential real estate brokerage, free entry can be consistent with established firms earning economic rents, although some of the rents may be wastefully dissipated through nonprice competition and business stealing effects.

A market failure is a necessary condition for regulation to be optimal, but it is not always sufficient. Market imperfections must be weighed against the imperfections of the legislative and regulatory institutions responsible for rulemaking and enforcement. This motivates turning to a discussion of the main laws and institutions of US financial regulation.

9.4   The Main Laws and Institutions

The core of modern federal financial regulation is formed by four laws passed during the Great Depression: the Securities Act of 1933 (the "1933 Act"), the Securities Exchange Act of 1934 (the "1934 Act"), the Investment Company Act of 1940 (the "1940 Act"), and the Investment Advisors Act of 1940.[26] These four acts each regulate a stage in the value chain previously discussed: respectively, they regulate the issuance of securities,[27] the brokerage and secondary trading of securities and the ongoing disclosure requirements of their issuers, investment companies (open and closed-end mutual funds),

---

26. This brief overview of securities regulation draws heavily on Coffee and Seligman (2002), who I refer readers to for more detail.
27. Along with the 1933 Act, the Trust Indenture Act of 1939 also governs the issuance of bonds.

and investment advisors (including both advisors who manage client assets directly as well as those who manage the assets of investment companies).

The 1933 Act requires the registration of securities with the SEC (subject to certain exemptions, e.g., for private placements that are not made available to the public) and requires the delivery of a prospectus to investors. Given that investors have a favorable cause of action if the issuer makes materially misleading statements or omissions in its offering documents, the disclosure in offering documents is generally much more extensive than ongoing disclosure by issuers. This generates two substantial costs to an initial offering of securities: (1) the fees and other costs associated with generating and delivering these documents, and (2) the competitive costs of the extensive disclosure of business information that is usually involved.

The 1934 Act establishes annual and quarterly disclosure requirements for companies, requires SEC preclearance of proxy statements for shareholder votes, and establishes a self-regulatory system for stock exchanges and brokers. The stock exchanges and the NASD, which self-regulates stockbrokers, are both overseen by the SEC. The 1934 Act (also referred to as the "Exchange Act") gives the SEC broad rulemaking authority to proscribe practices of broker-dealers as "manipulative, deceptive, or otherwise fraudulent." The 1934 Act has been amended by Congress multiple times—examples include the 1964 Securities Acts Amendments (which extended disclosure requirements to large over-the-counter [i.e., public, but not stock exchange–listed] firms); the 1970 amendment creating the Securities Investor Protection Corporate (which provides FDIC-like insurance for brokerage accounts); the Securities Act Amendments of 1975 (which deregulated brokerage commissions); the Foreign Corrupt Practices Act of 1977 (prohibiting bribery by public companies); the Insider Trading Sanctions Act of 1984 and Insider Trading and Securities Fraud Enforcement Act of 1988; the Private Securities Litigation Reform Act of 1995 (which sought to limit certain types of shareholder class action lawsuits); and the Sarbanes-Oxley Act of 2002 (SOX).

The Sarbanes-Oxley Act has been both controversial and an active current research topic and thus merits additional discussion. Most provisions of SOX appear to be a direct response to specific accounting abuses at firms such as Enron and Worldcom. SOX creates a self-regulatory body to regulate the accounting profession, restricts the provision of consulting and other services by an audit firm to an audit client, and requires the rotation of the lead audit partner every five years. For issuers, SOX requires audit committees to be composed entirely of independent directors and requires CEOs and CFOs to certify the firm's accounting numbers and face disgorgement of compensation and stock trading profits and criminal sanctions for misleading earnings or knowingly false statements. SOX requires the SEC to develop rules requiring companies to report on the adequacy of internal controls, rules requiring attorneys appearing before the SEC to report security laws violations, and rules governing the independence of security analysts. It also tightens rules on stock trading by directors and executives, extends the statue of limitations for securities fraud, and enhances protections for corporate whistleblowers.

SOX has been heavily criticized by the business community and some scholars for making external and internal auditing more expensive and onerous.[28] Eldridge and Kealey (2005) report that average audit fees for a sample of 648 Fortune 1000 companies increased from $3.5 million to $5.8 million from 2003 to 2004, and they attribute most of this increase to SOX. Leuz, Triantis, Wang (2008) and Carney (2006) argue that costs associated with SOX may have encouraged some firms to delist. Against this cost is the benefit firms with clean accounting received from a restored investor confidence. Li, Pincus, and Rego (2008) and Rezaee and Jain (2006) found positive stock price responses to the act. Engel, Hayes, and Wang (2007) find more positive event returns for larger firms, as one might expect given that the costs of SOX increase more slowly with firm size than the benefits.[29] This early evidence suggests that, for better or worse, SOX has significantly "raised the bar" for being a public company.

The 1940 Act regulates open- and closed-end mutual funds. Mutual funds are far more important than when the 1940 Act was passed: in 2003 equity mutual funds accounted for 19.7 percent of household equity holdings and money market funds accounted for 21.2 percent of household holdings of cash equivalents (demand deposits, time deposits, etc.).[30] The 1940 Act contains provisions designed to protect shareholders from dilution by fund managers. It requires that investment companies have a board of trustees, that they annually review the management contract for the fund, and that a majority of these trustees be independent of the investment advisor. It establishes the fiduciary duties of the trustees and the investment advisor. It also establishes rules governing transactions in shares of open-end mutual funds designed to ensure that investors transact at prices that reflect fair market values.

Although the 1940 Act does include some regulation of behavior, like the 1933 Act and 1934 Act, it relies primarily on disclosure. As Jackson (1997,

28. For example, Romano (2005) claims it ignored the findings of the empirical and accounting literature, attributes its passage to a media frenzy and the impending midterm elections, and calls it "Quack Corporate Governance."

29. Bushee and Leuz (2005) and Greenstone, Oyer, and Vissing-Jorgenson (2006) find analogous results for the 1964 Securities Acts Amendments, which extended disclosure requirements to firms traded on the OTC Bulletin Board: the disclosure requirements led some firms to delist (Bushee and Leuz) but was accompanied by positive event returns for those that remained (Greenstone et al.).

30. The money market mutual fund share of cash equivalents is calculated from lines two through five of table L.100 of the Flow of Funds Data for 2002. Mutual fund share of equity holdings is US mutual fund holdings of domestic stock estimated from the CRSP Survivor-Bias-Free Mutual Funds Database of $2.2 trillion divided by the sum of market capitalizations of equities listed in the CRSP Stock Price database of $11.3 trillion. Both of the later figures are year-end 2002.

535) puts it: "the 1940 Act relies on disclosure-based regulation more than any other comparable regulatory structure in the United States." This is notable in that whereas the 1933 and 1934 Act regulate securities markets where arbitrage ensures that sophisticated investors will have significant influence on asset prices, the 1940 Act regulates investments that are designed primarily for unsophisticated investors. Mutual funds cannot be sold short, and so market efficiency requires that full information and rationality be possessed by all investors, not merely a relatively small number with access to sufficient arbitrage capital.

Finally, the *Investment Advisors Act* requires registration of investment advisors managing a substantial amount of client assets in either investment companies or separate accounts. It also prohibits fraud and certain deceptive practices and limits the circumstances under which the advisor can receive incentive compensation. Until recently, SEC rules exempted advisors with a limited number of "accredited" (i.e., wealthy enough to be assumed to be sophisticated) clients from registration. The Dodd-Frank Act eliminated this exemption in 2012 and required sufficiently large advisors to hedge funds and other private funds to register with the commission.

The SEC has the primary responsibility for enforcing and promulgating new rules under these acts.[31] It is organized around these acts, with the Division of Corporate Finance having primary responsibility for the 1933 Act, the Division of Market Regulation for the 1934 Act, and the Division of Investment Management for the 1940 Act and Investment Advisors Act. These divisions support the commission in its two major channels for policymaking: the promulgation of new rules under the acts and responding to parties requesting that the commission take "no action" against a novel practice. Enforcement is handled by its own division, and these four divisions are supported by functional offices (the Office of General Counsel, Office of Chief Accountant, and Office of Economic Analysis).

The SEC grew considerably in the immediate aftermath of Sarbanes-Oxley, in terms of both staff and budget (figure 9.3). It also engaged in a significant amount of new rulemaking. A number of the more important new rules have involved increased disclosure by investment companies and advisors.[32] In some cases, enhanced disclosure requirements were adopted as a compromise in lieu of either direct dictation of practices (e.g., on fair

31. The SEC was also charged with enforcing the Public Utility Holding Company Act of 1935, which restricted interstate and nonregulated holdings of regulated utility companies, before its repeal by the Energy Policy Act of 2005. Even before then, Coffee and Seligman (2002, 70) had noted that this is "no longer an important statue because the SEC has largely deregulated the field" through rulemaking and enforcement policy.

32. For example, investment advisors are now required to disclose how they voted shareholder proxies (SEC Rule IA-2106). Investment companies are required to disclose their after-tax returns (33-8010) and to provide information about portfolio managers, including the factors used to determine their compensation (33-8458), about how the trustees determined the appropriateness of management fees (33-8433), about the availability of front-load commission discounts (33-8427), and about their policies regarding market timing, fair value pricing, and selective disclosure of portfolio holdings (33-8408).

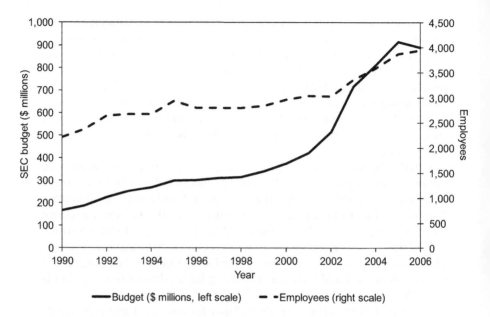

Fig. 9.3   SEC headcount and budget, 1990–2006
Note: Figures for 2005 and 2006 are budgeted, not actual.

value pricing) or more meaningful disclosure (e.g., of portfolio manager salaries, as opposed to the factors used to determine them). In addition, certain practices that were viewed as harmful to shareholders have been prohibited[33] and fiduciary duties have been clarified.[34] The SEC has promulgated rules as needed to implement SOX. It has also used rulemaking to implement decimalization, to relax short-selling rules (Regulation SHO), and to limit selective disclosure by companies, particularly to equity analysts (Regulation FD).

As mentioned before, the 1934 Act provides for the SEC to delegate primary regulatory authority to self-regulatory organizations (SROs): the stock exchanges self-regulate themselves, Finra (formerly the NASD) regulates its broker-dealer members, and the new Accounting Oversight Board created by SOX regulates the accounting profession. In each case, the SEC

33. For example, investment companies are now prohibited from directing brokerage commissions to firms as a reward for selling fund shares (SEC Rule IC-26591), as this was viewed as fund advisors using shareholders' assets to reward brokers for an activity that primarily benefits the advisor.

34. For example, SEC Rule IA-2106 requires that investment companies vote shareholder proxies in their own shareholders' interest. Although fund trustees already had a fiduciary responsibility to ensure that advisory and other fees charged to a fund were appropriate, and SEC Rule 33-8433 formally only requires additional disclosure of the basis of that decision, some have argued that in practice it is likely to reinforce trustees' fiduciary responsibilities in this area.

holds ultimate regulatory authority. A similar structure exists for derivatives, where the Commodity Futures Trading Commission (CFTC) acts as the ultimate regulator, but delegates self-regulatory authority to exchanges such as the Chicago Mercantile Exchange (CME). Generally, cooperation in this system is amicable, but there are exceptions, with the forced replacement of the NASD leadership following the Nasdaq market maker collusion scandal being a prime example.

Before modern federal securities regulation began in the 1930s, most states had their own regulations. These are often called "blue sky" laws, and they typically focus on the prevention of fraud by brokers, investment advisors, and securities issuers. They require registration by brokers and advisors and of newly offered securities, and the resulting registration fees provide a source of revenue that no states choose to forego. Apart from their revenue collection role, state securities laws declined in importance in the 1980s and 1990s, when a number of states dropped merit regulation of securities offerings, and the National Securities Market Improvement Act of 1996 preempted state registration requirements for exchanged listed securities. This trend has reversed in the last five years, particularly as former New York attorney general (NYAG) Eliot Spitzer has used the broad authority given him in New York State's Martin Act of 1921 to pursue allegedly fraudulent activity by equity analysts, mutual funds, and insurance companies.

The NYAG's activity in the last four years has created competition between state and federal regulators.[35] Whereas some states (e.g., Michigan) have explicitly rejected the suggestion that they investigate securities issues in parallel with the SEC, many others (e.g., California, Colorado, Kansas, Massachusetts, New Hampshire, New Jersey, North Carolina, West Virgina, and Wisconsin) have investigated in parallel or in advance of the SEC. Some have criticized the activities of New York and the other states, and indeed the Securities Fraud Deterrence and Investor Restitution Act of 2003 included language that would have preempted the Martin Act, had it passed (Macey 2005). At the same time, Eliot Spitzer and other state regulators have explicitly cited regulatory capture at the SEC in motivating action by the states.[36]

This revives a long-standing critique of the SEC and the SROs as reflecting the interests of industry, particularly in more aggressive enforcement action against misconduct by rogue individuals (broker fraud, insider trading) than against more systemic forms of misconduct (analyst conflicts, mutual fund compliance issues, earnings management). Those concerned about regulatory capture worry about two sources: top-down and bottom-up. A potential source of top-down is the natural political influ-

---

35. Romano (2001) discusses the potential benefits of competition across regulatory venues that issuers and investors could select (e.g., stock exchanges of different countries). The current competition between the state and federal governments is subtly different in that it involves competition between institutions to regulate the same venue.

36. See interviews of Eliot Spitzer cited by Abrams and Cohen (2004) and O'Brien (2005).

ence of so large an industry.[37] The partisan divide of the SEC over several recent regulators' proposals has also revived interest in the partisan political economy of the SEC (e.g., Zitzewitz 2002). A source of bottom-up capture is the staffing approach of SROs and the SEC. Turnover rates for attorneys, accountants, and compliance examiners at the SEC are more than twice those for comparable-level employees elsewhere in the federal government, including in bank regulation (Securities and Exchange Commission 2002). As Woodward (2001, 100) argues, the "best, and best by a wide margin, post-SEC employment opportunities [are] working for the regulatees."[38] A "revolving door" staffing model where employees work short tenures in the government and then transition to higher-salaried positions in industry can be successful in attracting talented individuals at a reasonable cost, but has been long regarded as a source of regulatory capture (Stigler 1971).

Following the abovementioned review of the scope of the securities industry, the economic rationale for regulation, and the main laws and institutions, I now turn to three recent issues in the regulation of financial services and markets that have parallels in other industries.

9.5   The Regulation of Pricing

In November 2003 in testimony before multiple congressional committees, Eliot Spitzer called attention to the "$70 billion in management and advisory fees" paid by mutual fund investors in 2002 that "are in addition to significant costs—such as trading costs—that are passed on to investors."[39] Spitzer cited the difference between advisory fees charged by the same firm to retail and institutional accounts reported by Freeman and Brown (2001), and he cited weak fund governance as the root cause of both the mutual fund share trading scandal and what he regards as an excessive level of fees: "We know that directors and managers breached their duties to investors in every conceivable manner. As regulators and lawmakers, our duty to investors is to investigate every manifestation of that breach and to return to investors any and all fees that were improper or inappropriate. This includes the fees that the managers received during the very time that they were violating their fiduciary duties to investors."[40] Spitzer proposed disclosure of the precise dollar amount of fees paid to each investor, a strengthening of fund trustee's

37. Opensecrets.org lists the securities industry as the fourth-largest political donor; it probably also accounts for some portion of the donations of the top industry, the legal profession. The securities industry's influence is not monolithic, and on many issues different parts of the industry have different interests (see, e.g., the analysis of interest group competition in Kroszner and Stratmann 1998).

38. A recent Government Accountability Office report (GAO-05-385, "Mutual Fund Trading Abuses: SEC Consistently Applied Procedures in Setting Penalties, but Could Strengthen Certain Internal Controls") found that the SEC did not have a system in place for ensuring that departing staff's next employer did not present a conflict of interest.

39. "Testimony of State of New York Attorney General Eliot Spitzer Before the United States Senate Banking, Housing, and Urban Affairs Committee," November 20, 2003, p. 2.

40. Ibid, 3.

fiduciary duties with respect to fees, most favored nations clauses preventing retail mutual funds from charging more than institutional accounts, and competitive bidding for advisory contracts. Lacking the jurisdiction to act on any of these proposals, Spitzer negotiated fee reductions with several mutual fund companies as part of subsequent settlements of share trading allegations.

The mutual fund industry and the SEC were not especially receptive to this line of argument. The SEC did not participate in the fee reduction portion of the mutual fund settlements, even when all other aspects of the settlement negotiations were coordinated. Regarding retail-institutional fee differences, the industry argued (convincingly) that servicing retail clients was more expensive per dollar invested than servicing institutional clients and (perhaps less convincingly) that this accounted for the entire difference in fees charged. Requiring the disclosure of fees paid by individuals was included at one point in a House of Representatives bill, but removed in committee. The SEC did require disclosure of trustees' rationale for the advisory fees charged, and some expect this to increase pressure from boards for fee reductions.

Any evidence of pressure created by this disclosure for lower fund expenses was slow to emerge from the data. The asset-weighted average expense ratio declined less than two basis points from 2002 to 2006 (table 9.4). While the combined market shares of Vanguard, Fidelity, and American Funds (three large fund families with lower than average expense ratios) increased from 27.3 to 35.2 percent from 2002 to 2006, this was offset by an increase in the average expense ratio charged by other funds in the industry. As discussed earlier, even if some investors became more sensitive to fees during this period and switched assets to lower expense ratio firms, if these were on average the most fee-sensitive clients at their original firms, their departure would have reduced the average fee sensitivity of clients at the other firms, increasing the optimal price. It is also possible that the increased regulatory activity during the 2002 to 2006 time period increased marginal (as opposed to fixed or sunk) costs and that this offset the effects of any greater fee sensitivity. In contrast, average fees did begin to decline after 2006, after the regulatory pressure on price had subsided.

Downward regulatory pressure on price, whether via the direct regulation of prices as in natural monopoly industries such as electricity or cable television or via indirect measures such as those proposed by the NYAG, is generally considered to have several potential side effects. First, if product quality is noncontractable and thus cannot also be regulated, price regulation can lead to lower-than-efficient levels of quality. For example, price regulation may encourage funds to substitute cheaper anonymous managers for more expensive star managers. Massa, Reuter, and Zitzewitz (2010) report that a trend toward anonymous team management is already in progress (driven, they argue, by a desire to avoid competition for star managers from the booming hedge fund industry) and that anonymous

Table 9.4   Mutual fund industry fees, 2002, 2006, and 2010 ($ millions)

Fund family	Expense ratio revenue	Total net assets	Asset-weighted average expense ratio (basis points)	Market share (%)
		2002		
Fidelity	4,593	658,704	69.7	11.6
Vanguard	1,413	568,286	24.9	10.0
American funds	2,570	332,297	77.3	5.8
Rest of industry	33,598	4,137,096	81.2	72.6
Total	42,174	5,696,383	74.0	100
		2006		
Fidelity	7,657	1,159,840	66.0	12.5
Vanguard	2,281	1,103,192	20.7	11.9
American funds	7,346	990,507	74.2	10.7
Rest of industry	50,371	6,044,359	83.3	65.0
Total	67,655	9,297,898	72.8	100.0
		2010		
Fidelity	7,588	1,322,583	57.4	12.3
Vanguard	2,545	1,445,017	17.6	13.4
American funds	7,581	985,509	76.9	9.1
Rest of industry	50,662	7,036,011	72.0	65.2
Total	68,376	10,789,120	63.4	100

Notes: Data are from the CRSP Survivor-Bias-Free US Mutual Funds Database. Total net asset figures are end of year. Expense ratio revenue is the expense ratio reported in the CRSP multiplied by total net assets. Variable annuity units and exchange-traded funds are excluded, but both index and actively managed open-ended funds are included.

teams manage less actively (as proxied by portfolio turnover) and produce slightly lower returns.

Alternatively, fund managers have other means of charging shareholders for their services, outside of the expense ratio. For example, rather than seeking out lower "execution only" commissions, they can place stock trades at brokers who provide benefits to the advisor. Examples of these benefits can be allocations of IPO (Reuter 2006), which are not always allocated to the funds whose trading produced them (Gaspar, Massa, and Matos 2006). Sales support for the advisor's funds, or "soft dollar" credits that are officially supposed to be used to finance purchases of research, but in practice have been used for office space, periodical subscriptions, computer equipment, and travel expenses. Benefits can also be given by the broker to the advisors' employees; the recently alleged excessive gift giving by Jefferies Securities to Fidelity employees provides an example.[41] Fund advisors can also divert shareholder assets by allowing stale price arbitrage trading in

41. See, for example, Craig Susanne and John Hechinger, "Entertaining Excess: Fishing for Fidelity Business, One Firm Employed Lavish Bait," *Wall Street Journal*, August 12, 2005, p. A1.

their funds, by engaging in cross-trades between portfolios at systematically advantageous prices, and by front running personal or favored-portfolio assets ahead of mutual fund trades. Most of these devices are either illegal or at least discouraged by regulators, but nevertheless, at least in principle one might worry that downward regulatory pressure on prices leads advisors to increase their use.

A second consequence of downward price regulation can be shortages. For mutual funds, which have high fixed costs at the firm level but low marginal costs, a "shortage" is most likely to take the form of a reduction in efforts to sell funds to shareholders with small account sizes. For investors who would not find their way to a less-aggressive marketer of (lower cost) funds, but would instead invest in cash equivalents such as bank deposits, this could lead to a welfare loss resulting from a lower than optimal exposure to equity markets.

This is, however, a commonly made argument that is easy to overstate. Expectations of the future equity premium that are derived from current valuations are lower than the historical US return premium commonly cited by industry. For example, Fama and French (2002) estimate a forward-looking equity premium of 2.5 to 4.3 percent as compared with a 7.4 percent premium calculated from historical returns. Suppose that the individual we are concerned with is a canonical mean-variance investor faced with dividing her portfolio between riskless cash/bonds at the risk-free rate and equities with normally distributed returns and a 3.4 percent (pre-expense) expected premium (taking Fama and French's midpoint). Suppose also that, if she can invest at comparable cost in either asset, she will want to hold an approximately market portfolio of 50 percent equities and 50 percent cash/bonds. It is straightforward to show that an advisor who places this investor in a 50/50 portfolio, but charges her 0.85 percent of her assets annually for the service, leaves her as well off in certainty-equivalent utility terms as if she had invested costlessly in cash on her own.[42] By comparison, the asset-weighted average expense ratio for "C class" shares for 2004 from the CRSP Mutual Funds data set is 1.75 percent.[43] Given these fees and expectations about the equity premium, it is hard to argue that the typical advisor is offering better certainty-equivalent utility than a bank CD that pays the risk-free rate.

42. The certainty equivalent utility of a mean-variance investor who invests s of their assets in a risky asset with normally distribution returns and $1 - s$ in the risk-free asset is given by $w[(1 + f) + sp - s^2 rv - e]$, where w is initial wealth, f is the risk-free rate, p is the expected equity premium, v is the variance of risk asset returns, r is a risk aversion parameter, and e is the expense ratio paid. For $s = 0.5$ to be optimal, p must equal rv. Assuming a p of 3.4 percent, $s = 0.5$ and $e = 0.85$ percent yields the same utility as $s = e = 0$.

43. C class shares are advisor sold, but compensate the advisor using a 12b1 fee that is included in the expense ratio, rather than using a front-end or back-end load. I focus on C shares since calculating the total annual fees paid to both fund manager and advisor does not require an assumption about holding period. Given their asset-weighted average loads and expense ratios of 5.0 percent and 0.93 percent, one would reach a similar conclusion about the overall fee levels of A shares if one assumed a holding period of six years.

A third, related consequence of downward price regulation can be exit. The increase in regulatory scrutiny in the last few years has increased fixed (as well as sunk) costs for mutual fund families and has probably also reduced the use of some of the non-expense-ratio sources of revenue described earlier. Thus one might expect some pressure for consolidation in the long run, but perhaps surprisingly there is not much evidence of this yet. The number of unique management companies offering funds captured by the CRSP data set has declined from 683 in 2000 to a low of 623 in 2004, but half percent of this decline was from 2000 to 2002 and thus was presumably more related to the stock market decline than to increased regulatory pressure.

The welfare costs of fund advisor exit depend crucially on what one assumes about consumer behavior. If we assume that consumers would like to maximize the risk-adjusted returns on their investments but do so imperfectly due to information and cognitive limitations, then we can analyze welfare by examining the implications of exit for shareholder returns. The firms most likely to be induced to exit by downward regulatory pressure on price are small, high-expense ratio firms, and studies of the determinants of fund returns find that these firms produce the lowest returns, even before deducting expenses (e.g., Carhart 1997). This suggests that in the mutual-fund context, regulatory-induced exit can be good for consumers. On the other hand, if consumers are fully rational and have perfect information about ex ante expected returns, then any fund they buy or continue to hold must be welfare maximizing for them.[44] The exit of a fund firm deprives its clients of their first choice and thus, by assumption, must reduce the welfare of these consumers.

Of course, even if one views returns as an adequate proxy for shareholder welfare, one might still have concerns about policies that induce exit and raise the minimum-required scale for entry in an industry. An increase in industry concentration might reduce competitive intensity in the industry, although concentration in this industry is low enough that one might not expect the exit of a small number of high-cost firms to significantly affect behavior.

On the other hand, increased entry barriers might also limit the future entry of innovative firms. The importance of this effect depends on the extent to which one views the industry as mature. Mutual funds appear to be relatively mature. A comparison of the ranking of top mutual fund families in terms of assets in the CRSP Mutual Funds database in 1992 and 2004 suggests that there has been little turnover (table 9.5). Six of the top seven in 1992 were also in the top seven in 2004 (Evergreen has replaced Merrill

---

44. For example, one reason why a customer might rationally buy high-expense funds with low ex ante expected returns is if the quality of services that are bundled with the fund are high. Collins (2005) argues that differences in service quality explain the price dispersion in index fund expense ratios reported on by Busse, Elton, and Gruber (2004) and Hortascu and Syverson (2005).

Table 9.5   Mutual fund families ranked by assets, 1992 and 2004

Rank	Firm	Assets in millions, 2004	Rank in 1992
1	Fidelity Management Research	913,209	1
2	Vanguard Group Investment Co.	889,955	2
3	Capital Research & Management Co.	650,119	5
4	Franklin Advisers Inc.	159,478	6
5	Evergreen Investment Mgmt. Company Inc.	151,759	76
6	Federated Investment Management Co.	146,990	7
7	Dreyfus Corporation	137,424	4
8	Barclays Global Fund Advisors	137,177	131
9	Charles Schwab Investment Mgmt. Inc.	135,962	26
10	Wells Fargo Bank	120,995	63

Lynch), although the order of families three through seven has changed slightly. Among the top twenty firms in 2004, Schwab and Barclays are the only firms that have moved up the rankings significantly other than through mergers. Hedge funds, in contrast, have experienced extremely rapid growth during this time period.

9.6   Antitrust

The best known financial services antitrust case is undoubtedly the case against the Nasdaq market makers in the mid-1990s. The case was initiated after Christie and Schultz (1994) reported that odd-eighths quotations (i.e., a market offering to trade a stock at 47 1/8 instead of 47 or 47 1/4) were extremely rare for a subset of Nasdaq stocks. After an investigation, the Department of Justice alleged that the avoidance of odd-eighths quotes was collusive behavior designed to increase average market maker spreads.

Several features of market making may have facilitated collusion. First, market makers observe each other's price quotations; cheating against any collusive arrangement would thus be readily detected. Second, avoiding odd-eighths was a focal arrangement that allowed for a distribution of quantity while minimizing the need for conferring. Avoiding odd-eighths quotations was particularly focal given that the minimum tick size on Nasdaq had only recently been reduced from one-quarter. Third, under preferencing agreements with sources of order flow (e.g., brokerages), many market makers had the right to handle any order flow at the current best bid and ask prices offered by any other market maker (the National Best Bid and Offer, or NBBO). This functioned as a "meet-or-release" clause; so long as the preferred market maker was willing to match, a market maker who undercut the current NBBO could not attract any of the preferenced order flow. This significantly reduced the returns to "cheating" on any collusive arrangement. Fourth, market makers competed in multiple markets, so cheating in one market could be punished in another. As Christie and Schultz (1995) discuss, an early response to an odd-eighths quotation was often a phone call to the trader's boss, where such punishments were reportedly explicitly threatened.

In addition, the average retail investor's understanding of the bid-ask spread component of transaction costs was limited, and many of the institutional investment managers, who presumably did understand bids and asks, had business units that were beneficiaries of any collusion. Furthermore, the rents from collusion were shared through a system known as payment for order flow. In exchange for signing the abovementioned preferencing agreements, sources of order flow (such as brokerages) received per share payments. Table 9.6 shows minimum tick sizes and average gross trading revenue and order flow payments per share for 1995 to 2003 for Knight Securities, the largest publicly traded pure-play market maker. In 1995 to 1996, Knight paid about one-third of its trading revenue for order flow.

As a result of the antitrust enforcement action, odd-eighths avoidance was abandoned, reducing the effective minimum tick size for stocks where there had been collusion. The collusion case also focused attention on the effects of tick size on investors' transaction costs and further reductions in minimum tick size followed, to 6.25 cents in June 1997 and to 1 cent in early 2001. As predicted by models such as Kandel and Marx (1998) that emphasized minimum tick size as source of market maker rents and payment for order flow, tick size reductions have reduced both market profitability and order flow payments (table 9.6).

Another market in which price transparency and multimarket contact potentially facilitate collusion is in underwriting and syndicated lending. Placing a new issue into the market requires access to a broad network of potential investors, especially since issuers prefer to place it with investors more likely to hold long term. As a result, several investment banks are usually required to manage and market an offering. Underwriting fees are

Table 9.6   Minimum tick size, payment for order flow, and market-making profits at Knight Securities (cents per share traded)

Year	Minimum tick size	Market maker trading revenue	Payment for order flow	Order flow payment share of revenue (%)
1995	12.5	1.47	0.55	37
1996	12.5	1.71	0.65	38
1997	Reduced from 12.5 to 6.25 in June	1.45	0.37	26
1998	6.25	1.03	0.21	21
1999	6.25	1.04	0.17	16
2000	6.25	1.03	0.16	15
2001	1	0.32	0.06	19
2002	1	0.15	0.03	22
2003	1	0.09	0.01	15

Source: Knight Securities S-1 and 10K statements.

typically a whole-number percentage of the funds raised (e.g., 7 percent for an initial equity offering, 3 percent for high-yield debt). Underwriting business is reportedly extremely profitable for the bank, and competition for it is typically hard fought, but nevertheless discounts from the standard underwriting fees are rare. Any underwriter who secured business through discounting underwriting fees would be unable to do so in secret, since underwriting fees are disclosed in offering documents. The amount of extra business an underwriter could gain through discounting would be limited by the issuer's desire for wide distribution. And competing banks could punish the discounter, by encouraging clients to exclude the discounter from other syndicates and by encouraging brokerage clients and asset managers (including any asset managers within the same firm) to avoid purchasing an issue whose underwriting business was obtained by discounting.[45]

The difficulties of discounting underwriting fees lead banks to compete along other dimensions. For example, issuers will demand that banks bundle low-margin products such as revolving credit lines to obtain the higher-margin underwriting business. Alternatively, commercial banks will demand inclusion in investment banking business as a condition of their lending. The latter practice is known as "tying," and the NASD has argued that it violates the Bank Holding Company Act Amendments of 1970, which prohibit banks from extending credit on the condition that borrowers engage in other business with the bank. Commercial banks have in turn argued that this form of tying is actually procompetitive in that it creates a nonprice means of competing for underwriting business.

Other forms of nonprice competition for underwriting business have allegedly included biases in analyst opinion and even presumably illegal bribes of management. Investment banks have also been accused of biasing their analyst coverage in order to win underwriting business, which would help explain the correlation between analysts' opinions and their firm's investment banking business found by Lin and McNichols (1998) and Michaely and Womack (1999). In the "spinning" cases, banks such as Credit Suisse First Boston were accused of allocating shares in underpriced IPOs to executives of firms in order to win their underwriting business.

Another example of collusion on one dimension of price being at least partly undone by competition on other dimensions is the pre-1975 era of fixed commissions. In the Buttonwood Tree Agreement of 1792 that formed the New York Stock Exchange (NYSE), the NYSE members agreed on

---

45. Some have argued that institutional investors avoided buying Google when it was offered because of their use of a Dutch auction process and a small number of underwriters and their negotiation of a 3 percent underwriting fee. Although Google used a modified Dutch auction that allowed it to price its shares below the market clearing price, creating an incentive for investors to participate in the offering, investment banks may have viewed a successful Dutch auction as a threat, since if it becomes the common mode of offering it would reduce the importance of underwriters' distribution networks.

minimum commissions: "We the Subscribers, Brokers for the Purchase and Sale of Public Stock, do hereby solemnly promise and pledge ourselves to each other, that we will not buy or sell from this day for any person whatsoever, any kind of Public Stock at a less rate than one-quarter percent Commission."[46] The NYSE and, after its 1908 founding, the American Stock Exchange maintained fixed commission structures. The 1934 Act gave the SEC oversight of brokerage commissions, but under the guise of self-regulation, the commission allowed the exchanges to exercise their authority over commissions.

Agreements on commissions only applied to trades on the stock exchanges, but the exchanges prohibited their members from off-exchange trading. Nevertheless, "third market" firms developed that specialized in handling off-exchange block trades for institutional investors at discounted commissions. This resulted in undesirable market fragmentation, leading the SEC to first press the exchanges to offer quantity discounts and then, in 1971, to require that commissions on large orders be set competitively (the ceiling was set at $500,000 in April 1971 and lowered to $300,000 in April 1972). The deregulation of large-trade commissions helped motivate a class of small investors to bring a class-action antitrust suit alleging that fixed commissions were price fixing in violation of the Sherman Act. In *Gordon v. NYSE* (1975), the US Supreme Court ruled that since the 1934 Act had explicitly given the SEC authority to regulate commissions, this superceded the antitrust laws. The decision was quickly made moot, however, by the fact that commissions were deregulated in 1975 by Congress (via the aforementioned Securities Acts Amendments of 1975) and the SEC.

During the era of fixed commissions, brokers engaged in nonprice competition by offering free research. In addition, institutional clients would negotiate "give ups," where, in lieu of a discount, a portion of their commission would be paid to another broker who in turn provided the investor with free services (such as research or computer services). A group of third-party research firms developed who earned most of their revenue from these give ups. At the time of commission deregulation, these third-party firms feared that investment managers' fiduciary duties would prevent them from paying commissions large enough to finance "give ups" and that managers would be unwilling to pay for research directly. In response to lobbying by asset managers and third-party research firms, Congress added a safe harbor, allowing asset managers to pay above-market commissions if they determine that the commission was reasonable given the combined brokerage and research services provided. "Give ups" were renamed "soft dollars," but their economic purpose changed. They were no longer a form of nonprice competition that undermined fixed commissions, but instead become a device for asset mana-

---

46. F. Eames, *The New York Stock Exchange 14* (1968 edition), quoted in *Gordon v. New York Stock Exchange* (1975).

gers to use client assets to purchase research (and other services) through a less transparent means than including its cost in the expense ratio.[47]

A consequence of the *Gordon* decision is that the extent to which the Securities Acts preempt the antitrust laws with respect to the securities industry is uncertain and depends crucially on the specific issue at hand. This question is important in part because regulatory capture theory would predict that enforcement of antitrust-related issues by a multi-industry regulator (like the DOJ or FTC) would be more aggressive than by a single-industry regulator (such as the SEC). In *Gordon*, the court found that Congress had explicitly discussed the stock exchanges' fixed commission agreements when writing the 1934 Act, and that their decision to give the SEC primary regulatory authority over commissions carried an implied antitrust immunity (Coffee and Seligman 2002, 646). In contrast, in the Nasdaq Market Makers case brought by the Department of Justice, which alleged practices that were not discussed by Congress when delegating authority to the SEC, the courts did not find that the antitrust laws were preempted.

9.7 Conflicts of Interest and Boundaries of Firms

> We have turned conflicts of interest into synergies.
> —Jack Grubman, former telecom analyst at Citigroup, in an e-mail, as quoted by Eliot Spitzer.

The proceeding discussion highlights some of the advantages for a firm participating in multiple financial services businesses. Many financial products are complements, and integrated providers should have incentives to provide them on more attractive terms for the usual reason (the elimination of double marginalization). There are also no doubt considerable synergies on the production side. Integration may make otherwise collusive markets more competitive, as if there is tacit collusion on one dimension of price, providing related products can increase one's ability to engage in nonprice competition. For example, a brokerage salesforce and research department give investment banks an advantage in competing for underwriting business, while the deposit base needed to finance lower-margin bank loans does the same for commercial banks.

At the same time, there are reasons for integration that are less benign from a regulatory perspective. Acting as an agent in industry A may create the opportunity to bias one's actions in order to generate business benefits in industry B, potentially at the expense of the industry A client. For example, asset managers can use their power to vote shareholder proxies as leverage

---

47. While most discussions of soft dollars find this problematic (e.g., Siggelkow 2004), Horan and Johnsen (2008) argue that the ability of managers to pass on the costs of research in a less-than-transparent manner is beneficial, in that it offsets what would otherwise be an incentive to underinvest in research.

in obtaining underwriting or other business (Davis and Kim 2007). In-house brokers or financial advisors can help sell an asset manager's funds instead of lower-fee or better-run alternatives. An in-house broker can allow an asset manager to internalize the benefit of commissions for trades done on behalf of their client, perhaps creating an incentive to overtrade a portfolio. In-house proprietary traders may be able to benefit from a brokerage or investment management business, by illegally front-running client portfolio trades, stepping in front of client limit orders,[48] or otherwise exploiting information gained from clients' trading activities. In-house proprietary trading can also benefit from improved execution quality resulting from the bundling of informed proprietary trading order flow with the presumably less-informed order flow from client's brokerage accounts or large managed portfolios, at the cost of worse execution for the less-informed orders. Furthermore, when punishing firms that defect against standard industry practices, it is helpful to be able to do so in multiple lines of business.

Most of this second category of synergies also represent conflicts of interest.[49] These conflicts involve the trade-off of one client's interests for the interests of either another, favored, client or the firm itself. In some cases, this trade-off of interests can be accomplished across firm boundaries through explicit payments. For example, "directed brokerage" was used as a substitute for fund selling by in-house brokers, and soft dollars, especially if used for nonresearch expenses, can be used to allow asset managers to internalize the profits from portfolio trading commissions. But bringing these trade-offs inside firm boundaries is helpful for several reasons. First, it eliminates the need for explicit payments that are potentially subject to regulatory or client scrutiny. Second, common ownership can provide a credible commitment to clients expecting favoritism that a contractual relationship might not. For example, an underwriting client expecting favorable opinions from an analyst is likely to be more assured of getting them if the analyst and the investment banker are employees of the same firm, as opposed to simply having a business relationship. Likewise, clients may invest in hedge funds run side by side with mutual funds because they expect the differences in fee structures to produce favoritism in their favor. Especially if hedge fund investors are more cognizant of the potential for such favoritism than mutual fund investors, firms running funds side by side may realize net marketing advantages.

Ironically, it was precisely these conflicts of interest that motivated the Glass-Steagall Act of 1933, which legally separated banking, securities, and

---

48. Suppose a client submits a limit order to buy at stock at $47.00 or better. A broker can "step in front" of this order by placing a limit order to buy at $47.01. If the broker's order is filled, the broker has the option to either hold the order and gain any market appreciation or, if demand for the stock weakens, sell to the client at $47.00.

49. For a useful taxonomy of conflicts of interest within and across financial services business lines, see Walter (2004).

insurance. While reversing the 1999 repeal of Glass-Steagall is not being widely contemplated, the trend toward convergence that the repeal reflected has certainly slowed, and perhaps even begun a reversal. In the summer of 2005, Citigroup swapped its asset management business for Legg Mason's brokerage business. The stated reason for the deal was to eliminate the regulatory risks arising from common ownership of asset management and brokerage. It remains to be seen whether this deal will begin a broader trend.

9.8   A Fourth Issue: Competition with Unobservable Quality

In many industries, competition can exacerbate problems that arise from the imperfect observability of product quality. Imperfect observability provides a rationale for minimum standards in industries as diverse as construction, food, pharmaceuticals, and transportation, particularly for dimensions of quality like safety, where quality affects the probability of rare but very adverse outcomes. Past work has shown that reputational concerns can act as a bond and limit the temptation to lower quality (e.g., Klein and Leffler 1981; Shapiro 1982), but that competition can exacerbate them by decreasing profits, and thus returns to maintaining reputations, as well as by increasing the return to lowering costs (see, e.g., Kranton 2003 on the general issue and Borenstein and Zimmerman 1988 and Rose 1990 on airline safety).

For example, in banking, depositors can observe the interest rate offered by a bank, but not the risk of losses due to bank failure. This problem is addressed by regulations mandating that banks provide deposit insurance, as well as by regulations limiting the riskiness of bank's investments. While banking is discussed in chapter 8, an analogous problem affects the investments that are the subject of this chapter. Investors can readily observe the past returns of an investment, as well as its realized past risk, as captured in variance of past returns. But investors often cannot observe unrealized risks. If an investment earns a higher return by accepting exposure to low-probability events, then investors may observe the returns without observing the risk, and competition for returns may exacerbate pressures to take such risks.

Two examples that arose in the financial crisis are credit and liquidity risk. During the middle of the decade, AAA-rated structured debt securities offered higher yields than Treasuries or AAA-rated corporate bonds. As we all know now, and as many knew at the time, flawed assumptions about levels and correlations of default risks made by rating agencies allowed tranches of pools of risky loans, such as residential subprime mortgages, to be rated AAA even when they carried substantial default risk (e.g., Coval, Jurek, and Stafford 2009). Because AAA-rated structured yields were often above borrowing costs faced by investment vehicles, it was possible to increase current yields further using leverage.

One example of a mutual fund that did so was the Oppenheimer Core Bond Fund, which was included as the conservative option in many state "529" college savings plans. The fund had very low variance returns in its twenty-year history prior to 2008, and held largely highly rated bonds. It clearly was judged as low risk by the states that included it as an investment option. Yet it lost almost 50 percent of its value during the financial crisis. The fund charged higher than average fees for its category, thus to maintain an attractive yield, it needed exposure to higher yielding credits, which it added using total return swaps on mortgage-backed securities. Competition on an observable dimension (yield net of fees) may have exacerbated the temptation to reduce quality on an unobservable dimension. The SEC later disciplined Oppenheimer for not adequately disclosing this added risk, although the $35 million settlement was less than 2 percent of investor losses, which totaled approximately $2.5 billion.[50]

Even if holdings disclosure requirements are complied with, they may not adequately inform investors about risk. One issue with holdings disclosures is that they are periodic, giving managers the opportunity to "window dress" their portfolios around disclosure dates. For example, Morey and O'Neal (2006) find that bond mutual funds' exposure to credit risk, as measured using correlations of fund returns with bond indices, decreases around portfolio disclosure dates, suggesting that funds shift out of risky bonds in order to reduce their apparent exposure to credit risk.

For hedge funds, which are not required to disclose holdings other than long positions in equities, the primary means of inferring risk is from the variance of monthly returns. Particularly in asset classes that trade infrequently or with wide bid-ask spreads, opportunities exist to smooth returns (Goetzmann et al. 2002; Getmansky, Lo, and Makarov 2004; Bollen and Pool 2009).[51] Smoothing of returns may not only mislead investors about past realized risk, but can also create incentives for redemption after a market decline, as investors who anticipate smoothing will expect managers to overvalue assets temporarily after a market decline. This has obvious averse implications for systemic risk. The refinement of policies affecting risk disclosures and portfolio valuation is likely in the years to come.

50. See "Oppenheimer Funds to Pay $35 Million to Settle SEC Charges for Misleading Statements during Financial Crisis" (available at http://www.sec.gov/news/press/2012/2012-110 .htm). Investor loses of $2.5 billion are from June 2008 to March 2009, and are measured by multiplying beginning of month assets by monthly returns. Both the settlement and the investor loss figures also cover a second fund (Oppenheimer Champion Income Fund), which was accused of similar practices. Oppenheimer also paid $100 million to settle a class action lawsuit over the same issues (see https://www.oppenheimercoresettlement.com// and https:// www.oppenheimerchampionsettlement.com//).

51. While papers on hedge funds are limited to analysis of return time series, Cici, Gibson, and Merrick (2011) show more directly that bond mutual funds smooth returns by switching between valuing bonds using bid and bid-ask midpoints.

9.9   Conclusion

Financial regulation has been basically reactive in the last decade. Sarbanes-Oxley, Dodd-Frank, and many of the significant SEC rules have been adopted in response to revelations of specific abuses, such as accounting fraud, mutual fund late trading, selective disclosure, insider trading, and market maker collusion. Even the most noteworthy deregulation, the gradual relaxation and finally repeal of the Glass-Steagall Act, was partly a response to a series of mergers between the industries the act was designed to keep separate. Given the increasing emphasis on compliance in most financial services firms in the last few years, the rate of revelation of new scandals is likely to slow. This should create the opportunity to think more proactively about what financial regulation should be attempting to accomplish.

Could thinking proactively in 2005 have yielded a less severe financial crisis? Some have characterized the financial crisis as an unexpectedly toxic combination of known problems. For example, in their dissent to the *Financial Crisis Inquiry Report*, Hennessey, Holtz-Eakin, and Thomas (2011), while generally more skeptical about regulation than the authors of the majority report, highlight the role played by a lack of transparency about holdings and risk exposure. They also note that while "credit rating agencies erroneously rated mortgage-backed securities and derivatives as safe investments, . . .buyers failed to look behind the credit ratings and do their own due diligence" (418). They noted that these buyers were "in theory, sophisticated investors" (426), but they left unsaid the fact that these buyers were almost entirely managers of third-party assets, and thus that agency problems might be behind the lack of due diligence.

Compulsion of due diligence by regulators is impractical, of course. The larger question is whether a lack of due diligence arises from competition over past returns that create temptations for exposures to risk. Competition over past returns is natural among active managers, while for passive managers competition is equally naturally more over fees and other costs. As discussed in sections 9.2 and 9.3, many investors pay a financial planner to sell them a mutual fund or annuity, pay the fund manager management and administration fees, and pay commissions and transactions costs for active management that is, on average, both aggressive and unsuccessful in generating positive risk-adjusted returns. Perhaps the largest and most controversial outstanding question about financial regulation is whether this represents an efficient market outcome or a market failure, and, if the latter, whether regulation should do more to correct that failure.

If one decides that it should, the next question would be how: how to change laws to correct existing market failures without creating new ones, and how to reform institutions so that they reinforce rather than undermine this goal. The first question is nontrivial. Disclosure about fees and conflicts of interest appears ineffective in influencing the behavior of many investors. On fees, the strengthening of mutual fund boards' fiduciary responsibilities to aggressively negotiate on investors' behalf also does not appear to have led to a significant reduction, at least in the short term. This raises the question of whether more direct regulation of price levels is desirable, either through outright price limits or through the strengthening of suitability requirements for broker recommendations. This hinges in large part on whether it could be implemented without the side effects that accompany it in other contexts.

But the more difficult question is arguably the institutional one. Both the approach of self-regulatory delegation and the staffing model for the SEC lead these institutions to reflect the interests of the industries they regulate. These interests may be well aligned with the public interest in disciplining the behavior of rogue individuals, but are likely to be much less so in correcting systemic market failures that are also sources of economic rents. Both the contrast with Eliot Spitzer over the last few years and the aggressive prosecution of the Nasdaq price fixing case by the DOJ in the 1990s suggest that multi-industry regulators might be less prone to capture. The SEC is currently organized around the industries it regulates, and while this specialization is no doubt useful for building industry expertise, a more generalist-oriented staffing model, in which staff develop expertise that creates future employment opportunities in multiple parts of the securities industry, may reduce at least some of the forces contributing to capture.

A second large and controversial question is whether regulation should continue to encourage, or instead discourage or attempt to reverse, convergence. Many financial services are complements in both their production and consumption, and convergence should allow for many genuine synergies: in production, product innovation, the reduction of search costs via one-stop shopping, and the potential elimination of double marginalization. At the same time, the presence of agency relationships in most services means that convergence may frustrate the policing of conflicts of interest by bringing them inside firm boundaries. Is it optimal to locate in the same firm the underwriters of securities and the third-party managers charged with deciding whether to invest in them? Do the problems associated with convergence outweigh the benefits? Research enumerating and economically sizing them would be especially helpful in answering this question.

As the length and recentness the bibliography that follows demonstrates, the postbubble and postfinancial crisis years have seen the popular interest in refining financial regulation matched by academic interest. Like policy, academic research is often reactive, exemplified by the many papers that usually follow a major policy change such as SOX, Regulation Fair Disclosure, and Dodd-Frank. By helping policymakers understand the economics of the securities business, including the nature of competition and the incentives faced by firms and agents, however, academic research can help policymakers prospectively identify changes that would lead to better outcomes.

Competition, incentives, and the effects of regulation are central issues in industrial organization (IO). While research in and debate about securities regulation is often dominated by specialists, given the centrality of what are essentially IO issues, the generalist readers of this volume are likely to also have a contribution to make.

References

Abrams, Robert, and Joel Cohen. 2004. "Explaining Eliot Spitzer: Eliot Spitzer the New York State Attorney General Understands How to Use Power," *Barron's,* March 22, 52.
Akerlof, George. 1971. "The Market for 'Lemons': Qualitative Uncertainty and the Market Mechanism." *Quarterly Journal of Economics* 84:488–500.
Alexander, Gordon J., Jonathan D. Jones, Peter J. Nigro. 2001. "Regulating Mutual Fund Investor Knowledge: Policy Fantasy or Reality?" In *Restructuring Regulation and Financial Institutions,* edited by James R. Barth, R. Dan Brumbaugh Jr., and Glenn Yago, 141–94. Santa Monica: Milken Institute.
Bagnoli, Mark, Michael Clement, and Susan Watts. 2004. "The Timing of Earnings Announcements Throughout the Day and Throughout the Week." Unpublished manuscript, Purdue University.
Barber, Brad, Terry Odean, and Lu Zheng. 2004. "Out of Sight, Out of Mind: The Effect of Expenses on Mutual Fund Flows." *Journal of Business* 78:2095–120.
Barberis, Nicholas, and Richard Thaler. 2003. "A Survey of Behavioral Finance." *Handbook of the Economics of Finance,* vol. 1, chapter 18. Amsterdam: Elsevier.
Baumol, William, Stephen Goldfeld, Lilli Gordon, and Michael Koehn. 1990. *The Economics of Mutual Fund Markets: Competition vs. Regulation.* Boston: Kluwer.
Bergstresser, Daniel, John Chalmers, and Peter Tufano. 2009. "Assessing the Costs and Benefits of Brokers in the Mutual Fund Industry." *Review of Financial Studies* 22 (10): 4129–56.
Bernheim, Douglas, and Michael Whinston. 1990. "Multi-Market Contact and Collusive Behavior." *RAND Journal of Economics* 21:1–26.
Bollen, Nicolas, and Veronica Pool. 2009. "Do Hedge Fund Managers Misreport Returns? Evidence from the Pooled Distribution." *Journal of Finance* 64 (5): 2257–88.
Borenstein, Severin, and Martin Zimmerman. 1988. "Market Incentives for Safe Commercial Airline Operation." *American Economic Review* 78 (5): 913–35.
Bushee, Brian J., and Christian Leuz. 2005. "Economic Consequences of SEC Disclosure Regulation: Evidence from the OTC Bulletin Board." *Journal of Accounting and Economics* 39:233–64.
Busse, Jeffrey, Edwin Elton, and Martin Gruber. 2004. "Are Investors Rational? Choices among Index Funds." *Journal of Finance* 59:261–88.
Busse, Jeffrey A., and T. Clifton Green. 2002. "Market Efficiency in Real-Time." *Journal of Financial Economics* 65:415–37.
Carhart, Mark M. 1997. "On Persistence in Mutual Fund Performance." *Journal of Finance* 52:57–82.
Carnahan, Ira. 2003. "Looting Mutual Funds." *Forbes.com,* March 19.
Carney, William J.. 2006. "The Costs of Being Public after Sarbanes-Oxley: The Irony of Going Private." *Emory Law Journal* 55:141–60.

Chevalier, Judith, and Glenn Ellison. 1997. "Risk Taking by Mutual Funds As a Response to Incentives." *Journal of Political Economy* 105:1167–200.

Choi, James, David Laibson, and Brigitte Madrian. 2010. "Why Does the Law of One Price Fail? An Experiment on Index Mutual Funds." *Review of Financial Studies* 23 (4): 1405–32.

Christie, William, and Paul Schultz. 1994. "Why Do NASDAQ Market Makers Avoid Odd-Eighth Quotes?" *Journal of Finance* 49:1841–60.

———. 1995. "Policy Watch: Did NASDAQ Market Makers Implicitly Collude?" *Journal of Economic Perspectives* 9:199–208.

Christofferson, Susan, Richard Evans, and David Musto. 2005. "The Economics of Mutual-Fund Brokerage: Evidence from the Cross Section of Investment Channels." Unpublished manuscript, McGill University.

Cici, Gjergji, Scott Gibson, and John Merrick. 2011. "Missing the Marks? Dispersion in Corporate Bond Valuations across Mutual Funds." *Journal of Financial Economics* 101 (1): 206–26.

Cici, Gjergji, Scott Gibson, and Rabih Moussawi. 2006. "For Better or Worse? Mutual Funds in Side-by-Side Management Relationships with Hedge Funds." Unpublished manuscript, Wharton School.

Coffee, John, and Joel Seligman. 2002. *Securities Regulation: Cases and Materials*, 9th edition. New York: Foundation Press.

Collins, Sean. 2005. "Are S&P Index Funds Commodities?" *Investment Company Institute Perspectives* 11–03.

Council of Economic Advisers. 2003. *The Economic Report of the President*. Washington, DC: Government Printing Office.

Coval, Joshua, Jakub Jurek, and Erik Stafford. 2009. "The Economics of Structured Finance." *Journal of Economic Perspectives* 23 (1): 3–25.

Damato, Karen, David Reilly, and Karen Richardson. 2004. "Do Mutual Funds Really Need Directors? Other Countries Use Different Systems Where Overseers Do Not Determine Fees." *Wall Street Journal*, June 7, R1.

Davis, Gerald, and Han Kim. 2007. "Business Ties and Proxy Voting by Mutual Funds." *Journal of Financial Economics* 85 (2): 552–70.

DeBondt, Werner, and Richard Thaler. 1985. "Does the Stock Market Overreact?" *Journal of Finance* 40:793–805.

———. 1989. "A Mean Reverting Walk Down Wall Street." *Journal of Economic Perspectives* 3:189–202.

Del Guercio, Diane, Larry Y. Dann, and M. Megan Partch. 2003. "Governance and Boards of Directors in Closed-End Investment Companies." *Journal of Financial Economics* 69:111–52.

DellaVigna, Stefano, and Joshua Pollet. 2009. "Investor Inattention and Friday Earnings Announcements." *Journal of Finance* 64:709–49.

Dyck, Alexander, and Luigi Zingales. 2005. "The Media and Asset Prices." Unpublished manuscript, University of Chicago.

Eldridge, Susan, and Burch Kealey. 2005. "SOX Costs: Auditor Attestation Under Section 404." Unpublished manuscript, University of Nebraska.

Engel, Ellen, Rachel Hayes, and Zue Wang. 2007. "The Sarbanes-Oxley Act and Firm's Going-Private Decisions." *Journal of Accounting and Economics* 44 (1–2): 116–45.

Fama, Eugene, and Kenneth French. 2002. "The Equity Premium." *Journal of Finance* 57:637–59.

Freeman, John, and Stewart Brown. 2001. "Mutual Fund Advisory Fees: The Cost of Conflicts of Interest." *Journal of Corporation Law* 26:609–73.

French, Kenneth. 2008. "Presidential Address: The Cost of Active Investing." *Journal of Finance* 63 (4): 1537–73.

Gabaix, Xavier, and David Laibson. 2006. "Shrouded Attributes, Consumer Myopia, and Information Suppression in Competitive Markets." *Quarterly Journal of Economics* 121:505–40.

Gaspar, José-Miguel, Massimo Massa, and Pedro Matos. 2006. "Favoritism in Mutual Fund Families? Evidence on Strategic Cross-Fund Subsidization." *Journal of Finance* 61 (1):73–104.

Gennaioli, Nicola, Andrei Shleifer, and Robert Vishny. 2012. "Money Doctors." NBER Working Paper no. 18174, Cambridge, MA.

George, Lisa, and Joel Waldfogel. 2003. "Who Affects Whom in Daily Newspaper Markets." *Journal of Political Economy* 111:765–84.

———. 2006. "The *New York Times* and the Market for Local Newspapers." *American Economic Review* 96:435–47.

Getmansky, Mila, Andrew Lo, and Igor Makarov. 2004. "An Econometric Model of Serial Correlation and Illiquidity in Hedge Fund Returns." *Journal of Financial Economics* 74:529–609.

Goetzmann, William, Jonathan Ingersoll, Matthew Spiegel, and Ivo Welch. 2002. "Sharpening Sharpe Ratios." NBER Working Paper no. 9116, Cambridge, MA.

Goetzmann, William N., Zoran Ivkovic, and K. Geert Rouwenhorst. 2001. "Day Trading International Mutual Funds: Evidence and Policy Solutions." *Journal of Financial and Quantitative Analysis* 36 (3): 287–310.

Goshen, Zohar, and Gideon Parchomovsky. 2006. "The Essential Role of Securities Regulation." *Duke Law Journal* 55:711–82.

Greene, Jason, and Charles Hodges. 2002. "The Dilution Impact of Daily Fund Flows on Open-End Mutual Funds." *Journal of Financial Economics* 65:131–58.

Greenstone, Michael, Paul Oyer, and Annette Vissing-Jorgenson. 2006. "Mandated Disclosure, Stock Returns, and the 1964 Securities Acts Amendments." *Quarterly Journal of Economics* 121:399–460.

Greenwood, Robin, and David Scharfstein. 2013. "The Growth of Finance." *Journal of Economic Perspectives* 27 (2): 3–28.

Grossman, Sanford, and Joseph Stiglitz. 1980. "On the Impossibility of Informationally Efficient Markets." *American Economic Review* 70:393–408.

Harris, Lawrence, and Michael Piwowar. 2006. "Secondary Trading Costs in the Municipal Bond Market." *Journal of Finance* 61 (3): 1361–97.

Hennessey, Keith, Douglas Holtz-Eakin, and Bill Thomas. 2011. "Dissenting Statement of Commissioner Keith Hennessey, Commission Douglas Holtz-Eakin, and Vice Chairman Bill Thomas." In *The Financial Crisis Inquiry Report, submitted by the Financial Crisis Inquiry Commission*, 413–39. Washington, DC: Government Printing Office.

Henriques, Diana. 2004. "Basic Training Doesn't Guard Against Insurance Pitch to G.I.'s." *New York Times*, July 20, p. A1.

Horan, Stephen M., and D. Bruce Johnsen. 2008. "Can Third-Party Payments Benefit the Principal? The Case of Soft Dollar Brokerage." *International Review of Law and Economics* 28 (1): 56–77.

Hortascu, Ali, and Chad Syverson. 2004. "Search Costs, Product Differentiation, and the Welfare Effects of Entry: The Case of S&P 500 Index Funds." *Quarterly Journal of Economics* 119 (May): 403–56.

Hsieh, Chang-Tai, and Enrico Moretti. 2003. "Can Free Entry Be Inefficient? Fixed Commissions and Social Waste in the Real Estate Industry." *Journal of Political Economy* 111:1076–122.

Huberman, Gur, and Tomer Regev. 2001. "Contagious Speculation and a Cure for Cancer: A Nonevent that Made Stock Prices Soar." *Journal of Finance* 56:387–96.

Investment Company Institute. 2006. *Understanding Investor Preferences for Mutual Funds*. Washington, DC: Investment Company Institute.

Jackson, Howell E. 1997. "Strategies for Regulating Risk in Financial Intermediaries: General Approaches and their Application to Regulation of Investment Companies." In *The Financial Services Revolution: Understanding the Changing Role of Banks, Mutual Funds, and Insurance Companies*, edited by Clifford E. Kirsch, 527–64. Chicago: Irwin Professional.

Jegadeesh, Narasimhan, and Sheridan Titman. 1993. "Returns to Buying Winners and Selling Losers: Implications for Stock Market Efficiency." *Journal of Finance* 48:65–91.

Kacperczyk, Marcin, Clemens Sialm, and Lu Zheng. 2008. "Unobserved Actions of Mutual Funds." *Review of Financial Studies* 21 (6): 2379–416.

Kandel, Eugene, and Leslie Marx. 1998. "Payments for Order Flow on Nasdaq." *Journal of Finance* 54:35–66.

Khorana, Ajay, Henri Servaes, and Peter Tufano. 2005. "Explaining the Size of the Mutual Fund Industry Around the World." *Journal of Financial Economics* 78:145–85.

———. 2009. "Mutual Fund Fees Around the World." *Review of Financial Studies* 22 (3): 1279–310.

Kim, Y. Han, and Felix Meschke. 2011. "CEO Interviews on CNBC." Unpublished manuscript, Kansas.

Kitch, Edmund W. 2001. "Proposals for Reform of Securities Regulation: An Overview." *Virginia Journal of International Law* 41 (3): 629–52.

Klein, Benjamin, and Keith Leffler. 1981. "The Role of Market Forces in Assuring Contractual Performance." *Journal of Political Economy* 89 (4): 615–41.

Klibanoff, Peter, Owen Lamont, and Thierry A. Wizman. 1998. "Investor Reaction to Salient News in Closed-End Country Funds." *Journal of Finance* 53:673–700.

Kranton, Rachel. 2003. "Competition and the Incentive to Produce High Quality." *Economica* 70 (279): 385–404.

Kroszner, Randall S., and Thomas Stratmann. 1998. "Interest-Group Competition and the Organization of Congress: Theory and Evidence from Financial Services' Political Action Committees." *American Economic Review* 88 (5): 1163–87.

Lee, C. M. C., Andrei Shleifer, and Richard Thaler. 1991. "Investor Sentiment and the Closed-end Fund Puzzle." *Journal of Finance* 46:76–110.

Li, Haidan, Morton Pincus, and Sonja Olhoft Rego. 2008. "Market Reaction to Events Surrounding the Sarbanes-Oxley Act of 2002 and Earnings Management." *Journal of Law and Economics* 51 (1): 111–34.

Lin, H.-W., and M. F. McNichols. 1998. "Underwriter Relationships, Analysts' Earnings Forecasts and Investment Recommendations." *Journal of Accounting and Economics* 25:101–27.

Leuz, Christian, Alexander J. Triantis, and Tracy Wang. 2008. "Why Do Firms Go Dark? Causes and Economic Consequences of Voluntary SEC Deregistrations." *Journal of Accounting and Economics* 45 (2–3): 181–208.

Macey, Jonathan R. 2005. "Positive Political Theory and Federal Usurpation of the Regulation of Corporate Governance: The Coming Preemption of the Martin Act." *Notre Dame Law Review* 80:951–74.

Massa, Massimo, Jon Reuter, and Eric Zitzewitz. 2010. "When Should Firms Share Credit with Employees? Evidence from Anonymously Managed Mutual Funds." *Journal of Financial Economics* 95 (3): 400–24.

Michaely, Roni, and Kent Womack. 1999. "Conflict of Interest and the Credibility of Underwriter Analyst Recommendations." *Review of Financial Studies* 12: 653–86.

Miller, Gregory. 2006. "The Press As a Watchdog for Accounting Fraud." *Journal of Accounting Research* 44:1001–33.

Morey, Matthew, and Edward O'Neal. 2006. "Window Dressing in Bond Mutual Funds." *Journal of Financial Research* 29 (3): 325–47.

Mullainathan, Sendhil, Joshua Schwartzstein, and Andrei Shleifer. 2008. "Coarse Thinking and Persuasion." *Quarterly Journal of Economics* 123 (2): 577–619.

O'Brien, Justin. 2005. "The Politics of Enforcement: Eliot Spitzer, State-Federal Relations, and the Redesign of Financial Regulation." *Publius* 35 (3): 449.

Odean, Terrance. 1998. "Do Investors Trade Too Much?" *American Economic Review* 89:1279–98.

Organisation for Economic Co-operation and Development (OECD). 2005. *OECD Heath Data*. Paris: OECD.

Philippon, Tomas, and Ariell Reshef. 2009. "Wages and Human Capital in the US Financial Industry: 1909–2006." NBER Working Paper no. 14644, Cambridge, MA.

Reid, Brian, and John Rea. 2003. "Mutual Fund Distribution Channels and Distribution Costs." *Investment Company Institute Perspective* 09-03.

Reuter, Jonathan. 2006. "Are IPO Allocations For Sale? Evidence From Mutual Funds." *Journal of Finance* 61:2289–324.

Reuter, Jonathan, and Eric Zitzewitz. 2006. "Do Ads Tempt Editors? Advertising and Bias in the Financial Media." *Quarterly Journal of Economics* 121:197–227.

Rezaee, Zabihollah, and Pankaj Jain. 2006. "The Sarbanes-Oxley Act of 2002 and Security Market Behavior: Early Evidence." *Contemporary Accounting Research* 23:629–54.

Romano, Roberta. 2001. "The Need for Competition in International Securities Regulation." *Theoretical Inquiries in Law* 2:387.

———. 2005. "The Sarbanes-Oxley Act and the Making of Quack Corporate Governance." *Yale Law Journal* 114:1521–612.

Rose, Nancy. 1990. "Profitability and Product Quality: Economic Determinants of Airline Safety Performance." *Journal of Political Economy* 98 (5): 944–64.

Securities and Exchange Commission. 1992. *Protecting Investors: A Half Century of Investment Company Regulation by the Division of Investment Management.* Washington, DC: US Government Printing Office.

———. 2004. *Joint SEC/NASD Report on Examination Findings Regarding Broker-Dealer Sales of Variable Insurance Products.* http://www.sec.gov/news/studies/secnasdvip.pdf.

Seligman, Joel. 2003. *The Transformation of Wall Street: A History of the SEC and Modern Corporate Finance*, 3rd edition. Aspen Press.

Shapiro, Carl. 1982. "Consumer Information, Product Quality, and Seller Reputation." *Bell Journal of Economics* 13 (1): 20–35.

Shefrin, Hersh. 2002. *Beyond Fear and Greed.* New York: Oxford University Press.

Shefrin, Hersh, and Meir Statman. 1985. "The Disposition to Sell Winners too Early and Ride Losers too Long: Theory and Evidence." *Journal of Finance* 40: 777–90.

———. 1994. "Behavioral Capital Asset Pricing Theory." *Journal of Financial and Quantitative Analysis* 29:21–29.

Shiller, Robert. 2003. "From Efficient Markets to Behavioral Finance." *Journal of Economic Perspectives* 17:83–104.

Siggelkow, Nicolaj. 2004. "Caught Between Two Principals." Unpublished manuscript, Wharton School.

Solow, Robert. 1956. "A Contribution to the Theory of Economic Growth." *Quarterly Journal of Economics* 70 (1): 65–94.

Stigler, George. 1971. "The Theory of Economic Regulation." *Bell Journal of Economics and Management Science* 2:3–21.

Stone, Amey. 2002. "When Market Timers Target Funds." *Business Week Online*, December 11.

Tkac, Paula. 2004. "Mutual Funds: Temporary Problem or Permanent Morass." *Federal Reserve Bank of Atlanta Economic Review* 4:1–21.

Tufano, Peter, and Matthew Sevick. 1997. "Board Structure and Fee Setting in the US Mutual Fund Industry." *Journal of Financial Economics* 46:321–55.

United States Census Bureau. 2005. "Product Lines: 2002." *2002 Economic Census, Finance and Insurance, Subject Series*.

United States House of Representatives. 1933. Report No. 85, 73rd Congress, First Session.

Walsh, Lori. 2004. "The Costs and Benefits to Fund Shareholders of 12b-1 Plans: An Examination of Fund Flows, Expenses and Returns." Unpublished manuscript, Securities and Exchange Commission.

Walter, Ingo. 2004. "Conflicts of Interest and Market Discipline in Financial Services Firms." *European Management Journal* 22 (4): 361–76.

Woodward, Susan. 2001. "Regulatory Capture at the Securities and Exchange Commission." In *Restructuring Regulation and Financial Institutions*, edited by James R. Barth, R. Dan Brumbaugh Jr., and Glenn Yago, 99–117. Santa Monica: Milken Institute.

Zingales, Luigi. 2004. "The Costs and Benefits of Financial Market Regulation." ECGI-Law Working Paper no. 21/2004.

Zitzewitz, Eric. 2002. "Regulation FD and the Private Information of Analysts." Unpublished manuscirpt, Stanford University.

———. 2003. "Who Cares About Shareholders? Arbitrage-Proofing Mutual Funds." *Journal of Law, Economics, and Organization* 19:245–80.

Contributors

Severin Borenstein
Haas School of Business
University of California, Berkeley
Berkeley, CA 94720-1900

Dennis W. Carlton
Booth School of Business
University of Chicago
5807 South Woodlawn Avenue
Chicago, IL 60637

Gregory S. Crawford
Department of Economics
University of Zurich
Blümlisalpstrasse 10
CH-8006 Zurich

Patricia M. Danzon
Health Care Management Department
The Wharton School
University of Pennsylvania
3641 Locust Walk
Philadelphia, PA 19104

Jerry Hausman
Department of Economics, E17-238A
MIT
77 Massachusetts Ave.
Cambridge, MA 02139

Paul L. Joskow
Alfred P. Sloan Foundation
630 Fifth Avenue, Suite 2550
New York, NY 10111

Eric L. Keuffel
Fox School of Business
Temple University
1801 Liacouras Walk
Philadelphia, PA 19122

Randall S. Kroszner
Booth School of Business
University of Chicago
5807 South Woodlawn Avenue
Chicago, IL 60637

Randal C. Picker
University of Chicago Law School
1111 East 60th Street
Chicago, IL 60637

Nancy L. Rose
Department of Economics, E18-210
MIT
77 Massachusetts Ave.
Cambridge MA 02139

J. Gregory Sidak
Criterion Economics, L.L.C.
1000 Connecticut Avenue, NW
Suite 900
Washington, DC 20036

Philip E. Strahan
Carroll School of Management
Boston College
140 Commonwealth Avenue
Chestnut Hill, MA 02467

Frank A. Wolak
Department of Economics
Stanford University
Stanford, CA 94305-6072

Eric Zitzewitz
Department of Economics
Rockefeller Hall 6016
Dartmouth College
Hanover, NH 03755

Author Index

Page numbers followed by the letter *f* refer to figures.

Abramowitz, A. D., 121n77, 122
Abrams, B. A., 492n5
Abrams, R., 567n36
Acemoglu, D., 442
Acharya, V., 487, 534
Adams, C. P., 408
Adams, W. J., 180, 181f
Adrian, T., 534
Ai, C., 313, 333n22
Aitken, M., 434f
Akerlof, G., 555
Alexander, G. J., 556, 558
Ang, J. S., 497, 520
Aoki, M., 507
Armantier, O., 90, 120
Armstrong, M., 160, 181, 294, 300, 301n7, 302, 305, 310, 311
Arrow, K. J., 441
Asch, D. A., 464
Asquith, P., 500
Attaran, A., 439
Averch, H., 228, 305, 455
Awad, M., 248

Bacon, R. W., 333
Bagnoli, M., 559
Bailey, E. E., 2n3, 66n6, 67, 75n18, 76n20, 92, 121n76
Baily, M. N., 421, 423
Bakos, Y., 181, 182

Balleisen, E. J., 4n9
Bamberger, G., 51, 54, 90, 90n42, 120
Barberis, N., 557n18
Barnes, B. A., 86
Barnhart, C., 84, 118
Baron, D., 296, 300, 301, 305
Barth, J., 502, 524
Basso, L. J., 106n57
Baumol, W. J., 106n57, 121n76, 305, 451, 545n2, 546n3
Beales, J. H., 466
Becker, G., 34
Beesley, M., 305, 310, 348n8
Bekaert, G., 523
Bell, R. A., 419
Belobaba, P., 84
Belzer, M., 57
Benerjee, A., 160
Benmelech, E., 503
Bennett, C. L., 427
Benson, B., 37
Berger, A. N., 514n24, 519n29
Bergstresser, D., 558
Berndt, E. R., 417, 434f, 462, 463, 465, 466, 467, 468, 469
Bernheim, D., 562
Bernstein, J. I., 312
Berry, S., 65n3, 93n44, 165n43, 166n45
Bertram, G., 333, 334, 335f
Bertrand, M., 523n31

591

Besanko, D., 162, 168, 296, 301, 305
Besant-Jones, J. E., 333
Besen, S., 144n7
Beutel, P., 165
Bhargava, R., 499
Binder, J., 163n39
Bittlingmayer, G., 35
Black, S. E., 519, 524n35, 534
Blair, C. E., 507
Blalock, G., 98
Bliss, C., 356n23
Bohn, R. E., 282
Boiteux, M., 293
Bollen, N., 580
Bonacorrsi di Patti, E., 523n30
Bonchek, M., 28
Borenstein, S., 51, 52, 54, 65n3, 75n18, 82,
    83, 85n33, 88, 98n49, 107, 121n77, 122,
    122n79, 123n80, 126n84, 217, 243, 245,
    252, 254, 255, 256, 261, 579
Boyd, J. H., 498, 502n15, 504, 517n27
Boyer, K., 57
Bradford, D. F., 451
Braeutigam, R., 160, 293
Brantner, V. V., 408
Bratu, S., 118
Brennan, T., 160, 296, 305, 310
Bresnahan, T., 165n43, 165n44, 166n47
Breyer, S., 75n18, 75n19
Brown, S., 568
Brown, S. M., 121n77, 122
Brueckner, J. K., 106n57, 120, 126n84, 127
Brunger, W. G., 86
Brynjolfsson, E., 181, 182
Buchanan, J., 491n3
Burgess, G., 510n21
Burton, M., 55
Bushee, B. J., 564n29
Bushnell, J. B., 8, 14, 213, 217, 252, 254,
    255, 256, 261
Busse, J. A., 556, 559, 572n44

Cabral, L., 296
Cacciotti, J., 434
Calfee, J. E., 431, 469
Calomiris, C. W., 491n2, 493, 494, 502, 505
Caprio, G., 524
Caramanis, M. C., 282
Card, D., 74
Carhart, M. M., 558, 572
Carlton, D., 35n1, 50, 51, 54, 90, 90n42,
    120
Carnahan, I., 561n25

Carney, W. J., 564
Cartwright, H., 434
Cauley, L., 184
Cave, M., 346n1
Caves, D. W., 106n57
Caves, R., 66n6, 68, 68n10, 70, 71n13, 74,
    107, 437, 448, 458
Cetorelli, N., 523, 523n30, 524n36
Cevasco, M., 419
Chalmers, J., 558
Chao, L. W., 456, 457
Chaplin, A., 55
Chaudhuri, S., 439
Chevalier, J., 556, 556n16
Chintagunta, P. K., 467
Chipty, T., 177n66, 179
Choi, J., 556
Chressanthis, G. A., 464
Christensen, L. R., 106n57
Christie, W., 573
Christofferson, S., 554, 558
Chu, C. S., 174
Cici, G., 555, 580n51
Clark, J. M., 310
Clarkson, K. W., 458
Clement, M., 559
Clinton, P., 434
Cockburn, I., 460
Coffee, J., 546n3, 562n26, 565n31, 577
Coglianese, G., 5n10
Cohen, J., 567n36
Coleman, M. S., 424
Collender, R. N., 523n33
Collins, S. C., 65n3
Comanor, W. S., 444, 445
Corsi, T., 57
Corts, K. S., 164n40
Coval, J., 579
Cowan, S., 305, 310
Crandall, R. W., 144n7, 155, 166n45, 168,
    368n49, 375, 375n61, 379n75
Craswell, R., 431
Crawford, G. S., 138, 146, 155, 160n32,
    162n37, 164n40, 165n42, 166n45, 167,
    169, 169n55, 174, 177, 178, 179, 180,
    181, 183, 184
Crivelli, L., 453
Cullen, J., 180, 183
Cutler, D. M., 434f

Damato, K., 560
Dana, J. D., Jr., 82
Daniel, T., 57

Dann, L. Y., 560
Danzon, P. M., 418, 424, 425, 433, 437, 438,
    439, 439n13, 440, 446, 449, 450, 451,
    451n20, 453, 453n21, 455, 456, 457,
    461, 469
Darrow, R. M., 84
Dave, D., 468
David, G., 468
Davis, D., 55
Davis, G., 578
Davis, L., 8, 19
Dehejia, R., 494n6
Del Guercio, D., 560
Dell'Ariccia, G., 523n30
Della Vigna, S., 559
Demirguc-Kunt, A., 495
Demsetz, R. S., 517
Derthick, M., 2n1, 2n3
De Rus, G., 128n86
Desiraju, R., 467
Dick, A., 513f
Dillon, R. L., 98n49
DiMasi, J. A., 408, 409, 423, 423f, 424n6,
    427, 428n9, 432, 442
Dionne, G., 98
Dixit, A., 349n12
Doganis, R., 100n51, 101
Domah, P. E., 333
Donnenfeld, S., 162, 168
Donohue, J. M., 419, 468
Doucet, J., 307
Douglas, G. W., 66n6, 72, 95, 107
Dranove, D., 425, 425n8
Drucker, J., 150
Drucker, S., 521
Dubois, R. W., 471
Duggan, M., 15, 446
Dunne, T., 87n35
Dyck, A., 559

Eads, G., 66n6, 72, 74
Eames, F., 576n46
Economides, N., 492n5
Edlin, A., 54
Edwards, J., 507
Eldridge, S., 564
Elixhauser, A., 470
Ellig, J., 19
Ellis, D., 503
Ellis, R. P., 449
Ellison, G., 556, 556n16
Elton, E., 556, 572n44
Emmons, W., 155, 170

Engel, E., 564
Epstein, A., 451, 461
Estache, A., 304, 333
Evans, R., 554, 558
Evans, W. N., 122

Fabrizio, K., 8, 19, 261
Fan, T., 127
Farrell, J., 54
Faulhaber, G. R., 48
Feitler, J., 57
Ferrandiz, J., 449, 456, 457
Festa, P., 46
Feuille, P., 74
Fink, C., 439
Finkelstein, A., 424n7
Finsinger, J., 305
Fiorina, M., 31
Fischer, K., 507
Flannery, M., 504
Flynn, S., 440
Forbes, S. J., 90n40, 97n48, 118, 120, 125
Ford, G., 177
Forsyth, P., 100
Foster, A., 144n6
Frame, W. S., 511f
Frank, R. G., 435, 448, 462
Frankel, A., 35n1
Frankfurter, F., 41
Fraser, D. R., 499
Freeman, J., 568
Friedman, M., 502
Fruhan, W., 72
Fullerton, D., 5n10
Furchtgott-Roth, H., 155, 166n45, 168
Furukawa, M. F., 418, 433, 437, 438,
    453n21, 456, 457

Gabaix, X., 557n18
Gaggero, A. O., 83
Gallagher, J., 56
Gambera, M., 523
Gande, A., 521
Garber, A. M., 457
Gaspar, J.-M., 555
Gatev, E., 525n37
Gelband, H., 441
Gendall, P., 469
Gennaioli, N., 547n4
George, L., 561
Geradin, D., 381n84, 382n88, 392n125
Gerardi, K., 65n3, 83
Gertler, M., 502n15, 504

Getmansky, M., 580
Giannakis, D., 304, 312, 322
Giaume, S., 83
Gibson, S., 555, 580n51
Gilbert, R., 306, 432
Gilead, 440
Gillen, D. W., 108n60
Gilligan, T. W., 38, 55
Giordano, J., 57
Glaeser, E., 503
Goetzmann, W. N., 561n25, 580
Goldberg, L. G., 519n29
Goldberg, P., 439
Golec, J. H., 423
Gompers, P. A., 508
Good, D. H., 99
Goolsbee, A., 65n3, 82, 121n78, 124,
    166n45, 173
Gordon, R. J., 122
Gorton, G., 494, 535
Goshen, Z., 547n3
Grabowski, H. G., 408, 409, 421, 422, 423,
    423f, 424n6, 425, 428n9, 432, 435, 436f,
    437, 447, 448, 458, 460
Graham, D. R., 66n6, 67, 75n18, 92
Graham, S. L., 498, 517n27
Grajek, M., 15
Grande, D., 464
Green, T. C., 559
Greene, J., 561n25
Greenhut, M., 37
Greenspan, A., 510n21
Greenstone, M., 564n29
Greenwood, R., 547n4
Grimm, C., 55, 55n13, 56, 57
Grodinsky, J., 38
Gruber, M., 556, 572n44
Guillou, S., 83
Guner, A. B., 521

Hammond, B., 488
Hammond, C. J., 309
Hansen, R. W., 408, 409, 423, 423f, 424n6,
    428n9
Harrington, J. E., 199
Harris, L., 557
Harvey, C., 523
Hausdorff, W., 420
Hausman, J. A., 16, 347, 349, 349n12, 350,
    353n17, 355n21, 358n26, 359, 360n30,
    360n32, 361n33, 365n45, 369n54,
    375n62, 380n81, 392n123, 396n136,
    400n157, 401n160, 401n162

Hayes, R., 564
Hazlett, T., 146, 157f, 158n31, 164, 165n41,
    170, 170n57
Hellman, T., 515
Hemphill, C. S., 435
Henderson, R., 460
Hendricks, W., 73, 74
Hennessey, K., 581
Henriques, D., 557
Hewitt, S., 517n27
Hilton, G. W., 38
Hirsch, B. T., 74, 111, 112n63
Hirst, E., 217
Hodges, C., 561n25
Hoek, J., 469
Holcombe, R., 37
Hollis, A., 440
Holtz-Eakin, D., 581
Horan, S. M., 577n47
Hortascu, A., 572n44
Hsieh, C.-T., 562
Hubbard, R. G., 492n5, 519n28
Huberman, G., 559
Hughes, J. P., 519
Hunter, N. J., 57
Hurdle, G. J., 65n3, 121n77
Hurwitz, M. A., 437, 448, 458

Iizuka, T., 467, 468, 469
Ingraham, A. T., 379n75
Isaac, R. M., 296, 305, 310
Ivaldi, M., 55
Ivkovic, Z., 561n25

Jack, W. L., 439n13, 451n20
Jackson, H. E., 564
Jackson, J., 177
Jaffe, A., 163
Jain, P., 564
Jamasb, T., 304, 312, 313n12, 322
Jara-Diaz, S. R., 106n57
Jarrell, G., 199
Jayaratne, J., 515n25, 519, 524n34, 533n44
Jegadeesh, N., 558
Jenkins, D., 122
Jensen, M. C., 507n19, 508
Jha, A., 284
Jia, P., 65n3, 93n44, 439
Jin, G., 467, 468
Johnes, G., 309
Johnsen, D. B., 577n47
Johnson, B. E., 98n49
Johnson, L. L., 228, 305, 455

Jones, C. I., 457
Jones, J. D., 556, 558
Jordan, W. A., 66n6, 71
Jorion, P., 505
Joskow, P. L., 2n2, 2n4, 8n13, 12, 13, 19n14,
  73n15, 75n18, 76, 199, 201, 210, 211,
  261, 272, 293, 294, 298n6, 305, 306,
  309, 310, 318, 322, 332, 338, 339, 455
Jurek, J., 579

Kacperczyk, M., 558
Kadiyali, V., 98
Kahn, A. E., 5, 12, 18, 19n14, 20, 66n7, 71,
  75n18, 76, 145, 346n2, 357
Kahn, C., 491n2
Kahn, E., 261
Kamita, R. Y., 3n6
Kanafani, A., 66
Kanavos, P., 449
Kandel, E., 574
Kane, E., 495, 496n7, 502, 507, 518, 532
Kanter, D., 163
Kaplan, D. R., 66n6, 67, 75n18, 92
Kaufman, G., 502n15, 507n18
Kealey, B., 564
Keeler, T. E., 66, 71, 71n13, 72, 438
Keeley, M., 515, 517
Kennet, D. M., 98
Kerf, M., 381n84, 382n88, 392n125
Kesselheim, A. S., 435
Kessides, I. N., 122
Kessler, D. P., 5n10, 5n11
Ketcham, J. D., 453
Kettler, H., 421
Keys, B. J., 522
Khan, L., 3
Khorana, A., 560
Kilian, L., 19
Kim, H., 578
Kim, Y. H., 559
King, R., 522
Kitch, E. M., 547n3
Klein, B., 579
Kleit, A., 57
Klemperer, P., 432
Klevorick, A. K., 305
Klibanoff, P., 559
Klingebiel, D., 523, 535
Kohlberg, W. E., 358
Kolko, G., 41
Koziara, E. C., 74n16
Kranton, R., 579
Kravitz, R. L., 419, 466, 468

Kremer, M., 421
Kroszner, R. S., 491n2, 493, 493f, 496n7,
  497, 498, 498n12, 500, 502, 507,
  515n25, 517, 518, 520, 521, 523, 527,
  528, 529, 530, 533n44, 534, 535, 568n37
Kruse, G. B., 469
Kuhlik, B. N., 418, 432, 435, 437
Kwan, S., 495, 517n27
Kwast, M. L., 517n27
Kwoka, J., 296
Kyle, M. K., 451

Laderman, E., 517n27
Laeven, L., 495, 523, 535
Laffont, J.-J., 2n5, 8, 74n17, 224, 231, 293,
  294, 296, 297, 299, 300, 301, 302, 303,
  305, 311, 353n18
Laibson, D., 556, 557n18
Lakdawalla, D. N., 446, 449, 457
Lamont, O., 559
Landes, E., 35n1
Landes, W., 29
Landis, J. M., 41
Landy, M. K., 2n1, 5n10
Lanjouw, J. O., 439n13, 440, 451, 451n20
Lasagna, L., 425
Laxminarayan, R., 441
Lazarus, D., 3n7
Lederman, M., 85, 90, 90n40, 120, 122n79
Lee, B.-J., 201
Lee, C. M. C., 557
Lee, D., 122
Leffler, K., 465, 579
Legler, J., 491
Leimkuhler, J. F., 84
Leonard, G. K., 380, 380n81, 401n160,
  401n162
Lerner, J., 432, 508
Leuz, C., 564, 564n29
Levin, M. A., 2n1, 5n10
Levin, R. C., 46n6
Levin, S., 170
Levine, M. E., 66n6, 70n12, 71, 121
Levine, R., 522, 523n32, 524, 535
Levinsohn, J., 166n45
Levy, R., 432, 433
Lewis, T., 300, 301
Li, H., 564
Lichtenberg, F. R., 414, 427, 442
Lin, H.-W., 561, 575
Linn, J., 442
Littlechild, S., 305, 307, 310, 348n8
Lleras-Muney, A., 494n6

Lo, A. W., 3n8, 580
Longman, P., 3
Longman, R., 461
Loomis, C., 52
López-Casasnovas, G., 453
Loughran, T., 500
Loutskina, E., 510n21, 527, 535
Lown, C., 499, 517n27, 522
Lu, Z. J., 445
Luce, B. R., 470
Lundblad, C. T., 523
Lyon, T., 297

Ma, A., 449
Macey, J., 497n11, 506, 567
Macpherson, D. A., 74
Madden, B. J., 429, 429n10
Madrian, B., 556
Mahmoud, A., 421
Maillet, L. E., 125
Majumdar, S. K., 346n1
Makarov, I., 580
Make, J., 138, 180
Makinson, L., 529, 530
Malmendier, U., 521
Malueg, D. A., 439n13
Mangum, S. L., 57
Mansfield, E., 432
Mansur, E. T., 8, 14, 255, 261
Markowitz, S., 468
Marshall, W. J., 38, 55
Martinez, S., 313, 333n22
Marx, L., 574
Mason, J., 502, 505
Massa, M., 555, 569
Masson, A., 447
Matos, P., 555
Mayer, C., 97, 118, 124
McCartney, S., 95n45
McCubbins, M. D., 28, 293
McCullough, G., 55
McGowan, J., 144n6
McGuire, T. G., 449
McNichols, M. F., 561, 575
Megginson, W. L., 234
Meisel, J., 170
Melick, W., 493
Mello, M. M., 464
Meltzer, A., 17, 425, 425n8
Merrick, J., 580n51
Merton, R., 517
Meschke, F., 559

Messing, N. A., 464
Mester, L. J., 498
Metrick, A., 535
Meyer, J. R., 67
Mian, A., 522
Michaely, R., 561, 575
Miller, A. R., 54
Miller, G., 506, 561n24
Miller, J. C., III, 66n6, 72, 95, 107
Milner, M., 396n135
Mirrlees, J., 356
Mishkin, F. S., 504
Mitchener, K., 496n9
Moe, J. L., 421
Moran, M., 421, 441
Morey, M., 580
Morgan, D. P., 515n25, 524, 525, 525n38,
    533n44
Moretti, E., 562
Morrison, S. A., 51, 65n3, 75n18, 82,
    121n78, 124, 126n84
Morrison, W. G., 108n60
Morton, F. S., 446
Moskowitz, T., 503
Moss, D. A., 4n9
Mote, L., 502n15, 507n18
Moussawi, R., 555
Muehlegger, E., 19
Mueller, M. L., 45, 46
Mulcahy, A. W., 439, 440
Mullainathan, S., 557
Mullins, C., 412, 463
Mullins, D., 500
Münnich, F. E., 454
Murdock, K., 515
Mussa, M., 161
Musto, D., 554, 558
Myers, S., 392n123
Myerson, R., 300, 301

Nalebuff, B., 182
Narayanan, S., 467
Netter, J. M., 234
Neumann, L., 90, 90n42, 120
Neumann, P. J., 470
Neven, D. J., 99, 111
Nevo, A., 165n43, 166n45
Newbery, D., 306, 333
Ng, C. K., 99, 106n57
Nicholson, S., 461
Nigro, P. J., 556, 558
Niskanen, W., 491n3

Noll, R., 2n1, 2n4, 28, 49, 75n18, 76, 144n6,
    293, 491n3
Nordhaus, R., 260

O'Brien, J., 567n36
Odean, T., 558
Odoni, A., 84, 100n51, 102
O'Hara, M., 496n8
Okie, S., 427, 429
Olson, M. K., 427
O'Neal, E., 580
Orlov, E., 83
Oster, C. V., Jr., 98
Over, M., 441
Owen, B., 49, 147n16, 293
Oyer, P., 564n29

Pakes, A., 165n43, 166n45
Palia, D., 492n5, 519n28
Palmedo, M., 440
Palumbo, F. B., 412, 463
Panosian, C., 441
Panzar, J. C., 106n56, 121n76
Paquette, C., 442
Parchomovsky, G., 547n3
Partch, M. M., 560
Passmore, W., 510n21
Pate-Cornell, M. E., 98n49
Patrick, H., 507
Patrick, R. H., 214, 251
Pauly, M. V., 449
Peck, M., 144n6
Peltzman, S., 2n1, 34, 55n13, 76, 421, 426,
    444, 492, 504, 517, 531
Peoples, J., 73, 74
Percy, A., 450, 455
Pereira, N. S., 424, 461
Perloff, J., 51
Petersen, M., 531
Petrin, A., 166n45, 169n55, 173
Philippon, T., 547n4
Philipson, T., 417, 442
Piga, C. A., 83
Pincus, M., 564
Pindyck, R., 45n3, 349n12, 350, 360n30
Pirrong, S. C., 36
Piwowar, M., 557
Pizzica, V., 396n135
Pollet, J., 559
Pollitt, M., 304, 312, 313n12, 322, 326n14,
    333
Pool, V., 580

Posner, R., 29, 34, 45n4, 293
Prado, M. J. L., 122
Prager, R., 155, 163, 170
Prescott, E. C., 82
Puig-Junoy, J., 453
Pulvino, T., 110
Puri, M., 497n11, 520, 521

Quirk, P. J., 2n1, 2n3

Rabin, R. L., 39, 500
Rajan, R. G., 497, 498, 520, 521, 523, 531
Ramsey, F. P., 451
Raskovich, A., 177n66
Rea, J., 558
Reekie, W. D., 445
Regev, T., 559
Rego, S. O., 564
Reid, B., 558
Reilly, D., 560
Rennhoff, A. D., 183–84
Reshef, A., 547n4
Reuter, J., 559, 561, 569, 570
Rey, P., 178
Rezaee, Z., 564
Richard, O., 90, 120
Richards, D. B., 78
Richards, S., 468
Richardson, K., 560
Richardson, T., 497
Ridley, D. B., 421
Rime, B., 515n25, 524, 533n44
Riordan, M., 296, 368n49, 449
Ripley, W. Z., 41
Ritter, J., 500
Roberts, M. J., 87n35
Robinson, J., 522
Robinson, S., 37
Robinson, T., 309
Rodriguez-Pardina, M., 333
Roe, M. J., 508
Roettgers, J., 142n5
Röller, L.-H., 15, 99, 111
Romano, R., 11, 18, 564n28, 567n35
Romer, P. M., 457
Rose, N. L., 2n2, 2n4, 8, 12, 19, 65n3, 66,
    66n6, 71n13, 73, 76, 83, 88, 98, 163n39,
    261, 579
Rosen, S., 161
Rosenthal, M. B., 419, 467
Rossi, M. A., 304
Rouwenhorst, K. G., 561n25

Rubinovitz, R., 155, 167
Rudnick, H., 333
Ruzzier, C. A., 304

Saffer, H., 468
Saidenberg, M. R., 517
Salkever, D. S., 435, 448
Salop, S. C., 82, 368n49
Samolyk, K., 504
Sampat, B. N., 435
Samuelson, L., 87n35
Sappington, D. M., 160, 294, 300, 301,
    301n7, 302, 305, 310, 312, 313, 333n22
Saravia, C., 8, 14, 255, 261
Sathisan, S. K., 66
Scharfstein, D., 547n4
Schatz, A., 150
Scheinkmann, J., 503
Schenone, C., 521
Scherbakov, O., 160n32
Scherer, F. M., 446
Schmalensee, R., 201, 297, 298n6, 307, 309,
    310, 311, 322, 332, 338, 354n19
Schmidt, S., 55
Schnabl, P., 487, 534
Schoar, A., 523n31
Schöffski, O., 454
Schuermann, T., 525n37
Schulenburg, J.-M. Graf v. d., 454
Schultz, P., 573
Schumpeter, J., 522
Schwartz, A. J., 502
Schwartz, M., 439n13
Schwartzman, D., 465
Schwartzstein, J., 557
Schweppe, F. C., 282
Schwert, G., 163n39
Scott Morton, F., 15, 437, 444
Seabright, P., 99, 106n57
Searcy, D., 150
Seligman, J., 546n3, 562n26, 565n31, 577
Serfes, K., 183–84
Servaes, H., 560
Settle, R. F., 492n5
Sevick, M., 560
Shaffer, S. L., 523n33
Shapiro, A. H., 65n3, 83
Shapiro, C., 260, 432
Shapiro, M., 2n1, 5n10
Shaw, W., 496n8
Shcherbakov, A., 187
Shefrin, H., 557n18, 558
Shelanski, H., 353n17

Shepsle, K., 28
Sherlund, S. M., 510n21
Shiller, R., 534, 557n18
Shin, H. S., 534
Shirley, M. E., 234
Shleifer, A., 303, 547n4, 557
Shughart, W. F., II, 497n11
Shull, B., 498
Shum, M., 155, 160n32, 162n37, 165n42,
    167, 174
Sialm, C., 558
Sibley, D., 296, 305
Sickles, R. C., 99
Sidak, J. G., 349, 361n33, 368n49, 369n54,
    380n81
Siggelkow, N., 577n47
Silberson, Z., 432
Simon, D. H., 98
Sinai, T., 97, 118, 124
Singer, H. J., 379n75
Smith, B. C., 84
Smith, D. L., 441
Snider, C., 128
Snyder, C. M., 177n66
Sood, N., 449, 457
Spence, A. M., 160
Spiller, P. T., 106n57, 293
Spitzer, M., 146, 157f, 158n31, 164, 170n57
Stafford, E., 579
Starr, P., 46
Statman, M., 558
Stavins, J., 83
Steiner, C. A., 470
Steiner, R. L., 447
Stephenson, M., 31
Stewart, C., 108n60
Stigler, G., 34, 180, 199, 492
Stiglitz, J. E., 4n9, 20, 515
Stiroh, K., 519
Stoft, S., 217
Stone, A., 561n25
Strahan, P. E., 493, 493f, 496n7, 502, 504,
    510n21, 514n24, 515n25, 517, 518, 519,
    521, 524, 524n34, 524n35, 524n36,
    525n37, 527, 528, 529, 530, 533n44,
    535, 536
Stratmann, T., 498n12, 507, 568n37
Strong, J. S., 98
Suarez, G., 487, 534
Sufi, A., 499f, 500, 521, 522
Sullivan, K., 454
Surowiecki, J., 5n10
Sutton, J., 412

Sylla, R., 491
Syverson, C., 65n3, 82, 121n78, 124, 572n44
Szerszen, C., 74

Tate, G., 521
Taylor, C. T., 432
Tejwani, S. S., 424
Telser, L. G., 465
Temin, P., 426, 438, 444, 460
Thaler, R., 557, 557n18
Thesmar, D., 523n31
Thomas, B., 581
Thomas, K., 488n1
Thomas, L. G., 419, 421, 422, 450, 460
Tirole, J., 2n5, 8, 74n17, 178, 224, 231, 293,
    294, 296, 297, 299, 300, 301, 302, 303,
    305, 311, 353n18
Titman, S., 558
Tkac, P., 560
Torbenson, E., 103n55
Towse, A., 421, 439, 439n13, 440, 449,
    451n20, 456, 457
Tretheway, M. W., 106n57
Triantis, A. J., 564
Trottman, M., 118n73
Tsao, A., 434
Tufano, P., 558, 560
Tullock, G., 491n3
Twaddle, D., 333, 334, 335f

Unterberger, S. H., 74n16

Van Dender, K., 126n84, 127
Vellturo, C. A., 55, 401n160, 401n162
Ventola, C. L., 419
Vernon, J. A., 409
Vernon, J. M., 199, 421, 422, 423, 425, 432,
    437, 447, 448, 458, 460
Vickers, J., 305, 310, 311
Viscusi, W. K., 199
Vishny, R., 547n4
Vissing-Jorgenson, A., 564n29
Vogelsang, I., 305, 346n1

Waldfogel, J., 414, 561
Walker, H., 465
Wallis, J., 491
Walsh, P., 234
Walter, I., 578n49
Wang, L., 425, 451
Wang, T., 564
Wang, Y. R., 425, 451
Wang, Z., 564

Wardell, W. M., 425
Watal, J., 439
Waterman, D. H., 179n70
Watts, S., 559
Weiman, D. F., 46n6
Weingast, B. R., 28, 38, 55, 293
Weisman, D., 402n164
Weiss, A. A., 179n70
Weitzman, M., 305
Whalen, W. T., 120
Whinston, M. D., 65n3, 182, 437, 448, 458,
    562
White, E. N., 492n5, 493, 494, 497
White, L. J., 162, 168, 488, 498, 502, 511f
Wiggins, S. N., 421, 423, 425
Wildman, S., 147n16
Wilkes, M. S., 419
Williams, J. W., 128
Willig, R., 106n57, 121n76, 374n60
Wilson, W., 55
Winston, C., 2n2, 19, 51, 55, 55n13, 56,
    75n18, 126n84, 128n86
Wizman, T. A., 559
Wolak, F., 8, 19, 202n2, 204, 212, 213, 214,
    215, 216n5, 229, 237, 238, 241, 245n8,
    246, 248, 250, 251, 252, 254, 255, 256,
    258, 259, 260, 261, 266, 267, 269, 272,
    283, 284
Wolff, E., 500
Wolfram, C., 5n10, 8, 19, 66n4, 261
Womack, K., 561, 575
Woodcock, J., 426f
Woodward, S., 568
Wosinska, M., 467, 468

Yasuda, A., 521
Yellen, J. L., 180, 181f
Yin, W., 446
Yurukoglu, A., 138, 155, 177, 178, 181, 184

Zeckhauser, R., 449
Zhang, Z., 99, 111
Zheng, L., 558
Zimmerman, M., 98n49, 579
Zingales, L., 523, 555, 559
Zitzewitz, E., 555, 559, 560, 561, 561n25,
    568, 569
Zolezzi, J., 333
Zorn, C. K., 98
Zuckerman, L., 118n73
Zupan, M. A., 164, 165n41
Zweifel, P., 453

Subject Index

Page numbers followed by the letter f or t refer to figures or tables, respectively.

Adverse drug reactions (ADRs), 427
Agency decisions, 30–31
Agriculture, antitrust immunities and, 35–36
Airline Deregulation Act (1978), 6, 51, 64, 75–76, 102
Airline industry, 3, 5–6; alliances in, 51; Civil Aeronautics Board and, 15, 50–51, 64, 64n1, 66–72; code-sharing alliances, 90–91; competition in, 51, 54; computer reservations systems in, 53; concentration in, since deregulation, 51–52; demand volatility and, 108–10; deregulation issues in, 104–5; deregulation of, in US, 75–98; entry and exit in, 87–88; fare structures, 83–84; financial health of airlines, 52; flight frequency and connections, 92–95; fuel cost issues, 112–13; hub-and-spoke networks, 51, 89, 117–18; in-flight amenities, 95–96; infrastructure development/utilization issues in, 124–28; innovation issues, 117–21; international markets, 98–104; Internet use and, 86; intrastate markets of, 70–71; introduction, 63–65; as investment, 52; labor issues, 110–12; load factors, 95, 114–15; loyalty programs, 84–86; market fundamentals, issues of, 108–17; market power concerns in, 121–24; market structure in, 89–92; merger activity in, 51, 89–92;
networks in, 88–89; online ticketing, 86; "open skies" agreements, 64n2, 101, 103; outside of US, 98–104; oversales and, 96–97; price levels, 76–79; price variation across routes in, 79–84; regional jets flights, 94–95; regulation and antitrust policy, 50–54; regulation of, 66–74; safety/security and, 97–98; service quality, 92–98; Standard Industry Fare Level (SIFL) formula, 70, 77–79; sustainability of competition issues in, 105–8; travel times and delays in, 97; use of Internet and, 86; variation in cross-route prices, 79–82, 79n28; variation in prices across passengers on same route, 82–84; wages and, 73–74
Airline Tariff Publishing Company (ATPCO), 53
Allocative inefficiency, welfare loss from, 19–20
American Airlines, 54, 83, 84
Antitrust, 26; boundary definition in, 33–34; exemptions, 35–37
Antitrust immunities, 34–37
Area-specific regulation, 26
Aspen Skiing case, 50
AT&T, 46–47; antitrust action against, 49–50
Australia, generation capacity divestiture in, 267

Automated mitigation procedure (AMP) mechanism, 278–80
Automatic teller machines (ATMs), 530–31
Averch-Johnson (A-J) model, 12–13

Bank Holding Company (BHC) Act (1956), 492, 498, 507, 532; Douglas Amendment to, 492
Bank Holding Company (BHC) Act amendments (1970), 575
Banking Act (1933), 497
Banking Acts (1956 and 1970), 498
Banking industry, US: antitrust and, 573–77; boundaries of firms, 577–79; chartering restrictions, 491–92; competition in, 579–80; conflicts of interest in, 521–22, 577–79; deposit insurance and, 517–18; diversification in, 515–17; economic growth and, 522–24; expansion of activities, 520–21; geographic expansion restrictions and, 491–93; impact of deregulation on structure of, 509–15; lessons from 2008 crisis and, 533–37; product-line restrictions, 497–502; regulation of pricing in, 568–73; rise of alternative institutions in, 505–27
Banking regulation/deregulation, US, 11–12; of bank capital, 504–5; consequences of market adaptation, 505–27; deposit insurance and, 493–97; evolution of, 488–505, 489–90t; geographic expansion restrictions, 492–93, 493f; historical background of state and federal, 488–91; impact of, on bank risk, 515–18; impact of, on efficiency and pricing, 518–19; impact of, on growth and entrepreneurship, 522–24; impact of, on potential conflicts of interest, 520–22; impact of, on stability and business cycles, 525–27; impact of, on structure of banking industry, 509–15; introduction, 485–88; politics of deregulation, 527–30; pricing restrictions, 502–4; timing of deregulation, 530–33; usury laws, 503
Bank Insurance Fund, 496–97
Basel II accord, 505
Basic service, cable, defined, 142
Benchmarking: external, 451–52; incentive regulation and, 307–8; internal, 449–51
Bermuda agreements, airline industry and, 100–101

Biotechnology industry. See Pharmaceutical industry regulation
Bitstream access, vs. line sharing, 362–65
"Blue sky" laws, 567
Bolar Amendment, 432
Boundary definition, 33–34
Britain. See United Kingdom (UK)
British Telecom (BT), 381–92
Broadcast networks, defined, 141
Bundling, in cable markets, 180–85
Bureaucratic drift, problem of, 28
Bureau of Consumer Financial Protection, 4n9
Bureau of Corporations, 40, 42
Buttonwood Tree Agreement (1792), 575–76

Cable Act (1984), 145
Cable Act (1992), 145, 146–47, 148
Cable programming networks, defined, 141
Cable television industry, 2, 6–7, 140; bargaining breakdowns and, 186–87; broadband access regulations, 150; bundling issue, 180–85; cross-ownership entry, 150–51; duopoly vs. monopoly markets in, 170–72; econometric studies of effects of regulation of, 163–69; economic consequences of regulation/deregulation of, 151–59; horizontal concentration issue, 175–78; infrastructure investment, 142, 143f; introduction to regulation of, 137–39; mergers in, 149; must-carry/retransmission consent, 146–47; online video issue, 185–86; programming market regulations, 147–49; regulation, 6–7; regulation history of (1950–1984), 144–45; regulation history of (1984 to present), 145–46; revenues, 140f; rise of competition and its effects in, 169–75; satellite competition and, 172–74; satellite regulations, 151–52; telephone company entry, 150–51; theoretical models of price/quality choice under regulation, 160–63; vertical integration issue, 178–80. See also Multichannel video programming distribution (MVPD) industry
Cable television systems terminology, 139–44
Capital cost accounting, incentive regulation and, 306, 336

Carve-outs, regulatory, 33–34
Certificates of Deposit Account Registry
    Service (CDARS), 496
Chevron doctrine, 30–31
Chicago Convention (1944 International
    Convention on Civil Aviation), 100
*Cincinnati, New Orleans, and Texas Pacific
    Railway* case, 39
Civil Aeronautics Act (1938), 66, 66n5
Civil Aeronautics Board (CAB), 15, 50–51,
    64, 64n1, 66–72; deregulation and, 75–
    76. *See also* Airline industry
Clayton Act (1914), 42, 43
Colleges, antitrust immunities and, 36
Colt Telecom Group (COLT), 386
Commerce Court, US, 41
Commodity Futures Trading Commission
    (CFTC), 567
Competition, assigning responsibility for
    controlling, 27–37
Competition policy, 26–27
Competitive local exchange carriers
    (CLECs), 364, 366–67, 370–72, 378–80;
    in UK, 383–90
Computer reservation systems (CRS), 53,
    85–86
Consumption decisions, regulated price
    structures and, 19
Cost-based regulation, 348, 349; economic
    analysis with cost but not demand,
    355–60; simple model of, 351–55
Cost-of-service regulation, vs. price-cap,
    331–32

Deficit Reduction Act (2005), 497
Deposit insurance, banking regulation and,
    493–97
Deposit Insurance Fund (DIF), 497
Depository Institutions Deregulation and
    Monetary Control Act (DIDMCA),
    503–4
Deregulation. *See* Regulation; *and specific
    industries*
Digital services, defined, 142
Direct-to-consumer advertising (DTCA),
    pharmaceutical industry regulation
    and, 419; effects of, 465–69
Distribution market, defined, 140
Dodd-Frank Act, 565, 581, 582
Douglas Amendment, to Bank Holding
    Company (BHC) Act (1956), 492
Dual banking system, 488–91

Electricity industry, 2, 3, 7–8, 7n12. *See*
    Wholesale electricity industry
Elkins Act (1903), 40
European Medicines Agency (EMA),
    419–20
European Union (EU): deregulation of
    airline industry in, 102–3; overview of
    safety and efficacy regulation of phar-
    maceutical industry, 419–20
Expanded basic services, cable, defined,
    142
External benchmarking, 451–52

FDA Modernization Act (FDAMA, 1997),
    417–19
FDIC Improvement Act (FDICIA), 496
Federal Aviation Administration (FAA), 66
Federal Aviation Administration (FAA)
    Modernization Act (2012), 128
Federal Communications Commission
    (FCC), 4, 144, 145–46, 149, 346, 348,
    355, 363, 364, 369–70, 376–77
Federal Deposit Insurance Reform Act
    (2005), 497
Federal Energy Regulatory Commission
    (FERC), 209, 260, 274–77, 281–82
Federal Home Loan Mortgage Corporation
    (Freddie Mac), 510
Federal National Mortgage Association
    (Fannie Mae), 510
Federal Power Act (1930), 209–10
Federal Reserve, 498–99
Federal Reserve Act (1913), 491
Federal Savings and Loan Insurance Asso-
    ciation (FSLIC), 495
Federal Trade Commission (FTC), 31,
    42–43
Federal Trade Commission Act (FTCA,
    1914), 42, 43, 413
Financial Institutions Reform, Recovery,
    and Enforcement Act (FIRREA), 495
Financial Modernization Act (1999), 499,
    521
Financial services regulation, incentives
    and, 15–16. *See also* Banking industry,
    US; Banking regulation/deregulation,
    US; Retail securities and investments
    industry
First Bank of the United States, 488
Fishing industry, antitrust immunities and,
    35–36
"Flow control" system, 126

Food and Drug Administration, 10
Food, Drug, and Cosmetics Act of 1938 (FDCA), 412–13; Kefauver-Harris Amendments (1962), 413
Foreign Corrupt Practices Act (1977), 563
Formal performance based regulation mechanisms, 310
France, pharmaceutical industry regulation in, overview of safety and efficacy of, 419

Garn St Germain Act (1982), 532
Generic drugs: entry of, and patent length, 432–38; prices of, and pharmaceutical industry regulation, 447–48. *See also* Pharmaceutical industry
Give ups, 576–77
Glass-Steagall Act (1933), 497, 498, 499, 506–7, 581
Gordon v. NYSE, 576, 577
Government-sponsored enterprises (GSEs), 510, 510n21
Gramm-Leach-Bliley Act (GLBA), 499
Great Britain. *See* United Kingdom (UK)

Hamilton, Alexander, 488
Hatch-Waxman Act (1984), 417–18, 431, 432, 435, 447, 448
Hepburn Act (1906), 40
Herfindahl-Hirschman Index (HHI), 51–52, 511–13
High Density Rules, 124, 125

Immunities, antitrust, 34–37
Imperfect markets, imperfect regulation and, 18–21
Incentive regulation, for electric distribution and transmission networks, 8–9; application, 336–37; benchmarking and, 307–8; capital cost accounting issues, 306, 336; contract menus and, 307, 338; cost-of-service regulation and, 336–37; data collection and, 338; dichotomy between incentive contracts and price setting, 337–38; early applications, 309–10; formal performance based regulation mechanisms, 310; implementation issues, 306–9; introduction, 291–93; literature review on theory of, 299–306; performance of mechanisms of, 332–36; portfolio of mechanisms, 338–39; price cap mechanisms, 310–13; profit-sharing mechanisms, 309–10;

regulation of National Grid Company (NGC) in England and Wales, 326–31; service quality incentives for electric distribution companies in UK and US, 322–26; service quality issues, 306–7; sliding scale mechanisms, 309–10; theoretical and conceptual foundations of, 293–99; UK implementation of basic price cap mechanism for electric distribution companies, 313–22; UK service quality incentives for electric distributions companies and, 322–26
Incentive regulation mechanisms, 308–9, 339–40
Incentives, firm behavior and, 14–16
Incumbent local exchange carriers (ILECs), 349, 362, 366, 368–69
Innovation, regulation and, 16–18
Insider Trading and Securities Fraud Enforcement Act (1988), 563
Insider Trading Sanctions Act (1984), 563
Institutions, importance of, 12–14
Internal benchmarking, 449–51
International Air Transport Association (IATA), 64
International Commission on Harmonization (ICH), 420
International Convention on Civil Aviation (Chicago Convention, 1944), 100
Internet: airline industry and, 86; cable systems and, 142; "over-the-top" (OTT) delivery of video programming over, 142–44
Interstate Commerce Act (1887), 25, 37–38; interaction with Sherman Act, 38–40
Interstate Commerce Commission (ICC), 40–41, 43, 66
Investment Advisors Act (1940), 562, 565
Investment Company Act (1940), 562, 564–65

Japan, pharmaceutical industry regulation in, overview of safety and efficacy of, 419

Kahn, Alfred, 75, 76
Kefauver-Harris Amendments (1962), 413
Kelly Air Mail Act (1925), 66
Kingsbury Commitment, 46

Labor, antitrust immunities and, 37
Legislation, creating, 28–31
Line sharing, vs. bitstream access, 362–65

Local exchange carriers (LECs), 150–51
Local market power mitigation (LMPM) mechanisms, 259–60; lack of effectiveness, 267–69
Loyalty programs, airline, 84–86

Managed care, promotion of, and marketing of pharmaceuticals, 470
Mann-Elkins Act (1910), 41
Market Risk Amendment (1996), 505
Marquette National Bank v. First Omaha Service, 503
McFadden Act (1927), 492
MCI, 46–49
Medicare Modernization Act (MMA, 2003), 435
Medicare Part D drug benefit, 443
Meltzer's "law," 17
Motor Carrier Act (1935), 55, 56
Multibank holding companies (MBHCs), 492
Multichannel video programming distribution (MVPD) industry, 141; innovation and, 142. *See also* Cable television industry
Multichannel video programming distribution (MVPD) markets, 137, 140; bargaining breakdowns and, 186–87; bundling and, 180–85; horizontal concentration in programming markets, 175–78; online video distribution and, 185–86; vertical integration and foreclosure, 178–80
Multiple system operators (MSOs), 148
Mutual Aid Pact (1958), 74, 74n16
Mutual fund industry, regulation of pricing and, 569–71, 570t

National Banking Act (1863), 488–91
National Cooperative Research Act (1984), 36
National Grid Company (NGC, England and Wales), 326–31
National Institute for Clinical Excellence (NICE, UK), 456
National Securities Market Improvement Act (1996), 567
Network industries, 27; modern approaches to, 43–58; railroads, 31–32
Network interface devices (NID), 362
Network unbundling, 39
New York Stock Exchange (NYSE), 575–76
New Zealand, 363–64; bitstream access

vs. line sharing in, 363–64; generation capacity divestiture in, 266; unbundling of telecommunications, 350, 392–99
Nodal pricing, wholesale electricity industry and, 282–84

Ocean shipping, antitrust immunities and, 36
Office of Gas and Electricity Markets (OFGEM, UK), 8–9, 313–31
Online ticketing, airline industry and, 86
Online video distribution (OVD), cable industry and, 185–86
"Open skies" agreements, 64n2, 101, 103
Orphan Drug Act (1983), 414–15, 415f

Patents, pharmaceutical, 431–41; industrialized vs. developing countries and, 438–41; length of, and generic entry, 432–438; literature on, 432; regulation and, 431–41; static efficiency loss and, 438–39
Patent Term Restoration and Competition Act (1984). *See* Hatch-Waxman Act (1984)
Pay-per-view networks, defined, 141
Pharmaceutical industry, 2, 10–11; managed care and, 470; pricing and competition in unregulated markets and, 444–47; profitability and rates of return for, 458–60; in UK, 445–46; unintended incentive effects in, 15. *See also* Generic drugs; Patents, pharmaceutical
Pharmaceutical industry regulation: accelerating R&D process and, 427; benefits of, 426–28; costs of, 421–26; in developing countries, overview of safety and efficacy of, 420–21; direct-to-consumer advertising (DTCA) and, 419, 466–69; effects of price regulation, 457; in EU, overview of safety and efficacy of, 419–20; forms of price and reimbursement regulation, 448–57; in France, overview of safety and efficacy of, 419; future research for price regulation, 457–58; industry structure and, 460–63; insurance reimbursement and, 441–44; introduction, 407–8; in Japan, overview of safety and efficacy of, 419; lessons learned from price regulation, 457–58; Medicare Part D drug benefit, 443; objectives of, 411–12, 412t; prices of generics and, 447–48; prices/profits

Pharmaceutical industry regulation (*cont.*) and, 441–44; promotion, international regulation of, 469; promotion, managed care and, 470; promotion of drugs and, 462–69; proposals for changing, 428–31; technological characteristics of, 408–11; in UK, overview of safety and efficacy of, 419; in US, overview of safety and efficacy of, 412–19

Premium programming networks, defined, 141

Premium services, cable, defined, 142

Prescription Drug User Fee Act (PDUFA, 1993), 415–17, 426–27

Prescription Price Regulation Scheme (PPRS, UK), 455

Price-cap mechanisms, incentive regulation and, 310–13, 337; for electric distribution companies in UK, 313–22

Price cap regulated prices, vs. rate-of-return (ROR) regulation, 348

Price cap regulation, 348; vs. cost-of-service regulation, 331–32; "RPI-X," 9

Price setting, 26

Principal-agent model: application of, to market design process for wholesale electricity industry, 222–25; described, 221–22

Principal/agent problem, 28

Private clearinghouse systems, 491

Private Securities Litigation Reform Act (1995), 563

Professional societies, antitrust immunities and, 36–37

Profit-sharing mechanism, 309–10

Programming market, defined, 140

Public utility commissions (PUCs), state, 274–76

Pure Food and Drug Act of 1906 (Wiley Act), 412

Railroad industry: as network industry, 31–32; regulation of, 32, 37–43, 55–56

Railway Labor Act, 74

Ramsey-Boiteux prices, 82

Ramsey pricing, 48

Ratchets, 308

R&D joint ventures, antitrust immunities and, 36

Reference price (RP) reimbursement systems, 452–54

Regulated price structures, consumption decisions and, 19

Regulation: boundary definition in, 33–34; costs and, 19; innovation and, 16–18. *See also specific industries*

Regulation Q controls, 17–18; elimination of, 11

Regulatory agencies, 5

Regulatory carve-outs, 33–34

Regulatory fallacy, 356–59

Regulatory lags, 308

Regulatory restructuring movement, challenges to, 2–3

Reigle-Neal Interstate Banking and Branching Efficiency Act (1994), 493, 510–11, 533

Reliability must-run (RMR) contracts, 268

Resets, 308

Retail securities and investments industry, 12; antitrust enforcement actions, 537–77; competition with unobservable quality and, 579–80; conflicts of interest and, 577–79; economic rationale for regulation of, 554–62; firm boundaries and, 577–79; introduction, 545–47; main laws and institutions of, 562–68; regulation of pricing in, 568–73; size and scope of, 547–54. *See also* Banking industry, US

Roosevelt, Theodore, 40–41

"RPI-X" price cap regulation, 9

Safety regulation, 10. *See also* Pharmaceutical industry

Sarbanes-Oxley Act (SOX, 2002), 545, 563–64, 581

Satellite Home Viewer Improvement Act (1999), 137, 151

Scalia, Antonin, 50

Second Bank of the United States, 488

Securities Act (1933), 562, 563

Securities Act Amendments (1975), 563

Securities and Exchange Commission (SEC), 12, 565–67, 569

Securities Exchange Act (1934), 562, 563

"Shadow banking," 507–8

Sherman Act (1890), 25, 26, 35, 37–38, 43; court vs. agency implementation of, 31–33; interaction with Interstate Commerce Act and, 38–40

Sliding scale mechanisms, 309–10

"Smart sunshine" regulation, 249–54

Smyth v. Ames, 32

Soft dollars, 576–77

Spitzer, Eliot, 567, 568–69

Sports leagues, antitrust immunities and, 36
Staggers Act (1980), 55
Standard Industry Fare Level (SIFL) formula, 70, 77–79
Standard principal/agent problem, 28–31
Stepping-stone hypothesis, 378–79, 387, 398
Sunk costs, role of, in telecommunications industry, 353–55
Surface Transportation Board (STB), 55, 56

Taft, William Howard, 41
Telecommunications Act (1996), 49–50, 137, 159, 346, 346n5, 349, 364
Telecommunications industry: conditions for prices independent of demand and, 351; early interconnection battles, 45–46; economic analysis with cost but not demand of cost-based regulation, 355–60; future of regulation, 400–404; MCI's entry into long distance, 46–49; role of common costs, 352–53; role of economies of scale, 352; role of economies of scope, 352–53; role of fixed costs, 352; role of sunk costs, 353–55; success of unbundling networks in, 360–72; Telecommunications Act's access rules, 49; *Trinko* case, 49–50
Telecommunications regulation: introduction, 345–51; possibilities of end of, 400–404; simple model of cost-based regulation of, 351–55
Television industry. *See* Cable television industry
Total element long-run incremental cost (TELRIC), 9, 346, 346n4, 349, 355, 361
Total service long-run incremental cost (TSLRIC), 9–10, 346, 346n4, 349, 355, 361
Trans-Missouri decision, 38–40; solving, 40–43
Trans-Missouri Freight Association, 38–40
Transportation Act (1920), 43
Trinko case, 49–50
Trucking industry: control of, railroads and, 55; deregulation of, 56–57; less than truck load (LTL) segment, 56–57; regulation of, 56–58; truck load (TL) segment, 56–57
"Tying" practices, 575

Unbundled network elements (UNEs), 348, 361, 362, 378–79

Unbundling, of networks, 350; New Zealand experience of, 392–99; rationales for, 365–72; success of, in telecommunications industry, 360–72; UK experience of, 381–92; US experience of, 372–81
Underwriting, antitrust and, 575–76
United Kingdom (UK): contract menus in, 307; deregulation of airline industry in, 101–2; generation capacity divestiture in, 266; Medicines Agency, 420; National Institute for Clinical Excellence (NICE), 456; overview of safety and efficacy regulation of pharmaceutical industry, 420; pharmaceutical industry in, 455–56; pharmaceutical industry regulation in, overview of safety and efficacy of, 419; Prescription Price Regulation Scheme (PPRS), 455; regulatory mechanisms in, 305; unbundling of telecommunications, 350, 381–92
United States (US): overview of safety and efficacy regulation of pharmaceutical industry, 412–19; unbundling of telecommunications, 350, 372–81
United States Court of Commerce, 41
Usury laws, US, 503
U.S. v. AMR et al., 54

Vaccine Compensation Fund (VCF), 431
Venture capital (VC) organizations, 507–8
Virtual bidding, wholesale electricity industry and, 284–85

Webb-Pomerene Act (1918), antitrust immunities and, 36
Wholesale electricity industry: active participation of final demand in, 241–46; basic technological features, 201–9; common market design flaws and their causes, 260–74; detecting/correcting market design flaws in, 254–56; dynamic pricing and, 285; economic reliability vs. engineering reliability of transmission networks, 246–48; future economic benefits from US restructuring, 282–85; historical review of US, 198–201; individual rationality constraint under government vs. private ownership, 230–34; individual rationality under market mechanisms vs. regulatory process, 225–30; interval metering deployment and, 285; intro-

Wholesale electricity industry (*cont.*)
duction, 195–98; market design process,
219–34; market design process, dimensions of, 234–48; market design process,
role of regulatory oversight, 248–60;
nodal pricing and, 282–84; oversight
of retail sectors, 257–58; oversight of
system operations, 256–57; oversight
of trading sectors, 257–58; oversight of
transmission networks, 256–57; protecting against harmful behavior and, 259–
60; regulatory challenges in, 218–19;
"smart sunshine" regulation and, 249–
54; theoretical framework of market
design process, 219–34; transition from
vertically integrated monopoly regimes
in US, 209–13; uniqueness of, 213–18;
US experience with restructuring, 274–
82; virtual bidding and, 284–85

Wiley Act (Pure Food and Drug Act of
1906), 412

Willis-Graham Act (1921), 46

Wilson, Woodrow, 41–42

Printed and bound by CPI Group (UK) Ltd, Croydon, CR0 4YY

23/04/2025

14661003-0005